W9-DAA-950

PRESIDENTIAL CAMPAIGN ACTIVITIES OF 1972

SENATE RESOLUTION 60

HEARINGS

BEFORE THE

SELECT COMMITTEE ON PRESIDENTIAL CAMPAIGN ACTIVITIES

OF THE

UNITED STATES SENATE

NINETY-THIRD CONGRESS

FIRST SESSION

WATERGATE AND RELATED ACTIVITIES

Phase I: Watergate Investigation

WASHINGTON, D.C., MAY 17, 18, 22, 23, AND 24, 1973

Book 1

Published By
THE LESLIE PRESS
111 Leslie St. — Dallas, Texas 75207

Source:
U. S. Government Printing Office
1973

SENATE SELECT COMMITTEE ON PRESIDENTIAL CAMPAIGN ACTIVITIES

(Established by S. Res. 60, 93d Congress, 1st Session)

★

SAM J. ERVIN, JR., North Carolina, *Chairman*
HOWARD H. BAKER, JR., Tennessee, *Vice Chairman*

HERMAN E. TALMADGE, Georgia
DANIEL K. INOUYE, Hawaii
JOSEPH M. MONTOYA, New Mexico
EDWARD J. GURNEY, Florida
LOWELL P. WEICKER, JR., Connecticut

SAMUEL DASH, *Chief Counsel and Staff Director*
FRED D. THOMPSON, *Minority Counsel*
RUFUS L. EDMISTEN, *Deputy Chief Counsel*

DAVID M. DORSEN, *Assistant Chief Counsel*
TERRY F. LENZNER, *Assistant Chief Counsel*
JAMES HAMILTON, *Assistant Chief Counsel*
CARMINE S. BELLINO, *Chief Investigator*
WAYNE H. BISHOP, *Chief Field Investigator*
EUGENE BOYCE, *Hearings Record Counsel*
R. PHILLIP HAIRE, *Assistant Counsel*
MARC LACKRITZ, *Assistant Counsel*
WILLIAM T. MAYTON, *Assistant Counsel*
RONALD D. ROTUNDA, *Assistant Counsel*
DONALD G. SANDERS, *Deputy Minority Counsel*
HOWARD S. LIEBENGOOD, *Assistant Minority Counsel*
H. WILLIAM SHURE, *Assistant Minority Counsel*
ROBERT SILVERSTEIN, *Assistant Minority Counsel*
LAURA MATZ, *Administrative Assistant*
CAROLYN ANDRADE, *Office Manager*
JOAN C. COLE, *Secretary to the Minority*

CONTENTS

HEARING DAYS

OPENING STATEMENTS

CHRONOLOGICAL LIST OF WITNESSES

Thursday, May 17, 1973

Friday, May 18, 1973

Tuesday, May 22, 1973

Wednesday, May 23, 1973

THURSDAY, MAY 24, 1973

INTERROGATION OF WITNESSES BY MEMBERS OF THE COMMITTEE AND COUNSELS

EXHIBITS

MATERIAL SUBMITTED FOR THE RECORD

PRESIDENTIAL CAMPAIGN ACTIVITIES OF 1972
PHASE I: WATERGATE INVESTIGATION

THURSDAY, MAY 17, 1973

U.S. SENATE,
SELECT COMMITTEE ON
PRESIDENTIAL CAMPAIGN ACTIVITIES,
Washington, D.C.

The Select Committee met, pursuant to notice, at 10 a.m., in room 318, Russell Senate Office Building, Senator Sam J. Ervin, Jr. (chairman), presiding.

Present: Senators Ervin, Talmadge, Inouye, Montoya, Baker, Gurney, and Weicker.

Also present: Samuel Dash, chief counsel; Fred D. Thompson, minority counsel; Rufus L. Edmisten, deputy chief counsel; Arthur S. Miller, chief consultant; Jed Johnson, consultant; David M. Dorsen, James Hamilton, and Terry F. Lenzner, assistant chief counsels; Barry Schochet, Ron Rotunda, and Marc Lackritz, assistant majority counsels; Eugene Boyce, hearings record counsel; Donald G. Sanders, deputy minority counsel; Howard S. Liebengood, H. William Shure, and Robert Silverstein, assistant minority counsels; Pauline O. Dement, research assistant; Eiler Ravnholt, office of Senator Inouye; Robert Baca, office of Senator Montoya; Ron McMahan, assistant to Senator Baker; A. Searle Field, assistant to Senator Weicker; John Walz, publications clerk.

Senator ERVIN. The committee will come to order.

OPENING STATEMENT BY SENATOR ERVIN OF NORTH CAROLINA

Senator ERVIN. Today the Select Committee on Presidential Campaign Activities begins hearings into the extent to which illegal and improper or unethical activities were involved in the 1972 Presidential election campaign.

Senate Resolution 60 which established the Select Committee was adopted unanimously by the Senate on February 7, 1973. Under its provisions every Member of the Senate joined in giving the committee a broad mandate to investigate, as fully as possible, all the ramifications of the Watergate break-in which occurred on Saturday, June 17, 1972. Under the terms of the authorizing resolution, the committee must complete its study and render its report on or before February 28, 1974. Of necessity, that report will reflect the considered judgment of the committee on whatever new legislation is needed to help safeguard the electoral process through which the President of the United States is chosen.

We are beginning these hearings today in an atmosphere of the utmost gravity. The questions that have been raised in the wake of the June 17 break-in strike at the very undergirding of our democracy. If the many allegations made to this date are true, then the burglars who broke into the headquarters of the Democratic National Committee at the Watergate were in effect breaking into the home of every citizen of the United States. And if these allegations prove to be true, what they were seeking to steal was not the jewels, money, or other property of American citizens, but something much more valuable—their most precious heritage: the right to vote in a free election. Since that day, a mood of incredulity has prevailed among our populace, and it is the constitutional duty of this committee to act expeditiously to allay the fears being expressed by the citizenry, and to establish the factual bases upon which these fears have been founded.

The first phase of the committee's investigation will probe the planning and execution of the wiretapping and break-in of the Democratic National Committee's headquarters at the Watergate complex, and the alleged coverup that followed. Subsequent phases will focus on allegations of campaign espionage and subversion and allegations of extensive violations of campaign financing laws. The clear mandate of the unanimous Senate resolution provides for a bipartisan investigation of every phase of political espionage and illegal fundraising. Thus it is clear that we have the full responsibility to recommend any remedial legislation necessary.

In pursuing its task, it is clear that the committee will be dealing with the workings of the democratic process under which we operate in a nation that still is the last, best hope of mankind in his eternal struggle to govern himself decently and effectively.

We will be concerned with the integrity of a governmental system designed by men who understood the lessons of the past and who, accordingly, established a framework of separated governmental powers in order to prevent any one branch of the Government from becoming dominant over the others. The Founding Fathers, having participated in the struggle against arbitrary power, comprehended some eternal truths respecting men and government. They knew that those who are entrusted with power are susceptible to the disease of tyrants, which George Washington rightly described as "love of power and the proneness to abuse it." For that reason, they realized that the power of public officers should be defined by laws which they, as well as the people, are obligated to obey, a truth enunciated by Daniel Webster when he said that "Whatever government is not a government of laws is a despotism, let it be called what it may."

To the end of insuring a society governed by laws, these men embodied in our Constitution the enduring principles in which they so firmly believed, establishing a legislature to make all laws, an executive to carry them out, and a judicial system to interpret them. Recently, we have been faced with massive challenges to the historical framework created in 1787, with the most recent fears having been focused upon assertions by administration of both parties of executive power over the Congress—for example, in the impoundment of appropriated funds and the abuse of executive privilege. Those challenges, however, can and are being dealt with by the working of the system itself—that is, through the enactment of powerful statutes by the Congress, and the rendering of decisions by the courts upholding the lawmaking power of the Congress.

In dealing with the challenges posed by the multitudinous allegations arising out of the Watergate affair, however, the Select Committee has a task much more difficult and complex than dealing with intrusions of one branch of the Government upon the powers of the others. It must probe into assertions that the very system itself has been subverted and its foundations shaken.

To safeguard the structural scheme of our governmental system, the Founding Fathers provided for an electoral process by which the elected officials of this Nation should be chosen. The Constitution, later-adopted amendments, and more specifically, statutory law, provide that the electoral processes shall be conducted by the people, outside the confines of the formal branches of the Government, and through a political process that must operate under the strictures of law and ethical guidelines, but independent of the overwhelming power of the Government itself. Only then can we be sure that the electoral process cannot be made to serve as the mere handmaiden of a particular administration in power.

If the allegations that have been made in the wake of the Watergate affair are substantiated, there has been a very serious subversion of the integrity of the electoral process, and the committee will be obliged to consider the manner in which such a subversion affects the continued existence of this Nation as a representative democracy, and how, if we are to survive, such subversions may be prevented in the future.

It has been asserted that the 1972 campaign was influenced by a wide variety of illegal or unethical activities, including the widespread wiretapping of the telephones, political headquarters, and even the residences of candidates and their campaign staffs and of members of the press; by the publication of forged documents designed to defame certain candidates or enhance others through fraudulent means; the infiltration and disruption of opponents' political organizations and gathering; the raising and handling of campaign contributions through means designed to circumvent, either in letter or in spirit, the provisions of campaign disclosure acts; and even the acceptance of campaign contributions based upon promises of illegal interference in governmental processes on behalf of the contributors.

Finally, and perhaps most disturbingly, it has been alleged that, following the Watergate break-in, there has been a massive attempt to cover up all the improper activities, extending even so far as to pay off potential witnesses and, in particular, the seven defendants in the Watergate trial in exchange for their promise to remain silent—activities which, if true, represent interference in the integrity of the prosecutorial and judicial processes of this Nation. Moreover, there has been evidence of the use of governmental instrumentalities in efforts to exercise political surveillance over candidates in the 1972 campaign.

Let me emphasize at the outset that our judicial process thus far has convicted only the seven persons accused of burglarizing and wiretapping the Democratic National Committee headquarters at the Watergate complex on June 17. The hearings which we initiate today are not designed to intensify or reiterate unfounded accusations or to poison further the political climate of our Nation. On the contrary, it is my conviction and that of the other committee members that the accusations that have been leveled and the evidence of wrongdoing that has surfaced has cast a black cloud of distrust over our entire society. Our citizens do not know whom to believe, and many of them have concluded that all the processes of government have become so compromised that honest governance has been rendered impossible.

We believe that the health, if not the survival, of our social structure and of our form of government requires the most candid and public investigation of all the evidence and of all the accusations that have been levelled at any persons, at whatever level, who were engaged in the 1972 campaign. My colleagues on the committee and I are determined to uncover all the relevant facts surrounding these matters, and to spare no one, whatever his station in life may be, in our efforts to accomplish that goal. At the same time, I want to emphasize that the purpose of these hearings is not prosecutorial or judicial, but rather investigative and informative.

No one is more cognizant than I of the separation of powers issues that hover over these hearings. The committee is fully aware of the ongoing grand jury proceedings that are taking place in several areas of the country, and of the fact that criminal indictments have been returned already by one of these grand juries. Like all Americans, the members of this committee are vitally interested in seeing that the judicial processes operate effectively and fairly, and without interference from any other branch of government. The investigation of this select committee was born of crisis, unabated as of this very time, the crisis of a mounting loss of confidence by American citizens in the integrity of our electoral process which is the bedrock of our democracy. The American people are looking to this committee, as the representative of all the Congress, for enlightenment and guidance regarding the details of the allegations regarding the subversion of our electoral and political processes. As the elected representatives of the people, we would be derelict in our duty to them if we failed to pursue our mission expeditiously, fully, and with the utmost fairness. The aim of the committee is to provide full and open public testimony in order that the nation can proceed toward the healing of the wounds that now afflict the body politic. It is that aim that we are here to pursue today, within the terms of the mandate imposed upon us by our colleagues and in full compliance with all applicable rules of law. The Nation and history itself are watching us. We cannot fail our mission.

I would like to put in the record at this time the Rules of Procedure* and a copy of the resolutions and guidelines of the committee.

I would like to recognize at this time other Senators so they may present their statements and first I recognize the vice chairman of the committee, Senator Howard Baker, who has been most alert and most cooperative in the work of the committee.

OPENING STATEMENT OF SENATOR BAKER OF TENNESSEE

Senator Baker. Mr. Chairman, thank you very much. I believe there is no need for me to further emphasize the gravity of the matters that we begin to explore publicly here this morning. Suffice it to say there are most serious charges and allegations made against individuals, and against institutions. The very integrity of our political process itself has been called into question.

* See p. 415.

Commensurate with the gravity of the subject matter under review and the responsibilities of this committee and the witnesses who come before it, we have a great burden to discharge and carry. This committee is not a court, nor is it a jury. We do not sit to pass judgment on the guilt or innocence of anyone. The greatest service that this committee can perform for the Senate, the Congress, and for the people of this Nation is to achieve a full discovery of all of the facts that bear on the subject of this inquiry. This committee was created by the Senate to do exactly that. To find as many of the facts, the circumstances and the relationships as we could, to assemble those facts into a coherent and intelligible presentation and to make recommendations to the Congress for any changes in statute law or the basic charter document of the United States that may seem indicated.

But this committee can serve another quite important function that neither a grand jury investigation nor a jury proceeding is equipped to serve, and that is to develop the facts in full view of all of the people of America. Although juries will eventually determine the guilt or the innocence of persons who have been and may be indicted for specific violations of the law, it is the American people who must be the final judge of Watergate. It is the American people who must decide, based on the evidence spread before them, what Watergate means, about how we all should conduct our public business in the future.

When the resolution which created this committee was being debated on the floor of the Senate in February of this year, I and other Republican Senators expressed concern that the inquiry might become a partisan effort by one party to exploit the temporary vulnerability of another. Other congressional inquiries in the past had been conducted by committees made up of equal numbers of members from each party. I offered an amendment to the resolution which would have given the Republican members equal representation on this committee. That amendment did not pass. But any doubts that I might have had about the fairness and impartiality of this investigation have been swept away during the last few weeks. Virtually every action taken by this committee since its inception has been taken with complete unanimity of purpose and procedure. The integrity and fairness of each member of this committee and of its fine professional staff have been made manifest to me, and I know they will be made manifest to the American people during the course of this proceeding. This is not in any way a partisan undertaking, but, rather it is a bipartisan search for the unvarnished truth.

I would like to close, Mr. Chairman, with a few thoughts on the political process in this country. There has been a great deal of discussion across the country in recent weeks about the impact that Watergate might have on the President, the office of the Presidency, the Congress, or our ability to carry on relations with other countries, and so on. The constitutional institutions of this Republic are so strong and so resilient that I have never doubted for a moment their ability to function without interruption. On the contrary, it seems clear to me the very fact that we are now involved in the public process of cleaning our own house, before the eyes of the world, is a mark of the greatest strength. I do not believe that any other political system could endure the thoroughness and the ferocity of the various inquiries now underway within the branches of Government and in our courageous, tenacious free press.

No mention is made in our Constitution of political parties. But the two-party system, in my judgment, is as integral and as important to our form of government as the three formal branches of the central Government themselves. Millions of Americans participated actively, on one level or another, and with great enthusiasm, in the Presidential election of 1972. This involvement in the political process by citizens across the land is essential to participatory democracy. If one of the effects of Watergate is public disillusionment with partisan politics, if people are turned off and drop out of the political system, this will be the greatest Watergate casualty of all. If, on the other hand, this national catharsis in which we are now engaged should result in a new and better way of doing political business, if Watergate produces changes in laws and campaign procedures, then Watergate may prove to be a great national opportunity to revitalize the political process and to involve even more Americans in the day-to-day work of our two great political parties. I am deeply encouraged by the fact that I find no evidence at this point in time to indicate that either the Democratic National Committee or the Republican National Committee played any role in whatever may have gone wrong in 1972. The hundreds of seasoned political professionals across this country, and the millions of people who devoted their time and energies to the campaigns, should not feel implicated or let down by what has taken place.

With these thoughts in mind, I intend to pursue, as I know each member of this committee intends to pursue, an objective and even-handed but thorough, complete, and energetic inquiry into the facts. We will inquire into every fact and follow every lead, unrestrained by any fear of where that lead might ultimately take us.

Mr. Chairman, my thanks to you for the great leadership you have brought to this committee in its preparatory phases, and my thanks to Mr. Dash, who has served with distinction as chief counsel to the committee and Mr. Thompson, who serves as minority counsel to the committee. I believe we are fully prepared to proceed with the business of discovering the facts.

Thank you very much.

Senator Ervin. Thank you for that statement.

Senator Talmadge, do you have a statement?

OPENING STATEMENT OF SENATOR TALMADGE OF GEORGIA

Senator Talmadge. Mr. Chairman, this committee was created by the U.S. Senate by unanimous vote for investigating any election irregularities during the 1972 campaign. The vote of the Senate was nonpartisan, being unanimous. This committee has been organized on a nonpartisan basis. Its staff is operating on a nonpartisan basis. Every vote that this committee has cast to date has been nonpartisan. In my judgment, this committee must get the facts, the full facts, and all of the facts on a totally objective, nonpartisan basis and let the chips fall where they may. I am confident that this committee will do so.

Senator Ervin. Senator Gurney.

OPENING STATEMENT OF SENATOR GURNEY OF FLORIDA

Senator GURNEY. Thank you, Mr. Chairman.

This committee begins today history hearings which may well turn out to be the most significant hearings ever conducted by any committee of the Congress. This fact should weigh heavily upon the work of both the Senators and the staff. The eyes and ears of the citizens of this Nation are watching and listening and so, too, are people around the world. Here at home there is desire that the wrongdoing be thoroughly exposed and the wrongdoers brought to justice. This is being done now. Already in recent weeks 15 key people have left this administration because of Watergate and allied scandals, several have been indicted, two of these are former high Cabinet officers. We can all take heart that our system of government is working and working well and rapidly now even though a slow and faltering start was made in the beginning. Between the work of prosecutors, grand jury, excellent investigative reporting and this committee, Watergate is going to be cleaned up.

However, there is another great overriding issue which will be present with us in these hearings, an issue which is troubling people not only all over this Nation but also people and leaders of other nations around the world. What will Watergate do and what will these hearings do to the office and institution of the Presidency? That is the question that is uppermost in people's minds and gnawing away in the pits of their stomachs. What is of great concern is the effect that Watergate may have on the American Presidency.

I see this concern in daily mail I receive. I hear this concern in my conversations with people. It is evident in the media reaction at home and abroad. The signs are in the stockmarket, in the price of gold and dollars. This concern is part and parcel of foreign policy, in NATO, Southeast Asia, the Middle East and its oil and in the trade and SALT talks. The absence of comment from seats of government and power throughout the world brings to mind the old saying "Don't rock the boat lest we capsize," and I think this is indicative of the national concern.

Why is this? The world is intertwined today, interdependent, no one nation can go it alone. Indeed, to a more-or-less degree we are in the same boat. Thus, the rocking of the boat by Watergate, its catastrophic effect upon the institution of the Presidency, is indeed the object of serious concern of everyone at home and abroad.

What then must we do here in this committee room in the ensuing weeks?

Someone once said, and I quote: "The present is fraught with the future," and so it will be with these hearings. The future cannot be unaffected by what we do and say in this room. It becomes imperative that this committee, the committee staff, and the press and public alike be continually aware that the committee's task is to investigate and present the facts of the investigation failure. This committee was not created to try any individual. It was not created to pass judgment on any individual. Our purpose is to seek the truth, and our methods and motives must never be suspect or we will fail in our task. The sense of history certainly rides with these hearings. And this thought should guide our work to the ends that it be thorough, yes, completely thorough, but always careful, deliberate, responsible statesmanlike to the end that the system of government and justice of a free and a democratic society, these United States will work its will in a fair and impartial and objective manner. By doing that the committee hopefully can make its greatest contribution and that is, regardless of the consequences to reaffirm, to reassure, to reestablish the faith of the people in their Government and its leaders.

Senator ERVIN. Senator Inouye.

OPENING STATEMENT OF SENATOR INOUYE OF HAWAII

Senator INOUYE. Mr. Chairman, the hearings which we begin today may be the most important held in this century. At stake is the very integrity of the election process. Unless we can safeguard that process from fraud, manipulation, deception, and other illegal or unethical activities, one of our most precious rights, the right to vote, will be without meaning. Democracy will have been subverted.

Mr. Chairman, as I see it, our mission is twofold. First, to thoroughly investigate all allegations of improper activities in the 1972 Presidential election so that the full truth will be known and, second, to take steps to prevent future occurrences of such activities. Our efforts should not be directed toward punishing the guilty—there are judicial processes with that aim underway in at least four cities—but to initiate a nationwide public debate on our elections and are they working or have they failed to work?

Like most Americans I have been truly shocked by the revelations and allegations of the scandal which is unparalleled in our country's history. The sins of the spies or the saboteurs, the manipulators or moneymen, the burglars or the buggers must be purged from the very heart and soul of the election processes.

Mr. Chairman, I must add a word of caution. We have heard many sensational charges in the past several months and undoubtedly we will hear many more in the weeks and months ahead. It is vital that hasty judgments not be made before we have all the facts. This country will be ill served by another period of McCarthyism. These hearings should serve to enlighten and to reform. They should lay the groundwork for a reaffirmation of faith in our American system.

Senator ERVIN. Senator Weicker.

OPENING STATEMENT OF SENATOR WEICKER OF CONNECTICUT

Senator WEICKER. Mr. Chairman and members of the committee, the gut question before this committee is not one of individual guilt or innocence. The gut question for the committee and country alike is and was how much truth do we want? A few men gambled that Americans wanted the quiet of efficiency rather than the turbulence of truth. And they were stopped a yard short of the goal by another few, who believed in America as advertised.

So the story to come has its significance not in the acts of men breaking, entering, and bugging the Watergate, but in the acts of men who almost—who almost—stole America.

Senator ERVIN. Senator Montoya.

OPENING STATEMENT OF SENATOR MONTOYA OF NEW MEXICO

Senator MONTOYA. Thank you, Mr. Chairman. Briefly, I want to say that we bear a heavy responsibility to conduct this inquiry fairly, justly, and most judiciously. I am confident that we will pass this test and assume this challenge. While a legislative inquiry is different from a court proceeding, I know that we will be respectful of the rights of individuals, but at the same time, we will be intent on searching out the truth of all evidentiary components which ostensibly have posed a threat to our constitutional processes, in particular, our concept of freedom and our electoral process. With these facts, we hope to alert the conscience and the vigilance of our citizens and restore their faith in our electoral process. We hope that this concern of all Americans will hover over all of us as a mandate for legislation and other remedies to insure against any future sinister invasions of the sanctity of our democratic institutions.

Senator ERVIN. Counsel will call the first witness.

Mr. DASH. Will Mr. Robert Odle please come to the witness table?

Senator ERVIN. Mr. Odle, stand up and raise your right hand.

Do you swear that the evidence you shall give to the Senate Select Committee on Presidential Campaign Activities shall be the truth, the whole truth, and nothing but the truth, so help you God?

Mr. ODLE. I do; so help me God.

Mr. DASH. Mr. Odle, I understand you have a brief statement that you wish to read to the committee.

TESTIMONY OF ROBERT C. ODLE, JR., FORMER DIRECTOR OF ADMINISTRATION, COMMITTEE FOR THE RE-ELECTION OF THE PRESIDENT

Mr. ODLE. Thank you. I would like to use this opportunity to make just one brief point. I joined the staff of the Committee for the Re-Election of the President more than 2 years ago because I believed in President Nixon and in his hopes and dreams for America. I still do.

During my association with the committee, I came into contact with more than 400 members of its national staff, salaried and volunteer. It now appears tragically that some of those people have acted unethically. Indeed, two former members of the staff have been convicted of crimes and if others are guilty, I hope that they will be exposed and prosecuted. These hearings will help in that purpose.

The point I want to make is this, that when we discuss the committee, we should remember that in addition to those who did wrong and who did act unethically, there were a million volunteers across the Nation and 400 people at national headquarters who did nothing unethical or illegal. They joined in the campaign because they believed in the President, a President who opened a door to China, all too long closed, a President who traveled to Russia and signed substantive agreements while there; a President who brought an end to the longest war in our history. I found those hundreds of people with whom I worked for 2 years, most of them, to be among the finest, most decent, hard working Americans I have ever met and I was proud to be associated with them in the cause of reelecting a man who I feel will ultimately be regarded as one of the greatest Presidents this Nation has ever known.

I want to associate myself with the spirit and the substance of the opening statements of the Senators which I just heard. I have been and want to continue to be of assistance to the Senate select committee in any way I can and I appreciate the opportunity to make this statement.

Mr. DASH. Now, Mr. Odle, for the record, would you please state your name and address?

Mr. ODLE. Robert C. Odle, Jr., 309 North St. Asaph Street, Alexandria, Va.

Mr. DASH. What is your present occupation?

Mr. ODLE. I am presently a consultant to the Committee To Re-Elect the President.

Mr. DASH. Prior to that time, what position did you hold with the Committee To Re-Elect the President?

Mr. ODLE. I was director of administration for the committee from May 1, 1971, until approximately May 1, 1973.

Mr. DASH. Can you tell us when the Committee for the Re-Election of the President was set up?

Mr. ODLE. Yes, sir; it was set up and announced, I believe, on May 11, 1971.

Mr. DASH. Can you state briefly—for what purpose the Committee for the Re-Election of the President was set up?

Mr. ODLE. Yes, sir. In the year 1971, a number of people began to look at the 1972 campaign. There was the thought that people would have to be getting to work full time to the President's campaign. They did not want those people to remain on a government payroll or on a White House payroll. They did not want that activity at the Republican National Committee, because at that point, it appeared the President might have competition in the primaries from two Congressmen and it would be particularly inappropriate for the RNC to house Presidential campaign activities. Therefore, the Committee for the Re-Election of the President was set up in May of 1971.

Mr. DASH. Now, Mr. Odle, who were the initial persons who came over and formed the Committee To Re-Elect the President or give it its start?

Mr. ODLE. There was Mr. Jeb Magruder, Mr. Harry S. Flemming, Mr. Hugh W. Sloan, Jr., myself, Dr. Robert Marik, Mr. Herbert Porter, and a number of secretaries who went there to assist us.

Mr. DASH. Now, of those persons, could you identify who had positions at the White House before they came over to the committee?

Mr. ODLE. Yes, sir; Mr. Porter, Mr. Magruder, Mr. Flemming had been at the White House; he left the White House and went into private business and then came to the committee, but he had been there before, and Mr. Sloan, and myself.

Mr. DASH. Now, Mr. Odle, will you please go to the chart.*

Have you seen that chart prior to this hearing?

Mr. Odle, would you first state what that chart purports to be?

*See exhibit No. 5, p. 11.

Exhibit No. 5

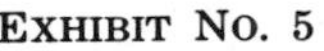

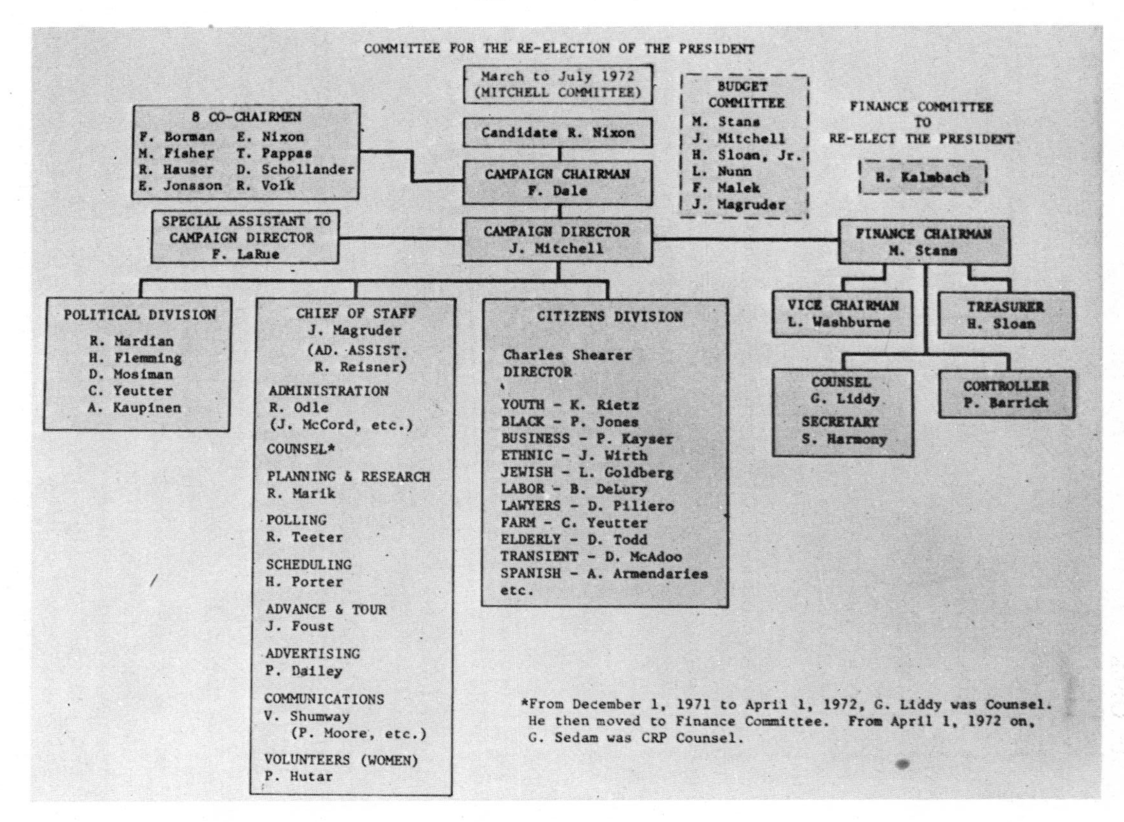
COMMITTEE FOR THE RE-ELECTION OF THE PRESIDENT
March to July 1972 (MITCHELL COMMITTEE)
Candidate R. Nixon
CAMPAIGN CHAIRMAN F. Dale
CAMPAIGN DIRECTOR J. Mitchell
8 CO-CHAIRMEN
F. Borman E. Nixon
M. Fisher T. Pappas
R. Hauser D. Schollander
E. Jonsson R. Volk
SPECIAL ASSISTANT TO CAMPAIGN DIRECTOR F. LaRue
BUDGET COMMITTEE
M. Stans
J. Mitchell
H. Sloan, Jr.
L. Nunn
F. Malek
J. Magruder
FINANCE COMMITTEE TO RE-ELECT THE PRESIDENT
H. Kalmbach
FINANCE CHAIRMAN M. Stans
VICE CHAIRMAN L. Washburne
TREASURER H. Sloan
COUNSEL G. Liddy
SECRETARY S. Harmony
CONTROLLER P. Barrick
POLITICAL DIVISION
R. Mardian
H. Flemming
D. Mosiman
C. Yeutter
A. Kaupinen
CHIEF OF STAFF
J. Magruder
(AD. ASSIST. R. Reisner)
ADMINISTRATION
R. Odle
(J. McCord, etc.)
COUNSEL*
PLANNING & RESEARCH
R. Marik
POLLING
R. Teeter
SCHEDULING
H. Porter
ADVANCE & TOUR
J. Foust
ADVERTISING
P. Dailey
COMMUNICATIONS
V. Shumway
(P. Moore, etc.)
VOLUNTEERS (WOMEN)
P. Hutar
CITIZENS DIVISION
Charles Shearer
DIRECTOR
YOUTH - K. Rietz
BLACK - P. Jones
BUSINESS - P. Kayser
ETHNIC - J. Wirth
JEWISH - L. Goldberg
LABOR - B. DeLury
LAWYERS - D. Piliero
FARM - C. Yeutter
ELDERLY - D. Todd
TRANSIENT - D. McAdoo
SPANISH - A. Armendaries
etc.
*From December 1, 1971 to April 1, 1972, G. Liddy was Counsel.
He then moved to Finance Committee. From April 1, 1972 on,
G. Sedam was CRP Counsel.

Mr. ODLE. Yes; this is a chart of the Committee for the Re-Election of the President until 1972, the initial part of 1972.

Mr. DASH. Up until what time?

Mr. ODLE. Up until July 1972.

Mr. ODLE. Yes, sir; it is a part of the records that the campaign staff had asked for.

Mr. DASH. Did you help prepare that chart?

Mr. ODLE. Yes, I did.

Mr. DASH. Does that chart accurately reflect the structure of the committee?

Mr. ODLE. Yes, it does.

Mr. DASH. Could you please point out the particular persons on the chart and the roles that they played for the committee?

Mr. ODLE. Yes, sir.

Mr. Dash, the other point I was going to make is this also shows the Finance Committee To Re-Elect the President in addition to this committee and the budget committee between the two committees.

Mr. DASH. What was the difference between the Committee To Re-Elect the President and the Finance Committee To Re-Elect the President?

Mr. ODLE. The essential function of the Finance Committee To Re-Elect the President was to raise the necessary funds for the campaign, to account for them, to keep records, to allocate the funds. The job of the Committee To Re-Elect the President was to conduct the national campaign activities. The budget committee between the two committees was made up of representatives of each and the function of the budget committee in effect was to decide how campaign dollars ought to be allocated—in other words, how the pie was sliced.

Mr. DASH. Now, would you point out principally the key persons on that chart and just briefly state what their position was in the committee?

Mr. ODLE. Mr. Francis Dale, who was president and publisher of the Cincinnati Enquirer. He was chairman of the Committee for the Re-Election of the President. Mr. Mitchell, formerly Attorney General, was campaign director. Mr. La Rue was special assistant to campaign director. There were eight cochairmen under Mr. Dale, who served, distinguished citizens from around the country. There were three divisions. The political division contained five political coordinators. Their job was to divide the 50 States among them and to organize State reelection committees in each State—the various other national programs under Mr. Magruder. Mr. Reisner was his administrative assistant.

Do you want me to go through all these?

Mr. DASH. No, just the names.

On that chart, you have Mr. Magruder and Mr. Reisner as the appointment secretary. What was the role of Mr. McCord who appears on that chart?

Does he in fact appear on that chart?

Mr. ODLE. Yes, sir, he does; he appears here under me. Mr. McCord was one of about five assistants who worked for me. His job was office security.

Mr. DASH. Now, do you have——

Mr. ODLE. That is what he was hired for, office security.

Mr. DASH. Now, do you have Mr. Liddy appearing on that chart?

Mr. ODLE. Yes, sir. Actually, what was done here is an asterisk was used. Mr. Liddy was general counsel of the Committee for the Re-Election of the President from December 1 to April 11, 1972. About the time that the new campaign legislation was taking effect, Mr. Liddy moved from here to here, the finance committee, where he became general counsel of that. He was replaced here on April 1.

Mr. DASH. Now, did Mr. Sloan appear on that chart?

Mr. ODLE. Yes; Mr. Sloan was treasurer of the finance committee.

Mr. DASH. And do you have Mr. Stans appearing on that chart?

Mr. ODLE. Mr. Stans was chairman of the finance committee.

Mr. DASH. And I see Mr. Kalmbach above, in a little box above Mr. Stans.

Would you explain what Mr. Kalmbach's relation was on that chart?

Mr. ODLE. Mr. Kalmbach was associate chairman on the finance committee until April, the predecessor of the finance committee, the Finance Committee for the Re-Election of the President. I do not believe he had an official role in the campaign after April, although I believe he assisted Mr. Stans.

Mr. DASH. Now, do we have the chart, the finance committee chart?*

Now, could you find Mr. Liddy on that chart?

Mr. ODLE. Yes; he was counsel.

Mr. DASH. What period did that chart represent—the role of the finance committee?

Mr. ODLE. I would say basically from April to November.

Now, within that time period, various changes were made in individuals, but that is the basic structure of the finance committee as I understand it from April 7 until November.

Mr. DASH. Now who was Sally Harmony appearing in that chart?

Mr. ODLE. Mrs. Harmony was Mr. Liddy's secretary.

Mr. DASH. Would you just go back now to the first chart for the moment? Does Mr. La Rue appear on that chart?

Mr. ODLE. Yes; Mr. La Rue is right here, special assistant to the campaign director.

Mr. DASH. Is Mr. Mardian on that chart?

Mr. ODLE. At that time, Mr. Mardian was a political coordinator, one of the five in the political division.

Mr. DASH. Does Mr. Malek appear in that chart?

Mr. ODLE. No; Mr. Malek was not a full-time member of the staff at that time.

Mr. DASH. Would you of your own knowledge or opinion—and if opinion, express how you have that opinion—those of the original shift from the White House to the committee? How Mr. Magruder came over to the committee? Who appointed the various persons who came over to the Committee for the Re-Election of the President?

Mr. ODLE. My understanding at that point in time was that Mr. Haldeman and Mr. Mitchell had asked Mr. Magruder to assume that position.

Mr. DASH. Who appointed Mr. Sloan, to your knowledge?

Mr. ODLE. I believe at that point, Mr. Haldeman asked Mr. Sloan to come over. I can't say, sir, that I know who appointed him but my best knowledge at that point was that Mr. Haldeman had asked Mr. Sloan to come to the committee.

---

*See exhibit No. 6, p. 15.

Mr. DASH. Is it your opinion that Mr. Mitchell and Mr. Haldeman were playing principal roles in selecting key people for the committee?

Mr. ODLE. Yes.

Mr. DASH. I have no further questions.

Mr. THOMPSON. Mr. Odle, you may be seated. Referring back to your first chart, the chart which depicts your organization when Mr. Mitchell was director of the committee, your budget committee, I believe you said your budget committee was comprised of members of both the finance committee and the Committee To Re-Elect; is that correct?

Mr. ODLE. Yes, sir, it is.

Mr. THOMPSON. What about Mr. Malek? Where was he employed?

Mr. ODLE. Mr. Malek came to the committee on a full-time basis July 1 as his deputy campaign director. He, in addition to that, before exercised some supervisory function over some of the citizens groups and also sat in on budget committee meetings.

Mr. THOMPSON. Was he at the White House prior to this time?

Mr. ODLE. Yes.

Mr. THOMPSON. Did he sit in on budget committee meetings at some time when he was at the White House?

Mr. ODLE. I believe so.

Mr. THOMPSON. Your name is not within this box here, but did you in fact come to budget committee meetings?

Mr. ODLE. Yes; I did.

Mr. THOMPSON. Who presided over those meetings?

Mr. ODLE. I would say the campaign director and the finance chairman jointly. That would have been Mr. Mitchell up until July 1, Mr. MacGregor thereafter, and the finance chairman, Mr. Stans.

Mr. THOMPSON. With regard to Mr. Stans, was his role limited to raising money or did Mr. Stans also participate in the decision as to how money would be allocated?

Mr. ODLE. I think that Mr. Stans, in the budget meetings, certainly kept an eye on where the money was going. He sometimes challenged expenditures. He would say, for example, do we really need to spend this amount of money on television advertising this next week. Yes; he was an active participant in the budget committee meetings.

Mr. THOMPSON. He voiced his opinion and took some participation in how the money was being spent, as well as raising money?

Mr. ODLE. Yes; he generally tried to put a brake on the spending, questioning whether expenditures in various categories were needed.

Mr. THOMPSON. Were all expenditures approved by him, or all major expenditures approved by him?

Mr. ODLE. I would say that in the budget committee sessions, his agreement was necessary before we could allocate a great deal of money, say, for television advertising the following week; yes, those kinds of major decisions.

Mr. THOMPSON. How large a sum of money would he have to be talking about before he would normally concern himself?

Mr. ODLE. Sir, I couldn't put a number on it. It would be difficult to do that. It would depend on the kind of thing we are talking about.

Mr. THOMPSON. Mr. Odle, in looking at your chart, is it fair to assume that from this organization chart, that when Mr. Mitchell was director, he had more direct control or day-to-day control over the

EXHIBIT No. 6

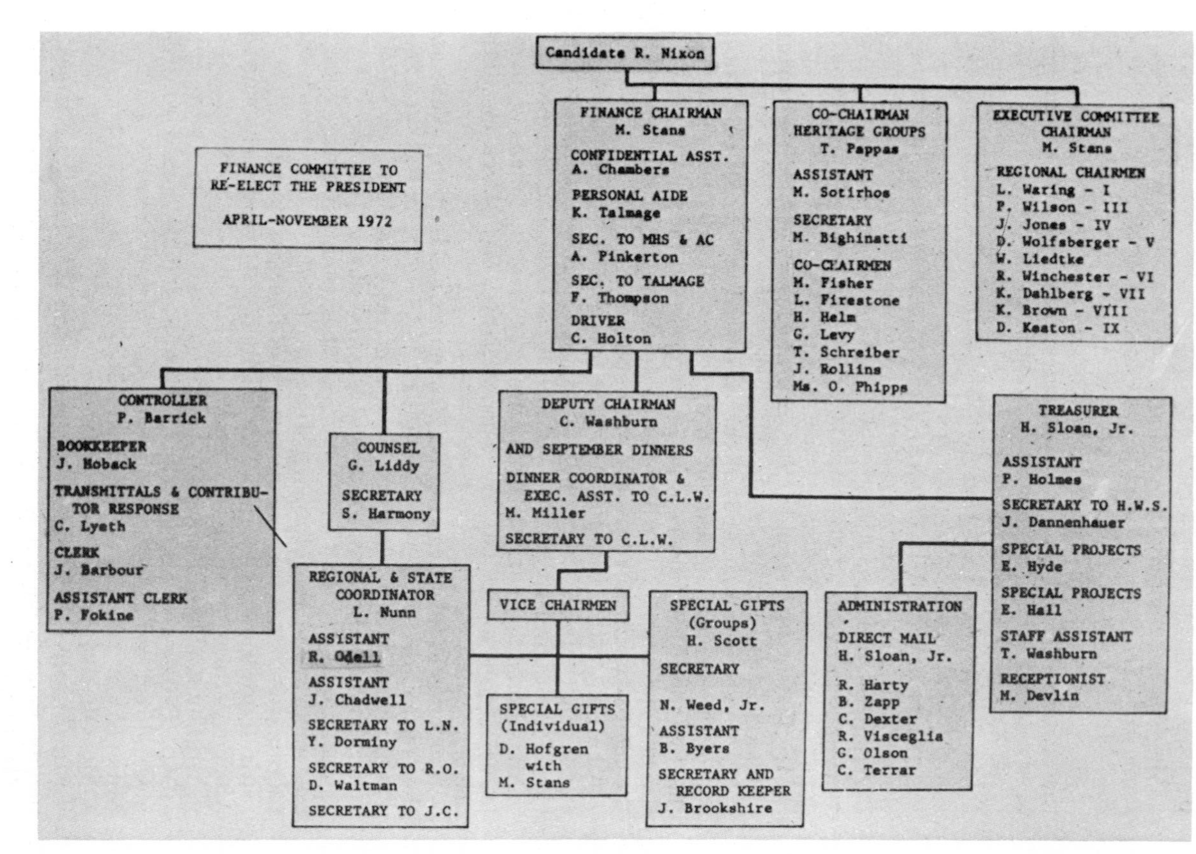
Candidate R. Nixon
FINANCE COMMITTEE TO
RE-ELECT THE PRESIDENT
APRIL-NOVEMBER 1972
FINANCE CHAIRMAN
M. Stans
CONFIDENTIAL ASST.
A. Chambers
PERSONAL AIDE
K. Talmage
SEC. TO MHS & AC
A. Pinkerton
SEC. TO TALMAGE
F. Thompson
DRIVER
C. Holton
CO-CHAIRMAN
HERITAGE GROUPS
T. Pappas
ASSISTANT
M. Sotirhos
SECRETARY
M. Bighinatti
CO-CHAIRMEN
M. Fisher
L. Firestone
H. Helm
G. Levy
T. Schreiber
J. Rollins
Ms. O. Phipps
EXECUTIVE COMMITTEE
CHAIRMAN
M. Stans
REGIONAL CHAIRMEN
L. Waring - I
P. Wilson - III
J. Jones - IV
D. Wolfsberger - V
W. Liedtke
R. Winchester - VI
K. Dahlberg - VII
K. Brown - VIII
D. Keaton - IX
CONTROLLER
P. Barrick
BOOKKEEPER
J. Hoback
TRANSMITTALS & CONTRIBUTOR RESPONSE
C. Lyeth
CLERK
J. Barbour
ASSISTANT CLERK
P. Fokine
COUNSEL
G. Liddy
SECRETARY
S. Harmony
DEPUTY CHAIRMAN
C. Washburn
AND SEPTEMBER DINNERS
DINNER COORDINATOR &
EXEC. ASST. TO C.L.W.
M. Miller
SECRETARY TO C.L.W.
TREASURER
H. Sloan, Jr.
ASSISTANT
P. Holmes
SECRETARY TO H.W.S.
J. Dannenhauer
SPECIAL PROJECTS
E. Hyde
SPECIAL PROJECTS
E. Hall
STAFF ASSISTANT
T. Washburn
RECEPTIONIST
M. Devlin
REGIONAL & STATE
COORDINATOR
L. Nunn
ASSISTANT
R. Odell
ASSISTANT
J. Chadwell
SECRETARY TO L.N.
Y. Dorminy
SECRETARY TO R.O.
D. Waltman
SECRETARY TO J.C.
VICE CHAIRMEN
SPECIAL GIFTS
(Individual)
D. Hofgren
with
M. Stans
SPECIAL GIFTS
(Groups)
H. Scott
SECRETARY
N. Weed, Jr.
ASSISTANT
B. Byers
SECRETARY AND
RECORD KEEPER
J. Brookshire
ADMINISTRATION
DIRECT MAIL
H. Sloan, Jr.
R. Harty
B. Zapp
C. Dexter
R. Visceglia
G. Olson
C. Terrar

operations of the committee than when Mr. MacGregor was running it?

Mr. ODLE. From all the outward appearances that there were, I think Mr. MacGregor shared equally in the role as campaign director that Mr. Mitchell did.

Mr. THOMPSON. When Mr. MacGregor took over, it appears that the citizens division and the political division were then answerable to Mr. Malek, then the campaign director?

Mr. ODLE. Yes, sir.

Mr. THOMPSON. That was not Mr. Mitchell's situation, was it?

Mr. ODLE. No; it was not. What happened there was to take the two groups of national programs, the two kinds of field programs, the citizens programs could be called horizontal—the field programs and the political programs, the State by State select committees—what you might call vertical programs and they were merged under a second, deputy campaign director.

Mr. THOMPSON. Would it be accurate to say that all department heads reported directly to Mr. Mitchell?

Mr. ODLE. I would say that they reported to Mr. Mitchell through one of the two deputy campaign directors generally. In other words, the director of the political division reported to the campaign director through the deputy. The director of the polling operation reported to the campaign director through the deputy.

Mr. THOMPSON. But the deputies are part of the division themselves, aren't they? So would not the division heads themselves, in effect, report directly to Mr. Mitchell on substantive matters?

Mr. ODLE. Sir, can we clarify who we have got here as division heads? If you mean that Mr. Magruder and Mr. Malek are division heads; yes, sir.

Mr. THOMPSON. All right. What about Mr. Mardian? What about the political division? Mr. Flemming?

Mr. ODLE. Which chart are we looking at right now?

Mr. THOMPSON. I am looking at the first chart.*

Mr. ODLE. The first chart, yes, at that point in time, those five men reported to the campaign director directly. Those five political coordinators. That was before there was a second deputy.

Mr. THOMPSON. All right, that situation was not present when Mr. MacGregor was campaign director?

Mr. ODLE. That is correct.

Mr. THOMPSON. So, in effect, there was more direct control or more direct relationship between the division heads when Mr. Mitchell was director, according to the chart.

Mr. ODLE. In that sense, yes.

Mr. THOMPSON. Normally, were all decision memorandums ultimately going through Mr. Mitchell when he was campaign director?

Mr. ODLE. Yes.

Mr. THOMPSON. Of course, this chart does not reflect any formal relationships with the committee or the members of the committee.

Mr. ODLE. No, it is an organizational chart.

Mr. THOMPSON. Mr. Liddy here is under the finance committee. He was with the Committee To Re-Elect previous to what, December 10?

*Chart, exhibit 5 appears on p. 11.

Mr. ODLE. From sometime in December until approximately April 1, correct.

Mr. THOMPSON. Do you know the reasons for his transfer from the Committee To Re-Elect to the finance committee?

Mr. ODLE. I think there were two reasons, principally. First, was that the finance committee found itself a great deal busier because of this new Federal campaign legislation. The recordkeeping and the work that had to be done of an administrative nature became very great and Mr. Stans felt a full-time counsel was needed at that point in the finance committee. Mr. Liddy found an office on the second floor and he was down there working and it was just kind of a natural thing for him to become this new counsel. In addition to that, I do not think that he and Mr. Magruder were exactly on the best of terms at that point.

Mr. THOMPSON. Was the finance committee physically separated from the Committee To Re-Elect?

Mr. ODLE. Initially everyone occupied one suite. Later on the finance committee remained in that suite and everybody else moved to different floors, and so at that point in time the finance committee did occupy a separate suite.

Mr. THOMPSON. I have no further questions, Mr. Chairman.

Senator ERVIN. Can you tell me, I think it was stated but I did not quite get it, how many men came from the White House staff to the Committee To Re-Elect the President?

Mr. ODLE. Initially, sir?

Senator ERVIN. Yes.

Mr. ODLE. Initially, in May of 1971 there would have been Mr. Magruder, Mr. Flemming, Mr. Sloan, Mr. Porter, myself, and two secretaries.

Senator ERVIN. Who subsequently came from the White House staff to the Committee To Re-Elect the President?

Mr. ODLE. Well, sir, a number of the people we see on those charts did. I could point them out for you.

Senator ERVIN. Suppose you go to the chart and identify the ones who subsequently came from the White House staff to the Committee To Re-Elect the President.

Mr. ODLE. I probably should use this chart.

Mr. Magruder——

Mr. DASH. Identify that chart for us.

Mr. ODLE. I am sorry, this is the July 1 chart. Is that the chart you would like me to review, Senator, the second chart?*

Senator ERVIN. Yes.

Mr. ODLE. Mr. MacGregor was counsel to the President for Congressional Relations, Mr. Flemming, I mentioned before, Mr. LaRue had been a consultant, I had been at the White House, Mr. Faust had been in the scheduling office at the White House, Mr. Timmons was still there, he never was a member of the staff but just exercised sort of supervisory responsibility for the convention. Mr. Shumway had come from the White House as I said earlier, Mr. Porter had come from the White House. Mr. Malek had come from the White House, Mr. Chotiner had come from the White House.

Senator ERVIN. Where does his name appear on the chart?

Mr. ODLE. Pardon?

---

*See exhibit No. 7, p. 19.

Senator ERVIN. The last person.

Mr. ODLE. Mr. Chotiner, he was director of ballot security. Mr. Compitan, one of our regional directors came from the White House. I believe that is all.

Senator ERVIN. Is it correct to say that most of the people in positions of authority, of the highest authority in the Committee To Re-Elect the President, came originally from the White House staff?

Mr. ODLE. Well, the campaign director, his chief deputies certainly did. Most of the people from the finance committee did not, and I would say that among the most divisions that reported to the two deputy campaign directors it is about evenly split.

Senator ERVIN. The head of the committee was former Attorney General John Mitchell, who occupied the office of Attorney General until about March 1972, did he not?

Mr. ODLE. Yes, sir.

Senator ERVIN. And then he became the chairman of the Committee To Re-Elect the President?

Mr. ODLE. Yes, sir.

Senator ERVIN. And you know when he actually assumed supervision of the committee?

Mr. ODLE. He, I believe, resigned as Attorney General in February and came to the committee in March, but he took a vacation in Florida, I do not believe it was until around April that he became involved in the campaign.

Senator ERVIN. Did he have anything to do with the committee prior to the time of his resignation as Attorney General?

Mr. ODLE. Major decision memorandums were sent to him for decision.

Senator ERVIN. Decision memorandums were subject to his approval?

Mr. ODLE. Yes.

Senator ERVIN. Before he left the Attorney General's office?

Mr. ODLE. Yes.

Senator ERVIN. Now, what relationship, if any, did Mr. Bob Haldeman have with the Committee To Re-Elect the President?

Mr. ODLE. No official relationship, of course, but Mr. Haldeman was assistant to the President and he, I know, was interested in what the committee was doing, what its programs were and how it was helping in the reelection of the President.

Senator ERVIN. Did he ever give instructions to anybody on the committee that you know of?

Mr. ODLE. Well, he did not become involved directly in that he had an assistant who worked for him who from time to time, was in touch with members of the committee.

Senator ERVIN. Who was the assistant?

Mr. ODLE. Mr. Gordon Strachan.

Senator ERVIN. Do you know John Dean III?

Mr. ODLE. Yes, sir.

Senator ERVIN. Did he have contacts with the committee from time to time?

Mr. ODLE. I believe that he did.

Senator ERVIN. Who had authority to direct the expenditure of money on the Committee To Re-Elect the President?

EXHIBIT NO. 7

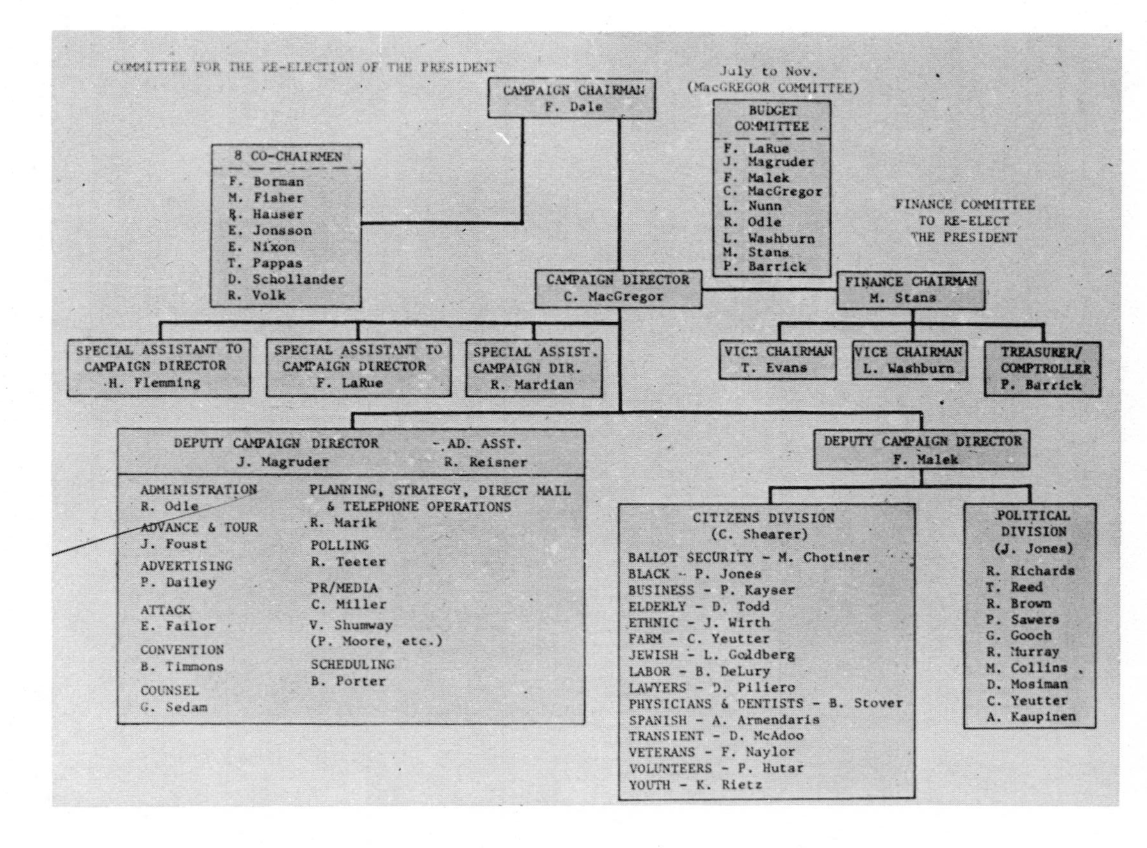
COMMITTEE FOR THE RE-ELECTION OF THE PRESIDENT
July to Nov.
(MacGREGOR COMMITTEE)
CAMPAIGN CHAIRMAN
F. Dale
BUDGET COMMITTEE
F. LaRue
J. Magruder
F. Malek
C. MacGregor
L. Nunn
R. Odle
L. Washburn
M. Stans
P. Barrick
8 CO-CHAIRMEN
F. Borman
M. Fisher
R. Hauser
E. Jonsson
E. Nixon
T. Pappas
D. Schollander
R. Volk
FINANCE COMMITTEE TO RE-ELECT THE PRESIDENT
CAMPAIGN DIRECTOR
C. MacGregor
FINANCE CHAIRMAN
M. Stans
SPECIAL ASSISTANT TO CAMPAIGN DIRECTOR
H. Flemming
SPECIAL ASSISTANT TO CAMPAIGN DIRECTOR
F. LaRue
SPECIAL ASSIST. CAMPAIGN DIR.
R. Mardian
VICE CHAIRMAN
T. Evans
VICE CHAIRMAN
L. Washburn
TREASURER/ COMPTROLLER
P. Barrick
DEPUTY CAMPAIGN DIRECTOR
J. Magruder
AD. ASST.
R. Reisner
ADMINISTRATION
R. Odle
ADVANCE & TOUR
J. Foust
ADVERTISING
P. Dailey
ATTACK
E. Failor
CONVENTION
B. Timmons
COUNSEL
G. Sedam
PLANNING, STRATEGY, DIRECT MAIL & TELEPHONE OPERATIONS
R. Marik
POLLING
R. Teeter
PR/MEDIA
C. Miller
V. Shumway
(P. Moore, etc.)
SCHEDULING
B. Porter
DEPUTY CAMPAIGN DIRECTOR
F. Malek
CITIZENS DIVISION
(C. Shearer)
BALLOT SECURITY - M. Chotiner
BLACK - P. Jones
BUSINESS - P. Kayser
ELDERLY - D. Todd
ETHNIC - J. Wirth
FARM - C. Yeutter
JEWISH - L. Goldberg
LABOR - B. DeLury
LAWYERS - D. Piliero
PHYSICIANS & DENTISTS - B. Stover
SPANISH - A. Armendaris
TRANSIENT - D. McAdoo
VETERANS - F. Naylor
VOLUNTEERS - P. Hutar
YOUTH - K. Rietz
POLITICAL DIVISION
(J. Jones)
R. Richards
T. Reed
R. Brown
P. Sawers
G. Gooch
R. Murray
M. Collins
D. Mosiman
C. Yeutter
A. Kaupinen

Mr. ODLE. Basically, of course, the budget committee, and then various divisional managers could, within the confines of that which had been approved by the budget committee, authorize things. I authorized for most of the staff members reimbursement for travel expenses and that sort of thing. Ultimately it would have been the deputy campaign director, campaign director and the finance chairman.

Senator ERVIN. As I understand from your testimony, Mr. Kalmbach was on the Committee To Re-Elect the President prior——

Mr. ODLE. Sir, there were two finance committees. When Mr. Stans resigned as Secretary of Commerce he came to the committee. There was a Finance Committee for the Re-Election of the President. Mr. Kalmbach was associate chairman of that committee. Then as the April 7 deadline approached at the time when the new legislation went into effect, Mr. Stans, I believe, was anxious that a new committee begin with a fresh start and I do not believe Mr. Kalmbach served as an officer of that new committee which was known as the Finance Committee To Re-Elect the President.

Senator ERVIN. There was no association between the Committee To Re-Elect the President and the Republican National Committee was there?

Mr. ODLE. Well, technically, no. In advance of the convention, but most everybody at the Republican National Committee was anxious that the President be reelected and obviously there was a great deal of work back and forth.

Senator ERVIN. But they were in effect separate organizations?

Mr. ODLE. Oh, yes, sir.

Senator ERVIN. Now, did Mr. Magruder have any authority to direct anyone to disburse funds?

Mr. ODLE. Yes.

Senator ERVIN. Can you tell me which members of the Committee To Re-Elect the President had such authority?

Mr. ODLE. Well, you would have—let me start explaining it this way. Any one of the directors and in any one of these various divisions had the responsibility to initiate requests for expenditures of funds and they would pass up through the deputies and up to the campaign director.

Senator ERVIN. And the actual authorization for expenditure did not come from the heads of divisions, however? They merely made the requests though, the recommendations?

Mr. ODLE. I would say, Senator, a little of each quite honestly. Let us say, for example, that the director of one of these various divisions wanted to purchase a hundred briefcases for his 50 State chairmen and vice chairmen to put materials in for their programing. He would theoretically fill out a check request form and that would go to his divisional head and then possibly, if I were involved in that, to the treasurer's office and the check would be written.

Senator ERVIN. Now, who had authority to direct the outlay of substantial sums of money? I would like to have all of the names if you can give it to us.

Mr. ODLE. Well, I really cannot answer that. I really do not know, Senator.

Senator Ervin. Mr. Hugh Sloan was the treasurer of the finance committee, was he not?

Mr. ODLE. Yes, sir.

Senator ERVIN. And he was the man who actually disbursed sums when substantial sums were called for, did he not?

Mr. ODLE. As I understand, sir.

Senator ERVIN. Do you know what control Mr. Stans had over the disbursement of funds?

Mr. ODLE. Mr. Stans was the finance chairman.

Senator ERVIN. In the normal course the finance chairman would be concerned with the collection of campaign contributions. Did he have authority, any authority in respect to the disbursement of them?

Mr. ODLE. Ultimately, I think that authority would be his. If I were to speculate on how much he used the authority that would just be purely speculation on my part.

Senator ERVIN. What about Mr. Mitchell?

Mr. ODLE. Well, Mr. Mitchell would not have disbursed any money, because he had no money, I mean, he had no custody of any money.

Senator ERVIN. Did he have authority or did he exercise authority to direct expenditure of funds?

Mr. ODLE. Yes; I think with Mr. Stans he would have had authority to directly disburse funds. Whether or not he exercised or not would be pure speculation.

Senator ERVIN. What about Mr. Jeb Stuart Magruder?

Mr. ODLE. Magruder. I would think in his capacity as deputy campaign director he would have.

Senator ERVIN. How many employees do you say the Committee To Re-Elect the President had on the books at the time?

Mr. ODLE. Over 400.

Senator ERVIN. Well, I would like to state that so far as I know, the committee has no evidence to contradict the assertion that the overwhelming majority of the men and women who worked on the Committee To Re-Elect the President were law abiding, conscientious citizens, and also would like to say as far as I know, that the statement of Senator Baker to the effect that we have no information thus far that either the Democratic National Committee or the Republican National Committee had any personnel who had allegedly committed any wrongs or alleged unethical action, in fairness I commend that statement of Senator Baker.

Senator Baker.

Senator BAKER. Mr. Chairman, thank you very much. I think counsel has done a very thorough job of inquiring of the witness of the details of the CRP organizational chart during relevant times in the 1972 Presidential campaign. I will not burden these proceedings by trying to elaborate on them or to extend into other areas, but there are other areas, Mr. Odle, that we would like to talk to you about, and I understand that you are agreeable to returning to this committee so that we might discuss other aspects of your knowledge of other matters.

Mr. ODLE. Absolutely.

Senator BAKER. With that understanding, then, and without implying any sinister purpose, but rather with the full understanding that you will return, there are other questions on other matters that

I want to discuss with you later but I will forego that so that we can continue with the description of the organization of the Committee To Re-Elect the President.

Senator ERVIN. Senator Talmadge.

Senator TALMADGE. Mr. Odle, you may be seated, I have only two or three very brief questions.

Are you aware of any actual political campaign experience in Mr. Magruder's background?

Mr. ODLE. Yes, sir, I believe he was involved in the 1968 campaign in southern California.

Senator TALMADGE. How about Mr. Sloan?

Mr. ODLE. Yes, sir, he was involved in the national finance committee in 1968 in New York.

Senator TALMADGE. How about Mr. Mardian?

Mr. ODLE. Bob Mardian. Yes, he was, I cannot remember his exact title. He was very actively involved, I believe in the 1968 campaign.

Senator TALMADGE. Mr. Flemming?

Mr. ODLE. Yes, Mr. Flemming was, too. He was one of the regional directors of the 1968 campaign. He also was active in Virginia politics. He was elected in Virginia.

Senator TALMADGE. Mr. Porter?

Mr. ODLE. I do not know. I do not think so.

Senator TALMADGE. Was that political activity of the gentleman you mentioned similar to the committee organization that you had in the Committee To Re-Elect the President?

Mr. ODLE. Did they do similar things?

Senator TALMADGE. Yes; was the election experience in previous campaigns similar to what you had?

Mr. ODLE. Some of them were. In the cases of Mr. Flemming and Mr. Mardian, yes, in the case of Mr. Magruder, I do not think so.

Senator TALMADGE. You testified in response to a question, that this has little relationship, if any, between the Committee To Re-Elect the President and the Republican National Committee. In view of that fact would it be fair to say that the Committee To Re-Elect the President was in fact the campaign instrument solely under the control of the President and his top White House staff?

Mr. ODLE. I would say that the Committee for the Re-Election of the President was formed exclusively to reelect the President. It had that as its one concern and its one goal.

Senator TALMADGE. Since there was no cooperation between the——

Mr. ODLE. Oh, yes, sir; there was close cooperation between the two.

Senator TALMADGE. I thought you stated in response to a previous question there was very little cooperation.

Mr. ODLE. I meant, what I think I said and what I hoped to say was there was no technical or legal relationship between the two. It eventually would have been improper but I also said I think that everybody at the National Committee was doing everything they could for the President and that, in fact there were relationships between the two committees.

Senator TALMADGE. Why was it necessary to have two committees then?

Mr. ODLE. Because, the President was but a candidate for the nomination prior to the convention. Now I do not think there was any, there was very much doubt that the President would triumph but there was, there was a distinct possibility of a challenge from Congressman McCloskey and challenge from Congressman Ashbrook and there were contradictions. I do not think it would have been proper for a body to work for a candidate, for President Nixon with two other challengers.

Senator TALMADGE. Was there any doubt as to his nomination?

Mr. ODLE. We hoped not. We were working so it would not be, but if you recall we were faced with—we were looking back at a situation, we were looking back at Senator McCarthy's challenge to President Johnson in 1968 in New Hampshire and how effective that challenge was.

Senator TALMADGE. It has been my experience, it is difficult enough to keep one campaign committee straight. When you have two in the field, it only complicates the problem. I repeat the question. You have testified that a multiplicity of people came from the White House direct to the Committee for the Re-Election of the President. Is it fair to say that that committee was set up, organized, and directed from the White House?

Mr. ODLE. I would say this: That I would say that those people who were at the White House had influence over the committee, they gave it direction, they assisted it but the campaign director of course was not at the White House, he came from the Justice Department. And so—[laughter]—I do not mean to try to get around your question, Senator, I am just saying that it was not exclusively a White House vehicle, I do not believe.

Senator TALMADGE. There was no doubt as to where the ultimate authority lay in that committee was there?

Mr. ODLE. No, sir.

Senator TALMADGE. Thank you, Mr. Chairman.

Senator ERVIN. Senator Gurney.

Senator GURNEY. Thank you, Mr. Chairman.

Mr. Odle, pursuing the line of questioning that Senator Talmadge was engaged in, do you know whether at any time the Committee To Re-Elect ever received any instruction from Robert Dole, the chairman of the Republican National Committee?

Mr. ODLE. Well, Senator Dole was actively involved, of course, in the campaign and I know he worked very closely with Mr. Mitchell and Mr. MacGregor. I do not know that Mr. Dole, Senator Dole would instruct Mr. Mitchell or Mr. Mitchell would instruct Senator Dole but they certainly worked together.

Senator GURNEY. But he was not actively involved in the Committee To Re-Elect the President?

Mr. ODLE. No, sir, he was chairman of the Republican National Committee.

Senator GURNEY. Do you know whether any Republican National Committee people were brought over to the Committee To Re-Elect the President?

Mr. ODLE. Yes, sir, there were people from the National Committee working at the committee in later stages.

Senator GURNEY. Do you recall how many?

Mr. ODLE. I do not think a great number, I would say less than 10.

Senator GURNEY. Do you recall what positions they had?

Mr. ODLE. To the best of my knowledge, they were working in the political field.

Senator GURNEY. Do you recall whether any people who were key people on the Committee To Re-Elect the President had ever been public officeholders before?

Mr. ODLE. Well, Mr. MacGregor, of course, was. He was a Congressman from Minnesota.

Senator GURNEY. Aside from him.

Mr. ODLE. Mr. Flemming was, I think, the first Republican ever elected to the Alexandria Council. Mr. Mardian has been active in Arizona and California politics. I don't know that he has been elected. I don't see any other names I recognize.

Senator GURNEY. Was the Committee To Re-Elect the President involved in any other political campaigns in 1972, the reelection of Republicans, other than the campaign to reelect the President?

Mr. ODLE. It certainly did what it could, I believe, to be of assistance.

Senator GURNEY. Well, could you amplify that? Did it directly involve itself in any other Republican campaigns?

Mr. ODLE. Well, I know that when Mr. Flemming became specia assistant to the campaign director after July, he actively worked with the Senate and House campaign committees, I believe, in support of other Congressmen, Republican candidates for high office.

Senator GURNEY. What did he do?

Mr. ODLE. I am not familiar, sir, with the specific activities.

Senator GURNEY. Well, were there any other—can you describe the policy meetings of the Committee To Re-Elect the President, where decisions were made what to do about the campaign, or discussions were had about the campaign?

Mr. ODLE. Sir, there was a strategy board. I did not attend those meetings.

Senator GURNEY. Who served on the strategy board?

Mr. ODLE. Well, there was Mr. Magruder, there was, I believe, Mr. Clifford Miller from California. I think Mr. Daly, I didn't go to the meetings and I can't remember all the people who did.

Senator GURNEY. Well, wasn't Mr. Mitchell involved in the policy meetings?

Mr. ODLE. I don't believe he went to those sessions. I believe those were brought to him in the forms of memorandums.

Senator GURNEY. These are the only people that you know that engaged in any policy meetings?

Mr. ODLE. Well, those are the ones I can remember right now off the tip of my tongue who went to those. I think there were strategy meetings.

Senator GURNEY. How was strategy disseminated from these policy meetings?

Mr. ODLE. Sir, that was not my area. I am sorry, I can't answer that.

Senator GURNEY. Did you ever receive any instructions from anybody in the White House during your service on the Committee To Re-Elect?

Mr. ODLE. I talked from time to time to Mr. Strachan, who was the White House liaison. He made some suggestions and ideas. I believe he said at one time the switchboard was overloaded and overburdened and he had trouble getting in, would I please hire another telephone operator. That was the only instruction I remember. There may have been others.

Senator GURNEY. What was the nature of your discussions with him other than the switchboard?

Mr. ODLE. Well, just general things relating to my own activities. I was in charge of personnel and I was in charge of volunteers, and things like that.

Senator GURNEY. Were your conversations in the nature of a report to him?

Mr. ODLE. No, not really. We provided on several occasions reports and copies of memorandums to Mr. Strachan so he would know what was going on.

Senator GURNEY. Did you ever see, in the course of your duties, White House personnel in the Committee To Re-Elect office?

Mr. ODLE. Oh, yes.

Senator GURNEY. Who were they?

Mr. ODLE. Well, various people from the White House would come over into the committee from time to time. The committee was there for 2 years. The President came over one night and shook hands. There were a number of White House officials that came to the committee from time to time.

Senator GURNEY. Who made frequent visits?

Mr. ODLE. There was a convention strategy group that was looking into the convention that met at the——

Senator GURNEY. Who were they?

Mr. ODLE. It was made up of representatives of the Republican National Committee, the committee, and——

Senator GURNEY. I am talking about White House people.

Mr. ODLE. The White House people. That is what I was going to get to. Mr. Timmons came over from time to time.

Senator GURNEY. Anybody else in connection with the convention?

Mr. ODLE. Mr. Carruthers, Mr. Goode.

Senator GURNEY. What other people came over from time to time?

Mr. ODLE. I just can't remember right now, Senator, exactly who it was who came to the committee from the White House. It was a very busy time.

Senator GURNEY. Well, did you ever see Mr. Haldeman in the office to Re-elect?

Mr. ODLE. Only once. That was when the President came to shake hands with staff members.

Senator GURNEY. And what about Mr. Ehrlichman?

Mr. ODLE. I never—I saw him there once.

Senator GURNEY. Do you know what his mission was at that time?

Mr. ODLE. No.

Senator GURNEY. Or did you just see him come in?

Mr. ODLE. Yes, sir, I just saw him.

Senator GURNEY. And Mr. Dean? Did you ever see him come there?

Mr. ODLE. Yes, I saw Mr. Dean a couple of times.

Senator GURNEY. Do you know what his purposes were when he visited?

Mr. ODLE. No, I do not.

Senator GURNEY. Do you know anything about the surveillance operations that may have been conducted by the Committee To Re-Elect the President?

Mr. ODLE. Absolutely not.

Senator GURNEY. Do you know anything about any of the sabotage operations that may have been conducted by the Committee To Re-Elect the President?

Mr. ODLE. Only what I have read in the newspapers.

Senator GURNEY. I have no further questions.

Senator ERVIN. Senator Inouye?

Senator INOUYE. Thank you, Mr. Chairman.

Mr. Odle, this morning's Washington Post suggests that Mr. Charles Colson organized at least 30 groups of supporters of President Nixon to "attack" network news correspondents through write-in, telephone, and telegram campaigns to their local stations. I know that one of your committee charts lists an E. Failer and shows that his area of responsibility is designated as "attack." Who is Mr. E. Failer and what was he?

Mr. ODLE. Mr. Edward Failer was basically, as the chart suggests, in the attack operation. The idea there was, as I understand it, and I was not close to it. The idea was to see what the opposition candidate was saying that day or that week to get an idea what his line was. what his pitch was that day and then to mobilize some of the other campaign activities against that, to criticize them, in effect, to say, no, you are wrong, Senator, it ought to be this way.

That was the basic idea. For example, he would maybe talk to a couple of his surrogates, who were members of the Cabinet and others who were speaking up for the President around the country. He would say, look, maybe we ought to use this line this week in attacking Senator McGovern. Or then he might go to the press office and say, maybe we should put out a press release doing thus and so.

That generally is my idea of what he was involved in.

Senator INOUYE. He was not involved in the attack of news correspondents?

Mr. ODLE. Well, not to my knowledge.

Senator INOUYE. Mr. Odle, press reports have indicated that you participated in the destruction of committee records following the June 17 break-in at the Democratic national headquarters. What was your part, if any, in the destruction of these records?

Mr. ODLE. I am glad you brought that up, Senator, because I appreciate the chance to respond to that. There was a story in the newspapers that I shredded documents the Sunday after the Watergate. In point of fact, I was not even in the District of Columbia the Sunday after the Watergate. How that story got there, I do not know. But I did not even enter Washington, D.C., that day.

Now, there was another report later on and that report said that I made a file search and then shredded documents. Again in point of fact, as administrative officer of the reelection committee, the agents from the FBI would come to me from time to time and they would ask me for various documents. Initially, they wanted Mr. McCord's W–4 forms and all sorts of documents that the committee had. And I did search files in response to those legitimate requests from the U.S. Attorney and the FBI. I then handed over those documents to the

FBI. I did not shred one document in relation to this campaign, in relation to any of these things.

Senator INOUYE. Did you have a shredding machine in your office?

Mr. ODLE. No, sir.

Senator INOUYE. Where was the shredding machine?

Mr. ODLE. There were shredding machines located on most of the floors, in a convenient point.

Senator INOUYE. As administrative officer, you were not involved in any shredding?

Mr. ODLE. I did not shred; no, sir, I was not. I did not go around after the Watergate break-in and participate in what was termed a housecleaning. I did not do that.

Senator INOUYE. Mr. Alfred Baldwin stated that he delivered copies of "bugged conversations" to the committee offices. Were you ever the recipient of reports of bugged conversations?

Mr. ODLE. Absolutely not. If you look back at that, what happened was that Mr. Baldwin testified that he at one point had sent memorandums from Mr. McCord, the security director, to me about office security, and that is quite true. And I have turned all of those over to the grand jury, to the Democratic National Committee, to Common Cause, to just about everybody else that asked for them.

He also testified that he turned over convention memos, that Mr. Baldwin saw convention memos. But somehow, that got garbled and when it came out, it came out in the press that for some reason, Mr. Baldwin took over logs to me and to other individuals.

That is absolutely untrue and as Mr. McCord's deposition shows, what really happened was that he wrote Mr. Liddy's name on that log and brought it to the building.

Senator INOUYE. Were you in any other way involved in bugging activities?

Mr. ODLE. Absolutely not.

Senator INOUYE. Is it true that you hired Mr. McCord?

Mr. ODLE. Yes, it is.

Senator INOUYE. Were you aware of his activities on June 17?

Mr. ODLE. I was not. I first heard that there was a burglary on Saturday afternoon, after I finished a meeting about—oh, I do not know, midafternoon. And somebody came by the door and said, "Have you heard there's been a burglary at the Democratic National Committee?" I said, just to some people who were in that meeting, not at that meeting, they were just there, "That could never happen here, because I have this guy working for me named Jim McCord, and he has got this place really tight and all I can say is I am glad McCord works for me."

And then, of course, it became apparent what had happened. But no, sir, I did not.

Senator INOUYE. Then you were not aware of his associations with Mr. Liddy or——

Mr. ODLE. No sir, I was not.

Senator INOUYE. I notice also listed there is a John Caulfield, John J. Caulfield?

Mr. ODLE. Yes, sir.

Senator INOUYE. Do you know Mr. Caulfield?

Mr. ODLE. Yes, sir, I do. He was the security director of the 1968 campaign. He recommended Mr. McCord.

96-296 O—73——bk. 1—3

Senator INOUYE. Press reports indicate that Mr. Caulfield tried to pressure Mr. McCord to remain silent on the Watergate break-in. My question is during what period was Mr. Caulfield employed by your committee?

Mr. ODLE. Very briefly, perhaps a month, and it was in the summer of 1972, I believe, perhaps in May—perhaps in April, it was.

Senator INOUYE. Did he, to your knowledge, try to pressure Mr. McCord in behalf of your committee?

Mr. ODLE. Pressure him?

Senator INOUYE. Pressure him to remain silent?

Mr. ODLE. Well, I just have no knowledge of that. Not to my knowledge at all. I haven't seen Mr. Caulfield since last summer.

Senator INOUYE. Would you describe the functions of your political division?

Mr. ODLE. Yes, sir, the function of the political division was to divide the States among the various political coordinators, or, as they become known later, the regional directors, and to set up State reelect committees in each State and to monitor the success of those committees.

Senator INOUYE. We hear much about dirty tricks and sabotage. Where did it come in your chart, or did it come in your chart?

Mr. ODLE. Sir, unfortunately, the chartmaker, when he made those charts, was not aware of those things.

Senator INOUYE. Were you aware of those things?

Mr. ODLE. No, sir, I was not.

Senator INOUYE. Mr. Chairman, I request an order to place in evidence a list of all the employees of the Committee To Re-Elect the President and the finance committee and the dates of their service and their prior employment.

Senator ERVIN. Would you furnish the committee that?

Mr. ODLE. Yes, sir, I think the staff has already requested it and I think it has been turned over, but if not, I will be glad to do that.

Senator INOUYE. Thank you.

Senator ERVIN. I understand if you have not supplied it to the committee, you will.

Mr. ODLE. If we haven't, we will, yes, sir.*

Senator ERVIN. Senator Weicker.

Senator WEICKER. Thank you, Mr. Chairman.

Mr. Odle, you refer to the fact that you were not in Washington, D.C., on June 18, is that correct?

Mr. ODLE. Um-hum.

Senator WEICKER. Did you participate in the emptying of Mr. Magruder's desk with Robert Reisner on June 17?

Mr. ODLE. Yes, sir, Mr. Magruder asked Mr. Reisner and myself to take certain things home over the weekend, because at the time, it appeared that he was concerned for the security of them. My best recollection is that I took home a file folder and he took home some other file folders and brought them back the following Monday or sometime.

Senator WEICKER. Would you be good enough to describe to the committee as to how you were alerted on June 17, exactly what you

---

*See p. 437.

did in responding to the alert, and your activities within the offices themselves and when you left—on June 17?

Mr. ODLE. Yes; my greatest concern, first of all—first of all, when we found out that McCord was involved in this thing, I was extremely concerned. I mean, here was our security director in jail because he had gone into somebody's office in the middle of the night. My first thought was that I was suddenly in charge of the guard force, I was suddenly in charge, directly and personally, in charge of all the office security. I remember one of the things I did that day was to call the security supervisor to make certain that we would have a guard come in that night to relieve the day guard. I was very concerned about that.

I remember thinking about what we would do to replace Mr. McCord. We needed somebody in that capacity.

It was a very serious day. I mean, when you find a man that you trust and respect is in jail for doing something and that man worked for you, it is quite a serious thing.

Is there some other area that you are interested in?

Senator WEICKER. Well, now, first of all who requested that you come over to the committee?

Mr. ODLE. I had been there, Senator. I was at a meeting that morn ing that started about 9 a.m. and ended in midafternoon. I had been there.

Senator WEICKER. Now, who made the suggestion that Mr. Magruder's desk be emptied?

Mr. ODLE. Well, I don't—first of all, I am not exactly sure of the chronology of events. I don't believe that anybody made the suggestion that the desk be emptied, although he expressed concern over the telephone from California——

Senator WEICKER. Who was "he"?

Mr. ODLE. He was Magruder.

Senator WEICKER. What time did he express concern?

Mr. ODLE. It would have been sometime late that afternoon.

Senator WEICKER. Did you talk personally with Magruder?

Mr. ODLE. Yes.

Senator WEICKER. Will you give the committee your best recollection of that conversation?

Mr. ODLE. My best recollection is that he was extremely concerned that we might be subject to similar activities, that there might be retaliation, that he was concerned for the security of the office building and the files and the papers, and he wanted certain things to be taken home over the weekend.

As I remember it, Mr. Reisner took home a lot of advertising matters, I believe.

Senator WEICKER. Well, if we can stop there for a minute. Was Mr. Reisner on the phone also?

Mr. ODLE. For a time he was, for a time I was, but my best recollection of it was I went out of the room for a while, I think.

Senator WEICKER. Did Mr. Magruder say, "clean out my whole desk"?

Mr. ODLE. No; I don't believe he did, because I don't believe that was done.

Senator WEICKER. Then he must have specified what was to be cleaned out?

Mr. ODLE. I believe he did. I don't believe he did that to me. I believe he may have. I just don't remember the exact chronology of all the things that happened that day.

All I know is the way it ended up is that I had a file and Mr. Reisner had some files and we brought them back the next week.

Senator WEICKER. But did you know what was in the files?

Mr. ODLE. No, sir, I did not.

Senator WEICKER. So in other words, it was a general, not a specific order, that was given to clean out the whole desk; is that correct? I mean, how would you know that you cleaned out the right things?

Mr. ODLE. I didn't take it, sir. I believe Mr. Reisner took that and then he gave it to me.

Senator WEICKER. And, you did not clean out Magruder's desk?

Mr. ODLE. No; I did not.

Senator WEICKER. Your participation in this matter was to receive files——

Mr. ODLE. A file.

Senator WEICKER. A file from Mr. Reisner?

Mr. ODLE. I believe, yes.

Senator WEICKER. Then what did you do with that file?

Mr. ODLE. I put it in my briefcase, I took some files from my own desk, that I was concerned about their own safety——

Senator WEICKER. What kind of files did you take?

Mr. ODLE. Budget committee files. The various minutes of the sessions that I described earlier. I was concerned for their security and I took them home with me over the weekend.

Senator WEICKER. Now, what did you do when you took this file home?

Mr. ODLE. Just left it at home.

Senator WEICKER. Put it anywhere?

Mr. ODLE. I think I may have put it in the closet or something, I am not exactly certain.

Senator WEICKER. And——

Mr. ODLE. The briefcase, I think I put in the closet.

Senator WEICKER. I beg pardon?

Mr. ODLE. I think I put the briefcase in the closet.

Senator WEICKER. The briefcase with the film in the closet?

Mr. ODLE. Yes.

Senator WEICKER. Then, what happened to the file?

Mr ODLE. Then, on Monday I returned it.

Senator WEICKER. You returned the file?

Mr. ODLE. Yes.

Senator WEICKER. To whom?

Mr. ODLE. To Mr. Magruder.

Senator WEICKER. To Mr. Magruder himself?

Mr. ODLE. To the best of my recollection, yes.

Senator WEICKER. Now, Mr. Odle, a few more questions. You mentioned the fact that you came into contact with Mr. Strachan from time to time.

Mr. ODLE. Yes, sir.

Senator WEICKER. Could you give me an elaboration of what from time to time means.

Mr. ODLE. I talked to Mr. Strachan probably two or three times a week, maybe two times a week. It is hard to say, sir.

Senator WEICKER. Did Mr. Strachan participate rather actively in matters over at the Committee To Re-Elect the President?

Mr. ODLE. Yes, sir.

Senator WEICKER. Can you tell me why, what his specific mission was?

Mr. ODLE. Mr. Haldeman obviously was worried a lot with a lot of other things besides the campaign. He was the Chief of Staff at the White House and a very busy man working on Government substantive policies and he was assisting the President. Mr. Strachan was there to devote himself more to what was going on politically so if Mr. Haldeman wanted to be aware of what was going on politically and simply asked Mr. Strachan, Mr. Strachan was simply the eyes and ears, you might say.

Senator WEICKER. I beg pardon?

Mr. ODLE. I suppose you might say he was the eyes and ears of the committee.

Senator WEICKER. Mr. Strachan was the eyes and ears of who?

Mr. ODLE. Mr. Haldeman. He was liaison to the committee.

Senator WEICKER. So any matters that went on in the Committee To Re-Elect the President, would it be fair to say they were reported back to Mr. Haldeman by Mr. Strachan?

Mr. ODLE. Well, that was Mr. Strachan's role which was to try to find out all of the things that were going on at the committee and make Mr. Haldeman aware of them, yes.

Senator WEICKER. Did Mr. Strachan attend the strategy sessions?

Mr. ODLE. I think that he may have, yes. I did not attend those meetings. It is hard for me to say exactly who did.

Senator WEICKER. All right.

Now, Mr. Odle, did you ever see in the hallways of the Committee To Re-Elect the President electronic equipment which would be electronic equipment for either bugging or debugging?

Mr. ODLE. Mr. McCord at least had a machine for a while which was a defensive measure, as I understand it, that went around to check for electronic eavesdropping in our building and I believe I have seen that, yes.

Senator WEICKER. So you did see this equipment which you believed to be debugging equipment, is that correct?

Mr. ODLE. I am pretty positive of it, yes.

Senator WEICKER. That it was debugging?

Mr. ODLE. Well, it was not debugging, it was collecting for countermeasures, yes.

Senator WEICKER. And this equipment was quite visible out there in the hall?

Mr. ODLE. I do not believe, sir, it was in the hall. It was a portable unit that I believe was in his office at one point, sir.

Senator WEICKER. Now, with respect to the citizens division, is it not true that Fred Malek became the head of that division between March and June?

Mr. ODLE. He exercised supervisory control over the citizens division. It was by no means a full-time occupation.

Senator WEICKER. When you say full-time occupation, do you use as a criteria his appearance on the payroll, is this what causes you to indicate he was not full time?

Mr. ODLE. No, I would use the criterion, hours spent.

Senator WEICKER. In hours spent he was part-time capacity?

Mr. ODLE. Very much so.

Senator WEICKER. You say he spent part of the time between the Committee To Re-Elect the President and part of his time at the White House?

Mr. ODLE. There was a guest office that he used from time to time when he was at the committee and I would say from September 1, when he resigned at the White House and came to the committee he spent most of his time at the White House.

Senator WEICKER. Most of his time at the White House, but also some time at the committee.

Mr. ODLE. Yes, sir.

Senator WEICKER. Mr. Odle, were Jean Roberts and Vicki Chern secretaries to Jeb Magruder?

Mr. ODLE. Yes, sir.

Senator WEICKER. Was Sylvia Panarites a secretary for both Bob Reisner and yourself?

Mr. ODLE. She was the receptionist and she worked for both of us, that is correct.

Senator WEICKER. She did work for both of you?

Mr. ODLE. Yes, that is correct.

Senator WEICKER. Now, under the advertising section is it not true that the November Group was a New York corporation operating out of the Committee To Re-Elect the President with Peter Dailey at the head and Paul Muller as treasurer and Glenn Sedam as secretary, is that correct?

Mr. ODLE. I can testify to the first two. I did not realize that Mr. Sedam was secretary.

Senator WEICKER. Now, just two more questions. In Ken Reitz' function here which I believe is listed as youth, was Tom Bell one of his assistants? Do you know his table of organization of people who worked for him?

Mr. ODLE. Yes, Mr. Bell was one of Mr. Reitz' assistants and was one of the first to join his staff.

Senator WEICKER. Was Bob Podesta one of his assistants?

Mr. ODLE. Yes, sir.

Senator WEICKER. Were Marilyn Johnson and Connie Cudd his secretaries?

Mr. ODLE. Yes, sir.

Senator WEICKER. Did Ken Smith and Eve Auchincloss work for Reitz on the speakers bureau?

Mr. ODLE. I am not sure of the speakers bureau. They worked for Mr. Jigg.

Senator WEICKER. Was George Gorton college coordinator under Reitz?

Mr. ODLE. Yes, sir.

Senator WEICKER. Was Angella Miller in charge of Nixonettes?

Mr. ODLE. Yes, sir.

Senator WEICKER. Did Angela Harris work on press for Reitz?

Mr. ODLE. She was in the press office but she spent most of the time working on youth activities.

Senator WEICKER. Now, in conclusion, I have prepared a chart,* Mr. Odle, which fills in some additional slots, and I wonder if you

* See exhibit No. 8, p. 33.

EXHIBIT NO. 8

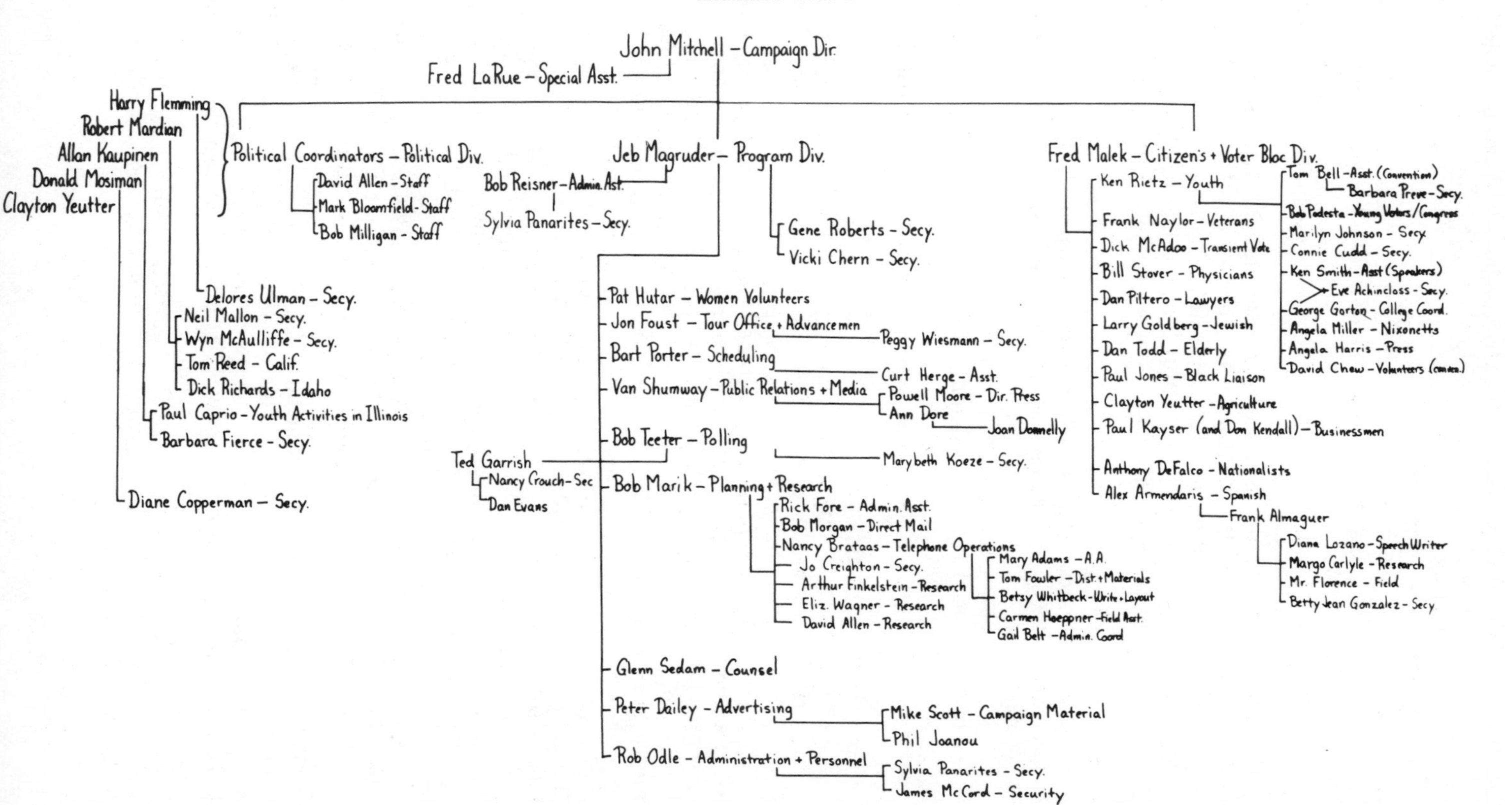
John Mitchell – Campaign Dir.
Fred LaRue – Special Asst.
Harry Flemming
Robert Mardian
Allan Kaupinen
Donald Mosiman
Clayton Yeutter
Political Coordinators – Political Div.
David Allen – Staff
Mark Bloomfield – Staff
Bob Milligan – Staff
Delores Ulman – Secy.
Neil Mallon – Secy.
Wyn McAulliffe – Secy.
Tom Reed – Calif.
Dick Richards – Idaho
Paul Caprio – Youth Activities in Illinois
Barbara Fierce – Secy.
Diane Copperman – Secy.
Jeb Magruder – Program Div.
Bob Reisner – Admin. Asst.
Sylvia Panarites – Secy.
Gene Roberts – Secy.
Vicki Chern – Secy.
Pat Hutar – Women Volunteers
Jon Foust – Tour Office + Advancemen
Peggy Wiesmann – Secy.
Bart Porter – Scheduling
Curt Herge – Asst.
Van Shumway – Public Relations + Media
Powell Moore – Dir. Press
Ann Dore
Joan Donnelly
Bob Teeter – Polling
Marybeth Koeze – Secy.
Ted Garrish
Nancy Crouch – Sec
Dan Evans
Bob Marik – Planning + Research
Rick Fore – Admin. Asst.
Bob Morgan – Direct Mail
Nancy Brataas – Telephone Operations
Jo Creighton – Secy.
Arthur Finkelstein – Research
Eliz. Wagner – Research
David Allen – Research
Mary Adams – A.A.
Tom Fowler – Dist. + Materials
Betsy Whitbeck – Write + Layout
Carmen Hoeppner – Field Asst.
Gail Belt – Admin. Coord.
Glenn Sedam – Counsel
Peter Dailey – Advertising
Mike Scott – Campaign Material
Phil Joanou
Rob Odle – Administration + Personnel
Sylvia Panarites – Secy.
James McCord – Security
Fred Malek – Citizen's + Voter Bloc Div.
Ken Rietz – Youth
Tom Bell – Asst. (Convention)
Barbara Preve – Secy.
Bob Podesta – Young Voters/Congress
Marilyn Johnson – Secy.
Connie Cudd – Secy.
Ken Smith – Asst (Speakers)
Eve Achincloss – Secy.
George Gorton – College Coord.
Angela Miller – Nixonetts
Angela Harris – Press
David Chew – Volunteers (conven.)
Frank Naylor – Veterans
Dick McAdoo – Transient Vote
Bill Stover – Physicians
Dan Piltero – Lawyers
Larry Goldberg – Jewish
Dan Todd – Elderly
Paul Jones – Black Liaison
Clayton Yeutter – Agriculture
Paul Kayser (and Don Kendall) – Businessmen
Anthony DeFalco – Nationalists
Alex Armendaris – Spanish
Frank Almaguer
Diana Lozano – Speech Writer
Margo Carlyle – Research
Mr. Florence – Field
Betty Jean Gonzalez – Secy.

might not go ahead and take a look at this chart and tell me whether it is accurate and if it takes time to do that. Mr. Chairman, I would be perfectly glad to go ahead and have Mr. Odle look at it and for the record, report back to the committee.

Senator ERVIN. That is perfectly all right.

Mr. ODLE. I will be glad to go over it right now with you if you like.

Senator WEICKER. I do not want to rush you or have you make any mistakes.

Mr. ODLE. Sure, shall we start and go through it? Mr. Mitchell was campaign director, Mr. LaRue was special assistant. You have the five political coordinators here and that is correct.

Senator ERVIN. It might be helpful for the record when you refer to the person instead of referring then as mister, will you give the names?

Mr. ODLE. All right.

Senator WEICKER. I would be perfectly satisfied, Mr. Chairman, to have Mr. Odle do this at his leisure so he makes sure of each person on the chart.

Mr. ODLE. I have no hesitation.

Senator ERVIN. I understood him to say he can answer the questions about that chart now.

Mr. ODLE. Yes, I have no hesitation of going over it with you if you would like.

Now, Senator, obviously——

Senator ERVIN. It might be, Senator, it might be helpful if he would bring it around over here and put it on the stand and take a ruler and point out things as he sees them.

Mr. ODLE. OK, we have Mr. Mitchell here as campaign director; Mr. LaRue was his assistant, that is correct. We have the five political directors coordinators at that time and that is correct. I believe Diane Copperman did not work for him, the same about Barbara Fierce, she did work for Mr. Caprio, Paul Caprio, sir, I do not believe related to Mr. Kaupman and I thought that he was in the Illinois campaign and Mr. Caprio was the regional director, and he did have Illinois as one of his States so possibly Mr. Caprio did but it was not at the national headquarters, to the best of my knowledge.

Delores Ullman was Mr. Flemming's secretary and did work for Mr. Mardian, and Tom Reed was from California, Dick Richards, I believe, was from Utah, rather than Idaho, but he did report, I think he was one of the political coordinators.

David Allen, Mark Blumfeld were all on that staff. Bob Reisner was administrative assistant to Mr. Magruder but Vicki Chern was really more his secretary than Mr. Magruder's, although she did work for both.

Gene Roberts, Sylvia Panarites, Pat Hutar was in charge of women's volunteers; Jon Foust, this is correct, Peggy Weismann was a secretary, Bart Porter was in charge of scheduling, Van Shumway, public relations and media, Powell Moore, and Ann Dore, Joan Donnelly, yes; they all work for him.

Mr. Herge did work for Mr. Porter. Bob Teeter had these two assistants, Ted Garrish, Dan Evans and Nancy Crouch was the name of the secretary as was Marybeth Koeze.

Bob Marik was in charge of research and planning. Breck Fore was administrative assistant, he later went to the political division. Bob Morgan was in charge of direct mail and answered telephones. David Allen moved from here to here both places so that is correct It may not be correct, I do not know that he did work there. I think that may be incorrect. These people all did report to Nancy Brataas, Mr. Sedam was the counsel.

Senator ERVIN. Pardon me, I think when you say "these people" did report, you should give the names to the reporter because he has to take them down.

Mr. ODLE. Glenn Sedam was counsel, Peter Dailey was in charge of advertising, Mr. Phil Joanou, Mr. Mike Scott, were two people who reported to Mr. Dailey. I was in charge of administration and personnel and these two people did report to me. Sylvia——

Mr. DASH. Which two people did you mean, Mr. Odle? The reporter has to have the names.

Mr. ODLE. Sylvia Panarites and James McCord.

Over the citizens and voter block group Ken Rietz was in charge of youth, he was assisted by Tom Bell, Barbara Preve, Bob Podesta, Marilyn Johnson, Connie Cudd, Ken Smith, Eve Auchincloss, George Gorton, Angella Miller. As I said before, Angela Harris technically was in the press office but she did spend the majority of her time on youth activities. David Chew, Frank Naylor, veterans; Dick McAdoo, transients; Bill Stover, physicians, Dan Piltero, lawyers; Larry Goldberg, Jewish; Dan Todd, elderly; Paul Jones, black; Clayton Yeutter; Paul Kayser, was head of the business operations, Mr. Kendall was the national chairman, Mr. DeFalco was at First Nationalists and he later left the staff, Mr. Armendaris, Spanish; assisted by Frank Almaguer, Margo Carlyse; Florence, I do not remember that name but it is probably correct. Betty Jean Gonzalez, of course, there was, Shearer was over here, too, as well as at the top of the citizens operation.

Senator WEICKER. Thank you, Mr. Odle.

Now, the last question on the subject of advertising, the approving of advertisements, was this done by the Committee To Re-Elect the President or was the final say-so given at the White House?

Mr. ODLE. I think that Mr. Haldeman had an interest in advertising without any question, and I think that in that case that both the campaign director, Mr. Mitchell, or Mr. MacGregor and Mr. Haldeman jointly made decisions on advertising. I would say that was the one area in which he had an interest more than others.

Senator WEICKER. Would you also say that in the area of polling?

Mr. ODLE. Yes, sir.

Senator WEICKER. So this again was a joint matter between Mr. Mitchell and Mr. Haldeman?

Mr. ODLE. There, I would think Mr. Mitchell was the campaign director, he had final authority, I would say that was the second area in which Mr. Haldeman was the most interested. That is my guess, Senator.

Senator WEICKER. Thank you very much, Mr. Chairman.

Senator ERVIN. Senator Baker omitted one question he wished to ask. It is not your turn but since the examination has gotten wider in the field, without objection, I am going to give Senator Baker an opportunity at this time to ask a question which he expected to ask at a subsequent hearing.

Senator BAKER. Senator Montoya has not had an opportunity. I will wait until he has asked questions.

Senator ERVIN. Excuse me, Senator Montoya.

Senator MONTOYA. Thank you, Mr. Chairman.

Mr. Odle, by way of preliminary foundation, will you give us your entire job classification and duties which you perform as head of the administration and personnel?

Mr. ODLE. Yes, sir.

I was basically in charge of office management and that would include procurement of office space, assignment of office space, procurement and assignment of office supplies, installations of office equipment, desks, furniture, telephones, switchboards, all of the kind of things that you would expect one to do in the capacity of office manager. In terms of personnel I was partially responsible for hiring and firing, particularly at the lower levels, secretarial recruitment was one of my jobs, finding secretaries.

Senator MONTOYA. Would that include hiring of secretaries for the directors?

Mr. ODLE. If they requested a secretary, yes.

Senator MONTOYA. Did you hire any secretaries for any of the directors?

Mr. ODLE. What do you mean?

Senator MONTOYA. For instance, Mr. Liddy.

Mr. ODLE. Yes; I did not. Somebody in our operation found, I believe, Mrs. Harmony and she was hired as Mr. Liddy's secretary after Mr. Liddy interviewed her.

Senator MONTOYA. Did you arrange for the interview?

Mr. ODLE. No.

Senator MONTOYA. What about Jeb Magruder's secretary?

Mr. ODLE. No; they came with him from the White House.

Senator MONTOYA. Did you arrange for the allocation of space?

Mr. ODLE. Yes.

Senator MONTOYA. Now, please explain how much space you had at that particular building and was the entire operation under the roof of one building?

Mr. ODLE. At what point in time, Senator, say, in the heat of the campaign?

Senator MONTOYA. Let us say from the time that Mr. Mitchell went onboard as campaign director.

Mr. ODLE. We had a suite on the second floor, we had a suite on the fourth floor. The campaign director had a suite on the fourth floor. We later, after Mr. Mitchell came aboard, took the entire third floor, we took the suite on the fifth floor, the suite on the eighth, the suite on the ninth and suite on the 11th.

Senator MONTOYA. When you speak of suites do you mean the entire floor?

Mr. ODLE. No, sir, we only had one entire floor in that building and everything and that was the third. We had suites from as many as five private offices, say, to 25. That is what I mean when I say suite.

Senator MONTOYA. Where did you have the file room?

Mr. ODLE. What?

Senator MONTOYA. Where did you have the file room?

Mr. ODLE. I do not believe we had a file room, sir.

Senator MONTOYA. Did you have files in different offices?

Mr. ODLE. Yes, sir.

Senator MONTOYA. Now, when you speak of files that I made available to the FBI, why were you called upon to make these files available?

Mr. ODLE. The subpenas from the FBI were directed to Clark MacGregor or his authorized representative, and Maurice Stans or his authorized representative. I turned out to be the authorized representative.

In addition to that, I was the administrative person of the committee, the administrative officer and it was sort of natural since I knew the building fairly well and knew the people fairly well, that I would be asked to assume that role.

Senator MONTOYA. Did you have keys to all these files?

Mr. ODLE. No.

Senator MONTOYA. Did you have keys to the files which you opened for the FBI?

Mr. ODLE. No.

Senator MONTOYA. How did you get those keys?

Mr. ODLE. I did not necessarily open all the files. What I would do is they would ask for certain kinds of information and I would go to the people who had custody of that information and with them try to find it.

Senator MONTOYA. All right, who had custody on that occasion?

Mr. ODLE. Well, many of the files they wanted were financial matters so the custody was maintained by the finance committee and I went to the people in the finance committee to get those files.

Senator MONTOYA. Let us go the Mr. Magruder's desk. You stated you opened his desk pursuant to a telephone call.

Mr. ODLE. No, sir, I did not. I only had a key to Mr. Magruder's desk, I did not open his desk.

Senator MONTOYA. Whose files did you take from whose desks and that you took home?

Mr. ODLE. Mr. Magruder's files, but the desk drawer had been opened by Mr. Reisner, I assume.

Senator MONTOYA. So, was that desk opened most of the time?

Mr. ODLE. No; I do not believe it was. It probably was not when I was there.

Senator MONTOYA. How do you know it was opened by Mr. Reisner?

Mr. ODLE. I do not. I said I suppose. I know I did not open it because I do not have the key.

Senator MONTOYA. Did you have keys on some of the file cabinets?

Mr. ODLE. I had keys to my own file cabinets.

Senator MONTOYA. Did the others?

Mr. ODLE. Other people would have keys to their file cabinets, yes.

Senator MONTOYA. Where were the secret documents filed and in whose office?

Mr. ODLE. Sir, I did not know that there were secret documents.

Senator MONTOYA. Well, you did procure a secret document for the FBI, did you not?

Mr. ODLE. No. No; they wanted things——

Senator MONTOYA. There were certain documents, stated documents, and you were told where those documents were. Is that right?

Mr. ODLE. No; they asked me to produce certain documents as the Senate committee has done and I went around and tried to find them for him.

Senator MONTOYA. Well, then you had availability to most of the files if you went around——

Mr. ODLE. Well, I went to people who had custody of files and asked them if I might have, if they did have this, and——

Senator MONTOYA. All right. Now, what kind of arrangement did you have with Mr. McCord and what was his job classification?

Mr. ODLE. Mr. McCord was hired as security consultant to the committee beginning in October 1971. He was part time and he was to be a part-time security consultant. He then became——

Senator MONTOYA. What did you perceive to be his duty as security consultant?

Mr. ODLE. In the broad range, from the time that he began until—well, he would have, of course, you know, stayed on. A number of areas. To go through them, the physical security of the building. We were concerned——

Senator MONTOYA. Was that his prime duty?

Mr. ODLE. It was his only duty, physical security of the building and the people in it.

Senator MONTOYA. And did you ever pay him any money by way of reimbursement for travel out of Washington?

Mr. ODLE. Once he went to New York to inspect the offices of the November Group and once I believe he went to Chicago to look at our direct mail warehouse. When he came back, I believe he submitted expense vouchers, a weekly expense form. I initialed those, signed them, to reimburse him for his plane fare, and then he would have been paid; yes. That was customary.

Senator MONTOYA. Did you authorize him to go to those places for that specific purpose?

Mr. ODLE. Yes, sir, I authorized him to go to New York to inspect the offices of the November Group, to Chicago to inspect our direct mail warehouse.

Senator MONTOYA. Did he go anywhere else from which he received reimbursement from the committee?

Mr. ODLE. He went to Miami to look at the Hotel Doral, and I suspect he would receive reimbursement for that; yes.

Senator MONTOYA. You had to okay all his reimbursements, did you not?

Mr. ODLE. Theoretically.

Senator MONTOYA. Unless he was paid in cash by some other individual who had available cash for that purpose. Did anyone have such cash available?

Mr. ODLE. Not that I knew of, never.

Senator MONTOYA. Are you aware that any of them, any employee of the CRP, could have disbursed funds for Mr. McCord's travel to other places other than the ones which you have named?

Mr. ODLE. No. I was not and when I read in the newspapers that he had cash, I was very surprised, because the way the system was set up, those things would go through me.

Senator MONTOYA. What kind of work or consultation transpired when Mr. Colson would vis t the committee offices and on how many occasions did he visit?

Mr. ODLE. I do not remember seeing Mr. Colson at the committee, sir.

Senator MONTOYA. Well, are you aware that anyone was in touch with him at the White House at any time?

Mr. ODLE. Yes, sir. People from our committee met with him.

Senator MONTOYA. Did you ever see Mr. Howard Hunt in that particular building?

Mr. ODLE. Sir, I have never seen Mr. Howard Hunt to this day.

Senator MONTOYA. Are you aware that he was in touch with any individuals in the building or the employees of the committee?

Mr. ODLE. I never heard his name, even, until after June 17.

Senator MONTOYA. How long did you keep Mr. McCord on the payroll after the Watergate bugging?

Mr. ODLE. About 1 minute.

Senator MONTOYA. How were you employed to go to the CRP?

Mr. ODLE. I was asked by Mr. Magruder.

Senator MONTOYA. What were you doing at that time?

Mr. ODLE. I was a staff assistant at the White House.

Senator MONTOYA. And where are you now employed?

Mr. ODLE. I am consultant to the committee.

Senator MONTOYA. Were you employed in any other position after the election?

Mr. ODLE. Yes, from May 1st until May 7th, I was a consultant for the Department of Agriculture.

Senator MONTOYA. Who recommended you for this job?

Mr. ODLE. People at the White House.

Senator MONTOYA. Who specifically?

Mr. ODLE. I am not exactly certain who initiated the call over there. I suspect the White House personnel office, which would have done it.

Senator MONTOYA. Did you receive any communiques or any other memoranda which were taken as a result of the bugging of Watergate and the Democratic National Committee?

Mr. ODLE. Never.

Senator MONTOYA. Were you aware that any of this might have been stored in the building over which you were the administrator?

Mr. ODLE. No, sir; I was not.

Senator MONTOYA. Did you ever discuss with Sally Harmony any of the memos which she typed for Mr. Liddy relating directly to the Watergate?

Mr. ODLE. No, sir; I did not and have not.

Senator MONTOYA. Now, you mentioned a few moments ago that there was communication between the CRP and the Republican National Committee.

Mr. ODLE. Yes, sir; there was cooperation and communication.

Senator MONTOYA. What kind of liaison went on between the two committees?

Mr. ODLE. Well, sir; I would say, for example, that the people in our political division would work with the people at RNC's field operations division. The people in our press office would work with people with their communications office, that sort of thing. I worked with the administrative guy there.

Senator MONTOYA. Did you have people going back and forth between the two?

Mr. ODLE. You mean back and forth between payrolls or visiting?

Senator MONTOYA. No, not on payrolls, but communication between people. Did you have people going back and forth between the Republican National Committee and the CRP?

Mr. ODLE. Oh, yes, yes.

Senator MONTOYA. How close were you to each other?

Mr. ODLE. They are here on Capital Hill and we were at 17th and Pennsylvania.

Senator MONTOYA. You mentioned also that some of the major decisions were made by Attorney General Mitchell while he was at the Justice Department.

Mr. ODLE. I presume they were. Decision memos were sent to Mr Mitchell from time to time.

Senator MONTOYA. What kind of memoranda were sent to Mr. Mitchell and what kind of major decisions did you have in mind that you made?

Mr. ODLE. Well, it was not I who had them in mind, sir, because I was not at that level of the campaign. But, for example, we were involved at that point in staffing and some of the decisions were whom should we bring aboard to do this job or that job and things like that? It is hard to think back. That is almost 2 years ago. But I would sav the major campaign decisions.

Senator MONTOYA. I will read you this memorandum and ask you if you know anything about it. It is from the citizens for the reelection of the President, Washington, July 3 1972, styled "confidential." Memorandum for the Attorney General. Subject. grantsmanship.

Mr. ODLE. Subject what?

Senator MONTOYA Grantsmanship. Do you know what that means?

Mr. ODLE. I am not certain.

Senator MONTOYA. That means the business of making grants in government for a political consideration and for political credit. And it reads as follows:

> Enclosed is a copy of a proposal to insure that the President and his Congressional supporters get proper credit for Federal Government programs. This proposal was written by Bill Horton in Fred Malek's office with the assistance of Bill Gifford, OMB, and Peter Millspaugh, in Harry Dent's office.
>
> If implemented, this should be an effective method of insuring that political considerations are taken into account.

Signed, Jeb S. Magruder, his initials. And the enclosure is the memorandum.

Mr. DASH. Could the memorandum be given to the witness, please?

Senator MONTOYA. You will now be presented with the memorandum.

Mr. ODLE. I recognize the form, sir, of the memorandum, our stationery, of course. I do not recognize this exact memorandum. I don't believe I have seen this one. But this is—I don't mean the subject matter is a similar subject matter, but this is the kind of way memorandums might have been transmitted to Mr. Mitchell.

Senator MONTOYA. Did you then or did you see similar memoranda going out of the office of which you were in charge of administration?

Mr. ODLE. My memorandums, for example, would have asked Mr. Mitchell if it would have been proper to take more office space.

I remember one time when we found that none of our people could find cabs very easily in the streets, if it would be all right if we leased a car or something like that; yes.

Senator MONTOYA. How far back was the committee or its administrator sending memoranda or memorandums to Mr. Mitchell at the Department of Justice?

Mr. ODLE. I believe after it was there for a while and had been staffed up. I would say May 1971.

Senator MONTOYA. And you still presume that he was making some major decisions in the Department of Justice prior to the time he resigned as Attorney General?

Mr. ODLE. Of course, yes.

Senator MONTOYA. That is all.

Mr. DASH. Can I have that exhibit back and can we have it entered in the record?

[The document referred to was marked exhibit No. 1.*]

Senator ERVIN. I will recognize Senator Baker at this time so he can ask the questions which he refrained from asking when he originally questioned the witness.

Senator BAKER. Mr. Chairman, thank you very much. I had first understood that we were going to cover only the organization chart with this witness and the various interrelationships from that standpoint. I must say I am delighted that we have gone further into the substance of the subject matter and we have covered a great deal of testimony that might have been covered in a later appearance by this witness.

But in view of that, it seems to me that it is appropriate at this time to pursue some of the things that I might otherwise have asked earlier on.

Mr. Odle, I am particularly interested in June 17. If you don't mind, and without great length, tell us where you were on June 17.

Mr. ODLE. At the committee offices.

Senator BAKER. Did you come there at 9 o'clock in the morning?

Mr. ODLE. Approximately, yes, sir.

Senator BAKER. Did you stay there all day?

Mr. ODLE. I stayed there most of the day; yes.

Senator BAKER. Was there any irregularity in the procedure of the office or anything that caused you concern at that time with reference to the activities at the office?

Mr. ODLE. Oh, yes, obviously.

Senator BAKER. Would you begin describing in your own way what happened on June 17?

Mr. ODLE. Let me give you some examples. The security office telephoned me.

Senator BAKER. Who?

Mr. ODLE. One of the guards in the security office.

Senator BAKER. Do you know who that was?

---

*See p. 449.

Mr. ODLE. I am sorry, I don't.

Senator BAKER. Tell me what happened, then.

Mr. ODLE. He said, Mrs. McCord is on the telephone. She is looking for a lawyer. We don't know who she is looking for, can you help her?

I said, I didn't think I could, but put her up to me.

She said something to the effect that Jim has been involved in a project that has failed and he is in jail.

Senator BAKER. Jim has been involved in a project which has failed and what else?

Mr. ODLE. And that he has been in the Watergate, and I can't remember the exact words.

Senator BAKER. It is important that you try.

Mr. ODLE. I know it is important, because it was reported in the papers as her saying, your project has failed, and Senator, she did not say that.

Senator BAKER. "She" being who?

Mr. ODLE. Mrs. McCord.

Senator BAKER. The statement of Mrs. McCord as you recall was that Jim's project has failed?

Mr. ODLE. Jim has been involved, something along those lines.

Senator BAKER. What was your reaction?

Mr. ODLE. Well, one of real shock.

Senator BAKER. Did you ask her what project?

Mr. ODLE. No, I didn't go into it, because I had been down—I had heard earlier from someone in the press office that there was a possibility that McCord was involved in it, too.

Senator BAKER. Go back a step and tell me what you heard in the press office.

Mr. ODLE. Well, I had heard from the press officer that day that it appeared that McCord was somehow involved in this thing.

Senator BAKER. In what thing?

Mr. ODLE. In the Watergate thing.

Senator BAKER. The Watergate break-in?

Mr. ODLE. Yes, sir.

Senator BAKER. Can you tell me who told you?

Mr. ODLE. Mr. Paul Moore, who was the press officer that day.

Senator BAKER. What did he say?

Mr. ODLE. He just kind of insinuated, he didn't say a great deal more, that McCord had been involved in that activity.

Senator BAKER. Did he say he was in jail?

Mr. ODLE. He suggested it.

Senator BAKER. What do you mean, he suggested it?

Mr. ODLE. Senator, I can't remember it exactly, in all fairness, I can't remember it.

Senator BAKER. Did you come away from that interview with the impression that Mr. McCord was in jail?

Mr. ODLE. With the suspicion, yes, sir.

Senator BAKER. Did you ask that press officer what had happened or why McCord was in jail?

Mr. ODLE. Later on after I had talked with Mrs. McCord, I believe I did.

Senator BAKER. But you don't remember——

Mr. ODLE. I have a very hard time reconstructing the chronology of that day.

Senator Baker. You left the press office and went to your office?

Mr. ODLE. Yes, sir, I received a call from Mrs. McCord in my office.

Senator BAKER. Is that the first call you received?

Mr. ODLE. I only talked with Mrs. McCord once.

Senator BAKER. Was that the first call you received after you arrived at your office on June 17?

Mr. ODLE. Sir, I can't answer that. I just don't know.

Senator BAKER. You have no recollection of any other call?

Mr. ODLE. That is correct.

Senator BAKER. And the switchboard operator put you through to Mrs. McCord and Mrs. McCord said, Jim's project has failed and he is in jail?

Mr. ODLE. That is when it hit, Senator. I guess what I am saying is—that is when I realized that the man I felt very strongly about was in prison. I guess that is when it hit.

Senator BAKER. What happened, then?

Mr. ODLE. Well, she wanted to know if he was employed by the committee as a paid full-time member of the staff or if he was a consultant, because I think a bail bondsman was asking.

So, I checked and found that he was a full-time member of the staff. I told her that. Then she wanted to know about a lawyer and I just didn't know who the lawyer was.

Senator BAKER. What do you mean, about a lawyer?

Mr. ODLE. She wanted to know if she could reach a certain lawyer. She gave me a name. I said I couldn't help her because I didn't recognize the name.

Senator BAKER. Can you tell me the name?

Mr. ODLE. It started with an "R." It could have been Raftern or Rafferty.

Senator BAKER. Did she tell you why that particular name?

Mr. ODLE. No, sir, because that was a name that appeared in the paper a few days later. That was the first time I heard that name.

Senator BAKER. Have you since learned who that lawyer was?

Mr. ODLE. No, sir.

Senator BAKER. Did she ask you to recommend a lawyer?

Mr. ODLE. No, sir.

Senator BAKER. Did she ask you for money?

Mr. ODLE. No, sir.

Senator BAKER. Did she ask you for assistance?

Mr. ODLE. No, sir.

Senator BAKER. Did she ask you for anything?

Mr. ODLE. Only the information as to whether or not he was an employee or a consultant.

Senator BAKER. That she was at a bail bondsman's office and the bail bondsman wanted to know if he were a full-time salaried employee of the Committee To Re-Elect the President.

Mr. ODLE. Something along the latter lines and exactly what she should say.

Senator BAKER. And you indicated that he was, she mentioned the lawyer's name, and that was the end of the conversation?

Mr. ODLE. That is right.

Senator BAKER. All right, what next happened on June 17?

96-296 O—73——bk. 1—4

Mr. ODLE. Again, I have a hard time with the chronology.

One of the things that happened—I very honestly don't know if it happened before or after the phone call—was that I saw Mr. Liddy as I testified at the trial.

Senator BAKER. Did he call you or did you call him?

Mr. ODLE. No, sir, nobody called anybody. I saw him in the hall.

Senator BAKER. I see.

Mr. ODLE. He asked me where the paper shredder was.

Senator BAKER. The what?

Mr. ODLE. The paper shredder. The paper shredder was a very famous big paper shredder.

Senator BAKER. Was there a big paper shredder and a baby paper shredder, too?

Mr. ODLE. Pardon?

Senator BAKER. Was there more than one?

Mr. ODLE. Yes, sir.

Senator BAKER. He asked where the big paper shredder was?

Mr. ODLE. Yes, sir.

Senator BAKER. Did you ask him why he wanted to know?

Mr. ODLE. No, sir, I didn't. I said, it is in there.

Senator BAKER. Did he have anything with him?

Mr. ODLE. Not at that time. He later came out and said, how do you work it? I said, you press the button.

Then later on I saw him with a pile of papers, perhaps a foot high.

Senator BAKER. What was he doing with them?

Mr. ODLE. He was on his way into the shredding room.

Senator BAKER. Did you see him shred any papers?

Mr. ODLE. No; but I assumed he was going to shred them.

Senator BAKER. Do you shred papers of that sort or that quantity regularly?

Mr. ODLE. No, sir, I don't.

Senator BAKER. Does anyone?

Mr. ODLE. Well, I would say this, that there was a concern for security and people's—let me put it this way, Senator. It didn't seem that highly unusual at that point. What seemed—in retrospect, I recognize the importance of it. I see what was going on.

Senator BAKER. But at that time, you didn't inquire why he wanted to know where the big shredder was?

Mr. ODLE. No, sir.

Senator BAKER. You didn't inquire what that foot high stack of documents was?

Mr. ODLE. Pardon?

Senator BAKER. You didn't inquire what that foot high stack of documents was?

Mr. ODLE. No, sir, I did not.

Senator BAKER. But he shredded it?

Mr. ODLE. Yes, sir.

Senator BAKER. Did you help him shred them?

Mr. ODLE. No, sir.

Senator BAKER. But you did tell him how to operate the machine?

Mr. ODLE. Yes, sir.

Senator BAKER. What happened next on June 17?

Mr. ODLE. Well, let me work backwards from the time I left.

Senator BAKER. Before you do, you made a statement just now that you were not overly concerned at the moment about this destruction of documents, but now in retrospect, you see their importance, but you were concerned for security. I think that is a paraphrase, a fair paraphrase of your testimony.

Mr. ODLE. Um-hum.

Senator BAKER. Why were you concerned about security? What sort of security? Against what?

Mr. ODLE. Sir, I wasn't concerned—I didn't mean to say I was concerned about security at that time with respect to Mr. Liddy. I said I was concerned about security in the context of the campaign. That is why we had a big paper shredder. We were concerned about that. That was my job.

Senator BAKER. Was that security concern heightened by the events that far on June 17?

Mr. ODLE. For a time, it was. I was concerned personally that I would find myself in a position where I was directly and personally responsible for running a guard force and protecting the offices and people in those offices and I didn't have a background in security and I didn't quite know—I didn't have the guy to rely on that I had in the past.

Senator BAKER. What was the general atmosphere in the office at that time? Were lots of people running around shredding papers?

Mr. ODLE. No, sir, that was just the one occurrence.

Senator BAKER. Now, what happened next on June 17?

Mr. ODLE. Well, later on in the day, there was a man that visited the committee. He asked to speak to somebody in authority, and I was around there and I talked to him. He identified himself as a plainclothesman from the Police Department and he said that he just wanted us to know that Mr. McCord was in jail.

Senator BAKER. What did you say?

Mr. ODLE. I said, I know Mr. McCord is in jail.

Senator BAKER. Was there any further conversation?

Mr. ODLE. I don't believe that there was. He felt badly about it. It was brought up to me a while ago in an interview.

Senator BAKER. You say he felt badly about it?

Mr. ODLE. He felt badly about it, yes, he did. I guess that he perhaps, when demonstrations or potential acts of violence were going to occur, he was Mr. McCord's contact with the Police Department.

Senator BAKER. Go ahead with the sequence of events on the 17th.

Mr. ODLE. I think that was about it. I think that after that, we removed the files, put them in the briefcase.

Senator Baker. What files did you remove?

Mr. ODLE. The ones we described previously. Mr. Reisner took some files and I took the one file.

Senator BAKER. Now, let's examine that just for a moment. Was there a telephone conversation between you, Reisner, and Magruder on that date, a three-way phone call?

Mr. ODLE. Yes, sir, there was.

Senator BAKER. Can you tell us firsthand of your own knowledge of the substance of that conversation? And first, what time was it?

Mr ODLE. Late afternoon.

Senator BAKER. On the 17th of June?

Mr. ODLE. Yes.

Senator BAKER. Tell us as best you can the substance of that telephone conversation.

Mr. ODLE. I really——

Senator BAKER. Did it involve the files?

Mr. ODLE. Yes, it did, I am trying to think of something else it involved to give you a feel for the conversation. I really cannot do that. All I remember is that at the conclusion of the conversation, it was decided that I should take a file and Bob Reisner should take some other files.

Senator BAKER. Mr. Odle, I do not mean to impede the examination, and I honestly do not mean to try to intimidate you.

Mr. ODLE. I understand, Senator.

Senator BAKER. But this is an extremely important point.

Mr. ODLE Yes, sir.

Senator BAKER. Let me ask you a few questions about the conversation itself.

Did someone refer to the McCord arrest?

Mr. ODLE. I think that we probably discussed it on the phone, yes, sir.

Senator BAKER. Do you know who initiated that topic? Was it you or was it Reisner or was it Magruder?

Mr. ODLE. I am sorry, I do not.

Senator BAKER. But there was a conversation about the fact that McCord had been arrested?

Mr. ODLE. Oh, yes, sir. By that time, I believe, it was being discussed through the committee. It was a very serious thing.

Senator BAKER. Did you discuss the fact that others were also arrested and in jail?

Mr. ODLE. Well, we knew that there were a group of them.

Senator BAKER. Did you discuss what the relationship of these people was to the Committee for the Re-Election of the President?

Mr. ODLE. Well, we knew that Mr. McCord was security director.

Senator BAKER. I know you knew it, but I am asking you whether or not there was any conversation about it?

Mr. ODLE. Others, no, I do not believe there was.

Senator BAKER. What I am saying to you, Mr. Odle, to short circuit the thing a little, is was there any conversation like, McCord's in jail, he is our security director, what are we going to do about it? Was there anything like that?

Mr. ODLE. That is what I said. I said something to the effect, my God, I have got to find a new guy. Mr. Magruder said something to the effect, you sure do, something like that.

Senator BAKER. Did you say anything about paper shredding?

Mr. ODLE. No, sir.

Senator BAKER. Did you say anyting like about getting McCord out of jail?

Mr. ODLE. No, sir.

Senator BAKER. Did you say anything about getting him a lawyer?

Mr. ODLE. No, sir.

Senator BAKER. Did you relay the conversation you had with Mrs. McCord?

Mr. ODLE. I may have.

Senator BAKER. But you are not sure?
Mr. ODLE. But I am not sure.
Senator BAKER. Were there instructions given or was there an agreement reached on what you were going to do about removing material from any place in the Committee To Re-Elect the President office?
Mr. ODLE. Sir, to the best of my knowledge, the only material that was removed were the things that Bob Reisner and I took and we brought them back on Monday.
Senator BAKER. Who told you to?
Mr. ODLE. I guess Mr. Magruder did. That is pretty obvious from the way I, as I reconstruct the conversation.
Senator BAKER. Who initiated the idea?
Mr. ODLE. It must have been Mr. Magruder.
Senator BAKER. Are you sure?
Mr. ODLE. Yes, I would think I would be.
Senator BAKER. Can you remember what Mr. Magruder told you to do?
Mr. ODLE. No, I cannot remember his words.
Senator BAKER. But can you remember the substance of his language?
Mr. ODLE. The substance of the instruction was that that file, which I for some reason called the strategy file——
Senator BAKER. Called the strategy file?
Mr. ODLE. Which I called the strategy file, I guess. And the advertising files.
Senator BAKER. Now, wait a minute. Did Magruder or Reisner mention a file by name, by category or classive indication, a strategy file or any other file?
Mr. ODLE. I thought that the word "strategy" was used, yes.
Senator BAKER. Did you know what he was talking about?
Mr. ODLE. No.
Senator BAKER. Did you know where it was?
Mr. ODLE. No.
Senator BAKER. All right, what further information was referred to Magruder or gained during that conversation?
Mr. ODLE. Just that that file and the advertising files were to be removed and brought back on Monday. There was a concern, I believe, on his part and certainly on my own, for the security of that building.
Senator BAKER. Removed and brought back on Monday.
Mr. ODLE. Yes.
Senator BAKER. By whom?
Mr. ODLE. By me and by Mr. Reisner.
Senator BAKER. Obviously, somebody has to have had described, as Senator Weicker indicated earlier, what was to be removed.
Mr. ODLE. Mr. Magruder, I believe, did that, because Mr. Reisner was Mr. Magruder's administrative assistant and reconstructing it in my mind, he would have done that. I did not know how Mr. Magruder's desk was organized, or his files. I did not have a key to it.
Senator BAKER. You did not participate in the gathering together of the files to be removed over the weekend?
Mr. ODLE. Technically, no.
Senator BAKER. What do you mean by that?

Mr. ODLE. Technically, I did not participate in the gathering of the files, because I did not gather the file, I did not take the file. It was given to me, in effect.
Senator BAKER. Did you go pick them out?
Mr. ODLE. No.
Senator BAKER. Were they gathered together in one place?
Mr. ODLE. I am not totally certain. I am not totally certain where the advertising files were kept.
Senator BAKER. Well, at some point, I take it that you mean these files that were to be taken out over the weekend were gathered up and parceled out and you took one of them?
Mr. ODLE. Um hum.
Senator BAKER. Did you know in advance which one you were going to take?
Mr. ODLE. No, sir.
Senator BAKER. Who gave it to you?
Mr. ODLE. I believe Mr. Reisner did.
Senator BAKER. Did he do it with any particular emphasis or was it a random choice of files?
Mr. ODLE. No, I do not think it was a random choice.
Senator BAKER. Do you think he gave it to you as a specific file he wanted you to keep?
Mr. ODLE. That Mr. Magruder wanted me to keep, yes.
Senator BAKER. Would you describe the file?
Mr. ODLE. It was a gray file folder, much like the one I have here.
Senator BAKER. Would you hold it up so we can see it?
You are describing what I would call a letter size, light gray file folder.
Mr. ODLE. Legal size.
Senator BAKER. Legal size light gray file folder?
Mr. ODLE. That is correct.
Senator BAKER. Was it sealed or tied in any way?
Mr. ODLE. No, much like this.
Senator BAKER. What was its thickness?
Mr. ODLE. I would say possibly—gosh, I do not know. An inch and a half.
Senator BAKER. What did you do with it when it was given to you?
Mr. ODLE. It was in my briefcase and I am not just sure whether I put it in my briefcase or Mr. Reisner put it in my briefcase, but it was put in my briefcase.
Senator BAKER. What time was this?
Mr. ODLE. I do not know. Late afternoon now.
Senator BAKER. 5 o'clock?
Mr. ODLE. Maybe 6 o'clock, around there. It is hard to say. Then I took some files from my desk which were important to me and files I was concerned about. Those were our budget files.
Senator BAKER. Why were you concerned about them?
Mr. ODLE. Because those are the most important files I maintained. If there was a problem with our own office or if there was any security problem, I certainly did not want, you know, those to be published in the newspaper.
Senator BAKER. All right, back to the file that was placed or that you put in your briefcase. Did you put anything else in your briefcase?

Mr. ODLE. Those budget files and the other file. Just those.
Senator BAKER. Was that two or three files?
Mr. ODLE. I believe there would have been two budget files—there were three ultimately. I think there were just two at that time.
Senator BAKER. Were they all gray?
Mr. ODLE. Yes, sir.
Senator BAKER. Not a blue one in the bunch?
Mr. ODLE. No, sir. Not——
Senator BAKER. Do you know what I am talking about?
Mr. ODLE. Yes.
Senator BAKER. What am I talking about?
Mr. ODLE. Well, there was a blue file. And it contained the things that Liddy, Mr. Liddy, had given Mr. Magruder.
Senator BAKER. When did you find that out?
Mr. ODLE. When I read the newspapers.
Senator BAKER. Did you look in that file?
Mr. ODLE. No sir, I did not.
Senator BAKER. Are you certain?
Mr. ODLE. Absolutely certain.
Senator BAKER. Did you open the cover?
Mr. ODLE. No, sir.
Senator BAKER. Did you count pages?
Mr. ODLE. No, sir.
Senator BAKER. Did you sign a receipt for it?
Mr. ODLE. No, sir.
Senator BAKER. You took it home. Where did you put it?
Mr. ODLE. I believe I put my briefcase in the closet.
Senator BAKER. Did you lock it?
Mr. ODLE. Did I lock the closet?
Senator BAKER. Or the briefcase.
Mr. ODLE. I might have locked the briefcase.
Senator BAKER. Did you inquire of anyone why you should take home that particular one?
Mr. ODLE. No, I gathered it was an important file, just like the budget files were very important to me; I guessed that file was very important to Mr. Magruder.
Senator BAKER. Did anybody mention to you the word "Gemstone"?
Mr. ODLE. No, sir.
Senator BAKER. Do you know what the word means?
Mr. ODLE. I do not know what it means. I have seen the word in the newspapers recently.
Senator BAKER. Have you ever seen a document like this? [indicating].
Mr. ODLE. No, sir, I have not.
Senator BAKER. I am showing you a letter-sized document that is bordered, approximately 8 by 10 inches, it says "Gemstone" on the top, "Source", "Date", "Exdis", "No Disem". Other words at the bottom. Have you ever seen a document like this?
Mr. ODLE. No, sir.
Senator BAKER. Let the clerk hand it to him.
[Witness is handed document.]
Mr. ODLE. No, sir.
Senator BAKER. Mr. Chairman, might the record note this as an exhibit?

Senator ERVIN. Yes; mark it exhibit No. 2.
[The document referred to was marked exhibit No. 2*]
Senator BAKER. Do you know what that is?
Mr. ODLE. Well, it is speculation, sir.
Senator BAKER. I do not want your speculation. Do you have any information, did you have any information at that time about the content of that file that might relate to that document, Gemstone?
Mr. ODLE. No, sir.
Senator BAKER. Did you ever later learn what was in that file?
Mr. ODLE. No, not until very recently.
Senator BAKER. Well, do you know now what was in it?
Mr. ODLE. Well, I can speculate what was in it.
Senator BAKER. You suspect that the Gemstone material was in it?
Mr. ODLE. I suspect that things which have no place in a political campaign were in it; yes, sir.
Senator BAKER. Now, once again, Mr. Odle, I am not trying to trap you. I am trying to establish the contents of that file. You told us that on June 17, you did not know, that over the weekend following June 17, you did not look. My question is did you later learn of your own knowledge what was in that file that you took home with you?
Mr. ODLE. Oh, no, never of my own knowledge; no sir.
Senator BAKER. Were you ever told by a responsible official on the Committee To Re-Elect the President?
Mr. ODLE. No.
Senator BAKER. Or by anyone else?
Mr. ODLE. No.
Senator BAKER. Did Reisner—was Reisner ever requested to take that particular file home?
Mr. ODLE. I do not know. I do not know how it happened. Maybe it——
Senator BAKER. In the course of that three-way conversation, was there a suggestion that Reisner take it and did he decline?
Mr. ODLE. I am not certain. That could—well——
Senator BAKER. What is your best recollection on it?
Mr. ODLE. I do not think he declined, no. I do not think he declined. I think he said his briefcase was full of the advertising files and that I should take this one or something like that.
Senator BAKER. Did you ask how come you were the one that was going to take that one home?
Mr. ODLE. No, sir, I would have if I had known what was in it.
Senator BAKER. I am about through, Mr. Odle. I have a few other questions, but not very many.
In a Washington Post story on January 11, 1973, it is alleged that as personnel director for CRP, you spent the weekend—I assume the weekend following the Watergate incident—moving from office to office inside the headquarter's inventoring files, perhaps removing some. According to one source, whenever Odle would go into McCord's office, he would order everyone else out of the area.

> No records were actually destroyed until after Mardian and LaRue returned from a West Coast trip on Monday, June 19.

That is from the Washington Post, page A-1, dated September 9, 1972.

---

*See p. 450.

Do you have any knowledge of that newspaper account? Can you confirm it or deny it?

Mr. ODLE. I believe I can deny it. I believe the reporters who wrote it would deny it today, too, if they were asked.

I do not know how that all came to be. I destroyed no piece of paper, not one shred of paper in connection with the Watergate.

Now, let me make a couple of things perfectly clear [laughter] I did not enter the District of Columbia on that Sunday and I did not shred any papers that Saturday and I did not conduct a file search and shred anything the next week. What I did was o be as helpful as I could to agents of the FBI and the grand jury and since then, Common Cause, the Democratic National Committee, the Senate select committee, and a lot of other committees, to go through the committee files and provide documents.

Last night, for example, one of the staff members of the committee said, I know you are busy appearing before the select committee tomorrow, but before you do at 10, would you go to the files and get me floor plans for 10 different floors, because we need them for the committee's function.

That is an example of what I have been doing since last June.

Senator BAKER. We thank you for it.

Mr. ODLE. I am glad to be cooperative. I have become a professional witness lately and a bit of a professional file finder and that is fine. But when one goes through offices and finds files, that does not necessarily mean that he takes those files and shreds them. It could mean that he turns them over to the grand jury.

In going into Mr. McCord's office—Mr. McCord did not have a private office. It was a security office. There were a lot of guards sitting around, drinking coffee and whatever. There came a time with the FBI agents when they wanted to go into that office and they wanted to meet one of the men in there to talk with him and then they wanted to go through the files. And sure, we asked all the people to leave the room.

But Senator, it is just incredible the number of times those things have been in the newspaper. If I could just mention one example which is kind of typical and this is not the fault of anyone here or anybody else. I do not think it is even the fault of the reporters, because I do not think they have been malicious.

There was a story in the Post, a column, saying a diary was found belonging to Eugenio Martinez and that in it the initials R.O., H.P., and J.M. This could be coincidence, but those are probably the initials of Robert Odle, Mr. Porter, and Jeb Magruder.

What happened was that that diary was captured by the FBI agents on June 26th after the burglary. Those were the initials of the FBI agents who had initiated it for their own purposes of evidence. Yet the retraction if it ever appeared in Washington, is not one that I saw. As we go through this thing, we find time and time again where people who have tried to be helpful have found themselves in newspapers for totally innocent acts, acts which we undertook to be of assistance.

Senator BAKER. Mr. Odle, I think you have been extremely cooperative and the reason I am asking you about these acts is precisely what you speak of, because so far, the people of the United States have based their judgment, if they have a judgment, on newspaper accounts, television and radio reports, as they properly should. The press has done us a billion dollars worth of staff work investigating. But one legitimate function of this committee, it seems to me, is to find out what witnesses say about particular allegations made in the press.

Mr. ODLE. That is right.

Senator BAKER. I have only one other question I would like to ask in that respect. I refer to an article in the Washington Post on September 23, 1972. The synopsis of it is that Robert C. Odle gave to Jeb Magruder an internal confidential/eyes only memo of the President's Re-Election Committee dated 2 days after the June 17 Watergate break-in purporting to list all the committee payments to McCord and lists no amount resembling the $3,500 allegedly paid for the radio receiver. The memo, from Nixon committee personnel director Robert C. Odle to deputy campaign director Jeb S. Magruder, lists 18 separate payments to McCord, the highest being $1,091.56 for security services.

Mr. ODLE. Sir, that memorandum was a copy of a memorandum that I prepared for the FBI, that I turned over to the attorney, and that I testified to for the grand jury. It is merely a copy for information.

One of the first requests of the Bureau was for a complete listing of every check that has gone to McCord and McCord associates. I went down to the finance committee and went through the files and we found all the checks and made a list. We put a list together and I sent that to the U.S. attorney and I sent a copy to Mr. Magruder, saying this is a copy of what I have given to the U.S. attorney.

Again, there is an example of where we try to be helpful and we find ourselves put in a difficult position.

Senator BAKER. Mr. Odle, you have been a cooperative witness, I thank you for your help and it has been a long time now. I have no further questions.

Mr. ODLE. Thank you.

Mr. DASH. Mr. Odle, as counsel, I want to state that you have been very cooperative with this committee, but certain of these questions have come out that would have to come out at another time and we would have had to ask you to come back before this committee. I think it is appropriate that we complete this line of questioning.

Following up Senator Baker's question concerning the telephone conversation which you had together with Mr. Reisner and Mr. Magruder shortly after the break-in, were you on an extension line with Mr. Reisner and Mr. Magruder and did you hear Mr. Magruder's telephone conversation?

Mr. ODLE. As I reconstruct it, yes, there were two telephone instruments in Mr. Magruder's office. I believe I was on one and Mr. Reisner was on the other.

Mr. DASH. I know you are trying to recall back a considerable period of time, now, but you used the term the instruction to get a "strategic file."

Could the conversation have been get the sensitive file? Could that have been the term used?

Mr. ODLE. I don't believe that term was used. And I also, sir, believe that the "strategy file" was my term, I think I was applying it to that.

Mr. DASH. And you were on the line with Mr. Reisner?

Mr. ODLE. Yes.

Mr. DASH. Listening to Mr. Magruder?

Mr. ODLE. Yes.

Mr. DASH. Is it then your testimony that you did not hear Mr. Magruder say to Mr. Reisner with you on the line, get the Gemstone folder?

Mr. ODLE. Oh, no, sir.

Mr. DASH. Did you have a conversation with Mr. Robert Houston around this time concerning the files that Mr. McCord kept in the security room?

Mr. ODLE. Yes; not at that time, I don't believe. I believe the following week.

Mr. DASH. And can you tell us what that conversation was?

Mr. ODLE. I was curious as to what was in the files and what was down there.

Mr. DASH. Have you asked Mr. Houston or discussed with Mr. Houston removal of anything from that file?

Mr. ODLE. No; Mr. Houston indicated that there were some personal effects belonging to Mr. McCord, pictures and the like, that he was going to return. He mentioned that to me. I don't remember any other discussion of removal of anything else.

As I say, I did sort of go through there to see what was in it. Mr. McCord no longer being with us, it was sort of my responsibility to do that.

Then I also looked through the files at some length with FBI agents, I believe.

Mr. DASH. And when you went through McCord's file, was this a file that was open or was this a locked file?

Mr. ODLE. It would have been kept locked at night, probably. It was open when I went through it, I believe.

Mr. DASH. Could you just briefly describe what was in the file when you went through it? What kind of files?

Mr. ODLE. Oh, security reports, things like that; the ID system that we maintained. When people left papers out of their desk or forgot to lock their file cabinets, there were security reports, normal kinds of things.

Mr. DASH. Did you notice any electronic equipment?

Mr. ODLE. Yes; there was electronic equipment, but it was basically the kind of stuff that we used, the committee, for example, the alarm system. The various doors of the committee offices were alarmed. There was a central alarm system there so if one of them was opened in the middle of the night, it would ring and that sort of thing, and closed-circuit television. It is possible that that machine he used to check for countermeasures would have been there.

Mr. DASH. Were you aware of any tapes that were in the files?

Mr. ODLE. No.

Mr. DASH. Did you see any tapes?

Mr. ODLE. You know, that is an interesting question.

Mr. DASH. To your best recollection?

Mr. ODLE. I don't think so.

There might have been, but I don't remember.

Mr. DASH. Now, do you recall Mr. Houston ever discussing with you or telling you that he removed that material from Mr. McCord's file?

Mr. ODLE. The things he talked about were Mr. McCord's pictures and his personal diplomas and certificates and memorabilia.

Mr. DASH. And you do not know of your own knowledge whether or not he did remove these things, the materials you discussed, the electronic equipment or any other materials from the file?

Mr. ODLE. No; there may have been some things belonging to Mr. McCord personally which he removed, you know.

Mr. DASH. What kind of things are you talking about?

Mr. ODLE. Again, I don't know. He just said he was going to return Mr. McCord's personal things to him. I saw no problen with that. I just said we were going to return these things.

Mr. DASH. As administrator, did he ever give you a report or an inventory of what he took out of that file to return to Mr. McCord?

Mr. ODLE. No; there was a 4-page listing of things in the room that I saw at one point, but those were not the things——

Mr. DASH. Now, do you know the name Gary Bittenbender?

Mr. ODLE. That is the policeman that came by that day.

Mr. DASH. Have you ever known him before?

Mr. ODLE. No; I never met him.

Mr. DASH. Did he ever come again?

Mr. ODLE. No; I have never seen him since.

Mr. DASH. Now, the chart that you described shows Mr. McCord actually working under you, is that correct?

Mr. ODLE. Oh, yes.

Mr. DASH. The chart you showed to the committee shows Mr. McCord working under your supervision?

Mr. ODLE. Yes, sir.

Mr. DASH. To your knowledge, did there come a time when Mr. McCord was assigned to work under Mr. Liddy's supervision?

Mr. ODLE. No, sir.

Mr. DASH. Did you have any knowledge that he was working under Mr. Liddy's supervision?

Mr. ODLE. Absolutely not.

Mr. DASH. Did you ever see Mr. McCord and Mr. Liddy together at the committee?

Mr. ODLE. Not really. I have seen them in the hall from time to time.

Mr. DASH. Now, you have mentioned, and I think you have already identified, a memoradum from the committee on committee stationery to the Attorney General back in 1971. I think you have already indicated that Mr. Haldeman, Mr. Strachan kept a fairly constant liaison with the committee.

Mr. ODLE. Yes.

Mr. DASH. Are you aware of memoranda from the White House to the committee discussing the political campaign program and strategy from time to time?

Mr. ODLE. That is fairly broad, Mr. Dash.

Mr. DASH. Well, let me show you a particular memorandum of 1972 from the White House and see if—would you just read the—not the material but what that memorandum is captioned—who it is from?

Mr. ODLE. It is from Mr. Ted Malek to Mr. Magruder, coordinating functions for the campaign organization.

Mr. DASH. And on what stationery is that?

Mr. ODLE. White House stationery.

Mr. DASH. What date is that?
Mr. ODLE. February 9, 1972.
Mr. DASH. And you were at the committee at that time, were you not?
Mr. ODLE. Oh, yes.
Mr. DASH. Are you familar with that kind of memorandum that would come over from the White House?
Mr. ODLE. I have not read this memorandum but I would not think it unusual for somebody at the White House to say to the committee what their thoughts were with respect to the campaign structure organization. People at the White House wanted to see the President reelected, and I do not see, I would not, I do not know that there were hundreds of such memoranda but without reading it I could not——
Mr. DASH. Would you want to read that memorandum to yourself?
Mr. ODLE. Yes, it is a memorandum describing—it is entitled "Coordinating Functions to the Campaign Organization." I think it is a fair description of what it discusses.
Mr. DASH. Does it relate to the role of the Attorney General in the strategy?
Mr. ODLE. Yes, it does.
Mr. DASH. Would you say that memorandum is merely a suggestion or does it go further than that?
Mr. ODLE. I would say it is a strong suggestion. I think Mr. Malek and Mr. Magruder at that time were; I do not think either one of them was in a position to instruct the other.
Mr. DASH. I think so that we now know what is in that memorandum, would you please read it into the record, please, sir?
Mr. THOMPSON. Mr. Dash, before he does that, would you mind if I saw a copy and read that myself?
Senator BAKER. Mr. Chairman, I think, if you do not mind, that neither the record nor the committee presumably have seen this rather lengthy memorandum and I wonder if counsel would supply a copy to us so we get the full burden and thrust of what you are talking about and then if we want to break for lunch or some such, we could take up this question later.
Mr. DASH. Fine.
Senator BAKER. I am sure I cannot follow what the witness is talking about at this point and I would like to see a copy of this or any other exhibit that is handed by counsel before we proceed to it.
Mr. DASH. Senator Baker, we will make copies and follow that procedure.
Now, by the way, in going over the chart, what was the role Mr. Bob Porter played?
Mr. ODLE. Mr. Porter was the director of scheduling.
Mr. DASH. Mr. Powell Moore?
Mr. ODLE. Mr. Powell Moore was the assistant director of public affairs.
Mr. DASH. And now, at the time—have you met or do you know or did you ever work with Mr. Krogh in the White House?
Mr. ODLE. I know Mr. Krogh at the White House; yes.
Mr. DASH. While you were at the White House did you ever attend a Justice Department task force meeting with Mr. Krogh, Mr. Mardian, and the FBI?

Mr. ODLE. No, sir.
Mr. DASH. Mr. Chairman, for the time being those are the only questions I have.
Mr. THOMPSON. Mr. Chairman, I have no further questions.
Mr. DASH. Could you, Mr. Odle, come back right after the lunch recess so that the members of the committee can see this memorandum and perhaps inquire into it?
Mr. ODLE. What time would that be, Mr. Chairman?
Senator ERVIN. I might state this gavel was given to me by the Chief of the Eastern Band of the Cherokees to preside over this meeting.
The committee will take a recess until 2 o'clock.
[Whereupon, at 12:40 p.m., the hearing was recessed, to reconvene at 2 p.m., this same day.]

AFTERNOON SESSION, THURSDAY, MAY 17, 1973

Senator ERVIN. The committee will come to order.
Counsel was asking questions of Mr. Odle.
Mr. DASH. Will you please give this memorandum to Mr. Odle?
Now, Mr. Odle, I think all members of the committee have received a copy of the memorandum, and if there is no objection, I would like for you to read that into the record.
Senator BAKER. Mr. Chairman, I might say I have no objection to the memorandum. I did not know what to think before we recessed for lunch and indicated my desire to have a copy which counsel has now supplied. You understand, Mr. Dash, this material was supplied in response to subpena duces tecum on the Committee To Re-Elect the President.
Mr. DASH. Yes, and Mr. Vice Chairman, it was received last night and that particular memorandum was given to me by my staff just prior to my asking a question.
Senator BAKER. I have no objection and I am sure we will have copies in advance hereafter.
Mr. DASH. Yes, we certainly will.
Senator BAKER. Thank you, Mr. Dash.
Mr. DASH. Mr. Odle, will you please read it and in reading it, will you please indicate the classification that apparently appears on that memorandum.
Mr. ODLE. It says: "Confidential, eyes only memorandum for Jeb Magruder from Fred Malek, subject, 'Coordinating Functions for the Campaign Organization.'" It is dated February 9, 1972.*

I have given further thought to our conversation of last night and to your February 7 memorandum to the Attorney General. Since I do not yet have an in-depth knowledge of the campaign operation, it is difficult for my observations to be precise. Nevertheless, I do have some reservations about the recommendations contained in that memorandum which can best be expressed in writing.
Planning: My reservations on your recommendations pertain mainly to the suggested planning process, but also to the responsibility for implementation.

Do you want me to read the substance of the entire memorandum?
Mr. DASH. Yes, please. Just comment on it.

* Later entered as exhibit 3, p. 58.

Mr. ODLE: [reading]:

Planning process: As you know, the Attorney General has asked me to devise a management audit system by which he can track overall progress and identify major problem areas for corrective action. Naturally, an integral part of such a system is the establishment of benchmarks by which progress is to be judged, or in short, a plan. Based upon my preliminary thinking on this, I have tentatively concluded that the planning system should incorporate the following characteristics:

The principal focal points of the planning should be the States (with the emphasis given to key States) rather than the functional areas such as voter bloc activities, telephone, direct mail, et cetera. Planning by State will help to highlight and direct management attention to progress on building voter support to carry individual States—the key to victory.

Planning of the functional activities within a State should be based upon a clearly defined strategy for obtaining the needed votes for carrying that State, spelling out, for example, the needed vote margin by distinctive geographical areas and the organizing and persuasion tactics which will be utilized.

As is implicit in the above two points, the planning should provide a sound basis for tracking progress and identifying problem areas for corrective action.

The line officials who will be held accountable for results, principally the State chairmen, should feel as though they have the lead in developing the plans affecting their areas of responsibility. Naturally, exercising quality control, the national campaign organization must ensure the plans fit the overall re-election strategy and capitalize upon polling information.

From our conversation, I would say you generally agree with this. However, from reading your memorandum your position on these principles is not clear. I believe they should be clarified prior to proceeding with development of a planning system.

Responsibility for implementation: I believe there is a strong argument for having Bob Marik perform this function in view of his sound knowledge of the campaign operations and his access to research information. However, it is also important for the "controller" to be intimately involved since these plans will provide the basis for tracking progress and identifying problems. To do this effectively, the "controller" must ensure that the plans provide a sound basis for monitoring campaign effectiveness. Also, he must be thoroughly familiar with their content. Perhaps we can meet the needs and capitalize on the strengths of both individuals by also giving the "controller" a definite part of this responsibility.

Formal decision-making process:

I really wonder whether the sort of staff secretariat operation which you suggest is necessary. Such a procedure has undoubtedly been helpful up to now, since the Attorney General has not been present and responsibilities have been shifting with the growth of the organization. However, with the Attorney General coming on board full-time soon, with him taking a more direct supervisory role over field operations, and with the division of responsibilities between the principals being clarified, I question the need for a staff secretariat system.

In fact, it may be counterproductive. Such systems are inevitably cumbersome and, therefore, not conducive to the need for fast decisions as the campaign heats up. Also, due to the sensitivity of the information and the need for speedy action, many of the decisions will undoubtedly be handled verbally, particularly toward the end of the campaign. This would undermine the staff secretariat's ability to coordinate effectively.

I recognize the abuse which can be perpetrated without such a system. However, given the nature of campaign management the answer lies in appointing competent division managers and making sure they have a clear understanding of their respective responsibilities rather than creating a cumbersome staff secretariat system. Of course, the Attorney General should, and will decide this matter. I believe it would be a disservice, however, to try to persuade him to lean on a staff secretariat system rather than bringing in the most competent managers possible, clearly laying out their responsibilities and then holding them fully accountable for results.

These are, of course, my initial reactions based on quite limited knowledge. Please note that I am not stating how it should be done, but merely laying out possible problems that need to be addressed before we get locked in.

Because of the above reservations, I recommend you either pull back the memorandum or ask the Attorney General to delay action on it pending further coordination with me. Another option would be for me to inform the Attorney General of my reservations and ask him to defer the decision. However, I do not think this is desirable and would prefer that you and I work it out in the spirit of cooperation that must become our trademark.

Frankly, I was taken by surprise last night. After our discussion on Friday about the need for teamwork and my openly discussing my role, I was surprised that you unilaterally submitted to the Attorney General recommendations having a profound impact on my area of responsibility and my working relationship with him. This was the reason for my rather vigorous reaction. In any case, we covered that ground fairly thoroughly last night, and I am confident that in the future we can work together on matters of this sort and resolve or spell out any differences prior to submitting recommendations.

Mr. DASH. I will not ask you any further questions on that memorandum, Mr. Odle. It was not your memorandum but I just put it to you on the questioning of the memorandum that had come from the White House and the format. Would that memorandum be identified as an exhibit?

Senator ERVIN. It will be marked as an exhibit and will be assigned the proper number.

Mr. DASH. Will the reporter assign the appropriate number to it?

[The document referred to was marked exhibit No. 3.*]

Mr. DASH. I only have one further memorandum and question for you. Now, Mr. Odle, you have before you a copy of a memorandum that has the word "sample" above it.

Mr. ODLE. Yes.

Mr. DASH. With the letterhead of Committee for the Re-Election of the President. Have you seen this sample memorandum prior to today?

Mr. ODLE. Yes. This is—we had in the committee staff manual, and it talked about everything, about how to make coffee about how to make memos, how to use the telephone and watch-lights and so on.

Mr. DASH. All right. This being a sample part of the staff manual that is showing how, would it be fair to say, this was a part of the staff manual and a sample directing a memorandum from Mr. Haldeman and how one would direct that?

Mr. ODLE. This is correct. This was just showing if someone in the committee were going to write a memorandum to Mr. Haldeman or someone else in the White House, this is the form they would use.

Mr. DASH. Does it show in the bottom a copy would be sent to Mr. Ehrlichman?

Mr. ODLE. It does but only as a sample, this whole memorandum is a sample. No; it would not have been that all memoranda to Mr. Haldeman would be sent to Mr. Ehrlichman.

Mr. DASH. Will it not indicate that the memorandum from the Committee for the Re-Election of the President to the White House at least went in sufficient number that you required a sample of a form to use so that you would have a routine method?

Mr. ODLE. Yes. We did want to have a routine method, and because of all the new secretaries who were coming on board and all the various new people on the campaign staff. We did want to have some sort of standard memorandum format which everyone used.

Mr. DASH. All right. Will you pick up the memorandum?

[The document referred to was marked exhibit No. 4 for identification only.**]

*See p. 451.
**See p. 454.

Mr. DASH. That is all I have, Mr. Odle.

Mr ODLE. All right.

Mr. THOMPSON. Mr. Odle, one or two questions. As I understand the significance of the first memorandum, the February 9 memorandum is first of all a memorandum which came from the White House to the committee and secondly, it refers to the fact that the Attorney General asked Mr. Malek to devise a management audit system at the time when he was still Attorney General on February 9. As I understand, he resigned March 1st as Attorney General, and it does reflect those two facts, is that correct?

Mr. ODLE. Yes, sir. It would seem to me to be my impression that the Senator is interested in the memorandum rather than the substance of the memorandum.

Mr. THOMPSON. The fact that something was sent.

Mr. ODLE. It went back and forth, which is a perfectly natural thing.

Mr. THOMPSON. That is all. Those are all the questions I have.

Senator BAKER. Mr. Chairman, I have no further questions but I cannot resist the temptation to say Mr. Odle has been a very good witness. He has been very forthcoming, he has testified at great length and it was brought to my attention a few minutes ago that when his testimony was interrupted for us to go to lunch one of the networks played "To Tell The Truth." [Laughter.]

Mr. ODLE. Well, Senator, I appreciate that comment very much. I would say this. In fact, if I said I would be happy to be here completely, I would be committing perjury.

Senator ERVIN. Mr. Odle, I have a question or two. You stated this morning that G. Gordon Liddy and Jeb Stuart Magruder were not on the best of terms.

Mr. ODLE. Yes, sir, that was my impression.

Senator ERVIN. Do you know what was the cause of their lack of goodwill?

Mr. ODLE. Well, I think of one reason and it is probably not that important, but I moved Mr. Liddy's office at one point from the fourth floor to the eight floor and Mr. Liddy very vigorously objected to that and tried to get me to change it and I said I was not going to do that, I cannot, I need the space, and he appealed that to Mr. Magruder and Mr. Magruder said "I do not want to get involved in office space. What Odle says about office space is what I am going to do about it."

They had a number of serious battles about the location of Mr. Liddy's office. That is just one example. I think Mr. Liddy was a little bit older than Mr. Magruder and possibly did not like to receive it from a younger man, but that is probably speculation on my part.

Senator ERVIN. You talked this morning about a shredder.

Mr. ODLE. Yes, sir.

Senator ERVIN. A shredder is a machine that is used to destroy documentary matters in such a way that like Humpty Dumpty they cannot be put together again, is that not so?

Mr. ODLE. Yes, sir, it is.

Senator ERVIN. It is used to destroy useless papers and it is also used to destroy papers which the destroyer wishes to have concealed from identification and reading, is it not?

96-296 O—73——bk. 1—5

Mr. ODLE. Well, I would suppose so. It was used primarily during the campaign so that people would not come into our offices and maybe copy the papers. You know that happened in the 1968 campaign to the Nixon campaign in that very same building, a columnist in Washington came in and talked to the team people and said "We would like your waste paper", and so that was one way of seeing that that columnist did not get our waste paper.

Senator ERVIN. In other words, you did not want the general public, the great purpose of a shredder is to make it certain that the documents cannot come to the attention, the contents of the documents cannot come to the attention, of anyone who might be interested outside of the organization, in reading those documents.

Mr. ODLE. I would think that would be a fair statement, especially with those people who at that time we were running against.

Senator ERVIN. Ordinarily, the purpose of a document is to preserve a record of what the document records, isn't it?

Mr. ODLE. I would suppose so.

Senator ERVIN. And what is the purpose of making a record and then destroying that record?

Mr. ODLE. Well, sir, I don't know that there was. I would think the basic purpose of that shredding machine we were talking about was to pick up the wastepaper in the evening and not the documents.

Let me say just one thing. We tried from the beginning to save documents because we thought that this campaign was, despite these other situations, was a fairly organized, well run, fairly thrifty campaign. [Laughter.]

That seems funny now, I know, but we did think that. We wanted to save the documents because we thought it might be interesting for a scholar to go back in 100 years and [laughter].

I can only tell you about our intention. In the light of recent events, that might appear funny, but I think the point I am making you will find interesting. But we did save documents. We saved many of them. Do you know, right now, there are 1,500 cubic feet of committee documents that have been available at various times to the U.S. attorney, the FBI, the grand jury, Common Cause, the Democratic National Committee, and the Senate select committee. We have been working with all those committees and panels making those documents available.

But you know, the thing that did not happen after the election was that we took out those documents and shredded them. We took them out, put them together, they are housed in one location pretty much right now and they are there. They were not destroyed or shredded.

Senator ERVIN. In the course of normal events, a man or organization who is proud of his good deeds and wants them recorded in history preserves documents, doesn't he?

Mr. ODLE. Yes, sir.

Senator ERVIN. And has no use for a shredder.

Mr. ODLE. Well, I don't know that I could agree with that. For example, let's say I was preparing a document for the budget committee's review and analysis and in the course of preparing that document, I made a lot of notes and those notes went into the thing and I threw the notes away.

Senator, in the middle of that campaign, I would not have wanted those notes on the front page of the Washington Post, because that would have given away some of our campaign strategy.

Senator ERVIN. Well, you could have locked them in a filing cabinet, couldn't you?

Mr. ODLE. Wastepaper? You could have. I know a Senate campaign did that, rented a warehouse——

Senator ERVIN. But you could not have put them in the wastepaper basket and put them in the shredder while you——

Mr. ODLE. This is a case where I might be writing a memorandum up or making up something that I would be sending to the budget committee and I would be having all these notes and taking things from the notes and putting them in, then I would throw the notes away. I am talking now about the wastepaper.

The basic purpose of the shredder was not to dispose of documents or records, it was to dispose of wastepaper.

Senator ERVIN. And to destroy wastepaper in such a manner that its contents could not be resurrected?

Mr. ODLE. Yes, sir.

Senator ERVIN. Now, I believe you said on the 17th, G. Gordon Liddy came into the offices of the Committee To Re-Elect the President and asked whether there were shredders?

Mr. ODLE. Yes, he asked where the large shredder machine was located, yes, he did.

Senator ERVIN. Was he the man ordinarily charged with the duty of disposing of wastepaper?

Mr. ODLE. No, sir. [Laughter.]

Senator ERVIN. Well, you told him where the shredder was, you said?

Mr. ODLE. Yes, sir.

Senator ERVIN. And he took the shredder and he shredded some documents, did he?

Mr. ODLE. Yes.

Senator ERVIN. Do you know where the documents came from that he shredded?

Mr. ODLE. No.

Senator ERVIN. Did he shred any documents that were in your custody?

Mr. ODLE. Absolutely not.

Senator ERVIN. Now, he was the man that was supposed to be in charge of intelligence operations, wasn't he?

Mr. ODLE. That is what it appears to be.

Senator ERVIN. Do you think it is reasonable to draw the inference that the documents he was shredding were documents that related to the intelligence activities?

Mr. ODLE. I do now, sir, today; I did not then.

Senator ERVIN. Now, who else was present at that time?

Mr. ODLE. Who else?

Senator ERVIN. Who else heard him ask for the shredder or saw him use the shredder?

Mr. ODLE. I don't think anybody was there.

Senator ERVIN. Were there any papers after that shredded by anybody else?

Mr. ODLE. I didn't see any shredding that day besides that.

Senator ERVIN. Yes, but subsequently. Was Robert Mardian present at that time?

Mr. ODLE. No, sir. I believe he was in California.

Senator ERVIN. And how long after this event was it before he returned from California?

Mr. ODLE. I believe he returned the following week.

Senator ERVIN. Do you know anything about any shredding of papers after his return?

Mr. ODLE. No, sir, I do not. I have read in the newspapers as you have that he and one other individual shredded papers. I have no knowledge of that and I did not see them shred papers.

There was something called a—referred to as a housing cleaning. If that existed, I did not see it.

Senator ERVIN. And you know nothing about any other papers being shredded after the break-in?

Mr. ODLE. That is exactly correct.

Senator ERVIN. Do you know whether anybody kept any records in the division as to the amounts of money that was disbursed for intelligence work?

Mr. ODLE. No, sir; I don't. I assume the finance committee people whose job it was to keep records kept records. I was not involved in that area.

Senator ERVIN. Have you found in your searches in assisting the FBI and the various committees you mentioned, have you found any papers which disclosed how much money was paid G. Gordon Liddy or E. Howard Hunt?

Mr. ODLE. No, sir; I have not.

Senator ERVIN. Any further questions?

Senator GURNEY. I have a few.

Mr. Odle, we worried the meat off the bone of that phone call at quite some length this morning, but there are one or two other questions I would like to ask you about. I am referring to the phone call between Mr. Magruder and you and Mr. Reisner.

Who initiated the phone call?

Mr. ODLE. I don't know. I can't remember. It could have been me, it could have been Mr. Reisner.

Senator GURNEY. Was it initiated from Washington?

Mr. ODLE. I believe it was.

Senator GURNEY. And why was it initiated?

Mr. ODLE. I guess just to discuss the state of the situation at that point, sir.

Senator GURNEY. You mean to discuss the Watergate break-in?

Mr. ODLE. Yes, I guess, and the fact that our security officer was involved in it.

Senator GURNEY. I understand the phone call was made from Mr. Magruder's office, is that right?

Mr. ODLE. Yes, that is right.

Senator GURNEY. How far is that from your office?

Mr. ODLE. It is about 20 feet from door to door.

Senator GURNEY. How is it that you and Mr. Reisner happened to be together at the time this phone call was made?

Mr. ODLE. Sir, I can't reconstruct that. It certainly wasn't unusual for us. Mr. Reisner's office, Mr. Magruder's office, and my office all opened onto a common area, a hall.

Senator GURNEY. Well, but it was a very unusual phone call, and of course, it is the most important piece of testimony you have given today.

Mr. ODLE. Yes, I know that, Senator, and I am trying to be helpful. But you know, to reconstruct events that didn't seem at that point that important is a difficult thing. I mean at that point, the most important concern that I had was, you know, what are we going to do about this guard force and do we have men coming on in the morning, and what are we to do for the replacement of McCord? That was my concern. That was my problem at that point. That is what seemed very significant to me. I suddenly found myself very personally in charge of something I didn't know a great deal about.

Senator GURNEY. Isn't that why you called Mr. Magruder, to discuss those matters with him?

Mr. ODLE. We probably discussed that with him. I think I probably said, well, I will have to hire somebody, and he said, yes, you will.

Senator GURNEY. You said the phone call was made later in the afternoon?

Mr. ODLE. I believe so.

Senator GURNEY. Had Mr. Reisner been with you all of the day?

Mr. ODLE. No.

Senator GURNEY. When did he join you?

Mr. ODLE. I saw him for the first time late in the afternoon on that Saturday.

Senator GURNEY. Did he come to see you or did you go to see him?

Mr. ODLE. Sir, our offices were in an area almost the size of that conference table.

Senator GURNEY. Well, you didn't discuss any matters with him until late in the afternoon?

Mr. ODLE. I don't believe so.

Senator GURNEY. Well, was the matter that you saw him about late in the afternoon, let us make a phone call to Mr. Magruder?

Mr. ODLE. At some point it seemed appropriate to call Mr. Magruder. I just can't reconstruct, Senator, exactly why.

Senator GURNEY. But that, as I understand it, is the reason why you and Mr. Reisner got together late in the afternoon?

Mr. ODLE. Well, that suggests that we decided in advance of that that we must get together and call Mr. Magruder, and on the scale of important things that day, that was pretty low. I can see in retrospect what you are driving at and I do appreciate, Senator, the importance of it.

Senator GURNEY. How long was the phone call?

Mr. ODLE. I don't——

Senator GURNEY. Was it a short phone call, a long phone call?

Mr. ODLE. Maybe 5 or 10 minutes.

Senator GURNEY. And the discussion initiated was a recount to Mr. Magruder about the Watergate break-in and Mr. McCord and all of the events that you knew at that time?

Mr. ODLE. He probably read it in the wire stories, possibly. I mean that might have been what could have happened.

Senator GURNEY. How did the discussion about the files come up? Who brought that up in the conversation?

Mr. ODLE. I can't recall, but I assume it was probably that Magruder did. I believe I was out of the office for a time and I came back in.

Senator GURNEY. You mean you were out of the office during the time of the phone call?

Mr. ODLE. Part of the phone call, as I said before, yes.

Senator GURNEY. You were not on the phone call at the time, then?

Mr. ODLE. That is correct.

Senator GURNEY. And you feel that it is after you came back into the office that the files were mentioned?

Mr. ODLE. I don't know when the files were mentioned. The message I got from the phone call was, as I said, that that one file was to be removed and that the advertising files were to be removed.

Senator GURNEY. Well, now, then, you received that information, you and Mr. Reisner. You were in Mr. Magruder's office. Then what happened? Was an immediate search made for the files?

Mr. ODLE. No, I don't think so. I think that probably what happened was that Mr. Reisner, who was more familiar with the way in which Mr. Magruder's desk was organized, would have taken the file. He either gave it to me or put it in my briefcase, something like that.

Senator GURNEY. Well, is it your testimony that—well, let's go back a little. How did Mr. Magruder pose this question about the file? Did this seem to be a matter of urgency or a routine matter, or how did it appear?

Mr. ODLE. He was concerned about it.

Senator GURNEY. Why was he concerned?

Mr. ODLE. He was concerned about it because he feared the security, he said, of our building.

Senator GURNEY. Well, now, of course, the break-in was done by one of your people—I say your people; one who was working for the Committee To Re-Elect the President.

Mr. ODLE. Yes.

Senator GURNEY. Was there some feeling of apprehension that more of your people would raid your own files?

Mr. ODLE. Sir, I don't know. I was possibly concerned about retribution. I was just concerned about general security. We had nobody any longer who could handle it for us. I guess his feeling was that it would just be best if the file was out of the office until he returned.

Senator GURNEY. But why? There must have been some reason?

Mr. ODLE. Well, we were concerned. I mean, you know, I took, as I said, my budget files home with me for the weekend.

Senator GURNEY. Was any mention made by Mr. Magruder about perhaps the issuance of a search warrant by anybody?

Mr. ODLE. Not that I recall.

Senator GURNEY. Naming these files?

Mr. ODLE. No.

Senator GURNEY. Had files ever been taken home before this discussion?

Mr. ODLE. I always used to take some files home to work on Sunday.

Senator GURNEY. Were you working on somebody else's files?
Mr. ODLE. No, no sir, no.
Senator GURNEY. All right. Now the phone conversation is finished and the important part of that was these files, the security of them, obviously a very important point. What happened after the phone conversation was over?
Mr. ODLE. Well I assume either Mr. Reisner gave me the file, put it on my desk or something like that.
Senator GURNEY. Well, I know but there you are you have got a phone and Reisner has got a phone and you put them down and then something happens, has happened.
Mr. ODLE. Senator, I am trying to be as cooperative as I can but to answer that question is to try to invent something.
Senator GURNEY. I understand. Well, was a search made for the files immediately?
Mr. ODLE. I do not think a search of that was necessary, Mr. Reisner was pretty familiar with the way in which Mr. Magruder's desk was organized.
Senator GURNEY. Did he go to the desk and open a draw or something?
Mr. ODLE. Senator, if I knew, if I could remember, that I would tell you. It is very hard to reconstruct today, that it is almost a year ago. I have told you, you know everything I can think of that relates to that activity.
Senator GURNEY. Well, let me ask you this then. You have no recollection about the search for the file, that is your testimony?
Mr. ODLE. Yes. I have no recollection of that, right. I did not go through his desk and search his file cabinet.
Senator GURNEY. Well, were you in—how long did you stay in the room after the phone call?
Mr. ODLE. Sir, I just do not know.
Senator GURNEY. Well, let me ask you this. Do you think it was 5 minutes or an hour?
Mr. ODLE. Well, it was probably a lot closer to 5 minutes than it was to an hour.
Senator GURNEY. Did you come back later and receive the file that you were going to take home from Mr. Reisner?
Mr. ODLE. It is possible, and another possibility is Mr. Reisner brought it into my office.
Senator GURNEY. Well, can't we pin it down better than a possibility?
Mr. ODLE. Well, I just, you know, can't quite exactly recollect how it happened. I think that he gave it to me standing there, he gave it to me in the office, something like that, he sent it to my office.
Senator GURNEY. Is it your testimony then that you had left the office, Magruder's office and returned to your own after the phone call and that the file was brought to you there by Mr. Reisner?
Mr. ODLE. I am not sure. Senator, I am just not sure.
Senator GURNEY. When did you go home that day?
Mr. ODLE. I went with my wife to a play that night, to dinner afterwards.
Senator GURNEY. I say when, when did you leave your office?
Mr. ODLE. Seven o'clock, I think.

Senator GURNEY. And the phone call was when?
Mr. ODLE. Late afternoon.
Senator GURNEY. What about the size—I understand there were two files, one that you took and one Mr. Reisner took, is that correct?
Mr. ODLE. I believe he took more than one. I think he took a number of, advertising files. I believe that he kind of filled up his briefcase and also——
Senator GURNEY. Why is that recollection, why did you have that recollection. Did he have these files in his hands at the same time he had the file that you were going to take in the other hand?
Mr. ODLE. No, I think what happened, he had mentioned at one point that his briefcase was full of these files.
Senator GURNEY. Was this when he was in your office?
Mr. ODLE. Or when I was in Mr. Magruder's office with him.
Senator GURNEY. When you were in Mr. Magruder's office?
Mr. ODLE. It could have been. Probably it was then.
Senator GURNEY. That he said what now?
Mr. ODLE. I think his indication was that I was asked to take another file home because his files were filling up his briefcase.
Senator GURNEY. But wasn't there a discussion about these files being taken home earlier in the phone conversation with Mr. Magruder?
Mr. ODLE. Yes; and I think that is the reason. Because when he had these advertising files they were filling up his briefcase and——
Senator GURNEY. Was it your understanding of the phone call that you were going to take part of the files too, is not that right?
Mr. ODLE. Well, I think they had been discussing that and——
Senator GURNEY. You all had been?
Mr. ODLE. Yes; that is right, and I had gone out of the office and I believe come back in.
Senator GURNEY. So it really was not a matter of a lot of files in one briefcase, it was a matter of both of you were going to take some files home?
Mr. ODLE. Yes; but I think that perhaps the reason for that was that he had all the files he could carry or he felt he could carry.
Senator GURNEY. What did he say to you when he handed you the file that you were going to take home, do you recall? Did he say anything?
Mr. ODLE. No.
Senator GURNEY. Well, did he say guard them carefully? What did he say?
Mr. ODLE. I have no recollection of that.
Senator GURNEY. Did you understand you were to guard it carefully?
Mr. ODLE. I felt it was an important file.
Senator GURNEY. And my recollection is that you carried the file home and put it in a closet with the briefcase?
Mr. ODLE. Yes.
Senator GURNEY. And it stayed there during the weekend?
Mr. ODLE. Yes.
Senator GURNEY. And then you brought it back Monday morning?
Mr. ODLE. Yes.
Senator GURNEY. Describe that now, what happened when you brought it back?

Mr. ODLE. I brought it back, and Mr. Magruder was there, I gave it to Mr. Magruder.

Senator GURNEY. Mr. Magruder was where?

Mr. ODLE. I gave it to Mr. Magruder in his office.

Senator GURNEY. This is the first thing Monday morning?

Mr. ODLE. I do not know. It was sometime Monday. I do not know that he was back the first thing Monday morning.

Senator GURNEY. It was sometime Monday morning?

Mr. ODLE. I believe it was sometime Monday.

Senator GURNEY. You do not know whether it was morning or afternoon?

Mr. ODLE. No; I do not, whenever he got back and asked for it.

Senator GURNEY. Well now, can you describe the circumstances surrounding the return of the file? Here is a file that you were protecting over the weekend because this is important, you bring it back Monday morning and it seems to me that you would be concerned about what to do with it. So tell us about it?

Mr. ODLE. Well, I believe he, in the course of being in his office with me, he asked me for the file and I went and got the file and gave it to him.

Senator GURNEY. In other words, you had it in your office and did not return it to his office until he asked for it, is that correct?

Mr. ODLE. I believe that is what happened.

Senator GURNEY. What did he say when he asked you for the file?

Mr. ODLE. "The file you took home, you know, may I have it," and I said "Yes."

Senator GURNEY. Did he go to your office and ask you?

Mr. ODLE. No; I believe I was going to see him that day and I believe he had seen a couple of other people before he had seen me and when I got to see him about some other matters that subject came up.

Senator GURNEY. Then can you tell us anything further about what happened when you handed over the file to him? Did he make any comment, remark or anything?

Mr. ODLE. I do not believe so.

Senator GURNEY. Did he seem relieved, elated or depressed or otherwise?

Mr. ODLE. I do not recollect that. I think he felt it was, you know, I mean I think he felt it was a serious file.

Senator GURNEY. Did he look at the file?

Mr. ODLE. No.

Senator GURNEY. Put it on the desk, was that it?

Mr. ODLE. I suppose.

Senator GURNEY. You do not know, you do not recall?

Mr. ODLE. No.

Senator GURNEY. You mentioned that you were a consultant now with the Committee To Re-Elect. What is that job?

Mr. ODLE. I am working on winding down the committee offices, working on some of the bills that are to be billed, sell furniture, and that sort of thing, attempting to wind it down. I have also been spending a great deal of time, as I say, you know with various committees looking into these matters and providing documents and things.

Senator GURNEY. Does your job as consultant mean you are no longer a paid employee?

Mr. ODLE. No; I am salaried on a daily basis.

Senator GURNEY. Just one other question: Did you handle any cash payments at all during your time with the Committee To Re-Elect the President?

Mr. ODLE. Yes. At one point in time during the time after the President had mined the harbor of Haiphong and the campaign committee was organized in support of that activity, totally. Incidentally, I received $3,000 or $4,000 from Herbert Porter, who, which was money that I transferred to a couple of people.

Senator GURNEY. Who were they?

Mr. ODLE. Well, I remember one of them is Paul Jones, the director of our black voters division, I think. One of the problems during the Haiphong thing was that we were spending money for things like buses and box lunches and other things like that.

Senator GURNEY. What were the buses being used for?

Mr. ODLE. The buses were being used to bring people to Washington to support—to rally in support of the President's mining of Haiphong which as you know at that point was a very major issue.

Senator GURNEY. What did these people do after they came to Washington?

Mr. ODLE. Well, I assume they rallied and they went home. [Laughter.]

Senator GURNEY. Where did they rally?

Mr. ODLE. There was a rally on the Capitol steps and some other activities in the metropolitan area. There was a vigil, I remember, in the Capitol building in support of that—that Haiphong thing.

Senator GURNEY. Who was in charge of that?

Mr. ODLE. Well, everybody was working on it, sir. The entire campaign apparatus that week went to work in support of what had happened. It was a very crucial time in the campaign, that policy was of great importance and future policy and everybody was working on it.

Senator GURNEY. You mean all 400 people?

Mr. ODLE. Yes, sir, absolutely. We did it publicly, and we did it overtly and we did it outwardly. Incidentally, there is one thing, there has been some suggestion that what was done there in support of the President's mining of Haiphong was a dirty trick or something we tried to hide, something like Watergate. It certainly did not seem that way to us. We did it openly, publicly, we set up a staff about it. We called people on the telephone and if they felt the way we did, they sent a telegram, we did not order anybody to do it. I do not think there was anything wrong about it, and the campaign committee had to keep together that week, everybody worked hard, pulled hard. We did not have that opportunity in the Presidential primaries and we did not have that much of an opportunity to test our State organizations out in the field and that event gave us an opportunity to do that.

Senator GURNEY. Was not some one person in overall charge of this operation?

Mr. ODLE. Well, I think the campaign director probably was at that point.

Senator GURNEY. No other person than that?

Mr. ODLE. Than the campaign committee?

Senator GURNEY. Than the campaign director.

Mr. ODLE. I am sorry. I would say that since the entire campaign was involved with this activity that the campaign director, Mr. Mitchell would have been in ultimate charge of that. Jeb Magruder of course was working on it, I worked on it full time.

Senator GURNEY. What did you do about it?

Mr. ODLE. I had meetings, I organized things, I went around to different people to check up and see how they were doing, and I helped to write the reports on what we were doing, that sort of thing.

Senator GURNEY. Now back to the cash payments that we started out on, you mentioned one cash payment was made to a Paul Jones, and as I understand that was in connection with this Haiphong operation?

Mr. ODLE. Yes; it was.

Senator GURNEY. Who was the other cash payment to?

Mr. ODLE. Well, there could have been other cash payments, in other words, it could have been that Mr. Jones got all of it or part of it, I can't remember anybody else that I actually gave the cash to. We were only talking about $3,000 to $4,000 and I know that—I believe, and I could be, you know, giving Mr. Jones what he does not deserve because it could have been somebody else and I gave Mr. Jones the check that I would have obtained from the finance committee but my best recollection is I did give him some cash and he used that cash to charter buses.

Senator GURNEY. Did you get a receipt for it?

Mr. ODLE. No.

Senator GURNEY. Why, all other disbursements were made by you—as I understand it—by check is that right?

Mr. ODLE. I never signed checks. The finance committee was the disbursing office. They signed the checks, they made the cash disbursements. We had the power of authorization.

Senator GURNEY. You would authorize payments to be made?

Mr. ODLE. Yes, sir.

Senator GURNEY. You actually did not make them?

Mr. ODLE. Correct.

Senator GURNEY. And you cannot remember to whom else you may have made the cash payments?

Mr. ODLE. Of that $4,000?

Senator GURNEY. Yes.

Mr. ODLE. No.

Senator GURNEY. I do not have any further questions.

Senator ERVIN. Senator Inouye?

Senator INOUYE. Thank you, Mr. Chairman.

Mr. Odle, as I recall the testimony this morning that prior to the Watergate break-in you had never heard of E. Howard Hunt?

Mr. ODLE. Yes, sir.

Senator INOUYE. Am I to presume from that that he was not on the payroll of the committee?

Mr. ODLE. Yes, sir, we were asked about that and we checked and found he was not.

Senator INOUYE. And you have no official relationship with him?

Mr. ODLE. I had never seen him, met him, talked to him or had any other kind of conversation with him.

Senator INOUYE. You have never met him?

Mr. ODLE. Never met him.

Senator INOUYE. It has been reported that the former Secretary of the White House Domestic Counsel has indicated that you were an occasional visitor to Mr. Hunt after the break-in?

Mr. ODLE. What? I am not aware of that—that it has ever been reported, but it is not true.

Senator INOUYE. You have never——

Mr. ODLE. Are you referring to—there was a story in the Post a long time ago about a secretary who worked for Mr. Liddy and Mr. Hunt at the White House, and that she was trying to describe telephone conversations between the White House and between that office, and I think she may have mentioned my name, that was a story. She was also the secretary, just before that, to one of my best friends, who worked down at the White House and perhaps that is what she is thinking of. I am saying, sir, categorically, I have never talked to Howard Hunt, met him, seen him, written a memorandum to him, received a memorandum from him.

Senator INOUYE. So, to this date you have never seen Mr. Hunt?

Mr. ODLE. To this date I have never seen Mr. Hunt, and the truth as to Mr. Liddy, I met him at the same time in December at the campaign committee.

Senator ERVIN. Senator Weicker?

Senator WEICKER. Thank you, Mr. Chairman.

Just a few questions, Mr. Odle. I know you have been very patient and very good and I am trying to refresh your recollection as to the 17th.

Let me see whether or not I might not be of some assistance in that regard.

Is it true that on that particular evening, you and other members of the staff were in Magruder's office watching the news on television?

Mr. ODLE. We did watch, yes; we watched the evening news.

Senator WEICKER. And, just so that we can—I am trying to be helpful in placing the phone call.

Mr. ODLE. I understand.

Senator WEICKER. Is it true that the phone call took place after the television news? Do you recall that?

Mr. ODLE. It could have, sir. I thought it took place before. But it could have taken place afterwards.

Senator WEICKER. Who was present when the call was made?

Mr. ODLE. I think just Mr. Reisner and myself.

Senator WEICKER. When you were watching the television show, was anybody else in the room with you?

Mr. ODLE. I think one of the secretaries was, who was working that day, yes.

Senator WEICKER. And, so, when the call was made, was Mr.—Mrs. Odle present in the room while you were watching the television show?

Mr. ODLE. She may have been. I do not believe she was. She arrived a little later.

Senator WEICKER. In any event, when the call was made, it was just you and Mr. Reisner in Mr. Magruder's office?

Mr. ODLE. Yes.

Senator WEICKER. Now, did you ask Mr. Reisner what he was doing there at that time? It was rather late in the evening?

Mr. ODLE. I do not remember that I did, no.

Senator WEICKER. I know that you do not recall the reference to Gemstone, but does, or do, the words "sensitive material," does that ring a bell?

Mr. ODLE. Sensitive—no, sensitive material does not. Sometimes we used the word—"sensitive" does. I mean sometimes you might label a memorandum in government or the committee, I suppose, confidential sensitive, possibly, but not sensitive material.

Senator WEICKER. Now, did Mr. Magruder make the request that these particular files that he was searching for at the particular time that you were on the phone with him?

Mr. ODLE. Again, I——

Senator WEICKER. In other words, at the same moment in time that you and Mr. Reisner were to call Mr. Magruder, was that the point in time that a request was made for a search of the files, and did a search go on while Mr. Magruder was on the line?

Mr. ODLE. I do not think so, no. But that recollection is pretty hazy.

Senator WEICKER. Is there any recollection that you indicated to Mr. Magruder during that phone conversation, the files which he referred to, in fact, were now in hand, they have been found?

Mr. ODLE. Sir, I do not think that they were lost. I mean, I think that Mr. Reisner was fairly familiar with the way in which Mr. Magruder's office was organized. I do not think that they had been misplaced or anything. I do not think it would have been difficult for him to locate the files he was referring to.

Senator WEICKER. So you have no recollection whatsoever, then, of searching for a particular file while you were on the phone——

Mr. ODLE. No.

Senator WEICKER [continuing]. With Mr. Magruder?

Mr. ODLE. I do not have a recollection of that.

Senator WEICKER. You have no recollection as to the fact that there was a question as to what sensitive material was being referred to by Mr. Magruder?

Mr. ODLE. No, I do not remember that term, sensitive material, being used.

Senator WEICKER. All right, then. One last question.

In the hiring of a high-level personnel on the Committee To Re-Elect the President, who was involved in the clearances?

Mr. ODLE. Could you name an example? That would—you know, there was not any great strategy or set of circumstances by which people were hired. I think it would depend on the person as to how it went.

Let us say, for example, that it was in the political division. The process would be much different than if it were in some other division.

Senator WEICKER. All high-level personnel, would you say that they were interviewed or cleared by either Mr. Malek or Mr. Strachan?

Mr. ODLE. No. No; not necessarily. I think Mr. Strachan may have interviewed a number of them, yes. But I do not think that that would have applied in all situations.

For example, in the political division, I do not think that Mr. Strachan would have interviewed those people that were brought in under the regional director. He could have, but I do not think so.

Senator WEICKER. Was an example Mr. Reisner?

Mr. ODLE. Yes; that is another area that that is very possible.

Senator WEICKER. What is possible?

Mr. ODLE. It is very possible that Mr. Reisner might have been interviewed by Mr. Strachan.

Senator WEICKER. Who was in overall charge of the hiring of personnel for the Committee To Re-Elect the President?

Mr. ODLE. At what point in time?

Senator WEICKER. At the period—let us take March, April, May, June?

Mr. ODLE. 1972?

Senator WEICKER. Right.

Mr. ODLE. I would say Mr. Magruder, Mr. Mitchell, and I would say in many cases, those people would be cleared by Mr. Strachan.

Senator WEICKER. And under the chain of command which you referred to before would be—could one make the assumption that clearance by Mr. Strachan did involve Mr. Haldeman, or was this an independent function of Mr. Strachan?

Mr. ODLE. I would say that Mr. Strachan would be looking out for Mr. Haldeman's interests in the clearance process, yes.

Senator WEICKER. I have no further questions, thank you.

Senator ERVIN. Senator Montoya.

Senator MONTOYA. Just one or two questions, Mr. Chairman.

In view of the testimony which you have adduced with respect to the meeting that you had with Mr. Reisner to try to get the files that were in Mr. Magruder's desk, let us reconstruct that scene again. As I understand it from this morning's testimony, you and Mr. Reisner went to Mr. Magruder's desk. Is that correct?

Mr. ODLE. We were in Mr. Magruder's office and we were each on the telephone. I do not have a recollection of going to Mr. Magruder's desk, although I could have been sitting at his desk on the telephone.

Senator MONTOYA. When I questioned you this morning, you did not recall who had the key to Mr. Magruder's desk or whether it was locked. Is that correct?

Mr. ODLE. No, no; Mr. Reisner would have had a key to Mr. Magruder's desk.

Senator MONTOYA. Well, was it locked or did Mr. Magruder open it in that instance?

Mr. ODLE. I do not know. I do not know.

Senator MONTOYA. All right. Now, you had been told during the conversation that these files were very important and that you should get them out of his desk. It that correct?

Mr. ODLE. No; not that I should get them out of his desk, that they should be taken out, and Mr. Reisner, who knew how the desk was organized——

Senator MONTOYA. Well, who gave the instructions or who vocalized the expression that the files were important and they had to be taken away from there for security reasons?

Mr. ODLE. Mr. Magruder, I suppose, would have.

Senator MONTOYA. Well, did he do this in the telephone conversation?

Mr. ODLE. I suppose that he did, yes.

Senator MONTOYA. Well, were you not engaged in that telephone conversation on another phone with him?

Mr. ODLE. For part of the time, yes.

Senator MONTOYA. Well, did you hear him say that?

Mr. ODLE. I do not have a recollection of him using specific words to say that, Senator, but I do remember that——

Senator MONTOYA. Well, would that be the connotation of what he said?

Mr. ODLE. I think that is a fair statement.

Senator MONTOYA. All right. Now, when you and Mr. Reisner decided to divide the files, he decided, or did you both decide, that you should take the file which was styled "Strategy"?

Mr. ODLE. That was my style—I mean, that was my word. I——

Senator MONTOYA. Why did you call it the strategy file?

Mr. ODLE. I do not know. I assume because it was very important.

Senator MONTOYA. Well, did you read it?

Mr. ODLE. No, sir, I did not read it.

Senator MONTOYA. You did not read it at that moment?

Mr. ODLE. No, sir, I did not.

Senator MONTOYA. Why did you call it the strategy file?

Mr. ODLE. Well, because something must have been said in the course of the telephone conversation that made it clear to me that it was a very important, strategic kind of file.

Senator MONTOYA. What do you recall was said during the conversation that led you to believe that it was a strategy file?

Mr. ODLE. I do not know. I do not know, I am sorry. Maybe Mr. Magruder said it was a strategy file. We did have strategy meetings and maybe it was a file that contained minutes of strategy meetings.

Senator MONTOYA. Did it turn out to be a strategy file?

Mr. ODLE. Sir, I do not know what it turned out to be, because I never looked at it.

Senator MONTOYA. Give me a description of that file and give me a description of the briefcase in which you transported it to your home.

Mr. ODLE. Well, I would say it was a file similar to the one I have here. It was a legal size. It was gray in color, light gray. The briefcase was a standard large briefcase.

Senator MONTOYA. And all you knew about this file was that there was something strategic, of strategic importance in it?

Mr. ODLE. Yes, sir.

Senator MONTOYA. And that it was important?

Mr. ODLE. Yes, sir.

Senator MONTOYA. And that it had to be guarded?

Mr. ODLE. Well, not guarded in a sense, but Mr. Magruder was concerned for the security of it.

Senator MONTOYA. All right. And you took it home in your briefcase?

Mr. ODLE. Yes.

Senator MONTOYA. And it was an open file and you did not read it?

Mr. ODLE. No, sir, I did not. I did not even read my budget files that weekend.

Senator MONTOYA. Are you a very curious man, Mr. Odle?

Mr. ODLE. I was not very curious about reading it that weekend. I was more interested in reading the Washington Post to find out what was going on down at the committee.

Senator MONTOYA. Were you not interested in the file in view of the extreme interest manifested by Mr. Magruder?

Mr. ODLE. I do not know that the interest was extreme. I did not read the file. I do not know why. Maybe I should have.

Senator MONTOYA. And you never found out what was in it?
Mr. ODLE. Well, no, but I can speculate.
Senator MONTOYA. Well, tell me what was in it from your speculation?
Mr. ODLE. Well, I do not know that that would fair to other people, Senator. Well, if you ask me to—I have been reading the newspapers.
Senator MONTOYA. All right, I will withdraw the question. I will be fair with you.
Mr. ODLE. Well, it is just——
Senator MONTOYA. I will be fair with you.
Now, you say that you disbursed $4,000 in cash?
Mr. ODLE. Yes.
Senator MONTOYA. And that for only part of it can you account at the present time?
Mr. ODLE. Well, my best recollection is giving cash to Mr. Jones. I cannot remember if I gave him $2,000 or $4,000.
Senator MONTOYA. All right, that is fine. Now——
Mr. ODLE. If I gave him the $4,000, the rally report, that accounts for it all.
Senator MONTOYA. Who gave you the cash?
Mr. ODLE. Mr. Herbert Porter.
Senator MONTOYA. Had you requested this cash or were they given to you for a specific purpose without your request?
Mr. ODLE. I requested it.
Senator MONTOYA. What did you request it for?
Mr. ODLE. To charter buses and bring people to Washington to participate in the rally.
Senator MONTOYA. Were you paying these people to——
Mr. ODLE. No.
Senator MONTOYA [continuing]. To come to Washington?
Mr. ODLE. I did not disburse the funds beyond to the one person or the two people. But I do not believe the money went to the people, sir, I believe it went to the cost of the buses and things.
Senator MONTOYA. To your knowledge, they were not paid to come to Washington?
Mr. ODLE. Yes, sir, to my knowledge, they were not.
Senator MONTOYA. So, therefore, on the matter of the Haiphong supporters, is this all you gave them, a boxlunch and a ride on the bus?
Mr. ODLE. To the best of my knowledge, sir, yes. I was not the one that actually did that.
Senator MONTOYA. That is all.
Thank you, Mr. Chairman.
Senator ERVIN. Let the record show that the charts which were identified by the witness, are made exhibits, and also, if Senator Weicker has no objection, we will also make his chart an exhibit. The reporter will mark them appropriately.
[The charts referred to were marked for identification as exhibits Nos. 5, 6, 7, and 8, and can be found on pp. 11, 15, 19, and 33, respectively.]
Senator ERVIN. Mr. Odle, I want to thank you on behalf of the committee for the very, the total cooperation you have given this committee in its investigation and I also wish to commend you for the forthrightness of your testimony and to say that in my judgment, I have known nothing or heard nothing that has occurred that reflects in any way whatever upon you.

Mr. ODLE. Thank you, Senator. I appreciate that.

Senator ERVIN. Thank you very much.

I would like to say to the committee that we have one witness this afternoon who has an engagement to be in a golf tournament tomorrow, Sergeant Leeper. And since he is to testify only upon the apprehension of people caught in Watergate, I am going to suggest that we be as expeditious as possible in our questions, since that proposition has been well established.

First, we have another witness before Mr. Leeper, but I just want to say I want to do all I can to facilitate his getting to the golf tournament tomorrow.

Call the next witness.

Mr. DASH. The next witness is Mr. Bruce Kehrli.

Senator ERVIN. Mr. Kehrli, hold up your right hand, please.

Do you swear the evidence you are to give to the Senate Select Committee on Presidential Campaign Activities to be the truth, the whole truth, and nothing but the truth, so help you God?

Mr. KEHRLI. I do.

Mr. DASH. Do you have a statement you want to give to the committee?

TESTIMONY OF BRUCE A. KEHRLI, SPECIAL ASSISTANT TO THE PRESIDENT

Mr. KEHRLI. I have no opening statement, but I do have a statement I may want to give.

Mr. DASH. Please give your name and address.

Mr. KEHRLI. My name is Bruce Arnold Kehrli. My address is 738 South Lee Street, in Alexandria.

Mr. DASH. What is your present employment, Mr. Kehrli?

Mr. KEHRLI. I am employed at the White House.

Mr. DASH. What is your position?

Mr. KEHRLI. My title is Special Assistant to the President.

Mr. DASH. Now, how long have you had such a position?

Mr. KEHRLI. I have had the title since January of this year. My position is actually that of staff secretary, which I have had since January 1 of 1972.

Mr. DASH. And to whom do you report, Mr. Kehrli?

Mr. KEHRLI. Right now to General Commander Haig.

Mr. DASH. And prior to that time, to whom did you report?

Mr. KEHRLI. H. R. Haldeman.

Mr. DASH. Now, a chart has been placed upon the easel to my left. Have you seen that chart before or something like it?

Mr. KEHRLI. Yes, I have.

Mr. DASH. And did you assist our staff in the preparation of that chart?

Mr. KEHRLI. Yes, I did.

Mr. DASH. Did you want to make some comment?

Mr. KEHRLI. Yes, I would like to make a statement now about the chart itself.

Senator ERVIN. The reporter will mark this chart with the appropriate exhibit number.

[The chart referred to was marked exhibit 9 and appears on p. 77.]

Mr. KEHRLI. The organization chart was prepared by the committee and checked with me for accuracy. It is accurate as far as it goes, but it could be misleading in two ways. First, it shows only those people about whom information was requested. It does not give an idea of the many hundreds of people who worked on or around various White House staffs, some of which, like the Domestic Council and the National Security Council, are themselves administratively separate and independent entities. There are also the working relationships with members of the Cabinet and with other people in the various departments and agencies of the executive branch. In other words, the chain of command is not nearly so small or so closely integrated as the few dozen boxes and names on this chart might indicate.

Second, there are often rearrangements within the White House staff which is in fact a fairly dynamic organization. This is partly a function of the nature of the work which involves not only long-range responsibilities but also, literally scores of short-term projects and informal ad hoc relationships.

Since many individual staff members have a wide range of responsibilities and each area of responsibility could conceivably have a different reporting relationship, some common denominator had to be chosen as the basis for the chart. The criterion chosen was the formal administrative chain of command.

This chart describes, then, the fundamental relationships which existed in the White House during the months it covers and the dates in parentheses upon which the individuals left the White House payroll. I shall be glad, to the extent of my knowledge, to answer any questions the committee may have about it.

Mr. DASH. Now, will you please go to the chart and take a pointer?

Now, Mr. Kehrli, taking your statement in consideration, if at any time in the explanation you make, you feel that it is important to describe any other function or any other role of the White House personnel, please feel free to do so, because the purpose of the chart is to relate to the resolution of our committee. But please do not feel constrained to the chart if you feel a full explanation requires you to do otherwise.

Mr. KEHRLI. Fine.

Mr. DASH. Now, on that chart, you will find Mr. Haldeman?

Mr. KEHRLI. Yes, Mr. Haldeman is right here. He is in charge of White House operations. You will notice that under Mr. Haldeman, you will find a number of other suborganizations and as I said, because this chart was based on administrative relationships, this may be deceiving and that any number of these people at any point in time may have had a different reporting relationship, depending upon what project or what subject area they happened to be working in.

Mr. DASH. But basically, under the organization you have and to the extent that that chart is relevant, the people who are shown under Mr. Haldeman worked for Mr. Haldeman?

Mr. KEHRLI. Right, but let me give you an example. For instance, we have the speechwriters here. Mr. Ray Price is the head of that group. Now, at any point in time, the President may have called Mr. Price with a specific request, not one which went through Mr. Haldeman, and Mr. Price may have responded to that request without ever going through Mr. Haldeman.

Mr. DASH. Would you say he may have or would have?

EXHIBIT NO. 9

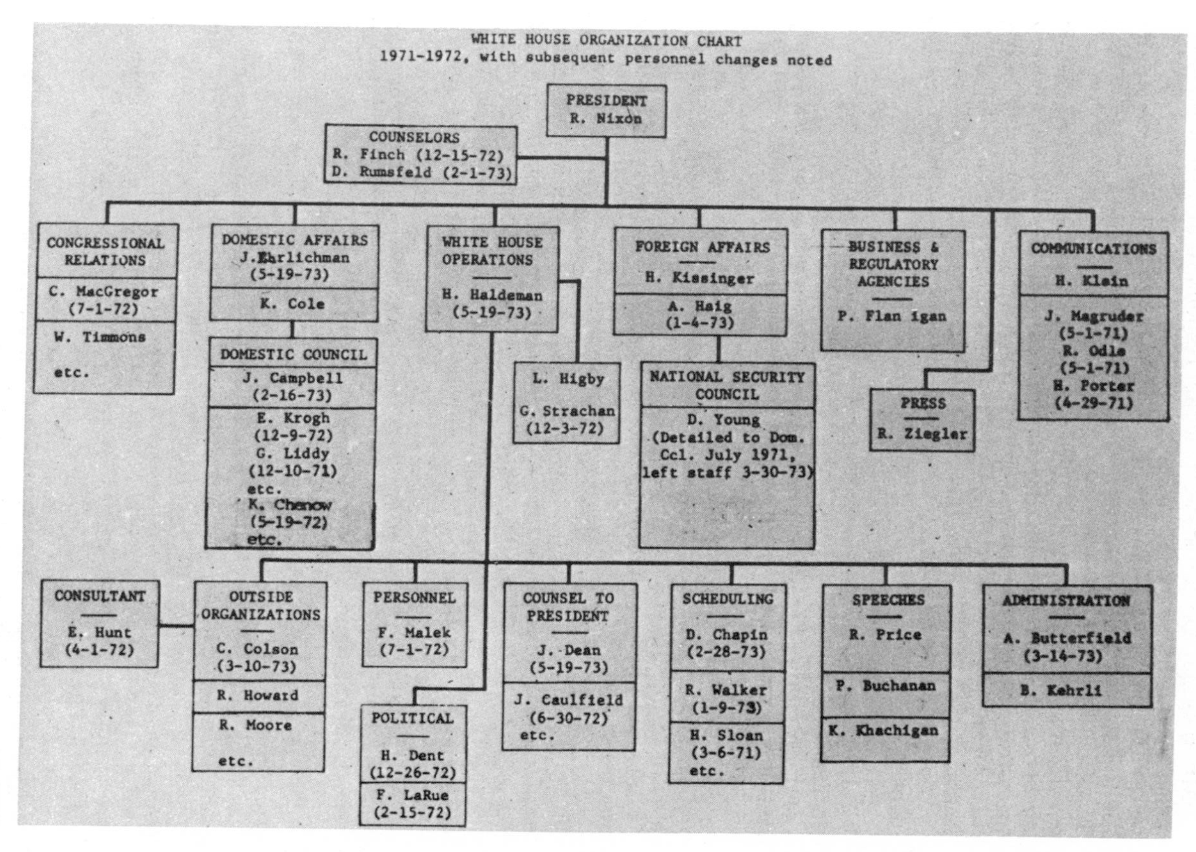
WHITE HOUSE ORGANIZATION CHART
1971-1972, with subsequent personnel changes noted
PRESIDENT
R. Nixon
COUNSELORS
R. Finch (12-15-72)
D. Rumsfeld (2-1-73)
CONGRESSIONAL RELATIONS
C. MacGregor (7-1-72)
W. Timmons
etc.
DOMESTIC AFFAIRS
J. Ehrlichman (5-19-73)
K. Cole
DOMESTIC COUNCIL
J. Campbell (2-16-73)
E. Krogh (12-9-72)
G. Liddy (12-10-71)
etc.
K. Chenow (5-19-72)
etc.
WHITE HOUSE OPERATIONS
H. Haldeman (5-19-73)
L. Higby
G. Strachan (12-3-72)
FOREIGN AFFAIRS
H. Kissinger
A. Haig (1-4-73)
NATIONAL SECURITY COUNCIL
D. Young (Detailed to Dom. Ccl. July 1971, left staff 3-30-73)
BUSINESS & REGULATORY AGENCIES
P. Flan igan
PRESS
R. Ziegler
COMMUNICATIONS
H. Klein
J. Magruder (5-1-71)
R. Odle (5-1-71)
H. Porter (4-29-71)
CONSULTANT
E. Hunt (4-1-72)
OUTSIDE ORGANIZATIONS
C. Colson (3-10-73)
R. Howard
R. Moore
etc.
PERSONNEL
F. Malek (7-1-72)
POLITICAL
H. Dent (12-26-72)
F. LaRue (2-15-72)
COUNSEL TO PRESIDENT
J. Dean (5-19-73)
J. Caulfield (6-30-72)
etc.
SCHEDULING
D. Chapin (2-28-73)
R. Walker (1-9-73)
H. Sloan (3-6-71)
etc.
SPEECHES
R. Price
P. Buchanan
K. Khachigan
ADMINISTRATION
A. Butterfield (3-14-73)
B. Kehrli

Mr. KEHRLI. On occasions, he would respond to Mr. Haldeman. On other occasions, he would not.

Mr. DASH. Now, under the direct line to Mr. Haldeman, who under that chart would be reporting, based on that chart, to Mr. Haldeman or through Mr. Haldeman?

Mr. KEHRLI. Well, any of these people at some point in time would report to Mr. Haldeman, but as I said before, on occasion, these people may have reported through another staff member—for instance, Mr. Dean, who is Counsel to the President, on a lot of legal matters reported to Mr. Ehrlichman.

Mr. DASH. Now, Mr. Hunt is listed there as a consultant on that chart?

Mr. KEHRLI. Yes, he is.

Mr. DASH. For what period of time, do you know, that he served in that role?

Mr. KEHRLI. I am sorry, I do not have his starting date. I was only asked to put the dates on on which they left the payroll.

Mr. DASH. When did he leave the payroll?

Mr. KEHRLI. That was on April 1, 1972.

Mr. DASH. And Mr. Colson—what was Mr. Colson's position? I do not think it is shown on the chart.

Mr. KEHRLI. Mr. Colson was in charge of liaison with outside organizations.

Mr. DASH. And Mr. Malek's role?

Mr. KEHRLI. Mr. Malek's role at this time was he had charge of the White House personnel office which was recruiting and placing people within the administration.

Mr. DASH. All right. Now, Mr. Dean, as you said, would either be reporting to Haldeman, but as indicated, he would also perhaps be doing quite a bit of his work with Mr. Ehrlichman.

Mr. KEHRLI. That is right.

Mr. DASH. So Mr. Dean's primary responsibilities were through Mr. Haldeman and Mr. Ehrlichman. Would that be true?

Mr. KEHRLI. Yes, it would.

Mr. DASH. And Mr. Chapin, what was his particular capacity and role?

Mr. KEHRLI. Mr. Chapin was in charge of scheduling the President which included any meetings within the White House, any trips, any meetings outside of the White House, generally on a long-range planning basis.

Mr. DASH. Now, going to Mr. Ehrlichman, Mr. Ehrlichman, I see is there on a line right next to Mr. Haldeman, is that true?

Mr. KEHRLI. Yes, he is.

Mr. DASH. And what was his official role?

Mr. KEHRLI. Mr. Ehrlichman was an adviser to the President as well as head of the domestic council.

Mr. DASH. Now, Mr. Krogh, what was his relationship to Mr. Ehrlichman?

Mr. KEHRLI. Mr. Krogh was a member of the domestic council staff. I might add at this point as I said in my opening statement I can only speak out of firsthand knowledge on the White House organization itself. The domestic council is a separate entity, has its own administrative procedures and its own administrative personnel.

Mr. DASH. Were you aware at that point in time that Mr. Liddy had worked in the White House staff under Mr. Krogh?

Mr. KEHRLI. I was aware only because I had heard his name mentioned. I can't verify that at this time or I couldn't at that point. I have since then checked and found he was on the domestic council and left on December 10, 1971.

Mr. DASH. Based on your check, Mr. Liddy did in fact work under Mr. Krogh?

Mr. KEHRLI. Yes, he did.

Mr. DASH. Did there come a time based on any check that you made in assistance in preparing this chart did Mr. Young from National Security Council and Kathleen Chenow work with Mr. Krogh and Mr. Liddy?

Mr. KEHRLI. Yes.

Mr. DASH. Do you know when that shift of relationship occurred?

Mr. KEHRLI. The National Security Council records indicate that David Young was detailed to the domestic council in July of 1971. We didn't have a specific date. Miss Chenow was on the domestic council staff at that point.

Mr. DASH. This chart does not show it. Are you aware of any time when Mr. Hunt worked with that group that later has become known as the "plumbers" by Mr. Krogh?

Mr. KEHRLI. Under Mr. Krogh, yes, sir.

Mr. DASH. Are you aware of that term?

Mr. KEHRLI. Yes, I am aware of it because I only read about it in the papers.

Mr. DASH. You are only aware of it because you read it in the papers?

Now, Mr. Strachan, who is Mr. Strachan and where does it appear on the chart?

Mr. KEHRLI. Mr. Strachan was on Mr. Haldeman's personal staff and it appears here.

Mr. DASH. What was his particular function with Mr. Haldeman?

Mr. KEHRLI. His particular function was liaison with the Republican National Committee and with the Committee To Re-Elect the President.

Mr. DASH. Now, are you aware of to your own knowledge as to how frequently Mr. Strachan was in touch as liaison with the Committee for Re-Election of the President.

Mr. KEHRLI. No, I am not.

Mr. DASH. But that was a main function of his, as you know.

Mr. KEHRLI. Yes.

Mr. DASH. And therefore he would be carrying back and forth for Mr. Haldeman, between Mr. Haldeman and the committee whatever messages Mr. Haldeman had for the committee or the committee for Mr. Haldeman.

Mr. KEHRLI. Carrying, I think, he may not or may not have carried them but they would have come through him at one point or another.

Mr. DASH. Mr. MacGregor at one point was a member of the White House staff as I see on the chart?

Mr. KEHRLI. Yes, he was.

Mr. DASH. I think you have him on the chart as leaving July 1, 1972. Do you know where he went from that?

Mr. KEHRLI. He went to the Committee To Re-Elect the President.

Mr. DASH. Mr. Magruder is shown on that chart on the other, on the right-hand side on the communications under Mr. Klein, staying until May 1, 1971.

Do you know where he went after that time?

Mr. KEHRLI. He went to the Committee To Re-Elect the President.

Mr. DASH. I think you have Mr. Odle and Mr. Porter working for Mr. Magruder and they left approximately, Mr. Odle May 1, 1971, and Mr. Porter April 29, 1971, according to the chart and do you know where they went when they left?

Mr. KEHRLI. They went to the Committee To Re-Elect the President.

Mr. DASH. Now, down towards the bottom you have Mr. Hugh Sloan under scheduling, and I take it under Mr. Dwight Chapin, and it appears in the chart that he left the White House on March 6, 1971.

Do you know where he went when he left the White House?

Mr. KEHRLI. He went either to the Committee To Re-Elect the President or the finance committee and I would have to check that.

Mr. DASH. And I see on the chart also at the bottom, I guess a line down from Mr. Haldeman to a box marked political H. Dent and under that Mr. LaRue, and a date of leaving February 15, 1972.

Do you know where Mr. LaRue went when he left the White House?

Mr. KEHRLI. I assume he went to the Committee To Re-Elect the President. I don't have that.

Mr. DASH. The facts would show that, I take it?

Mr. KEHRLI. Yes.

Mr. DASH. Now, are you of your own knowledge, and I know that we have asked you to come here to assist us in reconstructing the White House staff and the relationship around the time relevant to the 1971–72 period, that would cover the resolution in which we are engaged in dealing with the Watergate matter, and that this was the purpose of developing this chart.

Beyond being able to describe the various relationships of these people and their roles on the chart, do you have any further knowledge as to their relationship with the Committee To Re-Elect the President?

Mr. KEHRLI. No, I don't.

Mr. DASH. Do you know anything about the duties of Kathleen Chenow?

Mr. KEHRLI. No, I don't.

Mr. DASH. Mr. Chairman, I have no further questions.

Senator ERVIN. Mr. Thompson?

Mr. THOMPSON. Mr. Kehrli, if you would like to be seated I think perhaps it would be better. I have a few questions, Mr. Chairman.

Mr. Kehrli, I would like to ask you a few questions about Mr. John Dean, Counsel to the President.

According to your chart Mr. Dean is immediately responsible to Mr. Haldeman, is that correct?

Mr. KEHRLI. That is correct.

Mr. THOMPSON. And according to the chart he would not have direct access to the President as Ehrlichman, Haldeman, Kissinger, and these other men you have named would?

Mr. KEHRLI. Now, I should elaborate on that point. As I said, depending on the various issues or projects these people were working on they would have different channels of command. On some issues John Dean may have had direct access to the President.

Mr. THOMPSON. Could you categorize Mr. Dean's duties for us? What types of problems or situations would normally arise that would draw his attention and require his work?

Mr. KEHRLI. Basically he was responsible for seeing that anything that the President sent out in terms of an official document or proclamation, Executive order, things of this nature was correct legally. He also was an adviser to the President on legal matters and things like executive privilege. He also dealt with conflict of interest in terms of bringing people on board the staff and that was his responsibility.

Mr. THOMPSON. Would you say that his primary responsibility would be for providing legal opinions and approving legal documents?

Mr. KEHRLI. Yes, I would.

Mr. THOMPSON. I know you have here Mr. Finch and Mr. Rumsfeld as counselors to the President and I assume we can draw a strict distinction between counsel to the President, Mr. Dean, and counsellors to the President, Mr. Finch and Mr. Rumsfeld.

Mr. KEHRLI. Yes, Mr. Finch and Mr. Rumsfeld as counselors to the President performed a role that included their being spokesmen, they included special projects and they didn't have any set substantive responsibility but were free to move into any area the President may determine.

Mr. THOMPSON. You mentioned the area of executive privilege a moment ago, would Mr. Dean aid the President in formulating his legal position on executive privilege?

Mr. KEHRLI. He would advise him on it, yes.

Mr. THOMPSON. The President made a statement on March 2 pertaining to executive privilege, when he stated that the White House aides would not come down and testify before a committee formally, and another statement on March 15 of this year when he stated that Mr. Dean specifically had what might be referred to as double privilege.

Do you know whether or not Mr. Dean had any input with regard to the President's legal position on those two statements?

Mr. KEHRLI. I can't say that for a fact.

Mr. THOMPSON. Leaving that subject, Mr. Kehrli, I would like to ask you this: You mentioned the so-called "plumbers", Mr. Hunt, Mr. Liddy, who were in the White House at one time. As I understand it one time they were working on the so-called Pentagon Papers, the leaks pertaining to the Pentagon Papers situation, is that your understanding?

Mr. KEHRLI. My understanding is they were working on a project related to leaks the timing of it was such that I assume it had to do with the Pentagon Papers. I know David Young also worked on a commission on declassification that was set up.

Mr. THOMPSON. Well, reports have been that these papers concerned matters of national security.

Do you know why Hunt and Liddy in this particular project would operate out of the domestic council under Mr. Ehrlichman in this particular area if they were primarily national security problems?

Mr. KEHRLI. No, I don't.

Mr. THOMPSON. Does it seem like a logical situation to you or unusual situation to you, considering the nature of the domestic council and considering the nature of the work they were doing?

Mr. KEHRLI. Well, knowing the background of Mr. Krogh and Mr. Haldeman he was once counsel to the President and there were legal responsibilities dealing with the law and I don't think it was unusual to have an organization set up like that.

Mr. THOMPSON. Mr. John Caulfield is not on your chart, is he?

Mr. KEHRLI. Yes, he is.

Mr. THOMPSON. Is Mr. Caulfield on the chart? Is he under Mr. Dean?

Mr. DASH. He is under Mr. Dean.

Mr. THOMPSON. Did you mention in your testimony his relationship to Mr. Ehrlichman?

Mr. KEHRLI. Mr. Caulfield?

Mr. THOMPSON. Yes.

Mr. KEHRLI. No, I didn't.

Mr. THOMPSON. Would it be accurate to state that often he dealt with Mr. Ehrlichman on matters?

Mr. KEHRLI. No, I don't know.

Mr. THOMPSON. You don't know that.

I have no further questions, Mr. Chairman.

Senator ERVIN. Do you know Mr. Richardson?

Mr. KEHRLI. Yes, sir.

Senator ERVIN. What was his assignment?

Mr. KEHRLI. He was a writer.

Senator ERVIN. And he came in under Mr. Price or one of the writers with Mr. R. Price and Mr. Buchanan?

Mr. KEHRLI. Yes, sir.

Senator ERVIN Those are the only questions.

Senator BAKER. Mr. Chairman, thank you very much. Once again I understand that our operating format is to utilize this witness' testimony for the purpose of establishing an organizational chart within the White House. I have a number of questions that I wished to put to the witness that are not related to the organizational chart as such but in the interest of trying to conserve time and stick to that operating format, I would ask instead if the witness will agree to return at a later date so that we may ask him other questions that are not related to his testimony today.

Mr. KEHRLI. Yes, sir.

Senator BAKER. I might also ask, Mr. Kehrli, if, as an assistant to the President, you are appearing voluntarily or under subpena.

Mr. KEHRLI. I am appearing voluntarily.

Senator BAKER. Was there any intervention of a claim of executive privilege on your behalf?

Mr. KEHRLI. No, there was not.

Senator BAKER. Was there any instruction from the White House or anyone in it as to how you should conduct yourself with this committee, especially with respect to where you should cooperate or not cooperate?

Mr. KEHRLI. I was asked to, I was encouraged to cooperate.

Senator BAKER. Mr. Kehrli, so that you have some understanding of what I intend to ask you later, and once again I do not intend to pursue it today, when you return as a witness to testify at a later sequence of hearings I want to know particularly about the drilling and opening of Mr. Hunt's safe. I want to know what you found in it, I want to know what happened to it, and I want to know a number of other things related to it. But just so that you understand that I am not asking you those questions now in the interest of time and orderliness, I hope you will be prepared to respond when you do return.

Mr. KEHRLI. I do.

Senator BAKER. Thank you very much.

Senator ERVIN. Senator Talmadge.

Senator TALMADGE. Mr. Kehrli, who determined which people in the White House originally went to the Committee To Re-Elect the President?

Mr. KEHRLI. I don't think there was any one person who determined that. I think it was a joint decision based on the need of the White House and the committee. If the committee had a need and there was someone at the White House who was not in position or was in a position rather that they could leave and they felt that they could do a better job at the committee then they were able to go to the committee.

I don't think there was any one being that said you will go.

Senator TALMADGE. But there was more than one person who made the determination; who was it?

Mr. KEHRLI. I would say that, and I don't know for a fact, but I would imagine that it was probably made based on discussions between the head of the campaign committee and Mr. Haldeman, Mr. Ehrlichman, and other people on the staff.

Senator TALMADGE. Mr. Haldeman, Mr. Mitchell, and who else?

Mr. KEHRLI. Mr. Ehrlichman.

Senator TALMADGE. Mr. Ehrlichman.

Did you see any memoranda from the Committee To Re-Elect the President, circulating in the White House?

Mr. KEHRLI. The only thing that I saw that I can remember is one that came over with the committee's list of telephone numbers on it. We did circulate it.

Senator TALMADGE. That was the only one?

Mr. KEHRLI. Yes.

Senator TALMADGE. Did you ever see or have knowledge of any communication either written or oral between Mr. Mitchell and the White House staff prior to the time he resigned as Attorney General concerning the campaign activities?

Mr. KEHRLI. No.

Senator TALMADGE. Did you see any after July 1, the date Mr. Mitchell resigned as campaign chairman?

Mr. KEHRLI. Not that I remember.

Senator TALMADGE. Did you ever receive funds from the committee or the finance committee for campaign activities?

Mr. KEHRLI. No.

Senator TALMADGE. None whatever?

Mr. KEHRLI. I personally?

Senator TALMADGE. Yes.

Mr. KEHRLI. At one point I was the contact on the White House staff for payment of bills that were incurred by the President during the campaign. We went out of our way to a great degree to make sure that any travel, any events, anything whatsoever that the President did that could in the least way be construed as political were paid for by committee funds rather than appropriated funds.

Senator TALMADGE. The only funds you received then were the President's political activity and solely for that purpose?

Mr. KEHRLI. That is right.

Senator TALMADGE. And they were dispensed for that purpose. Was there ever any regular meetings held between the White House staff and committee officials?

Mr. KEHRLI. Not that I know of.

Senator TALMADGE. None at all?

Mr. KEHRLI. No; not that I know of, but, as I said, I was not in the mainstream of communication.

Senator TALMADGE. To your knowledge, never at any time under no conditions?

Mr. KEHRLI. That is right.

Senator TALMADGE. That is your answer?

Mr. KEHRLI. Yes, sir.

Senator TALMADGE. Thank you, sir.

No further questions.

Senator ERVIN. Senator Gurney.

Senator GURNEY. Thank you, Mr. Chairman.

Mr. Kehrli, I just want to talk a little bit about the White House organization and especially those people closest around the President most of the time more frequently than others.

Mr. KEHRLI. Mr. Haldeman.

Senator GURNEY. Who else?

Mr. KEHRLI. Mr. Ehrlichman.

Senator GURNEY. Who else?

Did Mr. Ziegler see him?

Mr. KEHRLI. Well, Mr. Ziegler, that is right. But beyond that there would be a tossup as to who was on the staff.

Senator GURNEY. How about Mr. Chapin?

Mr. KEHRLI. Mr. Chapin dealt primarily through Mr. Haldeman.

Senator GURNEY. What was Mr. Haldeman's previous employment?

Mr. KEHRLI. Pardon me, sir?

Senator GURNEY. What was Mr. Haldeman's previous employment?

Mr. KEHRLI. He was with the J. Walter Thompson Advertising Co.

Senator GURNEY. Where did Mr. Chapin come from before he came to the White House?

Mr. KEHRLI. The same company.

Senator GURNEY. Was he brought in by Mr. Haldeman?

Mr. KEHRLI. Yes; he was.

Senator GURNEY. Who was Mr. Ziegler with before he came to the White House?

Mr. KEHRLI. He was also with J. Walter Thompson.

Senator GURNEY. Was he also brought in by Mr. Haldeman?

Mr. KEHRLI. Yes; he was.

Senator GURNEY. What about Mr. Ehrlichman; was he ever with J. Walter Thompson?

Mr. KEHRLI. No; I don't think so.

Senator GURNEY. Was he a very close friend of Mr. Haldeman's?

Mr. KEHRLI. Yes; he was.

Senator GURNEY. What was their past friendship and association?

Mr. KEHRLI. Well, the only—only thing I can relate is what I read, they were evidently friends during college days.

Senator GURNEY. Who were you previously employed with?

Mr. KEHRLI. I was with J. Walter Thompson. [Laughter.]

Senator GURNEY. Who were the people who budgeted the President's time? I mean by that who were most responsible for those people who saw the President and those people who did not see the President?

Mr. KEHRLI. Mr. Chapin was responsible for the President's scheduling and that was done on a weekly and a daily basis, a long-range weekly scheduling followed up by a daily schedule. Mr. Butterfield was responsible for implementing that schedule.

Senator GURNEY. Who was Mr. Butterfield?

Mr. KEHRLI. Mr. Butterfield on the chart on the far right reported to Mr. Haldeman and he was—he had an office right outside the President's door and he was responsible for implementing the President's schedule on a daily basis making sure that the appoints were there on time, that when people came in they were positioned correctly.

Senator GURNEY. And he reported to Mr. Haldeman?

Mr. KEHRLI. Yes, he did.

Senator GURNEY. And Mr. Chapin reported to Mr. Haldeman?

Mr. KEHRLI. Yes, he did.

Senator GURNEY. Would anybody who had anything to do with budgeting the President's time report to anybody else but Mr. Haldeman?

Mr. KEHRLI. No.

Senator GURNEY. Are you familiar at all in your job in the White House with the people the President saw daily during your time there?

Mr. KEHRLI. You mean was I aware of his daily schedule?

Senator GURNEY. Yes, I mean would you be generally familiar with the people that he saw?

Mr. KEHRLI. I received a copy of his daily schedule so I saw the names of the people that he saw daily.

Senator GURNEY. I see.

Mr. KEHRLI. That were on the published schedule. Now, he often would call other people over and that wouldn't be on the published schedule calls obviously he couldn't keep it up on a minute to minute basis. It was issued during the morning and if it was changed during the day it wasn't worth issuing a new one for the staff.

Senator GURNEY. Would you generally be aware of the people who came to see him even though they were not on the regular schedule?

Mr. KEHRLI. No, I would not. My office is located in the basement of the White House, out of the traffic flow.

Senator GURNEY. Of those people that you are aware of who saw the President, because you did see the daily schedule, did many Senators ever visit the President?

Mr. KEHRLI. Yes, quite a few. And he also, he used to have, as I remember or he still does, breakfasts for Members of Congress.

Senator GURNEY. But I mean on a personal basis, talking to them in his own private office with him personally.

Mr. KEHRLI. I don't have an exact number but I do remember Senators and Congressmen on the schedule, yes, sir.

Senator GURNEY. Were these frequent visits?

Mr. KEHRLI. I really can't comment on the number of visits.

Senator GURNEY. How about Republican National Committee Chairman. Was he ever on the visitors list also?

Mr. KEHRLI. He was on the visitors list.

Senator GURNEY. Very often?

Mr. KEHRLI. It is difficult to say how often, he was in there more than once.

Senator GURNEY. Would you say frequently?

Mr. KEHRLI. I don't know, how would you term frequently?

Senator GURNEY. Well, you term it. I mean you saw the schedule, I didn't.

Mr. KEHRLI. I would say——

Senator GURNEY. Once a month?

Mr. KEHRLI. Once a month is probably correct.

Senator GURNEY. That would be about correct?

Mr. KEHRLI. That is right.

Senator GURNEY. What about other Republican Party people, State chairmen or other people whose work was within the party. Did you ever see them on the schedule?

Mr. KEHRLI. I may have but they weren't listed as a State chairman and I probably wouldn't recognize the names.

Senator GURNEY. Well, at any rate the people who saw the President were carefully screened by Mr. Haldeman and those people that we have talked about here who were brought to the White House by Mr. Haldeman, is that right?

Mr. KEHRLI. Mr. Haldeman was responsible for putting together the President's schedule, and based on, I am sure on, conferring with the President and what time was available and how it was to be used.

Senator GURNEY. Would you have any idea how many people on the White House staff, how many were there, total staff?

Mr. KEHRLI. Total on the White House staff approximately 500. Now there is a confusing point there and I am speaking only of the White House Office and the domestic council, for instance, the National Security Council, Council of Economic Advisers, all which are housed in the Executive Office Building, White House Office complex, are not included in that 500.

Senator GURNEY. I am talking about the 500 staff.

Mr. KEHRLI. Yes.

Senator GURNEY. Who recruited most of those people? Did you say?

Mr. KEHRLI. It was done—I can speak only from the time in November of 1970, when I came on the White House rolls, and they were recruited by the personnel office primarily.

Senator GURNEY. Who was in charge of that?

Mr. KEHRLI. Fred Malek.

Senator GURNEY. Who brought Fred Malek to the White House?

Mr. KEHRLI. I assume Bob Haldeman did, although I can't answer that for a fact, because I arrived almost on the same day that Fred Malek arrived.

Senator GURNEY. Is it fair to say that all people who came on board, regardless of who they were recruited by, were OK'd or turned down by Mr. Haldeman? Is that fair to say?

Mr. KEHRLI. Mr. Haldeman did want to be made aware, as he was responsible for them, of all members of the White House staff, all new members, and he was made aware of anyone, by anyone of the staff members if they wanted to bring an individual on.

Senator GURNEY. Did you ever hire anybody through your staff?

Mr. KEHRLI. No, I did not.

Senator GURNEY. Did you have a staff?

Mr. KEHRLI. I do now. Yes, my staff is primarily career employees. One of my basic responsibilities is the 280 or so career Government employees who serve the President, the Office of the President, year in and year out.

Senator GURNEY. I see.

Now, tell me, was one of your responsibilities the White House payroll?

Mr. KEHRLI. Yes. I was responsible for monitoring the White House payroll.

Senator GURNEY. What do you mean by monitoring?

Mr. KEHRLI. Well, whenever—for instance, any raises of professional employees were sent to Mr. Haldeman for approval; I approved all raises for people below that level—in other words, clerical types, secretaries.

Senator GURNEY. Did you ever handle any moneys that were paid to White House personnel that were not Federal payroll moneys?

Mr. KEHRLI. No.

Senator GURNEY. Did you ever handle any cash at any time?

Mr. KEHRLI. I did. We had, as I said when I was talking about, one of my responsibilities being making sure that anything that the President did or that his staff did in supporting him while he was participating in a political event was covered by funds from the Committee To Re-Elect the President as opposed to appropriated funds. We did have a problem at one point with, for instance, when the President would fly somewhere and they needed to start the plane, provision it with food. The way we had it set up was to have the military people go out and purchase the food, put it aboard the plane. Rather than having them, and most of them were low-level military people, put out money and have to be repaid, we brought over some cash and paid them in advance to buy this food.

Senator GURNEY. These were all moneys paid in direct support of the President?

Mr. KEHRLI. Absolutely.

Senator GURNEY. At any particular time.

And you testified that you made no cash payments to anybody other than in this area that you are now describing?

Mr. KEHRLI. To the best of my knowledge, yes.

Senator GURNEY. Well, now, what does that mean?

Mr. KEHRLI. Well, I can't remember.

Senator GURNEY. Do you think that you did?

Mr. KEHRLI. No.

Senator GURNEY. Do you know of any people on the White House staff who were paid moneys by anybody else that were not Federal payroll moneys?

Mr. KEHRLI. No, I do not; no.

Senator GURNEY. Were you responsible for the assigning of office space in the White House and also in the Executive Mansion?

Mr. KEHRLI. Yes, sir.

Senator GURNEY. What was the disposition of the office space assigned to Mr. Liddy and Mr. McCord and Mr. Hunt after they were removed from the White House payroll, do you recall?

Mr. KEHRLI. Mr. Hunt's office was in a block of space that had been assigned to Mr. Colson, but we do not assign specific offices within a staff. We assign a block of space to a staff and let them divide it up as they wish.

Senator GURNEY. And what about Mr. McCord and Mr. Hunt?

Mr. KEHRLI. I never knew Mr. McCord.

Senator GURNEY. How about Mr. Hunt?

Mr. KEHRLI. Mr. Hunt had an office in room 338.

Senator GURNEY. Is that the Executive Office?

Mr. KEHRLI. Of the Executive Office Building, that is right.

Senator GURNEY. What happened to his office after he was removed from the Federal payroll?

Mr. KEHRLI. It was left within the Colson operation. I do not know who was sitting in that now, Senator.

Senator GURNEY. Is that part of the block of offices of Colson's?

Mr. KEHRLI. He had people with various responsibilities within the Executive Office Building.

Senator GURNEY. After these people were removed from the Federal payroll, do you know whether they had access to their offices after that time?

Mr. KEHRLI. No, I do not.

Senator GURNEY. You do not know whether they used the telephones?

Mr. KEHRLI. No, I do not.

Senator GURNEY. What happened to their file cabinets?

Mr. KEHRLI. I know what happened to Mr. Hunt's file cabinets.

Senator GURNEY. That is all, Mr. Chairman.

Senator ERVIN. Senator Inouye?

Senator INOUYE. Thank you, Mr. Chairman.

Mr. Kehrli, according to that chart, Mr. Ehrlichman is presently the chief of the domestic section?

Mr. KEHRLI. Domestic council, yes, sir.

Senator INOUYE. And Mr. Haldeman is chief of the White House operation, Mr. Dean, counsel?

Mr. KEHRLI. Yes, sir.

Senator INOUYE. At this moment?

Mr. KEHRLI. No.

Oh, I see; yes, sir. That is right. They are still on the payroll through the 19th, which is this Sunday, and it was based on an agreement that was made in terms of trying to make sure that they had enough time to wind down their responsibilities on the White House staff, and that was determined that it was a reasonable amount of time to allow men with their responsibilities to phase out, get other people who were taking over their responsibilities briefed on what their responsibilities were and up to speed before they left.

Senator INOUYE. Following up on the matter of scheduling, you have indicated that Mr. Haldeman had final say as to who saw the President. Am I correct?

Mr. KEHRLI. On occasion, he would not have the final say. He would cover it with the President.

Senator INOUYE. Would this extend to telephone calls also?

Mr. KEHRLI. No, it did not. Mr. Chapin handled the telephone calls, as I remember it.

Senator INOUYE. Is it possible for a U.S. Senator to have called the President and been put through to him directly?

Mr. KEHRLI. I do not know. I am not that familiar with that setup.

Senator INOUYE. Your chart indicates that Mr. Colson was a liaison with outside groups.

Mr. KEHRLI. Yes, sir.

Senator INOUYE. Would you describe outside groups?

Mr. KEHRLI. Veterans groups, labor groups, groups of that nature.

Senator INOUYE. Are you aware of his activities with groups that have been mentioned in the press that you have not mentioned?

Mr. KEHRLI. For instance.

Senator INOUYE. It has been suggested that he has been involved in dirty tricks and——

Mr. KEHRLI. I am not aware of any dirty tricks.

Senator INOUYE. Do you know who Mr. Colson reported to?

Mr. KEHRLI. Mr. Colson reported to Mr. Haldeman for administrative purposes and on most of the things he did, he also reported to the President on occasion. I really can't give you a percentage breakdown, what percent he reported directly to the President or what percent he reported to Mr. Haldeman. I imagine on some occasions, he may have reported to Mr. Ehrlichman. Again, this is only something he knows.

Senator INOUYE. What was Mr. Gordon Strachan's role?

Mr. KEHRLI. Mr. Gordon Strachan was a staff assistant to Mr. Haldeman, who was in charge of liaison with the Committee To Re-Elect and the Republican National Committee.

Senator INOUYE. Did Mr. Ehrlichman get copies of all political memos as indicated in the exhibit* which was submitted earlier?

Mr. KEHRLI. I do not know.

Senator INOUYE. I have no further questions—oh, I do have one question.

Mr. KEHRLI. Yes, sir.

Senator INOUYE. Do you know a Mr. Roy Shepherd?

Mr. KEHRLI. No; I do not know him.

Senator INOUYE. Have you checked the files to see if he is on the payroll?

Mr. KEHRLI. I know for a fact that he is not on the payroll.

Senator INOUYE. If he is not on the payroll, how does one get admitted to the White House?

Mr. KEHRLI. I did some checking on Mr. Shepherd and he was admitted because he had a pass from another Government agency.

Senator INOUYE. What Government agency, sir?

Mr. KEHRLI. As I remember, it was the Department of Transportation.

Senator INOUYE. Is he on the payroll of the Department of Transportation?

Mr. KEHRLI. I do not know.

Senator INOUYE. But Mr. Shepherd is not on the payroll of the White House?

Mr. KEHRLI. That is correct.

---

*See exhibit No. 4, p. 454.

Senator INOUYE. Have you ever met Mr. Shepherd?
Mr. KEHRLI. No, sir.
Senator INOUYE. Were you aware that he visited one of the offices?
Mr. KEHRLI. Not before his name came up.
Senator INOUYE. Thank you, sir.
Senator ERVIN. Senator Weicker.
Senator WEICKER. Thank you, Mr. Chairman. Just a few brief questions.
Mr. Kehrli, when was the last time that you talked, either directly or on the telephone, with either Mr. Ehrlichman or Mr. Haldeman?
Let me ask the question first as to Mr. Ehrlichman?
Mr. KEHRLI. OK. I think I spoke with Mr. Ehrlichman last Friday or Saturday, and I do not remember which day.
Senator WEICKER. And what was the nature of this conversation—this was after he had left the White House?
Mr. KEHRLI. This was after the announcement of his resignation had been made and while he was winding down his activities at the White House.
Senator WEICKER. So this was directly, face to face?
Mr. KEHRLI. No, this was a telephone conversation.
Senator WEICKER. I see. Would you indicate the nature of that conversation?
Mr. KEHRLI. We were discussing the disposition of his papers that had been taken from the office and held in a room.
Senator WEICKER. What do you mean by the disposition of his papers? I do not follow you.
Mr. KEHRLI. This was at a time when they were turning back certain papers to the FBI.
Senator WEICKER. What was the purpose in your discussing this matter with him?
Mr. KEHRLI. Well, I wanted to make sure that he was aware of the fact that they were being turned back, since they were coming out of his files.
Senator WEICKER. In other words, the nature—was the phone conversation from you to Mr. Ehrlichman?
Mr. KEHRLI. That is right. And since one of my——
Senator WEICKER. To alert him that his files were being taken by an agent of the Federal Bureau of Investigation?
Mr. KEHRLI. That is right. One of my responsibilities is the preservation of Presidential papers and that includes filing systems in the White House and any file systems we have of special assistant papers.
Senator WEICKER. Can you give us any indication of his response when you so alerted him?
Mr. KEHRLI. He was aware of it and said he would check with Mr. Garment on it.
Senator WEICKER. That was the nature of the conversation?
Mr. KEHRLI. That was it.
Senator WEICKER. That he would check with Mr. Garment?
Mr. KEHRLI. Yes.
Senator WEICKER. And when was the last time that you talked to Mr. Haldeman?
Mr. KEHRLI. I think it was sometime last week. I do not have an exact date. We were discussing what he wanted to do with his retire-

ment benefits, whether he wanted to continue his health insurance, things of this nature, the official papers required when he resigned.

Senator WEICKER. Did you make a phone call to Mr. Haldeman to alert him that his records also were being commandeered by the Federal Bureau of Investigation?

Mr. KEHRLI. No; because they weren't.

Senator WEICKER. In other words, no papers of Mr. Haldeman's were taken by the Bureau?

Mr. KEHRLI. Not that I know of.

I think we are confusing something here. That is at one point in time, all the papers were taken and put in one area and there was extra security put on them. That was the initial movement. Then after that is the discussion that I had with Mr. Ehrlichman and these were the papers that were described in a couple of newspaper articles, FBI files.

Senator WEICKER. I am a little bit confused, too, on this point. Do not let me guide you, but in other words, was there some special reason why you alerted Mr. Ehrlichman as compared to Mr. Haldeman?

Mr. KEHRLI. Well, because we are talking about two different points in time. Immediately after Mr. Ehrlichman and Mr. Haldeman resigned, all of the papers within their offices and actually all of their working papers were taken and put in one room, as I understand it—I was only told this by Mr. Garment—so there would be no problem with any papers disappearing. That happened on the first of May, or about that time.

Now, we are talking about last weekend.

Senator WEICKER. Friday.

Mr. KEHRLI. When the FBI had requested some papers back that had been part of this group, and since they were included in Mr. Ehrlichman's files, I wanted to make sure that he was aware of the fact that they had been requested.

Senator WEICKER. Did you receive a request from the FBI to assist in this matter? Is that how it came to your attention?

Mr. KEHRLI. No; it came to my attention because I happened to be walking past the room where we kept the files and I noticed there were some people in the room making a manifest, making a log of the different papers, an inventory.

Senator WEICKER. And it was at that point in time you called Mr. Ehrlichman and let him know that his papers were——

Mr. KEHRLI. Yes; that is right.

Senator WEICKER. Now, in conversations that you have had with staff members of this committee, you have indicated—and you have also indicated on the chart—correct me if I am wrong—that there were basically five assistants to the President who reported directly to him. These men were John Ehrlichman, Bob Haldeman, Henry Kissinger, Clark MacGregor, and Peter Flanigan.

Is that correct?

Mr. KEHRLI. That is right.

Senator WEICKER. And you also indicated that the Special Counselors Robert Finch and Donald Rumsfeld also reported directly to the President but did not have specific operational responsibility to the White House?

Mr. KEHRLI. That is correct.

96-296 O—73——bk. 1—7

Senator WEICKER. Is it not true that the only people who had direct access to the President were Mr. Haldeman, Mr. Ehrlichman, and Dr. Kissinger, and that other people, including Clark MacGregor, Peter Flanigan, Finch, Rumsfeld, et al., saw the President but only at the sufferance of one of these three men?

Mr. KEHRLI. No; I would say that if they wanted to see the President, then a time would be set up based on the President's schedule and the President's priorities. And that was something that Mr. Haldeman was aware of and was able to set up.

On the other hand, the President at any time may have called for them or anybody else on the staff.

Senator WEICKER. But if the initiation of this contact was made by any of these individuals, they would have to go through one of the three that I have mentioned, Kissinger, Ehrlichman, and Haldeman?

Mr. KEHRLI. They would go to Mr. Haldeman to see what the President's schedule was in terms of time. Obviously, his time was more important than theirs. And in order to make sure that there was time available to see him, then they would go to Mr. Haldeman.

Senator WEICKER. In other words, do you consider as a practical matter Haldeman, Dr. Kissinger, Ehrlichman, Clark MacGregor, Peter Flanigan, Finch, and Rumsfeld equal as far as access to the President?

Mr. KEHRLI. I would not call them equals as far as access to the President, no, because each of them had different needs to see the President. The nature of Bob's, Mr. Haldeman's, job was such that he saw the President quite often. The nature of Mr. Rumsfeld's and Mr. Finch's jobs were such that they did not need to see the President that often. They did not request to see the President that often.

Senator WEICKER. Did Dr. Kissinger go through Mr. Haldeman?

Mr. KEHRLI. I do not think so, and I can't say that for a fact.

Senator WEICKER. Now, logs are kept, are they not, as to those persons that see the President and who telephone the President?

Mr. KEHRLI. That is correct.

Senator WEICKER. And who keeps those logs?

Mr. KEHRLI. Those logs are—actually, it is a compilation. The White House operators keep track of the phone calls and any number of people put together the log on who sees the President. It may be the military aide who is walking along and somebody may walk up to the President and shake his hand and start a conversation. So he would be the only one present, so he would be able to put that together.

The scheduling office keeps a log of his formal appointments. There is a secretary who sits outside his office who also keeps track of other people who are called in periodically. So actually, it is a combination of a number of different inputs that results in the final listing of people who saw the President.

Senator WEICKER. Does Mr. Nesbitt have the responsibility of keeping logs as to who sees the President?

Mr. KEHRLI. Mr. Nesbitt's responsibility is in terms of the daily diary, which is just what it says, a diary of the President's activities and phone calls for that particular day. He gains inputs from various sources and combines them so that the log shows not only phone calls, but also shows meetings and business.

Senator WEICKER. So this is, if there were any place, this is the one central place where you would have a fairly accurate description of both the personal meetings and the phone conversations with the President?

Mr. KEHRLI. It is one place. It is not the only place.

Senator WEICKER. Could you tell me what the other place is?

Mr. KEHRLI. Well, also within central files, which is the general filing organization, we have an organization that keeps track of who saw the President, when they saw him, and also what correspondence has gone back and forth between them. So, if a letter comes in to the President, we can pull the background information on him, letting him, or whoever is going to be drafting the response, know when this individual writing the letter saw the President last, when he wrote the President last, and what the response was, if any.

Senator WEICKER. All right, just two questions. First of all, where is Fred Fielding on this chart?

Mr. KEHRLI. Fred Fielding was the deputy counsel. He was John Dean's deputy.

Senator WEICKER. And on the chart here, he would be listed where?

Mr. KEHRLI. He would be listed below Mr. Dean.

Senator WEICKER. And have you ever worked with Mr. Fielding?

Mr. KEHRLI. Yes, I have.

Senator WEICKER. In what capacity?

Mr. KEHRLI. Well, in my capacity as staff secretary, one of my responsibilities is to make sure that any papers going to the President are thoroughly staffed, and that includes a legal opinion. Mr. Fielding was often the contact for these matters.

Senator WEICKER. And then my last question, Mr. Kehrli. At the time of the 1972 campaign, or prior to it, were there any changes of your duties, or any additional duties which were given to you, which were precipitated by the campaign?

Mr. KEHRLI. No. In January 1972, I changed jobs—January 1. That is when I went from being staff assistant to Mr. Haldeman into my present position as staff secretary.

Senator WEICKER. But at no time did you acquire any duties that related to the campaign?

Mr. KEHRLI. No.

Senator WEICKER. I have no further questions, Mr. Chairman.

Senator ERVIN. Senator Montoya?

Senator MONTOYA. Mr. Kehrli, how many people were separated or transferred to the Committee To Re-Elect the President from the White House?

Mr. KEHRLI. I do not have that exact figure with me. I can look that up.

Senator MONTOYA. Would you furnish it for the record?

Mr. KEHRLI. Yes, sir, I will.

[The following information was submitted by Mr. Kehrli in reference to the above:]

Persons separated or transferred from the White House to the Committee To Re-Elect the President

Name	*Separation date*
Sloan, Hugh W., Jr	Mar. 6, 1971
Harlowe, Jayne L. (Miss)	May 1, 1971
Magruder, Jeb S	Do.
Odle, Robert C., Jr	Do.
Roberts, Gene E. (Miss)	Do.
Jablonsky, D. Lea (Miss)	May 21, 1971
Duncan, Martha H. (Miss)	June 12, 1971
Kaupinen, Allan George	Oct. 29, 1971
Smith, Kenneth M	Nov. 9, 1971
Shumway, DeVan L	Jan. 14, 1972
Koon, Karen L. (Miss)	Feb. 12, 1972
Foust, Jon A	Apr. 1, 1972
Humphrey, Katherine J. (Miss)	July 1, 1972
Licata, Judith Ann (Mrs.)	Do.
MacGregor, Clark	Do.
Malek, Frederic V	Do.
Rausch, Doris (Miss)	July 18, 1972
Deane, John Russell, III	Aug. 4, 1972
Anderson, Stanton D	Aug. 19, 1972
Ochs, Valerie H. (Mrs.)	Do.
Jones, Jerry H	Apr. 7, 1972

Senator MONTOYA. How many people did you have at the White House during the course of last year? What was the largest number you had on the staff? You mentioned that now you have approximately 500 on board.

Mr. KEHRLI. Yes, sir; well, at one point, we were at around 510 and then we have our fiscal year 1974 budget is for 480 and we will be down to 480.

Senator MONTOYA. So you are effectuating a reduction of approximately 30 people?

Mr. KEHRLI. Yes, sir.

Senator MONTOYA. Do you have any on board from other departments?

Mr. KEHRLI. At this point in time?

Senator MONTOYA. Yes.

Mr. KEHRLI. Yes, sir.

Senator MONTOYA. How many, approximately?

Mr. KEHRLI. I do not have the figure on that. I can give you that figure.

Senator MONTOYA. Give me a round figure more or less?

Mr. KEHRLI. Oh, maybe 15.

Senator MONTOYA. What was the cause for the reduction in the budget request?

Mr. KEHRLI. The President's request that all parts of the Executive Office cut back and—that is basically it.

Senator MONTOYA. Now, during the course of the campaign, you were in charge of paying everyone on the White House staff, were you not? You were more or less the one who made the payroll?

Mr. KEHRLI. No, sir; well, I was indirectly in charge of the payroll. We have an accounting operation consisting of career Government employees who handle the payroll and details that go along with that.

Senator MONTOYA. How were those people from the White House staff who accompanied the President paid per diem when they remained in some places overnight during the political campaign?

Mr. KEHRLI. They were paid out of funds from the Committee To Re-Elect.

Senator MONTOYA. You had no—you did not authorize the payment of any funds to these people out of White House funds?

Mr. KEHRLI. Not that I know of. And again, as I said, we bent over backwards trying to make sure that anything that could come anywhere near being considered political was paid for out of the Committee To Re-Elect. In fact, I am sure that in many cases, there were events that were not political in any way, shape, or form, to avoid any appearance of paying for them out of Committee To Re-Elect funds.

Senator MONTOYA. Mr. Chairman, in view of the committee's policy that we not prolong the testimony of this witness because he was called for a different purpose other than for matters of substance, I will defer any further questioning, if he is going to appear again.

Senator ERVIN. Well, thank you very much. I understand you are willing to come back at some future time.

Mr. KEHRLI. Yes, sir.

Senator ERVIN. And also willing to comply with the record that the information which Senator Montoya asked you about a moment ago about, the number of people and the identity of people transferred from the White House staff to the Committee To Re-Elect the President?

Mr. KEHRLI. Yes, sir.

Senator ERVIN. Thank you very much.

Mr. KEHRLI. Thank you.

Mr. DASH. Would Sergeant Leeper come forward?

Senator ERVIN. Hold up your right hand. Do you swear the evidence you should give to the Senate Select Committee on Presidential Campaign Activities shall be the truth, the whole truth and nothing but the truth, so help you God?

Sergeant LEEPER. Yes, sir.

Mr. DASH. Sergeant Leeper, for the record, would you please state your name and address?

TESTIMONY OF PAUL W. LEEPER, SERGEANT, METROPOLITAN POLICE DEPARTMENT, WASHINGTON, D.C.

Sergeant LEEPER. My name is Paul William Leeper. I am a sergeant assigned to the Metropolitan Police Department. My address is 2301 L Street NW., Washington, D.C.

Mr. DASH. How long have you been a police officer, Sergeant?

Sergeant LEEPER. I am in my 12th year, sir.

Mr. DASH. And a sergeant?

Sergeant LEEPER. For the last 2½, 3 years, sir.

Mr. DASH. And what is your assignment in the Police Department?

Sergeant LEEPER. My assignment right now, sir, is I am in charge of the second district's casual clothes squad.

Mr. DASH. Where does that operate, what is the area, region of the city?

Sergeant LEEPER. In the area of the Watergate complex, the White House area.

Mr. DASH. Was that your position on June 17, 1972?

Sergeant LEEPER. Yes, sir. We were working that area.

Mr. DASH. Now, Sergeant, is the dress that you are presently wearing at this committee hearing the type of dress that you usually wear in your vocation?

Sergeant LEEPER. No, sir.

Mr. DASH. What is your usual dress?

Sergeant LEEPER. Well, we vary it from anything from old Army shirts, golf jackets, golf hats, casual clothes. I had a pair, on the night in question, a pair of blue slacks on, a blue jacket with a university written across the front of it, and a golf cap.

Mr. DASH. And in the police automobile that you use, is this a marked automobile or unmarked?

Sergeant LEEPER. No, sir, it is unmarked.

Mr. DASH. Was that the kind of automobile that you were in on June 17, 1972?

Sergeant LEEPER. Yes, sir.

Mr. DASH. Thank you.

Now, can we first have chart 5. While they are getting the chart, Sergeant, can you tell us did there come a time sometime early in the morning of or of June 17 or late in the evening, whatever time it occurred of June 16, that you received a call to come to the vicinity of the Watergate complex in Washington, D.C.?

Sergeant LEEPER. Yes, sir.

Mr. DASH. What was the nature of that call?

Sergeant LEEPER. Well, the call came out about 0152 hours on the morning of the 17th, Saturday, and the call originally came out for any scout car, which would be a marked car vehicle in the Police Department and official in it to respond to the Watergate, 2600 Virginia Avenue, to assist a special officer, the official vehicle would be a sergeant, lieutenant, or a captain's cruiser. These would be marked vehicles. No one answered that, and the dispatcher, the police dispatcher came over the air and asked if there was any TAC unit in the area.

Senator BAKER. Any what?

Sergeant LEEPER. They refer to us as casual clothes, tactical squads and they have other squads.

Senator BAKER. TAC unit.

Mr. DASH. Authority for tactical unit.

Sergeant LEEPER. Tactical unit. Yes, sir, and at this time I was working in cruiser 727, which is an unmarked police vehicle with Officer John Barrett and Officer Carl Shoffler.

Mr. DASH. Where were you located when you received that call?

Sergeant LEEPER. We were in the area of about K and 30th, Washington, D.C.

Mr. DASH. How close was it to the Watergate complex?

Sergeant LEEPER. Approximately a minute and a half, 2 minutes away.

Mr. DASH. If you can see the chart which is on the easel, and if not, can you go to it, do you recognize the photograph that appears on that easel?

Sergeant LEEPER. Yes, sir; it is of the Watergate complex.

Mr. DASH. What does it represent?
Sergeant LEEPER. The Watergate complex and the Howard Johnson across from it, the Kennedy Center on down from it and just the general area of the Watergate complex.
Mr. DASH. Is that where you went to with your automobile on that early morning of June 17?
Sergeant LEEPER. Yes, sir.
Mr. DASH. Can we have that photograph?
Senator ERVIN. Let the record show that photograph——
Mr. DASH. Will be marked as an exhibit.
Senator ERVIN [continuing]. Will be marked by the reporter as the appropriate exhibit.
[The photograph referred to was marked exhibit No. 10 and appears on p. 99.]
Mr. DASH. Sergeant, we are getting a little closer, what do you see there on that little one?
Sergeant LEEPER. That would be the Virginia Avenue side of the Watergate complex, 2600 block of Virginia Avenue NW.
Mr. DASH. All right. Can we have that next photograph now? Can the photograph which has just been exhibited be appropriately numbered by the reporter prior to making it an exhibit?
[The photograph referred to was marked exhibit No. 11 and appears on p. 100.]
Mr. DASH. Now, can we identify this drawing, Sergeant, as to the Watergate and the Howard Johnson, what does it show to you?
Sergeant LEEPER. It shows the Watergate, the sixth floor, Democratic National Committee in relationship to the Howard Johnson, which is located across the street from it.
Senator ERVIN. It will be marked by the reporter as the appropriate exhibit.
[The drawing referred to was marked exhibit No. 12 and appears on p. 101.]
Mr. DASH. Now, did you have anything to do with the Howard Johnson location, when you arrived in answer to that call?
Sergeant LEEPER. No, other than the fact when we were on the balcony of the Watergate.
Mr. DASH. What balcony was that, Sergeant?
Sergeant LEEPER. That was the sixth floor, the balcony of the Democratic National Committee.
Mr. DASH. Would that be where the space is on the left?
Sergeant LEEPER. Yes, sir. Where he has it marked, sir, directly across from the Howard Johnson.
Mr. DASH. Right. Why do we not hold that? Can we have the next exhibit? Sergeant do you recognize these drawings?
Sergeant LEEPER. Yes, sir.
Mr. DASH. You have seen them before?
Sergeant LEEPER. Yes, sir.
Mr. DASH. These drawings were used at the trial of the Watergate case in January?
Sergeant LEEPER. Yes, sir.
Mr. DASH. And you did testify at that trial?
Sergeant LEEPER. I did, sir.
Mr. DASH. When you did, you did use these drawings?

Sergeant LEEPER. Yes, sir.

Mr. DASH. And the numbers that appear on the right hand corner are the trial exhibits.

Now, of course, the letters show, can you identify that drawing and what it portrays?

Sergeant LEEPER. Yes, sir; that is the layout of the Democratic national headquarters, the sixth floor.

Senator ERVIN. Let the reporter mark it with the appropriate exhibit number.

[The drawing referred to was marked exhibit No. 13 and appears on p. 102.]

Mr. DASH. Now, can you, Sergeant, go to the exhibit? [Witness goes to exhibit.] All right, now, Sergeant, when you received the call and came to the Watergate complex—could you now indicate on the drawing where you arrived. Indicate your entry and indicate on the drawing what you and those officers accompanying you did?

Sergeant LEEPER. You want me to start, sir, from the time we arrived in front of the Watergate?

Mr. DASH. Yes, from the time you arrived in front of the Watergate.

Sergeant LEEPER [indicating on the drawing]. After the call came out we responded in the area of 30th and K, in front of the Watergate about seven car lengths from the main door going up into the lobby of the Watergate complex. At that time myself, Officer Barrett, and Officer Shoffler got out of the vehicle, went up the steps into the lobby where we were met by a special police officer who had put the call out.

Mr. DASH. Do you know his name, Sergeant?

Sergeant LEEPER. Wills, Burt Wills.

Mr. DASH. You say special police officer, was he an employee of the Watergate?

Sergeant LEEPER. No.

Mr. DASH. To your knowledge?

Sergeant LEEPER. No, he is employed for a guard service that is employed by the Watergate complex.

Mr. DASH. But his responsibilities, as you know it, were as a guard for the Watergate?

Sergeant LEEPER. Yes, sir.

Mr. DASH. All right. Continue, Sergeant.

Sergeant LEEPER. We conferred with him there in the lobby and at that time he brought it to our attention he had made his rounds about 20 or 30 minutes prior to this and found tape on one of the doors leading from the garage into the B–1 level.

Mr. DASH. When you say tape on one of the doors, could you explain that; what do you mean or what did he mean to you or what did you understand him to mean as tape on the door?

Sergeant LEEPER. Well, at that time, sir, we really did not understand what he meant by it. We responded down to the area where the tape was found and after looking at the door, the door had been taped with sort of a light colored masking tape. When the door would shut from all appearances the door would be locked but the lock is held in by the tape where the door was shut and it will not lock.

Mr. DASH. So this tape was on the edge of the door?

Sergeant LEEPER. Yes, sir.

EXHIBIT No. 10

EXHIBIT No. 11

Exhibit No. 12

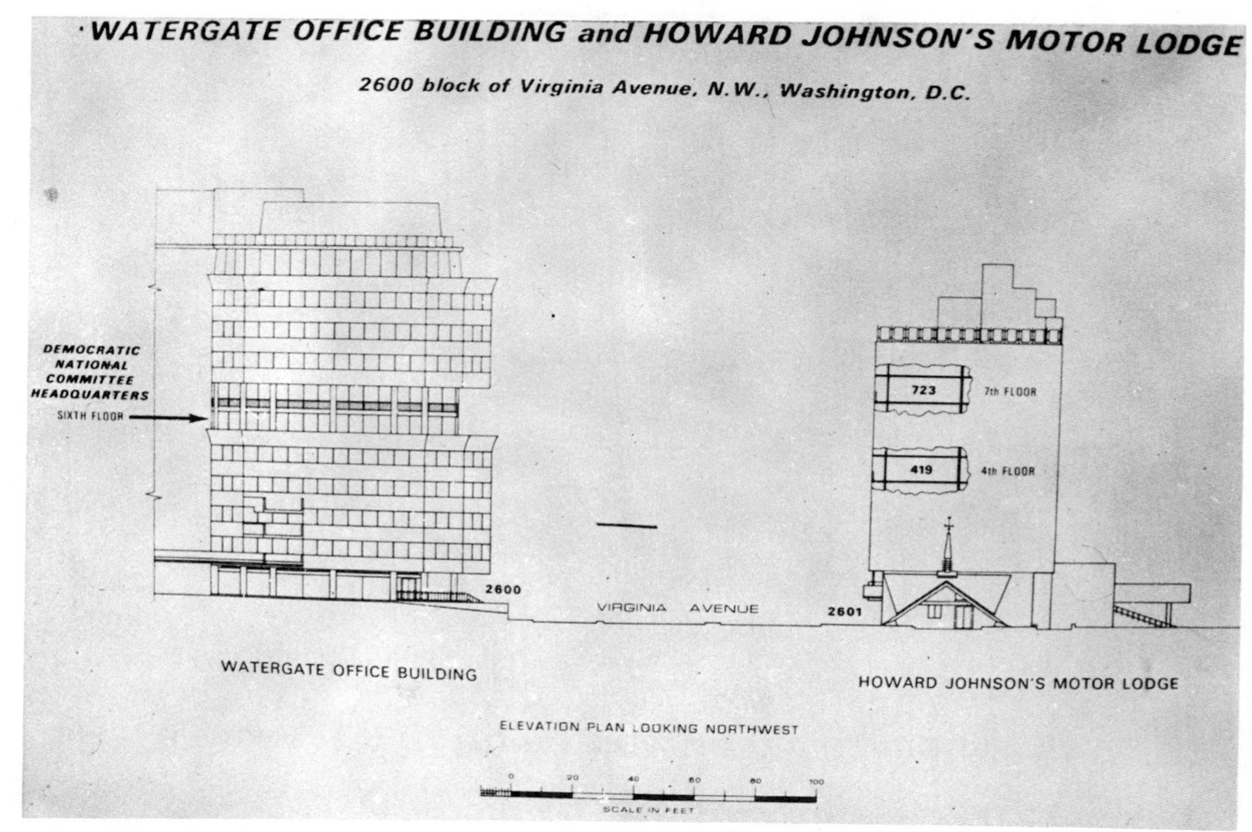

EXHIBIT NO. 13

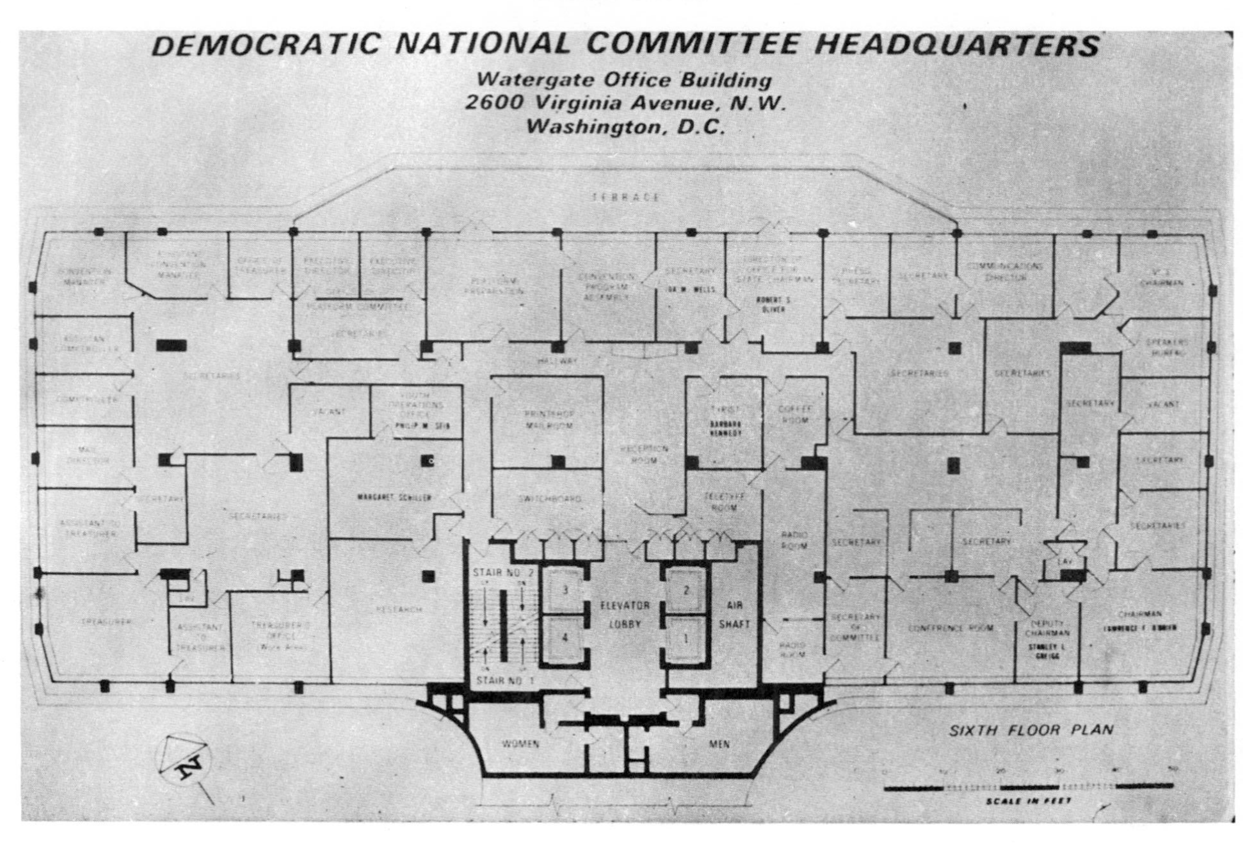

Mr. DASH. Forcing back the lock that would ordinarily spring and lock the door?

Sergeant LEEPER. Yes, sir.

Mr. DASH. And keeping it from being locked.

Sergeant LEEPER. Yes, sir.

Mr. DASH. What did you understand the purpose of that taping to be then?

Sergeant LEEPER. At that time it would give anyone who wanted to go in and out accessibility without having to use a key or a pick or something to unlock it.

Mr. DASH. Did you know whether these doors locked from the outside only or from both sides?

Sergeant LEEPER. With the lock in, you could not get in from the outside. I believe when we investigated that you could not get in also from the inside, a double locking type of service.

Mr. DASH. So if anybody who wanted to get inside and he was outside and he did not have a key he would have to tape the edge to get in?

Sergeant LEEPER. That is correct.

Mr. DASH. All right, proceeding, what did you do thereafter?

Sergeant LEEPER. At this point, after finding the door, it is not on this map here, I mean on this chart, but the door leading from the garage level into a small cubicle was taped, also the door leading from the cubicle into the stairwell was also taped, and not only the guard but we had prior knowledge from my crime reports that burglars and burglar attempts on the eighth and sixth floors of the Watergate complex, and the guard, I think brought it to our attention at that time they had some problem up there with attempted burglaries. So at that time, we sent the guard back to the area of the, where we had met him in the lobby in case, you know, we figured we had somebody inside at this time. We had a burglar going down on us, we sent him back to the lobby and myself and Officer Barrett and Officer Shoffler responded to the eighth floor by way of the stairwells. When we arrived at the eighth floor, which is the Federal Reserve Board, the door leading from the stairwell to the offices on the eighth floor was also taped in the same manner, same type of tape. There was a guard with us at that time, a guard by the name of Helms, who is a guard for the Federal Reserve Board, and his two assignments are the eighth floor and the B–1 level, which they had some offices on, the Federal Reserve Board.

We began a check of the eighth floor with that guard, he was supposed to have the keys to most of the offices. He could not get any of his keys to work in any of the office doors and all of them were locked. We found no other evidence of any tampering with any of the office doors leading off the main hallway on the eighth floor. At that time we responded back out to the stairwell. I directed that guard to respond back to the lobby to assist the other special officer in case anyone who was in the building could double back on us in any way. At that time Officer Barrett responded to the ninth floor and Shoffler and myself responded down to the seventh floor.

Mr. DASH. You were going down the stairwell, is that right?

Sergeant LEEPER. Yes, sir. We were in the stairwell right now, in the Watergate complex, it would be this stairwell here, these stairwells here, sir.

Mr. DASH. And going down from the eighth?

Sergeant LEEPER. Myself and Officer Shoffler are going down preparatory to checking the ninth floor.

The seventh floor door leading from the stairwell was locked. There was no evidence of any tampering of that door. We responded down to the sixth floor, the door leading from the stairwell had been taped in the same manner. At that time I responded to the corner stairwell and yelled for Officer Barrett to meet us——

Mr. DASH. When you use the term "responded" Sergeant, you mean you went in?

Sergeant LEEPER. I walked around about halfway up the seventh floor and yelled for Barrett. I said we have another door taped and responded here and come down here to assist us. At that time the three of us went into the sixth floor of the Watergate complex, which is the National Democratic Committee. We came in through here. We began a check of the offices that were open, some were opened, some were closed, when we got into this area we responded down to this area.

Mr. DASH. Officer, excuse me, when you went in was it dark, was it light, were there any lights on?

Sergeant LEEPER. There were some lights on, yes, sir, and we, as we checked each room we would flip the light switch on.

Mr. DASH. You were flipping lights on?

Sergeant LEEPER. Yes, sir, on and off. This door here was locked tight, we came back up this hallway and began a search of these floors here, myself and Officer Shoffler went into this room because this door here was propped open with a chair, which would, you know, which led us to believe we might have surprised somebody and ran out on the balcony. We went out on the balcony and began a search of the terrace.

Mr. DASH. You are now referring to the time you testified a little earlier?

Sergeant LEEPER. Yes, sir.

Mr. DASH. Going out on that balcony, that is the balcony you referred to?

Sergeant LEEPER. Yes, sir, that is the balcony right across from the Howard Johnson Motor Lodge.

Mr. DASH. What, if anything, did you see when you went out on that terrace?

Sergeant LEEPER. We searched the terrace with negative results but as we were coming back in Officer Shoffler said to me, he said, "Do you think that man," something to the effect "that man across the street who sees us," because at the time we had an—Officer Shoffler——

Mr. DASH. When you said across the street, do you mean on the pavement?

Sergeant LEEPER. No; at the Howard Johnson, on one of the balconies of the Howard Johnson.

Mr. DASH. Is that a level sort of parallel to the terrace where you were on?

Sergeant LEEPER. Yes, sir. And Officer Shoffler had his weapon out at the time, and he called it to my attention, he says that man across the street is watching us, I wonder if he called the police.

Senator BAKER. Just one second, just a second, I do not mean to unduly interrupt counsel, but just so I can keep the continuity in my mind, that man across the street was in the Howard Johnson?

Sergeant LEEPER. That is correct.

Senator BAKER. Where?

Sergeant LEEPER. He was out on the balcony. I did not see him, Senator. It was just called to my attention by Officer Shoffler.

Senator BAKER. But you knew he was watching you?

Sergeant LEEPER. Yes, sir.

Senator BAKER. How long did he watch?

Sergeant LEEPER. I do not know, sir. I did not even look over. I just——

Senator BAKER. You had your guns out?

Sergeant LEEPER. I did not have my gun out but Officer Shoffler had his weapon out.

Senator BAKER. And you were on the floor of the DNC, the Democratic National Committee?

Sergeant LEEPER. Yes, sir.

Senator BAKER. The balcony outside?

Sergeant LEEPER. Well, it is referred to as the terrace.

Senator BAKER. Who was that fellow?

Sergeant LEEPER. It was later found to be James Baldwin.

Senator BAKER. Do you know how long Baldwin watched?

Sergeant LEEPER. I think from the time we pulled up in front here, sir.

Mr. DASH. All right. Then, what did you do? Did you leave the terrace at that time?

Sergeant LEEPER. Yes, sir, we responded back in the area of the hallway and we met up again with Officer Barrett down to this area, checking the offices that were open as we came down the hallway, and we came into this room here through a glass door, Officer Barrett was the first man followed by myself and Officer Shoffler. Officer Barrett responded up to this area here and I started into this little secretarial cubicle here, Officer Shoffler was somewhere in this area and at this point I heard Officer Barrett yell: "Hold it, come out."

Mr. DASH. Where was that voice coming from?

Sergeant LEEPER. Officer Barrett?

Mr. DASH. Yes; where was that voice coming from?

Sergeant LEEPER. Right in this area here, Officer Barrett was right in this area. At this time I responded back out of the cubicle into this cubicle, jumped up on the desk, drawing my weapon and when I looked over this glass partition there were five men standing in front of a desk with their hands either raised above their heads or at least shoulder high wearing blue surgical gloves.

Mr. DASH. What, if anything, did you see them doing at the time that their hands were up when you had your guns out on them?

Sergeant LEEPER. Some of the gentlemen, sir, had tried to remove the gloves by using, you know, taking one hand and trying to throw it off with the other.

Mr. DASH. Did you notice any kind of equipment or paraphernalia in and around where you found the men?

Sergeant LEEPER. Yes, sir. One of the men had, was carrying an a.w.o.l. bag, an overnight bag, semilarge brown bag with his coat draped over it contained various items, cameras, bulbs, clamps for clamping the cameras to the desk, walkie-talkies, things of this sort.

Mr. DASH. Now, just going down toward the corner there from that room where you apprehended the men, the corner toward the bottom right corner, go all the way down to the large office in the corner there.

Sergeant LEEPER. Right in here, sir.

Mr. DASH. No; the large office in the corner, the very edge, whose office is that?

Sergeant LEEPER. That is the office of the chairman at that time of the Democratic Party was Lawrence F. O'Brien.

Mr. DASH. And was there entrance to that office from or access to it from where you found the men you apprehended?

Sergeant LEEPER. Yes, sir. As you can see by the chart, sir, you had access to that office.

Mr. DASH. And next to that office, to the left, whose office was that?

Sergeant LEEPER. That is the deputy chairman, sir, Stanley L. Gray.

Mr. DASH. Now, you at that point, what did you do with the men he apprehended at that point?

Sergeant LEEPER. We ordered them out from behind the desk and lined them up along the wall, facing the wall, hands on the wall, feet spread apart, and at that time I informed them who we were, they were under arrest for burglary and advised them of their rights and at that time, I directed Officer Barrett to begin a systematic search of each man.

Mr. DASH. Did you notice anything unusual about these men when you arrested them, the way they were dressed?

Sergeant LEEPER. They were well dressed, sir, in either suits, sport coats and ties.

Mr. DASH. Now, do you know the names of those people, did they give their names at that time to you?

Sergeant LEEPER. At that time, no, sir.

Mr. DASH. Did they give any names to you?

Sergeant LEEPER. Later, when they were booked in the precinct, taken to headquarters, 2301 L Street, they gave us names which later proved to be false names, aliases.

Mr. DASH. Did you later find out who they were?

Sergeant LEEPER. Yes, sir.

Mr. DASH. Could you name the persons who you arrested in that location by the names that later found out who they were to be?

Sergeant LEEPER. Frank Sturgis, Bernard L. Barker, James McCord, Eugenio Martinez, and I think it was Virgilio Gonzales.

Senator ERVIN. Virgilio Gonzales?

Sergeant LEEPER. I believe that is the way he pronounces his name.

Mr. DASH. Did you accompany them down to the station house?

Sergeant LEEPER. Yes, sir, we sent three of them down in a patrol wagon, one was transported, I think Mr. McCord, was transported in 83 scout and I transported Mr. Barker in the old clothes TAC unit, the unmarked cruiser.

Mr. DASH. At a later time did you come back and make any search of any room in the Watergate complex?

Sergeant LEEPER. I came back to the Watergate complex but the search was made by the Mobile Crime Unit. At the time we could get in touch with them they handled all the searching of the rooms and all the fingerprinting and processing.

Mr. DASH. What rooms were searched?

Sergeant LEEPER. Well, the Mobile Crime did a search of the whole complex—sixth floor complex. The conference room, all these rooms along here.

Mr. DASH. Were there any other rooms in the hotel or any other place of the complex that was also searched?

Sergeant LEEPER. Yes, sir. We obtained search warrants at about 2:30 in the afternoon, that would be Saturday afternoon on June 17, and went into rooms 214 and 314 of the Watergate Hotel.

Mr. DASH. What led you to get such search warrants?

Sergeant LEEPER. Well, we checked the guests, the register, to see who was registered at the Watergate and I think they also checked the Howard Johnsons across the street and some of the fictitious names these gentlemen had used were on the register of the Watergate Hotel.

Mr. DASH. Could you say briefly what, if anything, was found in the search of that hotel?

Sergeant LEEPER. More electrical equipment, more blue surgical gloves, about $4,200 in $100 bills, all in sequence, all brand new $100 bills; some electronic equipment. I guess that is it.

Mr. DASH. Sergeant, could you shed any light—were you present or do you have any knowledge of any check that was found on any one of these defendants or notebooks that had the name, E. Howard Hunt?

Sergeant LEEPER. I was on the search team that went into room 214 of the Watergate Hotel. It was myself and Detective Robert Dennell of our Department, Carl Shoffler, an agent from the Washington field office of the FBI; and also one of the men from Mobile Crime, Don Cherry, assisted us. At that time, it was called to my attention that they did find a book with the name——

Mr. DASH. Found what, sir?

Sergeant LEEPER. A small notebook, as you described it, with the names that you had brought out in it.

Mr. DASH. The name E. Howard Hunt? Is that the name?

Sergeant LEEPER. I believe it said, "E. Hunt, W.H.", on it, sir.

Mr. DASH. Are you aware of finding on the person of any defendant or anyone in the room any check that was signed by Mr. Hunt?

Sergeant LEEPER. No, sir, not to my knowledge.

Mr. DASH. Did you do anything else that evening or that morning or the following day with regard to the defendants?

Sergeant LEEPER. Well, I was at the second district headquarters when we began processing these men for court. I did not do actually any of the paperwork. We were assisted by some detectives, and Officer Barrett stayed on the scene out at the Watergate. He was trying to get in touch with somebody from the Democratic National Committee and later, Mr. Stanley Greigg came down. He was brought to the station with Officer Barrett, at which time, he was shown the five defendants to see if they had any right to be in the building, be in that area, the sixth floor, at which time he stated they did not.

Mr. DASH. At the time of the arrest, did you notice whether any of those persons apprehended were employed or had any relationship with the Committee for the Re-Election of the President?

96-296 O—73——bk. 1—8

Sergeant LEEPER. No, sir.

Mr. DASH. Did you learn at any time that any of them did?

Sergeant LEEPER. Well, after it hit the wire services and the press started picking it up, yes, sir.

Mr. DASH. You learned it from the press?

Sergeant LEEPER. Yes, sir.

Mr. DASH. I have no further questions.

Did you find any money on any of the indiv'duals that were apprehended?

Sergeant LEEPER. Yes, sir, we found quite a bit of money—well, not quite a bit. I would say about $3,600, all in $100 bills, all in the same sequence.

Mr. DASH. Was it $3,600?

Sergeant LEEPER I could give you a close est'mate, like——

Mr. DASH. Would you leave the chart now and go back to the table?

Now, would you refer to your records and give us a more specific statement as to the amount of money you found on any of the individuals and also in the hotel room?

Sergeant LEEPER. Also, from the defendant, Edward Joseph Hamilton, which would be Frank Sturgis, was approximately $215 in bills. From the defendant Frank Carter, which would be Bernard Barker, was approximately $230 in bills, two of which were $100 bills, and also Sturgis, two of the $250 he had was in $100 bills.

From the defendant Jean Valdez was $814 in bills, seven of which were $100 bills.

Mr. DASH. Who is Valdez?

Sergeant LEEPER. That would be Martinez, Eugenio Martinez.

Mr. DASH. From Earl Godoyn was $230 in bills, He would be, his real name would be Virgilio Gonzalez, was $230 in bills, two of which were $100 bills.

From Mr. McCord, using the alias of Edward Joseph Warren, no money was found on him.

Mr. DASH. Are you acquainted with how much money was found in the room, when the room was searched in the hotel, the apartment in Watergate?

Sergeant LEEPER. Yes, sir, there was $3,566.58. There was four packs of brandnew $100 bills, eight in a pack, so it would be $3,200 in $100 bills, all in the same sequence.

Mr. DASH. Did you or someone make a record of the serial numbers of those bills?

Sergeant LEEPER. Yes, sir, the Mobile Crime, which was Don Cherry, was on the scene with us.

Mr. DASH. Would you provide the committee with a list if we do not already have it of those numbers? It is not necessary to read them at this point in the record.

Sergeant LEEPER. Yes, sir.

[The list of serial numbers on $100 bills requested of the witness follows:]

C 03642257 A through C 03642264 A.
F 02457423 A through F 02457430 A.
F 02457433 A through F 02457440 A.
F 02457503 A through F 02457510 A.

Mr. DASH. Now, did there come a time when after the defendants were apprehended at the station, did any attorneys appear on their behalf?

Sergeant LEEPER. Yes, sir, and I will state to you these gentlemen refused to make any phone calls and refused to have us notify anyone at all.

Mr. DASH. So they did not make any phone call out that you know of?

Sergeant LEEPER. No, sir, it was around, probably around 9 or 9:30 Saturday morning, still in the a.m., that two attorneys did come to the second precinct headquarters at 2301 L Street and state that they were there to represent the five defendants.

Mr. DASH. Do you have their names, Sergeant?

Sergeant LEEPER. Their names were Douglas Caddy and Mr. Rafferty's name. I do not know his first name. It might be James Rafferty, I think.

Mr. DASH. Mr. Chairman, I do not have any further questions.

Mr. THOMPSON. I will defer to the Chair, Mr. Chairman. I do not have any questions.

Senator ERVIN. What was the name of the second lawyer?

Sergeant LEEPER. Mr. Rafferty, sir.

Senator ERVIN. What time did they appear?

Sergeant LEEPER. It was around 9 o'clock.

Senator ERVIN. They appeared notwithstanding the fact that no phone calls had been made by the persons arrested?

Sergeant LEEPER. That is correct, Senator. The defendants made no calls. In fact, they would not let us call anyone for them. They wanted no calls made.

Senator ERVIN. The serial numbers of these $100 bills were new bills?

Sergeant LEEPER. Yes, sir.

Senator ERVIN. And you took the serial numbers of all the bills down and you will supply the serial numbers to the committee?

Sergeant LEEPER. Yes, sir.

Senator ERVIN. I have no further questions. Senator Baker?

Senator BAKER. Mr. Chairman, thank you very much. I will try my best to be brief.

Sergeant, what time did you ordinarily work? What was your shift?

Sergeant LEEPER. We were working the 4 to 12 shift, sir.

Senator BAKER. 4 in the afternoon to 12 midnight?

Sergeant LEEPER. Yes, sir.

Senator BAKER. I take it you worked late this time?

Sergeant LEEPER. Very late, sir.

Senator BAKER. Was that on account of the workload or some other reason?

Sergeant LEEPER. Yes, sir; we have quite a few office buildings in our area. We have quite a few burglaries in these office buildings.

Senator BAKER. Is that part of the TAC squads or casual clothes squad's responsibility to canvass and protect these office buildings?

Sergeant LEEPER. Any type of crime, sir, mainly street robberies, commercial robberies, burglaries, larcenies of autos—we work over quite a bit.

Senator BAKER. This was 11:52 in the morning when you received the call. Was the call to you or did you volunteer to take the call?

Sergeant LEEPER. We volunteered to call when the dispatcher stated, "Is there any TAC unit in the area?" At that time, Officer Shoffler picked up the mike. He was riding on my right. I was driving. He stated, "We are a TAC unit and we have a sergeant on board." That is how we got into the affair.

Senator BAKER. I am not trying to imply anything, but this was almost 2 hours past your regular shift?

Sergeant LEEPER. Yes, sir.

Senator BAKER. Now, you have described for Mr. Dash at some length how you entered the building and went to the sixth floor, where the Democratic National Committee headquarters was then located, and I understand that you and who else were on the balcony? What was the name of the other officer?

Sergeant LEEPER. Officer Shoffler, Carl Shoffler.

Senator BAKER. At that time no one had been discovered inside?

Sergeant LEEPER. No, sir.

Senator BAKER. And you and Shoffler were on the Virginia Avenue side, facing the Howard Johnson Motel?

Sergeant LEEPER. Yes, sir.

Senator BAKER. And you or Officer Shoffler saw a man on the balcony across the street, at Howard Johnsons?

Sergeant LEEPER. I did not see the man, sir. It was brought to my attention by Carl. He said, "I wonder if that man over there is going to call the police."

Senator BAKER. What did you say to that?

Sergeant LEEPER. The way we were dressed, him having his gun out.

Senator BAKER. Was the gun clearly visible?

Sergeant LEEPER. It was described in court by Mr. Baldwin in much detail, yes, sir.

Senator BAKER. What did Mr. Baldwin do, do you know?

Sergeant LEEPER. I believe at that time, he was on a walkie-talkie, talking to one of the gentlemen who was down the hall from us.

Senator BAKER. Did you see that?

Sergeant LEEPER. No, sir. This is just what he has testified to in court.

Senator BAKER. That is what Mr. Baldwin said?

Sergeant LEEPER. Yes, sir.

Senator BAKER. Is Mr. Shoffler here with you, Officer Shoffler?

Sergeant LEEPER. No, sir.

Senator BAKER. Have you ever discussed with him whether he saw what Mr. Baldwin did or not?

Sergeant LEEPER. No, sir. I do not believe—once Mr. Baldwin had went off the balcony of the Howard Johnson, there would have been no way that Carl could have seen what he had done. As a matter of fact, we were moving pretty fast. We were coming off the terrace, going back in to Officer Barrett inside to search the rest of the building.

Senator BAKER. Was there any doubt in your mind that Baldwin saw you and Shoffler on the balcony?

Sergeant LEEPER. No, sir. In fact, Senator, in court, he described my outfit almost to a "T", what I was wearing.

Senator BAKER. I think, Mr. Chairman, at some point—not today, obviously, but I would like to have Mr. Shoffler called as a witness. I would like to hear his firsthand testimony in that respect.

I have no further questions.

Senator ERVIN. Senator Talmadge?

Senator TALMADGE. Sergeant, let me ask you about the demeanor of the people you arrested. Did they seem alert, competent, sure of themselves?

Sergeant LEEPER. Yes, sir.

Senator TALMADGE. Did they act like they felt sure someone would take care of them?

Sergeant LEEPER. I will say this, Senator, they were probably five of the easiest lockups I have ever had.

Senator TALMADGE. Then you knew from the demeanor of the people you arrested, the prisoners, the sophistication of their equipment and their dress, that you did not have ordinary burglars on your hands, did you not?

Sergeant LEEPER. Yes, sir.

Senator TALMADGE. From the time you arrested the suspects on, did you ever have any contact with FBI agents or the U.S. attorney's office personnel?

Sergeant LEEPER. Yes, sir, and the FBI agent that worked closest with us on this case was Special Agent Lano, Angie Lano. At the time of the search warrants, when we went down and got the search warrants and served the search warrants, we were assisted by Chuck Work, assistant U.S. attorney. He assisted us in the search warrants and assisted us when we served the search warrants on the two rooms at Howard Johnson and the vehicle located in the basement—I am sorry, the Watergate and the vehicle locked in the basement of the Watergate.

Senator TALMADGE. Did you have any further contact thereafter?

Sergeant LEEPER. Well, when we went to court on the case, sir, the case was handled by U.S. Attorney Earl Silbert, Mr. Donald Campbell, and Mr. Seymour Glanzer.

Senator TALMADGE. Thank you, Mr. Chairman.

No further questions, sir.

Senator BAKER. Mr. Chairman, might I impose on my colleague just for 1 minute? There is one question I wanted to ask. It will not take me but a second.

You testified, Sergeant, as I recall, that no telephone calls were made by the prisoners?

Sergeant LEEPER. That is affirmative, sir.

Senator BAKER. But the next morning at 9 a.m. or something or other, two lawyers appeared?

Sergeant LEEPER. Yes, sir.

Senator BAKER. Did anyone else besides lawyers appear?

Sergeant LEEPER. No, other than Mr. Stanley Greigg, who we brought down to the station in order to—was used as a complainant on the 251, which is a police report. And, of course—well, there was a lot of police. You mean, other than police personnel?

Senator BAKER. Yes, other than police personnel. Did anybody appear to make bond for them or to talk to them or to represent them whether they were lawyers or anyone else?

Sergeant LEEPER. No, sir, not to my knowledge.

Senator BAKER. Who would know that?

Sergeant LEEPER. Well, I was there from the time of the arrest until 7 o'clock Saturday night and I had no occasion to meet anyone, you know, other than the two lawyers who came in. In fact, I did not talk to them, they talked to Assistant Chief Wright.

Senator BAKER. So you are assuming that no one else talked to these prisoners from the time you took them to the station house until 7 o'clock in the evening of June 17, except the two lawyers which you have identified, other than police officials, FBI officials——

Sergeant LEEPER. Yes, sir.

Senator BAKER. Anybody else?

Sergeant LEEPER. No, sir.

Senator BAKER. Thank you.

Thank you, Mr. Chairman.

Senator ERVIN. Senator Gurney?

Senator GURNEY. Sergeant, did you or any of the other police at the station house find out how these lawyers knew these people were there under your custody?

Sergeant LEEPER. No, sir. I believe when they came in—I did not talk to them when they came in, but I understand they said to the station clerk, the first police officer they had contact with, we are here to represent the five men who were locked up.

Senator GURNEY. No one asked who advised them?

Sergeant LEEPER. No; the officer did not. He should have asked them at that time what are their names, but he did not. He just referred them to Assistant Chief Wright, who talked to them from then on.

Senator GURNEY. Did you ever find out who did call them?

Sergeant LEEPER. No, sir.

Senator GURNEY. No further questions.

Senator ERVIN. Senator Inouye?

Senator INOUYE. Sergeant Leeper, you have indicated that the men you arrested all gave false names?

Sergeant LEEPER. Yes, sir.

Senator INOUYE. In a physical search, did you come across any identity papers, papers to identify these men?

Sergeant LEEPER. Well, Senator, Mr. Sturgis, Frank Sturgis who used the name of Hamilton, he had a visa from Mexico in an alias name. Mr. McCord, I am not sure on the driver's license. Also, Mr. Sturgis had a driver's license, I believe, either from New York State or Massachusetts, in a——

Senator INOUYE. Was it made out in their real names?

Sergeant LEEPER. No; he also used the name of Frank Fiorini. He had about three or four different aliases.

Senator INOUYE. And all of these identity papers were in their false names?

Sergeant LEEPER. Yes, sir.

Senator INOUYE. Did you check and see where they got these identity papers?

Sergeant LEEPER. No, Senator. After the arrests were made and the defendants booked, a lot of the leg work, so to speak, the investigative work was picked up by the Washington field office and our burglary squad. It was almost in reality taken out of our hands.

In other words, we did not go over to National Airport and find out what plane they had flown in on and things like that.

Senator INOUYE. Are these identity papers still available?

Sergeant LEEPER. Yes, sir. They are either held by the U.S. attorney's office, which is still, you know, involved in this case, or they would be down at our property office.

Senator INOUYE. Were they very professionally made?

Sergeant LEEPER. I couldn't comment on that, sir. I don't think I have the qualifications to say that, whether they were or they weren't.

Senator INOUYE. Mr. Chairman, may we request to have these identity papers?

Mr. DASH. I think we have some of the exhibits that were turned over by the police department.

Mr. Thompson, do we have that?

Senator INOUYE. Mr. Leeper, you have indicated that in the service of your search warrant, you had an assistant U.S. attorney, Mr. Charles Work?

Sergeant LEEPER. That is affirmative, sir.

Senator INOUYE. Was it the usual procedure to have an assistant U.S. attorney in a burglary case?

Sergeant LEEPER. No, sir, but it being where this burglary had occurred, the dress and manner of these men, we felt that it was just a little bit bigger than the average burglary. That is all I can say.

Senator INOUYE. And the District of Columbia Police Department requested the arrest——

Sergeant LEEPER. Yes, sir, I think Inspector Charles M. Monroe was the night inspector who assisted us on it and I think he requested the chief U.S. attorney——

Senator INOUYE. You also testified that you had a meeting with Mr. Silbert.

Sergeant LEEPER. I have had many meetings with him, yes, sir.

Senator INOUYE. What is the nature of the conversations?

Sergeant LEEPER. Preparing myself, Officer Barrett, Officer Shoffler, for the case that went to court.

Senator INOUYE. It has been reported that when Mr. McCord was taken to the station, he was recognized by several officers. Is that true?

Sergeant LEEPER. Senator, I didn't leave that station, just for on and off, you know, maybe to go down to the Watergate to serve the search warrant, until 7 o'clock the next night. I didn't go to court with Mr. McCord. He may have been recognized down there. I can't answer that, sir.

Senator INOUYE. What happened to the property that was taken as a result of the search warrant?

Sergeant LEEPER. Well, like I stated before, Senator, some of the property is down at our property office and I understand some of it is being used by the U.S. attorney's office in the processing of the case.

Senator INOUYE. Well, this list was made on Saturday, wasn't it, after the search?

Sergeant LEEPER. Yes, sir.

Senator INOUYE. Why is it that it wasn't available until the 19th at 5 p.m.? I was told that an official of the Democratic National Committee wanted to have a list of those things that are—were taken out and the police department could not furnish him with this until 5 p.m. on the 19th.

Sergeant LEEPER. I couldn't answer that, sir. Once the property left our hands, it is handled by Mobile Crime. That is their purpose. They have officials down there and you would have to go through them.

Senator INOUYE. Who had charge of the investigation by the D.C. Police Department?

Sergeant LEEPER. Inspector Prete, who was at that time inspector. He is deputy commander of the CID.

Senator INOUYE. During the handling of this case, did you ever receive any special instructions or advice from anyone?

Sergeant LEEPER. No, other than what I have said before. We had meetings with the U.S. attorney's office, just preparing us to go to court on the case, which is just the normal—if you have any type of case, you usually meet with the U.S. attorney prior to your going into the courtroom.

Senator INOUYE. When was the investigation discontinued by the Police Department?

Sergeant LEEPER. Well, for us, Senator, it was almost discontinued other than testifying in court that Saturday. In other words, the investigation, the running down of the different leads, was handled by our burglary squad and, of course, the field office. As far as Officers Barrett, Shoffler and myself, other than testifying in court, that ended on Saturday.

Senator INOUYE. Is this case closed as far as the D.C. Police Department is concerned?

Sergeant LEEPER. I couldn't answer that right now, sir.

Senator INOUYE. I understand that the chief FBI agent in charge, Mr. Lano——

Sergeant LEEPER. Yes, sir.

Senator INOUYE [continuing]. Called your department on June 22 complaining of leaks of information to the press. Did he make such a call?

Sergeant LEEPER. I don't know, sir. He didn't make such a call to myself.

Senator INOUYE. Thank you very much.

Senator ERVIN. Senator Weicker?

Senator WEICKER. Thank you, Mr. Chairman.

Just a few very brief questions, one for Sergeant Leeper and then one for Officer Barrett.

Sergeant, do you think that the result would have been any different if it had been uniformed police in a marked car that had arrived to take care of this matter?

Sergeant LEEPER. Yes, sir; I don't think there would have been an apprehension.

Senator WEICKER. Why do you say that?

Sergeant LEEPER. Well, because of the fact that Baldwin would have made a marked car. It has "Police" written on it in six places. It has a domelight on top of it. The officers would have been dressed in full uniform. There would have been no doubt that it was police. I think that just gave us an edge of, say, 5 minutes and Baldwin didn't make us until he seen Shoffler's gun on the terrace. Then at that time, I don't think he really knew for sure if we were police or not, but he felt it was probably some type of security force, you know, maybe the security force for the Democratic Party.

Senator WEICKER. Mr. Chairman, I would like to ask a question of Officer Barrett. I understand he is here; might he be sworn, Mr. Chairman?

Senator ERVIN. Yes. Maybe we had better get through with this witness before we have another one.

Senator WEICKER. Was it the intention to call Officer Barrett?

Senator ERVIN. Well, Mr. Barrett, will you stand up; hold up your right hand. Do you swear that the evidence which you shall give to the Senate Select Committee on Presidential Campaign Activities shall be the truth, the whole truth, and nothing but the truth, so help you God?

Mr. BARRETT. Yes; I do.

Senator ERVIN. John Barrett, what is your other name?

TESTIMONY OF JOHN BRUCE BARRETT, OFFICER, METROPOLITAN POLICE DEPARTMENT, WASHINGTON, D.C.

Officer BARRETT. John Bruce Barrett.

Senator ERVIN. John Bruce Barrett, and you might state your residence and occupation for the record.

Officer BARRETT. I am a policeman assigned to Second District Headquarters, 2301 L Street NW.

Senator WEICKER. Officer Barrett, were you the first one to actually apprehend or see the group of individuals in that room?

Officer BARRETT. Yes, sir.

Senator WEICKER. At that moment in time did you hear anything that might have been a conversation coming over a walkie-talkie?

Officer BARRETT. No, sir; I did not hear anything, I just saw something.

Senator WEICKER. What did you see?

Officer BARRETT. I saw an arm; I stopped in the position before I entered the secretary's office outside of Chairman O'Brien's and I hesitated there for several minutes because it was dark back in the partitioned area, and while hesitating at that partition I saw a man down in a crouched position as if hiding by stooping—when the shadow passed my face, I was startled and that began the whole mess.

Senator WEICKER. And, just in conclusion, were these individuals in possession of a walkie-talkie?

Officer BARRETT. Yes, sir; Mr. Barker had a walkie-talkie in his possession.

Senator WEICKER. Did any communication come through that walkie-talkie at any time?

Officer BARRETT. There may have been some communication; I did not personally hear anything. I was too concerned.

Senator WEICKER. Sergeant Leeper, did you hear any communication come over the walkie-talkie?

Sergeant LEEPER. No, sir.

Senator WEICKER. I have no further questions, Senator Montoya.

Senator MONTOYA. I just have one or two questions, in order to clear the record. Would you state for the record the names of the individuals that were apprehended that night and also the different aliases that applied to each one?

Sergeant LEEPER. All right, Senator. James McCord, Jr., used the alias of Edward Martin. Bernard L. Barker used the alias of Frank Carter. Frank Sturgis used the alias of Joseph E. Hamilton and also Frank Fiorini. Eugenio Martinez used the alias of Jean Valdez; Virgilio Gonzalez used the alias Raul Godoyn.

Senator MONTOYA. And you indicated, I believe, that they were registered there at the Watergate Hotel under their aliases.

Sergeant LEEPER. I do not think all four of them had signed the—I would have to look back at the duplicates we have.

Senator MONTOYA. How many rooms did they have?

Sergeant LEEPER. They had two rooms at the Watergate—214 and 314.

Senator MONTOYA. Just one more question. What happened to the man across the street—Mr. Baldwin? Did you make any move or did the Police Department make any move to investigate what was going on in that particular room or did you communicate any suspicion to the burglary staff at the Police Department to follow through on that?

Sergeant LEEPER. Not at that time; no, sir.

Senator MONTOYA. When was this done?

Sergeant LEEPER. We made no communication with any Washington field office or our burglar squad with reference to this man. We had seen no significant matter at that time, you know, it did not mean anything to us at the time.

Senator MONTOYA. You did not include that in your report?

Sergeant LEEPER. No, sir.

Senator MONTOYA. That is all, Mr. Chairman.

Senator ERVIN. The committee will stand in recess until 10 o'clock tomorrow morning.

Thank you very much.

Sergeant LEEPER. Thank you, sir.

[Whereupon, at 5:15 p.m., the hearing was recessed, to resume at 10 a.m., Friday, May 18, 1973.]

FRIDAY, MAY 18, 1973

U.S. SENATE,
SELECT COMMITTEE ON
PRESIDENTIAL CAMPAIGN ACTIVITIES,
Washington, D.C.

The Select Committee met, pursuant to recess, at 10 a.m., in room 318, Russell Senate Office Building, Senator Sam J. Ervin, Jr. (chairman), presiding.

Present: Senators Ervin, Talmadge, Inouye, Montoya, Baker, Gurney, and Weicker.

Also present: Samuel Dash, chief counsel; Fred D. Thompson, minority counsel; Rufus L. Edmisten, deputy chief counsel; Arthur S. Miller, chief consultant; Jed Johnson, consultant; David M. Dorsen, James Hamilton, and Terry F. Lenzner, assistant chief counsels; Barry Schochet, assistant majority counsel; Donald G. Sanders, H. William Shure, and Robert Silverstein, assistant minority counsels; Joan C. Cole, secretary to the minority; Pauline O. Dement, research assistant; Eiler Ravnholt, office of Senator Inouye; Robert Baca, office of Senator Montoya; Ron McMahan, assistant to Senator Baker; A. Searle Field, assistant to Senator Weicker; Marc Lackritz, Ron Rotunda, assistant counsels; Eugene Boyce, hearings counsel; John Walz, publications clerk.

Senator ERVIN. I address these remarks to the committee members. It has been suggested by several members of the committee that when the Senators question the witnesses in the first go-around they limit themselves to 10 minutes and have as many rounds as they want to, but that is so each Senator gets the opportunity, a reasonable time for questioning.

If there is no objection I would ask unanimous consent that the Chair be allowed to limit each go-around to not more than 10 minutes questioning, with the understanding you can come back later as many times as you want to.

Will counsel call the first witness?

Mr. DASH. Officer Shoffler.

Senator ERVIN. Do you swear that the evidence you shall give to the Senate Select Committee on Presidential Campaign Activities shall be the truth, the whole truth, and nothing but the truth, so help you God?

Mr. SHOFFLER. Yes, sir.

Mr. DASH. For the record, Officer Shoffler, will you give your full name, address, and what your present occupation is?

TESTIMONY OF CARL M. SHOFFLER, OFFICER, METROPOLITAN POLICE DEPARTMENT

Officer SHOFFLER. Carl M. Shoffler, police officer.

Senator GURNEY. Officer, if you would pull the mike a little closer to you I think we would hear better.

Mr. DASH. Will you repeat your name?

Officer SHOFFLER. Carl M. Shoffler, sir. Police officer assigned to special services bureau, address is 300 Indiana Avenue NW.

Mr. DASH. Were you on duty in the early morning hours of June 17, 1972?

Officer SHOFFLER. Yes, sir.

Mr. DASH. And what particular outfit or unit were you assigned to?

Officer SHOFFLER. Second district tactical squadron, casual clothes unit.

Mr. DASH. Were you at that time traveling with Sergeant Leeper?

Officer SHOFFLER. Sergeant Leeper and Officer Barrett and I were partners that particular evening.

Mr. DASH. Did you answer with those other officers a call to come to the Watergate complex?

Officer SHOFFLER. Yes, sir.

Mr. DASH. I have no further questions of the witness, Mr. Chairman. I think Senator Baker has some questions.

Mr. THOMPSON. One or two questions.

Officer Shoffler, do you recall when you received the word from headquarters to answer this call at the Watergate? Were you in the car with Sergeant Leeper?

Officer SHOFFLER. Yes, sir.

Mr. THOMPSON. Do you know, do you remember whether or not you responded to the effect that a uniform car should not be sent?

Officer SHOFFLER. On runs on a casual unit response, if a casual clothes unit takes the run normally a uniform car stays out of the area. I do not recall if particular instructions were given to them on that evening to stay out of the area.

Mr. THOMPSON. But it would not have been unusual for you to make such a request?

Officer SHOFFLER. No, sir.

Mr. THOMPSON. What time of the morning was this?

Officer SHOFFLER. Approximately 1:52 a.m.

Mr. THOMPSON. Were you working past your regular duty hours on that occasion?

Officer SHOFFLER. Yes, sir.

Mr. THOMPSON. What were your regular duty hours?

Officer SHOFFLER. 4 p.m. to 12 p.m., sir.

Mr. THOMPSON. Why were you working overtime that particular night?

Officer SHOFFLER. Our tactical squadron deals with whatever particular crime problem is—a problem at that time. We were having, we were experiencing a problem with office larceny and burglaries in the downtown area, and felt that working over may produce results.

Mr. THOMPSON. When you got there at the Watergate who did you meet at the Watergate complex?

Officer SHOFFLER. The guard, Mr. Frank Wills.

Mr. THOMPSON. What did Mr. Wills say to you at that time?

Officer SHOFFLER. Mr. Wills stated that he had discovered the doors had been taped in a manner as to allow entrance.

Mr. THOMPSON. Did he state anything else to you?

Officer SHOFFLER. I asked him if there had been any prior burglaries. We were aware of prior burglaries in the building but not at the particular floors. Mr. Wills related to us there had been burglaries, I believe, on the sixth and eighth floors.

Mr. THOMPSON. What prior burglaries were you personally aware of besides what Mr. Wills told you?

Officer SHOFFLER. We were just aware of burglaries from our crime sheet at that particular address. I do not believe any of us were aware of any details.

Mr. THOMPSON. Did you observe tape on the locks of the doors at the Watergate complex?

Officer SHOFFLER. Yes, sir.

Mr. THOMPSON. Which doors?

Officer SHOFFLER. We went down to the garage level with Mr. Wills, so he could explain to us what he had discovered, and the doors at the garage level both had tapes on the locks.

Mr. THOMPSON. What did you perceive as you entered the Watergate?

Officer SHOFFLER. When we originally arrived at the scene?

Mr. THOMPSON. Yes.

Officer SHOFFLER. Through the front door, the lock.

Mr. THOMPSON. You went down, through the front door, down to the B–2 garage level. Did Mr. Wills go with you to show you that tape?

Officer SHOFFLER. Yes, sir.

Mr. THOMPSON. All right. After that, what did you perceive?

Officer SHOFFLER. At that time myself, Sergeant Leeper, and Officer Barrett responded up to stairwell, we ascertained from the guard that the stairwell and the elevators were the only ways out of the building so we felt that it would be best if we went up the stairwell, we might possibly surprise someone in the stairwell.

Mr. THOMPSON. Did Mr. Wills go with you?

Officer SHOFFLER. I believe Mr. Wills at that point responded to the elevator and I believe he went to get the guard to the eighth floor because he had keys for the doors.

Mr. THOMPSON. Guard for the eighth floor?

Officer SHOFFLER. Yes, sir.

Mr. THOMPSON. Was there a guard especially designated to guard the eighth floor?

Officer SHOFFLER. It was my understanding there was a guard for the eighth floor, yes, sir.

Mr. THOMPSON. Did you find tape on the door of the eighth floor leading from the stairwell?

Officer SHOFFLER. Yes, sir.

Mr. THOMPSON. How many other doors did you find tape on?

Officer SHOFFLER. We made a fast search of the eighth floor and were able to determine there were no signs of forceful entry into any of the offices on the eighth floor and we immediately, within a few minutes responded back down checking the stairwell as we went down and found tape on the sixth floor door.

Mr. THOMPSON. What is located on the eighth floor?

Officer SHOFFLER. The National Democratic Committee.

Mr. THOMPSON. On the eighth floor?

Officer SHOFFLER. On the eighth floor, Federal Reserve.

Mr. THOMPSON. And it was on June 17th?

Officer SHOFFLER. That is right.

Mr. THOMPSON. And on the sixth floor the Democratic National Headquarters or was at that time?

Officer SHOFFLER. Yes, sir.

Mr. THOMPSON. Is that correct? You checked the eighth, went down to the sixth, found tape on the door of the sixth and proceeded inside, is that correct?

Officer SHOFFLER. Yes, sir.

Mr. THOMPSON. Were you the officer who went on to the balcony there?

Officer SHOFFLER. Yes, sir.

Mr. THOMPSON. Did you observe anything across the way at the Howard Johnson motel across the street?

Officer SHOFFLER. I noticed a gentleman about our level that appeared to be observing us.

Mr. THOMPSON. What caused you to reach that conclusion? Was he just looking in your direction?

Officer SHOFFLER. He was looking in our direction, yes, sir.

Mr. THOMPSON. Was he by himself?

Officer SHOFFLER. Yes; to the best of my knowledge.

Mr. THOMPSON. Was he conspicuous, were there any other persons out there?

Officer SHOFFLER. No, sir.

Mr. THOMPSON. Could you determine his features?

Officer SHOFFLER. At that particular time because of the fact we were moving in more or less a hurried pace, the only thing that I really did pay attention to was the fact that there was a subject over there. I was interested in this, in the fact that my dress and the fact that I had at that point my weapon out——

Mr. THOMPSON. What I am really getting at is what in your mind could he, to make you very well——

Officer SHOFFLER. I believe he saw us very well.

Mr. THOMPSON. The room where you were there on the balcony, was it light?

Officer SHOFFLER. Yes, sir.

Mr. THOMPSON. What was your dress at that time?

Officer SHOFFLER. It was casual clothes, I believe I had a cutoff army jacket on, sir.

Mr. THOMPSON. Could you tell whether or not this man across the way had a walkie-talkie?

Officer SHOFFLER. No, sir.

Mr. THOMPSON. You could not tell. Was this because of your haste or because of the lack of light where he was?

Officer SHOFFLER. More so probably because of our haste.

Mr. THOMPSON. Because of the light?

Officer SHOFFLER. Because we were in a hurry.

Mr. THOMPSON. Because you were in a hurry.

Did you observe him closely enough to tell in your mind that he was probably observing you?

Officer SHOFFLER. Yes, sir.

Mr. THOMPSON. Did you make some comment to your fellow officers about that?

Officer SHOFFLER. Because of our dress, I felt that he may possibly call the police and they might with sirens and lights respond.

Mr. THOMPSON. Do you know the dispatcher who took this call this night from Mr. Wills or whoever it was there at the Watergate and called in this particular burglary?

Officer SHOFFLER. This will be from my recollection of our interview approximately a few weeks after the burglary and at that time I believe the dispatcher told me that the guard had placed the call.

Mr. THOMPSON. The guard placed the call. Do you know the name of the dispatcher?

Officer SHOFFLER. I will have the name shortly, sir.

Mr. THOMPSON. All right. Are those calls recorded in any manner?

Officer SHOFFLER. Yes, sir, for a period of 2 months.

Mr. THOMPSON. Do you know whether or not there was more than one call made that night?

Officer SHOFFLER. I do not know, sir, I believe there was only one call made from our conversation.

Mr. THOMPSON. Are those records of those calls periodically destroyed by the police department?

Officer SHOFFLER. As I said, sir, I believe they keep them for 2 months and then destroy the tape.

Mr. THOMPSON. Unless a special request is made that they be retained; do you know whether or not they were retained in this instance?

Officer SHOFFLER. I believe that the U.S. attorney's office requested a transcript of the statement.

Mr. THOMPSON. Have you seen the transcript yourself?

Officer SHOFFLER. No, sir.

Mr. THOMPSON. But I think it may be available in the district attorney's office.

Officer SHOFFLER. Yes, sir.

Mr. THOMPSON. All right. Did anyone request you to work overtime that night?

Officer SHOFFLER. No, sir.

Mr. THOMPSON. I have no further questions.

Senator ERVIN. Any further questions?

Senator BAKER. Yes, sir, I have a few.

Thank you, Mr. Chairman.

Mr. Thompson, I believe, has covered the events of that night very carefully and I have only a few questions to ask, a few further questions to ask.

When you arrived at the sixth floor, how many doors were taped?

Officer SHOFFLER. To the best of my recollection at this point, only the door leading from the stairwell into the floor, the entrance.

Senator BAKER. The stairwell to the fire escape or the stairs that lead from the sixth floor to the lower floor?

Officer SHOFFLER. That would be the stairwell that leads from the sixth floor to the lower floors.

Senator BAKER. Yes, is that also the fire escape?

Officer SHOFFLER. Both stairwells are together. I imagine that is the fire escape also, yes, sir.

Senator BAKER. Yes, do you have to have a key to get through that door to the fire escape as well as to get into the building, into the floor?

Officer SHOFFLER. It is necessary to have a key to gain entrance to the floor from the stairwell, but it is not necessary to have a key to get from the floor to the stairwell.

Senator BAKER. Was there any other door taped that you have any recollection of?

Officer SHOFFLER. On that floor?

Senator BAKER. Yes, sir, the door to the DNC, the Democratic National Committee, was not taped?

Officer SHOFFLER. The two glass doors around the other side there, you mean?

Senator BAKER. Yes, sir.

Officer SHOFFLER. No, sir, not to my knowledge.

Senator BAKER. Or any doors inside the DNC?

Officer SHOFFLER. No, sir.

Senator BAKER. So with the tape on the door from the stairway to the main sixth floor, if you assume for the moment that it was taped for a sinister purpose, you would only need to have a tape to get into the sixth floor, you would not need a tape to get out from the sixth floor?

Officer SHOFFLER. I believe that is correct, sir, yes.

Senator BAKER. Now, you went out on the balcony on the sixth floor, is that correct?

Officer SHOFFLER. Yes, sir.

Senator BAKER. Did you have a flashlight?

Officer SHOFFLER. Yes, sir.

Senator BAKER. Was it lighted?

Officer SHOFFLER. I believe I used it on the corner of the ledge. I had gone out on the ledge.

Senator BAKER. Were you clearly visible on that balcony?

Officer SHOFFLER. I believe—I imagine you are referring to from the Howard Johnsons.

Senator BAKER. That is what I am referring to.

Let me short circuit the inquiry by saying that I am trying by this line of questioning to establish these things: That you were on the balcony; that the balcony is across the street from Howard Johnsons; that a man was over there who we later learned was named Baldwin; that you were clearly visible, that you had a flashlight, that you had your pistol; that Baldwin was there and in your judgment, he saw you. If all those things are so, you may say so.

Officer SHOFFLER. All those things are so, yes, sir.

Senator BAKER. What did Baldwin do?

Officer SHOFFLER. What did I later find out he did?

Senator BAKER. No, what did you see him do?

Officer SHOFFLER. Oh, he just stood there, Senator.

Senator BAKER. When did the additional police arrive? When did the uniformed police and the police marked cars arrive? How long after you arrived?

Officer SHOFFLER. I would imagine it would have been approximately a half hour after the arrest.

Senator BAKER. Do you know who made the call on that, or did it arrive in the ordinary course of events?

Officer SHOFFLER. Sergeant Leeper requested transports.

Senator BAKER. Did he do that after you went into the Watergate or while you were still in your patrol car?

Officer SHOFFLER. Oh, after we had made the arrest. That is——

Senator BAKER. Oh, I see, after you had made the arrest?

Officer SHOFFLER. Yes, sir.

Senator BAKER. Now, when you got inside and made the arrest—by the way, who made the arrest, who made the first discovery of the intruders in the Democratic National Committee offices?

Officer SHOFFLER. Officer Barrett first.
Senator BAKER. Were you with him at the time?
Officer SHOFFLER. Yes, sir.
Senator BAKER. Was there any communication by walkie-talkie or—by walkie-talkie, that you heard or know of?
Officer SHOFFLER. I heard none, no, sir.
Senator BAKER. The name of the building guard was——
Officer SHOFFLER. Mr. Frank Wills.
Senator BAKER. Mr. Wills. And you met Mr. Wills in the lobby of the Watergate?
Officer SHOFFLER. Yes, sir.
Senator BAKER. What was his state of mind or appearance? Was he agitated or calm?
Officer SHOFFLER. Mr. Wills is a type of person that is very hard to judge his demeanor.
Senator BAKER. What did he tell you?
Officer SHOFFLER. He was saying about he felt there was somebody inside possibly, that at one time he had seen tape on a door and he removed the tape and later on, he saw the tape was back, and——
Senator BAKER. Did he say what floor that was on?
Officer SHOFFLER. He kept indicating, I believe he kept indicating the garage door at the B–2 level, because when we asked him to show us, that is immediately where he took us.
Senator BAKER. Did he ever speak of the tape on the sixth floor or the eighth floor?
Officer SHOFFLER. At this time, I have no recollection of him speaking of tape on those particular doors, sir.
Senator BAKER. Did Mr. Wills make any reference to the Democratic National Committee?
Officer SHOFFLER. I do not believe, as again my recollection, I do not believe he at any time indicated what he knew was on the sixth floor except I think he informed us that there were burglaries on the sixth floor and he was aware of that.
Senator BAKER. Did he make any indication as to why he did not call you when he first found the doors taped, but rather only after they were retaped?
Officer SHOFFLER. I believe when I interviewed him later, he told me that his suspicion was aroused only after the second time, because he had thought that possibly employees of the building or someone doing work in the building, as a convenience, taped the doors to keep them open.
Senator BAKER. I believe that is all, Mr. Chairman, thank you.
Senator ERVIN. Any further questions?
Mr. DASH. Just to clarify the record, Senator Baker asked you a question concerning whether or not the tape was needed if one was inside the room in order to get out and I think you said that one did not. Sergeant Leeper yesterday testified that these doors were locked both inside and out, so that if you were inside, you would need a key to get out, and therefore, it was his testimony that the tape was necessary to get out. Do you have information on that?
Senator BAKER. All right, now, Mr. Chairman, just a second.
You know, we are not in a court of law. We don't proceed by evidentiary rules, but the witness testified yesterday very clearly in one

respect and this witness has testified very clearly today. I think we ought not to try to lead the witness into a different statement. I think both statements stand on their own merit and we ought to leave it there.

Mr. DASH. I am just asking the question, Senator, as to whether he knows these doors are locked from inside and out.

Senator BAKER. He has already testified that you need a tape in order to gain entrance but you do not need the tape to get out.

Senator ERVIN. I see no harm in the question. I think we can probably let him answer.

Mr. SHOFFLER. There was, even at the time of the arrest and the small investigation we did after, we weren't able to determine too much about the door. This morning I placed a call to clarify it and was informed that certain offices in that building, you do need a key for both ways. But they have a buzzer system because of the fire regulation to get out of the office. That particular office didn't have a buzzer system and you could have free access from the floor to the stairwell.

Senator BAKER. So you did not have to have a key to get out?

Officer SHOFFLER. No, sir.

Mr. DASH. Thank you.

Senator ERVIN. Senator Weicker?

Senator WEICKER. Officer Shoffler, how long were you on the balcony?

Officer SHOFFLER. I would estimate 3 or 4 minutes.

Senator WEICKER. And how long after you believed Baldwin to have seen you when you apprehended the defendants?

Officer SHOFFLER. It would have had to have been within 5 or 6 minutes, 5 minutes at the absolute most. We went immediately from the balcony to the hallway, down the hallway, the three of us, then Officer Barrett observed movements behind a screen and the arrests were made.

Senator WEICKER. So the time was, the time from when you say you believed Baldwin to have seen you, to the time that you apprehended the defendants was 5 minutes?

Officer SHOFFLER. At the most, yes.

Senator WEICKER. At the most. And the time that you were actually on the balcony, again about 2 or 3 minutes?

Officer SHOFFLER. Yes, sir.

Senator WEICKER. Could you give me an answer on that?

Officer SHOFFLER. I would think that the whole time, from his observation of me on the balcony to the arrest, would have been 5, 6, 7 minutes at the most.

Senator WEICKER. And the actual time spent on the balcony.

Officer SHOFFLER. Two to three minutes.

Senator WEICKER. Two to three minutes.

I have no more questions.

Senator ERVIN. Thank you, Mr. Shoffler.

Call the next witness.

Mr. DASH. Mr. James McCord.

Senator ERVIN. Mr. McCord, raise your right hand.

Do you swear that the testimony you shall give to the Senate Select Committee on Presidential Campaign Activities shall be the truth, the whole truth, and nothing but the truth, so help you God?

Mr. McCord. I do, sir.

Mr. Dash. Mr. McCord, will you bring the microphone closer to you so we will hear you.

Now, for the record, will you first state your name and address?

TESTIMONY OF JAMES W. McCORD, JR.; ACCOMPANIED BY BERNARD FENSTERWALD, JR., COUNSEL

Mr. McCord. James W. McCord, M-c-C-o-r-d, Jr., the address is No. 7 Winder, W-i-n-d-e-r, Winder Court, Rockville, Md. 20850.

Mr. Dash. Are you accompanied with counsel this morning?

Mr. McCord. I am.

Mr. Dash. Will counsel please identify himself?

Mr. Fensterwald. Yes, my name is Bernard Fensterwald, Jr. My business address is 810 16th Street NW., Washington, D.C.

Mr. Dash. Mr. McCord, prior to your testimony, do you have any preliminary statement to make, that you wish to make to the committee?

Mr. McCord. Yes, there is. I would like to state, as I did when I appeared at the executive session of this committee, that I would like to be as accurate as I can, that some of the dates that I will refer to—there are approximately 75 to 100 different dates—I will try to recall to the best of my memory. Some may be in error.

As I stated when I first appeared, some matters go back some 12 or 14 months and some of the matters that are of interest to this committee I have therefore set forth in writing, attempting to reconstruct my memory to the best of my ability. I may refer to some of those memoranda during this meeting and to other notes that pertain to dates, and I hope you will bear with me and understand my reasoning in that regard.

I state finally that my participation in the Watergate operation on my part, for whatever reasons I may have had at the time, whatever rationale I may have had at the time, was an error, was a mistake, a very grave mistake, which I regret.

I am ready to proceed with the questions.

Mr. Dash. All right.

Now, is it a fact now, Mr. McCord, that you presently stand convicted on a multicount Federal indictment charging burglary, electronic surveillance and conspiracy arising out of the break-in of the Democratic National Committee headquarters at the Watergate?

Mr. McCord. That is correct.

Mr. Dash. Are you now awaiting sentence on that conviction?

Mr. McCord. That is correct.

Mr. Dash. What is your professional background, Mr. McCord?

Mr. McCord. I was born in 1924 in Waurika, Okla. I worked first for the Federal Bureau of Investigation in 1942, 1943, in Washington, D.C., in New York City. I, subsequently from 1943 to 1945, was an Army Air Corps officer. From 1948 to 1951, I worked as a special agent for the Federal Bureau of Investigation in San Diego and San Francisco, Calif. I worked from 1951 to 1970 with the Central Intelligence Agency as a security officer. I retired from that agency in August 1970 after 25 years Federal service.

Mr. Dash. Now, officially, during your service with the CIA and FBI, did you receive any awards or commendations for your service?

Mr. McCord. I received on retirement in August 1970 the Distinguished Service Award for outstanding performance of duty with CIA. I received some others.

Mr. Dash. Now, prior to your arrest, indictment, and conviction relating to the Watergate incident, were you ever arrested, charged with a crime, or the subject of any complaint or disciplinary proceeding in your life?

Mr. McCord. I have had traffic violations in the Washington area; yes, sir.

Mr. Dash. Is that all?

Were you an employee of the Committee To Re-Elect the President?

Mr. McCord. Yes.

Mr. Dash. What position did you hold and what were your duties?

Mr. McCord. I came aboard first as a security consultant part time in September of 1971.

Mr. Dash. By the way, how did you get that job?

Mr. McCord. I was introduced initially by Mr. John Caulfield and Mr. Odle, the Director of Administration who testified yesterday, and based on that interview was employed part time and then full time in January, the first of January 1972.

Mr. Dash. Now, what were your duties in that position as security chief?

Mr. McCord. The duties were essentially the function of the protection of the property and the lives of the personnel of the committee in that facility there and subsequently in the facility at Miami, Fla., that the committee and some of the White House staff would occupy during the Republican Convention in August of 1972. The duties were primarily those of physical security protection of personnel security, some document security, and some protective work for the family of John Mitchell.

Mr. Dash. Now, were those duties, and that assignment that you have just described under whose direction did you work?

Mr. McCord. Primarily under the direction of Mr. Robert Odle who was my immediate supervisor in the committee. The responsibility with Mr. Mitchell and his family, I received directions from him, from Mrs. Mitchell, from Robert Odle and Mr. Liddy.

Mr. Dash. Did there come a time when you worked under the direction of Gordon Liddy?

Mr. McCord. Yes, I did.

Mr. Dash. What was Mr. Liddy's position at that time?

Mr. McCord. He was at first from December until about March 19—December 1971 to about March 1972—general counsel for the Committee To Re-Elect the President. Thereafter he was—occupied the same position with the finance committee for the reelection of the President.

Mr. Dash. When did this arrangement begin or, in which capacity did you work under his direction, Mr. McCord, with Mr. Liddy?

Mr. McCord. The first discussions of the arrangements began sometime in January 1972. Early January.

Mr. Dash. Could you briefly state for the committee, Mr. McCord, what it was that Mr. Liddy wanted you to do?

Mr. McCord. I can give a bit of a background if you want that. When he first came aboard the committee in December 1971 he began to—we struck up an acquaintance, we had had a contact on it, and he began to question me regarding the state of the art of certain technical devices, for one thing. Listening devices and so on which appeared to be at that point in time a professional interest, a normal professional interest of someone who had worked in the field of law enforcement. We discussed as well the common topic of common interest to him and to me, and to others who were senior on the staff of anticipated demonstrations and possible violence that might be coming up in San Diego, Calif., which was originally scheduled to be the convention site for the Republican Convention in 1972 in August. The discussions——

Mr. DASH. Could you raise your voice a little if you can, Mr. McCord.

Senator BAKER. It might help—if I can interrupt just for a minute, Mr. McCord—I believe it might help if the panel operator might give us some advice in that respect if you could be a little further away from the microphone and talk a little louder because we are having a difficult time up here trying to hear you.

Mr. MCCORD. I think I am a little hoarse; if you can turn up the volume it might help.

Mr. DASH. Would you continue?

Mr. MCCORD. Yes.

Gradually the discussion in December, January, February of 1972 with Mr. Liddy, gradually developed into more and more conversation on his part with me in the offices of the Committee for the Re-Election of the President regarding technical devices and political matters pertaining to the forthcoming convention and that became apparent that he had an interest in several areas of intelligence gathering pertaining to the Democratic Party and the Democratic Convention, and in which it was contemplated or planned by him and by others whom he referred to in these conversations as John Mitchell, John Dean, counsel to the President, Jeb Magruder then in January the interim director of the Committee To Re-Elect the President, in which it appeared that those men, the four of them, were in the, by late January, the planning stage in which political intelligence was to be discussed at meetings at the Attorney General's office, Mr. Mitchell's office, and in which Mr. Liddy was seeking from me certain information regarding the costs and the types of electronic devices that could be used in bugging. That the part of the budget proposal which he was working, working on, the second part dealt with photography operations, clandestine photography operations, and a third party dealt with the broad area of political espionage, political intelligence.

Mr. DASH. Specifically, Mr. McCord, when you speak of political activity, political intelligence, bugging activities, what do you mean in terms of how that was to be attained; try to be as specific as you can, from your knowledge of what Mr. Liddy told you.

Mr. MCCORD. The area of political espionage and intelligence—I can set that one aside very quickly. He did not elaborate on in many details at all to me personally. Apparently others were involved with him which I can refer to later in the conversation—specifically Mr. Hunt, E. Howard Hunt.

The topic of photography, clandestine photography, in which he was preparing the budget and preparing to meet with the gentlemen I have referred to before, in planning sessions, dealt with photographic equipment and the cost of photographic equipment and specific items of equipment that would be used against the Democratic Party, the Democratic hierarchy in Washington primarily, but also in Miami, Fla. The electronic devices which he referred to specifically, were of a variety of types.

Mr. DASH. I am not asking specifically what the types were, but how were they to be used, where were they to be placed from your understanding?

Mr. McCORD. The initial interests specified by Mr. Liddy in this regard were, No. 1, against Mr. Larry O'Brien, then chairman of the Democratic National Committee in Washington, D.C., at his residence and subsequently at his office in the Watergate office building; perhaps other officers of the Democratic National Committee. The McGovern headquarters in Washington, D.C., were mentioned quite early in 1972. And there was some general reference to the Democratic National Convention facility or site wherever it might be located at this convention in the summer of 1972.

Mr. DASH. All right now, Mr. McCord; in connection with this assignment, in which you were having these discussions with Mr. Liddy, did you come to associate yourself with Mr. E. Howard Hunt, Bernard Barker, Eugenio Martinez, Frank Sturgis, and Virgilio Gonzales?

Mr. McCORD. Yes; I did.

Mr. DASH. And as a result of that association and your agreement with Mr. Liddy, did you with Mr. Barker, Sturgis, Martinez, and Gonzalez illegally enter the Democratic National Committee headquarters on two occasions one on or about May 30, 1972, and the other in the early morning hours of June 17, 1972?

Mr. McCORD. I did.

Mr. DASH. On the first occasion on or about May 30, 1972, you installed two telephone interception devices or wire types on two office telephones; one on the telephone of Spencer Oliver and the other on the telephone of Lawrence O'Brien?

Mr. McCORD. I did.

Mr. DASH. Leaving aside for the time being why you broke into the Democratic National Committee headquarters at the Watergate on the second time on June 17 and what circumstance led to your arrest, you were in fact arrested by plainclothesmen of the District of Columbia Metropolitan Police shortly after you entered; is that true?

Mr. McCORD. That is correct.

Mr. DASH. Is that the arrest which led to your reconviction?

Mr. McCORD. That is correct

Mr. DASH. Will you tell the committee, Mr. McCord, why, after a lifetime of work as a law enforcement officer without, as you have testified any blemish on your career, did you agree with Mr. Liddy to engage in his program of burglaries and illegal wiretapping and specifically the two break-ins on May 30 and June 17 of the Democratic National Committee headquarters at the Watergate?

Mr. McCORD. There were a number of reasons associated with the ultimate decision of mine to do so. One of the reasons, and a very important reason to me was the fact that the Attorney General himself, Mr. John Mitchell, at his office had considered and approved the operation, according to Mr. Liddy.

Secondly, that the counsel for the President, Mr. John Dean, had participated in those decisions with him. That one was the top legal officer for the United States at the Department of Justice, and the second gentleman the top legal officer in the White House and it was a matter that had currently been given——

Senator BAKER. Stop there, if you will, just for a second. I know you said you had approved according to Liddy, did you have personal knowledge of Mr. Dean's participation or was this also according to Mr. Liddy?

Mr. McCORD. Mr. Dean's participation came to me through two sources, one was Mr. Liddy, one was Mr. Hunt, E. Howard Hunt, in discussions which subsequently came to me, yes, sir.

Senator BAKER. I might say if I may, Mr. Chairman, that we have no desire to try to impede the progress of the testimony or to try to adhere strictly to the rules of evidence, such as the hearsay rule, which would otherwise apply in a court of law, but it would be helpful to me and I believe to the committee, if in each instance when the information you give us is not of your own personal first-hand knowledge, you identify it as such and give us the source.

Mr. McCORD. Yes, sir: I believe I was responding to the question of counsel, what were my reasons which involved in my case, a conclusion and motivation and intent as opposed to what someone had told me.

Senator ERVIN. We will adhere as much as possible to the rules of evidence which have been established and used in all the courts and I would say that your testimony is to the effect that you were assured by Mr. Liddy that John Mitchell and John Dean and Jeb Magruder had approved Mr. Liddy's proposed operations, and you also received assurance not only as to Mr. Dean from Mr. Liddy but also from Mr. Hunt. That was based on what you were told by Mr. Liddy and Mr. Hunt.

Mr. McCORD. That is correct, sir.

Senator ERVIN. I would say that under the rules of evidence this, at the present stage of this hearing, will not be admissible to show any connection with this matter by John Mitchell, John Dean, or Jeb Magruder but that the testimony which Mr. McCord is giving is relevant to show the motives which prompted Mr. McCord to participate in the matter.

Mr. McCORD. Yes, sir; I am explaining, I am not a lawyer, I am a layman, I will try to give the information of my knowledge, whether it is first hand or second hand for the benefit of this committee and you can stop me at what point you may feel is proper to do so.

Senator BAKER. Mr. Chairman, if I might just elaborate at that point, I thoroughly agree with the statement made by the chairman, I associate myself with him as to its content and form and, once again, I am not trying to impede your testimony. But it would be very helpful to us when your information is not first-hand information you can identify it as such for our record.

Mr. McCORD. Yes, sir.

Senator BAKER. Thank you.

Mr. DASH. Did you have any knowledge, directly or indirectly, that would lead you to believe or have information that the CIA was involved in this plan?

Mr. McCord. I had just the contrary, that there was no indication, no intelligence, no statements to me that this was a CIA operation, that quite the contrary, that it was an operation which involved the Attorney General of the United States at that point in time. Subsequently he became the director of the Committee To Re-Elect the President, involved the counsel to the White House, involved Mr. Jeb Magruder and Mr. Liddy, who was then general counsel, at that point in time of the Committee To Re-Elect the President and subsequently, was the finance committee general counsel, therefore, in my mind there was an absolute certainty that the CIA was not involved, neither did I ever receive any statement from any of the other codefendants at any point in time up to June 17 or subsequently, that this was a CIA operation.

Mr. Dash. For the record, your restatement of your belief that the Attorney General, Mr. Magruder, other than Mr. Liddy, was hearsay based on what Mr. Liddy told you and Mr. Hunt?

Mr. McCord. That is correct.

Mr. Dash. Now, would you have acted any differently with regard to this plan if you believed that Mr. Liddy was masterminding these plans on his own?

Mr. McCord. Yes, I would.

Mr. Dash. And what would you have done?

Mr. McCord. At the proposal for the operation that Mr. Liddy or Mr. Hunt or any other individual acting separately and apart from the White House and the Department of Justice, I would not have participated, I have a personal opinion that some others would not have participated but that may not be relevant to your question. My question is a categorical answer to that, I would say that the decision made to participate was not one made immediately but only after I saw that the gentlemen involved given careful consideration to this operation over a period of time, including a 30-day waiting period which to me was highly significant.

Mr. Dash. Now, Mr. McCord, did you engage in any other break-ins or wiretaps on your own or with Mr. Hunt, Mr. Liddy, or others such as the break-in in Mr. Ellsberg's psychiatrist's office?

Mr. McCord. I did not.

Mr. Dash. Now, after your arrest which you testified to, did you receive any money?

Mr. McCord. Yes, I did.

Mr. Dash. From whom did you receive that money?

Mr. McCord. From the wife of E. Howard Hunt, Mrs. Hunt.

Mr. Dash. Can you tell us how much money you did receive?

Mr. McCord. Yes, I received legal fees of $25,000 for the payment of lawyers. I received a continuation of salary from July through January at the rate of $3,000 a month, which the others were receiving as well.

Mr. Dash. Did you have knowledge, information, and belief as to where this money came from?

Mr. McCord. I was told that it came from the Committee To Re-Elect the President by Mrs. Hunt.

Senator Ervin. The same thing applies, the same rule, that it would be hearsay as to the committee and would not at this stage of the hearing be evidence to connect the committee with it.

Mr. DASH. Now, after your arrest and at the time of the indictment, after the trial or during the trial, did you receive any pressures, suggestions from any person concerning what you should do about that trial with regard to your plea, behavior, or conduct?

Mr. McCORD. Yes; I did.

Mr. DASH. Would you now please state to the committee from whom you received such directions or pressures, and what it was?

Mr. McCORD. Yes; it extended over a period of time beginning, to the best of my recollection, in late September or early October 1972, and it continued through the night before my conviction on January 29, 1973. The persons who communicated information to me, which I construed as political pressure, included Mr. E. Howard Hunt, Mrs. Hunt speaking for Mr. Hunt, she stated, my attorney, Mr. Gerald Alch, Mr. John P. Caulfield——

Mr. DASH. Will you please repeat again the name of your attorney that you just said?

Mr. McCORD. Mr. Gerald, G-e-r-a-l-d, Alch, A-l-c-h, and Mr. John Caulfield, C-a-u-l-f-i-e-l-d, who had originally hired me for the position, or who had interviewed me for the position with the Committee To Re-Elect the President.

Mr. DASH. Now, with Mr. Hunt, and with Mrs. Hunt, recognizing that you are dealing with hearsay, when you heard that said, what another person said, what was communicated to you by his presence?

Mr. McCORD. In regard to Mrs. Hunt or Mr. Hunt?

Mr. DASH. Well, first, Mr. Hunt.

Mr. McCORD. Conversations with Mr. Hunt began, to the best of my recollection, in late September or early October 1972, when I was seeing him at the courthouse on various pretrial exercises or events, motions, that were transpiring, in which we would talk about various matters, including the situation that we were in, what the trial appeared to be at that point in time—that is, what the future looked like for us; and in telephone conversations, with him to me. In other words, both in person and by telephone, Mr. Hunt stated that the defendants were going to be provided with, given Executive clemency after a period of time in prison, if interested, if they would plead guilty, and were sentenced, in a plea of not guilty, that they were going to be given financial support while they were in prison; that is, their families would be; and that rehabilitation, not specified, but rehabilitation, perhaps a job, would be provided for the men after the release from prison.

Mr. DASH. All right. Let us leave out for the moment Mrs. Hunt. Would you now proceed to any conversations you had leading up to contacts with Mr. Caulfield and what Mr. Caulfield did state to you?

Mr. McCORD. I have a statement, sir, in this regard.

Mr. DASH. Do you have copies of that statement for the committee?

Mr. McCORD. Yes.

Could you please, Mr. Fensterwald, provide copies for the committee?

Mr. FENSTERWALD. Yes.

Senator MONTOYA. Mr. Chairman, I would like for the witness to summarize the record just briefly, if he will—I mean, summarize the statement, unless he is going to read it in full.

Mr. DASH. He wants to read it.

Mr. McCord, what led you to prepare the statement? Why have you prepared that statement?

Mr. McCord. I prepared it, sir, for accuracy's purpose because of the nature of the information that is contained therein, as I have done with some previous statements to this committee, where I felt that my best recollection, as best I can recall it, set down in writing, would be the most accurate way of doing it rather than, in effect, under the pressure of lights and cameras and what have you, make statements that might either be misconstrued or might be inaccurate on my part, and in order to set it forth as briefly as I know how.

Mr. Dash. All right.

Now, will you please read the statement, and will you read it clearly so we can all hear it now?

Mr. McCord. I will state as a preliminary that the dates of the telephone calls that I refer to in this statement are to the best of my recollection; they may be inaccurate by a day or two, but they are the best recollection I have of the dates on which the calls occurred.

The subject is political pressure on the writer to accept Executive clemency and remain silent.

Political pressure from the White House was conveyed to me in January 1973 by John Caulfield to remain silent, take Executive clemency by going off to prison quietly, and I was told that while there, I would receive financial aid and later rehabilitation and a job. I was told in a January meeting in 1973 with Caulfield that the President of the United States was aware of our meeting, that the results of the meeting would be conveyed to the President, and that at a future meeting there would likely be a personal message from the President himself.

Senator Ervin. I would like to state at this point that the testimony of Mr. McCord as to what was told to him by John Caulfield would not be accepted in a court of law to connect the President with what Mr. Caulfield was doing, but it is admissible to show whether or not Mr. Caulfield was a party to any agreement to connect the President for any information on what is known as the Watergate affair, but it is not received in connection to the President at this stage.

Senator Gurney. I think it ought to be pointed out at that time that at this time, January 1973, it is my understanding that Mr. Caulfield was not in the White House at all, but was employed, I think, by the Treasury Department.

Mr. Dash. That is right.

Senator Gurney. I hope we can correct these things as we go along. You have all kinds of inferences here that are inaccurate and are casting aspersions that are going to damage peoples' reputations.

Mr. McCord. I only say in my statement that political pressure was conveyed to me by Mr. Caulfield which he attributed to the White House without citing——

Senator Baker. May I ask the counsel if Mr. Caulfield is under subpena?

Mr. Dash. Mr. Caulfield is under subpena and will be brought right after this witness.

Senator Baker. Is he under subpena at the present time?

Mr. Dash. His counsel has been informed that he wants to testify and he will accept a subpena.

Senator Baker. The answer is that he is not under subpena, and my request of the chairman is that a subpena be issued in standard form for Mr. Caulfield to testify and that he be scheduled to testify immediately next succeeding this witness.

Mr. DASH. This was our understanding.

Senator BAKER. Mr. Chairman, will you take care of that request?

Senator ERVIN. Yes, I will sign it as soon as I can get somebody to prepare it.

Mr. DASH. We have contacted his counsel and have been told by him that he is prepared to accept the subpena.

Will you please proceed with your reading of the statement, Mr. McCord.

Senator ERVIN. I would like to reiterate that what Mr. McCord says Caulfield told him is admissible to show what Caulfield did and said to you, sir, as a witness taking action or a friend taking action. It is not relevant to prove any connection with the White House or the President.

You may proceed now.

Mr. MCCORD. The sentence which follows the last sentence which I read from the memorandum reads, "The dates of the telephone calls set forth below are the current"—and that word is mistyped. It should be correct dates—"to the best of my recollection."

The second paragraph is: On the afternoon of January 8, 1973, the first day of the Watergate trial, Gerald Alch, my attorney, told me that William O. Bittman, attorney for E. Howard Hunt, wanted to meet with me at Bittman's office that afternoon. When I asked why, Alch said that Bittman wanted to talk with me about "whose word I would trust regarding a White House offer of Executive clemency." Alch added that Bittman wanted to talk with both Bernard Barker and me that afternoon.

I had no intention of accepting Executive clemency, but I did want to find out what was going on, and by whom, and exactly what the White House was doing now. A few days before, the White House had tried to lay the Watergate operation off on the CIA, and now it was clear that I was going to have to find out what was up now. To do so involved some risks. To fail to do so was in my opinion to work in a vacuum regarding White House intentions and plans, which involved even greater risks, I felt.

Around 4:30 p.m. that afternoon, January 8, while waiting for a taxi after the court session, Bernard Barker asked my attorneys and me if he could ride in the cab with us to Bittman's office, which we agreed to. There he got out of the cab and went up toward Bittman's office. I had been under the impression during the cab ride that Bittman was going to talk to both Barker and me jointly, and became angered at what seemed to me—I can finish the statement, sir, if you want. I am giving opinion. If you want opinion, I will finish the statement. If you want me to delete opinion, I will not finish the statement. I am setting forth the facts and what was going through my mind at the time.

Mr. DASH. Continue to read the statement, please.

Senator BAKER. I think it is fine, Mr. McCord, for you to go ahead and read the statement, but once again, to the extent that you can, would you identify as you go along those things attributed to other people that you do not know at firsthand? I have no objection, of course, to your stating what went through your mind. Your statement is significant in terms of your conduct, not necessarily in terms of the facts themselves. And it is relevant to this committee's inquiry as it relates to your conduct at one point or the other.

The request I made a few moments ago was that while some of your testimony will be hearsay in the strict sense, simply identify those parts, that information which you give us in this statement, which you received secondhand.

Mr. McCORD. Most respectfully, sir, I shall try to do so. What I am reading now is firsthand.

Senator BAKER. Thank you.

Mr. McCORD. The sentence that I began: Around 4:30 p.m. that afternoon, January 8, while waiting for a taxi after the court session, Bernard Barker asked my attorneys and me if he could ride in the cab with us to Bittman's office, which we agreed to. There he got out of the cab and went up toward Bittman's office. I had been under the impression during the cab ride that Bittman was going to talk to both Barker and me jointly, and became angered at what seemed to me to be the arrogance and audacity of another man's lawyer calling in two other lawyer's clients and pitching them for the White House. Alch saw my anger and took me aside for about a half hour after the cab arrived in front of Bittman's office, and let Barker go up alone. About 5 p.m. we went up to Bittman's office. There Alch disappeared with Bittman, and I sat alone in Bittman's office for a period of time, became irritated, and went next door where Bernard Shankman and Austin Mittler, attorneys for me and Hunt respectively, were talking about legitimate legal matters. I might add at this point parenthetically no knowledge whatever that either Bernard Shankman or Austin Mittler had any knowledge of whatever of the events which I am discussing in this memorandum.

Alch finally came back, took me aside and said that Bittman told him I would be called that same night by a friend I had known from the White House.

Senator BAKER. Now, at that point, I take it that that is secondhand information?

Senator ERVIN. That is testimony of what he says that his lawyer told him Mr. Bittman said. Of course, as far as Bittman is concerned and the White House is concerned, it is hearsay, but it is his own knowledge.

Senator BAKER. I entirely agree, Mr. Chairman. The point I am making is I want to separate the wheat from the chaff and what his lawyer told him clearly is primary evidence. What his lawyer told him that someone else told him is clearly hearsay after that. But once again, I am not trying to exclude it. I wish simply to identify it as we go along.

Mr. McCORD. I believe I stated it, sir, as it occurred, which was that this was a statement by Mr. Alch.

My statement was that: Mr. Alch finally came back, took me aside, and said that Mr. Bittman had told him that I would be called that same night by a friend I had known from the White House.

I assumed this would be John Caulfield who had originally recruited me for the Committee for the Re-election of the President position.

About 12:30 p.m. that same evening, I received a call from an unidentified individual who said that Caulfield was out of town, and asked me to go to a pay phone booth near the Blue Fountain Inn on

Route 355 near my residence, where he had a message for me from Caulfield. There the same individual called and read the following message:

"Plead guilty.

"One year is a long time. You will get Executive clemency. Your family will be taken care of and when you get out you will be rehabilitated and a job will be found for you.

"Don't take immunity when called before the grand jury."

Mr. DASH. Now, Mr. McCord, did you recognize that voice at all? Do you know who was speaking to you on the telephone?

Mr. McCORD. I do not know who the man was, the voice I heard over the telephone before in previous calls.

Mr. DASH. And, therefore, it is not your testimony from your reading that statement, it was Mr. Caulfield who was speaking to you?

Mr. McCORD. That is correct.

Mr. DASH. And, therefore, it is somebody else telling you, you believe that he was repeating a statement Mr. Caulfield but not a direct statement to you from Mr. Caulfield?

Mr. McCORD. He so stated he was repeating a statement from Mr. Caulfield, and he repeated the statement twice, that is correct.

Mr. DASH. Right. Can we continue, please?

Senator GURNEY. Can we find out more about these other calls where he heard this same voice? What were they, what did they involve, what were they?

Mr. McCORD. Sir, I can give them to you now or at the end of the statement, as you prefer and I am willing to do either that the committee desires.

Senator GURNEY. Well, they are very important, I would like to have them now.

Senator ERVIN. Senator, if he reads the statement, he states in his statement, it is on the 8th of January and first he said that his lawyer, Mr. Alch, told him that, Bittman said he would receive a call from a friend he had known from the White House, and he said at 12:30 p.m., the same day, that is after midnight on January 8, that he received this phone call from an unidentified individual.

Senator GURNEY. Yes, Mr. Chairman, what he also said was that he recognized the voice because he had heard it in previous phone calls, and my question was when and what were these previous phone calls about. This is a very important matter.

Mr. McCORD. The previous phone calls, the story gets a bit complex, I will be glad to do it either way you prefer, I believe it would have more continuity if I finished that first.

Mr. DASH. To clarify it for Senator Gurney, do you know the voice, do you know the identity?

Mr. McCORD. I heard the voice before, I do not know the identity of the man who called.

Senator BAKER. I don't think it will take long to do what Senator Gurney wishes to do, what he is talking about. I think it would be better to go ahead with the question and I would request that Senator Gurney proceed at this time.

Senator GURNEY. Would you proceed.

Mr. McCORD. I would be glad to.

Sometime in July, 1972, shortly after I got out of jail, which was in June 1972, about mid-day there was a note in my mailbox at my residence and when I opened the letter, which had not been stamped nor sent through the mails it was a note from Jack Caulfield signed "Jack" which said, "Go to the phone booth on Route 355 near your home," and he gave three alternate times at which I could appear at the phone booth for a telephone call from him.

To the best of my recollection, one of those times was very shortly thereafter, an hour or two later, and another time was the next day and that seems to me that the third time was the following evening.

I went to the telephone, to that telephone booth on Route 355 that afternoon, the same afternoon, as I best recall, and I heard the voice that I have referred to in this memorandum of today. I do not know the individual's identity, he had an accent that I would refer to as a New York accent. He said that he had formerly worked for Jack Caulfield. He said, "I am a friend of Jack's, I formerly worked with him. Jack will want to talk with you shortly. He will be in touch with you soon."

I received a call subsequently from Mr. Caulfield. To the best of my recollection it came to my home first and it said, "Go to the same phone booth on Route 355," which I did, and there Mr. Caulfield told me that he was going overseas in a few days. He said, "If you have any problems" if you have any problems, "call my home and leave word and I will call you back from overseas to your residence."

He said, "When you call my home ask for Mr. Watson."

Senator GURNEY. Mr. Watson?

Mr. MCCORD. Watson. He said, also, "After my return if you ever need to call me at my office," he gave a number, the office number and he said, "Simply leave word that Mr. Watson is calling."

So it was a name that both of us were to use, my name and his name. I did not contact him during the next 30 days and I next heard from him, to the best of my recollection sometime in September 1972, on a Sunday afternoon.

I can't recall the exact date but I do recall that Mr. Clark MacGregor, then the head of the Committee for the Re-Election of the President, had just finished a television appearance on one of the talk programs such as Meet the Press, and Mr. Caulfield called me at home and again asked that I go to the telephone booth on Route 355, which I did. He stated that he had trouble getting my home number because it was an unlisted number, and he stated, "We are worried about you"—this is Mr. Caulfield's statement [laughter] and he went on then to read briefly the words of a deposition which he planned to give to the Democratic National Committee, I had read in the papers a few days before that he had been scheduled as a witness before the Democratic National Committee, and he read the deposition to me indicating that this was, in effect, what he planned to say in the deposition.

There was some reference during the conversation to something doing with a double agent in quotes; Mr. Clark MacGregor, as I recall, in his television appearance had referred to the possibility of there being a double agent in the Watergate operation and the inference was that it was Mr. Baldwin, and I told Mr. Caulfield that so far as I was concerned whoever had drawn that conclusion had drawn absolutely an erroneous conclusion, that I had seen absolutely nothing that would indicate such, and I simply wanted to go on the record with Mr. Caulfield to that effect.

Senator GURNEY. We do want to get back to the statement but, in sort, what you are saying is that Mr. Caulfield's friend Watson by name is the man whose voice you heard?

Mr. McCORD. No, sir, that, most respectfully—that is not what I said, sir.

Senator GURNEY. Go on.

Mr. McCORD. I believe Mr. Caulfield used the name Watson. It was not his friend.

Senator GURNEY. I see.

Mr. McCORD. Yes, sir.

Senator GURNEY. All right. Go on. How many times did you hear this unidentified voice?

Mr. McCORD. To the best of my recollection I heard the voice prior to the January call two or three times. I cannot be absolutely sure but at least twice before January.

Senator GURNEY. Were these in connection with contacts with Caulfield?

Mr. McCORD. Always.

Senator GURNEY. Yes. I just wanted to make sure.

Mr. McCORD. Yes, sir.

Senator GURNEY. Thank you.

Mr. DASH. Will you proceed with the statement from where you left off, Mr. McCord, and I guess the prior sentence so we can have continuity.

Mr. McCORD. I believe my last sentence that I read was: The same message was once again repeated, obviously read.

I believe that appears in the statement you have on page 3.

The next sentence was that: I told the caller I would not discuss such matters over the phone. He said that Caulfield was out of town.

On Wednesday evening, January 10, the same party, to the best of my recollection, called and told me by phone that Jack would want to talk with me by phone on Thursday night, the following night, January 11, when he got back into town and requested that I go to the same phone booth on Route 355 near the Blue Fountain Inn. He also conveyed instructions regarding a personal meeting with Mr. Caulfield on Friday night, January 12.

On Thursday evening, January 11, the same party called me at home and told me that Caulfield's plane was late and that he—speaking of Caulfield—wanted to meet with me personally the same evening, that is Thursday evening, after arrival. I told him that I would not do so but would meet with him Friday night if he desired. Later that evening, Thursday evening, about 9:30 p.m., Caulfield called me on my home phone and insisted on talking with me but my family refused to let him do so, since I was asleep.

On Friday night, January 12, from about 7 p.m. to 7:30 p.m. I met with Caulfield at the second overlook, that is overlooking the Potomac at the parking area for looking at the Potomac area on George Washington Parkway in Virginia.

Mr. DASH. Mr. McCord, how did you know to go there? How was it arranged?

Mr. McCord. I believe it was stated in the Thursday evening call at which this unidentified party said Caulfield would want to meet with me personally and on Friday night said go to the second overlook on George Washington Parkway and he specified the time and that is what I followed through. I met with Caulfield at the second overlook on George Washington Parkway, that is the second one leaving Washington and going out to Virginia and talked with him in his car, in his automobile. Caulfield advised that he had been attending a law enforcement meeting in San Clemente, Calif., and had just returned. I advised him that I had no objection to meeting with him to tell him my frame of mind but that I had no intention of talking Executive clemency or pleading guilty; that I had come to the meeting at his request and not of my own, and was glad to tell him my views.

He said that the offer of Executive clemency which he was passing along and of support while in prison and rehabilitation and help toward a job later "was a sincere offer." He explained that he had been asked to convey this message to me and he was only doing what he was told to do. He repeated this last statement several times during the course of the meeting we had then, and I might add during subsequent meetings which he and I had.

My response was that I would not even discuss Executive clemency or pleading guilty and remaining silent, but I was glad to talk with him, so that there was no misunderstanding on anyone's part about it.

I might explain that the trial was going on during this period, this was the first week of the trial which began on January 8.

Caulfield stated that he was carrying the message of Executive clemency to me "from the very highest levels of the White House." He said that the President of the United States was in Key Biscayne, Fla., that weekend, referring to the weekend following January 8, the following meeting that we were in then, and that the President had been told of the results of the meeting.

Senator Ervin. Now the same rule previously announced that this evidence is competent to show what, if anything, John Caulfield did to induce Mr. McCord to plead guilty and keep silent—it is not any evidence at the present state of the hearing that connects or that makes any indication whatever and has any relevancy as to the President.

Mr. McCord. Yes, sir.

Senator Ervin. Yes.

Mr. McCord. He further stated that "I may have a message to you at our next meeting from the President himself."

I advised Caulfield that I had seen the list of witnesses for the trial and had seen Jeb Magruder's name, appearing as a Government witness. I advised him that it was clear then that Magruder was going to perjure himself and that we were not going to get a fair trial. Further I told him that it was clear that some of those involved in the Watergate case were going to trial, and others were going to be covered for—I was referring to John Mitchell, John Dean, and Magruder—and I so named those individuals incidentally in the conversation, and I said that this was not my idea of American justice. I further——

Senator ERVIN. The same ruling applies so far as John Mitchell, John Dean, and Magruder are concerned, that is that it does not connect them legally speaking.

Mr. McCORD. Yes, sir.

I further advised Caulfield that I believed that the Government had lied in denying electronic interception of my phone calls from my residence since June 17, 1972, and that I believed that the administration had also tapped the phones of the other defendants during that time. I mentioned two specific calls of mine which I had made during September and early October 1972, which I was certain had been intercepted by the Government, and yet the Government had blithely denied any such tapping. These were my words to Mr. Caulfield.

I compared this denial to the denial that the Government had made in the *Ellsberg* case, in which for months the Government had denied any such impermissible interception of the calls and yet in the summer of 1972 had finally been forced to admit them when the judge ordered, by court order, a search of about a dozen Government agencies, and calls intercepted were then disclosed.

I might state separate from the record at this point, that as I have previously stated, I had no knowledge whatever of any activity, monitorially or what have you, of Mr. Ellsberg's calls as have previously come out—as have earlier come out in the newspapers in the past few days. It is purely coincidence that I happen to mention the *Ellsberg* case at that time, I had been following the case in the papers and I knew the history of the case.

To go on with the statement: I stated that if we were going to get a fiction of a fair trial, through perjured testimony to begin with, and then for the Government to lie about illegal telephone interceptions, that the trial ought to be kicked out and we start all over again, this time with all of those involved as defendants. At least in this way, some would not be more equal than others before the bar of justice and we would get a fair trial.

The Executive clemency offer was made two or three times during this meeting, as I recall, and I repeated each time that I would not even discuss it, nor discuss pleading guilty, which I had been asked to do in the first telephone call received on the night of January 8, from Caulfield's friend, whose identity I do not know. I told him, referring to Mr. Caulfield, that I was going to renew the motion on disclosure of Government wiretapping of our telephones.

Caulfield ended the conversation by stating that he would call me the next day about a meeting that same afternoon, Saturday, January 13, and that if I did not hear from him, he would want to talk with me by telephone on the evening of Monday, January 15, 1973.

I did not hear from Caulfield on Saturday but on Sunday afternoon he called and asked to meet me that afternoon about an hour later at the same location on George Washington Parkway. He stated that there was no objection to renewing the motion on discovery of Government wiretapping, and that if that failed, that I would receive Executive clemency after 10 to 11 months. I told him I had not asked anyone's permission to file the motion.

He went on to say that, the President's ability to govern is at stake. Another Teapot Dome scandal is possible, and the Government may fall. Everybody else is on track but you. You are not following the game plan. Get closer to your attorney. You seem to be pursuing your own course of action. Do not talk if called before the grand jury, keep silent, and do the same if called before a Congressional committee.

I might add that two congressional committees had, prior to January 8—prior to that date—been conducting investigations into this case. I believe it was the Patman committee and Senator Kennedy's committee.

My response was that I felt a massive injustice was being done, that I was different from the others, that I was going to fight the fixed case, and had no intention of either pleading guilty, taking Executive clemency or agreeing to remain silent. He repeated the statement that the Government would have difficulty in continuing to be able to stand. I responded that they do have a problem, but that I had a problem with the massive injustice of the whole trial being a sham, and that I would fight it every way I know how.

I should make a correction in the sentence I just read in saying the whole trial being a sham, because I did not at that point in time make any reference at any time to Judge Sirica to the contrary of his being anything but an honest and dedicated judge, and I do not want the sentence to be misread.

He—talking about Caulfield—asked for a commitment that I would remain silent and I responded that I would make none. I gave him a memorandum on the dates of the two calls of mine in September 1972 and October 1972 that I was sure had been intercepted, and said that I believed the Government had lied about them. He said that he would check and see if in fact the Government had done so.

On Monday night, January 15, 1973, Caulfield called me again at the phone booth on Route 355 near my residence. I informed him that I had no desire to talk further, that if the White House had any intention of playing the game straight and giving us the semblance of a fair trial they would check into the perjury charge of mine against Magruder, and into the existence of the two intercepted calls previously referred to, and hung up

On Tuesday morning, the next morning, about 7:30 a.m., Caulfield called my residence but I had already left for court.

On Tuesday evening, Caulfield called and asked me again to meet him and I responded not until they had something to talk about on the perjured testimony and the intercepted calls. He said words to the effect "Give us a week," and a meeting was subsequently arranged on January 25, 1973, when he said he would have something to talk about.

About 10 a.m., on Thursday, January 25, 1973, in a meeting lasting until about 12:30 a.m., correction—12:30 p.m.—we drove in his car toward Warrenton, Va., and returned—that is, we drove there and returned—and a conversation ensued which repeated the offers of Executive clemency and financial support while in prison, and rehabilitation later. I refused to discuss it. He stated that I was "fouling up the game plan." I made a few comments about the "game plan." He said that "they" had found no record of the interception of the two calls I referred to, and said that perhaps it could wait until the appeals. He asked what my plans were regarding talking publicly, and I said that I planned to do so when I was ready; that I had discussed it with my wife and she said that I should do what I felt I must and not to worry about the family. I advised Jack that my children were now grown and could understand what I had to do, when the disclosures came out. He responded by saying that: "You know that if the administration gets its back to the wall, it will have to take steps to defend itself." I took that as a personal threat and I told him in response that I had had a good life, that my will was made out, and that I had thought through the risks and would take them when I was ready. He said that if I had to go off to jail that the administration would help with the bail premiums. I advised him that it was not a bail premium, but $100,000 straight cash and that that was a problem I would have to worry about, through family and friends. On the night before sentencing, Jack called me and said that the administration would provide the $100,000 in cash if I could tell him how to get it funded through an intermediary. I said that if we ever needed it I would let him know. I never contacted him thereafter; neither have I heard from him.

That completes the statement.

Mr. DASH. That completes it. I have one more question, Mr. McCord.

Have you ever made that statement before this Select Committee other than when you appeared before minority counsel and myself a couple of days ago? Have you ever made that statement before this committee, before the grand jury, or before any investigating body until this time?

Mr. McCORD. No, sir.

Mr. DASH. Would you please state to the committee why, when you were making statements at earlier times before this committee, before the grand jury and other inquiring bodies, you failed to disclose that information?

Mr. McCORD. I will be glad to.

I will take the grand jury and get that one out of the way. When I appeared before the grand jury, I told them that—I raised the question about political pressure, any pressure that had been put onto me by the Hunts. I told them also that there was a personal friend who was involved also in political pressure against me; that personally, at that point in time, it was a very painful thing to go into it, that I would be glad to do it at a later time, that I hoped they would defer that question until subsequent questioning and I would be glad to answer it. They said they would do so.

I believe when I appeared before the committee on March 28, your Senators asked me the same question and I said, yes, there had been political pressure applied to me, that one such pressure had been by a Government—one of your Senators asked me if it were by a Government employee—I think Senator Montoya. I responded, yes. He asked me if it were anyone at the White House. I said, no.

He asked if it were from the Department of Justice, and I said, no.

It was clear, I think, to the committee that I would like to be able to answer that question at a later time. The reason for the delay was that I wanted to be as accurate as I could about the information, get it all together, because it involved the President of the United States, in my opinion, and it was a very serious matter and I wanted to be very careful about it and accurate.

Mr. DASH. I have no further questions, Mr. Chairman.

Senator ERVIN. Mr. Thompson?

Mr. THOMPSON. Thank you, Mr. Chairman.

Mr. McCord, I would like to limit my questions to one area. That is what you know about the planning of the Watergate break-in.

First of all, I would like to separate what Mr. Hunt told you someone said about it from what Mr. Liddy told you someone said about it.

Did Mr. Hunt indicate to you that he knew anything about these meetings that Mr. Liddy referred to with Mitchell, Magruder, and Dean?

Mr. McCORD. The question is, did Mr. Hunt indicate——

Mr. THOMPSON. Yes, sir.

Mr. McCORD. That he knew anything about the meetings?

Mr. THOMPSON. Yes, sir.

Mr. McCORD. Yes, he did.

Mr. THOMPSON. What did he say about those meetings? Did he indicate he was present at any of those meetings?

Mr. McCORD. I am trying to recall exactly the context of the discussion. Do you want me to go into that as well?

Mr. THOMPSON. Yes, sir.

Mr. McCORD. The meetings, as best I recall, in which these references by Mr. Hunt took place, took place in Mr. Hunt's office, in the Robert F. Mullen Co. offices at 1700 Pennsylvania Avenue. They took place in April and May of 1972. To the best of my recollection, Mr. Liddy was present in all of the discussions.

Mr. Liddy, during those discussions, as best I recall, would raise the topic that the planning and the progress of the operation itself was going forward, comments about what Mr. Mitchell was saying to him about what could be done in terms of the priorities of the operation; that is, which ones were to be done first and second.

Mr. Hunt's comments, his exact words I cannot recall, but his comments made to me—and not to me, made in three-way discussions that were taking place during that period of time, indicated to me that he had separate, independent knowledge, perhaps from Mr. Liddy, perhaps from other sources, of his own that Mr. Mitchell and Mr. Dean and Mr. Magruder had planned the operations in the Attorney General's office to begin with and that at least Mr. Mitchell and Mr. Magruder had had subsequent discussions after the first meeting in the Attorney General's office, and that Mr. Magruder and Mr. Mitchell had had discussions with Mr. Liddy in Mr. Mitchell's offices at the Committee To Re-Elect the President regarding the ongoing plans to carry out the operations.

Does this answer your question somewhat?

Mr. THOMPSON. Well, I think it naturally raises several other questions. What did he say, as best you can recall, to indicate to you that he had any independent knowledge other than what Mr. Liddy might have told him?

Mr. McCORD. I think he would refer to comments regarding this as you and I have discussed before.

Mr. THOMPSON. That would not fall in that category, would it?

Mr. McCORD. It would fall in that category.

Mr. THOMPSON. The things Hunt had learned separate and apart from what Liddy had told him?

Mr. McCORD. It would fall into two separate categories. I said one, what Mr. Liddy had told him before and second, what he had learned from others. I mentioned to this committee the name of another individual, but I will not mention it at this point, that Mr. Hunt referred to in conversations, in which they were talking about the Watergate operations and the planning for the operations and so on. The statement——

Mr. THOMPSON. I think you should refer to the name.

Mr. McCORD. He referred to the name of Mr. Colson. That was interjected into the conversation by Mr. Hunt in the meetings with Mr. Liddy and me in his offices, Hunt's offices, at 1700 Pennsylvania Avenue, and specifically, when Mr. Hunt had a plan, a typed plan, operational plan, for the entry of the Democratic National Committee headquarters.

Mr. THOMPSON. Do you recall anything that Mr. Hunt said to you about Mr. Colson's involvement or did you just get the general impression that Mr. Colson was involved in some way from what Mr. Hunt told you?

Mr. McCORD. I believe my previous testimony, which I will restate before this committee, was to the effect that when I had met Mr. Hunt in his offices at 1700 Pennsylvania Avenue with Mr. Liddy that he had referred to his previous work at the White House for Mr. Colson, referring to him as his superior; that during the session that Mr. Hunt, Mr. Liddy, and I had in Mr. Hunt's offices, Mr. Hunt had a typed plan that he had typed himself, step-by-step, for the entry of the Democratic National Committee headquarters; that at one point, he held this plan in his hands, and his words were, he interjected the name of Mr. Colson into the conversation at that point, words to the effect, "I will see Colson." And he held the paper in his hand in this sense.

From that statement, I drew the conclusion that he was going to see Mr. Colson and discuss our giving him the operational plan. That is a conclusion, but this is also the words as best I recall, with which Mr. Hunt raised the name of Mr. Colson.

Mr. THOMPSON. I am sure that will need to be pursued. But getting back to my original point, is that innocent of knowledge Mr. Hunt had of these meetings we referred to? He did not bring Mr. Colson into the conversation with regard to these particular meetings that you previously referred to, did he?

Mr. McCORD. I believe you asked me if he appeared to have knowledge. I said he appeared to have knowledge of the previous meetings of the Attorney General, in the Attorney General's office, of Mr. Liddy, Mr. Magruder, and Mr. Dean, and my response was to the effect that he had it from Mr. Liddy from what he told me, and I believed also that he had this information from others.

Mr. THOMPSON. Well, I do not want to belabor the point.

Mr. McCORD. I am glad to answer the questions.

Mr. THOMPSON. You say that you think he had independent knowledge, and, of course, this is a serious matter. I think we have to determine whether or not we are relying on Mr. Liddy, or Mr. Hunt and Mr. Liddy for this information, which of course, is extremely important information. Anything you can state that Mr. Hunt told you to indicate that he had any independent knowledge of these meetings, I think would be very relevant. You can do it now or supply—you have supplied several memorandums that are very helpful in that regard; if you want to do that at a subsequent time, I think that would be appropriate.

Mr. McCORD. I would be glad to submit the committee a memorandum if that would be helpful to you, and set it forth in exactly the detail as best I recall.

Mr. THOMPSON. All right. Anything Hunt told you indicating that he knew of these meetings independent of what Liddy told him.

Mr. McCORD. All right.

[The following information was submitted in reference to the above.]

RECOLLECTION OF E. HOWARD HUNT'S COMMENTS

My best recollection of Hunt's comments regarding meetings in the Attorney General's offices, those of John Mitchell, were that Mitchell, Dean and Magruder, along with Liddy were present in at least the first two meetings, and that these meetings were in January or February, 1972, at which time plans and discussions were held by those present regarding bugging, photography and political espionage operations to be conducted against Democratic installations during 1972. These comments were made to me by Hunt during meetings with him in April–June 1972 in which he stated that he had received this information independently from Liddy and other unnamed persons.

Mr. THOMPSON. Now, let us get back to the meetings in a little bit more detail, Mr. McCord. How many meetings did Mr. Liddy say there were when the overall surveillance operations were discussed?

Mr. McCORD. At what point in time?

Mr. THOMPSON. Well, how many meetings overall, up until June 17, did Mr. Liddy indicate that he, Mitchell, Magruder, and Dean, or any combination of these people, had to discuss generally?

Mr. McCORD. He did not say the number. It was stated to me in various and sundry meetings with Mr. Liddy between January and June 17, by Mr. Liddy that he had had several meetings with Mr. Mitchell, that there appeared to be ongoing meetings with Mr. Mitchell from the planning stage until the completion of the plans for the second entry operation on June 17, that there appeared to be continuous discussions between at least Mr. Liddy and Mr. Mitchell, and sometimes Mr. Magruder, according to statements which Mr. Liddy made to me and they began with the planning and they continued through the ongoing operation itself, the monitoring and the planning for the second operation and discussions at various stages according to Mr. Liddy of the various priorities of the bugging and photography operations, what was to come first, what was to come second.

Mr. THOMPSON. Did Mr. Liddy come to you after each important meeting or after each meeting where these plans were discussed and give you a summary of the meetings, what was discussed and what the conclusions were?

Mr. McCORD. Not after each meeting at all, but we would see each other regularly during the week. I would say not once a day but every other day, most weeks between January and June 17. Sometimes he would tell me, I am getting ready to go up to see the Attorney General to discuss this operation, referring to the Watergate operation, to discuss the operations that he had planned.

Sometimes he would tell me, I have just come back from that operation, concluding what we are going to do now.

Mr. THOMPSON. Were some of these meetings, according to what he told you, while Mr. Mitchell was still Attorney General?

Mr. McCORD. Yes.

Mr. THOMPSON. And some after he came to the Committee To Re-Elect?

Mr. McCORD. Yes.

Mr. THOMPSON. Were money figures discussed?

Mr. McCORD. Oh, yes.

Mr. THOMPSON. According to what he said—according to Mr. Liddy, what was the original proposed budget for the overall surveillance operation? I assume we are talking about the overall operation, not just the Watergate break-in; is that correct?

Mr. McCORD. We are talking about three categories—political espionage, photography operations, and electronic operations, and the original figure in February that Mr. Liddy proposed, as I saw it in writing, in a draft on his desk on one occasion and in a typed memorandum on a second occasion, was approximately $450,000.

Mr. THOMPSON. All right, according to him, was that budget approved?

Mr. McCORD. The sequence of the events were that there were planning meetings in January or February or both in the Attorney General's offices, in which Mr. Dean and Mr. Magruder, Mr. Liddy, and Mr. Mitchell discussed the original amount, the $450,000 amount, and subsequently, approximately 30 days after the first formal meetings that I heard referred to by Mr. Liddy, there was a figure of approximately $250,000, which he said had been approved for the operation. And he referred also to some additional funds which he had in the order of approximately $100,000, but that figure is not absolutely certain in my mind, with a total of something around $300,000 or $350,000.

Mr. THOMPSON. According to him, was this money problem the need for subsequent meetings? Was that a concern of the people involved? Was there quite a bit of discussion as to exactly how much money should be spent on this project?

Mr. McCORD. Money was a topic that he said was discussed. He said the individual operations were discussed—that is, specifically the three parts of his budget which he had prepared on charts, which he had taken to at least one of the meetings. That is the three parts of political espionage and photography and so on. It was not limited, the discussion was not limited to the matter of funding. My understanding was all aspects of the operation were discussed in those meetings by the four individuals.

Mr. THOMPSON. Let me just ask you this. Did he tell you that John Mitchell ever told him that this budget is just too high and you will have to do it for less or something to that extent?

Mr. McCORD. No; he did not.

Mr. THOMPSON. Did he ever tell you that they specifically discussed the Watergate operation in any of these meetings?

Mr. McCORD. Which meetings are you referring to?

Mr. THOMPSON. I am talking about any meetings which he had with the Attorney General, when any of these other people were present.

Mr. McCORD, Oh, yes, sure.

Mr. THOMPSON. That the Watergate break-in specifically was discussed?

Mr. McCORD. Very definitely.

Mr. THOMPSON. What did he say about that particular discussion?

Mr. McCORD. It was a contiguous discussion. He sat in with Mr. Magruder from the earliest planning session in January through the first entry operation, Memorial Day weekend and then even to the second operation in June and he talked to me at various times and it was clear from what he said that their committee, that Mr. Liddy was having such meetings, he stated they were having such meetings in which the Watergate operation was a part of, Watergate referring to the Democratic National Committee headquarters himself. So I would say there were many such discussions by Mr. Liddy with me in which he stated that meetings had occurred with Mr. Mitchell and Magruder specifically on this after February.

Mr. THOMPSON. You mentioned, I believe, that you had frequent contact with Liddy. Did you have frequent contact with Mr. Magruder at the Committee To Re-Elect?

Mr. McCORD. Yes, I did.

Mr. THOMPSON. Would you see him on a daily basis?

Mr. McCORD. We would see each other on a daily basis. We would speak hello, exchange greetings. My point of contact at the committee was his deputy, Mr. Odle. My business was transacted primarily with Mr. Odle, their offices were adjoining.

Mr. THOMPSON. Their offices were close together?

Mr. McCORD. So we would see each other frequently in that sense.

Mr. THOMPSON. Just to speak or did you ever discuss any substantive matters concerning the re-election of the President or the operation of the Committee To Re-Elect the President?

Mr. McCORD. We had some meetings, one particular meeting with the Attorney General and Mr. Magruder lasting over an hour in which we discussed overall security of the committee and the security of the Mitchell family.

Mr. THOMPSON. You had a meeting with the Attorney General and Mr. Magruder?

Mr. McCORD. Yes.

Mr. THOMPSON. Where was this meeting?

Mr. McCORD. In Mr. Mitchell's office on the fourth floor in the law office suite that he occupied.

Mr. THOMPSON. When did this meeting occur?

Mr. McCORD. Sometime in March 1972.

Mr. THOMPSON. March. This would have been after your discussions with Mr. Liddy?

Mr. McCORD. That is correct.

Mr. THOMPSON. Concerning what was going on with Mr. Liddy, Mr. Magruder, and Mr. Mitchell?

Mr. McCORD. That is correct.

Mr. THOMPSON. Was anybody else present besides yourself and Mr. Magruder and Mr. Mitchell?

Mr. McCORD. Just the three of us.

Mr. THOMPSON. Just the three men. Did you take that opportunity before you decided to engage in this particular operation to inquire of them as to whether or not this was, in fact, going on with their approval and, in fact, had been done pursuant to their plans?

Mr. McCORD. No; there are some reasons for that and I can tell you if you would like to know them.

Mr. THOMPSON. Yes, sir.

Mr. McCORD. One was at that point in time the operation itself had not been funded. That did not come until roughly a month later. It was not absolutely clear that the operation itself would in effect get off the ground. I think the general assumption on the part of Liddy and certainly me was that until the funding came through that there was really nothing that could be absolutely counted on in terms of something going forward. It would appear to me, it appeared to me, not only premature for me to discuss it if it were to be discussed but there were other reasons for my not discussing it with them which were essentially this. It was essentially this: That in the talking stages with Mr. Liddy of my participation in the operation, I told him that I would like to be—that I would like to convey to him a request that either Mr. Mitchell or Mr. Magruder be advised that I would be or might be a participant in the operation so that if I disappeared from the committee offices at some particular time and somebody in a senior position of authority would be aware that it might be in connection with this operation, and in specific wanted to be assured that Mr. Odle, if he came to Mr. Magruder or Mr. Mitchell, inquiring about my whereabouts that someone in authority would be in a position to say "He is off on some other business, don't worry about it."

I did not expect, however, that at that point in time or even later that they would acknowledge to me that they were aware of my participation. I think in terms of some other things I have said to this committee about deniability and so on I assume just the opposite, that they would not indicate overtly to me they were aware that I was participating.

Mr. THOMPSON. And you would be in a position of having to completely trust Mr. Liddy?

Mr. McCORD. That is correct.

Mr. THOMPSON. In seeing that he had informed them.

Mr. McCORD. Yes.

Mr. THOMPSON. Did he tell you in fact he had informed them?

Mr. McCORD. No; he did not tell me, he assured me that he did and that was sufficient for me at that point in time.

Mr. THOMPSON. But he subsequently told you that he told them about your involvement?

Mr. McCORD. That is correct.

Mr. THOMPSON. Did he indicate to you that they knew of your involvement?

Mr. McCORD. There never was any problem that indicated that they did not know, for example, that I participated. If there had been, I would have raised it as an issue at that point in time in order to get the matter sorted out. There never was any serious problem at any time that came up in accounting for my time, for example, which really did bring it to a head. Had it done so, I would have inquired. But there was no reason to doubt what I am saying, there is no reason to doubt Mr. Liddy's word.

Mr. THOMPSON. At that time in March you had pretty much made up your mind, I assume, that if the thing was funded you would participate for the reasons that you have given?

Mr. McCord. The decision process, I think, on my part took place after the 30-day delay that I referred to here in which it appeared that this whole matter was being considered, reconsidered, discussed and so on by Mr. Mitchell. It was also very material to me that he hâd considered it while in the Attorney General's office, that the discussion had taken place there and he apparently had approved it and so on, but I had some reasons for considering that 30-day delay important, and this was part of my motivation.

Mr. Thompson. One or two more questions. You say you saw Mr. Liddy often and you saw Mr. Magruder often and you had this one meeting with the two of them. Did anything they said to you or did anything that you overheard them say to other people, any telephone conversations that you might have accidentally heard, indicate to you that what Liddy was telling you was in fact true or did any of these things in your mind corroborate what Mr. Liddy was telling you?

Mr. McCord. About what, the meetings with the Attorney General in his office? Certainly the fact there were charts, for example, Mr. Liddy had some charts which I have described to this committee before, which he said cost some $7,000 to prepare in which he set forth the plans, as I understood it the cost of the operation, the fact that he would go to so much trouble and to so much expense it was obvious to me this was officially approved by somebody in the operation within the committee itself and the Attorney General in order for that amount of money to be spent for material of this sort to go to that much trouble.

Mr. Thompson. Pardon me, did you ever see the charts themselves?

Mr. McCord. Yes; I saw the charts when he brought them in the day before he said a meeting was scheduled with the Attorney General, he pointed to the chart and said "These are for the briefing with the Attorney General tomorrow. These are connected with the papers which I have shown to you," the draft and the type of budget draft that he had and showed to me on a day or two before. He did not unwrap the charts themselves. They were in brown wrapping paper. He said they had been prepared commercially, locally—not locally, he said they had been prepared commercially and he subsequently told me that he had been told by John Dean to destroy the charts, and because they cost so much he did not plan to do so.

Mr. Thompson. So again he told you he had charts and you saw what appeared to be charts in brown wrapping paper, is that correct?

Mr. McCord. I saw it, that is correct.

Mr. Thompson. And he told you how much the charts cost?

Mr. McCord. That is correct.

Mr. Thompson. And he told you he was using these charts in discussion with the Attorney General and others?

Mr. McCord. Correct.

Mr. Thompson. So far as conversations by these gentlemen concerning their participation, were there any conversations or anything that they said that you heard which indicated that what Mr. Liddy said about the meeting discussing these things was true?

Mr. McCord. By these gentlemen you are referring to?

Mr. Thompson. I am talking about Mr. Mitchell, Mr. Magruder or Mr. Dean.

Mr. McCord. That is correct. They did not discuss it with me.

Mr. Thompson. All right.

Did you find Mr. Liddy, in his actions—did you consider him to be a level-headed individual at all times, a man of good judgment?

Mr. McCORD. Mr. Liddy—I will answer the question this way—Mr. Liddy was obviously very busy at the committee and most of his work appeared to me to be occupied with committee legal matters for both the Committee for the Re-Election of the President and for the Finance Committee To Re-Elect the President. My understanding from the staff members around him was that he was a very competent lawyer, that there never was any question of his legal knowledge and his legal competence. Quite the contrary, I heard complimentary remarks about the fact that he was a very sharp lawyer, in fact, he had something to do with either the writing or perhaps not the writing of the campaign law, Federal campaign law, but in connection with its interpretation. I know he was called on to interpret the law, this I heard.

Mr. THOMPSON. Of course, I am not limiting you, you understand, to your opinion of his legal knowledge and legal ability. I am talking about him as a man, how you judge him. Did you ever hear, for example, that he had shot a pistol in a restroom?

Mr. McCORD. No; I did not.

Mr. THOMPSON. Did you ever hear, for example, that he had made a threat against Mr. Magruder, they were having difficulties?

Mr. McCORD. Never did.

Mr. THOMPSON. Were you aware that he and Mr. Magruder had any personality conflict?

Mr. McCORD. Oh yes, sure.

Mr. THOMPSON. You were?

Mr. McCORD. Yes, sir.

Mr. THOMPSON. What is the extent of your knowledge concerning that?

Mr. McCORD. Essentially there was a personality difference between the two men and that something had been worked out for him to take the position with the finance committee.

Mr. THOMPSON. That brought about his switch from the Committee To Re-Elect to the finance committee?

Mr. McCORD. Yes, sir.

Mr. THOMPSON. Thank you, Mr. McCord.

Mr. Chairman, I have no further questions.

Senator ERVIN. Mr. McCord, there is evidence here that the five men arrested in the Watergate on and after midnight on the 16th and 17th of June had some hundred dollar bills, new $100 bills in their possession or in their rooms. Where did that money come from, if you know?

Mr. McCORD. I do not know, sir.

Senator ERVIN. Did you have any of it?

Mr. McCORD. No, sir.

Senator ERVIN. Then, you say that from after the return of the bills every indictment in September down to the last day of the trial, that you were urged to plead guilty and remain silent by a number of people. Did Mr. Hunt ever urge you to plead guilty and remain silent? That is, E. Howard Hunt?

Mr. McCORD. Yes, sir.

Senator ERVIN. And Mr. Howard Hunt——

Mr. McCORD. I am trying to recall, sir, the exact words.

Senator ERVIN. Yes.

Mr. McCORD. The words most frequently used by Mr. Hunt with me was that Executive clemency would be available to me.

Senator ERVIN. Yes. How many times did he urge you to plead guilty? That is, Hunt.

Mr. McCORD. I mean to correct that statement. I do not recall Mr. Hunt using those words with me to plead guilty.

Senator ERVIN. Did he urge you to or not to remain silent?

Mr. McCORD. Not in the exact words; no, sir.

Senator ERVIN. What words did he use as far as you remember?

Mr. McCORD. He used words to the effect that, he used words stating that "Executive clemency is going to be made available to us" and he spoke in terms as though it already had been committed, I say already, already as of the time that he first mentioned it to me.

Senator ERVIN. Now, you stated that you were paid some money through the instrumentality of Mrs. Hunt, and also that your lawyer fees were taken care of, as I understood you?

Mr. McCORD. Yes, sir.

Senator ERVIN. Do you know who paid your lawyer fees?

Mr. McCORD. I was told that both moneys came from the Committee To Re-Elect the President.

Senator ERVIN. Do you know the amount of your lawyer fees?

Mr. McCORD. Yes, sir.

Senator ERVIN. What was it?

Mr. McCORD. The amount I received from the committee was $25,000.

Senator ERVIN. Now, did your lawyer urge you to enter a plea of guilty? I am talking about Mr. Gerald Alch.

Mr. McCORD. I do not recall that, no, sir.

Senator ERVIN. But he did go with you to Mr. Bittman's office?

Mr. McCORD. Yes, sir.

Senator ERVIN. And Mr. Bittman was the lawyer for Mr. Hunt, was he not?

Mr. McCORD. Yes, sir.

Senator ERVIN. And then after that, you did not talk to Mr. Bittman yourself?

Mr. McCORD. No, sir.

Senator ERVIN. But Mr. Alch did?

Mr. McCORD. Yes, sir.

Senator ERVIN. And after his conversation with Mr. Bittman he told you that Mr. Bittman urged you to plead guilty and remain silent and said you would get Executive clemency?

Mr. McCORD. I will correct that, sir, if I left that impression. I believe the words were that in the afternoon of January 8, Mr. Alch said that Mr. Bittman wanted to talk with me about "whose word I would trust regarding a White House offer of Executive clemency" and then at the meeting at his office Mr. Alch came back to me after a meeting with Mr. Bittman and told me that I would be contacted by "a friend I have formerly known in the White House," and contacted that evening. I believe that was the substance of that conversation.

Senator ERVIN. How long had you known—when did you first know John or Jack Caulfield?

Mr. McCORD. I first met him in early 19—early September, 1971. I had heard of him before.

Senator ERVIN. Where was he working at the time you first met him?

Mr. McCORD. At the White House.

Senator ERVIN. Did he have any connection later with—rather, I believe you stated that you were employed by the Committee To Re-Elect the President on the recommendation of Mr. Caulfield?

Mr. McCORD. Yes, sir.

Senator ERVIN. Did Mr. Caulfield later have any association with the committee?

Mr. McCORD. Yes, sir.

Senator ERVIN. And after that association did he go to one of the executive departments?

Mr. McCORD. I understood from him that he did, yes, sir.

Senator ERVIN. Do you know which Department?

Mr. McCORD. I believe it was the Treasury Department.

Senator ERVIN. Do you know what position he held there?

Mr. McCORD. It was a senior position with the, I believe it is called Alcohol Tax and Fire Arms Division of it.

Senator ERVIN. Was he working in the Treasury Department at the time that he had the meetings with you?

Mr. McCORD. He told me that, yes, sir.

Senator ERVIN. Yes.

As I recall, you met with him first on Friday, January 12, somewhere on the George Washington Parkway?

Mr. McCORD. It was that Friday, yes, sir.

Senator ERVIN. Did he give you any reason why he wanted to meet you on the George Washington Parkway instead of seeing you at his home or your home?

Mr. McCORD. No, sir.

Senator ERVIN. Who was present at that meeting?

Mr. McCORD. Just the two of us.

Senator ERVIN. And at that time he urged you to plead guilty, the case was still pending, was it not?

Mr. McCORD. Yes, sir.

Senator ERVIN. It was just about the time the trial started was it not?

Mr. McCORD. This was the first week of the trial.

Senator ERVIN. And he urged you to plead guilty and assured you that if you pleaded guilty you would receive Executive clemency and also be given a chance after you served a sentence, to help to be rehabilitated to a job, did he not?

Mr. McCORD. I believe all is correct except the words "plead guilty" and I will try to restate that for accuracy. The words "plead guilty" have been used over the telephone to me by this unknown unidentified individual whose voice I described and subsequently——

Senator ERVIN. That was prior to the meetings?

Mr. McCORD. Yes, sir.

Senator ERVIN. Now then—excuse me, do you have something further?

Mr. McCORD. Well, in the conversation on the 12th of January and in the two subsequent meetings the words "plead guilty" would come up in this general language. "Are you going to plead guilty?" Or, "How about pleading guilty?" Or "What is your feeling about pleading now?"

Senator ERVIN. Now, this meeting was arranged at his insistence, wasn't it?

Mr. McCORD. Yes, sir.

Senator ERVIN. Then you met him again on Sunday, January 14, on the George Washington Parkway?

Mr. McCORD. Yes, sir.

Senator ERVIN. What was the conversation with him at that time or rather was that meeting held at his instance?

Mr. McCORD. Yes, sir.

Senator ERVIN. What occurred at that time?

Mr. McCORD. Let me refer to my notes to be correct.

The discussion was that there was no objection to renewing the motion on discovery of government wiretapping and that if that failed I would receive Executive clemency after 10 or 11 months, and then the conversation went on to say that the President's ability to govern is at stake. Another Teapot Dome scandal is possible and the government may fall. Everybody else is on track but you, you are not following the game plan, get closer to your attorney.

Senator ERVIN. Did that conversation occur in the automobile or did you get out of the automobile?

Mr. McCORD. No, sir; it was out of the automobile and it would be 50 feet, I would guess, from his car where we walked down toward the Potomac River from the overlook, just the two of us were present.

Senator ERVIN. The first conversation was on Friday, January 12, and that all occurred in the automobile?

Mr. McCORD. The other two meetings were in his automobile.

Senator ERVIN. Yes.

And then on your second meeting on Sunday, January 14, you got out of the car and walked in the woods toward the Potomac River?

Mr. McCORD. Yes, sir.

Senator ERVIN. Now, after that time you got several phone calls from him urging that you meet him again, did you not?

Mr. McCORD. Yes, sir.

Senator ERVIN. And you told him you didn't know anything further, that you had already made up your mind you would not accept Executive clemency, that you thought that it would be impossible for you to get a fair trial, and that you had hopes that on account of that, your belief that you had been wiretapped that the trial might be set aside, did you not?

Mr. McCORD. Words to that effect, yes, sir.

Senator ERVIN. And so he kept insisting on you by phone to meet him and you met him on Thursday, January 25, 1973?

Mr. McCORD. Yes, sir.

Senator ERVIN. 1972?

Mr. McCORD. 1973.

Senator ERVIN. Now that is when you say you were in his automobile?

Mr. McCORD. Yes, sir.

Senator ERVIN. In a direction down towards Warrenton, Va.?

Mr. McCORD. Yes, sir.

Senator ERVIN. What did he say on that occasion?

Mr. McCORD. We had about a 2-hour conversation. There were repeated offers of at various times during the discussion of Executive clemency and financial support following prison rehabilitation. There were discussions about the game plan that we referred to. There were discussions about the two telephone calls, and his comment that that could possibly affect appeals if they found no records of them.

Senator ERVIN. You thought your telephone had been wiretapped and he told you he had investigated that and found out it had not?

Mr. McCORD. Yes, sir.

Senator ERVIN. Now, there was a time when he made a statement to you which you interpreted to be something in the nature of a threat, what was that?

Mr. McCORD. I believe the words were, the words were, it is not my belief, it is my recollection, that the words were "You know that if the administration gets its back to the wall it will have to take steps to defend itself."

Senator ERVIN. He told you in that conversation, in the previous conversations, did he not, that all of the other people involved, that had been arrested in connection with the break-in were going along with the way he wanted them to go but you were the only one who was not going along with the game plan?

Mr. McCORD. I believe the words were, "that everybody else is on track but you." Yes, sir.

Senator ERVIN. Now, did you ever discuss with Mr. Liddy the exercising of electronic surveillance over the office of Senator Muskie?

Mr. McCORD. Yes, sir.

Senator ERVIN. And——

Mr. McCORD. I will correct that, sir, we discussed the lease of a building, I don't recall electronic surveillance except in some broad general terms this might be a future target. There was nothing beyond that and this was stated in February 1972.

Senator ERVIN. Now, Senator Muskie was one of the candidates for the Democratic nomination for President at that time?

Mr. McCORD. Yes, sir.

Senator ERVIN. Did you rent any office near the Muskie headquarters?

Mr. McCORD. I did.

Senator ERVIN. Where were the Muskie headquarters?

Mr. McCORD. I believe the address was listed as 1972 K Street but it was next to 1978 K Street which was an office location that I leased at the request of Mr. Liddy.

Senator ERVIN. Where was this office located with reference to the headquarters of Senator Muskie?

Mr. McCORD. It was the next building to Senator Muskie's office.

Senator ERVIN. And I believe the lease was taken in your name and that of John B. Hayes?

Mr. McCORD. Yes, sir.

Senator ERVIN. Who was John B. Hayes?

Mr. McCORD. That was another name for Mr. Liddy.

Senator ERVIN. And later, Mr. McGovern took over these headquarters from Senator Muskie, didn't he?

Mr. McCORD. I think after June 17th, yes sir.

Senator ERVIN. Was there ever any discussion between you and Mr. Liddy about exercising any kind of surveillance over Senator McGovern's headquarters?

Mr. McCORD. There were, sir. They were in the context of the location on First Street primarily.

Senator ERVIN. And this room was rented for possible use of that commission, was it not?

Mr. McCORD. 1908 K Street was, yes sir.

Senator ERVIN. Now, do you remember how long the lease of the room continued?

Mr. McCORD. Yes, sir, it continued until July 1972, when I cancelled it.

Senator ERVIN. What was the amount of rent that was paid a month for the room?

Mr. McCORD. $275 a month.

Senator ERVIN. The total rent, then, was about $2,220 that you paid for, was it not?

Mr. McCORD. There was a settlement fee that I negotiated with the people who owned the lease, which I think included another month's or two payment after July.

Senator ERVIN. Did you ever make any effort to bug Senator Muskie's or Senator McGovern's headquarters?

Mr. McCORD. Never Senator Muskie's. Senator McGovern's, there was a visit to the office by me, I believe on two—on three occasions in toto, on one of which I had some electronic equipment with me but it was never installed because there were other people working there at the time.

Senator ERVIN. In other words, you never found any time that the office was empty?

Mr. McCORD. That is correct.

Senator ERVIN. You know who paid the rent on this office?

Mr. McCORD. Which one, sir?

Senator ERVIN. Up there by the Muskie and McGovern headquarters?

Mr. McCORD. The one at the Muskie office, Mr. Liddy furnished the funds for that and furnished a cashier's check to pay for it.

Senator ERVIN. Thank you very much. I believe I have used my 10 minutes.

Senator BAKER. Mr. Chairman, it is almost 12:15 now and I wonder if it might be better if we conferred further examination of the witness until this afternoon.

Senator ERVIN. What is the will of the committee?

The committee will stand in recess until 2 o'clock.

(Whereupon at 12:12 p.m., the committee recessed to reconvene at 2 p.m., the same day.)

AFTERNOON SESSION, FRIDAY, MAY 18, 1973

Senator ERVIN. The committee will come to order.

Senator Baker.

Senator BAKER. Mr. Chairman, thank you very much.

Mr. McCord.

Mr. McCORD. Yes, sir.

Senator BAKER. We have covered your testimony at rather great length, and we have had the questions now of counsel and of the chairman. I will try to confine my questions to an elaboration or an extension of those subjects that you have already covered, for the sake of developing either further information or a clearer understanding of those things that have already been touched.

Without trying to retrace your steps, I wish you would tell me if this is a fair summation and narrative of your testimony. That you worked for the FBI, that you worked for the CIA for 19 years, that you worked for the Committee for the Re-Election of the President, in a consultative capacity and then as their security officer, that you involved yourself in certain electronics surveillance operations under the direction of Mr. Liddy and Mr. Hunt and possibly others, that you were one of those found inside the Watergate complex, the Democratic National Committee headquarters in the early morning hours of June 17, 1972; that you were taken to jail; that you were subsequently released on bond, there were subsequent conversations by telephone from an unidentified person, and from a Mr. Caulfield with respect to how you should conduct yourself specifically suggesting that you should plead guilty; that you were led to believe, at least, that there would be a promise of Executive clemency, that your family would be taken care of while you were in jail, when you were released that you would have a job, that you pled innocent at the trial instead of guilty, one of the two who pled innocent; that you were convicted on a multicount indictment, that you are now awaiting sentence; that you have appeared previously with this committee in executive session and with the staff of this committee on previous occasions; that you now appear to testify before us without any grant of immunity from this committee, although you are convicted of crimes involving much of the material presumably about which you testified.

I do not mean that to be an absolute recapitulation of your testimony but is that generally a fair statement of your involvement?

Mr. McCord. I think basically, yes, sir.

Senator Baker. Could we start at the beginning, Mr. Hunt—and tell us what your job was with the CIA—I mean, Mr. McCord, I am sorry. [Laughter.] I do not know who I am sorry to but I am sorry.

Mr. McCord. My duties were generally in the security field as a security officer there with the agency and with which I served for some 19 years, under which I served in the United States and overseas that covered a wide variety of duties related to that function of that Federal agency. I am met, and I am at a loss how to proceed in detail on that activity because of the numerous secrecy agents which I signed and which I understand I am in violation of the National Security Act if I disclose in public testimony.

Senator Baker. What I am really driving at, Mr. McCord, is whether or not you were a director or the Director of Security for the CIA in terms of installation of security, protective measures against electronic surveillance and the like.

Mr. McCord. No, sir, I was not the Director of Security and I did not testify to that, sir. I said I was a security officer with them and I cannot go into details of the exact work that I was involved with there because it does involve a violation of the National Security Act, as I understand it.

96-296—73—bk. 1——11

Senator BAKER. I do not want to lead you into that but I guess what I am really reaching for was whether or not as a result of your previous experience at CIA or otherwise you were acquainted with and thoroughly familiar with electronic surveillance techniques and clandestine operations such as that which was conducted at the Watergate.

Mr. McCORD. I am still—basically still—in the same position, sir, respectfully, sir, in face of the split legality of this problem, one of trying to cooperate with you fully and the other one trying to comply with what I previously stated.

Senator ERVIN. It is a little difficult to hear you. I believe if you would move the microphone in front of you and just talk a little bit louder it would be better.

Mr. McCORD. Yes, sir, I will try to.

Senator BAKER. I am not going to spend much time on it but really all I am reaching for is whether or not you were familiar with electronic surveillance techniques, and with clandestine operations such as was conducted at the Watergate regardless of how you knew it.

Mr. McCORD. I learned some electronics from the FBI, sir. I think I can answer that question without violating the general problem, the other thing.

Senator BAKER. Fine. Did you enter the Watergate complex of the Democratic National Committee on one or more than one occasion?

Mr. McCORD. The Democratic National Committee?

Senator BAKER. Yes, sir.

Mr. McCORD. I believe I have testified that twice and that is correct, sir.

Senator BAKER. All right, sir. When was the first time?

Mr. McCORD. Memorial Day weekend.

Senator BAKER. Do you remember the date?

Mr. McCORD. 1972.

Senator BAKER. Do you remember the day?

Mr. McCORD. I can check it. The evening of May 27, 1972.

Senator BAKER. About what time?

Mr. McCORD. 1:30 p.m., that evening, or it could have been the following day.

Senator BAKER. Who was with you on this first break-in?

Mr. McCORD. The other—the seven Cuban Americans that I have testified to previously, I believe, in this committee.

Senator BAKER. What did you do?

Mr. McCORD. The entire group went into the Democratic National Committee through an entry into, the door itself. I went in and joined them to perform the work of the electronic assignment that I had as a member of the team.

Senator BAKER. What was the electronic assignment that you had?

Mr. McCORD. Installation of the technical bugging devices in the Democratic National Committee that were previously authorized by the Attorney General.

Senator BAKER. Did you have instructions as to where they should be placed?

Mr. McCORD. Yes.

Senator BAKER. Where?

Mr. McCORD. In the offices themselves in connection with senior personnel officers of the Democratic National Committee, and specifically, Mr. O'Brien's telephone extension.

Senator BAKER. How many bugs did you plant?

Mr. McCORD. Two.

Senator BAKER. And where were they?

Mr. McCORD. Two were in offices that face Virginia Avenue. I think you have a sketch up on the board.

Senator BAKER. One of them was on Mr. O'Brien's telephone?

Mr. McCORD. That was an extension of a call director, that was identified as Mr. O'Brien's. The second was Mr. Oliver's——

Senator BAKER. The second one was where?

Mr. McCORD. In a telephone that belonged to Mr. Spencer Oliver, who is an executive director of the democratic State chairmen of the organization.

Senator BAKER. Were you specifically instructed by someone to plant those two bugs or just the O'Brien bug? Would you give us some detail on that?

Mr. McCORD. Sure.

Mr. Liddy had passed along instructions from Mr. John Mitchell. He set the priorities. Mr. Mitchell had stated priorities of the installation were first of all, Mr. O'Brien's offices and such other installations as that might provide information of interest to Mr. Mitchell and to whoever else the monitoring was to go to beyond Mr. Mitchell.

Senator BAKER. So the Oliver phone was bugged more or less by your choice, then, as distinguished from the O'Brien phone?

Mr. McCORD. No, I think the basic choice was this; the wording from Mr. Liddy was that Mr. Mitchell wanted it placed in a senior official's office, if not Mr. O'Brien's office, some other; in other words, two such installations.

Senator BAKER. Did you tape the doors on this first break?

Mr. McCORD. No, I did not, Mr. Hunt did.

Mr. BAKER. But they were taped?

Mr. McCORD. That is correct.

Senator BAKER. Now, you weren't apprehended on this first occasion, Memorial weekend. What was the purpose of the second entry into the Democratic national headquarters?

Mr. McCORD. You want hearsay information again, of course.

Senator BAKER. Yes, as long as it is identified as hearsay.

Mr. McCORD. Mr. Liddy had told me that Mr. Mitchell, John Mitchell, liked the "takes" in quotes; that is, the documents that had been photographed on the first entry into the Democratic National Committee headquarters and that he wanted a second photographic operation to take place and that in addition, as long as that team was going in, that Mr. Mitchell wanted, had passed instructions to Mr. Liddy to check to see what the malfunctioning of the second device that was put in, second, besides Mr. Oliver's, and see what the problem was, because it was one of the two things—either a malfunction of the equipment or the fact that the installation of the device was in a room which was surrounded by four walls. In other words, it was shielded, and he wanted this corrected and another device installed.

He also said Mr. Mitchell wanted a room bug as opposed to a device on a telephone installed in Mr. O'Brien's office itself in order to transmit not only telephone conversations but conversations out of the room itself, beyond whatever might be spoken on the telephone.

Senator BAKER. Were the same people involved in the first break-in and the second break-in?

Mr. McCORD. Those associated with the second break-in were Mr. Hunt, Mr. Liddy, and me, and four of the seven Cubans that were on the first operation, Cuban-Americans.

Senator BAKER. All right, sir, would you describe for us then the responsibilities, if there was an additional responsibility, of those involved in the second break-in?

Mr. McCORD. Mr. Liddy was in overall charge of the operation. Mr. Hunt was his assistant. Mr. Barker was the team captain of the group going in. My job was that of the electronic installation and the others of the group, the other Cuban-Americans, had functions divided into two categories; one of photographing certain documents within the committee, a couple of men had the function of generally being lookouts while we were inside.

Senator BAKER. Thank you, Mr. McCord.

Who placed the tape on the locks on the door on the second occasion?

Mr. McCORD. I do not know.

Senator BAKER. Who replaced it after it was first removed?

Mr. McCORD. I do not know.

Senator BAKER. Did you know while you were inside the complex that the tape had been removed and replaced?

Mr. McCORD. Yes.

Senator BAKER. Can you recall who told you that?

Mr. McCORD. Well, I think it was apparent—well, the sequence of events simply was that the four men, four Cubans went upstairs to the Democratic National Committee to begin work on the door. I received a call from the Howard Johnson Motel in the room directly across from the DNC, from Mr. Hunt, stating that the door was now open, speaking of the basement door, and that I should come up and join the men, and I did so.

Senator BAKER. Mr. McCord, did you employ Mr. Baldwin?

Mr. McCORD. Yes, I did.

Senator BAKER. Did you contact him and ask him to come to Washington to discuss temporary employment which might ripen into permanent employment after the election?

Mr. McCORD. No, sir, it was not put in that vein.

Senator BAKER. Is that the general text of your conversation?

Mr. McCORD. No, sir, it is not.

Senator BAKER. All right. I am quoting from a Washington Post story of October 8, 1972, which in synopsis form says, McCord met Baldwin in the Roger Smith Hotel, emphasized that while his job might be temporary, that it might prove to be a stepping stone to a permanent job after Nixon's reelection.

Could you comment on that account, please?

Mr. McCORD. That part fits what—the question that you had before was not exactly the case.

I called Mr. Baldwin and asked him if he were interested in a job as a security officer for Mrs. John Mitchell, who we'd been asked to provide a security officer for. He stated that he would be interested.

I asked him to come to Washington the next morning and discuss the matters in connection with the discussions which took place that day between me and him and Mr. Fred LaRue, who made the subsequent interview of him. Mr. Baldwin raised the question of whether or not there might be employment later. My statement to him roughly was that the position here at that point in time was only through November and that my assumption was that if he did a good job on it, there might be something else for him but there was no promise by me or Mr. LaRue and I am sure Mr. Baldwin took it that way.

Senator BAKER. Did you supply Mr. Baldwin with a .38 pistol?

Mr. McCORD. No, I did not.

Senator BAKER. Did anyone supply him with a .38 pistol?

Mr. McCORD. Yes.

Senator BAKER. Who did?

Mr. McCORD. That was obtained, given to him by Mr. LaRue, who had the weapon in his office. It belonged to Mr. Jack Caulfield.

Senator BAKER. Was it done in your presence?

Mr. McCORD. I can't recall specifically. It may well have been. It was done subsequent to an interview of Mr. Baldwin with Mr. LaRue. One of two things happened. Either Mr. LaRue gave it to him directly or Mr. LaRue called me or one of the men up to his office and sent the gun down to him or gave it to him, or one of the other men did. In any case, I was quite aware that he had it.

Senator BAKER. Just one of two more questions.

I see the chairman looking at his watch over here and I don't want to run excessively long. I will have other questions as the second round of inquiries starts. But let me try to close out this line of questioning this way.

First, did you ever conduct electronic surveillance or clandestine activities against anyone other than the DNC, the Democratic National Committee, at the Watergate complex, and the McGovern headquarters which you have already described?

Mr. McCORD. No.

Senator BAKER. Mr. McCord, please tell me whether or not you knew that this sort of activity was illegal?

Mr. McCORD. I knew certain things that came to me at the beginning of the operation and early in the operation which indicated that it might be legal, may well be legal, and I was so advised.

Senator BAKER. By whom?

Mr. McCORD. First of all, if I may explain, coming through Mr. Liddy and coming through my knowledge of the Attorney General, who was then Attorney General, and that was that the Attorney General, first of all, had the authority on his own signature to approve wiretapping within the United States for either national security reasons or for domestic security reasons.

Senator BAKER. What was your motivation? Why did you do this?

Mr. McCORD. There were several motivations, but one of the basic motivations was the fact that this man, the Attorney General, had approved it in his offices over a series of meetings in which he had obviously given careful consideration to it, while he was the top legal officer of the U.S. Government, and that the counsel to the President had sat in with him during such discussions; the fact that I was advised that it was within the Attorney General's purview and authority to authorize such operations if it were in the national interest to do so.

Senator BAKER. Did you believe that?

Mr. McCORD. I believed that he had the authority to do it. I believed that several things—not only was I told certain things pertaining to some matters I previously testified to, to this committee regarding Las Vegas and an incident out there, but I was also aware that many things come over the Attorney General's desk that I was not privy to, that Mr. Liddy was not privy to, but which the Attorney General was privy to, matters which might come to him through highly sensitive sources, wiretap information, which might provide a justification for such an operation, a justification beyond what was known to me.

I can put it conversely as well. I knew that, I felt that the Attorney General in his position as the top legal officer, if this operation were clearly illegal, would turn it down out of hand, that he would have no trouble making a decision on the matter immediately. I knew from previous contact with him that he was a very decisive man, that he did not agonize over decisions, and yet apparently, he took this one under careful consideration and considered it for some 30 days in making the decision, and frankly, I had it, my conclusion was that he took it as well to higher authority and got a final approval from his superior before embarking upon this task.

Quite candidly and quite frankly, this is exactly my motivation, my reason, the basic motivation of mine for being involved.

Senator BAKER. This was your assumption or your basis for judgment that the Attorney General must have done that? Do you have any evidence or any information that he did do that?

Mr. McCORD. The evidence that the counsel to the President sat in with him, on the meetings of this and, therefore, both the White House was represented and the Attorney General of the United States were represented in this decision and that this 30-day delay to me, I drew the conclusion that the Attorney General himself had conveyed the decision to his own superior for final decision.

Senator BAKER. You spoke of a 30-day period in your earlier testimony. Is that the same 30-day period?

Mr. McCORD. That is right. It is a 30-day period.

Senator BAKER. In your previous testimony you indicated, I thought you had said, you thought about 30 days for it before you did it. But I am not sure this is the testimony. Is this the same 30-day period you are speaking of when you think the Attorney General looked into it 30 days before deciding?

Mr. McCORD. That is right, sir.

Senator BAKER. Mr. Chairman, I have other questions but I will defer to my colleagues for questions.

Senator ERVIN. Senator Talmadge.

Senator TALMADGE. Thank you, Mr. Chairman.

Mr. McCord, you have made some very serious charges implicating the President of the United States probably as an accessory after the fact, the former Attorney General of the United States as probably an accessory before the fact and perhaps guilty of a conspiracy involving the Watergate bugging, your testimony was predicated upon hearsay that would not be admitted in a court of law. If you told this committee what is authentic, I think that it would require a good deal of corroboration.

You testified this morning that Mr. Caulfield was purported to offer Executive clemency to you, is that correct?

Mr. McCord. Yes, sir.

Senator Talmadge. Anyone else approach you about Executive clemency besides Mr. Caulfield?

Mr. McCord. I mentioned Mr. Hunt.

Senator Talmadge. That is two. Anyone else?

Mr. McCord. Mrs. Hunt conveyed a message from Mr. Hunt. She was obviously not speaking for anyone but himself. She was conveying it for him and so stated.

Senator Talmadge. Anyone besides Mr. Hunt or Mr. Caulfield approach you on the question of Executive clemency?

Mr. McCord. Yes, sir.

Senator Talmadge. Who?

Mr. McCord. My attorney, Gerald Alch, A-l-c-h.

Senator Talmadge. Gerald Hawkins?

Mr. McCord. Gerald Alch.

Senator Talmadge. A-l-t?

Mr. McCord. A-l-c-h.

Senator Talmadge. A-l-c-h?

Mr. McCord. Yes, sir.

Senator Talmadge. Do you know who approached your lawyer about Executive clemency?

Mr. McCord. No, sir.

Senator Talmadge. Your testimony is that three different individuals approached you on the idea that you would plead guilty, and keep quiet and as a result thereof you could expect Executive clemency, is that correct?

Mr. McCord. Yes, sir, and I believe I mentioned a message conveyed, which mentioned Executive clemency by Mr. Alch on January 8 from another individual.

Senator Talmadge. Who was that individual?

Mr. McCord. Mr. William Bittman, B-i-t-t-m-a-n.

Senator Talmadge. William Bittman. Who is he?

Mr. McCord. He was the attorney for Mr. Hunt.

Senator Talmadge. You testified this morning about several different meetings and conversations with Mr. Caulfield. You also testified that Mr. Caulfield, I believe, placed in your mailbox a note that was not sent through the U.S. Postal Service nor post office and was signed "Jack", is that correct?

Mr. McCord. I believe, sir, that is basically correct. I think I said that the note was placed by another individual who said he was a friend of Mr. Caulfield.

Senator Talmadge. The note was not from Mr. Caulfield?

Mr. McCord. Yes, sir, the note was from Mr. Caulfield, but the individual who subsequently talked to me on the phone first, this unidentified stranger said that he himself, the stranger, had placed the note in my mailbox from Jack.

Senator Talmadge. From Mr. Caulfield, the note was signed "Jack"?

Mr. McCord. Yes, sir.

Senator Talmadge. And did you receive that note?

Mr. McCord. Yes, sir.

Senator Talmadge. Do you have that note now?

Mr. McCORD. No, sir.
Senator TALMADGE. Do you know where it is?
Mr. McCORD. No, sir.
Senator TALMADGE. Why did you destroy it?
Mr. McCORD. Quite frankly sir, I cannot recall. There have been so many events since that date, that I suspect it was simply thrown out in the trash.
Senator TALMADGE. What was the subject of that note?
Mr. McCORD. The subject said, "Please go to phone booth on Route 355 on one of three different times," that one day, the day of the note, and two alternate dates, the following date and another one.
Senator TALMADGE. You also implicated the former Attorney General, Mr. Mitchell, in your testimony had approved and had at least known of the plan and at least an accessory to the Watergate bugging. Did you ever have any conversations with Mr. Mitchell yourself about that operation?
Mr. McCORD. About the Watergate operation itself?
Senator TALMADGE. Or any other surveillance or espionage?
Mr. McCORD. No, sir.
Senator TALMADGE. Neither about Watergate nor any other espionage activity?
Mr. McCORD. No, sir.
Senator TALMADGE. How many different individuals talked to you and purported to speak for Mr. Mitchell about the Watergate operation or any other bugging operation?
Mr. McCORD. Speaking for Mr. Mitchell purportedly, Mr. Liddy only as speaking for Mr. Mitchell.
Senator TALMADGE. All right, Liddy is one.
Mr. McCORD. Yes, sir.
Senator TALMADGE. Who else besides him?
Mr. McCORD. And Mr. Hunt raised the name of Mr. Mitchell in the context that I have testified to this morning, sir.
Senator TALMADGE. Both Liddy and Hunt told you——
Mr. McCORD. Yes, sir.
Senator TALMADGE. That this operation had been approved by Mr. Mitchell?
Mr. McCORD. Yes, sir.
Senator TALMADGE. Any others besides those two?
Mr. McCORD. No, sir.
Senator TALMADGE. You testified this morning about a meeting in Mr. Mitchell's office. Was there more than one meeting with the Attorney General or only one?
Mr. McCORD. I just said there were more than one meeting.
Senator TALMADGE. In which you personally were involved?
Mr. McCORD. I did not attend but I was told by Mr. Liddy there was more than one meeting that took place. I had heard him mention two specifically.
Senator TALMADGE. Did you yourself ever attend a meeting in Mr. Mitchell's office?
Mr. McCORD. No, sir.
Senator TALMADGE. On any matter.
Mr. McCORD. I attended meetings, yes, in his office at the Commettee To Re-Elect the President when he subsequently came over and I visited at his offices at the Attorney General's office at the

Department of Justice in December on another matter but not to discuss these particular operations.

Senator TALMADGE. How many different visits or conversations did you ever have with Mr. Mitchell?

Mr. McCORD. Numerous, sir.

Senator TALMADGE. A dozen, 15, 20, more?

Mr. McCORD. I would guess 15.

Senator TALMADGE. Does he know you by your name?

Mr. McCORD. Yes, sir.

Senator TALMADGE. You know him?

Mr. McCORD. Yes, sir.

Senator TALMADGE. You called him Mr. Attorney General, I presume?

Mr. McCORD. Yes, sir.

Senator TALMADGE. What did he call you? [Laughter.]

Mr. McCORD. Before June 17th? [Laughter.]

Senator TALMADGE. Before and after.

Mr. McCORD. I haven't seen him since June 17th. He called me Jim, I believe.

Senator TALMADGE. He called you Jim so you were on a first-name basis with him. And that is the only evidence that you have that would involve either the President of the United States or the Attorney General?

Mr. McCORD. I am sorry, sir, I missed the question.

Senator TALMADGE. The evidence that you have just reported including the individuals that you have named, based on what they heard others say which is hearsay, is the only evidence that you had involving either the President or the former Attorney General, is that correct?

Mr. McCORD. No, sir, the charts, for example, that I have described here earlier.

Senator TALMADGE. I am sorry, I can't hear you, the what?

Mr. McCORD. The charts of Mr. Liddy which Mr. Liddy——

Senator TALMADGE. Targets?

Mr. MccORD. The charts.

Senator TALMADGE. The charts?

Mr. McCORD. Yes, sir, the cardboard charts, were one other evidence of his meetings with Mr. Mitchell, and subsequently the money which Mr. Liddy transmitted to me for use in the operation he stated came through the duties to the organization of Mr. Mitchell.

Senator TALMADGE. Those charts you are also relying on is hearsay testimony on that.

Mr. McCORD. That is correct, sir. That is correct, sir.

Senator TALMADGE. Now what made you think that either Mr. Caulfield or Mr. Hunt had authority to offer Executive clemency to you?

Mr. McCORD. Mr. Caulfield because he told me that he was conveying a message from the very top level of the White House.

Senator TALMADGE. You assumed when he said top level that meant the President of the United States?

Mr. McCORD. I assumed it meant one of three people, sir.

Senator TALMADGE. All right; name them.

Mr. McCORD. Mr. Haldeman, Mr. Ehrlichman, or the President.

Senator TALMADGE. And what made you think that Mr. Hunt had authority to offer Executive clemency?

Mr. MCCORD. I did not believe that he had the authority but I believe that the message he was conveying probably—that the message did originate with the White House because of several things: One, that I knew from conversations with him and with his wife that he was in touch with the attorneys for the Committee for the Re-Election of the President, for one thing.

Senator TALMADGE. Who was Mr. Hunt's immediate superior?

Mr. MCCORD. His immediate superior at the White House, as I understood it from him, was Mr. Charles Colson, if that is your question, sir.

Senator TALMADGE. Mr. Colson. He was counsel to the President?

Mr. MCCORD. I believe he was on the White House staff, this is prior to June 17.

Senator TALMADGE. You testified this morning about the rental of office space near the McGovern-Muskie headquarters, I think it was originally Senator Muskie's headquarters, and thereafter Senator McGovern's. Do you know who approved the rental of the office that you operated out of on 1908 K Street NW., directly adjacent to the Muskie-McGovern headquarters?

Mr. MCCORD. Mr. Liddy stated that in connection with the overall Watergate operation—correction—in connection with the overall operations that he was discussing with Mr. Mitchell that this space was desired and would I arrange to have it leased and I did so.

Senator TALMADGE. That was the reason you leased the space?

Mr. MCCORD. Yes, sir.

Senator TALMADGE. When was the day you attempted to enter the McGovern headquarters here in Washington?

Mr. MCCORD. I believe the first date would have been about May 15 when Mr. Hunt introduced me to a young man called by the name of Thomas Gregory, introduced me at, I believe, the Howard Johnson restaurant, and subsequent to that introduction at a luncheon we went to the McGovern headquarters, it seems to me in the afternoon or late afternoon, and took a brief walk through the building itself, going in the front, coming out the back door mainly to see the layout of the offices. It took perhaps 5 to 10 minutes.

Senator TALMADGE. Who else was involved?

Mr. MCCORD. Mr. Thomas Gregory who worked for Mr. Hunt.

Senator TALMADGE. Just you and Mr. Gregory?

Mr. MCCORD. That went in; yes, sir.

Senator TALMADGE. Who gave the orders to attempt to enter the building, the McGovern headquarters?

Mr. MCCORD. On that particular occasion Mr. Hunt did. It had been previously agreed to, directed—correction, had been requested by Mr. Liddy.

Senator TALMADGE. Why were you told that it was necessary to enter the Watergate complex on the weekend of June 17, 1972?

Mr. MCCORD. A twofold purpose, the first being to do for the time, the photography team, to do photocopy work of documents within the Democratic National Committee and, second, to install additional listening devices within the Democratic National Committee.

Senator TALMADGE. I believe my time has expired. I will yield at this time for other questions.

Senator ERVIN. Senator Gurney.

Senator GURNEY. Thank you, Mr. Chairman.

Mr. McCord, in response to a question from Senator Baker you said that you thought that what you were doing in this operation was legal. Now, of course you spent some years in the FBI, didn't you?

Mr. MCCORD. Yes, sir.

Senator GURNEY. And also in the CIA?

Mr. MCCORD. That is correct.

Senator GURNEY. You ran your own security company?

Mr. MCCORD. Yes, sir.

Senator GURNEY. You were charged at the trial with several counts, as I understand, conspiracy, intent to steal property, entering the Democratic national headquarters, attempted interception of telephone conversations and attempted interception of oral conversations as well as possession of a telephone listening device, and an oral communications device.

Now, is it your testimony that you thought that all of these acts there on June 17 were legal?

Mr. MCCORD. It is my testimony, sir, if I may repeat a portion of it, that the Attorney General had the authority to authorize it. It was my experience that he did, in fact, authorize wiretapping and other related activities that were within his purview. That he could, and would have turned it down out of hand at the very beginning of the operation itself if, in fact, it were clearly and beyond any question illegal, because I was advised that it was——

Senator GURNEY. But authorizations by the Attorney General for wiretapping made, of course, in connection with national security cases or crime, trying to find out about organized crime, all of this in the purview of the Attorney General's office, wasn't this authorization an operation which had to do with the Committee To Re-Elect the President; hasn't that been your testimony?

Mr. MCCORD. No, sir.

My testimony was that it appeared to be that this operation was really threefold; that it was set in motion while the Attorney General was Attorney General.

Second, that the White House was a party to the authorization itself, and to the justification for the operation, because the counsel to the President had sat in on it.

Third, the Committee for the Re-Election of the President was represented in those discussions and that they may have been the funding mechanism for it and fourth, because of a time delay here and my knowledge of the relationship of Mr. Mitchell with his immediate superior, my conclusion was that his immediate superior approved and set in motion that operation and, therefore, it had all of those implications to me, that it was just not simply a Committee for the Re-Election of the President operation because it began with the Attorney General while he was the Attorney General.

Senator GURNEY. The activities, though, that you were doing, as I understand this course of events, were supervised by Liddy and Hunt, is that correct?

Mr. MCCORD. They were agents, as I understand it, for the Attorney General and for the White House.

Senator GURNEY. Well, that is not the question I asked. I said that they were the ones that were supervising and guiding your activities, were they not?

Mr. McCORD. They were the immediate supervisors, but not by my understanding——

Senator GURNEY. And were they not working for the Committee To Re-Elect the President?

Mr. McCORD. Mr. Hunt never did, to my knowledge. I believe there has been testimony to that effect by Mr. Odle.

Senator GURNEY. Who was Mr. Liddy working for during this period of time we are talking about?

Mr. McCORD. Mr. Liddy had two responsibilities. One was general counsel originally for the Committee for the Re-Election of the President and the second was general counsel for the Finance Committee To Re-Elect the President.

Senator GURNEY. The activities that you have described—that is, bugging the Democratic National Committee and photographing, as I understand, documents there, as well as the McGovern and Muskie operations—those all had to do with a political campaign, did they not?

Mr. McCORD. I think what we have not discussed here are some of the other things that went into my motivations and to the explanation by Mr. Liddy to me of the reasons for undertaking this operation at Democratic National Committee, which included electronic, photography, those two operations specifically, but the overall operation was not limited to that, either in the original planning or in the authority by the Attorney General.

Senator GURNEY. Well, did anything you do in this area of bugging and electronic surveillance have anything to do with anybody or any activity other than a political campaign of somebody?

Mr. McCORD. It came into being because of the, one of the basic motivations of mine, which I had not been concerned with, the violence-oriented demonstrators that we have previously discussed in testimony before this committee.

Senator GURNEY. I do not want to interrupt and guide, but it would be helpful, Mr. McCord, if you were responsive to the questions. Did you do any electronic bugging or surveillance that had anything to do with anybody or anything that did not involve political activity?

Mr. McCORD. No, no, sir.

Senator GURNEY. You did not spy on the Russians, the Chinese, or anybody like that?

Mr. McCORD. No, sir.

Senator GURNEY. Well, do you not think that at some time, it might have occurred to you that perhaps these were illegal things and did not really have anything to do with national security?

Mr. McCORD. Oh, yes, it occurred to me at the time the matters were being planned and being discussed. It has occurred to me since, yes.

Senator GURNEY. Then, why did you go ahead with it?

Mr. McCORD. For basically the reasons I have stated, but those were not the only reasons. The fact that the Attorney General, the White House itself, and in my personal opinion, the President of the United States, I felt, had set into motion this operation. Because of the close relationship of Mr. Mitchell and Mr. Dean and the fact that Mr. Dean worked with the President.

Senator GURNEY. In other words, even though you—if I am expressing your thoughts correctly—you believed it to be illegal or were highly suspicious that it was, that nonetheless, because the Attorney General, in your opinion, was ordering this, then you ought to go ahead and do it? Is that a fair thing to say?

Mr. McCORD. Sure, it is a gray area, no question about it. But because the Attorney General in his position, and because the White House was involved in it, these matters were matters on which my decision turned. I realized the illegality under normal circumstances, but I also realized that the Attorney General can make matters legal by his signature on a piece of paper, or his oral authorization of it, which he does do in domestic subversion cases and national security cases where electronic surveillance is involved. And it has been done hundreds of times.

Senator GURNEY. I would like to ask a question about this memorandum that you presented to the committee today, entitled "Political Pressure on Writer To Accept Executive Clemency and To Remain Silent."

Now, as I understand it from your testimony contained in here and other things that you have said, you were very troubled by the fact that, one, you were presented with this business of Executive clemency and a promise of your family being taken care of, and also a job later. I guess you did not think this was the right thing to do, and perhaps you were not too convinced that it would happen and that you also were afraid that perjury was going to be engaged in in the trial.

Am I fairly stating your reactions about this?

Mr. McCORD. Somewhat, yes, sir.

Senator GURNEY. Well, it strikes me as very curious that you appeared before the grand jury, of course, before the trial. You were there at the trial. As I understand it, the judge himself expressed indignation during the proceedings at one time that he was not getting the full story.

You appeared, of course, before the Senate select committee some weeks ago for a whole afternoon and we were not able to cover all of the testimony, of course, you did promise us that you would come back and advise us fully of everything that you knew, that you would give us memorandums, as I recall. And yet this very important testimony here, which involves Executive clemency, including the President of the United States we just learned about 2 days ago. Why the lateness of this? Why did you not inform us before of this?

Mr. McCORD. I believe I stated the reason, because it involved directly, in my opinion, the President of the United States. I think I can answer some of your other questions that you raised here about why I—the reason I did not come forth before.

Senator GURNEY. I did miss a part, I am sorry.

Mr. McCORD. I said because it involved directly the President of the United States. It also involved an individual that I considered a personal friend, Mr. Jack Caulfield. I testified to your committee at the very beginning that this was a rather painful matter for me to come forward with at the particular time that you first interviewed me. I said I had no reluctance in giving the information, that I would do so subsequently, and I did do so subsequently. I disclosed it to your committee 2 days ago.

But I think primarily it is because it involved the highest officer in the land, the President of the United States.

Senator GURNEY. Let me ask something about the salary and money arrangements, Mr. McCord.

What was your salary with the Committee To Re-Elect the President for your security work?

Mr. MCCORD. The salary was a gross salary of $20,000 a year.

Senator GURNEY. Twenty?

Mr. MCCORD. Twenty.

Senator GURNEY. Twenty?

Mr. MCCORD. Twenty.

Senator GURNEY. That is the contract. That was the arrangement when you were engaged on what you were going to be paid, is that correct?

Mr. MCCORD. It was not the original salary. The original salary was $625 a month, approximately, when I was first engaged as a consultant.

Senator GURNEY. But that was for part-time work?

Mr. MCCORD. That is correct.

Senator GURNEY. But then when you came onboard full time, it was raised to $20,000?

Mr. MCCORD. Yes, sir.

Senator GURNEY. And when was that?

Mr. MCCORD. The first of January 1972.

Senator GURNEY. Now, then, as you have testified, you learned from Mr. Liddy his curiosity about electronic devices and this led, of course, to his asking you if you would participate in what we now know as the Watergate affair. And this occurred—what date was that now, approximately?

Mr. MCCORD. The conversation began in January and——

Senator GURNEY. I mean when you agreed to go into the Watergate affair?

Mr. MCCORD. Approximately somewhere between 30 days after the initial conversation with Mr. Liddy, when he said he was going to see the Attorney General in the Attorney General's office, approximately at that period.

Senator GURNEY. And that would be, as I recall, probably in March sometime?

Mr. MCCORD. Late February or March, yes, sir.

Senator GURNEY. Well, was there any raise or increase in salary around this time as far as your work is concerned?

Mr. MCCORD. There was none anticipated and none received.

Senator GURNEY. Did it ever occur to you that if you were going to engage in rather hazardous activity, and they certainly resulted in that finally, as we know, that perhaps a higher rate of pay would be something that would be fair and equitable as far as you are concerned?

Mr. MCCORD. Oh, yes. There was a provision in the budget which Mr. Liddy labeled as "overhead," which provided that compensation.

Senator GURNEY. Well, would you describe that to the committee, what that "overhead" was?

Mr. McCORD. Yes, approximately $2,000 a month during the period of time that the operation was underway.
Senator GURNEY. And that began when?
Mr. McCORD. April 1972.
Senator GURNEY. And how was that paid?
Mr. McCORD. In cash by Mr. Liddy.
Senator GURNEY. How many of those payments did you receive?
Mr. McCORD. There were payments through June. I think they totaled approximately $16,000. I do not recall specifically, but I have the notes here if I may refer to them.
Senator GURNEY. Now, then, would you describe to the committee the other pay arrangements after the break-in and after you were apprehended?
Mr. McCORD. Yes, sir. The payments were made by Mrs. Hunt.
Senator GURNEY. In what amounts and at what time?
Mr. McCORD. Calls came to me by Mr. and Mrs. Hunt in July.
Senator GURNEY. How much?
Mr. McCORD. We were paid in cash. There was a lump-sum payment in August—in July of 1972—for 5 months "salary," in quotes, at $3,000 a month, total of $15,000, and subsequently legal fees.
Senator GURNEY. And when was that?
Mr. McCORD. In November, as I recall it, of 1972, and subsequently——
Senator GURNEY. And how much was that?
Mr. McCORD. Total of $25,000 for legal fees.
Senator GURNEY. That was November, then?
Mr. McCORD. Yes.
Senator GURNEY. Go on.
Mr. McCORD. And then again in November, 2 months payment of $3,000 each, a total of $6,000.
Senator GURNEY. So it was $15,000, $25,000, and $6,000; is that correct?
Mr. McCORD. That is correct.
Senator GURNEY. And those all came from Mrs. Hunt?
Mr. McCORD. That is correct.
Senator GURNEY. Did anybody else pay you any cash?
Mr. McCORD. No.
Senator GURNEY. How much did you pay your lawyer?
Mr. McCORD. Approximately $30,000.
Senator GURNEY. Thirty?
Mr. McCORD. Thirty, yes, sir.
Senator GURNEY. Were there any other payments?
Mr. McCORD. There were other payments to another lawyer which I had and Mr. Rothblatt, which I made some payments to.
Senator GURNEY. I don't particularly want to pry into that unless you want to give the information?
Mr. McCORD. Whichever you prefer.
Senator GURNEY. I am interested in some other payments, though. Weren't there payments made as far as either purchase of equipment or expenses in connection with the electronic business?
Mr. McCORD. Oh, yes. I testified to that in executive session, sir, in which there was a total received of approximately $6,000, I believe, a total of $76,000 in all for equipment and other related costs, $61,000

as an initial payment and about $4,000 subsequent—$5,000 subsequently for additional equipment purchases.

Senator GURNEY. Now, did you say 61 and 5?

Mr. McCORD. Yes, sir.

Senator GURNEY. I thought you said——

Mr. McCORD. There is a total of $76,000 in all, which covered all payments for all purposes prior to June 17, 1972.

Senator GURNEY. There was another $10,000 payment later?

Mr. McCORD. No sir, there was an initial $61,000 plus $5,000 for equipment, plus another $11,000 subsequently, but a total of $76,000 prior to June 17, 1972.

Senator GURNEY. Now, I do not want to quibble, but I have 61, 5, and 11.

Mr. McCORD. That is a total of $76,000.

Senator GURNEY. Seventy-seven that brings to me. A total of $77,000?

Mr. McCORD. Sixty-one—I am sorry, sir; 61 and 4 are 65 and 11—the total amount was $76,000. I will get the figures.

Senator GURNEY. Sixty-one, 4, and 11, is that it?

Mr. McCORD. I can recite them for you. April 12, $61,000 plus $4,000, a total of $65,000; May 8, $4,000; Memorial Day weekend, two $1,000 amounts; in June, $5,000. A total after May 8th of $11,000. The total of that is $76,000.

Senator GURNEY. Now, then, how was this disbursed?

Mr. McCORD. In cash by Mr. Liddy.

Senator GURNEY. I mean how did you spend it?

Mr. McCORD. Would you like the expenditures? They were expended in cash for the most part. There were some by check for some walkie-talkie equipment.

Senator GURNEY. Do you have a detailed account of how you spent it?

Mr. McCORD. Oh, yes.

Senator GURNEY. Do you have it with you?

Mr. McCORD. Yes sir.

Senator GURNEY. Is it a long one? Will it take some time?

Mr. McCORD. Yes sir, it is rather lengthy. I can read it if you want.

Senator GURNEY. I wonder then, Mr. Chairman, if we could receive that for the record. I do not really see any point in going all through that.

Senator ERVIN. If you will let the committee have the account, we will make a copy and return your original to you.

Mr. McCORD. All right, sir, we can do that.*

Senator GURNEY. But my understanding is that the account which you are going to present the committee shows the complete disbursement and spending for $77,000, is that correct?

Mr. McCORD. $76,000, sir, as I recall it.

Senator GURNEY. $76,000?

Mr. McCORD. That is correct. There were budget receipts and so on that were prepared on this and were shown to Mr. Liddy, referring for all the payments.

---

*See p. 448.

Senator GURNEY. Just one other question. There was some discussion earlier this morning about the *Ellsberg* case. My recollection is that your testimony was that there is no connection between the *Ellsberg* case and Watergate. Is that correct?

Mr. MCCORD. No sir, that was not my testimony. My testimony was that I had no knowledge of the wiretapping that allegedly occurred in connection with the *Ellsberg* case, nor did I have any knowledge of the break-in in connection with the doctor's records of Mr. Ellsberg. That was the intent of my testimony. I will make that correction now if I misled you.

Senator GURNEY. Well, do you think there is some connection between your Watergate operation and the *Ellsberg* case?

Mr. MCCORD. There apparently is in the personnel that were involved, yes sir, as I understand it from the newspapers. You do not know for a fact.

Senator GURNEY. Not as far as you and the people under you were concerned?

Mr. MCCORD. I had no people under me except Mr. Barker.

Senator GURNEY. How about those in the Watergate affair?

Mr. MCCORD. I do not know the role of the others in the Watergate and whether they may or may not have been involved. They have been so reported in the papers, but I do not know for a fact.

Senator GURNEY. My reason for asking this, I understand there was electronic equipment which was obtained by, I think, Mr. Liddy and Mr. Hunt in the Ellsberg affair. And they, of course, did have supervisory control and authority over you to some extent. Did you use any of that electronic equipment? Or did you purchase all your own?

Mr. MCCORD. I do not know what electronic equipment was that you are referring to here, sir.

Senator GURNEY. Well, all I know is what I read in the newspapers on that, but did you purchase all of the electronic equipment devices that you used?

Mr. MCCORD. That I used, yes sir. I do not know what Mr. Hunt used.

Senator GURNEY. Thank you, that is all.

Senator ERVIN. Senator Inouye.

Senator INOUYE. Thank you very much.

Mr. McCord, I have been much impressed by your background, you have received two academic degrees from two different universities, you are a colonel in the Air Force Reserve, you have had very distinguished service of many years with the FBI, very distinguished service with the Central Intelligence Agency. From that I believe I can assume that you are better versed than the man on the street when it comes to what is legal and what is not legal, is that assumption correct?

Mr. MCCORD. I am not a lawyer, sir, as I testified to you. I have a working knowledge of the law, yes, sir.

Senator INOUYE. You are acquainted with what national security is all about?

Mr. MCCORD. I certainly am.

Senator INOUYE. I would assume that being involved in the Government all these years that your concern with our activities would be a bit more acute than the average citizen. For example, were you aware that Mr. Mitchell was the chief campaign manager in the 1968 election?

Mr. McCord. I believe I heard that, yes, sir.

Senator Inouye. Were you aware at the time that you were discussing the possibility of the clandestine activities that Mr. Mitchell was considering going over to the committee to become chairman of that committee?

Mr. McCord. Oh, yes, sir.

Senator Inouye. Were you aware at the time of your discussion when he was Attorney General that he was actually in control of the campaign activities?

Mr. McCord. I did not know the full extent to which he was in control. I knew there were meetings with him by senior people from the Committee for the Re-Election of the President.

Senator Inouye. You knew he was actively involved in matters political?

Mr. McCord. Yes, sir.

Senator Inouye. And you were aware that the Democratic National Committee was a political organization?

Mr. McCord. Beyond any question.

Senator Inouye. And you are aware that Mr. Muskie, Mr. McGovern were also political citizens?

Mr. McCord. Yes, sir.

Senator Inouye. That they were seeking the presidency of the United States?

Mr. McCord. Yes, sir.

Senator Inouye. You were also aware that Mr. O'Brien was a politician?

Mr. McCord. Yes; indeed.

Senator Inouye. I gather from your prior testimony that you had received instructions on taking pictures?

Mr. McCord. No, sir.

Senator Inouye. Someone in your group had instructions?

Mr. McCord. One of the members at least; yes, sir.

Senator Inouye. What sort of pictures did you take?

Mr. McCord. I do not know, sir, I did not see them.

Senator Inouye. You did not see any copies?

Mr. McCord. No, sir.

Senator Inouye. You did not hear of any instructions?

Mr. McCord. In a general sense, I do not know the specific targets, but yes, I heard them discussed by Mr. Hunt with the team members generally and I heard the team members refer to them but I do not have specifics as to what they are, what was copied.

Senator Inouye. Did you have any reason to suspect Mr. McGovern, Mr. Muskie, or Mr. O'Brien were involved in activities which were inimicable to the United States and contrary to the national security, more specifically to overthrow the Government?

Mr. McCord. When I previously referred to a comment that Mr. Liddy made to me in connection with the Las Vegas trip, two trips that he was making for this committee.

Senator Inouye. You had reason to believe that these men were involved in activities which would be dangerous to the existence of the United States of America?

Mr. McCORD. No, sir.

Senator INOUYE. Then, why did you carry on these activities? You were well aware of what national security was all about. Were they involved in syndicated criminal activity?

Mr. McCORD [conferring with counsel]. I can go into the reasons behind some of the motivations that I had if you want me to do so, sir, which pertain to testimony I previously had given relating to the——

Senator INOUYE. I believe it is very important because I for one would like to know why the sudden change of heart.

Mr. McCORD. In what, sir?

Senator INOUYE. In being concerned about justice and legality. Because I cannot believe that you were not aware of the illegality of all these acts and that these were political activities?

Mr. McCORD. Yes, sir, I have admitted that the acts were both wrong on my part, it was a mistake on my part, I stated that at the beginning and I restate it at this time but the motivation——

Senator INOUYE. Were you aware at the time you were on the sixth floor of the Watergate that it was illegal?

Mr. McCORD [conferring with counsel]. Yes; of course.

Senator INOUYE. Why did you, as one who has served his country so well, as a colonel in the Air Force, distinguished service in the FBI and CIA decide to carry out these illegal acts? The only thing you have done wrong so far is to receive a traffic ticket.

Mr. McCORD. Sir, I can repeat my situation that held me into the decision to join in this operation which involved a series of discussions, which involved the White House itself, the counsel to the President, that top lawyer, involved the top lawyer of the Committee for the Re-Election of the President and involved the Attorney General himself in his capacity as Attorney General of the United States who had the authority. I realize that acts are illegal, that these acts are illegal, under normal circumstances but that he has the power and authority to make them legal by his oral approval of it, and particularly, in particular, about what I was convinced was his approval.

Senator INOUYE. You knew the Attorney General was soon to become chairman of the Committee To Re-Elect the President?

Mr. McCORD. I was aware of it but I was also aware that the matter had been approved while he had been Attorney General, had been considered while he was Attorney General, had been considered jointly with the counsel to the President and while he was Attorney General.

Senator INOUYE. On all the front pages of the U.S. press you had comments about Mr. Mitchell to become soon the chairman of this party?

Mr. McCORD. Yes, sir.

Senator INOUYE. So you knew that his activities may be political in nature?

Mr. McCORD. They very well may be and part of the reason attributed to the operation was political, no question about it, but I had previously stated as well that I was convinced that over his, I knew over his, desk came many matters which I had no knowledge of and, in particular, I was concerned about violence and demonstrations, particularly violence which already were being reported to be occurring, that planned to occur, to take place, at the Republican National Convention in Miami. We had many reports of it, first of all, at the convention of San Diego upward of a quarter of a million people. I was also aware that the Attorney General in his capacity had very broad access to information which I felt I might not be privy to and Mr. Liddy might not be privy to, but which would, could, and would have a bearing, possibly would have a bearing upon the relationship of, association with, some of these demonstrators to certain members of either the Democratic National Committee or to the McGovern headquarters and in fact one of the groups now under indictment in Tallahassee, Fla., did in fact have an office within the Democratic National Committee.

Senator INOUYE. Was it your belief that people like Mr. O'Brien, Mr. McGovern, and Mr. Muskie were involved in a conspiracy to plan violence?

Mr. MCCORD. No, sir.

Senator INOUYE. Where was the national security involved as far as these three men were concerned?

Mr. MCCORD [conferring with counsel]. Sir, I can restate what I previously stated before this committee in terms of violence that had already occurred, which involve bombings in a couple of States, which involved violence and demonstrations against our committee, which involved bomb threats against the Committee To Re-Elect the President, which involved violence in the building, which involved threats to Mr. Mitchell and Mrs. Mitchell, and I recited those in considerable detail, concerning the violence that was planned for the Republican National Committee and some of which were reported as early as 1971 and targeted against the Committee for Re-Election of the President. There had been reports they were in both groups in McGovern headquarters and the Democratic national headquarters some of the staff members working closely with the violence groups and, as I believe I testified to, that part of these informations we expected to obtain are the wiretap itself would have to do with calls and conversations and coordination between such groups and staff members in the Democratic National Committee. That was not the only purpose of the wiretap; I understood that part of the purpose was political intelligence, political intelligence for the Committee for Re-Election of the President and the White House out at the Democratic National Committee and out at the McGovern headquarters, that was one factor.

Senator INOUYE. Do you want the committee to believe at the time you made the decision to be involved in these illegal acts you felt that men like McGovern, Muskie, and O'Brien were involved in this national conspiracy of bombing and inciting violence?

Mr. MCCORD. No, sir; I did not testify to that and I do not want the committee to believe that. I was just telling what my reason and motivations were at the time and what they surrounded which was the participating by the Attorney General.

Senator INOUYE. And yet you indicated that one of your projected plans called for the bugging of Mr. O'Brien's private residence; is that not so?

Mr. MCCORD. No, that it was initially proposed that that be done. That is what was never done, that his office was bugged, yes, sir, in the Democratic National Committee.

Senator ERVIN. Would the Senator pardon me.

Senator INOUYE. Yes, sir.

Senator ERVIN. It was the official position of the Department of Justice that they could bug to discover domestic subversion without a warrant, without applying for a warrant, and, by a strange coincidence, it was June 19, 1972, when the Supreme Court first handed down a unanimous decision rejecting that position of the Department of Justice.

Mr. McCORD. I think there is also, sir, if I may add at this point——

Senator INOUYE. I am aware of that, Mr. Chairman; I just want to have Mr. McCord to tell us that these men were involved in domestic subversion and Mr. McCord is not just another citizen. He is a colonel in the Air Force, holds two degrees from two universities, a very learned man of distinguished service with the FBI and CIA.

Changing the subject, sir, now, did you have a contingency plan in the event of arrest?

Mr. McCORD. Did I have—or did the group have?

Senator INOUYE. Did the group have.

Mr. McCORD. There were very general contingency plans, the main contingency planning was mainly access from the building itself in case the men were caught.

Senator INOUYE. What about attorneys?

Mr. McCORD. None that I knew of, no, sir.

Senator INOUYE. I gather from prior evidence that all of you had aliases.

Mr. McCORD. Yes, sir.

Senator INOUYE. One man had a Mexican passport made out under an alias, another one had a driver's license in New York made out in a phony name and another one from Massachusetts and likewise; where were these identity cards made?

Mr. McCORD. I do not know, sir.

Senator INOUYE. Where was yours made?

Mr. McCORD. I do not know, sir. It was given to me by Mr. Hunt and I have no idea.

Senator INOUYE. You did not ask?

Mr. McCORD. No, sir; I can explain how I received it, if that is any help to you.

Senator INOUYE. Was it a professionally made identity card?

Mr. McCORD. It appeared to be.

Senator INOUYE. Can you tell us how you got it?

Mr. McCORD. Yes; the evening of June 17 Mr. Hunt handed some identification to me and said, "Put this in your pocket in case you need it when you go by the guard, if you go by the guard, and he asks any questions concerning who you are."

I took it and glanced at it briefly and put it in my pocket. The identification was under the name of Edward J. Martin.

Senator INOUYE. You have indicated that your activities were limited to just two Watergate break-ins and an attempted one planned for the Muskie and McGovern headquarters, is that correct?

Mr. McCORD. That is correct.

Senator INOUYE. You were not involved in any other activity?

Mr. McCORD. No, sir.

Senator INOUYE. Was Mr. Odle aware of your activities?

Mr. McCORD. No, sir.

Senator INOUYE. Did you at any time discuss the possibility of other activities?

Mr. McCORD. To the best of my knowledge he was in no way involved in any of the Watergate planning or the operations himself.

Senator INOUYE. The highest officials that you have met, according to your statement, is Mr. Liddy and Mr. Magruder?

Mr. McCORD. Met in what connection, sir?

Senator INOUYE. Directly involved in this activity.

Mr. McCORD. Met with Mr. Liddy only. I had many meetings with Mr. Mitchell and Magruder.

Senator INOUYE. Did you have any contact with Mr. Dean directly?

Mr. McCORD. Yes, sir.

Senator INOUYE. Did you discuss this matter directly with Mr. Dean? Did you have any direct contact with the Attorney General?

Mr. McCORD. Oh, yes, sir.

Senator INOUYE. Did you discuss this matter?

Mr. McCORD. No, sir. I previously testified to that. I did not. I testified to the reason.

Senator INOUYE. Were you meeting the Attorney General at the time you were planning this Watergate activity?

Mr. McCORD. I did not meet with him in planning sessions. I saw him regularly during that period; yes, sir.

Senator INOUYE. You were not curious enough to bring it up with him.

Mr. McCORD. I trusted Mr. Liddy who said he would discuss it with him. I felt if the Attorney General cared to discuss it with me he would raise it.

Senator INOUYE. You had no desire to bring it up on your own?

Mr. McCORD. I had no reason to question that Mr. Liddy would not mention to him I was not participating. I had no desire to proceed beyond that. He said that he would and I accepted his word for it.

Senator INOUYE. Mr. Chairman, I believe my time has expired; thank you very much, sir.

Thank you, Mr. McCord.

Senator ERVIN. Senator Weicker.

Senator WEICKER. Thank you, Mr. Chairman.

Mr. McCord, who hired Al Baldwin?

Mr. McCORD. I did, sir.

Senator WEICKER. Did you hire him or was it a decision involving you and another person?

Mr. McCORD. His initial employment was in a sequence of an interview by me and a subsequent interview with Mr. Fred LaRue of the committee in which the final commitment was made by Mr. LaRue, that is the sequence.

Senator WEICKER. So actually the final decision as to Mr. Baldwin's employment was made by Mr. LaRue, is that correct?

Mr. McCORD. Yes, sir.

Senator WEICKER. Now, Mr. McCord, do you know Robert Mardian?

Mr. McCORD. Yes, sir.

Senator WEICKER. In what connection do you know him?

Mr. McCORD. I first met him when he came to the Committee for the Re-Election of the President.

Senator WEICKER. When you say you first met him, would you care to describe that meeting?

Mr. McCORD. I believe the first meeting with him was in May, late May as best I recall, when he came to, shortly after he came to, the committee and as I recall his driver was being employed by the committee as a driver and we had some discussion in that context at that time.

Senator WEICKER. You had discussions with Mr. Mardian or with his driver?

Mr. McCORD. With Mr. Mardian.

Senator WEICKER. Can you give me the substance of those conversations?

Mr. McCORD. That conversation was something to the effect that the driver was being considered as a driver for Mr. Mitchell, and I inquired about the man's background and he stated that he had been a very satisfactory driver for him and he felt he would do a good job for Mr. Mitchell.

Senator WEICKER. Did you know what position Mr. Mardian held at the time that you talked to him?

Mr. McCORD. Oh, yes.

Senator WEICKER. Could you please state to the committee what that position was?

Mr. McCORD. He was, as I recall, a special assistant to Mr. Mitchell and one of functions that Mr. Mitchell had for him for the committee.

Senator WEICKER. I beg your pardon?

Mr. McCORD. He was a special assistant to Mr. Mitchell.

Senator WEICKER. Will you describe what you understood his duties to be as a special assistant to Mr. Mitchell?

Mr. McCORD. I understood general assignments for Mr. Mitchell. I did not know the specific details of everything that he was involved with at all. We talked a bit about Miami and the Miami convention and our concern over security there and I knew that he had some functions in connection with that.

Senator WEICKER. At the time of our first executive session, Mr. McCord, I asked you a question in what connection did you know Robert Mardian, and you took the fifth during that sworn interview.

Is there any reason why you would not like to or go ahead and describe now why you thought it was necessary at that moment in time?

Mr. McCORD. I believe it was taken on the advice of counsel at that point in time. I can't recall the specific questions, question that was asked at that period. If it can be recited I can give you the reason.

Senator WEICKER. The specific question was, "Have you had any contact with Robert Mardian at any time?

"Mr. McCORD. Yes, sir.

"Senator WEICKER. Could you describe to the committee what that contact consisted of?

"Mr. McCORD. I will take the fifth on that."

Mr. McCORD. There had been—I can give you now my reasons as best I recall for that.

There had been an article in Time magazine, it seems to me in August or so, 1972, in which there was an allegation against Mr. Mardian, as I recall it, that he was not only in charge of the Watergate operation but that he had some other political intelligence activities that he was carrying on that he was involved with in the Committee To Re-Elect the President. I knew that I had no knowledge of his involvement in the Watergate operations themselves. I knew that he had some function in connection with the—some function in connection with the convention at Miami. And I believe that was the reason that I took the fifth at that time, as I recall.

Senator WEICKER. Did you or the Committee To Re-Elect the President receive reports from the Internal Security Division of the Justice Department?

Mr. McCORD. Yes, sir, I did.

Senator WEICKER. Was Mr. Mardian head of that division?

Mr. McCORD. He had been, sir.

Senator WEICKER. Did you receive copies of FBI reports?

Mr. McCORD. I can explain a partial answer to that, sir, if you want me to, an answer that involves FBI reports.

I have raised with, I believe, Mr. Odle the problem of receiving adequate information concerning violence in demonstrations that might affect the committee headquarters in Washington and subsequently, the committee headquarters in Miami, and I asked if there were any way in which there could be some type of liaison to receive information from the FBI specifically, because I knew that they would have information that was not available to us and we knew that such information was being made available to other parties for the convention itself if it directly affected those parties.

As I recall, he sent a memorandum to Mr. Mitchell asking for approval of my contact with that organization.

The next that I heard was a call from Mr. Mardian in which he referred to that memorandum and he stated that Mr. Mitchell had given approval to my contact to acquire that type of information and that I should go to the Internal Security Division of the Department of Justice where such information as did affect, might affect, the security of the committee would be made available to me some of which was as I have described in those reports, yes, sir.

Senator WEICKER. So you received data from the Internal Security Division of the Justice Department?

Mr. McCORD. I did.

Senator WEICKER. And you received data from the FBI?

Mr. McCORD. Not from the FBI directly, no, sir.

Senator WEICKER. From whom did you receive such data?

Mr. McCORD. From the Internal Security Division. I do not believe the FBI was ever aware of that.

Senator WEICKER. And from what individual did you receive such information?

Mr. McCORD. I believe it was through the Chief of the Evaluation Section. I believe his name was Mr. John Martin.

Senator WEICKER. I am sorry. I did not hear the name.

Mr. McCORD. John Martin.

Senator WEICKER. John Martin was your contact?

Mr. McCORD. Yes, sir.

Senator WEICKER. At the Internal Security Division of the Justice Department, is that correct?

Mr. McCORD. Yes, sir, that is correct.

Senator WEICKER. Would it be correct to say that Mr. Martin is chief of the analysis and evaluation section?

Mr. McCORD. Yes, sir.

Senator WEICKER. And where did you meet Mr. Martin?

Mr. McCORD. At his office in the Department of Justice.

Senator WEICKER. Who knew, aside from Mr. Martin, that you were receiving this material?

Mr. McCORD. His deputy at the evaluation section. I believe the name is Lisker, I am not absolutely certain.

Senator WEICKER. I am not anxious to have any names here unless there is to be some identification.

I have before me a position report on this Internal Security Division. Could you tell me whether or not the name listed as deputy there is a name that you recognize, where I stopped reading?

Mr. McCORD. That is correct, sir.

Senator WEICKER. Would you please give the name, then, for the committee?

Mr. McCORD. J-o-e-l, Joel, Lisker, L-i-s-k-e-r.

Senator WEICKER. All right, then, to repeat again the question we were working on, who knew you received the material, who else besides Mr. Martin and Mr. Lisker?

Mr. McCORD. Mr. Martin, of course. Mr. Mitchell had initialed the memorandum that I subsequently saw on this, Mr. Robert Odle; at least those persons.

Senator WEICKER. Mr. Odle?

Mr. McCORD. Mr. Odle, yes, sir.

Senator WEICKER. You say there was a subsequent memorandum?

Mr. McCORD. The memorandum which Mr. Odle wrote on this subject I subsequently received, which had Mr. Mitchell's initials on it.

Senator WEICKER. Do you feel or do you know whether or not similar information, similar access to this information was given to the Democratic Party?

Mr. McCORD. I understood that they did have through some channels some access to information of this type; whether it came from that office, I do not know.

Senator WEICKER. Was the information which you received the basis for the apprehension which you described in answering the questions of Senator Inouye relative to your activities?

Mr. McCORD. It added to my apprehension, sir. It was not the basis. It came some weeks after my decision, but it added to that apprehension, because it dealt specifically with violence at the Republican National Committee.

Senator WEICKER. Now, I would like you to describe for me as best you can the types of information, in further detail, that you received from the Internal Security Division. Did you receive from the Internal Security Division, for example, or from the FBI any information as it related to the candidates or their staffs?

Mr. McCORD. Yes, sir, there was one such report that I do recall specifically.

Senator WEICKER. Can you give me details on that report?

Mr. McCORD. One such report dealt with, as I recall, a funding operation that was reported in which the McGovern committee purportedly funded a so-called barn storming tour of several members of the Vietnam Veterans Against the War on the west coast, as I recall, starting from Los Angeles, Calif., and going up the coast. It came concurrently with some other information that that same group was planning violence at the Republican National Convention involving danger to, threats to life of individuals. I think that was succeeded very shortly, in a matter of days, by the indictment of members of the Vietnam Veterans Against the War at Tallahassee because of the violence that they did plan, including a number of things that would endanger the lives of the people at the Republican National Convention.

Senator WEICKER. I want to be most careful on the grounds that we are covering.

Mr. Chairman, let me say this, that I would like to proceed for a few more minutes if I might, with the idea that the committee should pay very close attention to what obviously is a very serious matter. It is certainly the first time that I think I have ever known that the Internal Security Division of the Justice Department and the FBI were participating rather actively in a campaign, and I think that the facts should be laid out most carefully.

Now, can you tell me precisely what the dates were on which this type of activity took place? In other words, when you first made your contact with Mr. Martin and started to receive this type of material?

Mr. McCORD. My best recollection would have been within the last 2 weeks of May 1972.

Senator WEICKER. In the last 2 weeks of May, 1972, and you received this material between May of 1972 and when you were caught at the Watergate, is that correct?

Mr. McCORD. June 17, yes, sir.

Senator WEICKER. Of 1972?

Mr. McCORD. 1972.

Senator WEICKER. Have you ever been on the fourth floor of the Triangle Building?

Mr. McCORD. I believe that is the offices of the evaluation section, sir, if my memory is correct.

Senator WEICKER. Well, the Triangle Building is at 9th and D Streets. Have you ever been on the fourth floor of that building?

Mr. McCORD. If that is the offices of the analysis and evaluation section, I have been there, yes, sir.

Senator WEICKER. And this, as you understood this, you were with the intelligence evaluation committee at that time, or with the officers of it?

Mr. McCORD. With the Internal Security Division, Mr. Martin's particular office there, yes, sir.

Senator WEICKER. And on how many different occasions did you get this material from Mr. Martin and was he the only one that passed this information on to you?

Mr. McCORD. It would have been either Mr. Martin or Mr. Lisker. It was normally done in their offices when I would visit their offices. I recall a few occasions on which there were phone calls from these gentlemen, one of the two of the gentlemen; when we had 60 to 75,000 demonstrators in Washington and there appeared to be some information of relevance affecting the possible fiscal security of our installations by demonstrators that were then in the city, and I would get a call in that connection from one of the two men, saying, in effect, we think you ought to be aware of thus and so information. I recall specifically one such call dealing with the bombing of the Pentagon at that time.

Senator WEICKER. Again, I just want to repeat my first questions. On how many different occasions did you receive this material?

Mr. McCORD. Almost daily, sir.

Senator WEICKER. Almost daily?

Mr. McCORD. Yes, sir.

Senator WEICKER. And the nature of the material given to you related to groups, is that correct, individuals?

Mr. McCORD. Yes, sir.

Senator WEICKER. Individuals?

Mr. McCORD. Yes, sir.

Senator WEICKER. Both political and nonpolitical?

Mr. McCORD. Yes, sir.

Senator WEICKER. Now, when you received this material, what did you do with it?

Mr. McCORD. If it were of sufficient consequence. I would pass it along to Mr. Mitchell's office, usually through Mr. Odle. Quite often, I would put it in a memorandum for him for distribution to those other staff members of the committee who would normally want to know of forthcoming demonstrations in the Washington area, some of which might affect the committee.

Senator WEICKER. Why did you feel this was—now, you would pass this on to Mr. Mitchell at the Committee To Re-Elect the President, is that correct?

Mr. McCORD. Yes, sir, and other staff members.

Senator WEICKER. Well, and other staff members. Who is "and other staff members"?

Mr. McCORD. About six of the senior staff members, which included Mr. Sloan, who passed it to Mr. Stans, included Mr. Liddy, included Mr. Odle, included the prospective officers for Mr. Mitchell's wife, Mrs. Mitchell, and two or three other division chiefs there under Mr. Mitchell.

Senator WEICKER. And this almost on a daily basis?

Mr. McCORD. Yes, sir.

Senator WEICKER. And this is material which you yourself received and you yourself distributed?

Mr. McCORD. Yes, sir.

Senator WEICKER. Well, Mr. Chairman, I have a lot of other questions, but I am afraid I am going to have to digest that one for a few minutes and I would like to defer to you to have other questioning take place. I would hope that there will be an opportunity to proceed to further questioning on this.

Senator ERVIN. I might state that Senator Inouye has to go at 4 o'clock and it might be advisable for us to recess at 4 and let the witness come back on Tuesday.

Senator WEICKER. I beg Senator Montoya's pardon and thank you, Senator.

Senator MONTOYA. Thank you, Mr. Chairman.

Mr. McCord, going back to the time that you were hired, I would like to ask you if you had a personal acquaintance with the President?

Mr. McCORD. No, sir.

Senator MONTOYA. Had you worked with him in any capacity? Either while he was Vice President or before?

Mr. McCORD. No, sir.

Senator MONTOYA. Had you done any work in his behalf while you were working for the CIA?

Mr. McCORD. I was a staff member of the CIA while he was Vice President. He may have had access to material or reports which I wrote.

Senator MONTOYA. Did you ever speak to him during those same times?

Mr. McCORD. I don't recall it; no, sir.

Senator MONTOYA. Who was the person who recommended you for this particular job assignment?

Mr. McCORD. Mr. John Caulfield.

Senator MONTOYA. And where did you meet him?

Mr. McCORD. At the Executive Office Building in Washington, D.C.

Senator MONTOYA. And where is that Executive Office Building with respect to the White House?

Mr. McCORD. It adjoins it. It is on the White House grounds.

Senator MONTOYA. How many visits did you have with Mr. Caulfield before you were hired?

Mr. McCORD. I believe it was three or four, sir.

Senator MONTOYA. And why did you have three or four visits? Were they extensive interviews and did you go into the details of your assignment?

Mr. McCORD. Yes, sir. They were twofold, for twofold purposes. They were an opportunity for Mr. Caulfield to interview me personally and learn more about me and my background, and secondly, an opportunity for him to discuss the nature of the job that would be coming up in the campaign.

Senator MONTOYA. Did Mr. Caulfield at that time discuss with you the clandestine nature of your assignment?

Mr. McCORD. No, sir.

Senator MONTOYA. When did you and Mr. Caulfield, if you did, engage in such a conversation?

Mr. McCORD. I believe it followed the June 17 break-in.

Senator MONTOYA. That is when he was discussing with you the possibility of clemency?

Mr. McCORD. Yes, sir.

Senator MONTOYA. Or shortly after the June 17 break-in and before the trial? Which was it?

Mr. McCORD. My first conversation with him was shortly after June 17, sometime in July or August.

Senator MONTOYA. And was he an employee of the White House at that time?

Mr. McCORD. No, sir.

Senator MONTOYA. Where was he employed?

Mr. McCORD. He was either employed or due to be employed at the Treasury Department in the position I mentioned earlier.

Senator MONTOYA. And what was that conversation about?

Mr. McCORD. This was a conversation about which I referred this morning, a telephone call in which he stated that he was making a trip overseas and that if I needed to reach him, to call his home and leave word and he would call me back.

Senator MONTOYA. Now, after you had your three interviews with him, who else did you see prior to being hired on a part-time basis in October of 1971?

Mr. McCORD. Mr. Robert Odle at the Committee for the Re-Election of the President, to make an initial interview with me, with Mr. Caulfield present.

Senator MONTOYA. And were you hired pursuant to this interview?

Mr. McCORD. Yes, sir.

Senator MONTOYA. And you became a part-time employee of the operation there?

Mr. McCORD. I did.

Senator MONTOYA. Did you at any time discuss with Mr. Odle the triple assignment which you related this morning was your assignment, or was the nature of the operation with respect to Mr. Liddy's involvement?

Mr. McCORD. No, sir; I did not discuss that with Mr. Odle.

Senator MONTOYA. Now, when you stated this morning that one of the assignments, or that the total assignment would involve getting photographic information, political espionage, and electronic surveillance, when did you first find out about the composition of your entire operation?

Mr. McCORD. I believe it would have been in April 1972, when I met Mr. Hunt for the first time.

Senator MONTOYA. And I believe you have previously stated that during the course of February, you were in touch with Mr. Liddy and other individuals with respect to planning for the clandestine operation which later turned out to be Watergate?

Mr. McCORD. Yes, sir.

Senator MONTOYA. And where did this take place?

Mr. McCORD. The first part of your question, sir, was when?

Senator MONTOYA. Where did the initial conversations with respect to the Watergate planning take place?

Mr. McCORD. In Mr. Liddy's office at the Committee To Re-Elect the President.

Senator MONTOYA. Was this in February?

Mr. McCORD. January and February initially; yes, sir.

Senator MONTOYA. And who else was in on this?

Mr. McCORD. No one else, sir.

Senator MONTOYA. And were you aware that a plan was being formulated?

Mr. McCORD. Yes, sir.

Senator MONTOYA. And were you also aware that the plan was being formulated for submission to the Attorney General?

Mr. McCORD. Yes, sir.

Senator MONTOYA. And did you provide any input into this plan?

Mr. McCORD. Oh, yes, sir.

Senator MONTOYA. What kind of input did you provide?

Mr. McCORD. In the nature of information Mr. Liddy sought about different costs of equipment, electronic equipment and the different components that he was interested in, the transmission devices and the receiving devices in particular.

Senator MONTOYA. And did you discuss with Mr. Liddy at that time as to manpower requirements and other necessary details to carry out the plans?

Mr. McCORD. Oh, yes, sir.

Senator MONTOYA. Give us the substance of those conversations.

Mr. McCORD. He was interested in the overall cost, first of all, of these types of operations, specifically referring to electronic operations, what the pieces of equipment would cost, what it took to receive them, what types of receivers were best. He was interested in the best type of equipment in this sense for this operation. He wanted to know how many pieces of equipment it would take for the Democratic National Committee, for example, to transmit and receive transmissions from the Democratic National Committee headquarters; secondly, in connection with the McGovern committee headquarters; and thirdly, in connection with the Democratic National Convention site in Miami, Fla.

Senator MONTOYA. What was the value of the equipment that you used at the Democratic National Committee?

Mr. McCORD. I would guess about $15,000 in total but I am not sure.

Senator MONTOYA. $15,000?

Mr. McCORD. Fifteen, yes, sir.

Senator MONTOYA. What was the value of the equipment that you used in Miami?

Mr. McCORD. I did not use any there, sir.

Senator MONTOYA. Were you contemplating using the same equipment from the National Committee at the National Convention in Miami?

Mr. McCORD. No, sir, that was separate equipment.

Senator MONTOYA. Where else were you going to use equipment?

Mr. McCORD. Those three places that I have stated—the McGovern committee headquarters, Democratic National Committee, and the convention site for the Democratic Party in Miami, Fla.

Senator MONTOYA. Doesn't it stand to reason that for the expenditure of $65,000, you were going to launch quite a few operations?

Mr. McCORD. There were three separate locations and it would take——

Senator MONTOYA. Well, at the rate of $15,000 apiece, you would have some equipment left for other operations.

Now, why was the budget so high?

Mr. McCORD. Well, I think to answer your question, sir, there was planned, for example, for the Democratic National Committee two separate operations there, not just the one that was initially planned. Mr. Liddy budgeted for what he felt was adequate equipment for all three locations and it would not simply take just—you asked the question of how much was the value of the equipment that was installed and I gave the figure of about $15,000.

The additional equipment that was taken in was an additional cost factor there.

Does that answer your question, or have I not?

Senator MONTOYA. Let me ask you this: Did you assume when you purchased this equipment for an approximate sum of $65,000 that it would be used solely for the three operations about which you had testified, or did you assume that this equipment would be used for other operations, to which you would not be related in involvement?

Mr. McCORD. Oh, yes, sir. This was a part of it.

Senator MONTOY . Sir?

Mr. McCORD. Yes, the walkie-talkie equipment, for example, was scheduled, as I understood it, for use in certain surveillance operations by the Cuban individuals referred to against demonstrators and violence-oriented groups in Miami, Fla. So that was an example of my reasons for answering yes to your question.

Senator MONTOYA. So then am I to assume that other than your own involvement, there could have been other involvements in other parts of the country, or even in Washington?

Mr. McCORD. The communications, the walkie-talkie equipment specifically, I knew of no other immediate planned use of the electronic equipment; such could have been possible.

Senator MONTOYA. How much telephone tapping equipment did you buy and was this just barely sufficient, or was this in surplus after you had serviced the needs for the three places which you had in mind at the time, namely, the Watergate, the Democratic convention in Miami, and the McGovern headquarters?

Mr. McCORD. In the neighborhood of $45,000 worth of equipment planned for those three locations and possible other use against demonstrators in Miami.

Senator MONTOYA. You had $20,000 left in equipment, would you say?

Mr. McCORD. Perhaps more than that, sir.

Senator MONTOYA. How much more?

Mr. McCORD. You are referring to the—I mentioned the, $15,000.

Senator MONTOYA. And then it stands to reason that you could reuse some of this equipment you were using at Watergate and that you intended to use at Miami and also at McGovern headquarters, is that not correct?

Mr. McCORD. No sir, I believe they were planned to be used concurrently.

Senator MONTOYA. Sir?

Mr. McCORD. I think it was planned to be used in three separate operations concurrently.

Senator MONTOYA. Did you have any other employees under you or under your direction who were performing any of the activities within the master plan that you worked on initially?

Mr. McCORD. Just Mr. Baldwin.

Senator MONTOYA. And you stated that one of the purposes or objectives was to gather photographic information. Now who was in charge of this division?

Mr. McCORD. Mr. Hunt.

Senator MONTOYA. And who was in charge of political espionage?

Mr. McCORD. Mr. Liddy, as I understand it, and Mr. Hunt were jointly involved in the two. I understood Mr. Liddy was in charge.

Senator MONTOYA. All right. Who was involved in electronic surveillance?

Mr. McCORD. I was.

Senator MONTOYA. All right.

Did you employ anyone to help you in this endeavor?

Mr. McCord. Mr. Baldwin only at that point in time.

Senator Montoya. Who employed the Cubans?

Mr. McCord. Mr. Hunt, to my understanding.

Senator Montoya. Now, do you know whether Mr. Hunt recruited them in Florida?

Mr. McCord. I do not know, sir.

Senator Montoya. How were the Cubans procured?

Mr. McCord. That I do not know, sir.

Senator Montoya. Did you also have something to do with working out the arrangements for the security of the Attorney General and Mrs. Mitchell at their home?

Mr. McCord. Yes sir.

Senator Montoya. What specifically did you do in that respect?

Mr. McCord. Myself was to secure at Mr. Mitchell's requests a security officer for Mrs. Mitchell beginning in March, May, April, 1972, and to generally oversee the security of their apartment at the Watergate Hotel, Watergate Apartments, and to insure that there was security protection for their daughter who was attending school, a young daughter, teenager in Washington, and specifically, in particular to see there was a security officer accompanying her when she traveled.

Senator Montoya. How many times did you visit the apartment?

Mr. McCord. Numerous times.

Senator Montoya. Did you converse with Mrs. Mitchell or the Attorney General during those visits?

Mr. McCord. Yes sir.

Senator Montoya. What did you converse about?

Mr. McCord. Mainly matters relating to those functions, the security functions and in particular a security officer to travel with her and security of their apartment.

Senator Montoya. So you were very well acquainted with Mr. Mitchell?

Mr. McCord. Yes sir.

Senator Montoya. Now, will you state, are you aware of what happened to Mrs. Mitchell in California?

Mr. McCord. No sir.

Senator Montoya. Did you manifest any concern in view of the fact that you had hired these people to guard her?

Mr. McCord. In connection with the California matter, you are referring to?

Senator Montoya. Yes.

Mr. McCord. I was in jail at the time.

Senator Montoya. You were concerned about yourself only at that time?

Mr. McCord. Yes sir.

Senator Montoya. Now you wrote a letter, Mr. McCord, to Judge Sirica in which you indicated a belief that retaliatory measures would be taken against you, your family, and your friends if you should disclose facts relating to the affair, and you stated in your letter such retaliation could destroy careers, income, reputations of persons who are innocent of any guilt whatsoever, whatever.

Now can you give us the basis or the foundation for this particular belief which you communicated to Judge Sirica?

Mr. McCord. I believe I have testified previously that it was primarily family concerns that were expressed by my wife that such could happen physically if I decided to talk, they were not concerns trying to deter me but simply a natural family concern for myself and my family which in turn were relayed to me.

Senator Montoya. Were any of these communications by known individuals or were they just relayed to your wife more or less secondhand?

Mr. McCord. They were relayed to me secondhanded. I think the other half of the answer is, has to do with, the statement I read this morning. I do not think it concerned me greatly but I know that it had some effect upon my wife.

Senator Montoya. Now when Mr. Liddy unfolded this plan to you did he indicate to you how you would be taken care of in case anything happened?

Mr. McCord. No sir.

Senator Montoya. Did you have any concern that something could happen and then what would they do in that case?

Mr. McCord. Perhaps I do not understand the question, sir.

Senator Montoya. Did you at that time when the plan unfolded before your very eyes, was unfolded before your very eyes by Mr. Liddy, did you feel any concern for what might happen and who would take care of the situation if it did happen?

Mr. McCord. Yes.

Senator Montoya. What kind of concern did you have?

Mr. McCord. I think the concerns that what did happen might happen.

Senator Montoya. Well, now, when you were arrested at the Watergate and taken to jail, two attorneys apparently appeared there the next morning. Who were those attorneys?

Mr. McCord. Mr. Rafferty and Mr. Douglas Caddy, C-a-d-d-y.

Senator Montoya. Who sent them there?

Mr. McCord. I did not know at the time. I have since understood that Mr. Hunt had a part in arranging for their appearance.

Senator Montoya. Was anyone—was anything said to you by these attorneys to keep quiet or not divulging anything or even the source of your employment?

Mr. McCord. There was a brief discussion with all of the defendants at that first meeting, if that is what you are referring to, at the place where we were arrested.

Senator Montoya. Where was this discussion?

Mr. McCord. In the Second District Precinct in Washington, police precinct.

Senator Montoya. Now, you also indicated that you visited other places. Now, during your employment with the committee, what places did you visit throughout the country other than New York about which Mr. Odle testified yesterday?

Mr. McCord. Chicago.

Senator Montoya. I believe he testified about Chicago. What other places did you visit?

Mr. McCord. Miami, Fla; Miami, Fla.

Senator Montoya. How long did you stay there?

Mr. McCord. Two or 3 days.

96-296—73—bk. 1——13

Senator MONTOYA. What was your mission there?

Mr. McCORD. It was along, that was along, with about a half dozen White House personnel to review the overall planning for the use of the Doral Hotel which was to be used in August 1972 as, for both offices and residences for the Committee for the Re-Election of the President staff and for the White House staff, both. My task there was to look over the security needs and to recommend measures to appropriate to those needs.

Senator MONTOYA. Who went to Miami to plan the security for the Democratic National Committee?

Mr. McCORD. The Democratic National Committee?

Senator MONTOYA. And the convention, you indicated you had an interest in that.

Mr. McCORD. I did not. I do not know, sir, I did not.

Senator MONTOYA. Did you not state that there would be some effort made to carry on a surveillance program at the Democratic National Convention?

Mr. McCORD. Yes, sir.

Senator MONTOYA. And who was assigned to that task, if you know?

Mr. McCORD. I knew Mr. Hunt had some activity in that regard.

Senator MONTOYA. Did he hire other people, to your knowledge?

Mr. McCORD. I believe he utilized some of the other men that were in the Watergate operation. I had understood that from him, I was not certain as to the exact nature.

Senator MONTOYA. You were on two payrolls, apparently, when Mr. Liddy hired you for this clandestine operation. You were on Mr. Odle's payroll as well as Mr. Liddy's, is that correct?

Mr. McCORD. That is correct, sir.

Senator MONTOYA. And you were receiving how much from Mr. Odle and how much from Mr. Liddy on a monthly basis?

Mr. McCORD. Approximately one-twelfth of the $20,000 a year salary from Mr. Odle; $2,000 from Mr. Liddy.

Senator MONTOYA. Did your attorney at any time communicate to you that there had been some offers of clemency, that is, your attorney, Mr. Alch?

Mr. McCORD. Yes, sir.

Senator MONTOYA. Will you state what you received by way of information in that respect?

Mr. McCORD. Yes, sir.

Senator MONTOYA. Please do so.

Mr. McCORD. It is my recollection that the date was in late September or early October 1972 when Mr. Alch was in town, came to a meeting, he said, with Mr. Bittman and stated that Executive clemency and financial support and rehabilitation would be made available to the defendants in the case, including me.

Senator MONTOYA. That is all, Mr. Chairman. Thank you.

Senator ERVIN. Senator Baker will ask you one question and then we will adjourn.

Mr. McCORD. Yes, sir.

Senator BAKER. Mr. McCord, it is 4 o'clock and we are going to adjourn shortly, and my question does not require an answer today. We can take it up when you return on Tuesday. What I am about to say in no way disparages your testimony because you have been meticulously careful, I believe, in your testimony; you have been very exact in the answers you have given to counsel and to members of the committee. I must say I am impressed with the thoroughness with which you prepared memoranda today, and previously in your testimony before this committee in executive session. All of those things are commendable and we thank you for them.

I practiced law for almost 19 years before I came to the U.S. Senate, and I had a lot of witnesses at one time or the other, and I came to recognize a syndrome that I think may be present today, and that is, sometimes I had a witness on the stand who would tell me the answer to the question I asked exactly, and sometimes if I did not know what question to ask I would not get an answer.

Now the judicial system of the United States is a marvelous thing. It is made up, really, of an adversary conflict between a defendant and a plaintiff or between the State and the defendant.

But this committee is not engaged in an adversary conflict. We are engaged in a fact-finding mission to get all of the information we can. I think you and Mr. Fensterwald, who is a very fine attorney, know the principal matters that we are trying to establish, and you have covered with very exact answers many of the items that deal with the subject of this inquiry.

My question to you is this: Based on your references to other motivations, based on your reference twice, I believe, to a trip to Las Vegas, based on your reference to other people from time to time, based on the fact that part of the information that you might seek to obtain was national security and part was political, based on a sketchy description of some of the things, some of the threats that were passed on to you by the Internal Security Division and the like, I am led to wonder if we do not have that situation where the committee does not know what to ask you, and really we do want to know.

So, would it be possible, Mr. McCord, for you and your attorney to return on Tuesday, and supply us any information you think relevant to the scope of this inquiry, whether we have got enough sense to ask for it or not. Would you be willing to try to do that by Tuesday?

Mr. McCord. I will.

Senator Baker. Thank you very much.

Senator Ervin. We will stand in recess until 10 o'clock Tuesday.

[Whereupon, at 4 p.m., the committee was recessed, to reconvene at 10 a.m., Tuesday, May 22, 1973.]

TUESDAY, MAY 22, 1973

U.S. SENATE,
SELECT COMMITTEE ON
PRESIDENTIAL CAMPAIGN ACTIVITIES,
Washington, D.C.

The Select Committee met, pursuant to recess, at 10:05 a.m., in room 318, Russell Senate Office Building, Senator Sam J. Ervin, Jr. (chairman), presiding.

Present: Senators Ervin, Talmadge, Inouye, Montoya, Baker, Gurney, and Weicker.

Also present: Samuel Dash, chief counsel; Fred D. Thompson, minority counsel; Rufus L. Edmisten, deputy chief counsel; Arthur S. Miller, chief consultant; Jed Johnson, consultant; David M. Dorsen, James Hamilton, and Terry F. Lenzner, assistant chief counsels; Barry Schochet, assistant majority counsel; Donald G. Sanders, H. William Shure, and Robert Silverstein, assistant minority counsels; Joan C. Cole, secretary to the minority; Pauline O. Dement, research assistant; Eiler Ravnholt, office of Senator Inouye; Robert Baca, office of Senator Montoya; Ron McMahan, assistant to Senator Baker; A. Searle Field, assistant to Senator Weicker; Marc Lackritz, Ron Rotunda, assistant counsels; Eugene Boyce, hearings counsel; John Walz, publications clerk.

Senator ERVIN. The committee will come to order.

Mr. DASH. Senator Baker will be opening the questioning of Mr. McCord. But before that, Mr. McCord, it has come to our attention that there is concern among a number of Cuban-Americans and others of Latin nationalities that in your reference during your testimony, and I am not suggesting that it is your intention to cast any aspersions but that you have referred to others who participated with you by their proper names but in your reference to those who are Cuban-Americans you have referred to them as Cubans. Would you in your testimony in the future when referring to the participants who worked with you, use their proper names and when not necessary not use a nationality or ethnic reference.

TESTIMONY OF JAMES W. McCORD—Resumed

Mr. MCCORD. I would be very glad to.

Senator BAKER. Mr. Chairman, thank you very much.

Mr. McCord and Mr. Fensterwald, I appreciate your agreeing on Friday to respond to rather general and even possibly ambiguous questions. But to reiterate the question, so it is in perspective for today's hearing, my purpose is this: I remarked that I felt your testimony had been very thorough and very exact. We are grateful for the several memorandums that you provided the committee and from which you have testified which I believe adds to the element of concern and the element of sensitivity to exactitude which is exhibited. I also express the concern that notwithstanding very thorough interviews and one executive session with the committee, I continue to have the feeling that there is still a substantial amount of information which you may not think is relevant to this inquiry but which, in fact, may be relevant in terms of other witnesses or in terms of the general pattern which emerges. I indicated, therefore, that I would be grateful if you would search your mind and recollect within the boundaries and framework of the jurisdictional qualifications of this committee and within the scope of the general areas of inquiry which we have probed so far.

As you probably know, the resolution, Senate Resolution 60, which was passed by the U.S. Senate, provides for an investigation into Presidential campaign activities in 1972, to ascertain whether or not there were illegal, improper, or unethical activities. Beyond that, Mr. McCord as you and Mr. Fensterwald can surmise this committee is interested in broad categories. We want to know, of course, of illegal activity or activity which is now known to be illegal, such as the break-in at the Watergate, the Democratic National Committee. The so-called coverup, the allegations that efforts were made by some to conceal the involvement or connections involved. The money that was involved in the campaign activities, the source, the accounting procedures involved, if any, and the disposition of those funds and for what purpose. We want to know who is involved and what their relationships are. Those are the general areas that we have probed so far. My reason for reiterating it is to put, I hope, your further reasons in perspective and to add one additional caveat. Not only do I not know what I might ask you in these respects beyond what you have testified, but I do not want to limit you by a description that I have made of the contribution that you can make to this committee. I believe you to be a very, very important witness, and I reiterate this is not an adversary proceeding.

You are not a defendant in this forum and I am not a prosecutor of a defendant.

So with that, Mr. McCord, if you have a further statement to make I would be grateful for it. That may or may not generate further questions that I will have as we proceed with the testimony.

Mr. McCORD. All right, sir. I will try to give as much information as I can. I realize the very large scope of the committee's activities. I realize that it is also possible that the committee may have an impression from me which I apologize for that I may have more information to offer than I really do. I think I will do my best to set forth in this memorandum today, this statement, things that have come to mind that it would appear you would be very interested in and to respond to questions therefrom and to do anything further that the committee may want to amplify what I have said or develop any further information that may be helpful to you.

Senator BAKER. Thank you.

Mr. McCORD. One of the statements that we did not get into on the last meeting, I think primarily because of the factor of time, was a memorandum which I had written to the committee dated May 4, 1973, the subject of pressure on the defendants to blame the Watergate operation on CIA, and other matters. I am prepared to go into that statement at this time if it has your approval.

Senator BAKER. Thank you very much. Is that letter a part of the record?

Mr. McCORD. No, sir.

Senator BAKER. Do you have a copy of it?

Mr. McCORD. Yes, sir.

Senator BAKER. Might it be introduced, Mr. Chairman, as an exhibit?

Senator ERVIN. Yes.

Senator BAKER. I understand copies have not been supplied to the committee but if there is no objection, I would like to ask it be made an exhibit in the record at this point.

Senator ERVIN. I think it might be well to have it printed in full at this point in the record.

Senator BAKER. Thank you.

Mr. McCORD. I will read the statement.

I have previously referred to political pressure which was applied to the seven Watergate defendants.

One area of pressure which was applied was that of December 1972, in which intense pressure was applied on some of the defendants to falsely claim for purposes of a defense during the trial in January 1973, that the Watergate operation was a CIA operation. This would have had the effect of clearing the Committee for the Re-Election of the President and the White House of responsibility for the operation.

In two separate meetings in December 1972, it was suggested that I use as my defense during the trial the false story that the operation was a CIA operation. I refused to do so.

I was subsequently informed by Bernard Barker just before the trial began in January 1973, that E. Howard Hunt and other unnamed persons in Miami had brought intense pressure to bear against the Cuban-Americans and by those—I will digress from the record to read to whom I was referring—and the identities of these persons came to me in conversations with Mr. Bernard Barker and some of the other individuals involved, specifically I was referring to Mr. Bernard L. Barker, to Mr. Eugenio R. Martinez, to Mr. Frank A. Sturgis, to Mr. Virgilio R. Gonzales—I will restate the sentence.

I was subsequently informed by Bernard Barker just before the trial began in January 1973, that he, Howard Hunt, and other unnamed persons in Miami had brought intense pressure to bear against the Cuban-Americans who were defendants to use the same story that it was a CIA operation, as their defense, that my stand taken against it had been the decisive factor causing this ploy to be dropped, and that Hunt was very bitter about it. Mr. Hunt's bitterness was later revealed early in the trial when the Cubans advised that Hunt had said that I "was responsible for our being in the plight we were in for not going along with the CIA thing."

At a later time, I heard from Barker that he had been told that Cuban money was suspected of being funnelled into the McGovern campaign. I have no knowledge that this suspicion was ever verified.

The two December 1972 meetings with me were on December 21, 1972, and on December 26, 1972. Present at the first meeting with me at the Monocle restaurant in Washington, D.C., were Gerald Alch and Bernard Shankman, my attorneys. Present at the second meeting was Gerald Alch, and the meeting was at his office in Boston, Mass. Alch stated that he had just come from a meeting with William O. Bittman.

In the first meeting, Alch stated that he had just come from a meeting with William O. Bittman, attorney for E. Howard Hunt, and I received the impression in the discussion that followed that Alch was conveying an idea or request from Bittman. There followed a suggestion from Alch that I use as my defense during the trial the story that the Watergate operation was a CIA operation. I heard him out on the suggestion which included questions as to whether I could ostensibly have been recalled from retirement from CIA to participate in the operation. He said that if so, my personnel records at CIA could be doctored to reflect such a recall. He stated that Schlesinger, the new Director of CIA, whose appointment had just been announced, "could be subpenaed and would go along with it." I had noted in the newspapers of that day, December 21, 1972, that it had been announced by the White House that Mr. Schlesinger had taken over as Director of CIA, and that it had been decided that Pat Gray would be supported by the White House to be permanent Director of the FBI.

Alch went on to mention testimony, or a statement, made to Federal authorities by Gary Bittenbender, a Metropolitan Police Department undercover police officer, whom I had seen at the courthouse, on June 17, 1972, when the five of us who were arrested were arraigned, in which Bittenbender purportedly claimed that I had told him that day that the Watergate operation was a CIA operation. I advised Alch that if Bittenbender had made such a statement under oath that he had perjured himself, and that I had not made such a claim. Bittenbender can be interviewed to determine the circumstances under which he had made such a statement, and whether his statement was, in fact, an honest error of impressions based on events which occurred in court on that day, which could have misled him. Those were that some of us were identified in the hearing in court as formerly connected with CIA.

Alch went on to mention the name of Victor Marchetti whom he was considering calling to describe CIA training in which its employees were trained to deny CIA sponsorship of an operation if anything went wrong and its participants were arrested. He also requested that I meet with him in Boston on December 26, 1972, which I did.

There he opened the discussion by showing me a written statement of an interview with Bittenbender in which Bittenbender claimed that on June 17, 1972, I had told him that the Watergate operation was a CIA operation. I repeated to Alch my earlier statement, that Bittenbender had either perjured himself, or had made a false statement to Federal authorities. I told Alch that I could not use as my defense the story that the operation was a CIA operation because it was not true. In addition, I told him that even if it meant my freedom, I would not turn on the organization that had employed me for 19 years, and wrongly deal such a damaging blow that it would take years for it to recover from it, and finally that I believed the organization to be one of the finest organizations of its kind in the world and would not let anyone wrongly lay the operation at the feet of CIA.

By now, I was completely convinced that the White House was behind the idea and ploy which had been presented, and that the White House was turning ruthless, in my opinion, and would do whatever was politically expedient at any one particular point in time to accomplish its own ends.

In addition, I earlier had determined to tell the true story of the Watergate operation, and it was now only a matter of a propitious time to do so.

On Friday, December 29, 1972, I visited Bernard Shankman's office in Washington, D.C., and let him read a statement which I had prepared, which I proposed to read to the press on December 30, 1972, releasing Alch as my attorney. I believed that although Shankman had been present at the first meeting he was not a party to the events previously described. Shankman suggested that I give Alch an opportunity to meet with me and explain why he had undertaken the course which he had, and such a meeting was set up for Tuesday, January 2, 1973, in Washington.

Alch failed to appear, and I delivered a letter to Judge Sirica, releasing Alch as my attorney. Alch immediately called, asked to meet with me on January 3, 1973, and asked to continue as my attorney. We met and Alch stated that he, in conveying the request made of me on December 21 and December 26, 1972, was acting out of what he felt to be my own best interests. By this time, I was convinced that the ploy to lay the operation at CIA's doorstep had been headed off, and agreed to give him a second chance.

By this time, I was also convinced that the White House had fired Helms in order to put its own man in control at CIA, but as well to lay the foundation for claiming that the Watergate operation was a CIA operation, and now to be able to claim that "Helms had been fired for it." There had been indications as early as July that the Committee for the Re-Election of the President was claiming that the Watergate operation was a CIA operation. Mrs. Hunt had told me in late July 1972 that Paul O'Brien had told Howard Hunt in July that the Committee To Re-Elect the President had originally informed him that the Watergate operation was a CIA operation. Mrs. Hunt said that her husband had denied to O'Brien that it was a CIA operation. By early December 1972, it appeared that the White House was beginning to make its move. The events of December 21 and December 26, 1972, only confirmed this in my mind.

Further, based on an earlier discussion with Robert Mardian in May 1972, it appeared to me that the White House had for some time been trying to get political control over the CIA assessments and estimates, in order to make them conform to "White House policy." One of the things this meant to me was that this could mean that CIA estimates and assessments could then be forced to accord with DOD estimates of future U.S. weapons and hardware needs. This could be done by either shifting an intelligence function to DOD from CIA, or by gaining complete control over it at CIA.

Among other things, this also smacked of the situation which Hitler's intelligence chiefs found themselves in, in the 1930's and 1940's, when they were put in the position of having to tell him what they thought he wanted to hear about foreign military capabilities and intentions, instead of what they really believed, which ultimately was one of the things which led to Nazi Germany's downfall. When linked with what I saw happening to the FBI under Pat Gray—political control by the White House—it appeared then that the two Government agencies which should be able to prepare their reports, and to conduct their business, with complete integrity and honesty, in the national interest, were no longer going to be able to do so. That the Nation was in serious trouble has since been confirmed in my opinion by what happened in the case of Gray's leadership of the FBI.

E. Howard Hunt has additional information relevant to the above. Hunt stated to me on more than one occasion in the latter part of 1972, that he, Hunt, had information in his possession which "would be sufficient to impeach the President." In addition, Mrs. E. Howard Hunt, on or about November 30, 1972, in a personal conversation with me, stated that E. Howard Hunt's attorney, William O. Bittman, had read to Kenneth Parkinson, the attorney for the Committee To Re-Elect the President, in which letter, Hunt purportedly threatened "to blow the White House out of the water." Mrs. Hunt at this point in her conversation with me, also repeated the statement which she, too, had made before, which was that E. Howard Hunt had information which could impeach the President.

I regret that this memorandum has taken this length to set forth. In view of the nature of the information which I had to furnish, however, it appeared that there was no other way to adequately set this material forth, and to do so in the proper context, without deleting material highly relevant to the events being reported. I shall be glad to appear and answer questions under oath on the material which appears in this memorandum. It has my signature.

I have a further addition relevant to that in the statement which I could read at this time.

The topic of it is the December 1972 letter to John Caulfield. This letter is relevant to the May 4, 1973, memo submitted to Senate Watergate committee and the Federal grand jury, on the subject of pressure to place the blame on CIA for the Watergate operation.

A letter was written to John Caulfield during the week of December 25, 1972; reference to this letter appeared in the press the last weekend. And geared—speaking of my own feelings and at the time the letter was written—and geared because of what appeared to me to be a ruthless attempt by the White House to put the blame for the Watergate operation on CIA where it did not belong, I sought to head it off by sending a letter to Caulfield. This letter was couched in strong language because it seemed to me at the time that this was the only language that the White House understood. The letter read in substance as follows, to the best of my memory:

"Dear Jack: I am sorry to have to write you this letter. If Helms goes and the Watergate operation is laid at CIA's feet where it does not belong, every tree in the forest will fall. It will be a scorched desert. The whole matter is at the precipice right now. Pass the message that if they want it to blow, they are on exactly the right course. I am sorry that you will get hurt in the fallout."

The letter was unsigned and did not contain any message requesting any contact with Caulfield, nor any request for the White House to get me off in the case. I, in fact, sought no such contact at any time. If I had wanted to talk with Caulfield, it would not have been necessary to go through any complicated arrangements and a trip to William Bittman's office as occurred on January 8, 1973. I need only have made a phone call to Caulfield's office or home. At no time did I ever initiate any such call to Caulfield.

Now, the above letter to Caulfield brings to mind another set of communications of mine on December 6, 1972. On December 4, 1972, Judge Sirica had stated in open court that the jury in January 1973, would want to know who had hired the men for the Watergate operation and why.

On December 6, 1972, the Washington Star carried an article which appeared to me to be an administration-planted story answering Judge Sirica's query stating that "Reliable sources state that McCord recruited the four Cubans and that they believed that they were working for the President on an extremely sensitive mission." This was untrue.

This appeared to me to be laying the groundwork for a false claim at the trial that I was the "ringleader" of the Watergate plot. This would draw attention away from Hunt and Liddy, and I believe possibly away from the White House, since both of them had formerly worked at the White House and I had not.

That same evening December 6, 1972, I sent telegrams to William O. Bittman, attorney for Hunt, and Bernard Barker's residence in Miami, Fla., stating that the story was untrue as they both knew, and I asked for comments by return mail from Barker. I also wrote Hunt a letter on the matter stating that as he also knew, the story was untrue and he could either correct it or I would do so. Copies of the telegrams can probably be obtained from the Western Union Co.

With the letter to Caulfield in late December 1972, I was trying to head off an effort to falsely lay the Watergate operation off on CIA. In the telegrams and letter to Hunt and the others in December 1972, that I have just referred to, I was trying to head off an effort to falsely lay the recruitment of the Cubans off on the writer which would, in turn shift the focus of the trial off of those formerly connected with the White House, namely, Liddy and Hunt than from those who in effect had actually recruited them, namely Mr. Hunt.

I have some other memorandums in the statements that I have here to read, and I can answer your questions at this point or proceed to the reading of the statement, as you would prefer.

Senator BAKER. If it is agreeable with the chairman, Mr. McCord, I would prefer that you go ahead and read the material that you have.

Mr. McCORD. Newspapers over the weekend have also referred to some calls to some local embassies. I will try to explain those in the statement that I will read at this time.

In July 1972, Mrs. Hunt had told me that Paul O'Brien, attorney for CRP, had told her husband that when the Watergate case broke in June, the Committee for the Re-Election of the President told O'Brien that the Watergate operation was a CIA operation, I believe I referred to this in the earlier statement. She said that Howard Hunt had exploded at this and told O'Brien that this was not true; that it was not a CIA operation. A few days later Mrs. Hunt told me that the CRP lawyers were now reporting that the administration was going to allege at the trial that Liddy had stolen $16,000 and had bribed Hunt and McCord to perform the operation. I told her that it looked like they were now changing their cover stories, referring to the administration and I would not sit still for either false story, and I shortly wrote my attorney, Gerald Alch, repeating this information and setting forth these same views of mine.

In September 1972, the indictments came out and no one was being indicted among the higher ups, so there looked like a further coverup to me.

Also in September and October 1972, there began to be a series of telephone anomalies on my phone that indicated to me that the phone had been tapped. Further I had read in August 1972 in Newsweek magazine, I believe that Ellsberg had tried for 5 months to get the Government to admit wiretapping of his phone calls, and those of his attorney and the Government denied such calls until a court order forced a search of 12 separate law enforcement agencies and turned up telephone interception of Leonard Boudin's calls to the Chilean Embassy.

I knew that the Government had also lied about wiretapping in the *Coplon* case and in the *Hoffa* case for several weeks until disclosure was forced from them. In an effort to test the truthfulness of the Government on a forthcoming motion for disclosure of wiretapping of the defendants' phones in the Watergate case, including my own, I made two calls in September and October 1972 to two local embassies. On October 10, 1972, I asked for the filing of a motion for Government disclosure of any interceptions and 2 weeks later the Government came back with a denial of any, saying a search of Government records had been made. I knew that 2 weeks was too short a time to search 12 different Government agencies for such records, and believed the Government was not telling the truth.

In January 1973, after Caulfield had initiated contact with me, I advised him of the perjury of Jeb Magruder and of the two telephone calls I have just referred to, plus the other indications to me of illegal interception of my phone calls, and asked Jack to check into both. He came back a few days later and said that the Government had found nothing on the phone calls. He did not say what he had done about the information of perjury by Magruder.

In January I also asked my attorney to renew the motion for discovery of interception of my calls so there could be such a motion on the record and I believe he did so on January 17, 1973. I knew that the two embassy calls would be insufficient to overturn the case, because all that would happen would be for the Government to take the information to the bench and for the judge to declare the information not relevant.

Furthermore the Government would state that the information would not be used against me in evidence anyway. I did believe that such disclosure would be a way of testing the truthfulness of the Government regarding such illegal interceptions and I was greatly concerned that there had been other illegal interceptions of my telephone conversations and those of the other defendants beginning June 17, 1972.

Further, I did believe that if sufficient illegal interceptions of my phone calls had occurred such would have a bearing on my case. I still believe there was such an interception just as Dr. Ellsberg believed that his own phone calls had been intercepted.

There is an attachment to this, the New York Times of today's date. The title of the article "Warning Against Blaming of CIA Laid to McCord."

Continuing on a separate subject in a statement, if that is your desire.

Senator BAKER. Yes, sir.

Mr. McCORD. The topic of this memorandum is "Sanction of the Watergate Operation."

John Mitchell, by virtue of his position as Attorney General of the United States, and John Dean, by virtue of his position as counsel to the President, by their consideration and approval of the Watergate operation, in my opinion, gave sanction to the Watergate operation by both the White House and the Attorney General's offices.

I had been accustomed to working in an atmosphere where such sanction by the White House and the Attorney General was more than enough. As with White House staffers, it was not my habit to question when two such high offices sanctioned an activity—it carried the full force and effect of Presidential sanction.

For the preceding 30 years I had been working in an environment where if there were ever any question of the legality of a matter or an activity it would always be sent to high legal officials for a legal decision on the matter, where if they sanctioned it, that was sufficient.

I can elaborate on this another way. Left alone, I would not have undertaken the operation. I had plenty of other things to do in connection with my security work at the Committee To Re-Elect the President. Liddy wanted help. He came to me seeking that help with the word that it had the approval of the Attorney General and the counsel to the President. He said that it was part of the CRP mission, in order to obtain information regarding not only political intelligence but also regarding violence-oriented groups who would be planning violence against the committee in Washington, and later at the August convention site, thereby endangering the lives and property of the committee and its personnel. My mission was protection of such lives and property. Uppermost in everyone's minds, at that point in time and certainly in mine, was the bloodshed which had occurred at the 1968 Democratic National Convention in Chicago, and I constantly sought intelligence from any source which might help forewarn us and help us avoid in 1972 that danger to the lives of our people.

The right to demonstrate, or the right of peaceful assembly is a right guaranteed by the Constitution. I took absolutely no issue with that. It was the 2 percent to 3 percent of the demonstrators who focused on violence, damage to life and property, that concerned me. In 1969 we had seen the bombing of the Capitol Building itself. In May 1972 we had seen the bombing of the Pentagon with the equivalent of 18 sticks of dynamite. In February 1972 there were four pipe bombs emplaced at a police station in Manchester, N.H., one of which went off prematurely, and mangled the arm of the young man who had reportedly emplaced them. Caught with him was a young lady who had in her possession four letters which said, "we have just bombed the offices of the Committee To Re-Elect the President in New Hampshire." Found in her apartment were the makings of other pipe bombs. It was clear to me and to others that the intentions of the two were to go on from the police station and drop off other bombs at the CRP offices in Manchester, where there had been demonstration and trouble a few days before.

Only their arrest preempted that action. A few days later in Oakland, Calif., another pipe bomb was emplaced on the first floor of the Republican county headquarters and blew out all of the windows and damaged a pillar to the building. Luckily no one was injured or killed. Already in February there was a pattern then of bombings beginning to develop against the committee and against Republican offices.

Subsequently, in Austin, Tex., the offices of Senator Tower were destroyed by a firebomb which, I believe, as I recall did a million dollars worth of damage and destroyed irreplaceable files. So the concern was not of a theoretical threat, but of a realistic threat of violence, and I wanted advance notice from anywhere I could receive it, of action planned against us of this sort—advance notice, advance warning, so we could take measures to protect against it and protect our people's lives. Property could be replaced. Lives could not.

Questions were on my mind like: Who are these people who bombed in New Hampshire, in Oakland, the Pentagon Building, the Capitol Building? How are they funded? Who are they working with? Is anyone in collusion with them, encouraging them, or funding them? The Vietnam Veterans Against the War was one violence-oriented group that was already saying in the spring of 1972, that they were going to cause destruction to life and property at the August Republican Convention, using in their own words, their own bodies and weapons as the spearhead of the attack there—these are their exact words, and some of them have since been indicted in Tallahassee, Fla., with additional plans to damage the life and property in the convention.

Later in the summer of 1972 the VVAW did in fact have offices in the DNC in Washington, as I understand. I had also received information from the Internal Security Division in May 1972, that some individuals in Florida planned to forge college press credentials to get into both the Democratic and Republican Convention sites, and blow up the communication centers of both parties there and cause havoc on the convention floor. That information was part of the basis for my going to Miami in June 1972, with members of the White House staff to survey and strengthen the security of the Doral Hotel where both the White House staff and the CRP staff were to have both offices and quarters for July and August 1972. Some 30 recommendations were made as a result of that survey, to help protect against such violence, and I believe that most were put into effect before the convention.

Now, we also had word from CRP sources alleging that the McGovern committee had "a pipeline" directly into the offices of the Committee To Re-Elect the President in Washington; allegedly, they were feeding out, on a regular basis, policy position papers, that is, plans and strategy, which were rather important to the success of a candidate's campaign. If the other side is reading your poker hand, he can negate your plans.

We had word that one of the volunteers at the Committee To Re-Elect the President had in fact prior to coming aboard the committee, threatened the life of John Mitchell and of other persons. This was at about the same time Governor Wallace was almost killed in an assassination attempt. There were numerous threats in writing and by phone against John Mitchell and his wife. One such call came to the unlisted telephone of Mrs. Mitchell at their apartment and got her greatly upset, as it would any woman, because it appeared that even the unlisted telephone number appeared then no longer safe.

We certainly had sufficient indications that violence-oriented groups were out to endanger both life and property. With some 250,000 demonstrators planning to go to the convention in early 1972 and there were statements that some would be out to commit violence. The questions were: Who are such people? Who is funding them—encouraging them? Who is in collusion with them? What are they planning next and where? Are any of them being supported and encouraged by any staff members of the McGovern committee or DNC? I had no indication whatever that Larry O'Brien or Senator McGovern had either any knowledge of or part in such—just the contrary, I was completely convinced that they did not. But I was not so sure that, without their knowledge, other staff members might not be working behind their backs to quietly encourage groups such as VVAW.

McGovern's early political base was with some of the radical groups. My questions were, What was the extent of such encouragement, if any, and how far did it go? Did they let such groups use their telephones and work in their offices? There were indications in the summer of 1972 that such groups actually did just that in California and in DNC headquarters, in Washington. These then were some of my concerns, in my role as security chief of the CRP; I felt that the Watergate operation might produce some leads answering some of these questions, and I had been advised that the operation had the sanction of the White House and of the Attorney General, while he was Attorney General.

In hindsight, I do not believe that the operation should have been sanctioned or executed, nor should I have participated. However, you asked me about some of my previous motivations and what some of the atmosphere was in Miami. Those are some of the things that make up my atmosphere and some of my motivations.

My next statement has to do with the Intelligence Advisory Committee I previously referred to in the CIA memorandum, which I referred to Mr. Robert Mardian.

In May 1972, Robert Mardian had told me that he, John Mitchell, Robert Haldeman and John Ehrlichman were key members of an "Intelligence Advisory Committee." I now assume that this was the Intelligence Evaluation Committee, referred to, I believe, in the New York Times of May 21, 1973.

I have previously submitted a tape to the Senate Watergate committee which I believe contains material which was the product of that committee, and which I obtained from the evaluation section of the Internal Security Division of the Department of Justice, a contact established through Mr. Robert Mardian, in May 1972.

I have no knowledge of the sources of that committee.

Robert Mardian, during a brief conversation in June 1972, stated that he was going to be "in charge of intelligence operations at Miami during the convention." He did not elaborate further.

The next item is headed "Las Vegas Matter," which was referred to in the previous testimony on Friday.

In January or February 1972, Gordon Liddy told me that he was going out to Las Vegas, Nev., in connection with casing the office of Hank Greenspun, editor of the Las Vegas Sun.

Liddy said that Attorney General John Mitchell had told him that Greenspun had in his possession blackmail type information involving a Democratic candidate for President, that Mitchell wanted that material, and Liddy said that this information was in some way racketeer-related, indicating that if this candidate became President, the racketeers or national crime syndicate could have a control or influence over him as President. My inclination at this point in time, speaking of today is to disbelieve the allegation against the Democratic candidate referred to above and to believe that there was in reality some other motive for wanting to get into Greenspun's safe.

Liddy told me one day in February 1972 that he was going out to Las Vegas, and might need my help if there was an alarm system in the offices, when an entry operation was mounted to enter a safe in Greenspun's offices to get the information. A few days later Liddy told me that he had been to Las Vegas and looked over the offices and that there was no such alarm system, and my services were not needed.

Subsequently in about April or May 1972, Liddy told me that he had again been to Las Vegas for another casing of Greenspun's offices. Liddy said that there were then plans for an entry operation to get into Greenspun's safe. He went on to say that after the entry team finishes its work, they would go directly to an airport near Las Vegas where a Howard Hughes plane would be standing by to fly the team directly into a Central American country so that the team would be out of the country before the break-in was discovered.

Around the same time Liddy made this last statement to me about the Howard Hughes plane, Hunt told me in his office one day that he was in touch with the Howard Hughes company and that they might be needing my security services after the election. He said that they had quite a wide investigative and security operation and asked me for my business card and asked if I would be interested. I said I would like to know more about what was involved, gave him a card, but never heard from him again on this subject. However, I did read in the newspapers after July 1, 1972 that Hunt had apparently handled a Howard Hughes campaign donation to the Committee To Re-Elect the President sometime in 1972. Gordon Liddy told me in February 1972 that he, too, had handled a Howard Hughes campaign check, a donation to the 1972 campaign. This is the extent of my knowledge on this matter.

That completes my prepared statement and I will be glad to answer any questions.

Senator BAKER. Mr. Chairman, thank you very much.

Mr. McCord, I am very grateful, I think you supplied a great deal of additional information and it raises a great number of new questions and I am sure my colleagues on the committee will want to pursue that or other questions, so I will not detain you long in this first series of questions.

I think that your further elaboration and extension of your state of mind or motives in the several operations and especially the Watergate operation now appears more clear, at least to me.

Let me try to paraphrase the essence of your motivation, if I may, and if I am wrong for goodness sakes tell me so, but I want to know if this is the general message that you are giving us.

One, you had a long background of experience with Government agencies, the FBI and the CIA. You had become accustomed to activities related to sensitive matters, security matters, and to taking direction and accepting at face value the representations of the orders or the purported orders of very high officials in the Government, particularly the Justice Department and the White House.

That for a variety of reasons, when you were called on to enter the Democratic National headquarters in Washington at the Watergate complex, for a variety of reasons, including your general knowledge of threats against Attorney General Mitchell and his family, threats against others, pipe bombings, fire bombings, threats of violence and the like, coupled with your concern for national security matters, if that is the proper way to characterize it, that you decided on the assumption that your authority was complete, that you no longer need to concern yourself with the legality of it, that based on this information that you had, and based on the assurances which were forthcoming, that it seemed appropriate that you would undertake that entry. Is that a fair statement of your general motivation at the time?

Mr. McCORD. I would think so, yes, sir.

Senator BAKER. Mr. McCord, did you have any motivation to enter the Democratic National Committee for political purposes as distinguished from security purposes? It is not important in terms of the facts and the proof but it is important in terms of your state of mind.

Mr. McCORD. Let me answer it in a couple of sentences, if I may. I was fully aware that others had such motivations. My own motivations I have stated here. I had a role to play in the sense of an electronic component of the team and I played that role.

Senator BAKER. Mr. McCord, speaking of electronic surveillance, do you know of or did you ever investigate the bugging of Republican headquarters of the Committee for the Re-Election of the President headquarters here, New York, or elsewhere?

Mr. McCORD. Yes, sir.

Senator BAKER. Would you describe that for the committee?

Mr. McCORD. It was a regular ongoing activity at the offices in Washington and at the New York arm of the Committee for the Re-Election of the President, which was referred to as the November Group; they had offices, I believe, on Park Avenue in New York. It was done on a regular basis. It was done frequently at the end of the day or the beginning of the day or during sensitive conferences that were going on, in order to determine if in fact there was any activity of this sort happening against the Committee for the Re-Election of the President.

Senator BAKER. Did you discover any incident of that sort?

Mr. McCORD. There was one incident on June 16 of some concern at the New York office of the Committee for the Re-Election of the President. There had been earlier signs of possibly some illegal activity

96-296—73—bk. 1——14

at those offices prior to June 16, which I would describe, if you would like.

Senator BAKER. I would like.

Mr. McCORD. On the afternoon of June 16, 1972, about mid-afternoon, I received a call from the head of the office of the November Group in New York City, who stated that he and his entire office staff were quite concerned about an incident that had just occurred. He went ahead to relate that one of the secretaries at the office had received a call from a male individual in Los Angeles, Calif., and that she had immediately told that party that she would call him back on the WATS line, which is a leased line, call him back on that line and immediately did so. She called him, as I recall, at the Beverley Wilshire Hotel, although I cannot be absolutely certain, at the phone booth there. And during the conversation that the two of them had, about a few minutes into the conversation there was a click over the phone which was heard by her and by the male on the other end of the line, and what appeared to be a tape recording was played over the telephone line which was, as she described it when I talked with her, an anti-Nixon and antiwar harangue.

Senator BAKER. Mr. McCord, could I interrupt you for a moment?

Mr. McCORD. Yes, sir.

Senator BAKER. I understand this to be a call that was initiated from New York on a WATS line; that is, a flat rate monthly telephone line all over the country?

Mr. McCORD. Yes, sir.

Senator BAKER. To a number in California?

Mr. McCORD. Yes, sir.

Senator BAKER. Can you say whether or not the situation you described does in fact constitute a tapping or an intrusion into that circuit by someone unauthorized?

Mr. McCORD. It clearly appeared to be. I had not the slightest doubt about it, and neither did the telephone company in New York when I called them that afternoon.

Senator BAKER. Did you ever locate the source of that tap?

Mr. McCORD. I can relate what we did, what incidents occurred.

Senator BAKER. Would you do that for me?

Mr. McCORD. I immediately called, after we heard of this, to the chief security officer in the New York Telephone Co. He had previously been contacted by the November Group offices, stated that they were working on the matter trying to trace the point of interception of the call, along the numerous points of access to the telephone line within or beyond the November Group offices themselves. That that investigation was to continue throughout the weekend and that reports would be forthcoming as to what they had learned about it. There appeared to be no doubt from what he was saying that they also considered it an illegal interception of telephone conversation.

Senator BAKER. Were there other incidents of telephone tapping against the Republican National Committee or the CRP or any other Republican-affiliated group brought to your attention or which you investigated?

Mr. McCORD. There were two earlier occasions at the November Group offices when I was called to the November Group offices from Washington in which they had highly suspicious telephone anomalies, as it is known. Telephone conversations within the office itself of when another person picking up a telephone extension on a different line, for example, not connected with the one in which the call was being made, could overhear the conversation that was going on. Other strange anomalies, clicks and so on of a wide variety that indicated some problems in the telephone area. They had, in turn, contacted the telephone company. The telephone company had made a search, made a search of the offices itself, of the phone system, so they stated, and I did further checking of my own at that point in time of both of the two previous events, and we found nothing within the telephone system within the offices itself. That did not eliminate the possibility that beyond the office anywhere within the system at which there were points of access to the telephone lines that someone might not have been monitoring the conversation.

Senator BAKER. Mr. McCord, I am not trying to create the impression that because there were apparently taps on the Republican phones, that that justifies taps on the Democratic phones. I do not believe that, but I am anxious to know your state of mind and the reason and rationale for your security operations, including the break-in into the Watergate.

Now, my final question in that respect is, did you ever discover the source or responsibility for any of these efforts at electronic interception on the Republican operations?

Mr. McCORD. No, sir. Specifically, the November Group, we did not know that it was continuing after June 16, and I did not, never received the results of that inquiry.

Senator BAKER. Did you once work for the Republican National Committee, Mr. McCord?

Mr. McCORD. Yes, I did during the same period I was with the Committee for the Re-Election of the President, which I previously mentioned to your committee.

Senator BAKER. Yes, sir. Can you give us the dates and circumstances and the nature of your employment?

Mr. McCORD. Yes. I was employed by them as a part-time consultant during the period of roughly October 1, 1971, concurrent with that of the Committee for the Re-Election of the President, and extending through June 17.

Senator BAKER. June 17, 1972?

Mr. McCORD. That is correct, June 17.

Senator BAKER. Can you tell us who employed you?

Mr. McCORD. Yes. The director of administration at the Republican National Committee.

Senator BAKER. Do you know who that was?

Mr. McCORD. Barry Mountain, M-o-u-n-t-a-i-n.

Senator BAKER. Was he the only one you talked about employment?

Mr. McCORD. I talked to others there but he was my principal point of contact.

Senator BAKER. Did you ever talk to the chairman of the RNC about your employment?

Mr. McCORD. I talked to the cochairman, Mr. Tom Bevens. I do not believe I had any contact—I talked to both cochairmen, I do not believe I had any contact beyond that.

Senator BAKER. Who was chairman at that time?

Mr. McCORD. I believe Senator Robert Dole.
Senator BAKER. Did you ever talk to him?
Mr. McCORD. No, sir.
Senator BAKER. Was there ever any clandestine, covert, illegal, improper, or unethical conduct involved in your security operations for the Republican National Committee?
Mr. McCORD. Absolutely none whatever.
Senator BAKER. I have a number of other questions, Mr. Chairman, but I have taken more than my time. I would ask if I may, a single last question and then I will yield to my colleagues.
You recognize the term Gemstone?
Mr. McCORD. Yes, sir.
Senator BAKER. Can you describe for us what it means?
Mr. McCORD. That term I first heard, first read about in the newspaper itself referring to, according to the newspaper accounts, referring to it as a code name for the monitoring, the typing of final monitoring logs of report or logs coming out of the National Democratic Committee. I did not as such know it during the operation but I know something about the nature of the paper that it was on. I think that code name had some reference to that.
Senator BAKER. Is it fair to say the term Gemstone is a code name that covers work product in the accumulation of information of yourself and your teams' efforts in the intrusion of the Democratic National Committee headquarters at the Watergate?
Mr. McCORD. So I have been led to understand.
Senator BAKER. Do you have tape recordings of your interceptions of the Democratic National Committee?
Mr. McCORD, No, sir.
Senator BAKER. Or do you have photographs or any other information that was gained by this entry?
Mr. McCORD. There is no tape recordings, there are no photographs, I can think of nothing else at the moment.
Senator BAKER. Are there any tape recordings of the telephone conversations?
Mr. McCORD. No, sir, none were ever made.
Senator BAKER. Where is the information that you gained? Is it in the Gemstone file? Does the U.S. Attorney's office have it? Where is it?
Mr. McCORD. The material which I had received from—Mr. Baldwin was doing the monitoring, Alfred Baldwin—was turned over, all of it, to Mr. Liddy, Gordon Liddy.
Senator BAKER. Thank you very much, Mr. McCord. I am very grateful. I think you responded in a very thorough and very eloquent way to the question I put on Friday and I am very grateful to you.
Senator ERVIN. Senator Talmadge?
Senator TALMADGE. Mr. McCord, among other things in your testimony this morning, you stated that many efforts were made to persuade you or to coerce you to state that the bugging operation on the Democratic National Committee was a CIA operation.
Will you state the individuals who urged you to do that? One you stated was Mr. Hunt. Am I correct?
Mr. McCORD. Sir, I believe I will correct that impression if I left it. I had heard from Mr. Bernard Barker specifically that Mr. Hunt had brought pressure to bear upon Mr. Barker and the Cubans to

use as their defense that this was a CIA operation. Mr. Hunt did not directly put that pressure upon me. Others did.

Senator TALMADGE. Barker reported to you that Hunt had urged you to do so, is that correct?

Mr. MCCORD. That is right.

Senator TALMADGE. Barker, as I understand it was one of the people involved in the Watergate operation, was he not?

Mr. MCCORD. Yes, sir.

Senator TALMADGE. Barker, I believe, has been granted immunity and has not been convicted. Is that correct?

He pled guilty and was convicted?

Mr. MCCORD. Yes, sir.

Senator TALMADGE. Now, who else besides Barker was involved in urging you to blame this on the CIA? You stated two other names. I think one of them was Bittman and the other one was named Alch?

Mr. MCCORD. Yes, sir, I referred to conversations with Mr. Gerald Alch and Mrs. Hunt.

Senator TALMADGE. Tell me who Mr. Alch is. Give me his full name.

Mr. MCCORD. Gerald, G-e-r-a-l-d, Alch, A-l-c-h.

Senator Talmadge. Now, who is Mr. Alch?

Mr. MCCORD. He was my defense attorney through the trial in January 1973, whose services I had engaged at that time.

Senator TALMADGE. And he had no connection with the Committee To Re-Elect the President, did he? He was your own lawyer?

Mr. MCCORD. Yes, sir.

Senator TALMADGE. And he urged you to blame it on the CIA, did he?

Mr. MCCORD. He urged me to use that as my defense.

Senator TALMADGE. All right, now. Mr. Alch and who else urged you to do that?

Mr. MCCORD. I believe I have stated in my testimony that stories were circulating earlier stemming out of the Committee for the Re-Election of the President that the committee lawyers themselves had been told that early in July——

Senator TALMADGE. Let's get specific now. I don't want stories circulating. I want you to name the days, names, and places. That is evidence. Rumors are not.

Mr. MCCORD. Yes, sir.

The details as I have related them in the memorandum which I have read this morning on the topic of the CIA, pressure to lay it at the feet of the CIA, covers the full extent of my knowledge, sir, of any pressure upon me and it came principally through the attorney himself. So insofar as I personally was involved, that was the source.

Senator TALMADGE. All right, now. You have named Mr. Barker.

Mr. MCCORD. That is right, sir.

Senator TALMADGE. And you have named Mr. Alch?

Mr. MCCORD. Yes, sir.

Senator TALMADGE. Who was your own lawyer?

Mr. MCCORD. Yes, sir.

Senator TALMADGE. And I believe in your own testimony in chief, the memorandum you read, you also referred to a man by the name of Bittman, did you not?

Mr. MCCORD. Yes, sir.

Senator TALMADGE. Now, who is Mr. Bittman?

Mr. McCORD. Bittman is the attorney, William O. Bittman, the attorney for E. Howard Hunt, one of the other defendants.

Senator TALMADGE. All right, did he have any connection with the Government in any way or any connection with the Republican National Committee or the Committee To Re-Elect the President?

Mr. McCORD. Not to my knowledge, sir.

Senator TALMADGE. What I am trying to get at is the source of this pressure that you have contended was brought upon you to blame this on the CIA. Thus far, you have not connected that either with the Committee To Re-Elect the President or the White House or any other individuals, to my knowledge. One was your own lawyer, one was engaged in the crime with you, and the third one was the lawyer for Mr. Liddy, was it—Bittman?

Mr. McCORD. Mr. Hunt.

Senator TALMADGE. Mr. Hunt?

Mr. McCORD. Yes, sir.

Senator TALMADGE. He was Mr. Hunt's lawyer. And those three individuals are the only ones that urged you to blame this on the CIA. Is that a fair statement?

Mr. McCORD. Yes, sir; that is essentially correct.

Senator TALMADGE. So no one else anywhere whatever urged you to blame it on the CIA except these three individuals, is that correct?

Mr. McCORD. None that I can recall at this time, no, sir.

Senator TALMADGE. Now, did Mr. Barker or the other of the so-called Cuban-Americans ever come to you during the trial and tell you that they had been offered Executive clemency by Mr. Hunt?

Mr. McCORD. Yes, sir.

Senator TALMADGE. Will you describe the attitude and the demeanor at that time?

Mr. McCORD. Yes, sir. Mr. Barker specifically—I can recall specifically during the first week of the trial and beginning on the first day, on January 8, Mr. Barker came to me in the corridor outside, I believe, the courtroom of the U.S. District Court Building in Washington during breaks in the court proceedings and proceeded to relate to me the pressure which he said was being imposed upon him and upon the other men who were defendants—Mr. Sturgis, Mr. Gonzales, Mr. Martinez, pressure that he stated was stemming from Mr. Hunt and other unnamed individuals, to plead guilty and to go off to jail or prison and ultimately to receive Executive clemency and to receive financial support for their families while they were in prison and promises—and he stated promises were made that they would be given help in obtaining a job or rehabilitation at the prison. Mr. Barker spoke to me several times during that week regarding that particular pressure upon him which he described as intense.

He stated first that he was planning not to plead guilty and then subsequently, as the days progressed during the week itself, he began to tell me that he was thinking more and more seriously about it, and as I recall, about Wednesday of that week, roughly, in that week sometime, he seemed to have his mind made up that he would go ahead and accede to the pressure and plead guilty, and he put it in, in just about those words, and to accept the Executive clemency.

He was in a pretty highly emotional state at one point in time, the first day or two, stating that he was fighting the pressure as best he was able and it was clear from his demeanor that he was very worked up and very emotionally overwrought, split between what he was being forced to do and what he felt perhaps he ought to do in going ahead to proceed with the case and to see if he could get a fair trial.

He was not the only one. His family, his wife, and his daughter, related the same pressure to me, sometimes in his presence.

Senator TALMADGE. Did any of the other so-called Cuban-Americans besides Mr. Barker relate similar pressure?

Mr. McCORD. Yes, sir, all of them.

Senator TALMADGE. Every one of them?

Mr. McCORD. Yes, sir.

Senator TALMADGE. Now, did Mr. Hunt or Mrs. Hunt ever give you any information that they were sent to you by the Committee To Re-Elect the President or the White House or anybody to do this?

Mr. McCORD. Executive clemency?

Senator TALMADGE. Yes.

Mr. McCORD. Yes, sir.

Senator TALMADGE. Will you relate that?

Mr. McCORD. Yes, sir; during the meetings, personal meetings and telephone meetings beginning in July 1972 concerning money beginning in about October 1972, concerning Executive clemency—the term "Executive clemency" I first heard, I believe, from Mr. Hunt in early October—late September or early October—when I would see him at the courtroom or when he would call me by telephone. Thereafter, he subsequently mentioned it in almost every call. His wife referred to it. In substance, what they were saying was that the defendants were being promised Executive clemency if they went off to prison and had to serve time. Sometimes the words "Executive clemency" would be followed or accompanied by other statements about financial support and rehabilitation.

Senator TALMADGE. Did Mrs. Hunt state who gave her authority to make such a promise?

Mr. McCORD. My recollection of her conversations were that she was saying that she was transmitting this word to me from her husband. She did not specifically mention that I can recall now who gave it to him. I can draw only one conclusion as to where it came from, because——

Senator TALMADGE. She did not state the source of her authority to make that promise, though?

Mr. McCORD. I can't recall such statements on her part.

Senator TALMADGE. Who did she say she was in communication with?

Mr. McCORD. With the attorneys for the Committee To Re-Elect the President, the attorneys for the committee.

Senator TALMADGE. Who specifically? More than one individual is involved with the committee. I want you to name specific names if you know.

Mr. McCORD. I can tell you what she stated, sir, if this is what you want.

Senator TALMADGE. Tell me what she stated. This is the question I asked you.

Mr. McCORD. Yes sir. She stated that she herself was in communication with Mr. Kenneth Parkinson, one of the attorneys for the Committee To Re-Elect the President. She stated that her husband, Mr. Hunt, had been in touch in July with Mr. Paul O'Brien, also an attorney with Mr. Parkinson for the Committee To Re-Elect the President.

Senator TALMADGE. Mrs. Hunt, I believe, was the intermediary that transmitted money to you?

Mr. McCORD. She was, sir.

Senator TALMADGE. How much did she transmit, all told?

Mr. McCORD. $46,000, as I recall, of which about half was attorneys' fees.

Senator TALMADGE. $46,000?

Mr. McCORD. Yes sir.

Senator TALMADGE. Of which about half was to be used to pay your attorney's fees?

Mr. McCORD. $25,000, yes sir.

Senator TALMADGE. And the other was to be used to pay your salary?

Mr. McCORD. Yes sir.

Senator TALMADGE. And your salary was $3,000 a month, I remember?

Mr. McCORD. Yes sir.

Senator TALMADGE. All paid in brand-new $100 bills, is that true?

Mr. McCORD. Most of it, sir.

Senator TALMAGDE. Any of it in checks?

Mr. McCORD. No sir.

Senator TALMADGE. All in cash?

Mr. McCORD. Yes, sir.

Senator TALMADGE. Can you state why they paid in cash and not by checks?

Mr. McCORD. No, sir.

Senator TALMADGE. Did you not think that was an unusual method of payment?

Mr. McCORD. Yes, sir.

Senator TALMADGE. Did it cause you to wonder about the circumstances of that involvement?

Mr. McCORD. Yes, sir.

Senator TALMADGE. And how long did your salary continue to be paid? When was the last time you received the $100 bills in payment of your salary of $3,000 a month?

Mr. McCORD. The last payment was December 2 and it was a payment for December through January.

Senator TALMADGE. In other words, you have been paid through January and not since that time?

Mr. McCORD. That is correct, sir.

Senator TALMADGE. My time has expired, has it, Mr. Chairman? I do not want to usurp the time of others.

Senator ERVIN. You used 13 minutes.

Senator TALMADGE. Then I yield at this point to my colleague.

Senator ERVIN. Senator Gurney?

Senator GURNEY. Thank you, Mr. Chairman.

Mr. McCord, one or two other questions about Mr. Barker. What was your relationship with Mr. Barker in the Watergate affair?

Mr. McCord. My relationship, again, about a week, 4 or 5 days, perhaps, before Memorial Day weekend, in which I first met him and he was described to me as the team captain for the group going into the Democratic National Committee. My relationship with him was as a member of the team that went in.

Senator Gurney. Was he in charge or were you in charge?

Mr. McCord. He was in charge, sir.

Senator Gurney. Did you see him much after that?

Mr. McCord. I saw him during that Memorial Day weekend. I saw him on the first meeting at the Manger-Hamilton Hotel about May 24, when I first met him. I saw him the June 17 weekend. I saw him occasionally at the courthouse in the fall of 1972, when we would be there for hearings. I saw him, of course, during the trial period that I have referred to in my testimony today.

Senator Gurney. Did you see him at all between the time of the break-in incident and when you went to court?

Mr. McCord. Yes, sir, I was in, during the first week, first 4 or 5 days after we were arrested, we were in the same accommodations in the D.C. jail.

Senator Gurney. What kind of man would you say he was—was he dependable?

Mr. McCord. I liked Mr. Barker.

Senator Gurney. So you would say he was a man of reliability and dependability?

Mr. McCord. In the things I did with him and worked with him, he was a reliable person.

Senator Gurney. When you had these discussions with him on the pressure on him to plead guilty and take advantage of this Executive clemency—and how many occasions did you and he discuss that?

Mr. McCord. It began on or about January 8 and continued for that first week, during the first week of the trial, most of the days in the trial—most of the first week. So it was roughly a week that these conversations would occur.

Senator Gurney. And they occurred every day, would you say?

Mr. McCord. I know that they occurred—my recollection is that they occurred each of the first 3 days of the trial and that something was said about them the following 2 days, Thursday or Friday. I can't recall specifically what, because I believe his mind was pretty well made up at that time. I do not think there was too much discussion after the first days.

Senator Gurney. What were his reasons for discussing this with you, to seek your advice or to ask you if you were receiving pressure too, or how did the conversation come up?

Mr. McCord. It was generally in the sense, "We were receiving this pressure, I am torn up in trying to decide what to do. What are you planning to do," and some advice was sought and what I thought about acceding to the pressure.

Senator Gurney. In other words, they were rather extensive and serious discussions; is that correct?

Mr. McCord. They would run, I would say, 5 to 10 minutes, maybe 15 during court breaks primarily.

Senator Gurney. Well, who did Mr. Barker say to you was applying the pressure to him?

Mr. McCord. My recollection is that he stated Mr. Hunt. He also referred to other unnamed persons and I do not know who they were.
Senator Gurney. Well, you mean he said, "There are other unnamed persons whom I do not know who are applying pressure to me," and he said there were some other people and that is all I heard. What were these other people doing?
Mr. McCord. Applying pressure, so he stated.
Senator Gurney. Well, were they talking to him?
Mr. McCord. So he said.
Senator Gurney. Where were they talking to him?
Mr. McCord. I do not know. He did not say.
Senator Gurney. Were they calling him on the phone?
Mr. McCord. He did not state, sir.
Senator Gurney. Now, during this time, I guess you were out of jail on bail, both you and Barker; is that true?
Mr. McCord. Yes, sir.
Senator Gurney. Do you know where he was living at this time?
Mr. McCord. I believe in Miami, most of the time. He was in Washington sometimes for court appearances.
Senator Gurney. But no other name was mentioned in these conversations except the name of Mr. Hunt?
Mr. McCord. Yes, sir, that is correct.
Senator Gurney. Did you ever ask him who was applying this pressure besides Mr. Hunt?
Mr. McCord. No, sir.
Senator Gurney. Weren't you curious?
Mr. McCord. I was curious but I assume quite frankly that it was someone closely connected with Hunt, somebody that Hunt was obviously very closely associated with, perhaps somebody that Barker and Hunt had known together, I do not—I did not pursue it beyond that point. My primary concern was with the fact that Mr. Hunt was doing it, and I expressed some views on that.
Senator Gurney. Now then, you mentioned also that pressure was being applied to the others who were apprehended in the Watergate, the four people Sturgis, Martinez, Gonzales; is that their names?
Mr. McCord. Yes, sir.
Senator Gurney. And then one other whose name has slipped me for the moment. Did they ever tell you who was applying pressure to them?
Mr. McCord. My recollection is that they stated Mr. Hunt. There was some, I have a vague recollection that the names of, it was put in the same context that Mr. Barker did that others were doing so. That is a very vague recollection. I can be sure only about the name of Mr. Hunt.
Senator Gurney. Well now, let's take them one by one. When and where did Martinez say to you that pressure was being applied to him?
Mr. McCord. In the corridors of the, I believe it is called the, outside the, Ceremonial Court Room of the District Court Building in Washington, D.C., to the best of my recollection on at least each of the first 4 days of the trial beginning on January 8, during breaks in the court session.
Senator Gurney. And in these conversations what names did Martinez mention?

Mr. McCord. Mr. Hunt.

Senator Gurney. Did he mention any others?

Mr. McCord. No, sir.

Senator Gurney. Did you ask him about any others?

Mr. McCord. No, sir.

Senator Gurney. What about Sturgis?

Mr. McCord. If I may explain usually Mr. Martinez and Mr. Gonzales were together during these conversations and the conversations were in the form of something like a three-way discussion between me, Mr. Martinez, and Mr. Gonzales. Mr. Sturgis, I would say, mentioned it to me perhaps at the most once or twice that week. The others mentioned it, I would say, the first 4 days of the first week of the trial.

Senator Gurney. But none of these men ever mentioned any other name other than Mr. Hunt?

Mr. McCord. No, sir.

Senator Gurney. And none of them ever either mentioned or speculated who was giving Hunt the authority to apply this political pressure or offer of Executive clemency to all of you?

Mr. McCord. No, sir. There, the focus of their concern was, it was in terms of what should they be really doing about it and what concern they had if they did not do it or if they turned it down what would be their future, what was going to happen during the trial, so there wasn't much at all in the way of who was doing it and where it came from. Our general context of our discussion was that everybody understood that there was only one place that Executive clemency can stem from so nobody had any reason for discussing it.

Senator Gurney. Yes, I would understand that, too, but of course this would be a very important matter.

Mr. McCord. I understand.

Senator Gurney. Pleading guilty and then serving a prison term and then of course being able to get out of the prison term by a pardon and I am curious that no one thought to inquire where this was coming from other than from Mr. Hunt.

Mr. McCord. Yes, sir.

Senator Gurney. But no one ever did?

Mr. McCord. Well, they may well have done so.

Senator Gurney. But they did not mention it to you?

Mr. McCord. They did not mention it to me.

Senator Gurney. You mentioned in the statement about the CIA, at least the statements were certainly very shocking. They involve a new man coming on board the CIA, a change from Mr. Helms to another man and the fact that the new man could be, could work with and dealt with and your records might have been able to have been doctored all in this so-called CIA coverup. Would you go into that at more length? Where did you get this information?

Mr. McCord. What I transmitted to you, sir, and this is the source of it, were the words as I best recall it transmitted to me, communicated to me, by Mr. Alch in the two meetings that I referred to, one at the Monocle Restaurant here in Washington, near a couple of blocks from here about, on December 21, and the second——

Senator Gurney. Now could you describe how that came up because this is extremely important.

Mr. McCORD. All right, sir.

Senator GURNEY. Why did you happen to go there with him in the first place?

Mr. McCORD. My recollection is that I had been called the day before by Mr. Alch when he had come into Washington to, prepared to, appear for a court hearing, something to do with a court hearing regarding some, I believe, admission or entry of tape recordings of Mr. Baldwin's statements to the press into the acquisition of those tapes by the court, and he had first stated that he was planning to see me the day before and then he subsequently called that day before and said, "No, we will meet tomorrow afternoon" or "We will meet tomorrow, and I will call you," and he did call me early in the afternoon of December 21 and said "Why don't you meet us for lunch at the Monocle Restaurant, I have got some things I want to talk with you about." So I came to the Monocle Restaurant.

Senator GURNEY. Who is us, did he have someone else with him?

Mr. McCORD. Well, he had Mr. Bernard Shankman, my local attorney. He did meet with us.

Senator GURNEY. But he did not mention to you the subject of the visit?

Mr. McCORD. No, sir.

Senator GURNEY. Did you ask him?

Mr. McCORD. I think he mentioned, to my best recollection, he said something we should be talking about our defense at this point at this time or in this meeting, something along this line.

Senator GURNEY. Go on.

Mr. McCORD. I do not remember exactly. So we met, I responded to his call and came down to the Monocle Restaurant. The three of us sat and he related questions in the statements I have read to you here. I do not recall Mr. Shankman participating in this substantive conversaton, he may have but I do not recall it.

Senator GURNEY. Now, would you recall again what he said specifically about the CIA?

Mr. McCORD. All right, sir. I have set it down in writing and I would frankly like to refer to it because I have spent a lot of time in putting it down.

Senator GURNEY. I wish you would because it is sometimes very hard to follow every word.

Mr. McCORD. I stated as I best recall, that he had just come from a meeting with William O. Bittman, attorney for Mr. Howard Hunt. He stated that he had a suggestion concerning what I use as my defense during the trial which was that I use as my defense that the Watergate operation was a CIA operation, I do not recall exactly what I said in response except to say something to the effect that you are my attorney, what is your counsel on this, do you think I should?

Senator GURNEY. Go ahead.

Mr. McCORD. And his response was, "Yes, I think so," and he proceeded to discuss, to ask some questions of me. He said, he asked whether I could be ostensibly recalled from my retirement. That is, a person once retired, can he be recalled, and I said, yes, he can, and he said, "Well, you can ostensibly, we could use as our defense you could ostensibly have been recalled to the CIA to undertake the Watergate operation, could you not?" and I said it is technically possible or words to that effect. That he said if so, then, my personnel records at CIA could be doctored to reflect such a recall, and this is my best recollection of the exact words.

Senator GURNEY. Well now, who was going to do that?

Mr. McCORD. He did not say.

Senator GURNEY. Did you ask him?

Mr. McCORD. No. I was listening to the rest of the story.

Senator GURNEY. Did you make any comment on the record being doctored at the CIA? After all, how long were you there, 19 years?

Mr. McCORD. Yes, sir.

Senator GURNEY. Did you make any comment on that?

Mr. McCORD. I think I have stated in my statement here the situation I was in which was essentially one of wanting to hear out the story, what it was all about and I was really trying to figure out sort of what is going on at this point in time.

Senator GURNEY. Go on.

Mr. McCORD. I wanted to hear the rest of the statement out. This statement, during the conversation, and it might not be in this exact sequence of the things I have stated here but these are the things that were said during the conversation, one statement may have been reversed with another but these statements were made. He said that Schlesinger, the new Director of CIA, whose appointment had just been announced, could be subpenaed and would go along with it, that was his quote.

Senator GURNEY. Schlesinger could be what?

Mr. McCORD. Could be subpenaed.

Senator GURNEY. Yes.

Mr. McCORD. And would go along with it.

Senator GURNEY. Did you ask him how he knew this would occur?

Mr. McCORD. No, sir.

Senator GURNEY. Did he offer any evidence as to how he knew that Mr. Schlesinger would "go along with it?"

Mr. McCORD. No, sir.

Senator GURNEY. Go on.

Mr. McCORD. He went on to mention some testimony. He did not have any paper with him but he went on to mention some testimony by Mr. Gary Bittenbender, and he recited testimony that he said Bittenbender had given in which Bittenbender purportedly claimed that I told him the day of the arrest that the Watergate operation was a CIA operation. My response was that if such a statement had been made it was perjured testimony or a false statement.

Senator GURNEY. Why did he bring that up, do you know?

Mr. McCORD. I can give you an impression if you want an impression.

Senator GURNEY. Yes.

Mr. McCORD. Which was that, and that impression stems from what I later saw in his office which was a written statement, my impression was that he had received access to some type of interview with Mr. Bittenbender in which such a statement was obtained, perhaps by the Federal authorities in some case.

Senator GURNEY. Go on.

Mr. McCORD. He said he could be interviewed—correction. He went on to mention the name of Mr. Victor Marchetti, who he referred to as writing a book about CIA and he said we could subpena Marchetti and have him testify about customs and traditions of CIA agents in case they are arrested, or caught wherein they are trained to deny any connection with CIA.

Senator GURNEY. Well now, how would this help you?

Mr. McCORD. My understanding of the reason he was saying it, and I recall so much of the part of the statement to the effect that this would lay the background if Mr. Marchetti were called to the stand and asked to testify he would furnish statements to this effect that it would lay a background during the trial itself for any denials that might come up either by CIA or by the defendants, that this was, in fact, a CIA operation, which, of course, it was not.

Senator GURNEY. Of course, if they were going to back you up through the Director itself they would hardly deny the story at the same time, would they?

Mr. McCORD. Well, not much went into—there was not much discussion of what in effect the CIA Director would or would not say either in responding to a subpena to testify hard in terms of testimony itself concerning the men.

Senator GURNEY. Mr. Chairman, my time is up. I wonder if I may ask one or two questions on another matter, I do not think it will take long.

The CHAIRMAN. If there is no objection, you may.

Senator GURNEY. Thank you.

Mr. McCord, how much were you being paid by the Republican National Committee for its work?

Mr. McCORD. $625 a month, as best I recall, $625 to $650, in the beginning of the period of October, of roughly October 1 through the same period of my employment with the Committee To Re-Elect the President. The subject of this employment at both locations was discussed with both men who I worked with, which included both Mr. Liddy and Odle.

Senator GURNEY. This was in addition to $20,000 a year by the Committee To Re-Elect plus the $2,000 a month hazardous pay when you entered into the Watergate operation, is that correct?

Mr. McCORD. That is correct.

Senator GURNEY. Did you receive any pay from anybody else for any activity during this period of time?

Mr. McCORD. I do not recall any, sir.

Senator GURNEY. You did not receive any?

Mr. McCORD. I do not recall any.

Senator GURNEY. Tell me, did you ever participate in any other electronic surveillance activity like this political surveillance of any kind?

Mr. McCORD. No, sir.

Senator GURNEY. How about in previous years, previous campaigns?

Mr. McCORD. No, sir.

Senator GURNEY. Did you ever discuss with anybody at the Committee To Re-Elect the President or the White House, for that matter aside from Mr. Liddy, this business of bugging the Watergate? My understanding was that your conversations were with him at first, that is correct, is it not?

Mr. McCORD. Yes, sir. The only two people they were discussed with were Mr. Hunt and Mr. Liddy and I have stated my reasons for so doing.

Senator GURNEY. But you did not discuss it at any time with anybody else?

Mr. McCORD. No, sir.

Senator GURNEY. Did you ever suggest to anybody at any time in 1971 or 1972, that this would be a desirable operation?

Mr. McCORD. Did I suggest it?

Senator GURNEY. Yes.

Mr. McCORD. Absolutely not.

Senator GURNEY. The idea came from Mr. Liddy and Mr. Hunt?

Mr. McCORD. That is the first time I heard it.

Senator GURNEY. Thank you very much.

Senator ERVIN. Senator Inouye?

Senator INOUYE. Thank you, sir.

Mr. McCord, you testified last week and this morning that you were receiving almost on a daily basis information from the Internal Security Division of the Justice Department and from the Federal Bureau of Investigation. Would I be correct in designating the type of information you received as classified?

Mr. McCORD. Sir, I can tell you how the information was described, to me, which is, I think, relevant to your question and I will do that if you would like.

Senator INOUYE. Would you please?

Mr. McCORD. The information, as I recall at this point in time, was described to me by the two men who made it available.

Senator INOUYE. Who are the two men?

Mr. McCORD. Mr. John Martin and Mr. Joel Lisker.

Senator INOUYE. What were their positions?

Mr. McCORD. Chief and Deputy Chief of the Evaluation Section of the Internal Security Division.

Senator INOUYE. Of the Justice Department?

Mr. McCORD. Of the Justice Department, yes, sir.

Senator INOUYE. Did they ever advise you as to whether they were authorized by higher authorities to provide you with this information?

Mr. McCORD. My best recollection, sir, of the answer to that question is that when Mr. Martin first talked with me, when I first went to see him after Mr. Mardian had told me, Robert Mardian had told me that arrangements, that he had made arrangements for me to have access to such information from the Internal Security Division, and I went to Mr. John Martin's office for the first time, my recollection is that he told me two things in that regard. One is that he had received some word from Mr. Mardian asking that I be given access and that he had checked it out with his people, referring to his superiors.

Senator INOUYE. Was the type of information received the type generally made available to the public?

Mr. McCORD. To the public?

Senator INOUYE. Yes, sir. Was it public information?

Mr. McCORD. I don't think so, sir. I don't believe so.

Senator INOUYE. Then it was classified information of some nature?

Mr. McCORD. I was told that it was unclassified information. I do not recall seeing classification stamps on any of the information.

I might add—I believe your first question was that I contacted the FBI on this type of information. I apologize if I left that impression. I never contacted the FBI. My only contact was through the Internal Security Division.

I do not recall classification stamps on the information. There may very well have been such. I do not recall it.

Senator INOUYE. At that time, were you legally and appropriately authorized to receive such information? Were you cleared to receive such information?

Mr. McCORD. I had a clearance, sir, top secret clearance in connection with position, reserve positions in the military.

Senator INOUYE. At the time of the receipt?

Mr. McCORD. Yes, sir.

Senator INOUYE. I have been advised that at the time of the break-in, you had in your employment a man named Louis Russell, is that correct?

Mr. McCORD. That is correct, sir.

Senator INOUYE. Was he near the Watergate during the time of the break-in?

Mr. McCORD. I would like to respond to that, because Mr. Russell has been very unfairly treated in terms of his name being raised in this case, and I will explain the circumstances as he has told them to me and which I believe, which are these.

He stated that he was not there the night of the break-in at the Howard Johnson Motel or anywhere in the vicinity. He told me that the night before, which would have been the night of June 16, I believe—June 15—the Thursday night—that he had gone to the Howard Johnson Motel restaurant to have dinner and that he had gone there with a woman companion, who—they on a regular basis ate at the Howard Johnson restaurant as a custom over some years; that she normally went to the Watergate hairdresser, one of them, for her hairdo, and they would go over to the Howard Johnson restaurant and have dinner.

Senator INOUYE. Was he in any way connected with the bugging?

Mr. McCORD. Absolutely none, in no form whatever.

Senator INOUYE. It has been reported that Mr. John Dean, formerly of the White House staff, wanted the bugging operation carried out in such a way as to provide the Attorney General, Mr. Mitchell, deniability.

Mr. McCORD. Yes, sir.

Senator INOUYE. Have you heard of this phrase?

Mr. McCORD. Yes, sir.

Senator INOUYE. What is your understanding of the meaning of this term, "deniability"?

Mr. McCORD. That if something goes wrong, a person can claim that he had no connection with the operation.

Senator INOUYE. Was this explained to you?

Mr. McCORD. The word was mentioned to me and I can describe how it was mentioned and the context, if you would like.

Senator INOUYE. Please do so.

Mr. McCORD. Which was to the best of my recollection, the day after Mr. Liddy met in January, I believe the first or second—either the first or the second meeting with the Attorney General, in the

Attorney General's office, which he came back from that meeting stating that, relating what had transpired during the meeting, and then saying that Mr. John Dean had contacted him after the meeting and told him that he thought the operation was going to be approved and that there would have to be some way of giving deniability to Mr. John Mitchell in connection with the operation. My recollection is that Mr. Liddy amplified that by some statement to the effect at that meeting that if anything ever blew the operation, Mr. Mitchell could claim that he had no part of it.

Senator INOUYE. How did you propose to accomplish this deniability?

Mr. MCCORD. He didn't state, but it appeared to me that that statement really had no validity at a later time, because from other statements of Mr. Liddy, there were continuous meetings of him and Mr. Mitchell, extending up through, say, the week of June 17, and that therefore, the statement was essentially meaningless, because had it been planned that Mr. Mitchell had deniability, the events that transpired after February, after the statement was made, essentially negated the opportunity for in any way that Mr. Mitchell could disclaim connection. If, in fact, for example, after that first one or two meetings he had no further connection with the operation with Mr. Liddy, then perhaps there would have been deniability. But by continuing to meet with Mr. Liddy as Mr. Liddy related to me on numerous meetings between February and June, there was essentially no valid claim that could be made to deniability.

Senator INOUYE. I recall some account of your relationship with embassies. I am a bit confused about that.

Did you call embassies in relation to Watergate or did you mention embassies to any other contacts?

I am curious, were embassies bugged, too?

Mr. MCCORD. I have no knowledge, sir, of any contact with embassies, bugging of embassies, or any clandestine operations directed against embassies by any members of the team, the seven members of the team or anyone else connected with them.

Senator INOUYE. You did not discuss the matter of surveillance of embassies with the committee staff?

Mr. MCCORD. In the statement this morning, two phone calls that I referred to after June 17. But I have no knowledge prior to June 17.

Senator INOUYE. What were these phone calls about?

Mr. MCCORD. I can answer it again, if I may, sir.

I have stated that, the fact that in September and in October 1972, I made two phone calls to two local embassies, made some very brief statements over the phone—I don't recall the nature of the inquiry of the first phone call.

The second one was a phone call lasting 2 or 3 minutes. The calls were made from my residence. The purpose of both calls of mine, these two calls, was possibly to test the truthfulness of Government response.

When the motion was filed 2 or 3 days later—that is, October 10, 1972—requesting Government disclosure of intercepted telephone calls of mine from any time during 1972, I was convinced that our calls were being intercepted from our phones in our home. I am still so convinced that that transpired, particularly in September and October 1972, when there were numerous indications of it.

Senator INOUYE. During the period April, May, and June of this year, according to your memo, you received the gross sum of $76,000 for expenses?

Mr. McCORD. In connection with the Watergate operation, yes, sir.

Senator INOUYE. This was over and above your pay, am I correct?

Mr. McCORD. This was money given to me by Mr. Liddy for the purposes of purchasing equipment and paying related expenses connected with the Watergate operation, yes, sir.

Senator INOUYE. Did this include your personal pay?

Mr. McCORD. This included a category of money that I said was referred to euphemistically as "overhead" which was supposed to cover my personal travel expenses and compensation for whatever time was involved in this and compensation for related expenses.

Senator INOUYE. Then your salary for the months of April, May, and June for the Watergate intrusion was $12,000?

Mr. McCORD. I believe that is correct. I have heard that figure before.

Senator INOUYE. Then you had legal fees of $18,800. Who received the $18,800?

Mr. McCORD. One of my attorneys.

Senator INOUYE. All $18,800?

Mr. McCORD. Yes, sir.

Senator INOUYE. I notice here under equipment, "miscellaneous purchases, $12,750".

Mr. McCORD. Yes, sir.

Senator INOUYE. Were they small purchases?

Mr. McCORD. That is a fairly large amount of money.

Senator INOUYE. Because I have noticed you have listed items costing $400 specifically.

Mr. McCORD. These were purchases from several different locations in New York City, in Chicago, and some in Washington. The exact names of the ones that I purchased equipment from, names of the stores and what have you, I listed where I could earlier in this thing. I could not recall all of them because there were about, I would say, 20 or 21 different firms that equipment was purchased from. And there was purchased out of this $12,000 that you have referred to here quite a number of accessories of different types, in equipment that we were using, in particular, some purchases in New York City from firms that I can't recall the names of at this point in time. I have tried to reconstruct the exact cost where I can and I put into this other category exact costs that I can't remember.

Senator INOUYE. They were not for personal expenses?

Mr. McCORD. No, sir.

Senator INOUYE. And in filing your income taxes, did you include $12,000 of your income?

Mr. McCORD. My income—I have asked for an extension of filing of income tax in order to be sure specifically that everything is included that should be included and just how I am to report the source of the money that I received; exactly who do I state gave me the money that we reported in that income tax.

Is it the Committee To Re-Elect the President? Is it somebody else?

Senator INOUYE. Do you have any knowledge of who prepared Mr. Liddy's $7,000 charts?

Mr. McCORD. No.

Senator INOUYE. Do you happen to know why they were so expensive?

Mr. McCORD. My understanding was that he wanted some professionally prepared charts and that to get them in a hurry, he had to pay some sort of a premium to get them as quickly as he wanted them.

Senator INOUYE. Do you know what happened to these charts?

Mr. McCORD. He stated that he had been told to destroy the charts by Mr. John Dean but that he did not plan to do so. He planned to stash them away because they cost so much money. What he did with them, I don't know.

Senator INOUYE. That is all I have.

Senator ERVIN. Senator Weicker?

Senator WEICKER. Thank you very much, Mr. Chairman.

Mr. McCord, I would like to clear up one technical point. You placed the actions of your former attorney, Mr. Alch, in what might be charitably called an unfavorable light and I assume that if this committee chooses to hear Mr. Alch's side of the story, you are not going to raise the point of attorney-client privilege, right?

Mr. McCORD. No, sir.

Senator WEICKER. Now, Mr. McCord, I would like to go back to the questioning that I started last week, and start at the beginning with your first visit to the Triangle Building.

Would you tell the committee who attended the meeting, the first meeting at the Triangle Building?

Mr. McCORD. I will state my recollection. I believe I was the only one from the Committee To Re-Elect the President who attended, along with Mr. Joel Lisker, Mr. John Martin, the two men I referred to as the chief and the deputy chief of that activity. We met in Mr. John Martin's office. We talked, I would guess, for probably 45 minutes. We talked on the general subject of access of mine to the reports. He repeated—stated the two matters that I repeated, that he had received a call from Mr. Mardian and that he had checked it with his superiors.

Senator WEICKER. Was Mr. Houston present at the first meeting?

Mr. McCORD. I don't recall that Mr. Robert Houston, who is one of my assistants, was present at the first meeting. He may have been. My recollection is that he was not. I think he appeared later when I had other duties to perform, I think particularly when I went to Miami to do the survey I referred to here.

Senator WEICKER. In other words, there were subsequent times when Mr. Houston might have been with you——

Mr. McCORD. Yes, sir.

Senator WEICKER [continuing]. At the Triangle Building? Is that right?

Mr. McCORD. Yes, sir.

I can recall a couple of times.

Senator WEICKER. Now, at this first meeting, would it be fair to say that the procedures were discussed by which you would have access to this information?

Mr. McCORD. I believe so; yes, sir.

Senator WEICKER. And were the procedures included—was access to this information in your going to the Triangle Building, is that correct?

Mr. McCORD. Primarily.

Senator WEICKER. Primarily.

Was it also discussed that this particular section, on its own initiative, could go ahead and contact you at the Committee To Re-Elect the President?

Mr. McCORD. Yes, sir.

Senator WEICKER. Now, you have had fairly extensive experience with both the FBI and the CIA. Is it possible for you to identify material that has been obtained from wiretaps, or is that an impossible situation?

Mr. McCORD. No, sir; I could not, and in answer to your question, if it refers to this group, that I saw nothing——

Senator WEICKER. No, no, please, my question is in a much more general sense. Is it possible—specifically is it possible for you with your background to identify which materials were obtained from wiretap?

Mr. McCORD. I would say it would be exceedingly rare that I would be able to do so.

Senator WEICKER. So it is also true, then, that in those circumstances, material set before you could or could not have been obtained from wiretaps, is that true?

Mr. McCORD. Possibly, yes, sir.

Senator WEICKER. Now, I know that you made an effort at the last hearing to state your recollection of what materials you received. Have you given any additional thought to that? Is it possible for you to be a little more complete than you were the last time as to what documents and types of information you received from this particular division of the Justice Department?

Mr. McCORD. I can recall one or two things specifically.

I believe I made reference in my earlier testimony today to information about the forgery of college press credentials in connection with plans of more than one individual to gain access to both the Democratic National Committee Convention site at Miami and the Republican National Convention site, and specifically to use such forged credentials for the purpose of getting access to the communications center and blowing up those centers. This report I distinctly remember seeing and passed some information on it along to my own superiors.

Senator WEICKER. Well, I don't intend to take up the time of the committee here, but I wish that you would, as best you can, think about this matter. If there are any other matters which came into your possession which you have not told the committee about, would you be good enough to supply the committee with memoranda on that?

Mr. McCORD. Yes, sir, I will do so.

Senator WEICKER. Let me ask you, do you still have in your possession any of the documents which you received from this division of the Justice Department?

Mr. McCord. No, sir.
Senator Weicker. What happened to this material, then? Was it destroyed?
Mr. McCord. I don't recall our taking any material at all from the Internal Security Division offices. I dictated a memorandum at their offices onto a tape of one report that I had read and turned that tape over to your committee sometime back.
Senator Weicker. Now, on what particular occasion did the Internal Security Division take the initiative and call you?
Mr. McCord. Particularly during the last 2 weeks of May 1971 when there were sizable numbers of demonstrators in Washington, and their plans were being formulated by some violence-oriented elements within whose demonstrators for confrontation with the police, confrontation with them. I recall one specific report where I received a call from one of those two gentlemen stating that there had been evidence come to light that the bombing of the, one of the, rooms in the Pentagon which had appeared, the evening in which it had appeared, in the paper the day before that this had been determined to be caused by what is known as a plastic C-4 explosive, the equivalent of about 18 sticks of dynamite, and he was alerting me that to the effect that there was this plastic explosive being used and, as a matter of essentially some forewarning that someone had in their possession this type of plastic explosive.
Senator Weicker. Mr. McCord, did you actually receive any FBI reports while at the Internal Security Division?
Mr. McCord. I saw some material that was attributed to the FBI. I did not take any with me. I made extracts of some of the material that was shown to me.
Senator Weicker. Now, is it possible for you to go ahead and segregate the FBI material from the other matters that you have been discussing here this morning? Is there anything that stands out in your mind that specifically could be attributed to the FBI?
Mr. McCord. I cannot recall in terms of what I testified to today that that material came directly from FBI sources. My memory on where it came from at this point in time is not that clear.
Senator Weicker. Now, those were the major calls from the Internal Security Division, were they again Mr. Martin and Mr. Lisker?
Mr. McCord. Primarily Mr. Lisker.
Senator Weicker. Primarily Mr. Lisker?
Mr. McCord. Yes, sir.
Senator Weicker. Were they always made to you?
Mr. McCord. To Mr. Houston and me, primarily.
Senator Weicker. But either you or Mr. Houston received these calls?
Mr. McCord. Yes, sir.
Senator Weicker. Now, in your journeys to the Internal Security Division, did you ever have occasion to meet Mr. Guy Goodwin, the Chief of the Special Litigation Division?
Mr. McCord. I do not believe so, sir. I do not recall that name.
Senator Weicker. You have indicated recently that the Vietnam Veterans Against the War had an office in the Democratic National

Committee or McGovern headquarters. Where did you receive that information?

Mr. McCord. I do not recall the source of it now, except that it came to me some time during the summer of 1972.

Senator Weicker. When you say in the summer of 1972, was it before June 17?

Mr. McCord. No, sir.

Senator Weicker. After June 17?

Mr. McCord. Yes, sir.

Senator Weicker. How many times were you personally in contact with Robert Mardian?

Mr. McCord. I can recall two or three times.

Senator Weicker. Was this when he was still at the Internal Security Division or at the time he had left that division and was working for the Committee To Re-Elect the President?

Mr. McCord. Only after he had come to the Committee To Re-Elect the President.

Senator Weicker. You say that you had two or three personal meetings with him?

Mr. McCord. Yes, sir.

Senator Weicker. Were there additional contacts with him by phone?

Mr. McCord. I think there was a call or two separate from the meeting, as I can recall one or two calls in connection with the driver that Mr. Mardian had that we were considering for use at the committee.

Senator Weicker. Now, can you give me an indication as to the matters which you and Mr. Mardian discussed?

Mr. McCord. I can recall the subject of the driver that I have just referred to.

Senator Weicker. You referred to that at the last hearing also?

Mr. McCord. Yes, sir.

Senator Weicker. So I think it is well placed on the record.

Mr. McCord. The subject of the access to the materials that we have been discussing at the Internal Security Division with one meeting in connection with that that I can recall. There may have have been one other meeting, I cannot be sure whether two or three meetings, but if it was it is the second or the third meeting, but the other two topics that have been raised in my memorandum, they were discussed.

Senator Weicker. At any time while you were at the Internal Security Division, did you see Gordon Liddy there?

Mr. McCord. I am sorry, I was not listening, what was the question?

Senator Weicker. At any time that you were at the Internal Security Division, did you see Gordon Liddy there?

Mr. McCord. No, sir.

Senator Weicker. Do you have any knowledge that Mr. Liddy ever was at the Internal Security Division?

Mr. McCord. I had no knowledge before June 17. After that I read in the papers that he had some access.

Senator Weicker. Now, just a few more questions. To move for a minute away from the Internal Security Division matter, in your letter to Judge Sirica dated March 19, 1973, you said that you could not feel confident in testifying before a grand jury whose U.S. attorneys work for the Department of Justice. Why did you make that statement?

Mr. McCord. Because I believed that because of the fact that the U.S. attorneys work for the Attorney General and the Attorney General works for the White House that whatever information I gave to the grand jury would be immediately passed to the White House, who it seems to me, at that point in time had an adverse interest in what I had to say.

Senator Weicker. Was there anything in their conduct, was there anything in their conduct toward you, that gave you a basis for that statement?

Mr. McCord. No, sir.

Senator Weicker. Now, lastly, did you have any conversation after June 17 with Alfred Baldwin?

Mr. McCord. Yes, sir.

Senator Weicker. How many conversations did you have?

Mr. McCord. I believe I had two telephone conversations with him, maybe three, immediately after, almost after our arrest, after I returned home from the District of Columbia accommodations at the jail, and then I saw him twice, I believe, at the U.S. Attorney's Office in July when he was planning to appear for testimony.

Senator Weicker. Can you give me the nature of your telephone conservations with Mr. Baldwin?

Mr. McCord. Yes, sir, I can, and I can tell you that it is my understanding those calls were taped or recorded otherwise. My best recollection is that when I returned home around the—somewhere around the 23d of June—that there was a note from Mr. Baldwin asking me to call him at his home in Connecticut, which I did, and during that call my recollection is that he told me that he had called the Committee To Re-Elect the President, and I believe he said he talked to Fred LaRue and told him that he had been involved in the Watergate operation, that Mr. LaRue had expressed surprise that he had been so involved and Mr. Baldwin said that he asked him some questions about what help he was going to get from the committee itself of any kind and I think particularly in terms of legal fees and so on. He asked me, I believe he said, I cannot separate the phone calls out at this point in time, I can give you the substance of them if you want me to state them.

Senator Weicker. All right. Just go on.

Mr. McCord. In those calls he said that, I believe one of the attorneys for the Committee To Re-Elect the President had subsequently come up to Connecticut to see his attorney there. He did not say what was discussed. He asked a question of what the committee was doing, what knowledge I might have of the submission of expense accounts which Mr. Baldwin had previously submitted for his travels, while a security officer with Mrs. Mitchell, and I told him that I really did not know what the committee had done about it and I could not recall at that point in time whether there were really copies of any of those expense vouchers in my safe at the office but that that he should recompute what he figured was going to be due him and to send it to the Committee To Re-Elect the President, which I felt would reimburse him, and I understand they subsequently did.

There was some discussion, I am sure, about what he planned to do in terms of pleading guilty or not. Some discussion about his request for appearance before the grand jury in July. I am sure there are other matters but I cannot recall them right now.

Senator WEICKER. Who initiated these phone calls, did Mr. Baldwin initiate them or did you initiate them?

Mr. McCORD. No, he left a note for me first of all, to call him, and then he gave me subsequent instructions as to some other numbers I was to call him at in Connecticut, two or three different numbers, and I called those numbers and sometimes I called him at home and he would say, "Call me at a couple of other numbers," and I would call him at those numbers. My belief was that they were either—at that time they were probably his attorneys' offices; I believe others there may have been some FBI offices involved in it who were monitoring the conversation.

Senator WEICKER. You believe that you were calling Mr. Baldwin at FBI offices?

Mr. McCORD. Well, I have so understood that the conversations were being taped at that time.

Senator WEICKER. Let us separate this; there are two statements made here and I want to be very careful and you want to be careful about what is being said. No. 1, you had made the statement that you believe these conversations had been taped, correct?

Mr. McCORD. Yes, sir.

Senator WEICKER. Now, No. 2, are you saying that you believed these conversations to have been taped at FBI offices?

Mr. McCORD. I would guess at this point in time that one or two things happened. That perhaps the calls were made at his attorney's offices with FBI agents present listening to the calls or perhaps that the calls were to an unlisted FBI phone.

Senator WEICKER. So, in other words, you believe there was FBI involvement either in the offices of his attorney or actually at FBI offices insofar as your phone calls to Baldwin are concerned?

Mr. McCORD. FBI or Government——

Senator WEICKER. Or Government?

Mr. McCORD. Yes.

Senator WEICKER. Government personnel were involved in these telephone calls?

Mr. McCORD. Yes, sir.

Senator WEICKER. You mentioned the other day in your testimony that you had read of the possibility of Mr. Baldwin being a double agent and that you had no evidence to that effect. Is that correct?

Mr. McCORD. That is correct.

Senator WEICKER. Where did this first come to your attention?

Mr. McCORD. I believe I testified that I first heard the allegation over the TV interview on a Sunday by Mr. Clark MacGregor of the committee. I think I also read some references to it in the newspapers at about that time that the committee was handing out the story that Mr. Baldwin was a double agent, and I believe I also testified Friday that I told Mr. Caulfield I felt this was absolutely untrue.

Senator WEICKER. You told who it was untrue?

Mr. McCORD. Mr. Caulfield.

Senator WEICKER. Why would you have told Mr. Caulfield?

Mr. McCORD. Because he called me that same day that Mr. MacGregor made his statement over the TV and it appeared an hour or two earlier and I was a little bit concerned that this sort of story would be floating and I told Caulfield I had no knowledge of it and I did not believe it.

Senator WEICKER. I have no further questions, Mr. Chairman.

Senator BAKER. Thank you, Senator Weicker.

It is 12:20 now. The chairman found it necessary to leave for other important business. I would like to continue with Mr. McCord to finish the questioning with Senator Montoya, which I hope we can conclude around 12:30. And then to ask Mr. McCord to return at 2, when the committee will reconvene when I understand that both the majority and minority counsels may have some additional questions, but I hope we are coming close to the end of your rather extended testimony.

Senator Montoya.

Senator MONTOYA. Thank you, Mr. Chairman.

Mr. McCord, with respect to your suspicion that your phone had been tapped at your home did you conduct any investigation around your premises to determine whether there was actually a phone tap?

Mr. McCORD. Yes, sir.

Senator MONTOYA. And what did you find?

Mr. McCORD. I had some equipment in September 1972 that normally when you go through a particular procedure with it if there is an extension, a telephone extension off of the phone you are testing or if certain types of devices are being used on the line there is an alarm that is sounded somewhat like a buzzer and I would make these tests periodically through the fall of the year and it would go into the alarm during some of the tests. There were also many phone calls that had some very unusual things would occur when a call would come in in which we would hear an extension be picked up shortly after the call and other things.

Senator MONTOYA. Permit me to ask you this question. Then, on the basis of your investigation, are you concluding definitely that your phone had been tapped?

Mr. McCORD. I had no doubt then, sir, and I have no doubt now.

Senator MONTOYA. Were you also under the impression that as you spoke to other parties that your conversations may have been recorded during the time you communicated with anybody?

Mr. McCORD. Yes, sir.

Senator MONTOYA. About this case?

Mr. McCORD. Yes, sir, about this case.

Senator MONTOYA. On how many occasions did you suspect this or were you certain that this occurred?

Mr. McCORD. I would say at least a half dozen times, perhaps more during September and October, particularly, of 1972.

Senator MONTOYA. And when you mentioned the occurrence of these things to Mr. Caulfield, I believe you indicated that you cited only two instances?

Mr. McCORD. I referred to the two specific calls I was concerned about but I told him also about all these other things that had been happening that led me to believe that the phone was tapped.

Senator MONTOYA. Did you complain to anyone else?

Mr. McCORD. I made a lot of complaints to my lawyer in terms of filing motions, to Mr. Bittman when I discussed it with him. These motions went in the record.

Senator MONTOYA. Did you allege these occurrences in your motions?

Mr. McCORD. Yes, sir.

Senator MONTOYA. Now, with respect to your statements in your previous testimony that you were under the impression that the President knew of the clemency offer, would you please refresh my memory as to the actual conversations that led you into this belief?

Mr. McCORD. Yes, sir. The information that, and knowledge that led me to believe stemmed with conversations, stemmed from conversations with Mr. Liddy—Gordon Liddy—in January and February of 1972, in which he told me about the meetings with the Attorney General in the Attorney General's offices with Mr. Dean present in which the operation was deliberately stated at length that the process and consequence of the operation were discussed by those present, presumably meaning the advantages and disadvantages of them in what appeared to be the deliberate consideration, careful consideration, given to the operation by the Attorney General. I believe I stated that there was a 30-day delay which to me seemed quite significant. I believe I stated that the Attorney General was in my opinion, a very decisive man.

Senator MONTOYA. Mr. McCord, I do not know whether you understood my question.

Mr. McCORD. All right, sir.

Senator MONTOYA. But we are going back to January of 1972, in relating what transpired there. My question was: What led you to believe that the offer of clemency had the endorsement or approval of the President?

Mr. McCORD. I am sorry, sir. I misunderstood the question. The statement from Mr. Caulfield to me.

Senator MONTOYA. Will you relate those statements again?

Mr. McCORD. Yes, sir.

Mr. Caulfield stated that he was carrying the message of Executive clemency to me.

Senator MONTOYA. Did he state so specifically?

Mr. McCORD. Yes, sir. "From the very highest levels of the White House," these were his exact words.

He stated that the President of the United States was in Key Biscayne, Fla., that he already had been told of the forthcoming meeting with me. This was, I believe, on Friday, January 12, that the President had been told about the forthcoming meeting with me and would be immediately told of the results of the meeting.

Senator MONTOYA. Did you check with Mr. Liddy after your meetings to ascertain whether or not the offer and your response had been communicated to the President?

Was there any followup on your part?

Mr. McCORD. With Mr. Liddy, sir?

Senator MONTOYA. With Mr. Caulfield.

Mr. McCORD. Mr. Caulfield? I would like to answer the question this way, if I may.

He told me that the results of the meetings would be communicated with the President, that meeting of January 12, that Friday, that the results of the meeting he and I were then having, was then having would be communicated to the President, and he said, "I may have a message to you at our next meeting from the President himself." This is an exact quote.

Senator MONTOYA. Did you ever receive a message through Mr. Caulfield purporting to be a communication from the President?

Mr. MCCORD. He came back to me at subsequent meetings discussing Executive clemency and a large number of other matters. He did not specifically state that the President said them.

Senator MONTOYA. Now, you mentioned that you received a note in your box from Mr. Caulfield which was signed "Jack". You also mentioned a letter that you wrote to Mr. Caulfield which you addressed "Dear Jack".

Now, were you on a first-name basis with Jack Caulfield?

Mr. MCCORD. Yes, sir.

Senator MONTOYA. How long have you known him?

Mr. MCCORD. I first met him when he contacted me about the job at the Committee To Re-Elect the President in September. That was my first meeting with him, the first time I met him.

Senator MONTOYA. Was he the only one connected either with the White House or the committee to ask you to come to work?

Mr. MCCORD. No, sir, the first person that contacted me conveyed a message to me that—the first person was an individual in the Secret Service that I had known and he said that there was a possibility of a position open in campaign security work during the 1972 campaign and did I have any interest. My answer was—this gentleman called me by phone in September 1972, in about a 1-, 2-minute conversation. My answer was that I would have liked to have heard more about it.

He said, well, you may be getting a call. I shortly did receive a call from Mr. Caulfield.

Senator MONTOYA. Who was that person in the Secret Service?

Mr. MCCORD. Mr. Alfred Wong.

Senator MONTOYA. Now, going to the matter of receiving reports from the Internal Security Division of the Department of Justice, I do not want to belabor this point, but how many reports did you receive from this Division?

Mr. MCCORD. I have a little bit of trouble answering this question, because, Senator, the number of meetings I had with him I could probably guess at. The number of reports I saw there, separate individual reports, would be a sizable number and I could not estimate.

Senator MONTOYA. How many meetings did you have with him?

Mr. MCCORD. It seems to me the meetings began in late May 1972, and continued until close to June 17. I was gone a portion of that period to Miami, Fla.

Senator MONTOYA. So how many meetings would you say that is?

Mr. MCCORD. I would estimate a half dozen.

Senator MONTOYA. And how many reports did you see; more or less?

Mr. MCCORD. Probably 25 or so.

Senator MONTOYA. How many copies of reports did you take back with you?

Mr. McCORD. I took none back with me, sir.
Senator MONTOYA. Did you make any notes?
Mr. McCORD. Yes, sir.
Senator MONTOYA. And what were these reports about generally? I do not want to go into the specifics.
Mr. McCORD. About planned violence in Washington and in Miami, Fla., specifically in connection with the Republican National Convention, some in connection with the Democratic National Convention, in which there were plans to forge the college press credentials that I have referred to.
Senator MONTOYA. Who did you deal with at the Internal Security Division?
Mr. McCORD. Mainly, Mr. Lisker, Joel Lisker.
Senator MONTOYA. Did you deal with others?
Mr. McCORD. Mr. Martin.
Senator MONTOYA. Now, did you have any access to any FBI reports?
Mr. McCORD. Some of the material which I saw was referred to or identified as FBI material.
Senator MONTOYA. By whom?
Mr. McCORD. I believe Mr. Lisker.
Senator MONTOYA. Did you check these particular reports and did you see any attribution to the FBI on the face of the reports?
Mr. McCORD. Yes sir, some of them.
Senator MONTOYA. Another question that I want to clear up. You mentioned the Las Vegas trip. You mentioned that there were two trips made, either by Mr. Liddy or Mr. Hunt—which was it?
Mr. McCORD. Mr. Liddy.
Senator MONTOYA. One was to case the Greenspun office to determine whether or not a break-in could take place. Is that correct?
Mr. McCORD. Yes, sir. I understood both trips were for that purpose.
Senator MONTOYA. All right. Was there any actual break-in?
Mr. McCORD. I do not know of any, sir.
Senator MONTOYA. And you went to work for the Republican National Committee in October and you worked with them and for them until January, is that correct, January 1972?
Mr. McCORD. No sir, the relationship continued until June 1972.
Senator MONTOYA. Then you were on their payroll at $600 a month?
Mr. McCORD. Approximately.
Senator MONTOYA. You hadn't mentioned this before, because I interrogated you about the payroll at the CRP. You were on their payroll, too, were you not?
Mr. McCORD. Yes, sir, I mentioned these matters in the executive session to the investigators and I apologize if I appeared to mislead you.
Senator MONTOYA. What was your salary with the CRP from January until June 17?
Mr. McCORD. Gross salary was——
Senator MONTOYA. On a monthly basis.
Mr. McCORD. Monthly basis, the net pay was about $1,250 a month.
Senator MONTOYA. Who employed you at the Republican National Committee?

Mr. McCord. Mr. Barry Mountain.

Senator Montoya. What is his capacity there or what was his capacity at that time?

Mr. McCord. Director of administration.

Senator Montoya. And how long did you work for the Republican National Committee again?

Mr. McCord. I was on their payroll through some part of June; approximately the middle.

Senator Montoya. Now, you mentioned also that in December, some of you or all the defendants got together somewhere for a strategy meeting with respect to the trial. Is that correct?

Mr. McCord. I can't recall that testimony, sir.

Senator Montoya. Did you get together at any time in December or before the trial with respect to a trial strategy?

Mr. McCord. Yes, sir, I did.

Senator Montoya. With the other defendants?

Mr. McCord. No sir, only a general discussion with Mr. Barker a day or two before the trial.

Senator Montoya. And did you discuss anything there with respect to the offer of clemency or any help from the individuals at the White House or in Government or at the CRP?

Mr. McCord. I can recall some conversations that took place at this meeting, at which Mr. Barker was talking about pleading guilty or not plead guilty. I can't be sure whether Executive clemency was mentioned at that point in time. I think now it was.

Senator Montoya. By whom?

Mr. McCord. By Mr. Barker, stating that Executive clemency had—he understood it had been mentioned by Hunt or promised to Hunt.

Senator Montoya. And were you in constant touch with Mr. Hunt during the course of the trial?

Mr. McCord. Not contact as such. I saw him during the first week of the trial, before he pled guilty. I did not see him thereafter.

Senator Montoya. Now, there was an article, a statement by Mr. Caulfield on Saturday, and I will read this statement quoting him. It was a press statement:

> I have briefly reviewed Mr. McCord's statement before the Senate Select Committee, and while it does not fully reflect my best recollection of the events which took place between he and I during January of this year, it is true that I met with Mr. McCord on three occasions in January and conveyed to him certain messages from a high White House official.

Now, do you have any dispute with that statement?

Mr. McCord. Do I have any what, sir?

Senator Montoya. Dispute with that statement?

Do you question the accuracy of that statement?

Mr. McCord. He apparently has a separate recollection than I do, sir, from his statement, so there must be some differences of opinion as to what was said. I do not know what he might mean at this point in time.

Senator Montoya. But in view of his statement, you still state that what you said to this committee was correct as far as you knew and as far as you recall?

Mr. McCORD. It is accurate and correct to the best of my recollection, yes, sir.

Senator MONTOYA. Why did you turn down the overtures toward Executive clemency?

Mr. McCORD. Well, there are a number of reasons. In the first place, I intended to plead not guilty. I intended to fight the case through the courts of appeal, and I never had any intention of taking Executive clemency or pleading guilty, either; both of which were usually connected together when the terms were used. In other words, if you plead guilty, there will be Executive clemency offered to you. My basic position was essentially that I would not even dispute it, either one.

Senator MONTOYA. That is all, Mr. Chairman.

Mr. BAKER. Thank you, Senator Montoya.

[Whereupon at 12:40 p.m., the committee recessed to reconvene at 2 p.m., the same day.]

AFTERNOON SESSION, TUESDAY, MAY 22, 1973

Senator ERVIN. The committee will come to order.

Counsel will proceed.

Mr. DASH. Mr. McCord, I just have a few questions. There were many questions put to you for the period of your testimony, and I just have a few, and I do understand Minority Counsel Thompson has some questions.

I think that one of the areas that has not been covered is the role of the person who was on the other side of the wiretap which you installed the end of May 1972. Now, did you employ Mr. Alfred Baldwin for that purpose?

Mr. McCORD. Yes, I did.

Mr. DASH. What was his particular assignment with regard to monitoring the wiretap?

Mr. McCORD. His assignment was to listen on a radio receiver that received the transmissions from the Democratic National Committee telephones, in which the electronic devices had been installed in connection with the two dates of Memorial Day weekend and June 17, 1972.

Mr. DASH. Where was he located when he was doing this monitoring?

Mr. McCORD. On the seventh floor of the Howard Johnson Motel across the street from the Democratic National Committee headquarters.

Mr. DASH. Now, Mr. McCord, can you see the chart on the easel there? [Exhibit No. 12, p. 101.]

Mr. McCORD. Yes, sir.

Mr. DASH. The drawing purports to show the Howard Johnson on your right and the Watergate Office Building on your left. Now, does it represent the room 723 which was used by Mr. Baldwin for monitoring of those telephones?

Mr. McCORD. Yes, it was.

Mr. DASH. And he was just right across the street in doing that?
Mr. McCORD. Yes, sir.
Mr. DASH. In his monitoring how was he recording what he was hearing?
Mr. McCORD. He was listening with headphones to the conversations that were being transmitted and would take down the substance of the conversations, the time, the date on the yellow legal-sized scratch pad, and then ultimately would type them up a summary of them by time, chronological summary, and turn that typed log in to me and I would deliver them to Mr. Liddy.
Mr. DASH. Did you deliver them to Mr. Liddy directly?
Mr. McCORD. Yes.
Mr. DASH. Now, did there come a time when you were delivering those logs that they were retyped?
Mr. McCORD. I know of at least one instance in which that occurred because I saw them being retyped.
Mr. DASH. Was it your understanding that that occurred on more than one occasion, even though you yourself may not know?
Mr. McCORD. Yes.
Mr. DASH. What was the purpose of retyping the log, did Mr. Liddy explain that to you?
Mr. McCORD. I believe some general explanation, in substance that he wanted them in a more final complete form for discussion with Mr. Mitchell and whoever else received them.
Mr. DASH. Now, who did this retyping?
Mr. McCORD. Sally Harmony, H-a-r-m-o-n-y, who was the secretary to Mr. Liddy at the Committee for the Re-Election of the President.
Mr. DASH. Did you have occasion to observe her typing the logs?
Mr. McCORD. Yes, I did.
Mr. DASH. Did you have occasion to talk to her while she was doing it?
Mr. McCORD. Yes, I did.
Mr. DASH. In that conversation you had with Sally Harmony, did she give you any indication that she understood what she was doing when she was retyping that log?
Mr. McCORD. Yes, she did.
Mr. DASH. As a matter of fact, could you briefly describe, without going into any of the contents what a log would be, what actually would be entered on the log which Mr. Baldwin would first type and then be retyped by Miss Harmony?
Mr. McCORD. It would be similar to any other telephone conversation that one person might make to another beginning with a statement on his log of the time of the call, who was calling who; a summary of what was said during the conversation itself, including names of persons who were mentioned that Mr. Baldwin apparently believed were of sufficient significance to set forth in the log.
Mr. DASH. Then it would be true that anybody reading that would have no difficulty knowing it came from a telephone conversation?
Mr. McCORD. That is correct.
Mr. DASH. I think you testified earlier, and I just wanted to get it clear for the record, that your discussions with Mr. Liddy concerning meetings he had with the Attorney General, indicated that Mr.

Liddy was actually meeting with the Attorney General with regard to this operation?

Mr. McCORD. That is correct.

Mr. DASH. All the way up to what time, what was the last date that Mr. Liddy indicated that he had a meeting with the Attorney General regarding this particular bugging operation?

Mr. McCORD. My best recollection is immediately before June 17 during—I would estimate, during that week, immediately preceding June 17.

Mr. DASH. Did Mr. Liddy indicate what the nature of that meeting was?

Mr. McCORD. All I can recall at this point is some conversation, as a general conversation to the effect that "We discussed getting ready for the operation that is coming up" and I think just the overall planning for the operation.

Mr. DASH. Going back very briefly to the information that you were getting from the Internal Security Division, was your trip to Miami related in any way to the Department of Justice's investigation of the Veterans Against the War in Vietnam?

Mr. McCORD. No.

Mr. DASH. Was any of the investigation that you engaged in with regard to that group related to the Department of Justice investigation?

Mr. McCORD. In Miami, you mean?

Mr. DASH. Or any other place.

Mr. McCORD. I am sorry, would you mind restating that question? I am not sure I quite followed.

Mr. DASH. I think in your testimony you indicated that information you were receiving from the Internal Security Division and other information related in some respects to activities of the Veterans Against the War in Vietnam?

Mr. McCORD. Yes.

Mr. DASH. Was your activity in getting that information for any investigation you were conducting on behalf of the committee related in any way to any investigation the Department of Justice was making of the same group?

Mr. McCORD. If by that it is meant that whatever information I was acquiring separate and apart from the Internal Security Division was being transmitted to them the answer would be "No." It was a one-way street, it was at that time.

Mr. DASH. Now, you have named in the second break-in in the Watergate four persons—in addition to the involvement of Mr. Liddy and Hunt and you—named Mr. Barker, Mr. Martinez, Mr. Sturgis, and Mr. Gonzales. I think you also mentioned that in the first break-in there were three additional persons.

Could you name them for the record, please?

Mr. McCORD. I don't know that I know the names for certain. I have been shown some photographs by the FBI, if you want me to relate that.

Mr. DASH. Have you identified photographs of persons who did accompany you in the first time?

Mr. McCORD. I have seen two photographs of men that I believe were in that first operation.

Mr. DASH. As a result of that identification did you then learn what their names were?

Mr. MCCORD. I heard the names, the names that I originally—what I am trying to say, the names I originally heard were apparently not the true names so I can't associate the two together that way but the photographs, one individual was, I believe, that I made a probable identification was a Mr. Felipe Diego, and the other name associated with the photograph that I identified was a Mr. Reinaldo Pico.

Mr. DASH. Now, Mr. McCord, I have placed at your table a telephone which is not connected to anything. What I would like you to do, because you testified to the particular bugging operation of the Democratic National Committee headquarters, if you would demonstrate to the committee the manner in which you placed the so-called bug in the telephone.

I would like to ask the party who has the custody of the receiver to please take the receiver over to the table.

Mr. MCCORD. My counsel asked for assurance that I will not be prosecuted on this installation.

Mr. DASH. As I said, the telephone is not connected and no conversation is involved.

Now, I also will show you an item which was entered as an exhibit, [Government exhibit 16(b)] at the trial, and I understand was taken from either your possession or in the vicinity of where you were when you were arrested. I think it is a miniature transmitter in a telephone and I ask you to identify that.

Mr. MCCORD. Yes; I believe this is the one entered into evidence.

Mr. DASH. Now, will you identify exactly what that is?

Mr. MCCORD. This is a radio, essentially a radio transmitter which is powered by the power within the telephone system, the telephone line itself, and that transmitter is, was connected or was for the purpose of being connected into the telephone itself for the purpose of transmitting those conversations over the phone.

Mr. DASH. When that transmitter is connected in the telephone, is it capable of picking up both sides of the conversation?

Mr. MCCORD. Yes.

Mr. DASH. And broadcasting it to another place?

Mr. MCCORD. Yes; it is.

Mr. DASH. Will you just demonstrate, not actually attaching it, how you would place that in the telephone that is before you?

Mr. MCCORD. The cover would be taken off the telephone——

Mr. DASH. Could you lift the base a little so that the Senate committee can see what you are doing?

Mr. MCCORD. The cover would be taken off the telephone and two of the wires connected with this would be interconnected in series with the wiring within the phone itself.

This is the antenna which would be concealed underneath the telephone mechanism. The device itself would be likewise concealed under some portion of the telephone mechanism—there are three or four places that it could be put—and essentially, that is the technique of the installation.

Mr. DASH. All right. Now, since you are talking about a transmitter in a broadcasting unit, would there be any wires going from that telephone to the receiving unit which Mr. Baldwin was monitoring so that he could hear what was going on in that telephone?

96-296—73—bk. 1——16

Mr. McCord. No; it would be in effect, a small radio transmitting station, comparable, perhaps, to a very small scale of a radio station transmitting to a receiver in your home.

Mr. Dash. I will ask you to look at the kind of large receiver which was placed on the table which was entered into the trial as an exhibit [Government exhibit 105] and is that the receiver that was used by Mr. Baldwin over at the Howard Johnson Hotel?

Mr. McCord. Yes.

Mr. Dash. I take it that you identified it as his?

Mr. McCord. Yes.

Mr. Dash. Now, could you tell us the value of the receiver and what its potential is?

Mr. McCord. It is a very sophisticated and complex receiver with what is called a very high degree of sensitivity; that is, it is capable of picking up very weak transmissions. Normally, it sells for about $6,500. This one, I believe, is a used version of that. It is capable of covering a wide span of megacycles—kilocycle-megacycle range, almost to the very lowest or the very highest radio transmission can normally operate on.

Mr. Dash. What was the range of the little transmitter that you would install in the telephone? How far would it transmit?

Mr. McCord. It is a very hard thing to state specifically because it depends on so many variables. But the distance from the Watergate from the Democratic National Committee headquarters to the motel room at the Howard Johnson Motel, that transmission for this particular type instrument is received very well by this type of receiver and comes through very well. In line of sight, that range, that distance, is a normal transmission for a radio transmission.

Mr. Dash. You have testified that the receiver is a very sensitive receiver. Why was it necessary in this case to use a very sensitive receiver?

Mr. McCord. Because the object was to, the technical objective was to get the very minimum transmission possible out of that particular location so that other persons cannot pick up those transmissions in other locations. Within the Washington area, it is a very high density area of transmissions and it would be very easy under normal circumstances for someone else to also hear the conversation being intercepted unless it was an extremely low-powered transmission.

Mr. Dash. Was that to avoid detection?

Mr. McCord. Yes.

Mr. Dash. And was the microphone to be used—transmitter—a low-powered transmitter?

Mr. McCord. Very low.

Mr. Dash. And yet you were able through that receiver to get a very clear sound when it was monitored by Mr. Baldwin?

Mr. McCord. Yes, it took us about 2 days to find it. It was so low in output, so weak a signal, that it took a great deal of work, yes.

Mr. Dash. Now, once you put such a transmitter in the telephone as you indicated, you could conceal it so that it is not readily visible, even though the telephone was opened. Once you put it in there with no wires attached, using the current of the phone itself, how long could that transmitter actually transmit to that receiver? Over what period of time?

Mr. McCord. Under normal circumstances, a lot of variables again, such as the quality of the components, it would transmit for some months. Perhaps a year or so.

Mr. Dash. Perhaps a year?

Mr. McCord. Um hm.

Mr. Dash. And this therefore could have gone on way beyond June 17, could it not?

Mr. McCord. That is right.

Mr. Dash. Now, when Mr. Spencer Oliver, who we understand, whose phone was one of the phones on which such a device was used, or Mr. O'Brien's phone or one of the extensions was used, if he lifted his telephone to make a conversation with that kind of device which you have just described installed in it, would he hear a deadening on the line or would he know or have any indication that his phone was bugged or tapped?

Mr. McCord. He would receive no indication.

Mr. Dash. Therefore, is it your testimony that a professionally tapped telephone does not give any indication to the person who is using the telephone that his phone is tapped?

Mr. McCord. There is a yes and no answer, depending on the type of devices installed and the professionalism of them, and some other things; yes, sir.

Mr. Dash. And actually using a transmitter in a telephone isn't the typical way of tapping a telephone, is that correct?

Mr. McCord. This is correct.

Mr. Dash. This was a very special procedure that you used for this particular occasion?

Mr. McCord. Yes, it was.

Mr. Dash. I have no further questions.

Senator Ervin. I have about two, which will be the first for this day.

Who made arrangements for you to receive what you received on a daily basis, the documents from the Internal Security Division of the Department of Justice?

Mr. McCord. Mr. Robert Mardian made the contact with, as I understood it, with the Internal Security Division, where he had formerly worked.

Senator Ervin. At that time you made the contact, he was working with the Committee To Re-Elect the President, having retired from his Justice Department job?

Mr. McCord. Yes, sir.

Senator Ervin. He had been the head of that particular Division in the Department of Justice before he was transferred to the committee?

Mr. McCord. So I understood, yes, sir.

Senator Ervin. Now, when Mr. Caulfield came to see you, or rather, when he met you on three occasions and took you out twice on the George Washington Parkway and one time toward Virginia, was he driving his own automobile or a Government-owned automobile?

Mr. McCord. I believe he was driving his own automobile, I am sure, yes, sir.

Senator Ervin. That is all.

Mr. Thompson?

Mr. THOMPSON. Yes, Mr. Chairman.

Mr. McCord, I know you have been here a long time and I appreciate that fact, but I do have a couple of rather pointed questions I would like to ask you. I don't fancy myself in a role as a prosecutor or a defense lawyer, but I feel there are a couple of things that I need to ask you about, in quest of clarity and I plan to do so in that spirit. I am sure you understand.

Mr. McCord, there was some testimony, some previous testimony concerning the use of tape on the locks of the doors of the Democratic National Committee, and you testified, I believe last Friday, in response to a question by Senator Baker:

"Who placed the tape on the locks of the door on the second occasion?"

You responded: "I do not know."

The second occasion being the June 17 break-in as opposed to the first occasion, which I believe you said was May 27.

According to the civil deposition that you gave on April 30, 1973, in a suit brought by the Democratic National Committee against you and others, on page 167 of that deposition, your testimony is related as follows:

> The reason for checking it—first of all—on the way over, I checked the backdoor of the DNC of the Watergate Hotel office building basement level. The reason for checking it is that at the earlier meeting, earlier that evening, it had been decided that I would be elected to go into the DNC and tape the doors, so there could be ready access for them to get in and the man at the locksmith wouldn't have to pick a series of doors to get in. I did that. It took perhaps ten minutes.

Could you explain that description for us?

Mr. McCORD. Sure, because I believe your question was who taped the lock on the second occasion. They were taped—at least I understood the question that way—the June 17, they were taped on two different occasions and my response, if it was not clear, was intended to convey this idea, that I taped it on the first occasion that they were taped on the evening of June 17 and that someone else did the second taping that evening, perhaps an hour or so later. Among the other four men, the other four defendants, just which one did so, I don't know. That is what I was trying to convey.

Mr. THOMPSON. I see.

How many doors were taped on the second time?

Mr. McCORD. I think there were several, because there are several doors that normally would be taped, perhaps a half dozen or more. There is about three down on the lower level and then there are some doors up entering the corridors from perhaps the fourth, fifth, sixth, seventh floors that I believe were taped that evening.

Mr. THOMPSON. Had the tape been removed from those doors?

Mr. McCORD. I do not know about the corridor doors. They were not removed when I saw them on the lower level doors, the three or four down there.

Mr. THOMPSON. Of course, there would be no need to retape them had not the tape been removed, would there?

Mr. McCORD. Let us see if I understand the question. There would be no reason to retape them?

Mr. THOMPSON. To retape the doors the second time if the first tape had not been removed.

Mr. McCORD. No, that is correct, that is correct.

Mr. THOMPSON. You heard Officer Shoffler, I believe, Mr. McCord, testify last week that when the doors were locked at the DNC one could get out of the office building without a key or without having the door taped. Could you explain, first of all, what was the need to tape the doors once you were inside and, secondly, why did no one seemingly have the presence of mind to remove the tape on the B–2 level, leaving it there for the officers to find?

Mr. McCORD. Well, I think you almost have to see the different doors involved to be able to understand that situation and it involves this: There are, there are some stairwells coming down off the different floors and even stairwells off of the different floors, six or seven that coiled down like a rope. That is, you may go on down into the stairwell off of the corridor from one exit and it will go down one stairwell and you go around the corridor and it will go down another one and you go down a separate stairwell, the two of them wind down. Some of those doors are at night locked from both sides, as I recall, so that—some are not, let me correct that. Some are locked from the inside. Those that were locked so that if you were trying to get out of the corridor down into a stairwell late at night you could not get into the stairwell. But you might be able to go up a couple of floors, say, to the eighth floor and I think there was a door open there, and you would have to come down and then go into, say you wanted to get down back to the sixth floor and get into the corridor, go into that door from the stairwell side you could get in. So that door, for example, would have to be taped if you had in mind getting out in a hurry and getting down, it would have to be taped from, you had to plan it from, the stairwell side first. Some of these other doors locked from both sides. It is a pretty——

Mr. THOMPSON. I believe you almost have to be there to understand.

Mr. McCORD. That is correct.

Mr. THOMPSON. Is this the reason the eighth floor door was taped on the 17th?

Mr. McCORD. Yes, sir.

Mr. THOMPSON. Did you personally check out the doors, check the situation to determine whether or not the tape would be needed in particular doors when you went in to tape those doors or did anyone check that?

Mr. McCORD. Well, we knew from the previous operation on Memorial Day that they would have to be taped if you were going to plan to leave in a hurry if you got caught there, for example, if the police came in on you before you got in, you would have to tape the doors, otherwise, you could not be sure that you could get out.

Mr. THOMPSON. What about the answer to the second part of my question: You are an experienced man, CIA and FBI, and evidently these other men were experienced in their own way, and yet the tape of the B–2 level, readily accessible to anyone coming by there to check as the officer did, was left on the door. You did not remove the tape. Why was that done and, secondly, why was the risk taken to go back up into the DNC with no means of escape? Evidently, once you were caught, after you had seen that someone had removed the tape, and for all practical purposes you had to assume that someone was aware that somebody was trying to get in or had already gotten in, why was that decision made to start with? Why was the decision made to go back in there after you knew someone had been tampering with that door?

Mr. McCord. It is a good question, because we had a lot of discussions on it later.

Mr. Thompson. Where?

Mr. McCord. In jail. [Laughter.]

We came by the lower level door that originally had been taped, assuming that the tape was still there when you could get right on in without any delay, this is all of the five men together, getting ready to go up into the Democratic National Committee headquarters and we found that that tape had been taken off and the door was now locked, speaking of the basement level, so we regrouped, so to speak, right below the restaurant in the Watergate Hotel and talked over what to do and it was agreed that the locksmith and, I believe one or two of the men, would go back over and make an effort to pick the lock to get in, and that——

Mr. Thompson. Why? Why was that decision reached after you knew that someone had detected your being there previously?

Mr. McCord. All right, let me add, the decision was there to send the locksmith back over and let him start to work in order that there not be any more delay in time, and for the other men, Barker and I believe one other, go back up to Mr. Hunt's room and discuss the situation with Mr. Hunt and Mr. Liddy in terms of whether they feel what we should do next, should they go ahead and pick them, try to pick the lock and get on in or should we call it off, and for me to go back over to the motel and wait for a word on what was to be done; understood, well understood, this was a calculated risk in sending them back over to begin picking the lock but, on the other hand, the more time that went by, the fewer people there would be around the Watergate Hotel and the more conspicuous the men would be and, therefore, that had some risk in terms of delaying the matter any further. So we sort of decided to go in both directions—to go ahead and start to go in, to go back up and talk it over with Hunt and Liddy and see what they wanted to do.

Mr. Thompson. Who made the ultimate decision as to whether or not you were going back in that night? You say that there was a risk in waiting, you mean waiting any later that night or waiting for another day or another week or what?

Mr. McCord. Well, there were risks in waiting any longer that night, for example.

Mr. Thompson. Why not call the whole thing off and come back in 2 or 3 nights?

Mr. McCord. Well——

Mr. Thompson. It looks like a pretty good idea now, doesn't it?

Mr. McCord. It does, very good. [Laughter.]

It was made on the basis that, first of all, as I say any further delay in time made five men stand out that much more that night, any delay of time that night, made five men stand out that much more around the hotel and around the Watergate Office Building and therefore rather than to lose that time the decision was to go both ways, to send the locksmith over and start to work with it and send the other men over to talk with Liddy and Hunt to see whether or not they wanted to proceed or not.

Mr. THOMPSON. Let me ask you another question in regard to another subject. As I understand your testimony, it has been that I believe on July 27 of 1972, you received the first payment from Mrs. Hunt of $15,000?

Mr. McCORD. Yes.

Mr. THOMPSON. And that was to do you through November, I believe?

Mr. McCORD. Right.

Mr. THOMPSON. That you received some additional money in December which was to be payment in advance for the rest of December and January?

Mr. McCORD. Yes; that is correct.

Mr. THOMPSON. Do you recall the date of the payment in December?

Mr. McCORD. I believe it was the 2d of December.

Mr. THOMPSON. December 2d?

Mr. McCORD. Yes, sir.

Mr. THOMPSON. You mentioned the letter that you wrote to Mr. Caulfield, the anonymous letter in December. Do you recall the date in December of that letter?

Mr. McCORD. No; I do not. I remember the week which was the week following Christmas, December 25.

Mr. THOMPSON. The latter part of December?

Mr. McCORD. Yes.

Mr. THOMPSON. So the letter to Mr. Caulfield was after you received the No. 2 payment?

Mr. McCORD. Yes, sir.

Mr. THOMPSON. What was that payment, how much money was it?

Mr. McCORD. It was one of the 2 months' payments for the salary, for December and for, I think, additional money, $13,000 for lawyers' fees.

Mr. THOMPSON. Was there some question in the latter part of November or during December as to whether or not additional money would be forthcoming?

Mr. McCORD. Yes; there was. It was a question on Hunt's part and Mrs. Hunt communicated that question to me, and I think that probably had something to do with the letter that he wrote and that I have described, a three-page letter that was read to one of the lawyers.

Mr. THOMPSON. Did it have anything to do with your letter that you wrote to Caulfield?

Mr. McCORD. None whatsoever. My letter had to do with my anger about this plan to lay this operation on CIA, and I think the letter sort of indicates that.

Mr. THOMPSON. Mr. McCord, you have stated that you were concerned from sometime shortly before the trial I believe up until recently, that the trial was a sham, that the trial was fixed, that there was a miscarrying of justice, and I assume you are talking essentially about the fact that some of the right people were not being prosecuted, and you were not being free to arrive at full disclosure by the Government; is that correct?

Mr. McCORD. If I can state it more precisely it was the fact there was perjured testimony at the trial itself by a key witness, and that key witness was Mr. Jeb Magruder, his testimony was perhaps the most important testimony in the whole trial.

Mr. THOMPSON. Pardon me just a moment, the basis on which you say his testimony was perjured, I assume, has to do with what Mr. Liddy has told you about Mr. Magruder; is that not correct?

Mr. MCCORD. Told me before June 17 and the comments we exchanged at the time Mr. Liddy—excuse me—Mr. Magruder was up on the stand stating that he knew nothing about the Watergate operation prior to June 17.

Mr. THOMPSON. So the answer to my question is "Yes."

Mr. MCCORD. Yes.

Mr. THOMPSON. All right. Go ahead; that was the basis of your statement.

Mr. MCCORD. No, not quite, not completely. There is also a factor that Mr. Magruder in addition to testifying that he knew nothing about the Watergate operation and his testimony being probably that of the most important witness in the trial, also could have named others who were principal in the case, specifically Mr. Mitchell and Mr. Dean, according to the information I had from Mr. Liddy in which I had no doubt about.

Mr. THOMPSON. You could have, too, could you not?

Mr. MCCORD. I could have too; right.

Mr. THOMPSON. Why didn't you?

Mr. MCCORD. I will be glad to talk that one over, too. Why did I not get on the stand?

Mr. THOMPSON. Yes.

I think that is a fair question. It seems to me again according to the statement of your attorney there at the time, Mr. Alch, your defense was essentially as you stated to Senator Baker here today, that you felt that because of violence in the country and so forth, that actually it posed a threat, possibly to your life and the lives of other people, that is in the record according to Mr. Alch.

Mr. MCCORD. Sure.

Mr. THOMPSON. I take it your defense was not that at that time part of your motivation was, as you have stated here before this committee that you thought you had the right possibly to go ahead without being in any legal difficulty because of Mr. Mitchell's involvement, part of Mr. Dean's involvement, which is part of what you told us. Evidently you didn't tell Mr. Alch that; Mr. Alch didn't use that as part of your defense. I am wondering in answer to those questions, why didn't you come forward at that time and why didn't you tell Mr. Alch what could have been an even more significant part of your defense at that time.

Mr. MCCORD. Well, I had many conversations with Mr. Alch about the facts in the case, and the other principals involved and the decision of mine as to when to come forward with the information which I did as basically my decision and it was a day at a time decision on my part as to when was the proper issuance time to tell the facts on this case.

Mr. THOMPSON. You waited until——

Mr. MCCORD. I waited until I had an opportunity to tell, No. 1, a man I believed to be an honest judge, Judge Sirica; No. 2, to tell this committee so there would be a proper forum for all of the facts to come out and to be discovered.

I felt, for example, during the trial itself that if I came forward and told the story at this point in time, in light of the nature of the information I had which some people have described as hearsay or secondhand, the rules of evidence as I understand it may have excluded some of that information being provided in testimony, or at least I felt that all of the facts would not be developed during the trial if I got up on the stand and related them. To me it was a matter of when was the right time to tell it and this was a most difficult decision. It was not influenced by money or anything else. It was influenced by basically my own reasoning as to when was the right time to tell the story so that there would be an adequate forum for development of all of the facts in this case. I think my decision has been the right one. I think I told Judge Sirica first and I told this committee second and I am fully convinced that was a right decision.

Mr. THOMPSON. Was there any doubt in your mind that you would come forward at that time to Judge Sirica, that he would not have taken the appropriate action that the matter would not have been handled? According to the trial transcript Judge Sirica practically pleaded with anyone to come forward and tell the truth. He states here on page 1499 of the trial transcript:

"If they know anything about this case, if they want to talk to the grand jury it is not too late. That is up to them. I mean I always operate under the theory that the truth never hurts anybody. If they wait until they are convicted and then they decide to talk well, I can't say anything about that but I think if they are going to talk, if there is anything in their mind along those lines, the time for them to do it is during the trial."

He was stating that.

Mr. MCCORD. Yes.

Mr. THOMPSON. Was there any doubt in your mind that you would be compromised in any way if you went forward and told Judge Sirica back in January?

Mr. MCCORD. Not Judge Sirica in the least. He is the lone man I felt like I could depend on in this case.

Mr. THOMPSON. He is also the man who would be sentencing you shortly.

Mr. MCCORD. That is true, too. That is true, too, but what I am saying about my belief is the man is honest and genuine but you asked my reasons, and my reasons were the ones I have stated, and I think that the decision as to the timing of saying what I did was right and I don't regret that decision; I believe I was upset, as I told you earlier, that quite frankly the facts would not have come out and been developed by this committee in the way that they have.

Mr. THOMPSON. But you were, of course, receiving money during this period of time also, were you not?

Mr. MCCORD. I was receiving money until December 2, but quite frankly, as I told the people who were sending me it, it had no bearing on what I was saying or was going to say.

Mr. THOMPSON. You told Mr. Caulfield that there was a possibility that you could get your case thrown out of court because of a wiretap. Did that enter into your decision to hold out?

Mr. MCCORD. No.

Mr. THOMPSON. And not come forward?

Mr. McCORD. No, it did not.

Mr. THOMPSON. Were you not trying at that time with Mr. Caulfield to get him to get the Government to admit an illegal wiretap so your case would be thrown out?

Mr. McCORD. Oh, yes. Let me repeat what I said before so things will be as clear as I know how to make them.

I said I thought the case was a sham, that the trial was a sham, because of the perjured testimony and because of withholding a pile of material, No. 1 by gentlemen who would be hurt, which would involve a number of higher-ups in the case, and No. 2, we were not getting a fair trial. I have said this in many ways, in fact. I thought the fact that we ought to have—justice, as far as I was concerned, demanded that the case be kicked out and started all over again on this thing and start all over in a circumstance that, No. 1, we get a fair trial. We were not getting a fair trial. Perjury was being committed by key witnesses.

Mr. THOMPSON. You were interested in your fair trial, of course, as your constitutional right.

Mr. McCORD. For all fair trials.

Mr. THOMPSON. In your eyes, did Mr. Magruder's failure to tell the truth about it prejudice your case?

Mr. McCORD. Of course. If he was a key witness and all other testimony seems to fall into place around his testimony and he was withholding the names of principals in the case itself, I would say that prejudices the case and it puts a completely, totally different light on the case.

In other words, the trial itself was appearing to indicate that Mr. Liddy was the sum total of this operation, that he was the leader, the director, the funder, the whole package, and that the case cut off at this level. It did not. Obviously, the case extended much higher.

Mr. THOMPSON. In other words, Mr. Magruder should have come in and implicated higher-ups so that you would not have to. Is that the way his testimony prejudices your case?

Mr. McCORD. And he could prove it.

Mr. THOMPSON. That is the way you looked at that, because—I assume there was no controversy over the fact that you were caught with four other men, huddled behind a desk, with burglary tools on you and eavesdropping equipment on you?

Mr. McCORD. No argument about that at all but I thought under any circumstances, at least a man deserves a fair trial.

Mr. THOMPSON. Absolutely.

Mr. McCORD. And that we were not getting it.

Mr. THOMPSON. Absolutely.

You mentioned your calls in September and October to the Chilian Embassy and the Israeli Embassy. Let me ask you this: What was the purpose of those phone calls?

Mr. McCORD. I think I previously stated—If not I will restate it—to try to test——

Mr. THOMPSON. Try to test?

Mr. CORD. Try to test the accuracy of the Government's response regarding intercepted conversations of mine. I was concerned that there had been wiretapping since June 17 of my telephone conversations, and this would provide a test to see if in fact, all the Government records of the Government, some 12 agencies, had in fact been searched; the inferences by the response of the Government 12 days, 14 days after a motion was filed was there is nothing on the record in the Government of any interception of Mr. McCord's calls anywhere, and I knew that as I have stated, it takes more than 14 days normally to search 12 different Government agencies for records of such telephone calls.

Mr. THOMPSON. How was this a test, Mr. McCord? Did you think or did you know that these embassies had been bugged?

Mr. McCORD. I had assumed that they were.

Mr. THOMPSON. You assumed that they were?

Mr. McCORD. Yes, sir.

Mr. THOMPSON. And you based this assumption on your motion alleging that you were the subject of illegal surveillance?

Mr. McCORD. No, that is not quite right. If I left that impression, I did not mean to.

Mr. THOMPSON. Let me ask you this: If you assumed that they were bugged, would it be incorrect to say that possibly you called those embassies in order to more or less pull yourself up by your own bootstraps and have your conversations intercepted and perhaps get the Government in a position where it would have to deny or admit that those embassies were in fact bugged and, therefore, might dismiss your case on that basis?

Mr. McCORD. Oh, yes, if I may answer your question, oh, yes, I stated that this morning. I read it in the statement.

But to finish the rest of the story. Let us suppose that any calls were intercepted at any point in time. The normal procedure would be for disclosure by the Government of those calls in camera before the judge himself and the judge to determine the relevancy of those calls. It was clear that those calls were not relevant to the trial itself and were not going to be entered in evidence. Therefore, the case could not be adjourned.

Mr. THOMPSON. I want to interrupt you at that point. Pardon me for interrupting.

Of course, this was a long time after the fact. Did you realize this point of law at the time you called these embassies?

Mr. McCORD. Oh, I have had a pretty clear knowledge of the law since June 17, through what is called jailhouse lawyers who do as much as anybody can.

Mr. THOMPSON. Did Mr. Liddy advise you?

Mr. McCORD. I think I talked with him, yes, quite a few of them, about the predicament we were in. But he did not discuss this particular point.

Mr. THOMPSON. What you are saying is that at the time you made these calls, you realized that they would be possibly intercepted. You realized even at that time that they possibly might be irrelevant.

Mr. McCORD. I knew they were irrelevant. There was no possibility in it.

But I had read, to finish the rest of it, I had read, for example, in the month before the Dr. Ellsberg situation, where the Government had for 5 months denied that there were any interceptions of Mr. Ellsberg's calls or calls of his attorney. Yet, it was not until the defense attorneys required, requested a court order be issued searching the records of 12 different agencies and some 30 to 45 days later, calls, intercepted calls of Mr. Boudin were then disclosed by the Government showing that calls actually had been intercepted when previously they had been denied.

Mr. THOMPSON. Calls to these two embassies?

Mr. McCORD. No.

Mr. THOMPSON. Why did you mention these two embassies? What made you assume that these embassies were bugged?

Mr. McCORD. At random.

Mr. THOMPSON. I beg your pardon?

Mr. McCORD. At random.

Mr. THOMPSON. You picked them at random?

Mr. McCORD. Um hm.

Mr. THOMPSON. Because you read in the papers that some people have alleged in times past that governments do these sort of things against one another. Is that what you are saying?

Mr. McCORD. Something like that.

Mr. THOMPSON. Let me ask you another question on another subject.

I beg your pardon?

Mr. McCORD. I believe my attorney says something like that.

Mr. THOMPSON. These FBI reports and Internal Security documents that we have been talking about now, could you tell me—are you talking about classified material that is improper to be disseminated to political parties, or are you talking about materials that you disseminated to both parties, local police chiefs and things of this nature? I understand the FBI does disseminate a certain amount of material. I do not know about the Justice Department, but perhaps you do. Could you give us some idea as to the nature of these documents that were talked about?

Mr. McCORD. Of course, Mr. Mardian, who headed that division, could give you an accurate statement of the facts. I am drawing a conclusion, and my conclusion now, this is not only an appropriate thing to do, I think it is a very necessary thing to do to both parties, for example, when a convention is forthcoming and there is violence anticipated.

Let me put it another way. I think to fail to disclose to either party prior to such a convention where violence is anticipated and lives may be lost is almost criminal dereliction where it could have been prevented by disclosure of anything of this type, that had they received it, they perhaps could have taken steps to prevent the loss of life or destruction of property. I thought it was entirely appropriate at that time.

Now, your question as to classification. I understood the material was, had been declassified or was not classified. My memory is not as clear as it should be. Some of it may well have been classified. I do not know. But I felt the propriety of it was entirely proper.

Mr. THOMPSON. At the time, you did not feel that you were dealing with classified documents or you were getting anything that was improper for you to get?

Mr. McCORD. I did not feel there was anything improper. Quite to the contrary, as you said, I felt to fail to get it is to fail to get information that protects the lives of people you are charged with protecting.

Mr. THOMPSON. Did you know, or did you have an understanding during this period of time as to whether or not the Democratic Party also had this material available to them?

Mr. McCORD. I had an understanding that the Democratic Party was getting some comparable type of information. From whom they got it, through what channels, I do not know.

Mr. THOMPSON. All right; one more question, Mr. McCord. You mentioned you discussed the logs in connection with just what I asked you about a moment ago. To whom were these logs sent?

The record is not clear about this and I think in fairness, you should set the record straight.

Specifically, I refer to a story printed in the Washington Post on one occasion, stating that supposedly Mr. William Timmons, Gene Sedam, and Mr. Robert Odle received these logs. Do you know whether or not on any occasion any of these men ever received the results of the wiretaps or the bugging that you were carrying out?

Mr. McCORD. I have—am perfectly certain in my own mind that none of them received it. I think something of Mr. Baldwin's memory was in error if and when he made such a statement. I can understand how he made it at the time. I have no knowledge that they did receive it, I do not know whether they did receive it. They certainly did not receive it from me.

Mr. THOMPSON. Do you know if they were involved in any manner in this?

Mr. McCORD. Absolutely not.

Mr. THOMPSON. Thank you, Mr. McCord.

Mr. Chairman, I am finished.

Senator ERVIN. Mr. McCord, Mr. Thompson asked you why you did not speak earlier. At the time the trial was in progress and until after the trial, you had knowledge or at least information that all of the people involved with you, including Mr. Liddy and Mr. Hunt, were receiving compensation from the Committee To Re-Elect the President?

Mr. McCORD. I believe that is accurate; yes, sir.

Senator ERVIN. And you had witnesses at the trial and you had seen and heard the deputy director or deputy chairman, or whatever they called him, of the committee, Mr. Magruder, give testimony which you believed to constitute perjury?

Mr. McCORD. I did, sir.

Senator ERVIN. You had been urged by your lawyer to keep silent?

Mr. McCORD. Well, my lawyer had communicated to me the matter of Executive clemency. I cannot recall that he tried to get me to keep silent.

Senator ERVIN. Now, Mr. Caulfield had come on the scene three times and urged you to keep silent?

Mr. McCORD. Yes, sir.

Senator ERVIN. And you felt at that time there was nobody else that you knew that knew anything about this that you thought was willing to speak at that time?

Mr. McCORD. No other defendants; no, sir.

Senator ERVIN. So if you had come out and said anything, you would have been the lone voice, would you not, as far as you could see?

Mr. McCORD. A two-part answer.

I communicated my concern to Mr. Caulfield, a law enforcement officer, an assistant director of the Alcohol and Tax Unit.

Senator ERVIN. Well, were you influenced by the criticisms of certain people who had asked you to postpone making any statements until later?

Mr. McCORD. Yes, sir; I was.

Senator ERVIN. I would like to make a statement on behalf of myself as an individual and member of the committee, not as the chairman. I would like to thank you for your cooperation with the committee in its effort to ascertain the facts about this matter.

Mr. McCORD. Thank you, sir. Can I respond?

Senator ERVIN. Yes.

Mr. McCORD. I think, sir, that this country at this point in time, in having the very distinguished Senators and the staff that we have, is extremely fortunate in having such great men here to probe into this without fear of where it is going to end and develop all the facts. I am grateful.

Senator ERVIN. You will be available for further testimony if this committee decides to call you?

Mr. McCORD. Yes, sir.

Senator ERVIN. Thank you.

Counsel will call the next witness.

Mr. DASH. Call Mr. John J. Caulfield, please.

Senator ERVIN. Mr. Caulfield, stand up, please.

Hold up your right hand.

Do you swear that the evidence that you give the Senate Select Committee on Presidential Campaign Activities to be the truth, the whole truth, and nothing but the truth, so help you God?

Mr. CAULFIELD. I do.

Senator ERVIN. Mr. Caulfield, as I understand it, you will be available to the committee later if it wants to get you or to get any information from you other than that which you may give on this occasion?

Mr. CAULFIELD. I understand, sir.

Senator ERVIN. Thank you.

Senator BAKER. Mr. Chairman——

Senator TALMADGE. Mr. Chairman, there is a vote going on.

Senator BAKER. Before we proceed, I note that signal lights indicate that there is a rollcall vote in progress in the Senate.

Might I suggest, Mr. Chairman, if the members of the committee agree, in the interest of time and expediency, that we might consider part of the committee going to vote now and part of it going at the 5-minute warning buzzer and permit this witness to begin, at least, with the reading of his statement?

Senator ERVIN. I think that would be very wise.

Mr. DASH. Mr. Caulfield, would you for the record, please state your full name and address?

TESTIMONY OF JOHN J. CAULFIELD, ACCOMPANIED BY JOHN P. SEARS, COUNSEL

Mr. CAULFIELD. My name is John J. Caulfield, I reside at 5205 Concordia Street, Fairfax, Va.

Mr. DASH. Are you accompanied at this hearing by an attorney?

Mr. CAULFIELD. Yes, I am.

Mr. DASH. Will the attorney please identify himself for the record?

Mr. SEARS. My name is John P. Sears. I am an attorney in Washington, D.C.

Mr. DASH. Mr. Sears, there is another microphone.

Mr. Caulfield, you have a statement which you wish to either submit to the committee or read to the committee?

Mr. CAULFIELD. I would prefer to read it, Mr. Dash.

Mr. DASH. Every member of the committee, I understand, has received a copy of that. Would you now commence to read your statement?

Mr. CAUFIELD. Yes, sir; I will.

My name is John J. Caulfield. I was born on March 12, 1929, in the Bronx, N.Y. I was educated at the local parochial elementary school and Rice High School in Manhattan. Upon completion of my high school education I received a partial scholarship for basketball at Wake Forest University.

After 2 years I was forced to leave college owing to the fact that my family could not supply enough additional funds for me to continue my education. For a short time thereafter I worked as a bank teller before joining the New York Telephone Co. in 1949 as a draftsman.

In November of 1950 I was drafted into the U.S. Army where I served in the Signal Corps until I was honorably discharged in November of 1952. Prior to being drafted, I had taken the civil service examination for appointment to the New York City Police Department.

While still in the Army, I received notification that I had passed the examination and on June 1, 1953, I joined the police department as a patrolman. In August of that year, having graduated from the Police Academy, I was assigned to a Bronx precinct where I walked a beat and was assigned to a sector car which covered one area of the precinct.

Owing to an award which I received for the arrest and conviction of a ring of seven people involved in a series of robberies, I was promoted to the position of detective on September 25, 1955. Between that time and June of 1966, I was assigned to the Bureau of Special Services where my duties consisted of monitoring the activities of terrorist organizations and frequent assignment to VIP protective duties.

My activities in regard to militant terrorist groups consisted of monitoring and compiling intelligence on their overt activities, newspaper research, interviewing informants, investigating what relationships existed between these groups, and generally familiarizing myself with the progress of their activities. Examples of the groups which I investigated included the Communist Party, Cuban militant organizations, as well as a variety of Latin domestic revolutionary groups who planned or were suspected of planning various kinds of unlawful activities. During this time I received a number of awards in connection with my work, some of which were:

1. In 1958, I received a Meritorious Police Award owing to the seizure of a store of contraband weapons destined for Ireland. I might add parenthetically that my father has not yet gotten over that.

2. In 1959, I received an Excellent Police Award for arrest and conviction, in cooperation with the FBI, of the prime Castro agent operating in the United States in 1958.

3. In December 1964, I received a Meritorious Police Award for the arrest of the perpetrators of the bazooka shelling of the United Nations.

4. In 1965, I received an award for participating in the arrest and conviction of a group of French-Canadians and domestic militants who had plotted to destroy the Washington Monument, the Statue of Liberty, and the Liberty Bell.

My protective duties in regard to VIP assignments consisted, among other things, of coordinating the activities of Secret Service agents with the New York City Police Department in the political campaign of 1960. During the 1960 campaign I was assigned to both candidates when they visited New York and I got to know Mr. John Sherwood who was in charge at that time of Vice President Nixon's Secret Service detail.

Senator BAKER. Mr. Witness, would you suspend for just a moment? The signal system indicates there is now 5 minutes before the end of the rollcall.

Might I ask the committee if there is any objection to the witness continuing to read this statement in the presence of counsel, even though Senator Weicker and I as the only two committee members remaining have to go out now and vote. If there is any objection on behalf of the committee or on behalf of the witness or his attorney, we will have to suspend. But inasmuch as your statement is 26 pages long and each member has a copy of it, if you have no objection, I suggest that we proceed.

Mr. SEARS. We have no objection.

Mr. CAULFIELD. May I proceed?

Mr. DASH. Yes sir, proceed on behalf of the committee.

Mr. CAULFIELD. In May of 1968, I received a letter from Mr. Sherwood indicating that there was a possible position in the upcoming Nixon campaign for the Presidency for a person to serve in the security area. I telephoned Mr. Sherwood and substantiated what he had said in the letter and he told me that Mr. H. R. Haldeman would interview me if I were interested. Mr. Sherwood arranged an appointment for me with Mr. Haldeman at 450 Park Avenue in New York, which was the campaign headquarters, and I was hired.

With the assassination of Robert Kennedy in early June, my duties changed and ultimately, starting with the end of the 1968 convention, I became responsible to Mr. John Ehrlichman for being sure that the staff quarters and working areas of the Nixon campaign traveling staff were secure as we moved from city to city during the campaign. Mr. Ehrlichman was pleased with my work during this time, and on election night in 1968 he told me that in view of my work he would be happy to recommend me if I had any interest in obtaining a position with the Federal Government in Washington.

A few days after the election I called Mr. Ehrlichman in Key Biscayne, Fla., and told him I wished to be considered for the position of Chief U.S. Marshal. He told me that he would speak to Mr. Haldeman about this and get back to me. Subsequently a meeting was arranged with Mr. John Mitchell at the Pierre Hotel in New York at which Mr. Mitchell told me that while my work was highly thought of, there had been a decision made to "semimilitarize" the U.S. Marshal's Office and therefore they were considering a retiring, high, military official for this post. Between December 1968 and April of 1969, I was interviewed for and pursued a variety of possible appointive jobs in Washington.

In late March 1969, I received a telephone call from Mr. Ehrlichman who asked me if I would visit him in his office a day or two later. I did so and at that meeting he asked if I would be willing to set up a private security entity in Washington, D.C., for purposes of providing investigative support for the White House. I told him that I would think this over but by the time I had returned home that evening, I had decided that I did not wish to do this. I called him the next day with a counterproposal, namely, that I join the White House staff under Mr. Ehrlichman and, besides providing liaison functions with various law enforcement agencies, thereby be available to process any investigative requests from the White House. I mentioned to him that if he agreed with my proposal I would intend to use the services of one Mr. Anthony Ulasewicz who was a detective with the New York City Police Department nearing retirement. He said he would think about it and get back to me.

A few days later I received a call from his office asking if I would come to Washington to discuss the matter and that meeting resulted in my appointment to the White House staff on April 8, 1969.

My duties at that time consisted of being a White House liaison with a variety of law enforcement agencies in the Federal Government, through arrangements worked out with Mr. Ehrlichman, Mr. Herbert Kalmbach, and Anthony Ulasewicz. Mr. Ulasewicz retired from the New York City Police Department and was paid on a monthly basis by the Kalmbach law firm, that employment commencing on July 9, 1969. During the next 3 years, first on orders from Mr. Ehrlichman and later in some instances, on orders from Mr. John Dean, Mr. Ulasewicz, under my supervision, performed a variety of investigative functions, reporting the results of his findings to the White House through me. I do not fully recall all of the investigations performed in this fashion but have available a list of those which I do recall if the committee wishes to examine it.

In July of 1970 Mr. John Dean became counsel to the President and Mr. Ehrlichman was named to the position of Presidential Assistant for Domestic Affairs. Thereafter I worked directly for Mr. Dean, but on occasion, Mr. Ehrlichman continued to call upon me directly for investigative work involving the services of Mr. Ulasewicz.

In the spring of 1971, I began to notice that, for some reason, the amount of investigation work handled by Mr. Ulasewicz through me had diminished. Much of the talk around the White House was beginning to center more and more on the 1972 Presidential election and I began to examine ways in my mind in which I might become involved. Since I had performed security duties in the 1968 election campaign, and realizing some of the security demands of a Presidential campaign, I wished to become involved in the security area of the campaign.

Toward that end, I composed a memorandum suggesting that an outside security capability be formed to handle the demand of the

1972 campaign. Such an organization would have a capability to perform various security functions to insure the security of the traveling staff, the Committee To Re-Elect the President headquarters, the convention site and would employ various guards and security people. In short, I was suggesting the formation of a capability to cover all the security needs of a Presidential campaign. The name I gave to this suggested operation was "Sandwedge."

I further suggested that I leave the White House staff and set up this security entity, if it were approved, and suggested a budget of approximately $300,000 to $400,000. I gave the memorandum to Mr. Dean and got the strong impression from him that it went to higher levels, but I have no knowledge of who saw it. During the summer of 1971, I had high hopes that my proposal would be accepted and had one other direct conversation at lunch about its contents with Mr. Dean and with Mr. Jeb Magruder. Between the end of June and October of 1971, I inquired of Mr. Dean as to the status of my proposal on numerous occasions but ultimately was told by Mr. Dean that he didn't think my suggestion was "going anywhere."

I was disappointed that my memorandum had been refused. I next spoke with Mr. Dean concerning obtaining a position as a personal aide to John Mitchell, when be became campaign director. Mr. Dean agreed to ask Mr. Mitchell if such a position was available; he did so, and on November 24, 1971, he accompanied me to an interview at Mr. Mitchell's office.

I explained to Mr. Mitchell that what I wanted was a position similar to that occupied by Dwight Chapin in relation to the President and that in addition to handling the kinds of activities that Chapin handled for the President, I could be of value to Mr. Mitchell as a bodyguard. Mr. Mitchell listened to what I had to say but was noncommittal as to what status I would occupy with him. He said, however, that we would "get that all straightened out when I arrived at the reelection committee." He was unsure as to when he would join the reelection committee but thought that it would be sometime in January or February of 1972. I left his office and walked back to the White House by myself. Mr. Dean remained and as I was walking through Mr. Mitchell's outer office I noted Mr. Gordon Liddy sitting with Mr. Dean evidently waiting to see Mr. Mitchell.

At that time, I was sure I had a position with Mr. Mitchell but the nature of my duties was quite unsettled. Ultimately, on the 1st of March 1972, I went to the reelection committee to commence my duties there. It soon became clear to me that Mr. Mitchell regarded me only as a bodyguard which was not what I had had in mind at all. During March I took two trips with Mr. Mitchell outside of Washington, one brief trip to New York City and the other to Key Biscayne, Fla. Since Mr. Mitchell regarded me as his personal bodyguard I carried a revolver in my briefcase.

By the time the trip to Florida occurred in late March, I was already in touch with a friend of mine at the Treasury Department about possible employment there. After being in Florida for approximately 2 to 3 days, I received word that my house in Fairfax, Va., had been burglarized and so I flew home to attend to my wife and family. Mr. Fred LaRue had joined us in Florida after our arrival and upon my departure, he asked that I leave my revolver in his possession since

Mrs. Mitchell would "feel better" if there were a revolver on the premises. I gave my revolver to him and ultimately received it back in May of 1972, after LaRue had given it to Mr. James McCord for safekeeping upon Mr. LaRue's return from Florida.

Once I returned from Florida I performed no more duties of any kind for Mr. Mitchell and had formally decided to seek employment at the Treasury Department which I ultimately obtained. On April 28, I started working for the Treasury Department and then became Staff Assistant to the Assistant Secretary of Treasury for Enforcement and on July 1, 1972, I became Acting Assistant Director for Enforcement, Bureau of Alcohol, Tobacco, and Firearms.

In September of 1971, I received a call from Mr. Barry Mountain of the Republican National Committee who informed me that John Ragan was leaving his duties as security officer for the national committee, the Republican National Committee.

He asked me if I knew of anyone who would be interested in the position and I said no, but that I would check around. I subsequently asked Mr. Al Wong, a Deputy Assistant Director of the Secret Service, if he knew of anyone to recommend for such a position. He told me that he could recommend highly a former colleague and retired CIA agent, Mr. James McCord, and gave me his telephone number. I then called Mr. McCord and invited him to my office for an interview. Mr. McCord provided me with a résumé and, as a result of my interview with him, I called Mr. Mountain and arranged for Mr. McCord to see Mr. Mountain. He did so, and was thereafter hired by the Republican National Committee.

Since before leaving his employment, Mr. Ragan had intended to handle security for the Committee To Re-Elect the President offices as well as the national committee, it was natural that Mr. McCord upon being hired by the national committee was soon interviewed by Mr. Robert Odle, the office manager of the Committee To Re-Elect the President and in late December or early January Mr. McCord was hired by the Committee To Re-Elect the President also. I had been consulted about him by the reelection committee and recommended him for this position also.

Between our original meeting in September of 1971, and June 1972, Mr. McCord and I grew to be personal friends even though we did not physically see each other frequently with the exception of the month of March 1972, when I saw him on a daily basis at the Committee To Re-Elect the President. During this period we casually discussed on some occasions the possibility of going into business together after the election campaign was over and Mr. McCord felt quite beholden to me since he felt that I had been responsible for placing him at the national committee and the Committee To Re-Elect the President.

In May of 1972, we had lunch together at the Hay Adams Hotel in Washington. I had just begun my assignments at the Treasury Department and we discussed my plans and hopes for expanding my duties and he stated at that time that I should "keep him in mind" if I were looking for consultant help in carrying on investigations.

In July of 1972, and that date may well be wrong and I don't know but my recollection of the date was July of 1972, in July of 1972, after his arrest, I had Mr. Ulasewicz call his home and tell him to go to a designated public telephone booth near his house where I would be calling him. I called him at that public telephone and simply asked him if there was anything I could do for him or his family at this time of personal difficulty. No one had asked me to make this call and I was motivated entirely by my own personal concern for his condition and that of his family.

To deviate a bit here I noticed Mr. McCord indicated here his conversation with me on that occasion coming of a story relative to a double agent Alfred Baldwin. I do recall him mentioning that, I did not when I made this statement, that is in fact correct.

I did not see or hear from Mr. McCord again until I received an anonymous letter at my home in December of 1972. It was typewritten, a note approximately two paragraphs in length and, to the best of my knowledge said:

> Dear Jack—I am sorry to have to tell you this but the White House is bent on having the CIA take the blame for the Watergate. If they continue to pursue this course, every tree in the forest will fall and it will be a scorched earth. Jack, even you will be hurt in the fallout.

I examined the letter and found that it was postmarked in Rockville, Md., and thereby believed that the letter was from James McCord because he lived in Rockville. I called Mr. Dean's office and spoke with Mr. Fielding, an assistant to Mr. Dean, and read the letter over the telephone to him. Thereafter I went to Mr. Dean's office and gave him the letter.

In early January of 1973, I was attending a drug conference in San Clemente, Calif. when I received a telephone call in my hotel room from Mr. John Dean. He asked that I go outside the hotel and call him back from a public telephone, which I did. He told me that he had a very important message which he wanted me to deliver to James McCord, that Mr. McCord was expecting to hear from me and McCord would understand what the message referred to. He said the message consisted of three things:

1. "A year is a long time;"
2. "your wife and family will be taken care of;"
3. "you will be rehabilitated with employment when this is all over."

I immediately realized that I was being asked to do a very dangerous thing and I said to Mr. Dean that I did not think it was wise to send me on such a mission since Mr. McCord knew, as many others did, that I had worked closely with Mr. Dean and Mr. Ehrlichman at the White House and therefore it might be quickly guessed that any messages I was conveying were probably from one of the two. The reason I raised this question with him was because, very frankly, I did not wish to convey the message. Mr. Dean asked if I could think of any other way to do it and I suggested that perhaps I could get Mr. Ulasewicz to convey the message over the telephone anonymously, stating that the message had come from me.

Mr. Dean felt this would be all right so I hung up the telephone and called Mr. Ulasewicz in New York. He did not wish to convey the message at first but I convinced him to do it merely as a matter of friendship to me. Mr. Ulasewicz called Mr. McCord's home, and presumably, delivered the same message which Mr. Dean had given to me. He then called me back in California, and reported that he had delivered the message and that Mr. McCord's attitude had been one of satisfaction. I was glad to hear this since I had felt this probably meant that Mr. McCord had been in some stage of negotiation about his status and that this message had probably relieved his mind.

At this point in time, my impression was that obviously there had been some negotiations going on between Mr. Dean's office and Mr. McCord in regard to Executive clemency, such negotiations probably being carried on through third parties and that Mr. McCord had wanted to hear the message which was transmitted to him through a reliable source, such as myself.

I called Mr. Dean and told him that the message had been delivered by Mr. Ulasewicz and that Mr. McCord had seemed satisfied.

The next day I received another telephone call from Mr. Dean at my hotel in which he said that Mr. McCord wanted to see me as soon as I got back. I objected to seeing Mr. McCord, but finally Mr. Dean got my concurrence to do so. My impression was that Mr. McCord wanted to say something to me and I was not instructed to say anything more than what had been in the message to him.

I called Mr. Ulasewicz and asked him to arrange a meeting with Mr. McCord the following evening when I was to arrive back in Washington. Mr. Ulasewicz called me back and said Mr. McCord had agreed to meet with me at the second overlook on the George Washington Parkway but that, different from Mr. Ulasewicz's last conversation with Mr. McCord, Mr. McCord sounded quite irritated and annoyed.

Owing to a delay in my airplane flight from California I was unable to meet with Mr. McCord on the night of January 11 as I had intended. When I arrived in Washington on the evening of January 11, I did attempt to call Mr. McCord but was told by a member of his family that he had retired for the evening. Mr. Ulasewicz had already conveyed instructions to Mr. McCord for holding our meeting on Friday night, January 12. At approximately 7 that evening I met with Mr. McCord at the second overlook on the George Washington Parkway. He joined me in my car and as I recall the conversation, I first apologized to him for my delay in getting to see him due to my presence in California and the late arrival of my airplane. I also said I was sorry if he had been irritated by receiving the anonymous calls from my friend.

He said something like, "OK, that's OK, Jack." I said, "I guess you received the message then?"

Mr. McCord then said words to the effect: Jack, I am different from all the others. Anybody who knew me at the CIA knows that I always follow my own independent course. I have always followed the rule that if one goes [I took this to mean going to jail] all who are involved must go. People who I am sure are involved are sitting outside with their families. I saw a picture in the newspaper of some guy who I am sure was involved sitting with his family. I can take care of my family. I don't need any jobs, I want my freedom.

I stated that I was only delivering a message and had nothing to do with its formulation or had no control over what was being done. I sympathized with Mr. McCord's situation and made remarks such as, I can't understand how this all has happened, I'd give anything if I had not recommended you for your two jobs with the Republican Party.

I did try to impress upon Mr. McCord that I was simply a messenger and was not too pleased to even be doing that. I did say that the people who had asked me to convey the message had always been honorable toward me and that I thought it was a sincere offer.

He asked me who I was speaking with at the White House and I said I could not reveal any names but that they were from the "highest level of the White House."

He continually said that all he was interested in was his freedom and that he was not pleased that others who he felt had been involved were not suffering the consequences that he was. In the context of demanding his immediate freedom, he said that he knew of a way in which his freedom could be obtained and asked me if I could convey his plan to the people at the White House with whom I was talking.

His plan, simply, was as follows: On two occasions, one in September 1972 and the other in October 1972, Mr. McCord told me that he had called telephone numbers at foreign embassies in Washington and he stated he was sure these embassies were subjects of national security wiretaps. On both occasions he had stated that he was a man involved in the Watergate scandal and, without giving his name, had inquired as to the possibility of acquiring visas and other traveling papers necessary to travel to these foreign countries.

It was Mr. McCord's theory that if the Government searched its wiretap records, it would find records of these two calls. Meanwhile, Mr. McCord and his attorneys would make a motion in court, aimed at dismissing the case against Mr. McCord because of the use of wiretap evidence by the prosecution. Mr. McCord's idea was that when the U.S. attorney was told that at least two of Mr. McCord's conversations had been intercepted over a national security wiretap, he would be forced to dismiss the case rather than reveal that the two embassies in question were the subject of national security wiretaps.

Mr. McCord was quite adamant in saying that he was sure the Government could secure his immediate release if they wanted to help him and, other than the publicity incumbent on the Government for being forced to dismiss the case against him, such an approach would save the administration any real embarrassment. He gave me a note with the dates of the two conversations that he referred to and told me that he knew this kind of thing had been done before, most recently in the *Ellsberg* case and that he saw no reason why the Government could not at least accomplish this for him. I told Mr. McCord that I would get back to him on the wiretap situation and would probably be calling him in a day or two to set this up. I agreed to carry this message concerning wiretaps back to the White House and the meeting ended.

At no time in our first meeting do I recall saying anything about the President but I specifically renewed the offer of Executive clemency, as indicated above and referred to it as coming from "the highest levels of the White House." At some point in the conversation Mr. McCord said to me, "Jack, I didn't ask to see you." This puzzled me since my clear understanding from Mr. Dean was that McCord had specifically asked to see me.

In any event, I called Mr. Dean on Friday night, January 12, and reported that Mr. McCord did not seem interested in accepting the offer made in Mr. Dean's original message to him, that Mr. McCord wanted his immediate freedom and that he, Mr. McCord, felt that he had a way to obtain that freedom. I then mentioned over the telephone, McCord's idea for securing his freedom because of the use of national security wiretaps and said that I wished to discuss this matter directly with Dean.

The following day I saw Mr. Dean in his office in the White House and explained to him Mr. McCord's suggestion for obtaining his freedom, as Mr. McCord had described it to me. Mr. Dean said, "Well, I'll check on that." He then turned the conversation back to the offer of Executive clemency. To the best of my knowledge he said, "Jack, I want you to go back to him—McCord—and tell him that we are checking on these wiretaps but this time impress upon him as fully as you can that this offer of Executive clemency is a sincere offer which comes from the very highest levels of the White House."

I said, "I have not used anybody's name with him, do you want me to?"

He said, "No, I don't want you to do that but tell him that this message comes from the very highest levels."

I said, "Do you want me to tell him it comes from the President?"

He said words to the effect, "No, don't do that; say that it comes from way up at the top."

I told Mr. Dean I would get back to Mr. McCord and that indeed, I had told Mr. McCord that I would.

At the meeting with Mr. Dean he also impressed upon me that this was a very grave situation which might someday threaten the President, that it had the potential of becoming a national scandal and that many people in the White House were quite concerned over it. Mr. Dean said that none of the other then-defendants in the Watergate burglary "were any problem," and that Mr. McCord "was not cooperating with his attorney."

I have been asked at the U.S. attorney's office and by Senate investigators, and have tried as best I can to recall what impressions I had at this particular point in time. As best as these impressions can be stated, I believed that I was going back to see Mr. McCord to again extend an offer of Executive clemency and that by my doing so I was doing a great service for the President of the United States in a very sensitive matter. At no time, either before or after this meeting with Mr. Dean did I ever speak to any other White House officials about this offer of Executive clemency. I specifically never spoke to the President of the United States and have no knowledge of my own as to whether he personally had endorsed this offer or indeed whether anyone had ever discussed it with him. Since I had worked extensively for Mr. Dean and Mr. Ehrlichman and had formed an impression that Mr. Dean rarely made decisions on matters of consequence without speaking to Mr. Ehrlichman, my guess was that when Mr. Dean referred to "high White House officials" he at least meant Mr. Ehrlichman. I know that he was in conversation with someone about my contacts with Mr. McCord since, when I was in his office on January 13, he received a telephone call and I heard him say, "I'm receiving a report on that right now" to the party on the other end.

At any rate, I then called Mr McCord and arranged a meeting with him, again at the second overlook of the George Washington Parkway early in the afternoon on Sunday, January 14. On this occasion we both got out of our cars and walked down a path from the overlook toward the Potomac River.

This meeting lasted only 10 to 15 minutes. I did most of the talking. I told Mr. McCord that the White House was checking into the wiretapping situation and that I had been asked to impress upon him once again that the offer of Executive clemency was a sincere and believable offer coming from the very highest levels of the White House. I explained to him that among the reasons why I believed that such a commitment would be kept were that the White House officials with whom I was in contact were extremely concerned about the Watergate burglary developing into a major scandal affecting the President and therefore such a promise would not be given lightly. I told him that the White House officials with whom I was talking were complaining because they felt that Mr. McCord was the only one of the Watergate burglary defendants who was refusing to cooperate. At no time on this occasion or on any other occasion do I recall telling Mr. McCord to keep silent if called before the grand jury or any congressional committees.

Senator ERVIN. Mr. Caulfield, we have another vote. I think maybe you had better pause until we get back.

[Recess.]

Senator ERVIN. The committee will resume.

Mr. DASH. Mr. Caulfield, you were in the midst of your statement. I suggest you go back a sentence or two so we will have continuity.

Mr. CAULFIELD. Yes, sir.

Mr. DASH. Actually, perhaps you should go back a little further.

Mr. CAULFIELD. I will pick up a couple of sentences, Mr. Dash.

I told him that the White House officials with whom I was talking were complaining because they felt that Mr. McCord was the only one of the Watergate burglary defendants who was refusing to cooperate. At no time on this occasion or on any other occasion do I recall telling Mr. McCord to keep silent if called before the grand jury or any congressional committees.

His response to my conversation was that he still wanted his immediate freedom and he felt strongly that if the White House had any interest in helping him secure that freedom that they could do something about the two telephone calls which he was sure had been intercepted. I told him I would check on this matter again and get back to him.

I was not attempting to exert pressure on Mr. McCord by telling him of comments I was hearing from the White House; merely, I was attempting to let him know the kinds of things I was hearing from Mr. Dean concerning the White House's attitude toward him if that would be of any assistance to him.

Later on Sunday I telephoned Mr. Dean to report on my meeting with Mr. McCord. I told him that in my opinion Mr. McCord has absolutely no interest in the offer of Executive clemency. I told Mr. Dean that Mr. McCord was still adamant in his belief that the White House had the power to have the charges against him dismissed if it would merely pursue the wiretaps which he had mentioned. Mr. Dean said that I should tell him that there wasn't much likelihood that anything would be done about the wiretap situation and, in response to my comments about McCord's refusal to consider Executive clemency he said something like, "Well, what the hell does he know, anyway?"

Mr. Dean told me to go back to Mr. McCord again and "commiserate" with him but he did not ask me to renew the offer of Executive clemency. I guessed that the reason why he wanted me to see Mr. McCord again was simply to maintain a friendly relationship with him in case there was a need for any further conversation with him through me. I probably would have met again with Mr. McCord anyway, since I felt badly about his predicament and I considered him a good friend.

In any event, on Monday, January 15, I called McCord to report that nothing seemed to be happening in regard to the wiretap situation. He became quite angry over the telephone and reaffirmed his belief that if the White House really wanted to help him they could do so by using the method he had suggested and that he knew that Mr. Magruder (who was then going to be a Government witness) was going to perjure himself. I also mentioned getting together with him but he said he had no interest in seeing me unless I had something more to talk to him about. He was quite upset so I did not pursue the matter further.

On Tuesday, January 16, I again called him in an attempt to meet with him and he again was highly irritated about the White House's failure to do something about the wiretap situation and again mentioned Mr. Magruder. I said I would inquire further about the wiretaps and I might have something for him "in a week or so."

Subsequently I called him and arranged to meet with him again, the exact date of this meeting being unsure in my mind. We again met at the overlook on the George Washington Parkway, he got into my car and we drove out the parkway, pursuing a course in the general direction of Warrenton, Va. I have no specific recollection as to how long we drove but I would say that it was an hour or two.

I would characterize this conversation as a very friendly one in which a large portion of the time was spent discussing our respective families, how my job at the Treasury Department was going, and various other purely personal matters. I gave him my private telephone number at the Treasury Department and told him that if he or his wife ever wanted me to do anything for them, they should feel free to call me. I told McCord that if he or his wife should decide to call me, to simply use the name "Watson" and I would know who it was. Frankly, this was merely a device to save me from any possible embarrassment.

I do not have a specific recollection as to how it arose, but I believe he asked me if he was still the only one of the Watergate defendants that the White House was concerned about. I said that I thought he was, but that I had no knowledge of what relationship existed between the White House and the other Watergate defendants. He said that the Cuban defendants were quite nervous and in his opinion, might make a statement at any time and that I "could pass that along for whatever it was worth."

I told him there was absolutely no hope, in my opinion, of the White House ever doing anything about the wiretap situation and asked him when he thought he might make a statement. He said that he had not decided that yet, but that he had spoken to his wife and family and that he felt free to make a statement whenever he thought the time was right.

I again asked if there was anything I could do for him. He said one thing that I could do was to see whether bail money could be raised for him pending an appeal in his case. I said I would check into this.

Toward the end of our conversation, realizing that he definitely was going to make a statement on the Watergate burglary at a time of his choosing and that such a statement would in all probability involve allegations against people in the White House and other high administration officials, I gave him what I considered to be a small piece of friendly advice.

I said words to the effect that, "Jim, I have worked with these people and I know them to be as tough-minded as you and I. When you make your statement don't underestimate them. If I were in your shoes, I would probably do the same thing."

I later called Mr. Dean and advised him of Mr. McCord's request for bail funding and he said words to the effect that, "Maybe we can handle that through Alch." Some time later, Mr. Dean called me and asked me to tell McCord that the bail money presented too many problems and that maybe consideration could be given to paying premiums. I later called McCord and reported this. His reaction was, "I am negotiating with a new attorney and maybe he can get it handled." This is the last conversation I had to date with James McCord.

Although this is a lengthy statement, I wish to make two further points: At no time in any conversations with Mr. McCord did I advise, pressure, or threaten him in an attempt to make him accept the offer of Executive clemency. I viewed my role simply as one of a messenger and while I tried to give both Mr. Dean and Mr. McCord the full flavor of what was going on at both ends of this message-transacting process, I actively refrained from injecting myself into the process at either end. I realized at the time of my first conversation in January that I was involved in questionable activity but I felt that it was important to me to carry this message for the good of the President.

I have previously testified before the grand jury and have spoken on two other occasions with the U.S. attorney's office and have spoken on two occasions as well with Senate investigators. Although I have discussed the matter of whether any of my actions could be viewed as violations of the criminal law with my attorney and have been advised of the availability of privileges and possible attempts of securing immunity from prosecution, at no time have I refused to answer any questions in regard to my conduct and I have felt that it is more important that I be able to speak freely about my involvement in actions herein, than to have whatever protection might be rightfully mine under my constitutional and executive privileges. I hope that what I have to say here today will assist the committee in its investigations and if, upon a hearing of all the facts, it is thought that I am guilty of some wrongdoing I will still feel that the truth is my best defense.

Senator BAKER. Mr. Caulfield, we thank you very much for your lengthy but very useful statement. It is now 4:10 in the afternoon. The chairman has been called to the floor of the Senate to participate in the debate on a matter now pending on which we will shortly vote. Before he left the committee he suggested that we conclude your prepared statement today on the condition that you and your attorney are agreeable to returning in the morning at 10 o'clock so that the committee and staff can proceed with interrogation. Is that satisfactory to you?

Mr. CAULFIELD. Absolutely, Senator.

Senator BAKER. Then, the committee will stand in recess until 10 o'clock tomorrow morning.

[Whereupon, at 4:10 p.m., the hearing was recessed, to reconvene at 10 a.m., Wednesday, May 23, 1973.]

WEDNESDAY, MAY 23, 1973

U.S. SENATE,
SELECT COMMITTEE ON
PRESIDENTIAL CAMPAIGN ACTIVITIES,
Washington, D.C.

The Select Committee met, pursuant to recess, at 10 a.m., in room 318, Russell Senate Office Building, Senator Sam J. Ervin, Jr. (chairman), presiding.

Present: Senators Ervin, Talmadge, Inouye, Montoya, Baker, Gurney, and Weicker.

Also present: Samuel Dash, chief counsel; Fred D. Thompson, minority counsel; Rufus L. Edmisten, deputy chief counsel; Arthur S. Miller, chief consultant; Jed Johnson, consultant; David M. Dorsen, James Hamilton, and Terry F. Lenzner, assistant chief counsels; Barry Schochet, assistant majority counsel; Donald G. Sanders, H. William Shure, and Robert Silverstein, assistant minority counsels; Joan C. Cole, secretary to the minority; Pauline O. Dement, research assistant; Eiler Ravnholt, office of Senator Inouye; Robert Baca, office of Senator Montoya; Ron McMahan, assistant to Senator Baker; A. Searle Field, assistant to Senator Weicker; Marc Lackritz, Ron Rotunda, assistant counsels; Eugene Boyce, hearings counsel; John Walz, publications clerk.

Senator ERVIN. The committee will come to order. I would like to reiterate what I stated yesterday that Mr. Caulfield is to return later and that the questions at this appearance will be restricted to matters dealing with the communications between him and Mr. McCord. In respect to the questions of counsel——

Senator GURNEY. Mr. Chairman, may I inquire what the plan of the committee is on the witness following Mr. Caulfield?

Mr. DASH. Yes, the witness following Mr. Caulfield will be Tony Ulasewicz who will be the individual who has been identified as the person who made the telephone call to Mr. McCord and that he will be called specifically to testify as to that role. He too will be available, Senator Gurney, to come back and to testify on other matters which he has to testify before this committee.

Senator GURNEY. Mr. Chairman, as I understand that last evening counsel interviewed the attorney, the former attorney, for Mr. McCord and that his statements were in startling conflict and contrast with what Mr. McCord had told us here the other day and I would think it would be extremely important that we get this witness on just as soon as possible and I, as one committee member, would like to see him on this afternoon and I think his testimony is in total conflict with what Mr. McCord said and I think he should be called just as soon as we can get him just before the recess before we call Tony.

Mr. DASH. We can do that, Mr. Chairman. It is true Mr. Alch did come in and did request he be called and we thought we would call him immediately after Tony Ulasewicz but there is no reason why he could not be called immediately after Mr. Caulfield.

Senator GURNEY. I wish he might.

Senator BAKER. Mr. Chairman, let me make a suggestion, if I may, I think Senator Gurney's point is well taken. However, in the interest of continuity and in keeping with the preparation of the committee let me make an alternative suggestion, if I may. Let us finish with Mr. Caulfield today, Mr. Chairman, I would suggest, which I think we can do in a reasonably short period of time since Mr. Caulfield, I understand, is agreeable to return and to explore other matters not related directly with the subject matter of his testimony thus far, that we go forward then with the next witness who is——

Mr. DASH. Tony Ulasewicz, which I think will only take about 10 minutes.

Senator BAKER. After we finish that we will call Mr. Alch and that will result in some continuity and then also be in accord with Mr. Gurney's request. I am sure Mr. Alch will be on the stand today.

Senator GURNEY. That is what I want to be sure, he does get on the stand. We have taken a good deal of time in the questioning, in fact, I have used my own fair share but I do think it is awfully important that we get Mr. Alch on today because his testimony is going to be in such sharp contrast and contradiction to what we learned from Mr. McCord earlier and I think we ought to get it to clear up some of these things that are hanging around the room here.

Senator WEICKER. Mr. Chairman, it is my understanding then that only so we might present a logical picture we will restrict our questions to the matters that Mr. Caulfield raised yesterday in his testimony but certainly that there are no restrictions and no bars as to future testimony and that he will be recalled for any questions we want to ask, is that correct?

Senate ERVIN. That is correct.

Senator WEICKER. Thank you very much.

Mr. DASH. Mr. Caulfield, because your statement was a lengthy one, and there was a recess over the evening, let me seek to briefly summarize the essential highlights of your statement that you gave to the committee, and please correct me if anything I say is not consistent with your understanding of your statement.

In December of 1972 you received an unsigned note which you understood came from Mr. McCord which complained of a White House effort to blame CIA for the Watergate and threatened that "all the trees in the forest will fall," if this effort continued.

In early January 1972, while you were in California, you received a telephone call from John Dean from Washington asking you to deliver the following message to Mr. Dean.

"1. One year is a long time. 2. Your wife and family will be taken care of. 3. You will be rehabilitated with employment when this is over."

You did not want to deliver the message but you thought that it could be delivered through Mr. Tony Ulasewicz and Mr. Dean agreed to do it that way.

TESTIMONY OF JOHN J. CAULFIELD—Resumed

Mr. CAULFIELD. Mr. Dash, can I interrupt a second, the correct pronunciation is Ulasewicz.

Mr. DASH. Ulasewicz.

Mr. CAULFIELD. Right.

Mr. DASH. You did call Mr. Ulasewicz and you asked him to deliver this message, and although he himself at first was reluctant he did agree to deliver the message and he did call Mr. McCord and reported back to you that Mr. McCord appeared satisfied and you reported this to Mr. Dean.

The following day you received another call from Mr. Dean informing you that Mr. McCord wanted to see you when you returned to Washington. You had Ulasewicz arrange the meeting which was set for Friday, January 12, at the second overlook on the George Washington Parkway. In substance you emphasized that you were only a messenger, that the offer you were conveying of Executive clemency was from the highest levels of the White House, and that it was a sincere offer. Mr. McCord's response in substance was that he wanted his complete freedom and even suggested a plan which involved proffering that the Government had wiretapped his telephone calls, that he had made two calls to foreign embassies whose phones he believed were wiretapped. You do not recall saying anything about the President to Mr. McCord but you did transmit an offer of Executive clemency to Mr. McCord which you told him came from the highest levels of the White House. You reported this meeting to Mr. Dean on the telephone. The following day you met with Mr. Dean and he told you to go back to Mr. McCord and impress upon him as fully as you could that the offer of Executive clemency was a sincere offer and when you asked if you should mention any names, such as the President, he said no, but told you that you should say that the offer came "from way up top." Mr. Dean also expressed his concern over this matter as a grave situation that could threaten the President and could become a national scandal. That none of the other defendants in the Watergate case were any problem and Mr. McCord was not cooperating with his attorney.

You again met with Mr. McCord at the second overlook on the George Washington Parkway on January 14 for a short while, and conveyed the message of concern over a national scandal which could threaten the President and that McCord was the only one of the defendants not cooperating. Again, McCord expressed his interest to you in securing his freedom and wanted you to do something about the wiretaps he had mentioned to you earlier.

You telephoned Mr. Dean that same day and told him that Mr. McCord was not interested in Executive clemency, and that Mr. McCord believed that the White House could help him get the charges dismissed by supplying proof of the wiretaps for him.

You had a final meeting with Mr. McCord on a date you cannot recall but about the third week in January where you picked him up in your automobile on the second overlook on the George Washington Parkway and drove for about an hour or 2. At this time you told him that the White House could not do anything for him about the wiretap problem and there was a lengthy conversation which for the most part involved other subjects than Watergate. You concluded during that conversation that Mr. McCord definitely was going to make a statement on the Watergate burglary and it would probably involve allegations against people in the White House and other high administration officials. You gave him what you indicated to the committee as friendly advice to the effect, "Jim, I have worked with these people and I know them to be as tough-minded as you and I. When you make your statement don't underestimate them. If I were in your shoes I would probably be doing the same thing."

You also had received from Mr. McCord some reference or request to do something about bail and you were not able to accomplish anything on the bail issue during further contacts with him. That at no time did you talk with the President about this matter or mention the President to Mr. McCord concerning the offer of Executive clemency but that you carried this message to Mr. McCord because you felt it was for the good of the President.

Is that basically a fair summary of the gist of the contacts with Mr. McCord and Mr. Dean that were contained in your statement?

Mr. CAULFIELD. Yes, sir.

Mr. DASH. Now, although you state that you made no mention of the President to Mr. McCord during the meeting, you do know, do you not, that the President is the only person in this country who can grant Executive clemency in a Federal criminal matter?

Mr. CAULFIELD. Yes, sir, I do.

Mr. DASH. Did you understand when you were speaking with Mr. Dean that Mr. Dean wanted you to transmit the message to Mr. McCord that the offer of Executive clemency was made with the proper authority?

Mr. CAULFIELD. Yes, sir.

Mr. DASH. Was it your intention during the meetings with Mr. McCord to leave him with the clear understanding that the persons with authority to make such a representation of Executive clemency were in fact extending this offer to him?

Mr. CAULFIELD. Just repeat that for me, Mr. Dash?

Mr. DASH. Yes.

Was it your intention during your meetings with Mr. McCord to leave him with the clear understanding that persons with authority to make such a representation as to Executive clemency were in fact extending this offer to him?

Mr. CAULFIELD. Yes, sir.

But, of course, I have not and did not at that time have any direct knowledge that the President had made such an offer, endorsed such an offer, or in any way was involved in that offer.

Mr. DASH. I understand that.

Mr. CAULFIELD. Right.

Mr. DASH. Looking back, Mr. Caulfield, what do you see your role to have been in this relationship and what did you think about it?

Mr. CAULFIELD. Well, as I have indicated in my statement, Mr. Dash, I viewed myself as a messenger between Mr. Dean and Mr. McCord, exchanging information back and forth on the ongoing negotiations, which obviously had been taking place prior to the time that I had received the telephone call in California.

Mr. DASH. And was it your understanding at that time, especially with the discussions you had with Mr. Dean, that there was serious concern at the White House, at least Mr. Dean was conveying to you, involving a possible scandal, that there was a real effort to get Mr. McCord to accept this offer because of the concern or trouble that probably he might be able to raise in the Watergate case?

Mr. CAULFIELD. That was my clear impression, Mr. Dash, yes, sir.

Mr. DASH. And you were being asked to do this because of your friendly relationship with Mr. McCord?

Mr. CAULFIELD. That is correct.

Mr. DASH. I have no further questions, Mr. Chairman.

Senator ERVIN. Mr. Thompson?

Mr. THOMPSON. Thank you.

Mr. Caulfield, as I understand it, you have been a personal friend of Mr. McCord's, is that correct?

Mr. CAULFIELD. That is correct, sir.

Mr. THOMPSON. Would you still say that relationship exists as far as you are concerned?

Mr. CAULFIELD. Yes, sir, I still consider Jim McCord my friend.

Mr. THOMPSON. As you were talking to him about the possibility of Executive clemency and he was responding to you, what would you say, according to what he told you, his primary interest was?

Mr. CAULFIELD. Very frankly, sir, as I reflect back upon the conversation, it is very clear in my mind that Jim McCord was concerned about his freedom and was taking the steps that he believed to gain that freedom totally. He was uninterested in any deals of a year is a long time or other statements like that. He, in that first conversation at the car, made it crystal clear to me that he was different from the others, that I could check it if I wanted to, that he wanted his freedom, period.

Mr. THOMPSON. In other words, he was not necessarily disinterested in any deals, but he was not interested in any deals that would not produce his freedom. Is that a correct statement?

Mr. CAULFIELD. That is correct. That is correct.

Mr. THOMPSON. As you state here in your statement, he continually said that all he was interested in was his freedom and he was not pleased that some of the others that had been involved were not suffering as he was suffering, is that correct?

Mr. CAULFIELD. That is correct.

Mr. THOMPSON. You referred also in your statement to his plan, a plan which he had which he thought would produce his freedom. I believe you referred to his two telephone calls in September and October of 1972 to two embassies.

Mr. CAULFIELD. Yes sir.

Mr. THOMPSON. According to what he told you, was it your impression that he believed that these two calls were made in order to ultimately produce his freedom, put the Government in an embarrassing position, and therefore produce his freedom?

Mr. CAULFIELD. Yes sir.

Mr. THOMPSON. All right, now. Let me ask you about your relationship with Mr. Ehrlichman for just a few moments.

How long did you work for Mr. Ehrlichman when he was counsel for the President?

Mr. CAULFIELD. From the day that I arrived at the White House on April 8, 1969, formally, through July 1970, when Mr. Ehrlichman moved over to the Domestic Council, and then on an informal basis from that time until the time I worked at the White House.

Mr. THOMPSON. Then after Mr. Ehrlichman left the Office of Counsel for the President, Mr. Dean was his successor; is that correct?

Mr. CAULFIELD. Yes sir.

Mr. THOMPSON. You remained, then, under Mr. Dean; is that correct?

Mr. CAULFIELD. That is right.

Mr. THOMPSON. Did you have any contact or any continuing relationship with Mr. Ehrlichman after Mr. Ehrlichman left to go to the Office of Domestic Affairs?

Mr. CAULFIELD. Well, only on rare peripheral matters relative to the investigations that I indicated in my statement.

Mr. THOMPSON. And while you were working for Mr. Ehrlichman directly, as I understand it, you had possibly more than one function with one of those to carry out certain investigations?

Mr. CAULFIELD. Yes, I had many other functions, sir, but that was one small part of my duties at the White House.

Mr. THOMPSON. And you continued to do some of these matters for him pursuant to his direction after you left that office?

Mr. CAULFIELD. On very rare occasions, sir.

Mr. THOMPSON. Would you on some occasions act as an intermediary between Mr. Ehrlichman and Tony Ulasewicz, for jobs which Mr. Ulasewicz would do?

Mr. CAULFIELD. Yes sir.

Mr. THOMPSON. Would you say that would be on frequent occasions?

Mr. CAULFIELD. That would be infrequent after July of 1970.

Mr. THOMPSON. But occasionally.

Mr. CAULFIELD. Oh, yes; yes sir.

Mr. THOMPSON. Now, Mr. Caulfield, in your statement here, you state that you were guessing that Mr. Dean probably was referring to Mr. Ehrlichman when he referred to high White House sources?

Mr. CAULFIELD. Yes, that was my guess.

Mr. THOMPSON. That was your guess at that time?

Mr. CAULFIELD. Yes sir.

Mr. THOMPSON. You also state, "I know he was in conversation with someone about my contact with Mr. McCord, because when I was in his office on January 13, he received a telephone call and I heard him say 'I am receiving a report on that right now'."

Were you referring to Mr. Ehrlichman?

Mr. CAULFIELD. No; what I am saying is that the call came in, that there were no names mentioned. Mr. Dean said, I am receiving—there was, apparently the party calling made some comments. Mr. Dean said "I am getting a report on that right now."

Mr. THOMPSON. Oh, I see, this conversation that you overheard was Mr. Dean with someone?

Mr. CAULFIELD. I mean in Mr. Dean's presence, Mr. Counsel.

Mr. THOMPSON. I see. And you assumed that that conversation perhaps was with Mr. Ehrlichman or possibly with Mr. Ehrlichman?

Mr. CAULFIELD. Possibly with Mr. Ehrlichman, but I have no way of knowing, sir.

Mr. THOMPSON. You feel very definitely in your mind that he was talking with someone else about it, is that correct?

Mr. CAULFIELD. I want to be careful there, sir, because I just do not know where the call came from. If it was coming from outside, it could have been someone else. If it was coming from within the White House, then it was someone in the White House. So—by that I mean, sir, there is an interoffice telephone system. Now, I do not know and have no way of knowing whether that was an interoffice call or whether or not it was a call coming from outside. So that is why I mentioned it that way.

Mr. THOMPSON. What would you say was the relationship between Mr. Dean and Mr. Ehrlichman during this period of time? Did Mr. Dean in many matters in effect report to Mr. Ehrlichman?

Mr. CAULFIELD. Yes, sir.

Mr. THOMPSON. Or answer to Mr. Ehrlichman?

Mr. CAULFIELD. Yes, sir; on many matters having to do with Mr. Dean's work as well.

Mr. THOMPSON. Did you ever talk with Mr. Ehrlichman about this matter, this business of possible Executive clemency for Mr. McCord with anyone?

Mr. CAULFIELD. No, sir.

Mr. THOMPSON. You never did?

Mr. CAULFIELD. No, sir.

Mr. THOMPSON. Did you ever talk to anyone there at the White House besides Mr. Dean?

Mr. CAULFIELD. Absolutely no one but Mr. John Dean.

Mr. THOMPSON. I have no further questions, Mr. Chairman.

Senator ERVIN. If there is no objection, I would like to exchange places for questioning witnesses with Senator Montoya and let him take my place and I will take his place.

Senator MONTOYA. Thank you, Mr. Chairman.

Senator ERVIN. There are no objections. You may proceed.

Senator MONTOYA. Thank you, Mr. Chairman.

Mr. Caulfield, I think we had better get your background and employment duties at the White House in better perspective. What exactly were you doing when you went to work at the White House in April of 1969?

Mr. CAULFIELD. My prime duties at the White House was to act as liaison primarily with the U.S. Secret Service and other Federal law enforcement agencies. As I indicated, I worked under Mr. Ehrlichman, Mr. Krogh was under Mr. Ehrlichman as well. From time to time, I would be assigned major projects that came up in the law enforcement area.

For example, shortly after coming to the White House, I was assigned to the then-emerging drug abuse task force that subsequently emerged as Operation Intercept.

Senator MONTOYA. Well, were you working directly under Mr. Ehrlichman? Or were you working under Mr. Dean?

Mr. CAULFIELD. No, Mr. Dean, sir, was not at the White House at that time. This is—you asked—I think the question was what were my duties when I went into the White House? When I went into the White House, Mr. John Dean was not yet there. He was at the Justice Department.

Senator MONTOYA. As I understand, you went to work at the White House in April 1969 and you worked there until March 1972.

Is that correct?

Mr. CAULFIELD. Yes, sir.

Senator MONTOYA. All right.

Were you on the payroll of the White House or were you being paid by someone else?

Mr. CAULFIELD. No; I was on the White House payroll, sir.

Senator MONTOYA. Did you ever get paid from the President's attorney?

Mr. CAULFIELD. No, sir.

Senator MONTOYA. And were you assigned to the White House payroll or were you on the Treasury payroll?

Mr. CAULFIELD. I don't quite understand.

Senator MONTOYA. Were you working or being paid from the payroll attributable to the Department of the Treasury or to the White House?

Mr. CAULFIELD. The White House payroll, sir.

Senator MONTOYA. All right.

Mr. CAULFIELD. Yes, sir.

Senator MONTOYA. Now, did you come in contact quite frequently with Mr. Ehrlichman?

Mr. CAULFIELD. In the course of my duties, yes, sir, not on a daily basis certainly but I would be working with his staff people, Mr. Egil Krogh when I first went in there, as I have indicated I would be assigned major projects. I was the White House representative for the Marihuana and Dangerous Drugs Task Force that began in the spring of 1969.

Senator MONTOYA. All right.

Now, in the course of your employment at the White House what relationship did you have with Mr. Dean when he came onboard?

Mr. CAULFIELD. Well, Mr. John Ehrlichman, when I was working for him coming aboard the White House was counsel to the President. When Mr. Ehrlichman became the Presidential assistant and headed up the Domestic Affairs Council, Mr. John Dean came in and became the counsel to the President, and I remained in the office of the Counsel to the President under Mr. Dean, my direct supervisor.

Senator MONTOYA. Did he assign many things to you?

Mr. CAULFIELD. Yes, sir.

Senator MONTOYA. Did Mr. Ehrlichman continue to assign things to you to do?

Mr. CAULFIELD. As I have indicated, Senator, only on rare occasions after Mr. Ehrlichman became Assistant to the President for Domestic Affairs.

Senator MONTOYA. Did Mr. Haldeman assign things to you?

Mr. CAULFIELD. On only one or two occasions that I could recall, Senator. Very rarely, in fact almost never.

Senator MONTOYA. All right.

You mentioned that you had interviewed Mr. McCord for his employment at the executive offices and recommended him to go to work for the Committee To Re-Elect the President. That is correct, isn't it?

Mr. CAULFIELD. Well, that is essentially correct, sir. The recommendation was for employment at the Republican National Committee initially and flowing from that Mr. McCord was hired by the Committee To Re-Elect.

Senator MONTOYA. How many interviews did you say you had with Mr. McCord?

Mr. CAULFIELD. I recall two. I recall a luncheon when it was already established that he was on board.

Senator MONTOYA. Who did you clear with at the White House before he recommended Mr. McCord for that appointment?

Mr. CAULFIELD. I didn't clear anybody, sir.

Senator MONTOYA. Who did you call at the Republican National Committee?

Mr. CAULFIELD. I called Mr. Barry Mountain who was the then deputy chairman for administration.

Senator MONTOYA. Had he asked you to recommend someone?

Mr. CAULFIELD. Yes, sir.

Senator MONTOYA. Was there a job classification for the individual that he wanted?

Mr. CAULFIELD. No. As I recall, the way Mr. Mountain explained it to me they wanted someone to come up and do a security survey and possibly following the survey the party who did the survey would be hired as a supervisor of security at the Republican National Committee.

Senator MONTOYA. Was there any discussion with respect to that classification that the man who would be chosen and the man that you might interview should be qualified in espionage activities for the party?

Mr. CAULFIELD. Absolutely not, sir.

Senator MONTOYA. Were you aware that that was one of the competencies that this man should have anyway?

Mr. CAULFIELD. No, sir.

In reviewing Mr. McCord's qualifications they appeared to me from a career experience in security work to be absolutely outstanding, and his credentials appeared to be impeccable.

Senator MONTOYA. What did you conceive with respect to the game plan that was going on at the time?

Mr. CAULFIELD. I beg your pardon?

Senator MONTOYA. Mr. McCord mentioned that you had told him that he was ruining the game plan. What did you conceive that to be?

Mr. CAULFIELD. Well, sir, I do not recall Mr. McCord saying "game plan" but it was obvious to me that there were negotiations going on with respect to this Executive clemency for Mr. McCord.

Senator MONTOYA. Then let me read to you from Mr. McCord's statement on page 9. I read as follows: "I refused to discuss it. He stated that I was fouling up the game plan. I made a few comments about the game plan." That was Mr. McCord's statement on page 9. Do you recall that conversation?

Mr. CAULFIELD. I do not recall those words, Senator.

Senator MONTOYA. Well, what words akin to that were uttered by you in the presence of Mr. McCord?

Mr. CAULFIELD [conferring with counsel]. Senator, I am a little confused on your asking me—I have no recollection of Mr. McCord—of me saying to Mr. McCord he was fouling up the game plan. My statement does not indicate that.

Senator MONTOYA. Well, let me read an extended text of that statement. On page 9 "About 10 o'clock a.m., on Thursday, January 25, 1973, in a meeting lasting until about 12:30 a.m. we drove in his car toward Warrenton, Va., and returned, and a conversation ensued which repeated the offers of Executive clemency and financial support while in prison and rehabilitation later. I refused to discuss it. He stated that I was fouling up the game plan. I made a few comments about the game plan."

Mr. CAULFIELD. Yes, sir.

Mr. MONTOYA. You recall that?

Mr. CAULFIELD. No, sir, I do not. As I indicated in my statement this trip here was one of friendly conversation between two friends. I have no recollection of offering him Executive clemency on that occasion. I have no recollection about stating that I was fouling up the game plan.

Senator MONTOYA. Did Mr. Dean tell you why he was calling you to get in touch with McCord?

Mr. CAULFIELD. When was that?

Senator MONTOYA. When he called you at San Clemente.

Mr. CAULFIELD. He indicated to me that he had a very important message that he wanted to be delivered to James McCord.

Senator MONTOYA. I understand that. But did he tell you why he had chosen you for that mission?

Mr. CAULFIELD. No, sir, he did not.

Senator MONTOYA. Did you ask him?

Mr. CAULFIELD. No, sir. He knew, of course, that I had known Jim McCord.

Senator MONTOYA. How did he know? Had you discussed Jim McCord with him?

Mr. CAULFIELD. I had been over to the committee. Eventually after he was hired I am sure I mentioned to Mr. Dean that this fellow McCord is hired, he appears to be outstanding. He was well aware that I knew Jim McCord; there was no question in anybody's mind.

Senator MONTOYA. Did you get in touch after Watergate with Mr. Dean to indicate to him about your friendship with Jim McCord?

Mr. CAULFIELD. Would you repeat that, Senator, please?

Senator MONTOYA. Did you get in touch with Mr. Dean and communicate your friendship with Jim McCord?

Mr. CAULFIELD. When, sir?

Senator MONTOYA. After the Watergate break-in.

Mr. CAULFIELD. We had conversations. I expressed shock on many occasions that James McCord was arrested at the Watergate.

Senator MONTOYA. No, but the point I am trying to make, Mr. Caulfield, is that you had two or three interviews with Mr. McCord; they were short in duration.

Mr. CAULFIELD. Yes, sir.

Senator MONTOYA. Preliminary to his being hired?

Mr. CAULFIELD. Yes, sir.

Senator MONTOYA. There were other people at the Republican National Committee and at the Committee To Re-Elect the President——

Mr. CAULFIELD. Yes, sir.

Senator MONTOYA [continuing]. Who knew Mr. McCord better than you did, presumably because he worked with them for a longer time and I am wondering why Mr. Dean selected you to carry on this mission of offering Executive clemency to Mr. McCord when there were other people within the organization of the national committee and the CRP who had developed a better and more intimate acquaintance with Mr. McCord.

Mr. CAULFIELD. Well, of course, I am sure that Mr. Dean trusted me, and in reading some of the things that might have gone on before there was apparently a need for someone from the White House to bring a message to him, and certainly Mr. Dean knew that I knew Jim McCord, and then I would like to reiterate that I received a letter in December which I had brought to Mr. Dean's attention wherein it was alleged that the White House was involved in attempting to place the blame on CIA. So all of these things Mr. Dean knew. Mr. McCord sent me the letter; Mr. Dean knew that.

Senator MONTOYA. Did you ever inquire of Mr. Dean when he was telling you just what to say to Mr. McCord, did you ever inquire from him as to the high sources and who they were?

Mr. CAULFIELD. Well, sir, in the first telephone call this was all just him asking me to go and deliver this message to Jim McCord. Subsequently, as I have indicated in my statement, we did have a conversation after the first meeting.

Senator MONTOYA. Now, you mentioned that Mr. Dean had instructed you to say that it comes from way up at the top.

Mr. CAULFIELD. Yes, sir.

Senator MONTOYA. What did you conceive that to be at the time?

Mr. CAULFIELD. Well, sir, in my mind I believed that he was talking about the President. Although, again——

Senator MONTOYA. How would you have interpreted that without any further explanation? The same way?

Mr. CAULFIELD. I do not understand, Senator.

Senator MONTOYA. You mentioned that it was your impression that it must have come from the President. Now, did you, when you reached that impression, question Mr. Dean any further about it?

Mr. CAULFIELD. No, sir.

Senator MONTOYA. My time has run out so I will not pursue that any further.

Thank you, Mr. Chairman.

Senator ERVIN. Senator Gurney.

Senator Baker?

Senator BAKER. Mr. Chairman, I would like to follow your example. I would offer to yield to Senator Weicker at this point. I believe that he may or may not wish to yield to Senator Gurney.

Senator WEICKER. Mr. Chairman, I just have two or three brief questions; then I will yield.

Mr. Caulfield, turn to page 19 of your testimony. You state there, "I have been asked by the U.S. Attorney's Office and by Senate investigators and am trying as best I can to recall what impressions I had at this particular point in time. As best as these impressions can be stated, I believed that I was going back to see Mr. McCord to again extend an offer of Executive clemency and that by my doing so I was doing a great service for the President of the United States in a very sensitive matter."

My first question to you, very simply, is this: Using your own words, I would like you to comment and explain to me why it is—why it is—that you thought you were doing a great service for the President of the United States?

Mr. CAULFIELD. Well, sir, to go back a little bit, it was a great honor for me to serve as a member of the President's staff. I had come from a rather humble background, a police officer. I did receive this great opportunity to serve on the President's staff. I felt very strongly about the President, extremely strongly about the President. I was very loyal to his people that I worked for. I place a high value upon loyalty. Now, out of the blue, I am injected into this scandal. I am being asked by one of my former superiors to deliver a message that I know to be Executive clemency. I tried to avoid it, as my statement indicates. I imposed upon my friend to do it, hoping that all parties would be satisfied. I was not successful.

I was brought back in again to it, now being asked to see Mr. McCord directly. I did go to see him.

Now I am becoming further implicated into this matter. I had this conversation with John Dean, who was the counsel to the President. I had been there 3 years. I know what the relations are and how they exist. I make certain judgments based upon those relationships. In my mind, I felt that the President probably did know about it.

Now, I am going out the door, to become more specific, and it crossed my mind that this conceivably was for the President. I believed it. I had to think about that. And based upon all of that background, I believed I was doing something for the President of the United States, and I did it, sir.

Senator WEICKER. Mr. Caulfield, you have lived a life dedicated to the law. In the very beginning of your statement, you cite a career, a very fine career, one that was recognized time and time again. Let me ask you this question.

I read on page 24 of your testimony, where you are talking to McCord and where you have given a friendly piece of advice, and you say, "Jim, I have worked with these people and I know them to be as tough-minded as you and I. When you make your statement, don't underestimate them. If I were in your shoes, I would probably do the same thing."

I read that, and you tell me if I am wrong, as the testimony of a man who is in conflict. On the one hand delivering a message to a friend; on the other hand, a man whose whole career has been dedicated to honesty and seeing the truth come out. Would that be a fair description of a conflict that was occurring within you at that time?

Mr. CAULFIELD. There was a definite conflict, Senator. You are absolutely right. I know when wrongdoing is occurring. I have indicated here that I knew that the offer of Executive clemency in this matter was wrong, yes sir, I knew that. But what I am saying to you, sir, is that my loyalties, and especially to the President of the United States, overrided those considerations.

Senator WEICKER. So actually, there was a conflict between your loyalties, and it is interesting that you used the very word that I had in a written question before you made your statement. Did you feel, at this moment in time, a conflict between your loyalties to the President and a life dedicated to law and the pursuit of truth?

Mr. CAULFIELD. Yes, sir. That is correct. And also that I was hopefully being able to help a friend.

Senator WEICKER. Then lastly, Mr. Caulfield, on page 25, you state: "That I realize that at the time of my first conversation in January that I was involved in questionable activity but I felt that it was important for me to carry this message for the good of the President." Was there a conflict in your mind between doing an act for the good of the President and an act that would be for the good of the country?

Mr. CAULFIELD. That is a tough question, Senator. All I can say is that I did what I did for the reasons that I have stated.

Senator WEICKER. I have no further questions.

Senator ERVIN. Senator Talmadge?

Senator TALMADGE. Mr. Chairman, at this time, I yield to the distinguished Senator from Hawaii, Mr. Inouye.

Senator INOUYE. Thank you very much.

Mr. Caulfield, am I to conclude from your responses to Senator Weicker, that you were aware that you were involved in a criminal act of obstructing criminal investigations?

Mr. CAULFIELD. Yes, sir.

Senator INOUYE. On your first call to Mr. McCord soon after the Watergate break-in, I notice from your testimony that you contacted Mr. Ulasewicz?

Mr. CAULFIELD. Yes, sir.

Senator INOUYE. For a man on the Kalmbach payroll doing espionage work, to go through some very secretive process to get in touch with him makes me ask: Why all this secrecy when, as you have stated, it was just to convey your sympathies to Mr. McCord? Why did you go through all this secret movement? Were you afraid that the phones were tapped?

Mr. CAULFIELD. Are you speaking about my call to, asking Mr. Ulasewicz to call James McCord, sir?

Senator INOUYE. Yes, why did you go through all that secret stuff to get in touch with Mr. McCord. According to your statement, all you wanted to say is I feel sorry for you, can I do anything for you. Is that right?

Mr. CAULFIELD. Yes, sir. To have spent a career in security work as I have, and as Mr. McCord had, and to watch the daily accounts of the Watergate developments from June 17 on, it certainly occurred to me, sir, that any conversations taking place over Mr. McCord's home telephone conceivably could have been the subject of some type of wiretapping by either governmental parties or other people who were concerned about Mr. McCord. Plus the fact, sir—well, I should go back a little bit.

That impression, and Mr. McCord, I undertstand, has indicated that he had the same concerns, indicated to me that a circuitous route, if I wanted to speak to him, would be the appropriate way to do it, sir.

Senator INOUYE. I would like to call your attention to page 16 of your prepared remarks, in which you describe Mr. McCord's plan. This plan called for Mr. McCord's calling two foreign embassies and telling the official in such embassies that he was a defendant in the Watergate case and requesting a visa. From this, did you gather that Mr. McCord was trying to blackmail the U.S. Government?

Mr. CAULFIELD. No, sir.

Senator INOUYE. Or were you aware that if he carried out this plan, it would place in jeopardy the national security of the United States of America?

Mr. CAULFIELD. That is a two-part question, now.

Are you asking did I think that this was a blackmail?

Senator INOUYE. Yes.

Mr. CAULFIELD. No, sir; I didn't think that this was a blackmail. I viewed this as an attempt on the part of a man who was distraught, who wanted his freedom and had come across a means of obtaining that freedom. I did not consider it to be blackmail, sir. I considered it, based upon my conversation with Mr. McCord, that he was distraught.

Senator INOUYE. Didn't you think that there was a risk of compromising the security apparatus of the United States? As he pointed out, the Government would have to dismiss the case or admit that there were taps on these two embassies.

Mr. CAULFIELD. Well, sir, again in passing these messages back and forth, and I passed this one back to Mr. Dean, certainly a matter of this type would, in my judgment, work its way up to any questions of policy and national security.

Senator INOUYE. Did you think that this was a reasonable plan?

Mr. CAULFIELD. I thought it was an interesting one, sir.

Senator INOUYE. You didn't think it was illegal or dangerous?

Mr. CAULFIELD. Sir, again, it is possible that these thoughts crossed my mind, but I have no recollection of it. And again, I am being put in a position of being a messenger and I was focusing on that. I wasn't giving consideration to all of the nuances, serious nuances, that would be included.

Senator INOUYE. Now as you sit here as a witness, do you consider that that plan was dangerous or illegal?

Mr. CAULFIELD. I can't judge that, Senator. It is certainly a serious matter.

Senator INOUYE. Do you think it is proper to set up a government in a trial like this?

Mr. CAULFIELD. No, I don't think it is proper to set up the government, sir.

Senator INOUYE. On page 24, this is one sentence that puzzles me. It says, "When you make your statement, don't underestimate them."

What did you mean by that?

Mr. CAULFIELD. Well, as I indicated in the statement, this was an extremely friendly conversation, Senator, I don't know if this has come through in my statement. We were talking now for an hour, an hour and a half about families, my boys, his children, his wife, my job. He gave me the suggestion that he might be able to help me in liaison with the Post Office, as I recall. This was all a very cordial conversation under very difficult conditions amongst friends.

Now, as I indicated, I was convinced in my mind that he was going to go ahead at some point in time and make a statement. And looking at the broad picture, I could envision an ordeal for him, significant ordeal. He could be effectively on the other side of the people that I was talking to.

I was a friend. I don't know if he fully appreciated that, but that was the intent of my remarks, to let him know.

Senator INOUYE. You were giving him friendly advice?

Mr. CAULFIELD. That is right, sir.

Senator INOUYE. You were giving him friendly advice?

Mr. CAULFIELD. Yes, sir. That is right, sir.

Senator INOUYE. Not to underestimate it, what did you mean?

Mr. CAULFIELD. Not to underestimate the tough-mindedness of all the players in this game.

Senator INOUYE. What did you think that the other side would do to Mr. McCord?

Mr. CAULFIELD. I had no idea. It is apparent that Mr. McCord apparently has misinterpreted that, looking at his statement but that was not the intention. I would say that to a friend that was about to make a major decision that would be tough and I did.

Senator INOUYE. I thank you very much, Mr. Chairman.

Senator ERVIN. Senator Gurney.

Senator GURNEY. Thank you, Mr. Chairman.

Mr. Caulfield, your testimony certainly has been very full and very clear. I just want to press home one or two points.

Referring to the previous testimony by Mr. McCord, at page 320 of the record, he had this to say about his conversations and meeting with you.

"Caulfield stated that he was carrying the message of Executive clemency to me from the very highest levels of the White House. He stated that the President of the United States was in Key Biscayne, Fla., that weekend," referring to the weekend following January 8, "following meetings that we were in then, and that the President had been told of the results of the meeting."

Did you ever learn that the President had learned of the results of any of your meetings with Mr. McCord?

Mr. CAULFIELD. Absolutely not, sir.

Senator GURNEY. He also stated this further on in the testimony on the next page. "Mr. McCord. He," meaning you, "further stated 'I may have a message to you at our next meeting from the President.' "

Did you ever tell him that?

Mr. CAULFIELD. No, sir.

Senator GURNEY. Did you ever have any communication with the President of the United States with regard to this so-called Executive clemency offer to Mr. McCord?

Mr. CAULFIELD. None whatsoever, sir.

Senator GURNEY. Did you ever hear Mr. Dean in any of your conversations with Mr. Dean ever refer to the fact that he had informed the President of any of these meetings?

Mr. CAULFIELD. No, sir.

Senator GURNEY. Did Mr. Dean ever say to you, "The President has instructed me to make this offer of Executive clemency to McCord through you," or through anybody else as far as that is concerned?

Mr. CAULFIELD. Absolutely not, sir.

Senator GURNEY. Did you ever apply any pressure to Mr. McCord in any of these meetings for him to do anything in regard to this upcoming trial?

Mr. CAULFIELD. No, sir.

Senator GURNEY. Did you ever urge him or advise him to plead guilty?

Mr. CAULFIELD. Never.

Senator GURNEY. This point has been covered but it is important because of Mr. McCord's testimony. My understanding is that your understanding about these calls to the Embassy and the wiretaps on the Embassies that this was his theory of defense, a way that he could get out of it by having the case dismissed if these wiretaps had occurred, is that correct?

Mr. CAULFIELD. That is correct.

Senator GURNEY. Did Mr. McCord ever discuss with you what other plans he might have if he were found guilty at the trial?

Mr. CAULFIELD. No, sir.

Senator GURNEY. One final question. You served for some time under Mr. Ehrlichman in the White House. For how long a period?

Mr. CAULFIELD. From April 8, 1969, through July of 1970.

Senator GURNEY. Did you see quite a bit of him during this time?

Mr. CAULFIELD. No, sir; I would not characterize my time under Mr. Ehrlichman as frequent visits. I would be working very closely with his staff people, primarily Bud Krogh, who had a variety of duties in the Federal law enforcement area, and I would work primarily through Mr. Krogh into Mr. Ehrlichman.

Senator GURNEY. But you were generally familiar with some of the missions or the work that Mr. Ehrlichman was carrying on in the White House, is that fair to say?

Mr. CAULFIELD. Generally familiar, yes, sir.

Senator GURNEY. Would you say that it was also a fair thing to say that Mr. Ehrlichman undertook a great many missions, a good deal of work in the White House, in his duties on his own, on his own independent carrying out, is that a fair thing to say?

Mr. CAULFIELD. Well, of course, I have no way of knowing that, Senator.

Senator GURNEY. Would that be your impression?

Mr. CAULFIELD. It is possible, Senator.

Senator GURNEY. I do not have any further questions, Mr. Chairman.

Senator ERVIN. Senator Talmadge.

Senator TALMADGE. Mr. Caulfield, are you still on the Federal payroll?

Mr. CAULFIELD. I am in what they call administrative leave status because of these developments with the Treasury; yes, sir, as of this moment, yes, sir, I am still on the Federal payroll.

Senator TALMADGE. Getting a check?

Mr. CAULFIELD. Yes, sir.

Senator TALMADGE. But you are on leave?

Mr. CAULFIELD. Yes, sir.

Senator TALMADGE. Did you call Mr. John Ehrlichman immediately after the break-in at the Watergate on June 17?

Mr. CAULFIELD. Yes, sir.

Senator TALMADGE. What did he say?

Mr. CAULFIELD. Well, I received a telephone call on the afternoon of June 17, which is the date of the break-in, the date of the break-in, about 3 or 4 p.m., as I recall, from a gentleman I worked with in the U.S. Secret Service, Mr. Patrick Boggs, and he called me and he said, "Do you know Jim McCord?" and I said "Yes, I know Jim McCord." And he indicated, he said: "Well, we have received a report that there is a break-in at the Democratic National Committee. We are concerned because of our protective capabilities or responsibilities, rather, in that area. We have some agents checking into it. Some of the people appear not to have given their correct names and we are getting a report that one of those not giving the correct name is Jim McCord."

He said "Now, do you want to call John Ehrlichman or should I call him?"

After I had recovered from the shock, I indicated: "Well, you go ahead and try and reach him and I will try to reach him as well."

And I called the White House board and I was told that he was en route to his residence. By the time that I did reach him Mr. Boggs had already contacted him. And I said to Mr. Ehrlichman, I said, "John, it sounds like there is a disaster of some type. Did you speak to Mr. Boggs?" He said, "Yes, what is this all about?" I said, "I haven't got the foggiest notion what it is all about but they are saying they believed Jim McCord, who works for the committee, has been arrested in a burglary at the Democratic National Committee."

He said, I forget what he said exactly, I think it was a long silence, as I recall, and I said, "My God, you know, I cannot believe it." He said, "Well, I guess I had better place a call to John Mitchell." I said, "I think that would be very appropriate." [Laughter.]

Senator TALMADGE. Who said it sounds like a disaster, you or Mr. Ehrlichman?

Mr. CAULFIELD. John J. Caulfield.

Senator TALMADGE. Why did you have Mr. Ulasewicz call Mr. McCord rather than calling McCord yourself?

Mr. CAULFIELD. In this July call?

Senator TALMADGE. Yes. This anonymous, mysterious call with the New York accent. [Laughter.]

Mr. CAULFIELD. Are we talking about the January call or the July call?

Senator TALMADGE. We are talking about the call with no name that Mr. Ulasewicz is alleged to have made at your request and the request of John Dean.

Mr. CAULFIELD. Oh, well again I did not want to make the call Senator. I knew how serious it was, how dangerous it was, I explained to John Dean that I did not want to do it. I had to focus completely on the seriousness of the misconduct but intuitively I knew that I was wrong, and I just did not want to do it, and as I have indicated in my testimony I tried to get out of it and I felt that because I had asked Mr. Ulasewicz previously to set up this telephone arrangement with Mr. McCord outside of his residence that he could, when Mr. McCord received a call he would, understand that it was coming from me.

This was my way of getting the message delivered without getting involved.

Senator TALMADGE. Whom were you working for at the time you relayed Mr. Dean's message to Mr. McCord?

Mr. CAULFIELD. In January?

Senator TALMADGE. Yes, sir.

Mr. CAULFIELD. I was the Assistant Director of the Bureau of Alcohol, Tobacco, and Firearms.

Senator TALMADGE. Now, on behalf of whom did you assume Mr. Dean to be speaking, talking of when he spoke of Executive clemency to Mr. McCord?

Mr. CAULFIELD. Well, as I have indicated coming from Mr. Dean, having worked with him, I assumed that there were others at the White House who were involved in this matter in terms of the offer.

Senator TALMADGE. Who did you think was the real author of the message, Mr. Dean or someone else?

Mr. CAULFIELD. Well, sir, again I believe that conceivably, very conceivably, that if we are going to talk about others that quite possibly Mr. Ehrlichman. I had no way of knowing that, Senator.

Senator TALMADGE. Mr. Chairman, I have no further questions, thank you, sir.

Senator ERVIN. Senator Baker?

Senator BAKER. Mr. Chairman, thank you very much.

Mr. Caulfield I won't take very long but necessarily I expect the points I want further elaboration on in the questions I have may be at least in part repetitious. Do you have any idea why Mr. McCord chose you to send that letter to?

Mr. CAULFIELD. Well, I do not—of course, I do not know but Jim McCord knew I worked at the White House. He knew that I had worked for Mr. Dean.

Senator BAKER. The answer is you don't know. Did Mr. McCord ever tell you why?

Mr. CAULFIELD. No, sir. He did not.

Senator BAKER. Did he confirm that he wrote the unsigned letter to you?

Mr. CAULFIELD. Yes. I think there was just a brief conversation about it in our first conversation in the car.

Senator BAKER. Did he indicate to you why he wrote the letter at all? You have told me now that he did not indicate why he chose you to write the letter—did he indicate to you why he wrote the letter?

Mr. CAULFIELD. I think in substance what he said was what was in the note, you know, the CIA, the White House will do this thing to the CIA, I am not going to stand for that.

Senator BAKER. Did he tell you why the White House was going to blame this on the CIA?

Mr. CAULFIELD. No, sir, I have no recollection of that as to why.

Senator BAKER. He didn't elaborate on that point at all?

Mr. CAULFIELD. No, sir.

Senator BAKER. Did you have any indication or evidence or suspicion that the White House was trying to "blame it on the CIA" independent of your conversation with Mr. McCord?

Mr. CAULFIELD. Senator, the whole letter was—upset me quite a bit. You know it was unsigned and I assumed it was Mr. McCord, and the last sentence bothered me.

Senator BAKER. Did you ask him why he felt they were going to blame it on the CIA?

Mr. CAULFIELD. No, sir.

Senator BAKER. Mr. Caulfield, it seems to me that a defendant in those circumstances or a suspect who had been arrested on charges such as Mr. McCord had been arrested, have three possible alternative courses of action. I am speaking now in the hypothetical sense: He can plead guilty; he can plead not guilty and defend himself on the facts; or third, he can try to contrive a way to create circumstances which would result in his exoneration separate and apart from the fact.

Would that be the range of possibilities that presented themselves to Mr. McCord at the time?

Mr. CAULFIELD. In my judgment?

Senator BAKER. Yes, sir.

Mr. CAULFIELD. Yes, sir.

Senator BAKER. Now let's focus on the third. Obviously he pled not guilty. This record has reference, extensive reference, to efforts allegedly to induce him to plead guilty and receive Executive clemency which he declined to do. He pled not guilty. He was convicted. But before his trial and conviction or at least during the time of his trial and before his conviction this conversation with you, as I understand it, and please excuse me for being repetitious but I want to fix it clearly in my mind in relation to the alternatives that were available to Mr. McCord, at the time of this conversation the trial was going on or at least he had not been convicted yet, is that correct?

Mr. CAULFIELD. That is my recollection, yes, sir.

Senator BAKER. The trial was actually in progress, was it not?

Mr. CAULFIELD. I am not absolutely certain, I believe it was but dates are——

Senator BAKER. And Mr. McCord told you he was not going to plead guilty. He was not interested in Executive clemency, he was not interested in the year, that that was a long time, that he wanted out free and clear, is that the essence of it?

Mr. CAULFIELD. That is the essence of it, Senator.

Senator BAKER. And that he wouldn't settle for anything less?

Mr. CAULFIELD. That is right.

Senator BAKER. And that to achieve that end he had arranged and contrived to phone two foreign embassies whose telephones he knew or suspected to be tapped, presumably illegally or at least embarrassingly to the U.S. Government so that those calls could be subpenaed by his attorneys and produced in court as evidence of illegal surveillance so that the prosecution against him would have to be thrown out or at least so that the Government would be so embarrassed by these alleged taps on foreign embassies that they would dare not prosecute him further, is that the fair intendment of what Mr. McCord told you?

Mr. CAULFIELD. Yes, sir.

Senator BAKER. Mr. McCord was holding hostage either the embarrassment of the U.S. Government with respect to wiretaps on foreign embassies or he was holding hostage the illegality of those taps on foreign embassies. Was that the thrust of his design for a defense at the time of that conversation?

Mr. CAULFIELD. That is my interpretation, sir, of his comments at that time.

Senator BAKER. Thank you very much.

Senator ERVIN. Now, the trial had begun at the time you had these meetings with McCord in January?

Mr. CAULFIELD. Yes.

Senator ERVIN. And presumably, McCord knew something about the conversations which are occurring between the defendants and their lawyers, did he not?

Mr. CAULFIELD. Presumably, Senator, yes, sir.

Senator ERVIN. And had you not heard alleged statements in the press or heard statements over the TV to the effect that since certain men, Barker and McCord, had previously worked for the CIA, that there was some suspicion that the CIA was involved?

Mr. CAULFIELD. I think probably in the minds of many people at that time, that was the suspicion. I do not know whether or not I suspected that. But, yes, sir.

Senator ERVIN. Now, McCord knew you were a lawyer for the President and also knew you were his friend, did he not?

Mr. CAULFIELD. Yes, sir.

Senator ERVIN. So he wrote you a letter which was susceptible of the interpretation that he was giving you a warning that there was no validity to the claim that the CIA was responsible for Watergate?

Mr. CAULFIELD. Yes, sir.

Senator ERVIN. And did you not entertain the opinion after receiving that letter that McCord probably wrote it believing that you would communicate its contents to Mr. Dean, at whose instance you had interviewed McCord?

Mr. CAULFIELD. Yes, sir; and I did just that.

Senator ERVIN. And you did that?

Mr. CAULFIELD. Yes, sir.

Senator ERVIN. Now, you testified under the questioning of Senator Weicker to the effect that your training in law enforcement had given you a conviction that it was wrong to attempt to suppress testimony by an offer of Executive clemency.

Mr. CAULFIELD. No question about that, Senator.

Senator ERVIN. And also that you had a sense of loyalty to the President?

Mr. CAULFIELD. That is correct, Senator.

Senator ERVIN. And also that you considered Jim McCord your friend and appreciated the fact that he was in a very unfortunate situation and you were motivated not only by your loyalty to what you thought, the loyalty to the President and by what assurance you had received from Mr. Dean that if McCord did not go along with the other defendants and cooperate with his lawyer, that there might be a scandal against the President?

Mr. CAULFIELD. That is exactly right, Senator.

Senator ERVIN. So you were compelled to choose between your loyalties, and that was the reason you were willing to carry the message from Dean to McCord, notwithstanding the fact that you did not approve of offering Executive clemency in return for suppressing the testimony?

Mr. CAULFIELD. Yes, sir.

Senator ERVIN. Well, it is proof of what my old philosophy professor told me, that the greatest trials we have in this world is when you are compelled to choose between different loyalties, some of which are conflicting. And you were trying to protect the President, you were trying to aid a friend, and you were trying to carry out a mission which you accepted somewhat reluctantly from the man that you knew—that is, John Dean—whom you knew to be the President's counsel and whom you knew would be actuated by the desire to protect the President against any scandal?

Mr. CAULFIELD. Absolutely correct, Senator.

Senator ERVIN. Now, when you performed this mission for John Dean on these three occasions, what did you expect or, rather, what did you understand was expected of McCord in return for Executive clemency?

Mr. CAULFIELD. I believed that in terms of the context of the message, a year is a long time, that it would be some time less than a year.

Senator ERVIN. Did you infer from your conversation with Dean that under Dean's statements, McCord was expected to plead guilty, keep silent, receive a short sentence, and then receive clemency?

Mr. CAULFIELD. If he accepted the offer, that would be the way I would interpret it, yes, sir.

Senator ERVIN. Now, you were asked a question if Mr. Ehrlichman did not do some things on his own accord, on his own authority.

For whom was Mr. Ehrlichman working?

Mr. CAULFIELD. Sir, he was working for the President of the United States.

Senator ERVIN. Did you know of your own knowledge of any time that Mr. Ehrlichman did things on his own accord, out of his own head and imagination?

Mr. CAULFIELD. I am sure he has many times, Senator.

Senator ERVIN. And you are unable to tell me whether he was acting on instructions or acting out of his own head and imagination?

Mr. CAULFIELD. No, sir. If I were given an assignment, I would go ahead and do it.

Senator ERVIN. And when you called Mr. Ehrlichman shortly after the break-in, in June, or sometime about in July, you think Mr. Ehrlichman told you he thought he had better call John Mitchell and you said you thought it would be a good idea?

Mr. CAULFIELD. Yes, sir.

Senator ERVIN. And John Mitchell had been Attorney General at that time, and had just resigned as director of the Committee To Re-Elect the President, a short time before?

Mr. CAULFIELD. Yes, sir.

Senator ERVIN. That is all I have.

Senator BAKER. Mr. Chairman, might I ask one more question?

Senator ERVIN. Yes.

Senator BAKER. Mr. Caulfield, you have testified at length and extensively about matters of great importance in which you had a direct involvement.

Mr. CAULFIELD. I beg your pardon, Senator.

Senator BAKER. Mr. Caulfield, you have testified at length and extensively about important matters in which you had a direct involvement?

Mr. CAULFIELD. Yes, sir.
Senator BAKER. You are aware of the nature of those transactions?
Mr. CAULFIELD. Yes, sir.
Senator BAKER. And the possible consequences from them?
Mr. CAULFIELD. Yes, sir.
Senator BAKER. Mr. Caulfield, have you ever been requested to or have you ever suggested that there be any claim of Executive privilege on your behalf?
Mr. CAULFIELD. No, sir.
Senator BAKER. Have you ever requested immunity from prosecution from this committee, a grand jury, or anyone else with respect to the information that you have given?
Mr. CAULFIELD. Absolutely not, sir.
Senator BAKER. Thank you, sir.
Senator ERVIN. I want to thank you for appearing before the committee and for your testimony, and with the understanding that you will return later at the request of the committee, you are excused at this time.
Mr. CAULFIELD. Yes, sir.
Senator ERVIN. Thank you very much.
Mr. DASH. Will Mr. Anthony Ulasewicz come to the witness table, please.
Senator ERVIN. Will you raise your right hand?
Do you swear that the evidence that you will give to the Senate Select Committee on Presidential Campaign Activities shall be the truth, the whole truth, and nothing but the truth, so help you God?
Mr. ULASEWICZ. I do.
Mr. DASH. Be seated, Mr. Ulasewicz.
Mr. ULASEWICZ. Yes.
Mr. DASH. Mr. Ulasewicz, for the record, would you please state your full name and your address.

TESTIMONY OF ANTHONY T. ULASEWICZ

Mr. ULASEWICZ. My name is Anthony, middle initial T. last name U-l-a-s-e-w-i-c-z. I reside in the town of Day, D-a-y, Saratoga County, in the State of New York.
Mr. DASH. And you are appearing alone, without an attorney?
Mr. ULASEWICZ. Yes, sir.
Mr. DASH. Mr. Ulasewicz, I understand that you have had a police career. Will you please give us that professional background?
Mr. ULASEWICZ. Yes. I was appointed to the New York City Police Department February 17, 1943, and left the department on or about July 9, 1969. I was a detective first-rate in a command known as the Bureau of Special Services and Investigations of the New York City Police Department. I spent 21 years in that command, 6 years without a uniform.
Mr. DASH. Could you briefly describe what your duties were in that assignment?
Mr. ULASEWICZ. The Bureau of Special Services conducted investigations regarding organizations or groups in the city who might be a problem at any time. These were groups, perhaps dissident groups with governments in their own background nations. We

provided security for visiting personages and any causes or demonstrations that might have resulted in difficulty to the city.

Mr. DASH. How long have you known Mr. John Caulfield?

Mr. ULASEWICZ. For about 10 years.

Mr. DASH. Did you meet him during your service in the police department?

Mr. ULASEWICZ. Yes, while I was in the Bureau of Special Services, Mr. Caulfield became part of the command for some time and then left for another command and that is how we started our friendship.

Mr. DASH. Now, in July of 1972, did you receive a call from Mr. Caulfield?

Mr. ULASEWICZ. In June of 1972.

Mr. DASH. In June of 1972. Can you just briefly tell us what the nature of that call was?

Mr. ULASEWICZ. Yes.

Mr. Caulfield called me somewhere about the 25th or 26th of June and asked me to come to see him in Washington, D.C., the next day on a personal matter. I met with him around noontime. He mentioned that he was thinking of contacting Mr. McCord, a friend of his, that he did not have his telephone number. It was unlisted, it had been changed. And he said would I assist him in arranging for an appointment so that he may speak—not me, but speak with Mr. McCord.

Mr. DASH. Then what did you do?

Mr. ULASEWICZ. I said, all right, if you do not know any other, if you want my help, I will do it. I did not question him in any way.

He asked me could I do it as soon as possible? I said, I will do it right now. I said, No. 1, you will have to give me some kind of identifying information, how will Mr. McCord know that it is you that is contacting him?

What I did was I wrote a note on a plain piece of paper and told Jack I would deliver that to Mr. McCord, setting up a telephone and he can then have his conversation. The purpose of this call, he said he wanted to help Mr. McCord, express his sympathy, et cetera, they had been such good friends in the past.

I wrote a note, arranged—I told Jack that I must have some identifying information so that this thing, that Mr. McCord would believe it is he. He said, well, there was an incident recently in which Mr. Caulfield left his raincoat somewhere, and I put that—that was the identifying information, that I am a mutual friend for whom you recovered a raincoat.

Mr. DASH. Did you, in fact, take that note?

Mr. ULASEWICZ. Yes.

Mr. DASH. Where did you deliver it?

Mr. ULASEWICZ. I proceeded immediately to the area where Mr. McCord resides. Mr. Caulfield had given me the address. I looked around through the area, located a place, a Blue Inn or something, which has a large parking lot, two telephone booths isolated by themselves.

I took the two telephone numbers of the booths, put them on the note, put two different times, like 2:30 and 4:30, and then wrote on the note about a mutual friend wishes to speak to you, or words to that effect; you recently recovered a raincoat of his. It was not signed.

I then proceeded—this telephone booth is within the vicinity, of course, of Mr. McCord's residence. I then took the note. I went to Mr. McCord's residence, placed it in the letter box, and walked away.

I then called from some area not too far, I called Mr. Caulfield and informed him that it was done.

Mr. DASH. Now, later, in January 1973, did you again receive a telephone call from Mr. Caulfield?

Mr. ULASEWICZ. Yes, I did.

Mr. DASH. Where—did you know or did he indicate he was calling from?

Mr. ULASEWICZ. He indicated he was calling from California. I think it was the San Clemente Inn in California.

Mr. DASH. And what, if anything, did he tell you in that telephone conversation?

Mr. ULASEWICZ. Well, he indicated to me that he wished another favor concerning Mr. McCord. He would like me to contact Mr. McCord and deliver a message. And as Mr. Caulfield says, there was a loud silence.

I said, "Jack, you realize that what you are asking is a very unusual request for many reasons—the timing; it is a different situation than it was in June, prior to it, et cetera."

He said, "Tony," or something like this in response, "you know I am here on meetings, I am conducting meetings, I am very busy, there is interruptions. I can't do a thing like this from here. It would be very inconvenient. I know that what I am asking is, I wouldn't do it except I know that you are a friend and I can ask you to do it."

He said, "I wouldn't ask anyone else, I don't know who else I can ask."

He said, "Things are being pushed on me. I don't want to get into it or I wouldn't ask you to do it."

I said something that, well, Mr. McCord, of course, being a good wireman, Jack, anything that is said to him, it can be expected it is probably recorded.

He said, "if this ever comes out, I will definitely admit that I asked you to do this, and under these circumstances and on a friendship basis."

Mr. DASH. What was the message that Mr. Caulfield asked you to give Mr. McCord?

Mr. ULASEWICZ. To the best of my recollection, the message was in five or six phrases. It was—let's see now. I don't have the original notes. I wrote the phrases lightly after I agreed. It was, "A year is a long time. No one knows how a judge will go. Your family will be provided for. Rehabilitation and job opportunities will be provided for."

During this conversation, which incidentally, occurred at a telephone booth in the town of Day, and the telephone system is not the best, it wasn't too clear and I thought Mr. McCord asked me to repeat something.

Mr. DASH. Right now, I am asking you to recall the message or the telephone call you had from Mr. Caulfield.

Mr. ULASEWICZ. Oh, to Mr. Caulfield?

Mr. DASH. What Mr. Caulfield asked you to tell Mr. McCord.

Mr. ULASEWICZ. Oh, well, I finished with Mr. Caulfield and he gave me the number and I then went in and made this call to Mr. McCord.

Mr. DASH. The message you gave to Mr. McCord was not your own message, was it?

Mr. ULASEWICZ. Oh, no, Mr. Caulfield's message.

Mr. DASH. I take it the message you gave to Mr. McCord was the same message you have given?

Mr. ULASEWICZ. Same message, yes, sir.

Mr. DASH. All right, then you can go ahead and say what you told Mr. McCord, but before that how did you contact Mr. McCord?

Mr. ULASEWICZ. Mr. Caulfield gave me a telephone number to Mr. McCord's residence. I did not have that number, so he provided me with the number, but I did have, I told him I did have, the number to the telephone booth and I had those and I contacted Mr. McCord at his residence.

Mr. McCord was not surprised at the phone call apparently and I said, "Go to the phone," and he did have the telephone where it was, identical with the June message.

Mr. DASH. Now Mr. McCord did call to the telephone booth. Did he call you or did you call him?

Mr. ULASEWICZ. No; I called Mr. McCord.

Mr. DASH. And you did reach him at the other end of the line?

Mr. ULASEWICZ. I did reach him, right.

Mr. DASH. What, if anything, then now did you tell him that Mr. Caulfield asked you to tell him?

Mr. ULASEWICZ. Right.

I told him I had a message from Mr. Caulfield and that I went into this message as I just said, "A year is a long time. No one knows how a judge will go. Your family needs will be provided for, rehabilitation and job opportunity will be provided for."

In the course of the conversation Mr. McCord said something I didn't quite understand, I repeated a phrase or two of this. And there was something about "Don't know whether he asked me to plead guilty or is that part of my message," and that is all I recall of the message.

Mr. DASH. Do you recall saying anything about immunity, did immunity come up in the discussion?

Mr. ULASEWICZ. I don't recall, it may very well have happened. I have heard Mr. McCord's testimony here, of course, as everyone has, and I searched my mind very strongly on the matter because I still believe Mr. McCord could have been taped and might have it on tape; I don't know, but knowing that possibility, I certainly searched my memory and this is the best I can remember.

Mr. DASH. And it is possible in your searching your memory that the idea of pleading guilty came up during the conversation.

Mr. ULASEWICZ. It is quite possible it might have been in it.

Mr. DASH. All right.

Now, what did Mr. McCord say after you gave him that message? By the way, when you gave him that message did he know who you were?

Mr. ULASEWICZ. No; I never met Mr. McCord in person prior—at any time.

Mr. DASH. Did you identify yourself by name?

Mr. ULASEWICZ. No; I went right into it, "I have a message from Jack Caulfield," and his response indicated to me that he was expecting a message apparently. I went right into it and he thanked me and seemed satisfied.

Mr. DASH. What did you do after that?

Mr. ULASEWICZ. I called Mr. Caulfield back in California and told him I relayed the message that he had given me, and that Mr. McCord did not seem surprised, and that he seemed satisfied.

Mr. DASH. Did you have any other contact with Mr. McCord on the telephone?

Mr. ULASEWICZ. The next day Mr. Caulfield called me again and asked me to once more deliver a message to Mr. McCord.

Mr. DASH. What was that message?

Mr. ULASEWICZ. That message was, Mr. Caulfield said to me that, to explain, to make sure that Mr. McCord realizes that he is in California, that he, Mr. Caulfield, is in California, that he will meet with him as soon as he returned, first order of business, from California, to set up a tentative, a meet on the second overlook on Washington highway or parkway, and to get that message to him and then call back and verify it.

Mr. DASH. Did Mr. Caulfield pick that particular location?

Mr. ULASEWICZ. Yes, he did, and he said he knew I was not familiar with that area but he said, McCord would know the area.

Mr. DASH. All right.

Then were there any other contacts you had on the telephone?

Mr. ULASEWICZ. Mr. Caulfield called me once more after that and he said that he had planned to leave a day earlier. His plane, however, was delayed, would I tell Mr. McCord that as soon as he landed that same evening he will contact Mr. McCord and try to meet him immediately rather than the following day as I originally conveyed my message.

Mr. DASH. What did Mr. McCord respond to that?

Mr. ULASEWICZ. Mr. McCord was very annoyed. He told me, he kind of brushed me off, said, "I have people here. I have my own family problems, I know you are doing what you think is right," something to that effect. He spoke kind of rapidly and he said: "You can tell Jack that I will meet only as originally scheduled," meaning the, originally the second call, the overlook on the Washington Parkway.

Mr. DASH. Did you report that back to Mr. Caulfield?

Mr. ULASEWICZ. No, I couldn't report that back to Mr. Caulfield.

Mr. DASH. That was the last contact?

Mr. ULASEWICZ. That was the last contact I had in this matter with either of the two gentlemen.

Mr. DASH. All right, I have no further questions, Mr. Chairman.

Senator ERVIN. Mr. Thompson.

Mr. THOMPSON. Mr. Ulasewicz, was not Mr. Ehrlichman responsible for your being hired originally at the White House?

Mr. ULASEWICZ. Yes, sir.

Mr. THOMPSON. Did he direct your work while you were at the White House?

Mr. ULASEWICZ. Mr. Caulfield directed my work.

Mr. THOMPSON. He did.

Was that at the direction of Mr. Ehrlichman? Did he direct Mr. Caulfield?

Mr. ULASEWICZ. That was my impression.

Mr. THOMPSON. Between the first telephone call that you made to Mr. McCord until after the trial, did you discuss the calls that you were making with Mr. Ehrlichman or anyone else at the White House?

Mr. ULASEWICZ. No, sir.

Mr. THOMPSON. You only discussed these matters with Mr. Caulfield?

Mr. ULASEWICZ. And no one at any time.

Mr. THOMPSON. All right.

Did you see your role as someone who was delivering certain words which you took down, say, in writing and repeated or did you see your role as someone who was supposed to engage in conversation with Mr. McCord and paint a picture for him, so to speak?

Mr. ULASEWICZ. Absolutely not, strictly as a messenger to give these phrases over to him, and I did not—I originally did not repeat them in their full context from Mr. Caulfield. My recollection is I gave phrases——

Mr. THOMPSON. All right. When Mr. McCord responded to those words did you engage in conversation with him then?

Mr. ULASEWICZ. No, sir.

Mr. THOMPSON. According to your best recollection, was there ever any discussion between Mr. McCord and yourself about the fact that he should not testify at the trial?

Mr. ULASEWICZ. I do not recall it.

Mr. THOMPSON. Was there ever any discussion, to the best of your recollection, between Mr. McCord and yourself that he should plead guilty?

Mr. ULASEWICZ. It may have been. I do not recall.

Mr. THOMPSON. Well, if it may have been, would this have been in your original message or would this have been pursuant to a conversation?

Mr. ULASEWICZ. No, it would have been in the original message which was that only time, only that first call.

Mr. THOMPSON. All right. This was not in your direct testimony. This was not a part of your direct testimony. Is it your opinion that it was not in your original message or that it possibly could have been?

Mr. ULASEWICZ. It could have been in the original message.

Mr. THOMPSON. So you do not remember what you told him?

Mr. ULASEWICZ. From the best of my recollection these three phrases are positive about the message would be about "a year is a long time, no one knows how a judge will go. Your family needs will be provided for, rehabilitation, and job opportunities". When there was a pause there may have been something on plead guilty or so but I was giving the message as rapidly as I could as I wanted to finish the matter.

Mr. THOMPSON. Pardon me, you say that may have come about or discussed when there was a pause?

Mr. ULASEWICZ. Yes. Mr. McCord said something that I did not quite understand so I repeated my message.

Mr. THOMPSON. This pause, would this still be part of your original message?

Mr. ULASEWICZ. Original message. These only came in the original—any discussion of the, regarding the, judge and all that business came only in the first conversation. The second conversation was to make the appointment, and the third conversation was to inform him that Mr. Caulfield would try to get to him a day sooner.

Mr. THOMPSON. You did not seek to interpret in any way what the message meant?

Mr. ULASEWICZ. No, sir.

Mr. THOMPSON. To Mr. McCord?

Mr. ULASEWICZ. No, sir.

Mr. THOMPSON. Did Mr. Caulfield ever tell you who was directing him in this matter?

Mr. ULASEWICZ. He did not.

Mr. THOMPSON. I have no further questions, Mr. Chairman.

Senator ERVIN. Did you not infer, in other words, you made the statement to Mr. McCord which Mr. Caulfield had asked you to make?

Mr. ULASEWICZ. Yes, sir.

Senator ERVIN. Was it not implicit in that statement that he would get these advantages if he entered a plea of guilty?

Mr. ULASEWICZ. I would assume so, yes, definitely.

Senator ERVIN. You certainly did not construe this statement he is going to be rehabilitated and given, serve——

Mr. ULASEWICZ. No, sir.

Senator ERVIN [continuing]. Serve only a year in jail and get this fine treatment if he fought the case?

Mr. ULASEWICZ. Absolutely. I did not mean to infer any such thing, definitely.

Senator ERVIN. Senator Baker. If not, I will pass directly to Senator Gurney, and then Senator Talmadge.

Senator GURNEY. Mr. Chairman, I do not have any questions of the witness.

Senator ERVIN. Senator Talmadge?

Senator TALMADGE. Mr. Ulasewicz, had you been aware of the Watergate affair at the time you were asked to make the call?

Mr. ULASEWICZ. Yes sir.

Senator TALMADGE. Why did you agree to serve as a contact in this situation?

Mr. ULASEWICZ. Because of my friendship with Mr. Caulfield and in his original call to me with my arguments as to why I did not want to—from his demeanor, his conduct, I could see it was very important to him. He was in some kind of a position that caused him great concern and as a friend I said I would do it.

Senator TALMADGE. Did you assume that Mr. Caulfield's authority was coming from higher authority in the White House?

Mr. ULASEWICZ. I assumed it was coming from at least Mr. Dean, somebody above Mr. Caulfield.

Senator TALMADGE. Did you believe that these White House sources would approve what you did?

Mr. ULASEWICZ. Yes, I suppose so.

Senator TALMADGE. Were you paid for your services in your contact with Mr. McCord?

Mr. ULASEWICZ. No sir. I was on no one's payroll at the time of these conversations in January. I was not in anyone's employ, I might say.

Senator TALMADGE. I have no further questions at this time, Mr. Chairman.

Senator ERVIN. Senator Weicker?

Senator WEICKER. No questions, Mr. Chairman.

Senator ERVIN. Senator Inouye?

Senator INOUYE. Thank you very much.

According to Mr. Caulfield's testimony you were a member of a "private security entity in Washington, D.C., providing investigative support for the White House" is that correct?

Mr. ULASEWICZ. That is correct.

Senator INOUYE. You worked under Mr. Caulfield but were on the payroll of Mr. Kalmbach?

Mr. ULASEWICZ. That is correct.

Senator INOUYE. What were you receiving as salary from Mr. Kalmbach?

Mr. ULASEWICZ. $22,000 a year plus expenses.

Senator INOUYE. Are you still on Mr. Kalmbach's payroll?

Mr. ULASEWICZ. No sir.

Senator INOUYE. When were you taken off the payroll?

Mr. ULASEWICZ. In 1971—well, to the end of the year of 1972.

Senator INOUYE. What was the nature of your work?

Mr. ULASEWICZ. It was supporting, as an outside supporting investigative to Mr. Caulfield.

Senator INOUYE. Will you describe some of your duties. One of the newspapers described you as the super spy. Is that a correct statement?

Mr. ULASEWICZ. The newspapers have painted quite a few pictures of me recently, but I was no spy, of course, of any kind. I did investigative work in support of whatever Mr. Caulfield related to me. I did no slanderous spying as the newspapers' allegations, et cetera. I could best put in its category is probably supporting anybody who is conducting legitimate investigations. I used no wiretaps, I never used any surveillance, et cetera.

Senator INOUYE. You considered your work to be legal?

Mr. ULASEWICZ. Absolutely legal, yes, sir. I took—when I left the police department, I left a fine ongoing career not to get involved in anything illegal and I made a stipulation at the time with Mr. Ehrlichman at the time the job was taken. Mr. Caulfield knew I would not go for it.

Senator INOUYE. In this special assignment you undertook from Mr. Caulfield to serve as contact with Mr. McCord, were you aware you were being an accessory to the crime of obstructing a criminal investigation?

Mr. ULASEWICZ. Yes, sir. I knew that it was wrong.

Senator INOUYE. You knew you were an accessory to a crime?

Mr. ULASEWICZ. Yes, sir.

Senator INOUYE. But as a matter of friendship you proceeded?

Mr. ULASEWICZ. Yes, sir.

Senator INOUYE. Did you have other assignments of similar nature?

Mr. ULASEWICZ. No.

Senator INOUYE. I have no further questions, Mr. Chairman.

Senator BAKER. Thank you, Senator Inouye.

I might say the question has not been asked you but I will put it now, while we are limiting our inquiry to a single set of events and circumstances, do I understand that you are willing to return and to testify further at the pleasure of the committee on other matters that you may have knowledge of?

Mr. ULASEWICZ. Yes, sir.

Senator BAKER. Very good.

Senator Montoya.

Senator MONTOYA. I have no questions.

Senator BAKER. Senator Montoya has no questions.

Let me ask one question or one line of questions, it really does not bear much on the matter at hand though; did I understand you to say McCord was a pretty good wireman?

Mr. ULASEWICZ. Well, from what I have read in the case and from the fact that Mr. Caulfield hired him, I would say he was one of the best wiremen in the business. [Laughter.]

Senator BAKER. I am not familiar with the term, what do you mean a pretty good wireman?

Mr. ULASEWICZ. Well, a wireman in police parlance would be anyone who is familiar with applying wiretaps, any type of surveillances by electrical means, and so forth in a room, on a person, in an automobile, in a tire, or any place and I would say he was a good man.

Senator BAKER. Is that a term of general usage in your trade?

Mr. ULASEWICZ. Yes, sir. However, I was never a wireman. [Laughter.]

While I was in the police department many of the functions that we did, of course, they were all legal with proper papers, et cetera, and judicial permission, we have some of the finest wiremen in the department. [Laughter.]

So it would be a thing of common knowledge to myself or anyone else.

Senator BAKER. You think your wiremen were better than McCord's wiremen?

Mr. ULASEWICZ. I will tell you, any old retired man in the New York City Police Department who would become involved in a thing like that, he thought he had to for whatever reason it was, he would not have walked in with an army, that is for sure. [Laughter.]

Senator BAKER. He would not have walked in with an army.

Would he have walked in with identification papers and serial numbered $100 bills and address book?

Mr. ULASEWICZ. He probably would have walked in like any decent common looking citizens, laid something in the right place and walked right out and that would have been the end of it for a long time. [Laughter.]

You see, I must be honest here, Senator. [Laughter.]

Senator BAKER. How could you have gained the information, how could you have gained the information that Mr. McCord obviously or apparently was seeking, that is, a telecommunication link with what was going on in the Democratic National Committee without going in there with an army and taping the doors and all the rest.

Describe to us how else that might have been done by a good man.

Mr. ULASEWICZ. Well, a wireman would only do wires. He might not necessarily be a good man for a different type of investigation. If it is a question of obtaining information from the Democratic Party, Republican Party, or anybody else the easiest way is to write a postal card asking them to mail you all their leaflets, they will put you on their mailing list and you will have everything. If it is all written they will do it.

Senator BAKER. Politicians are pretty anxious to add to their mailing list.

Mr. ULASEWICZ. Politicians are the most vulnerable people in the world, in my last 3 years of experience, to any kind of scandal, et cetera. I do not say they are guilty of it because I still have to come back here. [Laughter.]

But because of the type——

Senator BAKER. The last thing on earth I would want to do is to convert your testimony into self-serving purposes for this committee but you do not have any good wiremen on us, do you? [Laughter.]

Mr. ULASEWICZ. It looks like there are plenty of them here. [Laughter.]

Senator BAKER. You know that is not a very good answer. You are heightening my concern. [Laughter.]

Mr. ULASEWICZ. I have none on anybody. Thank you.

Senator BAKER. Thank you.

Senator ERVIN. I understand that you will come back when the committee requests you for further evidence?

Mr. ULASEWICZ. Definitely, Senator.

Senator ERVIN. Thank you, thank you very much.

I think it is almost recess time and it is better to recess until 2 o'clock and then start with the next witness.

[Whereupon, at 11:45 a.m., the hearing was recessed, to reconvene at 2 p.m., this same day.]

AFTERNOON SESSION, WEDNESDAY, MAY 23, 1973

Senator BAKER [presiding]. The committee will come to order.

The chairman has asked me to announce that he is on his way from a meeting of the Judiciary Committee which, as you know, is considering the nomination of Mr. Elliot Richardson to be Attorney General of the United States. That he and Senator Gurney, a member of the Judiciary Committee, will be here momentarily. He asked me, however, in the interest of time to convene the committee, and to proceed with the opening statement which we understand Mr. Alch is now prepared to give.

Mr. DASH. I see Mr. Gerald Alch is at the witness table. Will you, Mr. Chairman, swear the witness?

Senator BAKER. Mr. Alch, would you hold up your right hand?

Mr. ALCH. Yes, sir.

Senator BAKER. Will you please state your name?

Mr. ALCH. Gerald Alch.

Senator BAKER. Mr. Gerald Alch, do you solemnly swear that the testimony you are about to give before this committee will be the truth, the whole truth, and nothing but the truth, so help you God?

Mr. ALCH. I do.

Senator BAKER. You may be seated.

Mr. DASH. Now, the committee has been supplied 13 pages of a statement that Mr. Alch will be reading. Our committee staff has done the typing and reproducing of this for Mr. Alch, having supplied a copy of his statement, and the rest of it will be available to the committee during the course of the reading of the statement.

Mr. Alch, for the record, will you give your full name and address?

TESTIMONY OF GERALD ALCH, ATTORNEY

Mr. ALCH. Yes, sir.

My name is Gerald Alch, A-l-c-h. My address is 954 West Roxbury Parkway, Chestnut Hill, Mass.

Mr. DASH. And you did prepare a statement which you wish to read to this committee?

Mr. ALCH. Yes, sir.

Mr. DASH. Will you proceed reading that statement?

Mr. ALCH. Thank you, and I will.

May it please the honorable committee, in all candor, I am about to give testimony with a certain degree of regret. This is because those areas to which I shall address myself are areas which I, as a criminal defense attorney, believe to be somewhat sacred. They reflect conversation between a lawyer and his client, uttered in the course of a relationship wherein I was exerting my best efforts to protect the interest and welfare of James W. McCord. I take most seriously the well-established attorney-client privilege. Nevertheless, in my judgment, Mr. McCord, in his testimony before this honorable committee on Friday, May 18, 1973, and in other prior disclosures, both written and oral, has waived such privilege which I have been informed he has acknowledged. Mr. McCord has made allegations concerning my conduct in the defense of his liberty. These allegations are, in some instances, completely false and in other instances, have been twisted out of context into untruths, presumably to serve his present purpose, whatever that may be, but that impugn my personal standards of ethical and legal behavior. I accordingly believe it now to be my duty and responsibility to respond and I have accepted the invitation of this honorable committee so to do for which I am most grateful. Here, then, is a true narrative of my representation of Mr. McCord.

In July of 1972, my office received a telephone call from Mr. McCord requesting an appointment. On a Saturday morning during that month, I met with him for the very first time. He identified himself as one of those arrested in the Watergate building on June 17, 1972. He told me that he had taken a calculated risk in doing what he did and was prepared to face the consequences. Within that framework, however, he indicated he wanted the most effective legal representation possible and asked whether or not my partner, Attorney F. Lee Bailey, would be interested in representing him. I told him that I had advised Mr. Bailey of my appointment with him and that he, Mr. Bailey, was not interested in representing any defendants in this particular case.

Mr. McCord told me as a result of his impression of me, he desired my counsel. A fee of $25,000 plus expenses was quoted and agreed upon by Mr. McCord. Arrangements were made for the payment of this fee over a period of time, which arrangements were ultimately met by Mr. McCord, although over a longer period of time than originally agreed upon. I asked Mr. McCord to give me specific details attending the Watergate break-in, but he specifically declined to do so except to state his personal motivation for so acting, that is, as he told me at that first meeting, the protection of others. I explained to him that since he had been physically apprehended in the Watergate complex, he could obviously not deny that fact and inquired as to his motivation in so acting. He told me that as chief of security for the Committee To Re-Elect the President, he had received information to the effect that various antiwar demonstrations by groups which he described as "radical" were being planned for the upcoming Presidential election and that these demonstrations had, in the past and would invariably in the future, lead to violence or the threat thereof to various prominent Republican officials, including, but not limited to, members of the Committee To Re-Elect the President and including, but not limited to, the President of the United States. I told him that I would explore whether or not this motivation could, in any way, be embraced by a recognized legal defense. He told me that he wished me to come to Washington, D.C., and meet with an attorney by the name of Paul O'Brien, whom he described as one of the counsel to his employer, the Committee To Re-Elect the President. He desired that I contact Mr. O'Brien and advise him of his—Mr. McCord's—position.

Shortly thereafter, I traveled to the Capital and telephoned Mr. O'Brien for an appointment. Mr. McCord drove me to Mr. O'Brien's office, whereupon I met with Mr. O'Brien and a gentleman introduced to me as Mr. Kenneth Parkinson. I introduced myself, told Mr. O'Brien I had been retained to represent Mr. McCord and was here at Mr. McCord's direction to inform him as a representative of Mr. McCord's employer, the Committee To Re-Elect the President, that Mr. McCord was, as he had told me, prepared to face the consequences of his acts. Mr. O'Brien and I exchanged office telephone numbers and the meeting, which had lasted for approximately 15 minutes, terminated.

My first official act on behalf of Mr. McCord was to represent him at a pretrial indictment probable cause hearing before a superior court judge in the District of Columbia. All other defendants had waived such a hearing, but I decided to utilize it, as best I could, for discovery purposes. Mr. McCord was most impressed with my in-court presentation and he told me so. I subsequently accompanied him, his wife, and daughter before the Federal grand jury. At one point, prior to indictment, I was advised by the prosecutors, Mr. Earl Silbert and Mr. Seymour Glanzer, that they possessed independent evidence that equipment utilized in the monitoring of telephone conversations from the office of the National Democratic Committee had been delivered to Mr. McCord's home in the presence of Mr. McCord's wife on the night of June 17, 1972. They advised me of the possibility of Mr. McCord's wife being indicted as an accessory after the fact, but indicated this would not be done if the equipment was produced. I discussed this with Mr. McCord and he requested me to work out the best arrangement possible, but to do anything and everything to protect his wife whom he said had no involvement in his activities. Accordingly, an arrangement was agreed upon with the prosecutors, whereby the equipment was surrendered to them with the agreement that they would not divulge, during trial, the fact that this particular equipment was obtained from Mr. McCord. Mrs. McCord was not indicted and the Government kept its word with regard to the manner in which said equipment was introduced during trial.

In the ensuing weeks and months, during my many contacts with Mr. McCord, he continuously insisted that his only purpose in participating in the Watergate break-in was to protect his employers and other Republican officials from threats of violence. He would, almost daily, send to me clippings from various newspapers published throughout the country, reflecting reports of antiwar group activities which in some instances involved violence. In fact, at one point, he sent to me a typed memorandum reflecting this alleged motivation for his conduct, which memorandum included various legal citations of law, which he believed to be in support of the defense he wished me to present. I have made available to this honorable committee copies of three such memorandums, which was accompanied by a handwritten note from Mr. McCord which reads as follows: Dated July 13, 1972. "Gerald, I well understand that it is your job and not mine to work up a defense. Nevertheless, I have been putting together some ideas and collecting every newspaper clipping I can find which may be of help later. I am strongly oriented toward the grounds of self-defense and defense of others and of property as my defense. I believe we can make the strongest defense on these grounds. We both of course have to talk this out at length and you have the final say in this matter. With best regards, Jim."

I read this, may it please this honorable committee, to emphasize this fact: That Mr. McCord was from the beginning, in complete agreement with the defense ultimately presented in his behalf. At no time, did he ever state to me that he believed the Watergate operation to be legal as a result of the alleged involvement of the then Attorney General, the counsel to the President, or anyone else. As a matter of fact, during one of my many conversations with Mr. McCord on this subject, I told him that my legal research revealed that the defense of the protection of others required that the perpetrator not know he was breaking the law.

I said to Mr. McCord, "No jury will ever believe that a man with your background with the FBI and the CIA would not realize he was breaking the law in breaking into an office at night, wearing surgical gloves and armed with eavesdropping equipment."

He laughed and agreed that such a contention was, in fact, legally untenable. I further explained that the reason for his actions, as he had explained them to me, would be more properly embraced by the legal defense of "duress," wherein the perpetrator felt compelled to break a law in order to prevent a greater evil. Mr. McCord had explained to me his belief of a direct relationship between these potentially violent antiwar groups and the Democratic Party and that his participation in the Watergate burglary was accomplished in the hope of obtaining advance evidence of planned potentially violent demonstrations.

I advised that the law of "duress" allowed for the perpetrator to possess criminal intent, that is, to know that he was breaking the law and that therefore, based upon what he had told me with regard to his own motivation, this defense was not only compatible therewith, but in my opinion, constituted the only defense available. Mr. McCord wholeheartedly agreed. And I commenced to prepare the case on this basis.

I also received from Mr. McCord an outline of a proposed book he was in the process of writing entitled "Counter Espionage Agent for the Republicans—The True Story of the Watergate Case." It was an outline, listing such chapters titled "The Beginnings"; "The Committee To Re-elect the President"; "Background to Violence and Political Espionage"; "Jack Anderson, the Man Who Brought you the Eagleton Case"; "The Political Opposition"; "The Watergate Incident, The True Story"; "The Defendants"; "The Grand Jury"; "The Lawyers"; "The Investigators"; "The Congressional Committees"; "The October Phase"; "The News Media"; "The Final Story"; with a prolog, as the book goes to print, "If the Democrats Had Had Alarms and Guards."

Copies of this outline have also been provided to this honorable committee. All of these memorandums, I may add, gentlemen, were provided to me by mail directly from Mr. McCord.

In this regard, on September 19, 1972, one of my associates from my office, Mr. John Albert Johnson, appeared with Mr. McCord for arraignment with Chief Judge Sirica, since I had a court commitment in another State. Mr. McCord told Mr. Johnson that he was in the process of writing a book and desired our opinion as to whether he could have this book published prior to election day. He told Mr. Johnson that he felt that any publication after Presidential election day would not be worthwhile monetarily. Mr. Johnson reduced this conversation to a file memorandum, copies of which also have been presented to this honorable committee. When Mr. Johnson advised me of this, I told Mr. McCord that in my opinion, no such publication should be contemplated prior to trial. Mr. McCord, reluctantly it appeared to me, agreed to follow my advice.

There were other memorandums that I received from time to time from Mr. McCord which suggested for consideration other potential defense material which I rejected. One such memorandum, copies of which have been provided to this honorable committee, listed and discussed such topics as "the Mafia and Democratic National Committee Funds and Personnel"; "Flying Tigers and Anna Chenault"; "Israel and the Mafia." Said memorandum as you honorable Senators will note in the copies provided to you, also mentioned the names of other individuals and law firms, which names I choose not to bandy about in this public hearing.

On several occasions, Mr. McCord told me that he was convinced there existed a concerted effort on the part of his codefendants and their counsel to make him the "fall guy" of the Watergate operation. On one particular occasion, he mailed to me a memorandum, copies of which you also have. For the record, said memorandum reads as follows:

OCTOBER 17, 1972.

Subject: Shift of the Focus of Publicity.

Jerry, about a week ago, Newsweek Reporters told my men that the FBI had been leaking information to them relative to my case and some of the material would appear in the next two issues. Last week, one item appeared regarding an office of mine rented on K Street, D.C. This week's issue, October 23 date, carries for the first time an allegation that I was the "ring leader" of the Watergate operation. Instead of being fourth down the ladder from Liddy, Hunt, and Barker, I am now the "ring leader", according to the FBI. This had been predicted, that I would try to be made the focus in order to draw the attention away from the W.H. men, Liddy and Hunt. I could see it coming as early as August and more particularly, 2 weeks ago, when you and I talked. The FBI leaks to Newsweek are no accident. It is as predicted. Jim.

I advised Mr. McCord that I had kept abreast of newspaper coverage of the Watergate incident and that in all honesty, could discern no effort on anyone's part to foist upon him prime responsibility for the offenses charged. He disagreed with me and I told him that I would subsequently discuss the matter with other defense counsel.

At another time prior to January 1973, Mr. McCord advised that he had made telephone calls to the Israeli Embassy on September 19, 1972, and to the Chilean Embassy on October 10, 1972. He did not divulge the contents of these telephone conversations. He explained his purpose as follows:

He told me he was convinced that the Government had telephone taps on the phones of these Embassies, but would not admit to such activity. He was certain that his calls had been intercepted. He instructed that I make a motion in court requiring the Government to disclose any and all intercepted communications in which he was involved. His theory was that the Government, rather than reveal such activity, would dismiss the case against him.

I asked him what these calls were about. He told me that they were phone calls relative to the case. I now understand that these phone calls were not of any relative substance which fact Mr. McCord had not told me originally.

I received a letter from him dated August 23 reflecting these thoughts, copies of which I have made available to this honorable committee. It is a two-page letter and in the interest of expediency, I shall not read the letter in its entirety. It deals with the subject of the consequences the Government intercepting telephone calls. However, I would respectfully call to the attention of this honorable committee the last paragraph of the letter, which reads as follows:

"Enjoyed the visit with you and appreciated your visit. I have got a great lawyer and am well aware of that fact. With best regards, Jim."

In addition, I have provided this honorable committee with copies of undated memorandum from Mr. McCord, reflecting four telephone calls: one from Chile to McCord's office; another from Mr. McCord's office to the Chilean military attaché; a call to the Israeli Embassy from Mr. McCord's home, and a similar call to the Chilean Embassy.

I would respectfully invite the committee's attention to the fact that the first two of these calls occurred prior to my ever meeting Mr. McCord, before I ever represented the man. As a result thereof, I made an appropriate motion for disclosure of any Government electronic surveillance in any way pertaining to Mr. McCord. Mr. Silbert's response was that he had no knowledge of any such surveillance. Again, at my client's insistence, I made a second similar motion at the bench during trial, explaining to Chief Judge Sirica that I was doing so at my client's insistence that such calls had, in fact, been made and had been electronically intercepted.

The Government again stated its total lack of knowledge of any such activity and accordingly, no action was taken on my motion. My actions in this regard were consistent with and occasioned by my determination to defend my client to the best of my ability by utilizing any and all legal and proper means. In retrospect, I must conclude that my efforts were not, to say the least, appreciated.

With regard to opportunities presented to Mr. McCord to tell all that he knew with regard to the Watergate operation, I state the following:

On or about October 25, 1972, the Government conveyed to local counsel, my local counsel, Bernard Shankman of Washington, and my associate, Mr. Johnson, an offer to accept from Mr. McCord a plea of guilty to one substantive count of the indictment and in return for his testimony as a Government witness, a recommendation of leniency would be made to the court. The Government indicated, however, that it could not and would not recommend any type of sentence which would allow Mr. McCord to remain at liberty. This offer was transmitted to Mr. McCord and was unequivocally rejected.

In November of 1972, a second plea offer was received from the prosecutors. At this time, the offer was essentially similar to the first offer, except that Mr. McCord would have to plead to three counts of the indictment instead of one. The explanation for this change of position was that the Government's case had grown considerably stronger. This offer, which also involved Mr. McCord's testifying as a Government witness, was related to and again rejected by Mr. McCord.

I advised Mr. McCord after an in camera session with Chief Judge Sirica, during trial, that there still existed an opportunity for him to appear before the grand jury, even at that stage of the trial, to make full disclosure. I have been informed that the committee has been provided with a transcript of that in camera proceeding and I, therefore, will not attempt to paraphrase the words of Chief Judge Sirica, nevertheless, I relayed this information to Mr. McCord and this third opportunity was turned down. I take the liberty of bringing these three instances to the attention of this honorable committee since, in my opinion, Mr. McCord, in portions of his testimony before you on May 18, 1973, implied that I had pressured him to plead guilty and remain silent. Senators, I state to you that this is not so and respectfully refer you to the question asked of Mr. McCord by Senator Ervin on May 18, 1973 and I quote, Question. "Now, did your lawyer urge you to enter a plea of guilty? I am talking about Mr. Gerald Alch." Answer. "I do not recall that, no, sir." That portion, at least, of Mr. McCord's testimony, is accurate.

With regard to the allegations of Mr. McCord to the effect that I suggested that the CIA be brought into the case in a defense posture, I state the following:

As heretofore explained, I had decided to base Mr. McCord's defense on the theory of "duress" for two basic reasons. First, it was the only legally recognized defense that I felt was supportable; second, more importantly, it appeared to be the factual truth, based upon Mr. McCord's explanation of his own motive. In December of 1972, I attended one of several meetings of defense counsel, the purpose of which was to discuss various aspects of trial strategy. I proceeded to explain the defense that I was contemplating, duress. A discussion ensued wherein some of the other defense attorneys reasoned that this "security motive" and by that they were referring to my contemplated defense of duress based on what Mr. McCord had told me, would be applicable only to Mr. McCord in view of his position as chief of security for the Committee To Re-Elect the President. In the general discussion that followed, the question arose as to whether or not the CIA could have been involved. It was pointed out by others, and I emphasize by others because at this point my defense of Mr. McCord had been formulated based upon what he had told me, and with his concurrence, it was pointed out by others that all of the individuals apprehended in the Watergate complex had some prior connection with the CIA and that one of the Cuban-Americans had been in possession of what appeared to be CIA-forged documents.

Before the meeting went on to other topics, it was agreed that each lawyer would ask his respective client whether or not he had any knowledge of any CIA involvement. When the meeting terminated, I telephoned Mr. McCord at his office by prearrangement and asked him to meet with me and local counsel, Mr. Shankman, at the Monocle Restaurant for lunch. During lunch, which lasted for approximately 45 minutes, I asked Mr. McCord whether, to his knowledge, the CIA was in any way involved with the Watergate venture. He did not directly respond to this specific question, but did become quite upset at what he believed to be the antagonism of the White House against the CIA. He cited the dismissal of Helms—of Mr. Helms, as CIA Director and the appointment of Schlesinger in his place, as an attempted "hatchet job" by the administration against the CIA. He did venture his observation that if any CIA officials were subpenaed that they would not and could not comply with said subpena. Because of the brevity of the luncheon and because of the obvious need for more detailed pretrial preparation meetings, I asked Mr. McCord to come to Boston in a few days, which he agreed to do.

On or about December 26, 1972, Mr. McCord came to Boston and initiated our conversation by stating that the CIA was not involved and that he would have no part of any attempt to involve that agency. He asked that I relay this position to other defense counsel at our next meeting, which I agreed to do, and in fact did.

I did not, after advising other defense counsel of Mr. McCord's denial of CIA involvement, engage with other counsel in any further conversation of any potential defense involving the CIA. At no time did I suggest to Mr. McCord that the so-called CIA defense be utilized, for the defense of "duress" had already been agreed upon, but I merely asked him whether or not there was a factual basis for this contention. Mr. McCord's allegation that I announced my ability to forge his CIA personal records with the cooperation of then acting CIA director, Mr. Schlesinger, is absurd and completely untrue. I have never had the privilege of meeting Mr. Schlesinger nor the privilege of talking with the man. No such statement was ever made. I had no contact with the Director of the CIA, let alone an agreement involving the forging of documents.

My local counsel, Mr. Bernard Shankman, who was present at the Monocle, can corroborate that I did not say that. The remainder of my discussion with Mr. McCord in Boston was devoted to further analysis of the "duress" defense and when the meeting ended, I told him that I would keep in daily telephone contact with him until our next meeting which I tentatively scheduled for the first week of January 1973.

Between December 26, 1972, and the first week of January 1973, I attempted to contact Mr. McCord on several occasions by telephone, but each time that I called, I was told that he was not in and my requests for a return call were not answered. This puzzled me, for up to that point it was Mr. McCord's habit to return my calls immediately upon his receiving any message from me so to do. On or about January 2, 1973, I received a call from local counsel, Bernard Shankman, who advised me that Mr. McCord had or was about to deliver a letter to Chief Judge Sirica, dismissing me as his counsel. This was a shock to me, for at our last meeting in my office on December 26, 1972, we parted on a most cordial note, and in complete agreement upon the theory of his defense. I asked Mr. Shankman to advise Mr. McCord that I would fly into Washington on January 3, 1973, to speak with him on this matter. I did meet with Mr. McCord after I had learned that a letter of dismissal had, in fact, been given to Chief Judge Sirica and that Chief Judge Sirica's position was that I was still counsel of record and that this development would not afford a basis for a continuance. When I met Mr. McCord, he picked me up at the airport in Washington. I expressed astonishment at his action and asked him why he had acted in that way. Mr. Shankman had told me that one reason cited to him by Mr. McCord was the question regarding the CIA defense. I brought this up to Mr. McCord and said to him in substance, "I thought that issue was laid to rest during our last meeting in Boston when you denied any factual involvement on the part of the CIA." He agreed that it was, but said that was not the reason for his letter. He claimed that I had not been maintaining sufficient contact with him, and that he was unsure of my being adequately prepared for trial. I told him that in my opinion, this was not so; that he had the right to any lawyer of his choice and that if he wished to dismiss me, that was his prerogative; I pointed out what I had viewed as a most satisfactory attorney-client relationship based upon mutual trust and confidence, and suggested that if he had any grievance with me that he should advise me of the same, face to face, rather than refusing to answer my phone calls and unilaterally, without my knowledge, delivering to the judge a letter of dismissal. When I said this, he became defensive, apologized for what he described as a "lack of communication and misunderstanding," and expressed his desire to maintain me as counsel. Again, he voiced his confidence in me and extended his hand in affirmation of that confidence.

On January 8, 1973, the first day of trial, I learned that Mr. William O. Bittman's client, Mr. Hunt, had offered to plead to any and all counts of the indictment immediately prior to trial, but that Chief Judge Sirica had said that he would not entertain any change of plea until after jury selection and opening statements.

This appeared to me to be highly prejudicial to my client, for it would tend to give the jury the impression that after the Government's opening statement, one of the defendants had thrown in the towel, so to speak, overwhelmed with the weight of the evidence against him. I felt this could and should have been avoided by a change of plea being resolved prior to the commencement of trial, since this had been the request of defendant Hunt. I had told Mr. McCord that our routine, once trial began, would be for him to spend some time each day immediately after court with Mr. Shankman and myself to review what had gone on that day and to discuss what was to happen the following day. I wanted to discuss with Mr. Bittman the details of his client's proposed change of plea in order to ascertain whether or not there would be a basis for a mistrial. It was agreed that we would meet at his office immediately after court was concluded for that day. Mr. Shankman, Mr. McCord, and I hailed a cab and at the last minute, codefendant Barker asked if he could ride in the cab with us. Where at that time Mr. Barker was going, or why he was going to Mr. Bittman's office, as I eventually ascertained, I do not know.

There was no significant conversation with Mr. Barker in the cab. Mr. McCord has alleged that I told him that the purpose of going to Mr. Bittman's office was that Mr. Bittman wanted to talk with him, Mr. McCord, about "whose word he would trust regarding a White House offer of Executive clemency," and that Mr. Bittman wanted to talk to Mr. Barker as well. This is not true. I merely said to Mr. McCord that prior to the scheduled daily post-court meeting between he, Mr. Shankman and myself, that we would stop at Mr. Bittman's office, for I wanted to discuss with him the ramifications and details of Mr. Hunt's proposed change of plea. When we arrived at Mr. Bittman's office, Mr. McCord has alleged that I sensed his anger at Mr. Barker's presence, and therefore, delayed going up to Mr. Bittman's office for approximately 30 minutes. The simple truth is that I suggested when we got out of the cab that we three have a cocktail and Mr. McCord, Mr. Shankman, and I went into a restaurant directly across the street from Mr. Bittman's office for just that purpose.

When we arrived at Mr. Bittman's office, I went with Mr. McCord and Mr. Shankman to the firm's library and went back to Mr. Bittman's office to see if he was there. I had a discussion with him, Mr. Bittman, in which he confirmed the judge's refusal to entertain any change of plea by Mr. Hunt until after opening statements. At this point, I recall mentioning to Mr. Bittman that I felt my client was becoming a bit paranoid, that he felt he was being made the "patsy" or "fall guy." I mentioned it at that time since in my mind, that allegation made to me by Mr. McCord seemed inconsistent with Mr. Hunt's desire to plead guilty. After I mentioned Mr. McCord's apprehension, my recollection is that Mr. Bittman said in words or substance, "Tell Mr. McCord he will receive a call from a friend of his." Mr. Bittman did not mention the "White House" as alleged by Mr. McCord. The identity of this friend was not made known to me, nor did I make inquiry in this matter. I considered the possibility, without actually knowing, that the purpose of this call was to allay Mr. McCord's fears that his codefendants were turning against him, and that the caller could very well be Mr. Bittman's client, Mr. Hunt. This was surmised on my part. I considered this possibility in view of the context of the conversation immediately preceding Mr. Bittman's remark, that is, my statement in accordance with Mr. McCord's request, of his apprehension with regard to his codefendants. I subsequently told Mr. McCord just what Mr. Bittman had told me, that he would receive a call from a friend. I did not mention the words "the White House" because Mr. Bittman did not mention those words to me. Mr. McCord nodded, said, "OK" and had no further response to my statement.

Some time later, as the trial was in progress, Mr. McCord told me that he had been in contact with a man by the name of Caldwell.

That is how I remember it as he told me. He specifically stated that he did not wish to tell me who this man was or the subject matter of his conversation with him. In response, I told Mr. McCord that that was his prerogative. In this regard, I respectfully invite the attention of this honorable committee to Mr. McCord's letter to Chief Judge Sirica of March 19, 1973, of which I had no prior knowledge. I respectfully refer to the next to the last paragraph on page 2 of this letter and I have provided copies of this letter to this honorable committee, where, after alleging complaints of various topics, including, but not limited to, allegations of political pressure applied to the defendants to plead guilty and remain silent, Mr. McCord in the second to last paragraph on page 2 stated—and this letter was written without my knowledge, and I quote:

"I have not discussed the above with my attorneys as a matter of protection for them."

Mr. McCord has alleged that the subject of Executive clemency was discussed on this day, January 8, 1973. This is not true. In late 1972, during one of the pretrial meetings of defense lawyers in Washington, I had an occasion to say to Mr. Bittman, "Bill, what do you think our clients will receive as a sentence should they be convicted?" Mr. Bittman responded in substance, as if he were theorizing, "You can never tell, Christmastime rolls around and there could be Executive clemency." I scoffed at this notion and told Mr. Bittman that in my opinion, the President would not touch this case with a 10-foot pole, let alone exercise Executive clemency. This subject had not been on any agenda, but arose in what I characterize as "lawyers' talk." Subsequently, but not on the same day, I mentioned this to Mr. McCord in a most skeptic manner, and said to him, "Jim, it can be Christmas, Easter, and Thanksgiving all rolled into one, but in my opinion, the President would not touch this with a 10-foot pole, so do not rely on any prospect of Executive clemency."

Mr. McCord laughed and agreed with me. That was the only occasion that the words "Executive clemency" were ever mentioned by me to my client. I have neither met John Dean nor spoken to him in my life. I have neither met John Caulfield nor spoken to him in my life.

During the trial, I presented to Chief Judge Sirica my contemplated defense theory of "duress" supported by a memorandum of law. Several days later, after receiving a written response from the Government, the court ruled as a matter of law that this defense did not apply to this case, thereby precluding me from presenting evidence in support thereof and from relying upon it in closing argument.

After opening statements, Mr. Hunt and the four others—the four Cuban-Americans—pleaded guilty at which time I filed a motion for mistrial, which was denied.

When this happened, I explained to Mr. McCord that the only possible remaining defense was the general defense of "lack of criminal intent" but advised him that in my opinion, it had little or no legal merit for it was asking the jury to believe that he did not know he was breaking the law when he broke into the Watergate complex and that this, to say the least, was not very "salable". Mr. McCord indicated his understanding of our position, told me that he was, nevertheless, most pleased with my exerting my best efforts with regard to the proposed theory of "duress" and asked whether or not the judge's ruling could be a point of appeal in the event of conviction. I told him that it could and would be, that the record had been made in that regard, and he indicated his complete satisfaction with the then existing situation.

As the trial approached the completion of the Government's case, I conferred with Mr. McCord at one of our daily post-trial meetings and told him that a decision would have to be made regarding whether or not he would take the stand. I explained to him that if he elected to testify, it would be his obligation to answer any and all relevant questions. It was at this time that Mr. McCord told me that he had evidence to the effect that the Watergate operation had been approved by John Mitchell. I asked him the nature of the evidence and he told me he had been so advised by Mr. Liddy. I asked him if he had any other corroborative evidence and he told me he did not. I told him that although this was technically hearsay, it would be admissible as a declaration by one coconspirator to another and told him to understand beyond any doubt, that should he take the stand, that question would in my opinion be asked and an answer required. I told him that if he elected to take the stand, full disclosure would be necessary; that I was with him all the way, but that this crucial decision of whether or not to testify could only be his, I did advise him, however, to resolve this question as soon as possible and not advise me of his decision at the last minute, thereby precluding adequate time for preparation of direct and cross-examination.

As the trial progressed and the time for decision was at hand, Mr. McCord asked me what I thought the grounds of appeal would be in the event of conviction. I reviewed them with him mentioning such things as the court's denial of my motions for mistrial, based upon the timing of the change of plea by his five codefendants, as well as the ruling by Chief Judge Sirica precluding the defense of "duress". He told me that he had decided not to testify. I asked him if he had any reservations regarding that decision and he said he did not.

As the jury announced its verdict, I immediately asked the chief judge to be heard on the matter of bail, which request was denied. The court advised that the motion be put in writing so as to allow the Government to respond. I immediately set to work upon this, urged the prosecution to respond as quickly as possible and, several days later, a hearing was held, at which time bail was set at $100,000.

What I am now about to relate is not for the purpose of self-commendation, but is stated to show and emphasize the relationship that existed between Mr. McCord and I from the beginning to the end of the trial. There was not a day of trial that passed without Mr. McCord shaking my hand at the end of each day and telling me what a superlative job I had done. He used adjectives such as "terrific," "outstanding," and expressed his total and unequivocal satisfaction and appreciation for my efforts. I remember the day of final argument when present in the courtroom were Mr. McCord's wife, his son, his daughter, and his parents. After my final argument, they all came up to me and profusely thanked me for the words I had uttered on Mr. McCord's behalf. They said they were proud of my description of Mr. McCord and that they were "thrilled to sit there and hear it." Mrs. McCord had previously told me of her anxiety over what the effects of the trial might have on her son who was a student at the

Air Force Academy. On the day of the final argument, she asked if I could obtain for her a copy of the argument so that she could give it to her son. When the jury announced its verdict of guilty, Mr. McCord turned to me, he extended his hand and said, "There is no one that could have done a better job than you did. You are a terrific lawyer and I shall always be grateful to you." It was, to me, an emotional moment. My local counsel, Mr. Shankman, can be a witness to this.

To further demonstrate the status of my relationship with my client, I have provided this honorable committee with a copy of my letter to Mr. McCord dated February 6, 1973, while he was incarcerated at the District of Columbia jail. I specifically refer the attention of this honorable committee to the third paragraph of that letter which reads as follows, this is my letter to Mr. McCord: "I again reiterate to you that I shall continue to do everything possible on your behalf and shall stay with you in all that may lie ahead. Having a client convicted can never be a source of gratification to an attorney. I will, however, always remember your vote of confidence in me before, during, and after trial."

I immediately commenced my efforts to effectuate Mr. McCord's release on bail. The record will reflect that a petition to reduce the bail set by Chief Judge Sirica was filed in the Court of Appeals for the District of Columbia at the earliest possible time. I made several visits to Mr. McCord in the District of Columbia jail. I remember his expressing dissatisfaction at being placed in a maximum security area. I immediately spoke to the prison superintendant and asked if anything could be done. No commitment was made, but I was told that my request would be given every consideration. I remember that approximately a week after the trial ended, my wife and I went on a 4-day vacation to Jamaica and even then, I made at least one, if not two, daily phone calls to Mrs. McCord on the question of bail. My concern was to effectuate the release of my client as soon as possible.

I recall my first visit to Mr. McCord at the jail. When he first saw me, he was approximately 20 feet away. He broke out into a wide smile, extended his hand and accelerated his pace. He told me how glad he was to see me so that he might again express his gratitude for my efforts in his behalf. I told him of my immediate appellate action regarding bail and of my daily telephonic contact with his wife, and he thanked me profusely. I remember him telling me how fortunate he felt to have me working so hard as his attorney and he again reemphasized his belief that my job for him was beyond reproach.

He told me that his wife was contacting friends with regard to bail, but he specifically asked that I call a man by the name of Bernard Fensterwald, whom he said might be very helpful in raising bail. This was the first time I had heard the name. I did not ask who this man was, or what his relationship to Mr. McCord was, merely made note of his name and telephone number and called him from the pay phone at the jail, immediately after leaving Mr. McCord.

I introduced myself as Mr. McCord's attorney and told Mr. Fensterwald the purpose of my call. He told me that he thought he could arrange to meet the bail requirements within a matter of days; that he had friends with whom he was in contact; that these friends stated that things "looked good" and that I should stay in daily contact with him.

I immediately related this hopeful news to Mrs. McCord and she was understandably overjoyed at the prospect of her husband's imminent release. Daily phone calls were made to Mr. Fensterwald. I was not always able to reach him directly, but when I did, he would tell me that his friends were still working on it and to keep in daily contact. Several days passed. The word from Mr. Fensterwald was still inconclusive, that is, he was still waiting word from other people.

Then, during one of my telephone calls, he told me that these other contacts had fallen through, but that he was ready, willing, and able to personally borrow the full amount of $100,000 and that he could do so by "just going down to the bank and signing the note." He told me that his motive for so acting was that he was "outraged" at the high bond set by Chief Judge Sirica and felt this to be a gross injustice, which he was taking upon himself to rectify.

This was, I believe, in February of 1973. I told him I would call him the following day. When I did so, he told me that he had been refused by the bank, but that he was looking to another source for funds. He did not specify, nor did I ask the identity of the source. He did tell me, however, to ascertain from Mrs. McCord, how much she could raise through friends and relatives so that he could attempt to come up with the balance.

I again visited Mr. McCord and advised him of the progress. He had been in jail some 2 weeks now, and I sensed his anxiety was increasing. He told me that when I spoke to Mr. Fensterwald again, I was to be sure to relate to him his—Mr. McCord's—gratitude. I left Mr. McCord, went to the phone booth in the jail, called Mr. Fensterwald, and related McCord's thanks. Mr. Fensterwald's reply was, and I quote, "I don't see how he can send his thanks to me because I never even met the man." This seemed unusual to me, to say the least, that a man would be doing what Mr. Fensterwald said he was trying to do for someone he had never met, but I was not about to look a gift horse in the mouth. My sole concern was for my client, and my immediate objective was to effectuate his release on bail. Mrs. McCord subsequently advised that she was able to raise $60,000. I related this to Mr. Fensterwald who said he would be able to produce the remaining $40,000. This was shortly thereafter accomplished, and Mr. McCord was out on bail awaiting sentencing.

In the following days, I was involved with legal commitments which took me out of Boston, but kept in telephonic touch with Mr. McCord. Our relationship remained most cordial. When the date of sentencing arrived, I was engaged in trial in Federal court in Chicago, Ill., before the Honorable Judge Hoffman. I asked for and received permission to adjourn the trial for the day of sentencing, so that I might be present with Mr. McCord in court.

This was the day when Chief Judge Sirica read in open court Mr. McCord's letter of March 19, 1973, of which I had no prior knowledge.

When Chief Judge Sirica called a 20-minute recess immediately following his reading of the letter, I sat with Mr. McCord at the counsel table and asked him why he had not informed me of his intentions. He apologized for so doing and again repeated that he had not advised me of his allegations in the letter as a matter of my own protection. I asked him what he wanted me to do. He told me he wished to speak privately, with me being present, to Chief Judge Sirica regarding the allegations of his letter, and asked that I advise the court of this request.

During this conversation, a man approached Mr. McCord and said in what I can best describe as a whispered or hushed manner, "If you need an office, you can use mine right after court." Mr. McCord nodded, and I asked Mr. McCord who this man was. Mr. McCord identified the individual and introduced him to me as Bernard Fensterwald. This was the first time I had met the man with whom I had had so much telephone contact pertaining to bail. Mr. McCord said to Mr. Fensterwald, in my presence, "The one thing I feel sorry about is keeping Gerry in the dark and pulling this on him." Mr. Fensterwald replied, "Sorry hell, let it all hang out."

When court reconvened, I related to the chief judge Mr. McCord's request, which at that time was granted, and an in camera meeting was tentatively set up for the following week. I naturally was embarrassed at not having been advised by my client as to so crucial and dramatic a move—I'm talking about the letter to Chief Judge Sirica—but reasoned to myself that, after all, I had been away, engaged in trial, and Mr. McCord's apology seemed most sincere, and I, therefore, chose not to make an issue out of this failure of communication.

This, I recall, was on a Friday. It was on that day that Mr. Samuel Dash, of the Senate Select Committee, came to me, introduced himself, and asked if he could converse with Mr. McCord or said that he was interested in doing so. I told him that it was Mr. McCord's immediate request to speak with Judge Sirica, and that I would be happy to relay to Mr. McCord Mr. Dash's request. I then resumed my Chicago trial and in the newspapers read that Mr. McCord had begun to confer with Senate investigators. I found out about it that way, reading it in the newspapers.

Subsequently, Mr. McCord called me and said that since I was away on trial and that since things were "breaking so quickly," didn't I think it was a good idea for him to retain local Washington counsel. I said, yes, I thought it was a good idea. He asked me if I had any objection to Mr. Fensterwald, I said I had none, and Mr. McCord advised me this would be done.

My next contact with Mr. McCord was when he and I and Mr. Fensterwald met the night before our last court appearance before Chief Judge Sirica at which time in court that day, the sentencing was continued until June 16, 1973. Mr. McCord was extremely upset over what he believed to be unfair newspaper coverage of his disclosures. He kept smashing his fist on my suitcase. At this point, Mr. Fensterwald said to Mr. McCord, "The reporters have been asking me whether or not you or I had ever had any past relationship. I told them that we had." This was Mr. Fensterwald speaking. At this point, Mr. McCord looked up with a surprised expression. Mr. Fensterwald said, "Well, after all, you have in the past submitted to me checks which were donations to the Committee for the Investigation of the Assassination of the President." Mr. McCord smiled and said, "Oh, yes, that's right."

Prior to the court appearance of the following morning, at a meeting at Mr. Fensterwald's office, it was agreed that since my immediate trial schedule called for me to remain in Chicago for an anticipated period of 6 to 8 weeks, that Mr. Fensterwald would continue to represent Mr. McCord in my absence, both in the criminal matter and in all hearings before the grand jury and this honorable committee but that upon the completion of my trial duties, I would again assume my role as counsel in all matters. That morning, in court, I asked for and received a continuance of sentencing to June 15, 1973. I advised the court of Mr. McCord's desire to cooperate fully with both the grand jury and Senate committee, and further advised of Mr. McCord's preference to first testifying before the Senate committee. When court was over, I said to both Mr. McCord and Mr. Fensterwald that I would be happy to continue my representation of Mr. McCord, but asked that in the future, as long as I continued in that capacity, I at least be given the courtesy of being kept abreast of Mr. McCord's activities, so that I would not again be embarrassed.

Both Mr. McCord and Mr. Fensterwald agreed that this was proper, Mr. McCord again apologized to me and Mr. Fensterwald told me that he would call me "wherever I was every day," even if he had nothing to tell me. The meeting ended with all of us shaking hands, and I flew out of town. I have not seen either Mr. McCord or Mr. Fensterwald since that time.

Subsequently, while I was still on trial in Chicago, I did receive several phone calls from Mr. Fensterwald, although not daily as he had promised, and I might add, although not reflected in the memorandum, for the sake of accuracy, some of these calls I received when I was staying at the Holiday Inn on Lake Shore Drive in Chicago. Another of these calls I received when I was staying at the Sheraton Hotel in Chicago.

In one of these conversations, he said to me—this is Mr. Fensterwald talking—"what do you think of all that is going on?" referring to the disclosures being made by Mr. McCord to this honorable committee. I replied, "Whatever is right for Jim McCord is all right with me," Mr. Fensterwald replied, and I quote, "We're going after the President of the United States." I replied that I was not interested in any vendettas against the President but only in the best interest of my client, to which Mr. Fensterwald replied, "Well, you'll see, that's who we're going after, the President."

I might add at this point, Senators, although it is not contained in the memorandum, an investigator from my office was in my hotel room when this conversation took place. And I recall putting the phone down and turning to my investigator, whose name is John McNally and said to him, "You will never believe what I just heard on the telephone," and I told him.

His response to me was "Too bad you didn't have that recorded."

During another telephone conversation with Mr. Fensterwald, he stated that he was most displeased with the reaction of the Republican members of this honorable committee, to Mr. McCord's submitted memorandum and further stated that "I'll submit memorandums but I don't want the Republicans to see them."

During a third telephone conversation, he advised of Mr. McCord's intention to hold a national press conference. I replied that in my opinion, this would demean Mr. McCord's position and that he should stay within the framework of both the grand jury and the Select Committee. I further stated that to hold such a press conference could conceivably antagonize Chief Judge Sirica. Mr. Fensterwald replied that he would attempt to obtain approval of such a press conference from Senator Ervin, and that if such approval was obtained, this would be presented as a mitigating factor in the event of Chief Judge Sirica's displeasure.

Subsequently, my contact with Mr. McCord and Mr. Fensterwald diminished and I immediately, after the completion of my Chicago Federal case, commenced a 5-week murder trial in Cook County, Chicago. On May 8, 1973, my secretary gave me a message reflecting a call from the Los Angeles Times from a reporter whose name I recall to be Jackson, in regard to a four-page memorandum of Mr. McCord, involving the CIA that was about to be published the following morning. I called Mr. McCord that night, was told by his wife that he was not in, and I left a message for him to call me. He never did. The following day, the New York Times published a memorandum by Mr. McCord, alleging that I had stated that I could obtain forged CIA documents with the cooperation of the Director of the CIA. I again called Mr. McCord and his wife told me that he was at a meeting and that she would once again relay my message to him, but he never called.

At approximately 5:30 p.m. on May 8, 1973, I contacted Mr. Fensterwald by telephone and asked him to explain these false allegations made by Mr. McCord. Mr. Fensterwald stated, "I can only hazard the guess that it is the result of Mr. McCord's faulty recollection." He added, "I can tell you one thing, it's a terrible cliche, but I think you will agree with it, that there is no zealot like a convert." I have had no further contact from Mr. McCord.

Mr. McCord has accused me of exerting pressure upon him, but I respectfully request this honorable committee to take note of the following facts:

1. Mr. McCord did not plead guilty.
2. He admitted, under oath, in response to a question put to him by Senator Ervin, that I never urged him to enter a plea of guilty.
3. In his letter of March 19, 1973, to Chief Judge Sirica, in referring to his allegations of improprieties, including but not limited to political pressure, stated, and I quote: "I have not discussed the above with my attorneys as a matter of protection for them."
4. Mr. McCord proceeded to trial with a defense based upon what he told me to be the truth.

I have done nothing wrong and am, therefore, not afraid, but I am upset as a practicing criminal trial lawyer. I must confess that I am the type of criminal defense attorney who, rightly or wrongly, gets emotionally involved with his client's cause. I remain fully cognizant of the fact that a man's liberty is at stake, rather than a determination of dollars and cents. I ask my client to take me into his confidence and I reciprocate. I keep him constantly advised of my thoughts and theories. To me, this attitude of complete disclosure is based upon my interpretation of the duty I owe to the man that I am defending. How can a lawyer effectively represent his client when faced with the possibility that the man for whom he is working night and day is constantly making a record of privileged conversations with the intent of subsequently violating this privilege by making false accusations and by selectively extracting statements out of context and twisting them into untruths?

Can a defense attorney function properly under such circumstances? I have always made a practice not to comment on matters of which I have no knowledge. Mr. McCord has made accusations directed toward many men. I am in no position to judge his credibility in that regard. I do, however, have firsthand knowledge of his relationship with me, and in regard to his accusations against me, he is not telling the truth.

As I watched Mr. McCord on national television on May 18, 1973, and listened to him falsely accuse me of professional misconduct, which accusations are false in every respect, I immediately and vividly recalled his praise for me throughout the trial, his confidence expressed to me at the time of the guilty verdict, and his further expression of gratitude during the period of his incarceration, and I asked myself "What kind of a man is this?"

I stand ready to answer all questions.

Senator ERVIN. We have to vote in just a few minutes on the nomination of Mr. Richardson to be Attorney General, and this is a long statement and I think the committee, as I understand it, thinks it would be better to adjourn now and come back in the morning to begin the questions, so we will stand in recess until 10 o'clock in the morning.

[Whereupon, at 3:30 p.m., the hearing was recessed, to reconvene at 10 a.m., Thursday, May 24, 1973.]

THURSDAY, MAY 24, 1973

U.S. SENATE,
SELECT COMMITTEE ON
PRESIDENTIAL CAMPAIGN ACTIVITIES,
Washington, D.C.

The Select Committee met, pursuant to recess, at 10 a.m., in room 318, Russell Senate Office Building, Senator Sam J. Ervin, Jr. (chairman), presiding.

Present: Senators Ervin, Talmadge, Inouye, Montoya, Baker, Gurney, and Weicker.

Also present: Samuel Dash, chief counsel; Fred D. Thompson, minority counsel; Rufus L. Edmisten, deputy chief counsel; Arthur S. Miller, chief consultant; Jed Johnson, consultant; David M. Dorsen, James Hamilton, and Terry F. Lenzner, assistant chief counsels; Barry Schochet, assistant majority counsel; Donald G. Sanders, H. William Shure, and Robert Silverstein, assistant minority counsels; Joan C. Cole, secretary to the minority; Pauline O. Dement, research assistant; Eiler Ravnholt, office of Senator Inouye; Robert Baca, office of Senator Montoya; Ron McMahan, assistant to Senator Baker; A. Searle Field, assistant to Senator Weicker; Marc Lackritz, Ron Rotunda, assistant counsels; Eugene Boyce, hearings counsel; John Walz, publications clerk.

Senator ERVIN. The committee will come to order.

The committee has had a meeting this morning and decided to hold hearings in addition to those previously scheduled for the 12th, 13th, and 14th of June, to hold hearings on the 5th, that is Tuesday, the 5th day of June, Wednesday, the 6th day of June, and Thursday, the 7th of June.

The committee has received requests from Mr. McCord and Mr. Fensterwald for an opportunity to be heard before the committee. The committee is going to pursue the list of its scheduled witnesses. The committee will extend to Mr. McCord and Mr. Fensterwald an opportunity to furnish statements in writing of what they wish to testify to, under oath, under sworn statements, affidavits, and also give them an opportunity to meet with the staff and see what it is they want to testify. But the committee does not intend to get bogged down with the controversy between lawyers neither of whom, according to the evidence before the full committee, have any personal knowledge of the matters that the committee is investigating, except insofar as they gained it through the trial. So we will proceed at this time on the assumption that if Mr. Fensterwald and Mr. McCord wish to testify further before the committee they will first give us a sworn statement of what they propose to testify to and consult with the staff. We see no reason to put Mr. McCord on the stand to repeat anything he has already said before, and we see no reason to try to decide a controversy between the two lawyers with respect to their personal conversations at this time, and we will proceed with any further questioning.

Senator BAKER. Mr. Chairman, thank you very much. I might say I entirely concur with the statement that the chairman has made. I think it would not serve the purpose of moving these hearings with expedition to get into rebuttal, surrebuttal and rerebuttal. I do think that it is important that the rights and the reputation of every witness be protected. Therefore, I am delighted that the staff will conduct a further interview with Mr. McCord and will now interview Mr. Fensterwald in order to advise this committee on the desirability of having them as witnesses under oath at a later time but I think we ought to proceed and I am happy to concur in the statement of the chairman that we should proceed with the ordinary witness list and I am especially pleased that in the interest of reaching the facts as soon as possible that we are going to have this extra session so that we can proceed quickly.

Thank you very much, Mr. Chairman.

Mr. DASH. Mr. Chairman, just one further comment. Mr. Fensterwald did inform me just before the committee convened he would immediately after Mr. Alch's testimony file a sworn statement with the committee.

Now, Mr. Alch——

TESTIMONY OF GERALD ALCH, ATTORNEY—Resumed

Mr. ALCH. Yes, sir.

Mr. DASH. Could you again tell us, you indicated what fee you received from Mr. McCord. What was that fee?

Mr. ALCH. $25,000 plus expenses which expenses have not been received yet.

Mr. DASH. Yes.

Could you tell us in what form you received that money?

Mr. ALCH. Periodic payments in cash with the exception of the last two installments which were in the form of cashier's checks in relatively smaller amounts of $1,700. The bulk of the money received was in cash in $100 bills.

Mr. DASH. $100 bills.

Did you have any knowledge or information or belief as to where the money was coming from?

Mr. ALCH. No, sir, and I believe that in one of Mr. McCord's depositions he stated that at the time he paid me my fee he did not tell me where it came from except that it came from him.

Mr. DASH. Did you in October 1972 ever meet with Mr. McCord and urge him to urge the Committee To Re-Elect the President to give him more money so that you may have more additional fee?

Mr. ALCH. No, sir. There was a conversation where, as I explained yesterday, the original payment of fees, the schedule of the original payment of fees was not being adhered to by Mr. McCord, and I asked him whether or not, when I might expect more money in accordance with the schedule that he had told me. He told me that, to bear with him, that it would be forthcoming, and I told him that I would.

Mr. DASH. Now, it was obvious, Mr. Alch, from the length of your statement, and the manner in which you delivered it, that you were quite upset with your former client's statement.

What I would first like to do, and I think it would be helpful to isolate the specific statements made by Mr. McCord which you find and did find objectionable, and correct me if there are additional ones but I think there are two main areas that I have isolated in his statement and your statement.

One, his statement in his memorandum of May 4, 1973, that on two occasions, one in the Monocle Restaurant, and another time in Boston that you suggested that he base his defense on CIA involvement, and in that the reference to what you might be able to do with Mr. Schlesinger in terms of forged documents and things of that nature.

The second area of complaint is his statement that you participated in having him exposed to an offer of Executive clemency. These appear to me to be the two main areas of his statement which I think you find objectionable and that was covered by your statement.

Mr. ALCH. Yes, sir.

Mr. DASH. Right.

Now, as to Mr. McCord's first complaint that you suggested he use CIA involvement as a defense, it is true, is it not, that the question, at least of CIA involvement, was the subject of discussion between you and Mr. McCord on two occasions in December, one at the Monocle Restaurant and another time in your office in Boston?

Mr. ALCH. Why, this way, Mr. Dash. I specifically asked him whether or not there was any factual basis to the contention that the CIA was involved.

Mr. DASH. Yes. But there was that discussion. You did raise that?

Mr. ALCH. I said it just that way.

Mr. DASH. Right.

Did you on either occasion show Mr. McCord a statement from a D.C. police officer, Gary Bittenbender, indicating that Mr. McCord told Bittenbender that Watergate was a CIA operation?

Mr. ALCH. Yes, sir. That statement had been provided to me pursuant to my discovery motions filed in the case by the Government. It was a report in which it quoted a D.C. policeman, Mr. Bittenbender, by name, as saying that at the time of Mr. McCord's arrest, I believe at the District of Columbia jail, Mr. McCord said, referring to the other four men who had been arrested with him, "These are all good men, ex-CIA men." I naturally called that to my client's attention because there loomed a distinct possibility that that statement might be introduced against him at trial. In fact, it was not.

Mr. DASH. All right. Now, Mr. Alch, in the statement that you submitted to the committee, as you read it, that was not included in that statement; is that true?

Mr. ALCH. It was not, sir.

Mr. DASH. There is no reference to your mentioning to Mr. McCord that you did have that statement from officer Bittenbender?

Mr. ALCH. It was not, sir. I believe I mentioned it when I met with you the night before my testimony.

Mr. DASH. That is true; but is there any reason why that was left out of your statement?

Mr. ALCH. No, sir.

Mr. DASH. Did you ever mention during either of the two meetings at the Monocle Restaurant and in your office in Boston when you asked Mr. McCord about the CIA involvement, the name Victor Marchetti, who might be a witness on CIA training?

Mr. ALCH. I did mention the name Victor Marchetti, not in the context of his being a witness. It came up this way: In the course of discussing Mr. McCord's background with the CIA, I mentioned to him that I had recently heard that a man by that name had come out with a book about the CIA. I mentioned that to Mr. McCord. He said to me words to the effect that Mr. Marchetti was not in good grace with the CIA or any ex-members of the CIA. He said he did not think highly of the man and that was the extent of the conversation.

Mr. DASH. Did you know Mr. Marchetti at all?

Mr. ALCH. Never met the man in my life.

Mr. DASH. Was there any discussion as to whether Mr. Marchetti would be a good witness on CIA training to indicate that CIA men are trained to disavow any relationship with the CIA?

Mr. ALCH. There was a discussion with Mr. McCord with regard to his background with the CIA. In that context, I mentioned to him whether or not Mr. Marchetti's book might be a good reference point. He said it would not be.

Mr. DASH. Now, after your meeting of December 1972 at the Monocle Restaurant with Mr. McCord, did you call your partner, Mr. Bailey, and raise the question of the CIA defense?

Mr. ALCH. I did.

Mr. DASH. What was the nature of that call and what did Mr. Bailey have to say?

Mr. ALCH. I would constantly keep Mr. Bailey advised of the development of all cases that I was working on. In the course of my conversation, and this conversation took place after the meeting at the Monocle but prior to my meeting with Mr. McCord in Boston, I told him of the conversation that had taken place in the lawyer's office and told him that I had asked Mr. McCord whether or not there was any factual basis to the CIA involvement. As I told you yesterday, Mr. McCord did not specifically respond to that question. It was my impression that that topic was going to be raised at our next meeting in Boston.

Mr. Bailey told me that unless Mr. McCord or anyone else could come up with any factual evidence of any CIA involvement, that if Mr. McCord wished to pursue that defense without any such factual evidence, that I was to withdraw from the case and that I was to tell that to Mr. McCord.

When Mr. McCord met with me in Boston at our next meeting, he initiated the conversation by saying to me, there is no CIA involvement and I will have no part of anything that is going to put the blame on the CIA. That rendered my withdrawal direction from Mr. Bailey moot.

Mr. DASH. Right, but that was a significant discussion with Mr. Bailey, was it not, concerning the CIA involvement, or the defense of the CIA involvement?

Mr. ALCH. I would not say it was significant in the sense that I keep Mr. Bailey advised of all cases which I am involved in and which he is not involved in. He is the head of the office and his policy is that I let him know what I am doing all the time.

Mr. DASH. But it did raise the possibility of Mr. Bailey's suggestions to you that you might withdraw from the case if it was put?

Mr. ALCH. That was his suggestion to me. If there was no such defense rendered, fine.

Mr. DASH. But that was not put forth in your discussion with the committee?

Mr. ALCH. It was not.

Mr. DASH. In your statement on page 10, you say during the meeting with defendants in December, and prior to your Monocle meeting with Mr. McCord, "The question arose as to whether the CIA was involved."

Would you tell us how the question arose, who raised it?

Mr. ALCH. This was at the meeting in Mr. Bittman's office attended by the lawyers?

Mr. DASH. Yes.

Mr. ALCH. It was at that point that I wanted to announce to my—to the other defense counsel, what my contemplated defense would be. I did so. I told them that I was contemplating the defense of duress based upon what my client had told me. The reaction seemed to be that this would only be applicable to Mr. McCord in view of his being chief of security and that this particular defense could not inure to the benefit or could not be utilized by any other defendant. My response was, well, that is my contemplated defense; that is what I am going forward on.

It was at that point that the question was raised of whether or not there was any CIA involvement.

Mr. DASH. Now, do you know how that question was raised? Who raised it?

Mr. ALCH. I am not sure. It may have been Mr. Bittman. I cannot be positive. That is a possibility. But may I stress that when it was raised, it was raised in this type of way: Is there any CIA involvement in this thing? And at that point, it was pointed out, the fact that all defendants had some prior connection with the CIA and at least one of them had been found with documents which purported to be or were alleged to be forged CIA credentials.

Mr. DASH. Then, as I understand from your statement, each of you were going to contact your clients and ask that question of them?

Mr. ALCH. Yes, sir.

Mr. DASH. Now, were you aware, Mr. Alch, of every contact that may have been made with your client by others who may have suggested the defense of CIA involvement to them?

Mr. ALCH. No, sir. I only knew what he told me.

Mr. DASH. Therefore, any pressure that could have been visited upon Mr. McCord, you might not have been aware of, is that correct?

Mr. ALCH. Entirely. As I pointed out yesterday, Mr. Dash, I do not come before this honorable committee to offer any judgment or opinion on allegations of Mr. McCord which pertain to activity not involving me. I do not know about those things. I came here to refute what he said about me.

Mr. DASH. Now, for example, are you aware that in December, which is the very month you raised the question of CIA involvement with McCord, that Mr. McCord sent Mr. John Caulfield a note complaining of a White House effort to blame the CIA for Watergate and threatening "That all the trees in the forest would fall if this effort continued."

Were you aware of this?

Mr. ALCH. I was not.

Mr. DASH. So it is no fiction, really, that Mr. McCord was deeply concerned over what he believed was a conspiracy to have him implicate the CIA in the Watergate case?

Mr. ALCH. I have no knowledge to contradict that statement by Mr. McCord.

Mr. DASH. Actually, according to your own statement, when you first raised the CIA involvement with Mr. McCord in the Monocle Restaurant, you said he did not really respond to it, but launched into a complaint about how the White House was treating the CIA. I think that was your statement.

Mr. ALCH. That is correct.

Mr. DASH. Therefore, Mr. Alch, when you raised the question of CIA involvement with him for the very first time after the meeting with Mr. Bittman and the other lawyers, it is likely, is it not, taking into consideration the entire circumstances of Mr. McCord's concern, that Mr. McCord could have concluded that you had joined in the conspiracy he honestly believed existed to blame the CIA in the Watergate case?

Mr. ALCH. In my judgement, that would be giving him the benefit of a doubt to which I do not believe he is entitled, for this reason: I suppose, hypothetically speaking, that it is possible for a man to misinterpret a question put to him as to whether or not the CIA was involved on the one hand, and a suggestion that it was on the other. That is a point of discrepancy, in answer to a hypothetical question, could possibly be the subject of a misinterpretation.

However, on his allegation that I said to him words to the effect that I could cause his personnel records to be doctored and that the Director of the CIA would go along with it, it escapes me how that type of allegation can be a misunderstanding. I did not say it. You can't infer words of that nature unless they were said and I did not say it. And most fortunately, there was a third person present at this meeting.

Mr. DASH. All right.

Let us move now to the next area of complaint. That is Mr. McCord's indication or implication of you that you participated in having him exposed to the pressures to accept an offer of Executive clemency.

Mr. ALCH. Yes, sir.

Mr. DASH. Now, it is true, is it not, that you might have also been not aware of pressures from other sources or from Mr. Hunt or of any contacts from the Committee for the Re-Election of the President or the White House, concerning Executive clemency, and therefore, might not have been aware of all that might have been going on concerning the CIA?

Mr. ALCH. That is true. I may not have been aware of it because I had no knowledge of that if it, in fact, happened.

Mr. DASH. Now, were you, for example, aware that Mr. Hunt may have been in frequent contact with the Committee for the Re-Election of the President officials or White House officials?

Mr. ALCH. I was not. I rarely saw Mr. Hunt and, as you know, when the trial started and his plea of guilty was accepted by Chief Judge Sirica, he was out of it.

Mr. DASH. It is true, though, is it not, that you did go to the office of Mr. Bittman, Mr. Hunt's lawyer, with Mr. McCord on January 8, the first day of the trial?

Mr. ALCH. Yes, sir.

Mr. DASH. Then you had a private meeting with Mr. Bittman while Mr. McCord was in another part of the office?

Mr. ALCH. I had a meeting with Mr. Bittman, a discussion with Mr. Bittman. I hesitate to call it a private meeting because, as I explained yesterday, we walked into the office, came into the library of the office where other lawyers were seated. Mr. Bittman was not there. I walked back to his office to see if he was there. He was.

Mr. DASH. Was anybody else in the office?

Mr. ALCH. No, sir.

Mr. DASH. So you were alone with Mr. Bittman?

Mr. ALCH. Yes, sir.

Mr. DASH. In your statement you acknowledge that Mr. McCord was incensed, and I think in your words "paranoid," because he believed other defendants, including Bittman's client Hunt, were trying to make him the fall guy.

Did you think or did you not think that you were only adding to his concern by meeting with Mr. Bittman alone, not in Mr. McCord's presence?

Mr. ALCH. No, because I had told Mr. McCord why I was going to Mr. Bittman's office instead of immediately going back to my hotel where it was arranged that each day after trial he, I and local counsel would meet to discuss what had happened that day and was going to happen the next day. I told him why I wanted to speak with Mr. Bittman. I wanted to find out the ramifications of the proposed change of plea by Mr. Bittman's client, Mr. Hunt, which I felt could possibly be the predicate for a motion for a mistrial which I eventually filed.

Mr. DASH. How long did that meeting with Bittman last?

Mr. ALCH. Approximately 15 minutes at the most, maybe less.

Mr. DASH. And after that meeting or at the conclusion of it I understand from your statement that Mr. Bittman told you to tell Mr. McCord that he would receive a telephone call from a friend that night?

Mr. ALCH. That is correct.

Mr. DASH. Did you ask Mr. Bittman who would call your client or what the message would be?

Mr. ALCH. I did not.

Mr. DASH. Why not?

Mr. ALCH. I felt it was of no importance to me. I surmised in my mind that this call was in connection with Mr. McCord's fears that his codefendants were plotting against him. If I had to guess that who I thought was going to call I thought it may have come from Mr. Bittman's client, Mr. Hunt.

In any event, the remark was made as I was walking out of the office and I had said OK, went back to the library and relayed that message to Mr. McCord.

Mr. DASH. You did relay that message to Mr. McCord that he would get a call that night?

Mr. ALCH. No, not that night. I just said "Mr. Bittman said you would be getting a call from a friend," and I also told Mr. McCord, I said, "I went in there and told him at your request you are feeling that you were being ganged up on, so to speak, by your codefendants and Mr. Bittman said you will be getting a call from a friend."

Mr. DASH. Now, this committee has already received evidence, actually just prior to your testimony, that a call, in fact was made and was received by Mr. McCord, and that it originated from Mr. Dean in the White House to Mr. John Caulfield, to Tony Ulasewicz and set the stage for a meeting on the George Washington Parkway between Caulfield and McCord in which Caulfield extended an offer of Executive clemency to McCord "from the highest levels of the White House." That testimony has come before the committee.

Mr. ALCH. Yes, sir.

Mr. DASH. Did you know of that call or that meeting?

Mr. ALCH. I did not.

Mr. DASH. Then, therefore, since it was you, Mr. McCord's lawyer, who transmitted to Mr. McCord his first notice of a telephone call, he was to receive on the night of January 8, and that Mr. McCord knew you were conveying a message from Mr. Bittman, and it was that call which ultimately resulted in a meeting where an offer of Executive clemency was made to your client, presented as coming from the highest levels of the White House. Really, was it so unreasonable for Mr. McCord to conclude that you were involved in setting him up for such an offer of Executive clemency?

Mr. ALCH. If he made that conclusion it was factually false. But let us suppose he did make that conclusion. This was in a period of time, as the trial was just about to commence, where I enjoyed with him what I considered to be a very fine relationship. Why would he not have come up to me and asked me about it or told me something to the effect that pursuant to your message to me I got a call last night? That never happened.

Mr. DASH. Well, at that time perhaps he had begun to distrust you, Mr. Alch—that he needed you as counsel for his trial but after that call perhaps he had lost confidence in you.

Mr. ALCH. In response to that, Mr. Dash, from what I know of Mr. McCord, it would seem to me rather or highly unlikely that he would go to trial with a lawyer whom he did not trust.

Mr. DASH. He actually mentioned to you that he received a call from a man, you will recall, named Caldwell?

Mr. ALCH. Not the next day.

Mr. DASH. Not the next day?

Mr. ALCH. Yes, sir.

Mr. DASH. And then he refused to discuss that with you any further?

Mr. ALCH. That is correct.

Mr. DASH. Now, also Mr. Caulfield in his testimony before this committee stated that at one of his meetings——

Mr. ALCH. Mr. Dash, may I add one thing to the last question, if I may?

Mr. DASH. Yes.

Mr. ALCH. When Mr. McCord told me that he had received a call from a man named Caldwell, and specifically refused to tell me who he was or what the nature of the conversation was, what I did was to see whether or not there would develop any tampering or modification or interference with my advice to Mr. McCord as his counsel or whether or not I was suddenly going to be met with suggestion to change the trial strategy that Mr. McCord and I had already agreed upon.

Mr. McCord was free to see whomever he pleased but at no time did indications ever come to me that either Mr. McCord of his own doing or potentially as a result of being talked to by others was either disregarding my advice, modifying my advice, or introducing a new approach to the trial. That never happened.

Mr. DASH. In your relationship with Mr. McCord, did you find Mr. McCord a suspicious individual?

Mr. ALCH. I hesitate to use the word suspicious. There were times when I would communicate with him and ask him for positions or information on particular topics, and he would not give me immediate responses. His attitude would be or his response would be "Let me think about it" or words to that effect, and days would pass and then I would get a definitive response. Whether or not that can properly serve as a predicate for a conclusion of one being suspicious I hesitate or I can't say.

Mr. DASH. I think in your testimony and in your statement you have indicated that he really did not give you all the information that has now come forward. That he did not confide in you concerning everything about the case.

Mr. ALCH. That attitude commenced from my very first meeting with him but I might say in my experience as a criminal defense attorney complete disclosure by a client is not something that happens in every case.

Mr. DASH. Now, Mr. Caulfield, in his testimony before this committee, stated that at one of the meetings that he had with Mr. Dean during the time he was making offers of Executive clemency to Mr. McCord, that Mr. Dean told him, Mr. Caulfield, that Mr. McCord was "Not cooperating with his attorney." Could Mr. Dean have referred to or been referring to anyone other than you?

Mr. ALCH. Well, the fact is that I was Mr. McCord's attorney at that time, to my knowledge, and the only reason I add that caveat is this: I was informed that, when—I was not informed, when I read a transcript of, I believe, Mr. Caulfield's testimony, I believe he said that in one of his meetings with Mr. McCord prior to the completion of trial, that the subject of bail came up, and Mr. Caulfield stated, "Maybe your lawyer Alch can handle it," or words to that effect, to which, according to Mr. Caulfield, Mr. McCord replied, "Well, I am negotiating with another lawyer. Maybe he can handle it."

Now, this was before the trial ended. His present lawyer is Mr. Fensterwald. I had no contact or even knowledge that such a man existed until after Mr. McCord's incarceration. So I now think and ask myself, was Mr. McCord in any contact with any other attorney during the trial?

If that statement about "I am not cooperating with your attorney" or "Get close to your attorney" was directed toward me, I can't explain it because, as I have explained to the committee yesterday, Mr. McCord was cooperating with me every day.

Mr. DASH. Could it be explained, and again having already testified, I think twice that morning you were not aware of all contacts that might have been made by others concerning your client or others in the White House? That it could be or could it be likely that some contact by other defendants or their counsel were being made with the White House during which your representation of your client could have been discussed?

Mr. ALCH. Mr. Dash, it is possible only because I don't know.

Mr. DASH. You don't know and therefore——

Mr. ALCH. I am in no position to refute or confirm.

Mr. DASH. And you have no other explanation of why Mr. Dean might have made that statement?

Mr. ALCH. I do not. As I told the committee yesterday, I had never met the man nor spoken to him in my life.

Mr. DASH. I have no further questions, Mr. Chairman.

Senator ERVIN. Mr. Thompson?

Mr. THOMPSON. Thank you, sir.

Mr. Alch, let me ask you a few questions. Going back to your original testimony concerning the sequence of events as you described them, what evidently was going on in Mr. McCord's mind as he relayed these things to you—his thoughts about his own defense and those matters?

First of all, as I understand your testimony concerning matters which Mr. McCord considered to be important to his own defense, he raised the matters of the tapping of his line and the bugging of the lines of the Chilean or the Israeli Embassies.

Now, how did he explain this to you? How did you indicate that that could or would be a defense for him?

Mr. ALCH. He analogized that to a situation which he said arose in the Ellsberg case. That if I made a motion for disclosure of such intercepted telephone calls which he thought were intercepted, that the Government, because of embarrassment or national security reasons would refuse to divulge it and would, therefore, in lieu of divulging it dismiss the charge against him.

Mr. THOMPSON. According to what he told you did he consider this a complete defense for him, that this would extricate him from the situation and cause his case to be dismissed?

Mr. ALCH. Yes, sir, he didn't say it was a complete defense. He described it as a means of effectuating the dismissal of the charges against him.

Mr. THOMPSON. Did he indicate whether or not he placed the calls to those two embassies specifically for that purpose?

Mr. ALCH. He did.

Mr. THOMPSON. I believe you stated he also furnished you materials concerning the Mafia and the DNC, Israel and the Mafia, Jack Anderson and Government contracts, these matters. Did he indicate in any way that these could possibly be used as a defense for him or could help his defense in any way?

Mr. ALCH. When he gave me that material, he said, let us get on the offensive, let us make the Democrats—put the Democrats on the defense. He said, let us stir up something.

When he told me that and when he sent me the memorandum, I simply took no action on it.

Mr. THOMPSON. Concerning his book, Counter Espionage Agent for the Republicans, I believe you said was his proposed title, what was his reason, according to him, for wanting that book to be published before the election? Was it because he wanted the dissemination of information?

Mr. ALCH. No, sir.

Mr. THOMPSON. What was his reason, according to what he said?

Mr. ALCH. I had been advised by my associate, Mr. Johnson, who attended the arraignment of Mr. McCord in Washington, that Mr. McCord said to him, would it not be better monetarily for me if this book were published before the Presidential election?

Mr. THOMPSON. As time went on, you indicated that he had suspicion of the codefendants, he thought that he was going to be a fall guy, that he wanted to shift the focus of publicity?

Mr. ALCH. Yes, sir.

Mr. THOMPSON. I believe in December, you had your conversation when the business of the CIA was first broached, and in January, I believe you said you heard of a dismissal letter that he had filed.

Mr. ALCH. That is correct.

Mr. THOMPSON. And you were his attorney at that time; is that correct?

Mr. ALCH. I was and technically still am.

Mr. THOMPSON. You were attorney of record at that time?

Mr. ALCH. Yes, sir.

Mr. THOMPSON. Did he give you any notice of the fact that he was filing a letter of dismissal against you?

Mr. ALCH. None whatsoever.

Mr. THOMPSON. During the trial, you said things worked out between you, you said during the trial he praised you.

Mr. ALCH. Constantly.

Mr. THOMPSON. You said you never urged him to plead guilty?

Mr. ALCH. I never did.

Mr. THOMPSON. Now, after the trial, your first contact with Mr. Fensterwald, I believe you said, was when the bond situation arose.

Mr. ALCH. That is correct.

Mr. THOMPSON. And he indicated that he could take care of the entire $100,000?

Mr. ALCH. That is correct.

Mr. THOMPSON. And he finally came up with $40,000 of the $100,000?

Mr. ALCH. That is correct.

Mr. THOMPSON. Mrs. McCord taking care of the remaining part of it?

Mr. ALCH. Yes.

Mr. THOMPSON. Did Mr. Fensterwald indicate to you whether or not it was his own personal money or whether or not he was raising the money from other sources?

Mr. ALCH. He indicated he was raising the money from other sources which he did not designate.

Mr. THOMPSON. Do you know to this day where he got those funds?

Mr. ALCH. No, sir.

Mr. THOMPSON. The first day you met him was March 23 or 24?

Mr. ALCH. That was the day, whatever the day was that Chief Judge Sirica read Mr. McCord's letter.

Mr. THOMPSON. And again, the letter to Judge Sirica, you had no notice concerning that?

Mr. ALCH. None whatsoever.

Mr. THOMPSON. And in your conversation with Mr. Fensterwald, as I understand it, as he explained it to you, the reason for his releasing the statement concerning your trying to get him to blame it on the CIA, which again you had no notice of, as I understand, until it was brought to your attention——

Mr. ALCH. That is correct.

Mr. THOMPSON. That an L.A. Times reporter had been given the story back in December?

Mr. ALCH. Let me explain just exactly how that happened.

The day before the memorandum was published, on one of my office secretarial note pads, my secretary advised that a call had come in from a Mr. Jackson of the Los Angeles Times to the effect that a story was about to break, a memorandum alleging or talking about the CIA, Mr. McCord, and me.

Mr. THOMPSON. That is the first you heard of it?

Mr. ALCH. The very first.

I called up Mr. McCord, could not reach him. The next day, the memorandum appeared in the newspapers. I got a copy of the New York Times, read it, put another call in to Mr. McCord. I was told he was at a meeting and that the message for him to return my call would be given to him, and that is when I called up Mr. Fensterwald.

When I asked him about this, Mr. Fensterwald said, I had told Mr. McCord to tell you; I am surprised that he did not.

I asked him to explain the reason for this memorandum, which contained false allegations. Mr. Fensterwald told me something to the effect that Mr. McCord had given this story back in December.

Mr. THOMPSON. Before the trial?

Mr. ALCH. This was before the trial. He had given this information back in December and when he heard—when Mr. McCord heard that the story was about to be published, Mr. Fensterwald said that Mr. McCord wanted to beat the newspapers to the punch and submit his own memorandum in advance of publication.

Mr. THOMPSON. When Fensterwald told you that they were going after the President of the United States and repeated that statement, did you ask him if he had any information that McCord did not have that would implicate the President?

Mr. ALCH. I did not. My only response to him on the telephone was as I stated yesterday, I am not interested in any personal vendettas. At that point, after I ended the conversation, taking Mr. Fensterwald's statement at face value, he obviously was, to say the least, antagonistic toward the President. It appeared to me, and this was a surmise, that Mr. Fensterwald might be using Mr. McCord as a means for this particular goal or objective which he stated to me.

What I proceeded to do as best I could, being on a trial in Chicago, was to keep abreast of the newspapers to see the nature of the memorandum and the testimony that Mr. McCord was giving.

The first mention, to my recollection, of Mr. McCord referring to the President was when he referred to an alleged executive offer of clemency coming from the President last Friday.

Mr. THOMPSON. That is the first time in all of your dealings with Mr. McCord, throughout the trial and otherwise, of his mention of the President?

Mr. ALCH. Yes, sir, and I was in contact with one of Mr. Dash's assistants that night.

Mr. THOMPSON. Do you know how long Mr. McCord had known Mr. Fensterwald?

Mr. ALCH. I do not.

Mr. THOMPSON. Was there ever any discussion in your presence between the two of them as to what amount of time or any previous contact they might have had?

Mr. ALCH. The only discussion which might have been embraced by that question was one I referred to yesterday, in my hotel room the night before our last in-court appearance, where Mr. Fensterwald said that reporters had been asking him if he had any prior relationship with Mr. McCord. And he said, I told him I had. Mr. McCord looked up with a surprised look on his face.

And Mr. Fensterwald said, sure, don't you remember, there were checks that you donated to the committee to investigate the assassination of the President, words to that effect.

Mr. McCord countered by saying, oh, yeah, yeah, that is right.

Mr. THOMPSON. Do you know what relationship Mr. Fensterwald has to the committee to investigate assassinations?

Mr. ALCH. No sir.

Mr. THOMPSON. Did it not appear strange to you, did it not cause you then to inquire about any previous relationship or just exactly what Mr. Fensterwald's role was to be? You were attorney of record; you were supposed to be handling the case. Here is a man who comes to you indicating that he is a stranger to Mr. McCord, but he is trying to raise a hundred thousand dollars for him. He evidently has some connection with a committee to investigate assassinations. Did you not inquire into this situation?

Mr. ALCH. My first inquiry was when the name was mentioned to me and Mr. McCord told me that he was a friend who could help with bail. Mr. Fensterwald himself later told me the reason for his motivation or for his actions were to justify what he termed "an outrage." He was referring to the $100,000 bail.

At the point where this conversation came about to which I have just referred, the very next morning—it did bother me. Consequently, the very next morning, I called them both together outside the corridor of the courtroom, and I said, "Look, if you want me to remain as attorney of record, you have got to keep me abreast of everything that you are going to do. I do not want to be embarrassed again." I had been when the letter to Judge Sirica was delivered.

That was when Mr. Fensterwald said to me, "I will call you every single day even if I have nothing to tell you." Keeping in mind that prior to this, Mr. McCord had called me and said, "You are away on trial, I need someone local, do you have any objection if I retain someone in Washington?"

I said "I have none."

Mr. THOMPSON. Let me ask you one series of questions in a specific and isolated area as to your visit to Mr. Bittman's office.

Mr. ALCH. Yes sir.

Mr. THOMPSON. I am not going to second-guess your trial techniques or whatever. From the record, I think it appears that you did a very fine job when a client was caught redhanded. But some things just do not seem to fit together.

For example, would you tell the committee, when you came out of Mr. Bittman's office and spoke to Mr. McCord, told him he would receive a call, what other conversation did you have? What did you say, where did you go? Did you leave together?

Mr. ALCH. We went back to my hotel room, as we did, perhaps, with maybe one or two exceptions every day after the trial. That was the type of relationship we had. I insisted that each day after court, he would come back with me to discuss what went on. I would have the discovery material for the next day as far as witnesses were concerned, other matters that may come up. I would discuss this with him.

It was that type of thing. At that point, we were talking about jury selection and I recall the discussion that particular afternoon, after we left Mr. Bittman's office, over my displeasure—respectfully, as far as Chief Judge Sirica is concerned—at the proposed manner of jury selection. I didn't think there was enough time being given to——

Mr. THOMPSON. You didn't need your client to sit down with you and Bittman and the other lawyers to discuss this, did you? Couldn't you discuss it privately? Couldn't he wait in the motel room or whatever while the lawyers talked? Why didn't you send him on? Why did you have to bring him to Bittman's office with you?

Mr. ALCH. He had no car with him. He had gone to the courthouse in a cab. As the custom turned out to be, we would go back to my hotel room in a cab.

I said to him, "Jim, I want to go back and talk to Bittman about this matter of his client's change of plea; come on with me and as soon as I am through, I will tell you about it and we will go back to my hotel for further discussion."

That is the way it happened.

Mr. THOMPSON. And Barker just happened to get into the cab; he didn't indicate the reason he was getting into the cab?

Mr. ALCH. That was exactly the way it happened.

Mr. THOMPSON. What happened to him? Did he go to the office with you, did he leave with you?

Mr. ALCH. He walked into the building in which Mr. Bittman's office is. I did not. Mr. McCord, Shankman, and I went across the street to get a drink. When I came up to Mr. Bittman's office, I didn't see Mr. Barker. As to why he was going there, as to how long he stayed there, as to whom he saw there, I simply have no knowledge.

Mr. THOMPSON. Who was Barker's lawyer?

Mr. ALCH. At that time, it was Mr. Henry Rothblatt.

Mr. THOMPSON. Is Mr. Rothblatt's office in that building?

Mr. ALCH. I am not sure. I know Mr. Rothblatt had an office very close to Mr. Bittman's office. I know that because when it was decided, since there were out-of-town lawyers involved, where we would meet whenever we would meet, Mr. Rothblatt agreed to meet in Mr. Bittman's office because he had an office either in the same building or close to it. It may have been in the same building. I don't know.

Mr. THOMPSON. You were going in to discuss this situation which concerned you, Judge Sirica's ruling, with Bittman, which is essentially a conversation probably addressing itself to lawyers.

Why didn't you take Mr. Shankman, your associate, in to talk with you?

Mr. ALCH. No particular reasons. Mr. Shankman was privy to all of my trial strategy. What happend was we walked into the library, put our briefcases down, other lawyers were there. I just got up and said, "I want to go back and see if Bill's in his office." And I did.

Mr. THOMPSON. You found him there and left your cocounsel in the library with Mr. McCord?

Mr. ALCH. That is right.

Mr. THOMPSON. Did he ever see Bittman as far as you know that day?

Mr. ALCH. Who?

Mr. THOMPSON. Mr. Shankman.

Mr. ALCH. Mr. Shankman?

Mr. THOMPSON. Yes.

Mr. ALCH. I believe he may have said hello and goodby to him. It was not a long stay at Bittman's office.

Mr. THOMPSON. There was no particular reason why you wanted to talk to Mr. Bittman out of the hearing of anyone else?

Mr. ALCH. Absolutely not. As a matter of fact, I told Mr. McCord what the discussion was with Mr. Bittman.

Mr. THOMPSON. When Bittman said that he would receive a call from a friend, didn't you ask who that friend was?

Mr. ALCH. I did not.

Mr. THOMPSON. Didn't it concern you as a criminal defense lawyer? When anybody else is making a contact with your lawyer, whether it is another lawyer, a third party, another defendant, isn't that something that concerns a defense lawyer in the trial of a case?

Mr. ALCH. Mr. Thompson, as I say, in the context of that remark, my assumption was that it could very well have been a call from Mr. Hunt or some of the other codefendants. I don't know.

Mr. THOMPSON. Wouldn't that have concerned you? Codefendants sometimes have different interests, don't they?

Mr. ALCH. At that point in the trial, I was not aware of any conflict.

Mr. THOMPSON. But there is always the possibility, isn't there?

Mr. ALCH. When you are beginning a trial and your client and you are in complete agreement on a presentation of a defense, that was my main concern.

Mr. THOMPSON. And then coincidently, he did receive a call?

Mr. ALCH. So I am informed.

Mr. THOMPSON. So other testimony has proven.

Mr. ALCH. So other testimony has told me.

Mr. THOMPSON. Do you know how we can make this jump from Bittman's statement to you about a call from a friend to other testimony that he did receive a call shortly after that?

Do you know whether Bittman called Dean, or what is the answer to it? Did you make any inquiry?

Mr. ALCH. No, and I can't answer the question, because I have no knowledge of it.

Mr. THOMPSON. Thank you.

No further questions.

Senator ERVIN. I believe Sir Edward Coke said that one scratch of a pen is better than the slippery memory of a multitude of witnesses. Hasn't that been proven true in your practice as trial lawyer?

Mr. ALCH. I am not sure I understand the significance of the remark.

Senator ERVIN. Well, where two men communicate with each other by word of mouth, isn't there a two-fold hazard in that communication, in, first, that the man who speaks may not express himself clearly, may not say exactly what is in his mind? And if he does, the man who hears it may put a different interpretation on the words than the man who spoke them?

Mr. ALCH. Yes, sir.

Senator ERVIN. Yes. And that is very well illustrated by something that came out here this week. Mr. McCord testified that Mr. Caulfield told him that the President was interested in this offer of Executive clemency and Mr. Caulfield said he never mentioned the President's name, he merely said the highest levels of the White House. So, Mr. Caulfield meant one thing and Mr. McCord understood another from the words.

Mr. ALCH. Yes, sir.

Senator ERVIN. And I believe you made a little mistake yourself in your statement. You were talking about, you said that you understood Mr. McCord to say "Caldwell" when he was obviously talking about "Caulfield," which is quite a natural mistake.

Mr. ALCH. Yes, sir, that is my recollection.

Senator ERVIN. I think you are a little irritated with your client, I do not blame you, I got irritated with my clients when they did not take my advice and went around talking to other people.

Mr. ALCH. Senator, if I may, you as a lawyer can well appreciate the fact that you do your best for your client. If he is pleased, that is the ultimate goal. You cannot guarantee whether he is going to get convicted or acquitted. What upset me is how the man turned on me with what I have alleged and believe with all my heart to be false accusations in the manner, in the framework of which he did. Of course, I am upset.

Senator ERVIN. Well, the first thing, as you stated to Mr. Dash, you were offended by his apparent charge that you had suggested to him that they blame this on the CIA.

Mr. ALCH. That is correct.

Senator ERVIN. Let us see if there was not a little justification for him in making a mistake on that.

You testified you attended a meeting of all of the lawyers involved in the case.

Mr. ALCH. Yes, sir.

Senator ERVIN. As I understand, Mr. Bittman was appearing for Mr. Hunt. Mr. Henry Rothblatt was appearing for Sturgis and Martinez and Gonzales and Barker, and you were appearing for McCord and who was appearing for Liddy?

Mr. ALCH. Mr. Peter Margoulis.

Senator ERVIN. Yes. Now, there was a meeting of most of these lawyers and it had been pointed out in the press that Mr. Sturgis had apparently CIA credentials issued in the name of Mr. Martin, I believe.

Mr. ALCH. Yes, sir.

Senator ERVIN. It was also apparent, in that it came out in the press, that other members of those of the group who broke into the Watergate had false credentials?

Mr. ALCH. That is correct, sir.

Senator ERVIN. And the press had suggested since McCord had been involved in the CIA, and Hunt had worked for the CIA, and Barker had been in the Bay of Pigs operations, CIA and possibly others, that perhaps there was a CIA involvement. Was that not speculated in the press?

Mr. ALCH. In the press; yes, sir.

Senator ERVIN. And at this meeting, of course, the first thing a lawyer tries to find out from his client is what kind of defense, if any, he has got, is that not true?

Mr. ALCH. Of course.

Senator ERVIN. So the lawyers would be discussing at that time what possible defense they had, and it was suggested by one of the other counsel that perhaps they could get evidence that would sustain a defense that would lay this break-in on the CIA, was it not, at the meeting with lawyers?

Mr. ALCH. Yes, sir. But, Senator, I do not mean to split hairs but I do wish again to point out that it did not come out in the sense that "let us make this a CIA defense." It did not come out that way. It was not presented that way. The way it was presented was, could this be a CIA defense because of all of these things? Let us go back and ask our client. That is the way it happened.

Senator ERVIN. Well, the only way the lawyers can find out whether their clients have a defense is to discuss matters like this.

Mr. ALCH. Ask them.

Senator ERVIN. And try to investigate it.

Mr. ALCH. Of course.

Senator ERVIN. And it was suggested in this meeting of lawyers by some attorney other than yourself?

Mr. ALCH. Yes, sir.

Senator ERVIN. That the lawyers involved should try to ascertain from their clients whether the CIA was involved, whether they had any knowledge enough to implicate CIA, was it not?

Mr. ALCH. That is right.

Senator ERVIN. And immediately after that you went in and talked to Mr. McCord about it, did you not?

Mr. ALCH. Yes, sir.

Senator ERVIN. Asked him?

Mr. ALCH. Yes, sir.

Senator ERVIN. Now, do you not think that it is possible that a man who had read in the newspapers about the alleged involvement of the CIA or the suggestion involving the CIA, who is asked by his attorney about the matter might think that his attorney was indicating to him that that was a possible defense?

Mr. ALCH. No, for this reason: If it was that type of potential—if it was that type of potential misunderstanding, assuming arguendo this might be so. But in Mr. McCord's statement he brought this out under the general heading of pressure, my bringing pressure upon him, which to me negated or diminished the chances of it being a misunderstanding. To me, it implied more, it sounded more of intentional misrepresentation.

Senator ERVIN. Well, the word "pressure" is used by different people. There are all kinds of pressures, are there not? There are heavy pressures and light pressures.

Mr. ALCH. True.

Senator ERVIN. Now, it is in evidence here that Mr. McCord in December, previous to the time of the trial, had become so much concerned about the possibility of involvement of CIA that he had written a letter to Mr. Caulfield saying in effect, it would be a mistake to involve the CIA because if they did, all the trees in the forest would fall and there would be a scorched earth. Do you not know that Mr. McCord showed extreme loyalty to the CIA?

Mr. ALCH. Don't I know it now?

Senator ERVIN. Yes.

Mr. ALCH. I know that is what he says, yes.

Senator ERVIN. Did you tell Mr. McCord when you met with other lawyers that you all were discussing the possible defenses?

Mr. ALCH. I did.

Senator ERVIN. Now, in all fairness to Mr. McCord, do you not think it is possible that Mr. McCord thought that you thought they ought to see if they could involve the CIA? Just in fairness to him?

Mr. ALCH. I will answer it as fairly as I can in this manner, sir. I do not enjoy coming down asking to appear before this honorable committee for which I am most grateful, and in effect calling a man a liar. My nature is such that I do not enjoy doing it.

What you are suggesting is that there may have been, if I may take the liberty of interpreting your remark, that there may have been a misunderstanding on Mr. McCord's part about that particular aspect of it. With the exception of my objecting to him categorizing that as pressure, that may be. I am not looking to bury Mr. McCord. My presence here is a reaction, not an action. But I keep going back to this: You cannot interpret a lawyer saying "I am going to forge CIA documents with the assistance of the CIA Director," out of my saying "What do you want for lunch," or "see you in Boston," or "we are discussing a CIA defense." Either those words were said or they were not.

Now, when I watched television last night, Senator, I heard and saw Mr. McCord again reiterate that I said those words. I have already advised the committee that at this meeting there was another lawyer present, I invite you to contact him. However, I also saw Mr. Fensterwald deny that he said to me on the telephone, "We are out to get the President."

Senator ERVIN. Well now, wait a minute on that. Did Mr. McCord ever mention the President to you at any time in any conversation he ever had with you?

Mr. ALCH. No, sir.

Senator ERVIN. And Mr. McCord was not present so far as you know, and did not overhear any of the phone conversations between you and Mr. Fensterwald on that point?

Mr. ALCH. Not to my knowledge, but my record——

Senator ERVIN. So far as it appears down to this day, there is no evidence that Mr. McCord ever mentioned the President of the United States except he said that Mr. Caulfield mentioned the President of the United States in a conversation with him.

Mr. ALCH. That is correct. Except that when the remark was made to me by Mr. Fensterwald, he was Mr. McCord's counsel and he said we—he used the word "we".

Senator ERVIN. The minds of human beings are very fallible I found through a long practice of law—and also legislative bodies, and I have heard a lot about this, and read a lot in trying to prepare. I have got much information and misinformation about this matter and I do not know the precise source of all of these things.

Now, Mr. McCord says, someone, I believe he said you, suggested that if they changed the record at the CIA to show he had been called back to duty, there might be a chance to have a defense of that kind. You say you never said that?

Mr. ALCH. Mr. McCord said much stronger words than that, Senator. He said I told him that I could effectuate the forgery of his CIA records with the cooperation of the CIA Director. That is pretty strong talk.

Senator ERVIN. I do not believe that is the testimony Mr. McCord gave this committee.

Mr. ALCH. The record, of course, will clear it up.

Senator ERVIN. The record will speak for itself. My recollection, and I do not guarantee, but my recollection is that he said you, or somebody, said that by letting the record of the CIA show—wait a minute now, here is McCord's statement. He said "Alch said," that is you, "my personnel records at CIA could be doctored to reflect such a recall. He stated Schlesinger, the new Director of CIA, whose new appointment had just been announced, could be subpoenaed and would go along with it."

Mr. ALCH. Yes, sir.

Senator ERVIN. He did not accuse you of anything except saying that the records could be doctored, that you advocated that. You were just expressing a surmise?

Mr. ALCH. Well, Senator, perhaps through a lawyer's—and an experienced lawyer's—eyes, looking at it really close, dissecting it, that conclusion might be proper. But not to the average person who reads it on the street.

Senator ERVIN. Now let's see, you also, if I infer from your statement, you also took offense of the fact that Mr. McCord had stated that you had recommended he enter a plea of guilty. Am I correct in that?

Mr. ALCH. No, sir. I specifically pointed out that in response to your question, he said I did not.

Senator ERVIN. Let's talk about this plea of guilty a minute. You stated in your statement that you learned from Bittman that Hunt was contemplating pleading guilty?

Mr. ALCH. Yes, sir.

Senator ERVIN. And you also learned that later, a short time later, that Henry Rothblatt's clients were contemplating pleading guilty?

Mr. ALCH. Yes, sir.

Senator ERVIN. And you discussed with McCord the fact that this would be a very bad thing to happen to his defense?

Mr. ALCH. No, sir. I told him that I was of the opinion that it would prejudice him because of the reaction to the jury.

Senator ERVIN. Yes. Well, that would be prejudicial to his case, would it not?

Mr. ALCH. His case but not his defense.

Senator ERVIN. Now, as a matter of fact, the assistant district attorney in charge of the case three times approached you with a view to negotiating a plea of guilty?

Mr. ALCH. Two times.

Senator ERVIN. On the part of McCord?

Mr. ALCH. Two times to my recollection.

Senator ERVIN. And I would not criticize you a bit if you recommended a plea of guilty because you had a client who was caught redhanded at the burglary and the defense was on very precarious grounds at best, and so if he did say that you urged him to plead guilty, I think it would be a compliment to your intelligence as a lawyer rather than a reflection on it.

Mr. ALCH. With all due respect, I reject the compliment, for this reason, Senator: First of all, because he specifically said to you I never suggested that he enter a plea of guilty. The reason, when this proposition was put to me, or this offer was put to me by the Government, I practice this way, I do not—that is too important a decision for me to make. I simply take it back to the client and say: "Here it is; what do you say?" He said, "No."

Senator ERVIN. Well, you never recommend to a client?

Mr. ALCH. When I get an offer?

Senator ERVIN. I will have to confess that I have recommended to many clients that they plead guilty and I felt like I was serving their cause the best.

Mr. ALCH. I am not saying anything like that was improper. All I am saying, in this particular instance, Senator, I just brought it back to him and said, "Here is what is available to you."

Senator ERVIN. You are not taking any offense at any possibility that McCord may have said that you recommended to him that he should plead guilty?

Mr. ALCH. No, because he said just the opposite.

Senator ERVIN. Yes, good; so we will have no controversy over that. So you are not falling out with him on that?

Mr. ALCH. No.

Senator ERVIN. Let us go to Executive clemency. You did attend a meeting with Mr. Bittman?

Mr. ALCH. Yes, sir.

Senator ERVIN. Now, Mr. Bittman was representing Hunt?

Mr. ALCH. Yes, sir.

Senator ERVIN. You knew that Hunt had been a consultant in the White House or the Executive Office?

Mr. ALCH. I honestly was not just sure of what Mr. Hunt's position was.

Senator ERVIN. You knew he had been working for the Committee To Re-Elect the President, didn't you?

Mr. ALCH. That I did.

Senator ERVIN. And you do not know what contacts were had between Mr. Hunt and any of his former associates in the Committee To Re-Elect the President or between his counsel and any of those people?

Mr. ALCH. No, sir.

Senator ERVIN. But you did have a discussion with Mr. Bittman in which Mr. Bittman mentioned Executive clemency, did you not?

Mr. ALCH. Yes, sir, in the context that I described.

Senator ERVIN. In other words, when Mr. Bittman was discussing with you the fact that his client, Mr. Hunt, might plead guilty or had determined to plead guilty, I do not remember which, you discussed with him, not Executive clemency, but what?

Mr. ALCH. No, sir; I tried to make clear yesterday with Mr. Bittman where the words "Executive clemency" came up did not happen on January 8. It happened some time in late 1972 and when it happened, when I said to him just in a casual conversation, "What do you think our clients are liable to receive for a sentence if they are convicted?"

just like that, and that is when he said to me—and in not a very authoritative tone I might add—"You never can tell. Christmastime rolls around, Executive clemency might come into the picture. Forget it. The President won't go near it."

Senator ERVIN. You participated in the trial and heard the evidence.

Mr. ALCH. Yes, sir.

Senator ERVIN. And you know that it was proved on trial as shown on the trial or at least evidence tended to show that the notebook of Mr. Hunt which was introduced into evidence had the White House phone number on it, didn't you?

Mr. ALCH. If it was, I certainly don't recall.

Senator ERVIN. You don't recall it?

Mr. ALCH. Because Mr. Hunt's local counsel—I don't recall.

Senator ERVIN. Anyway when you asked Mr. Bittman what kind of sentences the clients might get if they were convicted he said, "Well, it might be Executive clemency," didn't he?

Mr. ALCH. He didn't say it that way.

Senator ERVIN. Well, he said Christmas was coming.

Mr. ALCH. That is right. [Laughter.]

Senator ERVIN. And he at least indicated that he thought parts of executive's hearts became kinder around Christmastime than any other season of the year.

Mr. ALCH. Senator, let me say this. He did not respond in this type of way, he did not say, "Now, look, Christmas is coming, they are going to get Executive clemency." It wasn't that type of conversation. What he said to me was in sort of a theorizing way, "Well, just as Christmastime comes around there may be Executive clemency," I immediately responded as I told you yesterday that "There is no chance of that happening, in my opinion."

Senator ERVIN. You said, on page 16 of your statement:

> I had occasion in late 1972 during one of the pretrial meetings of defense lawyers in Washington, I had occasion to say to Mr. Bittman, "Bill, what do you think our clients will receive as a sentence should they be convicted?" Mr. Bittman responded in substance as if theorizing, "You can never tell. Christmastime rolls around and there could be Executive clemency."

Mr. ALCH. Yes, sir. Those are his words, to the best of my recollection.

Senator ERVIN. So I think that was sort of right to have an idea that Christmas had some relation to Mr. Bittman's remarks.

Mr. ALCH. In the context of the way he uttered it.

Senator ERVIN. Well, now, you agree you left that meeting and then you saw Mr. McCord. Later you discussed the question of executive privilege with Mr. McCord, didn't you?

Mr. ALCH. I didn't discuss the question, I relayed to him the conversation I had with Mr. Bittman.

Senator ERVIN. Yes, and you relayed the conversation in which Bittman had said in effect that you can never tell, Christmastime rolls around and there could be Executive clemency.

Mr. ALCH. I did with a singular addition of my own.

Senator ERVIN. Yes, and you said it was absurd to expect Executive clemency, the President wouldn't touch it with a 10-foot pole or something like that.

Mr. ALCH. That is what I said.

96-296—73—bk. 1——22

Senator ERVIN. And McCord agreed with you?

Mr. ALCH. He did.

Senator ERVIN. Now, you, on one occasion, told Mr. McCord that Mr. Bittman, rather Mr. Bittman told you in one of these meetings of the lawyers, that Mr. McCord was going to receive a message, a telephone call.

Mr. ALCH. Yes, sir.

Senator ERVIN. And didn't you ask Mr. Bittman what business other people had—you had been talking about the case, hadn't you?

Mr. ALCH. At that particular point we had been talking about my client's apprehension that his codefendants were conspiring against him.

Senator ERVIN. Anyway he told you—your client—somebody else was going to communicate by telephone with your client?

Mr. ALCH. Yes, sir.

Senator ERVIN. And it was a short time after that, according to the evidence, your client did receive a telephone call and had three conferences with Mr. Caulfield.

Mr. ALCH. Not to my knowledge.

Senator ERVIN. Well, the evidence shows it although you don't know it.

Mr. ALCH. Yes.

Senator ERVIN. But you conveyed the message which Mr. Bittman gave you about Mr. McCord going to receive a telephone call, didn't you?

Mr. ALCH. I tried to tell my client everything.

Senator ERVIN. Yes.

Don't you think it is reasonable now, he got a call, and you told him in advance that he is going to get the call, and then he receives a call and had some negotiations, or conversations at least about executive privilege, you don't think Mr. McCord is liable because in his mind he associated those conversations he had pursuant to this telephone call with you? Can't you see where he would reasonably draw a deduction that the telephone call which resulted in this indicated that you knew something about Executive clemency?

Mr. ALCH. No, for this reason. I again reiterate how close we were in our contact and in what we would tell each other. If he thought, and he has now labeled this as improper conduct on my part, the question I keep asking myself is that if he did make the surmise and conclude that I was engaged in improper conduct, this was before the trial began, or was it before the trial began or whenever it happened, why wouldn't the man come up to me and confront me with it? That is what I don't understand.

Senator ERVIN. Well, you go and tell him that he is going to receive a phone call.

Mr. ALCH. Yes, sir.

Senator ERVIN. And he does receive a phone call.

Mr. ALCH. Yes, sir.

Senator ERVIN. And as a result of receiving a phone call, he has an offer of Executive clemency made to him.

Mr. ALCH. Yes, sir.

Senator ERVIN. And you say that it wasn't reasonable for him to infer from those facts that you knew about the offer of Executive clemency?

Mr. ALCH. I say it was not reasonable for him to infer or assume and later allege that that was in any way the basis of improper conduct on my part.

Senator ERVIN. Well, I don't infer it was, Mr. Alch.

Mr. ALCH. What, sir?

Senator ERVIN. I used to be a trial lawyer. I was always interested when I had a client, especially one who had no defense. I was always glad of the prospect of getting any kind of clemency. I do not see that it reflects on you. It might be a glory to your competence as a lawyer or to your judgment as a counsel to try to do so. It is no reflection on you. It is to your credit.

Mr. ALCH. No, sir. I did not know about it. If any type of legitimate, legal offer came from the Government that would benefit my client, I would put it to him. I certainly would not keep it from him.

Senator ERVIN. Just one question about the book. The Scriptures say, "Much study is a weariness to the flesh and of making books there is no end." It seems that everybody who gets into jail today wants to write a book about it.

When Mr. McCord talked to Mr. Johnson at the time about writing a book, he was out of a job, was he not?

Mr. ALCH. Not to my knowledge.

Senator ERVIN. You do not know that your client was out of a job?

Mr. ALCH. No, sir, he had electronic—not electronic—surveillance—McCord Associates.

Senator ERVIN. Do you know that he had been fired by the Committee To Re-Elect the President?

Mr. ALCH. Yes, sir, but he also told me that he had income from McCord Associates. I would call him sometimes at the office.

Senator ERVIN. But notwithstanding the fact that he was paying your fee, you did not suspect he might be in penurious circumstances?

Mr. ALCH. That was a possibility.

Senator ERVIN. I might say if Mr. McCord wanted to write a book about Watergate, he could make A. Conan Doyle turn green with envy.

Mr. Baker.

Senator BAKER. I thank the chairman for the opportunity to proceed now to inquire of this witness about matters that concern me very greatly.

The chairman has alluded a number of times to his distinguished career in North Carolina as a trial attorney and as a judge. I must say, Mr. Alch, that you are now in a position of having been interrogated by one of the best. I am not sure which interrogation it was, that of a lawyer or of a judge, but you know that you have been interrogated.

Mr. ALCH. I deem it an honor.

Senator BAKER. Now, not to try to emulate the sterling example of the chairman, but I also recall that when I tried cases in Tennessee, when proof was concluded, when the judge charmed the jury, he said something to this effect: He said, ladies and gentlemen of the jury, you will now take the evidence as adduced in the hearing room from all of the witnesses. If you find any testimony of witnesses in conflict, you will reconcile it if you can. If you cannot, then you will look to the testimony of other witnesses, the circumstantial evidence if available, the documentary evidence or demonstrative evidence if appropriate, and then you will weigh and balance that evidence and make your judgment as to where the truth actually lies.

Now, while that is a charge used in essence by the courts in my native State of Tennessee, I think it fairly summarizes the dilemma that we are faced with here as committee members. We are not judges and we are not a jury, but we most assuredly are after the facts, the truth, and it is now apparent that we are going to have to try to reconcile differences in testimony if we can; and if we cannot, look to the testimony of other people, demonstrative evidence to circumstantial evidence, to try to find where the truth lies.

Mr. ALCH. Yes, sir.

Senator BAKER. Now, in the time I have before me, still remaining to me, Mr. Alch, I want to suggest two or three things that appear to be in conflict, and I want you to suggest to us how we might go about reconciling those apparent discrepancies or how we might go about shedding additional light on the subject matter.

Begin with the allegation as I understand it of Mr. McCord as stated on page 2 of his testimony as follows: "There followed a suggestion from Mr. Alch that I use as my defense during the trial the story that the Watergate operation was a CIA operation." This is Mr. McCord speaking.

Mr. ALCH. Yes, sir.

Senator BAKER. "I heard him out on the suggestion, which included questions as to whether I could ostensibly have been recalled from retirement from the CIA to participate in the operation. He said that if so, my personnel records at CIA could be doctored to reflect such a recall. I stated that Schlesinger, the new Director of CIA, whose appointment had just been announced, could be subpeaned and would go along with it."

Mr. ALCH. Yes, sir.

Senator BAKER. You previously testified that you did not say that to Mr. McCord. Is that correct?

Mr. ALCH. That is correct.

Senator BAKER. Did anyone say that to Mr. McCord in your presence?

Mr. ALCH. No, sir.

Senator BAKER. Do you have any knowledge of anybody saying that to Mr. McCord?

Mr. ALCH. No, sir.

Senator BAKER. Then there is a conflict between your testimony and that of Mr. McCord. Do you have any suggestions as to how this committee can reconcile that apparently irreconcilable difference in proof and give us some indication of where the truth lies?

Mr. ALCH. Two.

Senator BAKER. Tell us.

Mr. ALCH. One, speak to the third party who was there.

Senator BAKER. Who was there?

Mr. ALCH. Mr. Bernard Shankman.

Senator BAKER. Is he under subpena, Mr. Counsel?

Mr. DASH. We have been interviewing Mr. Shankman.

Senator BAKER. Would you make a notation that I would like to speak to Mr. Shankman.

Would you go ahead, sir?

Mr. ALCH. If that should prove inconclusive with regard to this discrepancy and with regard to the discrepancy that Mr. Fensterwald denies that he told me that he was not going after the President——

Senator BAKER. No, no, we will get to that in a minute.

Mr. ALCH. Very well.

Senator BAKER. Confine yourself if you will to the allegation made by Mr. McCord, contained on page 2 of his statement, with respect to the defense of the recall of the CIA and the doctoring of his records to reflect that. Is there anything else except Mr. Shankman's possible testimony that you can suggest to us that might shed some light on that apparent conflict and the testimony of you and Mr. McCord?

Mr. ALCH. Yes, sir.

I suggest that both Mr. McCord and I, if he is willing, submit to a polygraph test conducted by a competent examiner, accredited by the American Polygraph Association. I state my willingness to do so.

Senator BAKER. Do you have any other suggestion?

Mr. ALCH. No, not at this time.

Senator BAKER. It is further suggested by Mr. McCord that on a number of occasions, intense pressure was brought to bear on him to involve the CIA. I do not have that page reference before me, but I hope that is a fair summation of the thrust and burden of Mr. McCord's testimony. You have denied the suggestion that you consider fabricating a defense of recall to the CIA. Can you shed any further light on whether there were other or give occasions on which you suggested that we "pack it off" on the CIA?

Mr. ALCH. I never did.

Senator BAKER. Did you ever bring intense or any pressure to bear on Mr. McCord on this or any other subject?

Mr. ALCH. I did not.

Senator BAKER. Do you have any suggestion on how this committee might reconcile that apparent conflict, how we might find the testimony of other witnesses, circumstantial evidence or demonstrative evidence, or other information that might tell us where the truth lies?

Mr. ALCH. As to pressure that I put upon him?

Senator BAKER. No, tell us if you know of any other information, save and except the testimony given to this committee by Mr. McCord and by you, that might shed some information on who is telling the truth, you or Mr. McCord?

Mr. ALCH. As to what particular point?

Senator BAKER. As to the point that intense pressure was brought to bear upon him repeatedly to try to make it appear to be a CIA operation.

Mr. ALCH. To my knowledge, my activity to which he points was that meeting at the Monocle Restaurant. You can correct me if I am wrong, but in my reading of Mr. McCord's testimony, that is the only instance in which he says that I pressured him with regard to CIA activity. I have already given you my two suggestions as to how to find out who is telling the truth. To my knowledge, he has not cited any other examples of my allegedly pressuring him to adopt a CIA defense falsely.

Senator BAKER. Moving then to another subject, it would appear to me a material conflict between your testimony and the statements of Mr. Fensterwald given publicly after our hearings on yesterday may produce for this committee a similar dilemma if, in fact, Mr. Fensterwald makes a statement or testifies. That relates your allegation that Mr. Fensterwald said, "We are out to get the President."

Mr. ALCH. Yes, sir.

Senator BAKER. I understand this question is premature. Therefore, I saved it till last. But in anticipation of the fact that Mr. Fensterwald may deny that, and I rather suspect that he may——

Mr. ALCH. I believe he already has.

Senator BAKER. I believe he has not here, but I believe he has publicly outside this hearing room——

Mr. ALCH. Yes, sir.

Senator BAKER. Would you now tell us what method you could suggest to bring the testimony of other witnesses to bear or other circumstantial evidence or any evidence, to try to find who is telling the truth in that respect?

Mr. ALCH. Polygraph.

Senator BAKER. Can you suggest anything else?

Mr. ALCH. It was a head-on conversation. To my knowledge, nobody was—I know nobody was listening in on my end. To my knowledge, nobody was listening in on his end. I do not know.

Senator BAKER. Did you tell the committee that you turned immediately and spoke to an associate?

Mr. ALCH. Yes; Mr. John McNally.

Senator BAKER. How soon did you do that? Was it immediately after the conversation?

Mr. ALCH. Yes, sir.

Senator BAKER. You are familiar with the term, res gestae?

Mr. ALCH. Yes, sir.

Senator BAKER. With reference to the hearsay rule?

Mr. ALCH. Yes, sir.

Senator BAKER. I do not know if it could serve your own purposes, but does it fall within the scope of that?

Mr. ALCH. It could very well.

Senator BAKER. Mr. Alch, there are other conflicts, but I will not go further with them at this point. We cannot try a case with one witness and certainly not with the testimony of a lawyer. I have never in my life been in a situation where two lawyers were potentially in a swearing contest, but that looks like where we are headed.

Now, I want to move on to another subject matter. The chairman has suggested that it might be a glory to your competency as a lawyer and your judgment as a counsel had you advised Mr. McCord to plead guilty, that after all he was caught, as the chairman put it, I believe, redhanded in Watergate. He was indicted on what—seven counts, or eight?

Mr. ALCH. Seven, I believe.

Senator BAKER. Did you ever consider advising him to plead guilty?

Mr. ALCH. I did not, for this reason. He told me from the beginning he did not want to. He told me he wanted to go to trial and he told me the defense he wanted to use based upon what he claimed to be the true motivation of his actions.

Senator BAKER. What did he tell you to be the true motivation of his actions?

Mr. ALCH. His attempt to obtain advance warning of planned violent demonstrations by radical antiwar groups, as he put it, which would, in his opinion, lead to violence to prominent Republican officials.

Senator BAKER. And he said that in relation to the entry into the Democratic National Committee?

Mr. ALCH. He did.

Senator BAKER. Not into the headquarters of the Weathermen or any other group, but the DNC, the Democratic National Committee?

Mr. ALCH. That is what he told me was his reason for doing what he did.

Senator BAKER. Did you advise him that that was or was not an available defense?

Mr. ALCH. I told him I would look into it. I did. He was talking and submitted memorandums to me under the topic of defense of others. My research told me or showed me that this particular defense did not permit the one claiming not to know that he was breaking the law.

I told him so.

Senator BAKER. Did you then tell him that the defense was not available?

Mr. ALCH. That particular one, but I also told him that there was a similar related defense which particularly allowed the perpetrator to know that he was breaking the law. That was the defense of duress. That defense was presented in his behalf and when Chief Judge Sirica ruled as a matter of law that it was not applicable to the facts, I made my offer of proof.

Senator BAKER. Did the U.S. Attorney's Office, did the Justice Department, or anyone else contact you to try to induce or even to discuss the matter of your client pleading guilty?

Mr. ALCH. Yes, sir.

Senator BAKER. When?

Mr. ALCH. As reflected in my statement, there were two times. The dates appear in my statement.

Senator BAKER. One to plead guilty on one charge of the indictment?

Mr. ALCH. And become a Government witness.

Senator BAKER. And the second time to plead guilty to three or four counts——

Mr. ALCH. Three, and become a Government witness.

Senator BAKER. Were there any other offers?

Mr. ALCH. From the Government, no, sir.

Senator BAKER. Were there any suggestions of Executive clemency?

Mr. ALCH. No, sir. The only other, and I do not want to characterize it as an offer. It was not an offer. But as a result of a meeting in chambers with Chief Judge Sirica during the trial, I came out and advised my client that it was not too late to go before the grand jury.

Senator BAKER. Mr. Alch, you have previously stated that the way you practice law, the decision on whether to plead innocent or guilty is too important for you to decide; it must be left to your client. I admire your rectitude in that respect, but I doubt your judgment. And I really wonder, and I put this to you in a very blunt and in a very,

very cruel way, I really wonder if there is not a balancing judgment to be made in the minds of the expert retained as counsel to advice him on the trial of his rights, on the one hand the likelihood of prosecution and conviction, and on the other hand, advantages of pleading guilty on one or four counts of the indictment.

Mr. ALCH. Senator, I was not moot on that point at all. My discussion—in my discussions with Mr. McCord, as we were talking about the defense which we ultimately used, I pointed out to him that, No. 1, it was the only possible legally recognizable defense I could think of; and also told him that in my opinion, the chances of success were less than 50–50.

Senator BAKER. All right. At that point, what was Mr. McCord's reply?

Mr. ALCH. "I want to go to trial on that defense."

Senator BAKER. On that defense?

Mr. ALCH. On that defense.

Senator BAKER. When did he then bring up the matter of his contrived wiretap, I mean conversations with embassies that he suspected or knew of wiretaps? Was it before or after your conversations with him about the possibility of pleading guilty either to one or four counts of the multiple count indictment?

Mr. ALCH. I am not sure.

Senator BAKER. All right, skip that. Tell me what your reaction was when Mr. McCord told you of the two embassy phone calls.

Mr. ALCH. I asked him what the phone calls were about. He told me they were phone calls relative to the case, no more.

Senator BAKER. Did he tell you that he suspected they were tapped?

Mr. ALCH. He did.

Senator BAKER. Did you ask him how he knew that?

Mr. ALCH. I did.

Senator BAKER. What did he say?

Mr. ALCH. "I know they are."

Senator BAKER. I know they are?

Mr. ALCH. Yes, sir.

Senator BAKER. Did you ask him anything else?

Mr. ALCH. I asked him, how do you know? He said there was a similar situation in the Ellsberg case.

Senator BAKER. When was the Ellsberg case tried and dismissed? That was a long time after this?

Mr. ALCH. No; he gave me a memorandum. I think it is one of the papers I submitted to the committee in which he cited the Ellsberg case.

Senator BAKER. When was that? Do you have——

Mr. ALCH. I do not have a copy with me, but it is one of the documents I submitted.

Senator BAKER. Mr. Counsel, do you have that?

Now, you are a lawyer. You are a member of the bar of the District of Columbia?

Mr. ALCH. No, sir.

Senator BAKER. Of the State of Massachusetts?

Mr. ALCH. Yes, sir.

Senator BAKER. Do you understand your obligations as an officer of the court?

Mr. ALCH. Of course.

Senator BAKER. Did you have the impression that your client was trying to manufacture and contrive a method by which the Government would be required to dismiss this case, notwithstanding his guilt or innocence?

Mr. ALCH. No, sir. I did not take this to be a frivolous attempt or action on his part. When he told me that these calls were relative to the case, at my client's instruction, I presented the motion.

Senator BAKER. Had he not told you the calls were relative to the case, what would you have done? Would you then have had an ethical dilemma as an attorney?

Mr. ALCH. Yes, sir. If I had thought in my own mind that, No. 1, the calls were not made or that, No. 2, they were made for frivolous purposes and of no consequence nor relation to the case, I certainly would have.

Senator BAKER. I have here a letter styled "Dear Gerald," dated August 23 of what year?

Mr. ALCH. It would have to be 1972.

Senator BAKER. I am going to read it into the record, Mr. Chairman. It won't take but a few minutes. The letter is signed "Jim" in pen. [Reading]:

Dear Gerald:

This case of *Russo and Ellsberg* v. *Byrne* was filed about an hour before I picked it up at the Supreme Court today. It appeared directly on target for us so made a copy.

Petitioners are making a pitch of course for government dismissal of the case, rather than disclose the Chilean Embassy foreign wiretap, in which Boudin's conversations were recorded.

Petitioner's reasons for granting the writ are directly relevant to our situation in that they are arguing that:

1. On constitutional grounds, the determination of the relevance of wiretapped conversations be made in adversary proceedings, rather than in camera.

2. The refusal of the lower court to compel discovery and to conduct an adversary hearing is in conflict with the provisions of the two wiretapping statutes—the Omnibus Crime Control and Safe Streets Act of 1968 and the Organized Crime Control Act of 1970.

3. Wiretaps for foreign intelligence purposes—and their constitutionality without a court order—are at issue and their legality needs to be determined by the Supreme Court in its October session, in order to set this case to rest one way or another.

Though Justice Douglas is in the minority, his comments set forth in the appendix are a pretty fair summary of the thinking of the court as expressed in its two recent decisions (June 19 and June 26th of this year) on the wiretapping issue.

In any case, I would bet my last dollar that the Supreme Court will rule that (a) the determination of the relevance of wiretapped conversations be made in adversary proceedings, rather than in camera, and the identity of the person or organization on whose phone the tap was made be made known to the defense and (b) the refusal of the lower court in the *Ellsberg* case to compel discovery and to conduct an adversary hearing is in conflict with the two wiretapping statutes cited above;

In my own case there are three possibilities relevant to the above:

1. In the Spring of this year, telephone calls were made from my office phone from a young Chilean employee of mine, to the Chilean military attaché's residence in D.C.; and calls were received from Chile (from members of his family), to him at my office phone at night. As an employee of mine, he would appear to stand in somewhat the same situation as the petitioner's consultants in the *Ellsberg* case (page 3 Jurisdiction), if those calls were tapped on national security grounds by the government.

2. If taps were placed on my home and/or office phones by the government on the authority of the Attorney General, without court order, during the first week

after my arrest on June 17th, they would be illegal, according to the Supreme Court decision of June 26th in the case of *U.S.* v. *U.S. District Court of Eastern Michigan*. There is a fair chance that there were such taps during that period on my phone because at that time, the stories in the press, and the bond hearings, were full of innuendo that the Watergate operation may have been a Latin-American or anti-Castro operation out of some type. A tap on domestic security grounds on the Attorney General's authorization only (now illegal) would be a fair likelihood.

3. Any calls by me, subsequent to June 17th, to any organization on whom there was a national security wiretap, would, on motion, have to be disclosed to the defense if any of the 3 arguments set forth in the Ellsberg writ, under reasons for granting the writ, prove successful before the Supreme Court. If not disclosed then prosecution would have to be dropped.

The two slip opinions in the *Celbard* Case (June 19th) and the *U.S.* v. *U.S. District Court of Eastern Michigan* (June 26th) were mailed to you about 3 weeks ago. I'll be copying the rest of the appendix to the Ellsberg writ of certiorari tomorrow and mail it to you. Hope you find some encouragement in this.

There are two things about that, Mr. Alch, if I may. It is an extraordinarily thorough legal document.

Would you admit that?

Mr. ALCH. If it came from a layman, yes, sir.

Senator BAKER. And second, that it would appear to you that your client was conveying to you the possibility that those telephone calls he made to the Chilean Embassy could form the basis for dismissal because of nondisclosure of wiretaps on those embassies of the U.S. Government.

Mr. ALCH. That is what he was conveying to me.

Senator BAKER. Did you then or do you now think of that as an effort to contrive defense?

Mr. ALCH. No, sir. Because I asked him if these calls were relative to the case. He told me that they were. When a client comes up to you and says, "I have been making calls which I believe were tapped, I think if the Government refuses to disclose them, it may result in the dismissal of the charges." After having been told by him that they were relative to the case, I felt it my duty to present a motion.

Senator BAKER. I won't proceed further except to say, Mr. Alch, are you telling this committee that the only thing that saves that situation from being a contrived defense which you should have objected to as counsel and as an officer of the court was the single representation by your client that the material was relevant?

Mr. ALCH. Not at all. Let's suppose those calls were intercepted. Let's suppose the divulging of those interceptions would have led to very, very material evidence or evidence which led to other evidence that the Government was going to introduce. That can only be ascertained by, No. 1, having the Government come forward and saying, yes, we did intercept some calls.

Then, according to my understanding, the judge looks at it, sees its relevancy, sees if it taints any other evidence.

Senator BAKER. I understand.

Mr. ALCH. It is quite important.

Senator BAKER. The distinction you make then, is that on the basis of filing a motion for discovery the representation of your client that the cause is relevant to his defense is sufficient, but to go forward beyond that you needed the substance of the messages as intercepted, if in fact they were intercepted.

Mr. ALCH. I had to know what they were in order to see what, if anything, can be done with them.

Senator BAKER. Thank you, Mr. Alch.

Mr. ALCH. Yes, sir.

Senator ERVIN. Senator Talmadge.

Senator TALMADGE. Mr. Chairman, it is perfectly obvious, of, course, to all members of the committee that the testimony of Mr. Alch varies significantly from that of Mr. McCord in any number of instances. I want all witnesses to be put on notice that at an appropriate time wherever there is any evidence of perjury, I expect to ask the staff of this committee to submit a transcript of that possible perjury to the appropriate prosecuting attorney for action as the situation may arise.

Now, Mr. Alch, how did it happen Mr. McCord selected you as his attorney?

Mr. ALCH. He called my office and requested an appointment. That is all I know about it.

Senator TALMADGE. You had never met him before?

Mr. ALCH. Never in my life, sir.

Senator TALMADGE. You do not know who suggested that he call your office?

Mr. ALCH. I do not, sir.

Senator TALMADGE. And when he called your office, you gave him an appointment?

Mr. ALCH. I did not, but whoever he spoke to set up one, and I kept it.

Senator TALMADGE. And then, he came to see you in Boston?

Mr. ALCH. Yes, sir.

Senator TALMADGE. And he employed you at that point?

Mr. ALCH. Yes, sir.

Senator TALMADGE. Now, did Mr. McCord ever tell you at any time that he thought he was acting legally in this matter because of the involvement of Mr. Mitchell or Mr. Dean?

Mr. ALCH. No, sir.

Senator TALMADGE. In a statement that you gave to the members of the staff of our committee on May 22, 1973, in the presence of Mr. Sam Dash, Mr. Thompson, Mr. Silverstein, Mr. Shure, Mr. Hamilton, Mr. Edmisten, I read the following: "As the trial progressed, a decision began to loom as to whether McCord would take the stand. I asked him what he could testify to. At that point he said that the Watergate operation had been approved by John Mitchell. I asked him how he knew this, and he said Liddy told him."

Mr. ALCH. Yes, sir.

Senator TALMADGE. How do you explain that discrepancy in your evidence?

Mr. ALCH. I respectfully submit it is not a discrepancy. When he told me that, he did not tell me that in any way implying that that justified the operation and made it legal. He never told me that because Liddy told him that Mr. Mitchell was involved that it was legal. He merely told me that that is what Liddy told him. At no time when he told me that was it in the context of him saying to me, "And, therefore, I think it is legal."

Senator TALMADGE. As a good lawyer, did you not pursue that question at that time, as to whether or not Mr. Mitchell was involved, and if it had been approved by him, it would have been legal, would it not?

Mr. ALCH. Because—I do not know—because from the very beginning I had specifically asked Mr. McCord in discussing the defense we ultimately arrived upon, whether or not he had acknowledged the fact that he knew he was breaking the law when he did what he did; he said he did not understand he was breaking the law.

Senator TALMADGE. Now, does the Attorney General have authority to authorize wiretaps?

Mr. ALCH. I believe he does through appropriate court order.

Senator TALMADGE. Does he have to have a court order?

Mr. ALCH. I believe he does.

Senator TALMADGE. I do not believe it required one at that time. I think if the Attorney General had authorized the wiretap and had directed Mr. McCord to carry it out, I think it actually would have been legal. I think the authority for authorizing the wiretap also carries with it the authority of breaking and entering. You did not further investigate that point that Mr. McCord suggested to you at that time, did you?

Mr. ALCH. No, sir, because, as I say, when he did give me that information, it was not in the context of him saying what I did was legal.

Senator TALMADGE. I have no further questions, Mr. Chairman.

Senator ERVIN. Senator Gurney.

Senator GURNEY. Mr. Alch, we have plowed and replowed about every point of contradiction between you and Mr. McCord many times, so I will not go into those. But there is one thing we have not discussed yet, though, and that is Mr. McCord's letter to Judge Sirica. That actually touched off the Watergate affair.

Mr. ALCH. Yes, sir.

Senator GURNEY. So I think we ought to discuss that perhaps just a moment or two here.

I have the letter before me, I will not read it all, but I will take up the various points that he brought out as to why he wanted to talk to the judge.

The first point he mentions there was political pressure applied to the defendants to plead guilty and to remain silent. Now, of course, we have touched upon that to a certain extent here in the questioning of you, but can you give us any further light on that?

Mr. ALCH. I cannot, sir.

Senator GURNEY. Did he ever discuss with you at any time, either from the time he first engaged you as his lawyer until the time he dismissed you as his lawyer, anything about any political pressure brought against any defendant in the Watergate affair?

Mr. ALCH. He did not, as I believe he stated in that letter.

Senator GURNEY. One thing that Mr. McCord did testify to earlier was that he had some conversations during the trial with Mr. Barker and also with Martinez, Gonzales, and Sturgis. As I understood the testimony, it was during recess periods or after the trial, he would see them in the corridor, he would talk to them, and that is when this business of political pressure came up; that is, the other defendants saying that political pressure was being brought on them, they did not know exactly what to do about it. His testimony seemed to indicate they were trying to find out what he was going to do. Were you with your client most of the time during this trial; what I am trying to find out was, of course, were you present at any of these talks, and were you with your client most of the time?

Mr. ALCH. I thought I was; as I review his testimony, there apparently was a great deal of activity on his part to which I was not privy either by being present or having knowledge.

Senator GURNEY. Well, on that score, Mr. Alch, would you describe to the committee how you and your client were together during the trial from the first time that you met in the morning or whenever the trial began until the end of the day? Would you describe that?

Mr. ALCH. Yes, sir. On most occasions he would pick me up at my hotel. We would drive to court. I cannot say that during every 5- or 10-minute recess I stayed by his side. I am sure there were many occasions when I conversed with others. At lunchtime, we would walk over to, I believe it is the museum near the courthouse; we would have lunch there. I did not always have lunch with Mr. McCord. On some occasions I did and on some occasions I did not. When the court would adjourn for the day, he and I and Mr. Shankman would take a taxicab to my hotel. Sometimes Mr. Shankman would come right up with us, other times he would go up to his office, which was directly across the street, to check on phone calls, and we would have a discussion on what happened that day, and what was about to happen the next day, and Mr. McCord would go home.

My next contact with him would be to repeat that procedure the following day.

Senator GURNEY. Were you with him at any time that he had discussions with Mr. Barker or these other men?

Mr. ALCH. No, sir.

Senator GURNEY. At no time did he mention to you anything about political pressure either before, during, or after the trial?

Mr. ALCH. The first time he mentioned it to me—well, he did not mention it to me when I turned to him about that letter and asked him specifically not about political pressure but why he had done this without telling me.

Senator GURNEY. What did he say to that?

Mr. ALCH. He orally repeated what he said in the letter. He had not told me because—for my protection.

Senator GURNEY. Why did he think you needed protection?

Mr. ALCH. I do not know.

Senator GURNEY. And not confiding in you as his attorney.

Mr. ALCH. I do not know.

Senator GURNEY. Then, the next point he makes here, No. 2—

> Perjury occurred during the trial in matters highly material to the very structure orientation and impact of the Government's case and to the motivation and intent of the defendants.

Did he ever discuss any perjury that he thought had been committed at the trial?

Mr. ALCH. No, sir. The closest he ever came to that was when Mr. Magruder was testifying and he leaned over to me and called, he swore at Mr. Magruder, period. When I cross-examined Mr. Magruder—this is why it sticks out in my mind—in trying to support my defense, I asked Mr. Magruder if he knew Mr. McCord, if he could observe his duties. He said he could, and he said—I asked him to give me his opinion or to describe the manner in which he carried out his duties and he had nothing but superlatives for him. That is it.

Senator GURNEY. In his testimony before the committee, as I recall, Mr. McCord had mentioned either before or during the trial he was afraid perjury was going to be committed but he never discussed this with you at any time?

Mr. ALCH. No, and again I referred to that admission of his in his letter.

Senator GURNEY. What about the motivation and intent of the defendants—did he ever discuss that with you?

Mr. ALCH. No, sir. Keeping in mind——

Senator GURNEY. Except his own, of course.

Mr. ALCH. Of course. But keeping in mind that after the first 2 or 3 days of trial, there were only two defendants.

Senator GURNEY. Yes. But he never discussed the motivation and intent of any of the people who were arrested in the Watergate affair?

Mr. ALCH. No, sir.

Senator GURNEY. Then, he goes on to say No. 3, "Others involved in the Watergate operation were not identified during the trail when they could have been those testified."

Did he ever say to you anything about that?

Mr. ALCH. He did, in this sense: During the trial, as I said yesterday, when we were talking about whether or not he would take the stand to testify, I asked him what the nature of his testimony would be, and that is when he told me that Mr. Liddy had informed him that Mr. Mitchell had known and/or approved of this operation.

Senator GURNEY. Now, on that score, why do you think he brought that up? I remember that you had discussions with him about it as to whether he would testify or not but why do you think he brought this up? What was his motivation?

Mr. ALCH. I can only guess. It happened when I asked him, when we were trying to decide whether or not he would take the stand. I said to him, "Now, tell me, when you get up there, you are going to have to tell all that you know, just what do you know about this thing?"

Our defense of duress had been turned down by the court. That is when he told it to me. Why he chose that time to tell it to me, I honestly do not know.

Senator GURNEY. Well, did you ask him, "Now, if Mr. Mitchell is involved in this, how is this going to help you in the defense that we are presenting to the court here?"

Was that discussed?

Mr. ALCH. I did tell him, first of all, I asked him, "Who told you?" He said Mr. Liddy. I said, "Do you have any other corroboration of this?" He said, "No." Well, you know that this is not a part of our defense, the defense of duress. It was not a part of, and the only actual defense we had, was just to argue a general lack of criminal intent, which I told him was not going to amount to much. It was in that respect that I told him that, but I did tell him that despite the relevancy or lack of relevancy to his preferred defense, that was going to come out in response to questions put to him if he elected to take the stand. He elected not to do so.

Senator GURNEY. No. 5, he says:

Such statements, some statements, were unfortunately made by a witness which left the court with the impression that he was stating untruths or withholding facts in his knowledge when, in fact, only honest errors of memory were involved.

Who was he talking about there? What was involved in that?

Mr. ALCH. I am not sure. But I believe he was talking about Mr. Baldwin, I am not sure. I believe he was talking about Mr. Baldwin when Mr. Baldwin said that he could not or thought that the letter or the man to whom he was to deliver the logs at the Committee To Re-Elect the President had a German-sounding name and at one point, whether it was before or after trial Mr. McCord mentioned to me that the log had, in fact been addressed to Mr. Liddy, and that this was an honest mistake in recollection on Mr. Baldwin's part. That may be what he was referring to.

Senator GURNEY. That was not discussed during the trial with you?

Mr. ALCH. Not to my knowledge.

Senator GURNEY. This was afterward?

Mr. ALCH. It may have been, I am not sure. It could be when Baldwin was testifying to that effect, Mr. McCord may have turned to me and advised me of that, that I think he is mixed up because I remember that the name on the envelope was Liddy and that there was a guard there with a German-sounding name and he is confusing it, he may have told me that at the time of Mr. Baldwin's testimony.

Senator GURNEY. Apparently it is not a very important point but something that he remembered about the course of the trial.

Mr. ALCH. Apparently.

Senator GURNEY. No. 6 in his letter to the judge says this:

My motivations were different from those of the others involved but were not limited to or simply those offered in my defense during the trial. This is no fault of my attorneys but of the circumstances under which we had to prepare our defense.

What can you tell us about his motivations being different from those of the others?

Mr. ALCH. I can only tell you two things: No. 1, he told me that his motivation, that is the protection of others, was peculiar to him. As to his reference to other areas which we did not pursue through no fault of any attorneys I don't know but I can only surmise he was making references to areas of which he had made no disclosure to me.

Senator GURNEY. Do you know if he wrote the letter or if anybody else wrote the letter?

Mr. ALCH. The letter to Chief Judge Sirica?

Senator GURNEY. Yes, what I am reading from.

Mr. ALCH. The only information that I have that could in any way be interpreted as an answer to that question is this: When I called up Mr. Fensterwald the night of the day that the memorandum came out alleging that I had told him about the forging of CIA documents, and I asked him why this had been done he made a reference—Mr. Fensterwald made a reference—in the telephone conversation, that "This was a bomb just like the one we dropped on you back before Judge Sirica."

It stuck out in my mind because of the use of the word "we." Whether it was intentional or nonintentional, I don't know. That is what was said.

Senator GURNEY. I take it what you are saying is that in your own mind you surmised that together they had drafted this letter which went to the judge.

Mr. ALCH. At that point, I did.

Senator GURNEY. Of course, at that point Mr. Fensterwald was not Mr. McCord's attorney, was he?

Mr. ALCH. No, sir.

Senator GURNEY. I mean to your knowledge.

Mr. ALCH. Well, I know this much, I don't know whether or not he was in contact but I had not yet entered his appearance as attorney of record.

Senator GURNEY. Yes.

Speaking of that you mentioned, I think at one time, and I can't remember now, but it was in the courtroom, you were coming out of the courtroom, that this unknown man rushed up and said to McCord, "You can use my office." When did that occur?

Mr. ALCH. In the 20-minute recess that Judge Sirica allowed us to more or less react to his reading of the letter. I stayed in the courtroom with Mr. McCord. It was at that time that Mr. Fensterwald came up and whispered to Mr. McCord, "If you need an office after this is over use mine."

Senator GURNEY. This was immediately after the letter affair?

Mr. ALCH. Immediately after that was read in court.

Senator GURNEY. Why did he do that?

Mr. ALCH. I don't know.

Senator GURNEY. Do you think he might offer an office to you?

Mr. ALCH. That would be more appropriate but as to why he made the offer to Mr. McCord I don't know.

Senator GURNEY. Did he, McCord, identify Fensterwald as Fensterwald at that time?

Mr. ALCH. When I asked who this gentleman was Mr. McCord said this is Mr. Fensterwald. I turned around and said, "Oh, I talked to you a great deal on the telephone, how do you do."

And that is when Mr. McCord said to him, "The only thing I am sorry about is pulling this surprise on Gery."

Mr. Fensterwald said, "Surprise, hell. Let it all hang out."

Senator GURNEY. The testimony before us shows, as you know, that McCord and Caulfield met on some occasions and talked about Executive clemency.

Mr. ALCH. Yes, sir.

Senator GURNEY. Did McCord ever discuss this with you at any meetings or conversations—or conversations he ever had with Caulfield?

Mr. ALCH. Other than to say that he had received a call from a man whose name I recall to be Caldwell, that he would not tell me who it was or what he was talking about. I told him that was his prerogative and as I explained this morning my concern was to see whether or not there would be any indication that my counsel to him was being disregarded, tampered with or modified.

Senator GURNEY. But he never mentioned Caldwell as you called him ever discussing Executive clemency with you?

Mr. ALCH. No, sir.

Senator GURNEY. One final question, Mr. Alch.

Back to the Bittman meeting, and Barker's going with you in the taxicab to the meeting. Did you ever have any discussion at any time with Mr. Barker about what came out of this meeting with Mr. Bittman?

Mr. ALCH. No, sir. I never saw Mr. Barker that day after he got out of the cab, and the reason in my statement I put down there was no significant conversation is because my recollection is that there was no conversation, and then it dawned on me I must have said "hello" and "goodbye" to him so I put down no significant conversation.

Senator GURNEY. But you never had any discussion with him either at any other time?

Mr. ALCH. No, sir.

Senator GURNEY. That is all, Mr. Chairman.

Senator ERVIN. Senator Inouye.

Senator INOUYE. Thank you very much.

Mr. Alch——

Mr. ALCH. Yes, sir.

Senator INOUYE. You have described Mr. F. Lee Bailey as the head of your law firm; isn't that correct?

Mr. ALCH. Yes, sir.

Senator INOUYE. You have also testified that as a matter of practice and procedure you consulted with Mr. Bailey on every step, every development in any case under your jurisdiction?

Mr. ALCH. Well, I would not say every step of every case but we do confer and I do give him more or less progress reports on the case.

Senator INOUYE. Does he also advise you as to what you should be doing?

Mr. ALCH. On occasion he tells me what in his opinion would be the right thing or the wrong thing to do.

Senator INOUYE. And is this a partnership?

Mr. ALCH. No, sir.

Senator INOUYE. Are you an employee of Mr. Bailey?

Mr. ALCH. Yes, sir.

Senator INOUYE. The fee that was received from Mr. McCord, the $25,000 going to the law firm or going to you?

Mr. ALCH. Unfortunately it goes to the law firm.

Senator INOUYE. It goes to the law firm.

You have testified, if I recall, that Mr. McCord really wanted Mr. Bailey to represent him; isn't that correct?

Mr. ALCH. That is what he told me.

Senator INOUYE. And that Mr. Bailey had indicated that he did not want the case?

Mr. ALCH. That is correct.

Senator INOUYE. But you decided to take the case.

Mr. ALCH. When I told Mr. McCord that Mr. Bailey did not want it, he said, "Well, you look all right to me, you impress me enough. Will you represent me?" and I said, "Yes."

Senator INOUYE. Do you know why Mr. Bailey did not want this case?

Mr. ALCH. No sir, it might have been his commitments, his lack of time, I do not know.

Senator INOUYE. Under ordinary circumstances, or shall I say in normal times, I would not be asking you the following questions. However, because of the bizarre nature and circumstance of the matter before this committee, I feel compelled to ask you these questions.

Mr. ALCH. I understand, Senator.

Senator INOUYE. No. 1, was Mr. Bailey indicted by a Federal grand jury?

Mr. ALCH. Yes, sir.

Senator INOUYE. When did this happen?

Mr. ALCH. To my knowledge, the indictment came down May 18, 1973.

Senator INOUYE. Did you discuss your appearance before this committee with Mr. Bailey?

Mr. ALCH. Only to the extent that I advised him that I had received a telegram from Mr. Dash marked "urgent" asking that I contact him, and I did so.

Senator INOUYE. Has this indictment in any way influenced your appearance before this committee?

Mr. ALCH. I do not see how it could.

Senator INOUYE. Have you been in contact with any person officially or otherwise connected with the Committee To Re-Elect the President or the administration?

Mr. ALCH. I have been in contact, as I explained yesterday, with Mr. Paul O'Brien who was introduced to me or who—to whom I was directed by Mr. McCord, and who was described by Mr. McCord as counsel to the Committee To Re-Elect the President.

Senator INOUYE. My question is have you been in contact since Mr. Bailey's indictment?

Mr. ALCH. No, sir.

Senator INOUYE. So the indictment has not in any way affected your testimony?

Mr. ALCH. Absolutely not, Senator.

Senator INOUYE. I thank you very much.

Mr. Chairman, I would like to, if I may, bring up another matter.

I concur with your statement, Mr. Chairman, that we should let the chips fall where they may, and the committee's investigation should go wherever the path leads. In the last few days, Mr. McCord has raised many serious charges, especially against several political organizations and members of the Democratic party. I believe these charges should be investigated, and that any Democrat involved in any illegal activity should be prosecuted or on the other hand if these charges have no substance the air should be cleared. As we all recall, Mr. McCord, in his testimony Friday, and Mr. Alch today, maintained that one of the major motivations for taking part in the bugging of the Watergate offices was his knowledge of "calls and conversation and coordination" between staff members of these political organizations and violence groups.

Mr. McCord has implied that his daily review of materials from the Internal Security Division may have fed his belief or at least did not refute his fear.

Therefore, Mr. Chairman, very respectfully I wish to recommend that the committee submit a formal request to the Justice Department, more specifically the Internal Security Division, that it provide this committee whatever evidence and information it has collected which indicates the existence of a criminal conspiracy or the involvement of the Democratic National Committee or any of the Democratic Presidential candidates named in Mr. McCord's testimony, to wit, Mr. Muskie or Mr. McGovern with any violence groups to carry out unlawful acts.

Senator ERVIN. As I understand it, the staff of the committee has been trying to investigate this field.

Apart from this, I would make an observation. Ever since I have been in Washington, I found there are a lot of people in authority in Washington who see subversives and dissenters and ghosts hiding under the beds and every rosebush and, unfortunately, some of them get into a security position but I certainly agree with you this should be looked into.

Senator INOUYE. Because I consider——

Senator ERVIN. I will ask the staff to prepare a letter to make that request to the Internal Security Division of the Department of Justice.

Senator INOUYE. I thank you very much, Mr. Chairman.

Senator ERVIN. Senator Weicker.

Senator WEICKER. I have no questions, Mr. Chairman.

Senator ERVIN. Senator Montoya.

Senator MONTOYA. I have a few questions, Mr. Chairman.

Mr. Alch, what were the exact words or the mental attitude of Mr. McCord when you confronted him with the offer to plead to one charge in exchange for him being a Government witness, assuming that you did not recommend it?

Mr. ALCH. He said words to the effect "no deal."

Senator MONTOYA. What else did he say?

Mr. ALCH. Just "Tell them I am not interested in that type of arrangement."

Senator MONTOYA. Now this was communicated to Mr. McCord as a result of your meeting in the office of Mr. Bittman, is that correct?

Mr. ALCH. Are we talking about—I may have misunderstood you, Senator, are you talking——

Senator MONTOYA. As I understood your testimony you went to Mr. Bittman's office on January 8?

Mr. ALCH. Yes sir.

Senator MONTOYA. You went into a private conference with him?

Mr. ALCH. Yes sir.

Senator MONTOYA. And you discussed with him the possibility that Mr. Hunt was going to offer a plea of guilty?

Mr. ALCH. Yes sir.

Senator MONTOYA. Now, did you at that conference ascertain or did you at that conference receive the suggestion or analyze the suggestion from the prosecutors as to what they might do if Mr. McCord would plead guilty?

Mr. ALCH. No sir.

Senator MONTOYA. Did you discuss it with Mr. Bittman?

Mr. ALCH. I did not.

Senator MONTOYA. I understand from your testimony, of course, that these conferences or offers by the prosecutors took place in the courtroom; is that correct?

Mr. ALCH. Either in the courtroom or at their office.

Senator MONTOYA. Yes.

Now, did you attend any other conferences in Mr. Bittman's office?

Mr. ALCH. Yes sir.

Senator MONTOYA. When was this?

Mr. ALCH. The exact dates I do not recall. I recall the purposes. One such purpose was to prepare motions, memorandums, affidavits in support of motions; one such occasion Mr. McCord accompanied me up there. The reason——

Senator MONTOYA. But you remained outside?

Mr. ALCH. No, no, he came in with me on this particular occasion to which I am referring because we were using Mr. Bittman's office and secretarial help because of logistics problems, whenever immediate typing had to be done.

Senator MONTOYA. Now, on what date did you and the lawyers for the other defendants meet to work out the strategy for the trial?

Mr. ALCH. There were several meetings. I cannot specifically recall the dates. I could tell you that there were, to my recollection, perhaps three or four in the late fall and winter—in the late months of 1972.

Senator MONTOYA. During what particular conferences did the matter of the CIA involvement being used as a defense occur?

Mr. ALCH. Mr. McCord claimed it was December 21, 1972. It could very well be. He may very well be right about that.

Senator MONTOYA. Well, with respect to that conference what transpired specifically?

Mr. ALCH. As I told the other Senators, I announced what my defense was going to be. The response was "Well, this applies to your man but it does not do us any good." At that point, the question was asked "Is this a CIA operation?" In the conversation that followed, it was pointed out that some of the defendants, if not all of them, had prior CIA connections, that one of them had been caught with documents which purported to be CIA-forged credentials, and each lawyer agreed to ask the client whether or not there was in fact a factual basis for CIA involvement and then we went on with the conference.

Senator MONTOYA. Who brought up the matter of using the CIA involvement as a defense?

Mr. ALCH. I have told the Senators, I am not sure. It may have been Mr. Bittman, it may have been one of the other defense attorneys. I just do not have specific recall.

Senator MONTOYA. Were any of the defendants present at this conference?

Mr. ALCH. I believe that—I believe Mr. Liddy was present.

Senator MONTOYA. Did you communicate specifically to the conference and those attending that Mr. McCord would have none of that?

Mr. ALCH. Not at that time because I hadn't discussed it with him. After I discussed it with him and he told me that—at a subsequent meeting, I did say to them, "Mr. McCord says there is no CIA involvement and he will have no part of any allegations to that effect."

Senator MONTOYA. When did you discuss it with him? More or less?

Mr. ALCH. It was late in the year.

Senator MONTOYA. Was that in December?

Mr. ALCH. December 21, I believe. And then a few days later in Boston.

Senator MONTOYA. Then Mr. McCord advised Mr. Shankman, your local participator in the defense, that he did not want to communicate with you for the reason that you were trying to get the CIA involvement in as a defense. That is correct, isn't it?

Mr. ALCH. That is what Mr. Shankman told me Mr. McCord told him.

Senator MONTOYA. And that is what you testified here.

Mr. ALCH. What I said, sir, was when I confronted Mr. McCord after the letter of dismissal had been given to Judge Sirica, I told him that Mr. Shankman had told me the reason for his being dissatisfied was this CIA-contemplated defense and I said to him in words or substance, I thought that was laid to rest at our last meeting, to which he replied, "That is not my reason. My reason is I don't think you are communicating with me enough, I don't think you are adequately preparing the case," et cetera.

Senator MONTOYA. Did you feel any time that Mr. McCord was not giving you all the material facts to present an adequate defense?

Mr. ALCH. Well, I knew from the very beginning by what he told me. When I asked him what is involved, he said, "I am just going to tell you what my motivation was."

Senator MONTOYA. Well, you indicated in testimony that he would not give you in many instances immediate responses.

Mr. ALCH. That is right.

Senator MONTOYA. And there would be days of lapse and then he would come back with defense answers.

Mr. ALCH. Yes, and mostly in written memorandums.

Senator MONTOYA. Well, did this not disturb you in trying to present an adequate defense?

Mr. ALCH. It puzzled me a bit, because when I——

Senator MONTOYA. Did it ever occur to you that in view of that attitude by Mr. McCord and his failure to respond to your questions and divulge all the necessary information, that you might consider withdrawing from the case?

Mr. ALCH. No, sir, for this reason. What I would ask him to give to me was corroboration of a lot of things. From the very beginning, he said, this is why I broke into the Watergate. And I would say to him, well, can you give me reasons documenting or corroborating your intention? And he would say, let me think about it.

Then I would get in the mail memorandums, some of which I have made available to this committee, outlining, here is my reason, here is the information I was receiving.

Senator MONTOYA. All right. Then during your meeting of January 8, you indicated that Mr. Bittman had told you when you expressed Mr. McCord's concern about what was going on, that he was being made the fall guy, you indicated that Mr. Bittman had told you, tell McCord that he will receive a call from a friend.

Mr. ALCH. Yes, sir.

Senator MONTOYA. Now, did you at that time ask Mr. Bittman what that call would be about?

Mr. ALCH. I did not.

Senator MONTOYA. Did it arouse your curiosity?

Mr. ALCH. To the extent I surmised that it had something to do with his fears or his suspicions that his codefendants were ganging up on him, because Mr. Bittman said it right after I made that remark to Mr. McCord.

Senator MONTOYA. You are an inquisitive lawyer. You didn't ask any questions as to who might be calling your client on that night?

Mr. ALCH. I did not. I assumed that it was going to be or could have been Mr. Hunt.

Senator MONTOYA. And did you ask Mr. McCord when you told him this who might be calling him that night?

Mr. ALCH. I did not.

Senator MONTOYA. Did you speculate as to what the call might be?

Mr. ALCH. Yes, sir.

Senator MONTOYA. What did you speculate to him about?

Mr. ALCH. The purpose—I didn't speculate to him. I speculated in my own mind that the purpose might be to allay his fears.

Senator MONTOYA. Now, after Mr. McCord spoke to this alleged friend, did you ask him the next day what the call was about?

Mr. ALCH. No, sir, it didn't come up the next day. It was some days later, and I don't exactly recall how many days it was.

Senator MONTOYA. And you had no curiosity in your mind about this thing at all?

Mr. ALCH. No, sir. I was preparing a case; we were selecting a jury. I had my hands full.

Senator MONTOYA. All right, now, when you discussed—or did you discuss with Mr. Bittman the offer of clemency?

Mr. ALCH. In the context that I have described, yes, sir.

Senator MONTOYA. Do you believe or did you have reason to believe Mr. Bittman was serious about this offer of clemency?

Mr. ALCH. In my opinion, he was not.

Senator MONTOYA. Did you discuss with Mr. McCord the possibilities of clemency in the event that he should plead guilty?

Mr. ALCH. No, sir, the only time I discussed clemency with him was when I relayed to him my discussion with Mr. Bittman, and I told him in words or substance, don't rely on it because it won't happen.

Senator MONTOYA. Now, at the time that you were advised that Mr. Hunt would plead guilty, did you ever entertain the notion, or was there ever any discussion to the effect that the plea would be in exchange for a later grant of Executive clemency?

Mr. ALCH. No, sir, because the reason given to me by Mr. Bittman was that Mr. Hunt was so emotionally upset over the death of his wife that he simply could not stand the rigors of the trial. That is what was told to me.

Senator MONTOYA. Were you aware or did you have any suspicions that Mr. McCord or any of the defendants were being offered clemency in exchange for a plea of guilty?

Mr. ALCH. No, sir.

Senator MONTOYA. Were you aware of any interest on the part of any people at the White House that in the event Mr. McCord would plead guilty, there would be some favoritism with respect or in the direction of clemency from the White House?

Mr. ALCH. No, sir, I don't know anybody at the White House.

Senator MONTOYA. Now, I recognize the two positions taken here from the testimony of Mr. McCord and you.

Mr. ALCH. Yes, sir.

Senator MONTOYA. Now, Mr. McCord has already pleaded guilty or has been found guilty by the court and jury, and he is up for sentencing. He has nothing at stake now except waiting for the mercy of the judge in the sentencing procedure.

Now, there is this obvious contradiction in the testimony. And I see that Mr. McCord's testimony will serve him no further except to say the truth.

Now, you have denied his testimony in your statement. My question to you is what would be the consequences to you as an attorney should the McCord allegations be found to be true?

Mr. ALCH. Are you talking about the allegations that I——

Senator MONTOYA. With respect to you.

Mr. ALCH. Well, what specific allegations? All allegations which I have denied, I say are not true.

Senator MONTOYA. Now, you have an interest in trying to dispel the veracity of Mr. McCord's allegations in that if they would be found to be true or credible, you would be subject to some ethical—some reprisals—from some grievance committee or from a court; would that not be true?

Mr. ALCH. Perhaps, as I look upon it now. My immediate reaction when I heard them, Senator, was that the man is telling things about me that are not true, that accuse me of improper, illegal conduct, and I want an opportunity to refute those allegations.

Senator MONTOYA. So you have a very specific interest—with which I do not quarrel—in appearing before this committee to dispel what has been said about you by way of casting aspersions on your integrity?

Mr. ALCH. Yes, sir.

Senator MONTOYA. That is all.

Senator ERVIN. I want to ask two or three questions.

Mr. ALCH. Yes, sir.

Senator ERVIN. Mr. McCord told you that he had been furnished information from the Internal Security Division of the Department of Justice and from other sources, which led him to believe that there might be some violence practiced against the President or his surrogates in the campaign, did he not?

Mr. ALCH. Yes, sir.

Senator ERVIN. And that was the kind of defense he wanted to interpose, was it not?

Mr. ALCH. Yes, sir.

Senator ERVIN. And you studied that defense and briefed it and Judge Sirica held, during the progress of the trial, that he would charge that that defense was unavailable, legally speaking?

Mr. ALCH. Yes, sir.

Senator ERVIN. Then the only defense you were left with was the defense of lack of criminal intent on the part of Mr. McCord?

Mr. ALCH. If it can be called a defense; yes, sir.

Senator ERVIN. Well, as you told him, that was a very weak defense, and I think that is because it is a rule of law, is it not, that every man is presumed to intend the natural consequences of his own acts, and the natural consequences of McCord's own acts was that he was caught in the Watergate?

Mr. ALCH. That is correct.

Senator ERVIN. Now, you suggested that you might solve some conflict in testimony by a polygraph test?

Mr. ALCH. Yes, sir.

Senator ERVIN. Do you not know, as a lawyer, that polygraph tests are not admitted in evidence in any court in the United States?

Mr. ALCH. I know—I believe that in some jurisdictions, Senator, if there is a stipulation by the adversary parties to the effect that whatever the results are, if the judge in the case determines that it is given by a competent examiner under proper circumstances, it is admissible.

I also know of recent Federal decisions. The reason I say this is because, as a defense attorney, we sometimes utilize that, both for investigation and to try to get it into evidence.

I am also cognizant of recent Federal decisions which have held that under certain circumstances, it is admissible.

Senator ERVIN. Do you not know, as a lawyer, that the overwhelming majority of all judicial decisions are to the effect that polygraph tests will not be received as evidence?

Mr. ALCH. Senator, I was asked by Senator Baker as to any suggestions I could offer as to how to resolve the question of credibility, which understandably, to me is most important. I gave the Senator that answer.

Senator ERVIN. My question had no relation to that. My question was do you not know, as a lawyer, that results of polygraph tests are not received as evidence by any court in the United States?

Mr. ALCH. I do not. I believe that there are certain jurisdictions now, today, there are opinions which state they are admissible. I believe, and this is just my opinion, that, as time goes on, they will eventually be admissible. But I think they are admissible in some jurisdictions today.

Senator ERVIN. My question is this: Do you not know, as a lawyer, that the overwhelming majority of all courts in the United States hold that polygraph tests are not admissible in evidence?

Mr. ALCH. Yes, but the trend, in my opinion, is beginning to go the other way. And I think it should. I have faith in them.

Senator ERVIN. There are 86 different Federal judges in the United States—district judges. No, more than that. There are 86 separate Federal districts in the United States and an old lawyer in St. Louis made a speech some time ago in which he said:

> Do not waste your time looking up the law in advance, because you can find some Federal district court decision that will sustain any proposition you make.

Mr. ALCH. Senator, I know from my own experience that a great many, if not all, prosecutors heavily rely on them.

Senator ERVIN. Yes. I happen to have made a study of polygraph tests, and I call them 20th century witchcraft. I think a guilty person who is calm can pass one without any difficulty, and a truthful person who is nervous could pass one with great difficulty.

Senator BAKER. I would like to say something, and I will say it either now or when you finish.

Senator ERVIN. Say it now.

Senator BAKER. To begin with, I did not bring up the question of the lie detector test—the polygraph test. I asked the witness very properly for any suggestions he had as to how we could arrive at the truth in a contradictory situation.

Mr. ALCH. Yes, sir.

Senator BAKER. This is not a court of law. We are not bound by the rules of evidence. If we were, we would not have gotten two-thirds of the testimony we have. We would have been out on the hearsay rule. But this is a factfinding group and I am not suggesting that we compel these witnesses to take a polygraph test. But I must say, Mr. Chairman, that if these people who are in conflict want to do that, I think we would do a disservice if we did not permit them to and receive that for whatever it is worth.

If I were a sitting judge and had to decide whether the results of that test were hearsay or not, I would be hard put to conclude that it was not hearsay or was not in violation of a constitutional guarantee against self-incrimination. But I am not a judge. I hope I never am a judge.

Senator ERVIN. Well, I have followed the rules of evidence so far as I can, because I think the experience of the rest and the administration of justice shows it is about the best way to ascertain truth.

Senator BAKER. Let me make a suggestion, Mr. Chairman, if you will listen to me for just a second. I would like Mr. Dash to hear it, too. And I do not have any idea what Mr. Fensterwald will say about that, about whether he wants to take a polygraph test or not. If he does not, there is nothing anybody is going to do about it. Nor is anybody, as far as I am concerned, going to make any comment on it. That is yet to be determined.

But if we are suddenly going to be bound by the rules of evidence, we have given them only the most glancing pass so far in this hearing. Then I would suggest as an alternative possibility, Mr. Chairman, that if it is indeed the embodiment of 20th century witchcraft—which I do not believe, because I think virtually every police department in the United States now uses it in its investigative work—I would suggest instead the possibility that the staff—that the staff as a part of its investigative technique, undertake those results and then this committee will decide whether it has any value or not.

Senator ERVIN. Did not Judge Sirica state several times during the course of the trial on criminal charges, that the lawyers on neither side of the case were asking the right questions in respect to who or whether the accused were hired to break into Watergate, and if so, by whom they were hired?

Mr. ALCH. My recollection, Senator, is that if those questions were asked by Chief Judge Sirica, they related to the prosecution.

Senator ERVIN. Yes. Now, as a matter of fact, did it not come out in the evidence that Sturgis, Barker, Martinez, and Gonzales had approximately $4,200 in bills whose serial numbers showed that they came from the campaign funds contributed to reelect the President?

Mr. ALCH. I have no specific recall. That may be correct.

Senator ERVIN. You do not recall that?

Mr. ALCH. Not specifically.

Senator ERVIN. Do you recall it otherwise than specifically? Do you not recall evidence to that effect?

Mr. ALCH. I do not recall the exact amount. I remember that there was money introduced.

Senator ERVIN. And do you not know that they were traced in the evidence, the serial numbers, to a bank in Miami taken out of the $114,000 deposited, $89,000 of which came out of the Mexican bank and $25,000 through a check of Mr. Dahlberg?*

Mr. ALCH. I believe that was the evidence.

Senator ERVIN. You were told by your client that John Mitchell was involved and he told you that he had been told that by Liddy, did he not?

Mr. ALCH. He did.

Senator ERVIN. And he knew that Liddy and McCord and Hunt had all worked for the Committee to Re-Elect the President?

Mr. ALCH. He did.

Senator ERVIN. Yes; and Mr. Magruder. Were any questions asked by anybody to indicate whether or not anybody other than those three were involved in the Watergate?

Mr. ALCH. By me?

Senator ERVIN. By anybody.

Mr. ALCH. I do not recall. I did not. Disclosure from Mr. McCord regarding what Mr. Liddy told him came after Mr. Magruder had testified.

Senator ERVIN. Now, as a matter of fact, did not the Department of Justice maintain, clear up to the Supreme Court of the United States, that the Attorney General had the right and power to exercise electronic surveillance over persons suspected of domestic subversion without getting an order of the court, or the President, acting through the Attorney General?

Mr. ALCH. I do not recall that. If you are referring, and I am asking this respectfully, are you referring, Senator, to when there was an appeal regarding whether or not the contents of the monitored calls should be divulged?

Senator ERVIN. Yes, but do you not know as a lawyer, talking about several district court cases on that point, some of which held that the President had the inherent power to wiretap without an order of the court in cases of domestic subversion, and others held to the contrary?

Mr. ALCH. Yes, sir.

Senator ERVIN. And finally, the Supreme Court of the United States, 2 days after the Watergate break-in, handed down the unanimous decision that that power did not exist?

Mr. ALCH. Yes, sir.

Senator ERVIN. The committee will stand in recess until 2 o'clock.

Mr. ALCH. Am I excused, Mr. Chairman or shall I return?

Senator ERVIN. We will excuse you, subject to recall.

[Whereupon, at 12:40 p.m., the hearing was recessed, to reconvene at 2 p.m., this same day.]

AFTERNOON SESSION, THURSDAY, MAY 24, 1973

Senator ERVIN. The committee will come to order.

Counsel, Mr. Hamilton, will call the first witness.

Mr. HAMILTON. Mr. Bernard L. Barker, please.

---

*Checks will appear as exhibits Nos. 21-25 in "Phase I, Watergate Investigation, Book 2."

Senator ERVIN. Mr. Barker, do you solemnly swear that the evidence you shall give to the Senate Select Committee shall be the truth, the whole truth, and nothing but the truth, so help you God?

Mr. BARKER. I do.

Senator ERVIN. Let the record show that the witness is testifying under an order of immunity entered by Judge Sirica pursuant to the resolution and request of the committee under sections 6002 and 6005 of title 18 of the United States Code.

You may take your seat, Mr. Barker.

Mr. HAMILTON. Mr. Barker, would you state your full name, please?

TESTIMONY OF BERNARD L. BARKER

Mr. BARKER. My name is Bernard L. Barker.

Mr. HAMILTON. And where do you reside, Mr. Barker?

Mr. BARKER. At present I am in Cell Block 4, District of Columbia Jail.

Mr. HAMILTON. And where is your home residence?

Mr. BARKER. 5229 Northwest Fourth Street, Miami, Fla.

Mr. HAMILTON. Mr. Barker, would you please give us the date and the place of your birth?

Mr. BARKER. March 17, 1917, Havana, Cuba.

Mr. HAMILTON. And were your parents American nationals?

Mr. BARKER. Both my parents were American nationals. My mother was an American national of Cuban descent.

Mr. HAMILTON. Now, Mr. Barker, did you serve in World War II?

Mr. BARKER. That is correct.

Mr. HAMILTON. And were you a prisoner of war?

Mr. BARKER. That is correct.

Mr. HAMILTON. Mr. Barker, do you now stand convicted in regard to your role in the break-in of the Democratic National Committee headquarters at the Watergate on June 17, 1972?

Mr. BARKER. I do.

Mr. HAMILTON. Did you also participate in a break-in of those headquarters on the Memorial Day weekend of 1972?

Mr. BARKER. I did.

Mr. HAMILTON. Mr. Barker, who recruited you for these activities?

Mr. BARKER. E. Howard Hunt.

Mr. HAMILTON. And was Mr. Hunt your supervisor in the Watergate operations?

Mr. BARKER. That is correct.

Mr. HAMILTON. And had Mr. Hunt also been your commanding officer in the Bay of Pigs operation?

Mr. BARKER. The words "commanding officer," I was Mr. Hunt's principal assistant in the Bay of Pigs operation.

Mr. HAMILTON. Mr. Barker, was the first Watergate-type affair that you participated in the break-in of the office of Dr. Ellsberg's psychiatrist in September of 1971?

Mr. BARKER. That is correct.

Mr. HAMILTON. Now, for these activities, the Watergate operations and the Ellsberg affair, were you paid by Mr. Hunt for your participation in these matters?

Mr. BARKER. No.

Mr. HAMILTON. Well, if you received no pay, Mr. Barker, what was your motivation for participating in these operations?

Mr. BARKER. The original operation was the Ellsberg operation. It was explained to me that this was a matter of national security. After this operation, the second operation was on Mr. Hoover's death and this was an operation to give assistance and to infiltrate a group of persons who were at the Capitol steps.

Mr. HAMILTON. Mr. Barker, would you put the microphone a bit closer to your mouth, please.

Mr. BARKER. The third operation was the first entry into the Watergate. There was a second entry at the Watergate when we were captured. At no time was I told any different from the original motivation for which I had been recruited.

Mr. HAMILTON. Mr. Barker, is it correct that part of your motivation for participating in these operations was to gain later assistance from Mr. Hunt and others in high places for a Cuban liberation operation, is that correct?

Mr. BARKER. Our team, which was composed of myself and Mr. Martinez, Mr. Sturgis, and Mr. Gonzales, to us this was our prime motivation.

Mr. HAMILTON. Mr. Barker, in the two Watergate operations was it your job to search for documents to be photographed?

Mr. BARKER. That is correct; that was my only job.

Mr. HAMILTON. And was it Mr. Martinez' assignment to handle the photography?

Mr. BARKER. Mr. Martinez' assignment, he worked as a team member with me. His assignment was to photograph the documents I gave him.

Mr. HAMILTON. What sort of documents were you primarily looking for in the Democratic headquarters?

Mr. BARKER. I was looking for documents that would involve contributions by a national and foreign agent to the Democratic campaign, especially to Senator McGovern, and possibly also to Senator Kennedy.

Mr. HAMILTON. Were you looking for documents reflecting contributions from any particular foreign government?

Mr. BARKER. The foreign government that existed on the island of Cuba.

Mr. HAMILTON. Were any documents of this particular type found during the first entry into the Watergate?

Mr. BARKER. No, sir.

Mr. HAMILTON. Now, after your arrest and transportation to jail did lawyers eventually arrive at the jail to assist you?

Mr. BARKER. Yes, a lawyer arrived at the District Jail.

Mr. HAMILTON. Would you tell the committee, please, the names of these attorneys?

Mr. BARKER. Mr. Caddy and Mr. Rafferty.

Mr. HAMILTON. Now, are those attorneys Douglas Caddy and Joseph Rafferty, is that correct?

Mr. BARKER. That is correct.

Mr. HAMILTON. Had you called these lawyers to come to the jail?

Mr. BARKER. No, sir.

Mr. HAMILTON. To your knowledge, had any of those arrested called his lawyers on the telephone?

Mr. BARKER. I believe not, no, sir.
Mr. HAMILTON. Do you know who supplied these lawyers to you?
Mr. BARKER. No; I do not know.
Mr. HAMILTON. Now did there come a time when you, for yourself and the others arrested, received certain moneys from Mrs. Hunt?
Mr. BARKER. That is true.
Mr. HAMILTON. Would you tell the committee the total amount of the moneys that you so received?
Mr. BARKER. The total amount of the moneys that I received to the best of my recollection included approximately $17,000 for bail bond money, of between $10,000 and $12,000 for expenses during the period to cover from that time until trial, and I received the amount of, to the best of my recollection of $18,000 of which $5,000 was for—I think it was, Mr. McCord's civil suit fee to Mr. Rothblatt and the other $13,000 was to cover Mr. Rothblatt's fees of the four Cuban-Americans involved.
Mr. HAMILTON. Mr. Barker, when was the last payment that you received from Mrs. Hunt?
Mr. BARKER. From Mrs. who?
Mr. HAMILTON. From Mrs. Hunt, the last payment that you received?
Mr. BARKER. I think the last payment I received was money—to the best of my recollection, is the money for the attorney's fees.
Mr. HAMILTON. And when was that, Mr. Barker?
Mr. BARKER. I would put it in the month of October, approximately.
Mr. HAMILTON. 1972.
Mr. BARKER. That is correct.
Mr. HAMILTON. Mr. Barker, were there any conditions attached to this money received from Mrs. Hunt that required you to either plead guilty or to remain silent?
Mr. BARKER. There were absolutely no conditions and the answer to either a plea of guilty or to remain silent is negative.
Mr. HAMILTON. Mr. Barker, were any offers of Executive clemency transmitted to you or threats communicated to you in order to induce you to remain silent?
Mr. BARKER. No.
Mr. HAMILTON. Would you tell this committee why you chose to plead guilty?
Mr. BARKER. I was guilty. I was caught inside the national Democratic headquarters at 2:30 in the morning.
Mr. HAMILTON. Mr. Barker, my final question: Do you have any knowledge that anyone higher up than Mr. Hunt or Mr. Liddy was involved in the Watergate operation?
Mr. BARKER. I knew Mr. Hunt by name, although I do not know Mr. Hunt under the code name of Edwardo in this operation as the same way we used that code in the Bay of Pigs operation.
I knew Mr. Liddy, the person I know now as Gordon Liddy, I knew him as George Leonard. I did not find out Mr. Liddy's name until after I was in jail and he was, to the best of my understanding, Mr. Hunt's superior. This can be indicative to this board that I knew of no one, absolutely, connected with this above Mr. Hunt by person and Mr. Liddy by the name of George Leonard.
Mr. HAMILTON. Mr. Chairman, no further questions.
Senator ERVIN. Any questions, Mr. Thompson?

Mr. THOMPSON. Yes sir.

Mr. Barker, was it your opinion at the time of the break-in of the Democratic National Committee headquarters at the Watergate that your operation was a CIA operation?

Mr. BARKER. I do not know the answer to that question.

Mr. THOMPSON. Was it your opinion at that time that it was a CIA operation?

Mr. BARKER. The only opinion that I can intelligently make is that it was a result of the operation in which I was involved. In the first operation in which I was involved, I was told, I'm speaking of the Ellsberg operation, that it was a matter of national security, of high sensitivity, that it involved a traitor to this country who had given information to a foreign embassy, he or his associates, and I proceeded on that assumption at that time. Since then, I have been told nothing different of any other organization.

It was explained at that particular time and place that national security was above FBI and CIA.

Mr. THOMPSON. Haven't you stated that the matter in which the operation was carried out, the person to whom you were responsible, your former superior, Mr. Hunt, the manner in which you were taken care of financially, all pointed toward the fact that it was a CIA operation?

Mr. BARKER. The methods utilized in the operation were the same methods utilized when I worked for Mr. Hunt in the Bay of Pigs invasion. This training I received with the rest of the Cubans from a Government agency. This does not mean that this was a CIA operation.

Mr. THOMPSON. But was it not your opinion at that time that it was, and was it not your opinion even after that time, when you were receiving this money, that it was a natural thing, it was an ordinary thing?

Mr. BARKER. The moneys that were received for the attorneys, for the expenses and for the family support was received in the same spirit and under the same conditions that would have been similar in a CIA operation. Comparatively, it is based on the following philosophy: If you are caught by the enemy, every effort will be made to retrieve you, all expenses will be taken care of, and your family will be provided for. This was true of the Bay of Pigs invasion; to my knowledge, some of those families of that time, are still being taken care of that I know of. And we expected this—we were not surprised, let us say, that this situation would come to pass.

However, there was a doubt in my mind at that time to the effect of what did it mean, what did national security mean as above FBI or CIA? And that question has still not been solved in my mind.

If it was a CIA operation, only the CIA would admit this, not I. I did not need to be told what it was. I knew the persons involved. Mr. Hunt had been my superior in the Bay of Pigs invasion and I would assume that Mr. Hunt, who was counselor at the White House, had the authority to order me at that time or to request for me to become involved in a matter of national security for which my training and my disposition was available at that time.

Mr. THOMPSON. Did you ever have any discussion with anybody about the possibility that if you went to trial and entered a plea of not guilty, that the Ellsberg break-in would be exposed?

Mr. BARKER. This has never been discussed. The Ellsberg break-in would never have been exposed by me.

Mr. THOMPSON. Not by you, but in the course of the trial, either by the prosecution in their case in chief, or the cross-examination of any of the other defendants, or in any manner? Was that a consideration that you had in entering the plea of guilty?

Mr. BARKER. A while ago, I explained that the methods of operation we used were the same as those we had learned. As a matter of discipline, of compartmentalization, and of habit, we do not discuss these operations with anyone or even among ourselves. This was a rule between our team and it is the type of training we have received. We have never discussed this, even among ourselves.

Mr. THOMPSON. Even with Mr. Hunt?

Mr. BARKER. Even with Mr. Hunt.

Mr. THOMPSON. So you never discussed it with—excluding your attorney. I am not speaking now of your attorney, of course. Attorney-client privileges might be present. But with anyone else, you have never discussed that with anyone else?

Mr. BARKER. Not to my knowledge, no.

Mr. THOMPSON. Let me ask you this: Do you recall a trip you took in a taxi to Mr. Bittman's office after a day of trial with Mr. McCord, Mr. Alch and Mr. Shankman?

Mr. BARKER. Yes, I recall.

Mr. THOMPSON. What is your recollection of that?

Mr. BARKER. I can only say to my best recollection, that I was in Washington at that time. To the best of my recollection, I had come up for a meeting of attorneys on some new motions that were going to be put in, and I had been asked by Mr. Rothblatt to meet him at Mr. Bittman's office. I saw Mr. Alch and Mr. McCord get in a cab and I asked them if they would drop me off at Mr. Bittman's office. I said Mr. Bitmann's office because this is how I thought of the office. Mr. Rothblatt, my attorney, had an office in a lower level of the same building where Mr. Bittman's office was and to the best of my recollection, I went there to meet Mr. Rothblatt. And to the best of my recollection, nothing was discussed, nothing was told to me about the meetings that the attorneys had that I can remember at this time.

Mr. THOMPSON. Did you ever go to Mr. Bittman's office that particular day?

Mr. BARKER. Did I ever what?

Mr. THOMPSON. Did you go to Mr. Bittman's office that day?

Mr. BARKER. I do not remember going to Mr. Bittman's office.

Mr. THOMPSON. Did you part company with Mr. McCord, and and Mr. Alch, and Mr. Shankman when you entered the building, or when?

Mr. BARKER. No, no. As soon as I arrived—there had been no conversation in the cab and as soon as I arrived, I thanked them for giving me the lift and I just went up to the office by myself.

Mr. THOMPSON. Where did they go?

Mr. BARKER. The last I saw them, they were in the cab. I do not know. When I reached the elevator, they were not there.

Mr. HAMILTON. Mr. Barker, would you identify your lawyer, please?

Mr. BARKER. My recollection of that meeting was that it was a pretrial——

Mr. THOMPSON. Mr. Barker, pardon me. Would you identify your attorney?

Mr. SCHULTZ. Daniel Schultz.

Mr. BARKER. That this motion was to be a pretrail motion that I am referring to. At that time, as far as the time element is concerned, that I recollect being in the cab. I do recollect being in the cab. I am a bit confused as to the time. It was to the best of my recollection that the time that I got in the cab with them was to meet Mr. — I remember it was to meet Mr. — my attorney. It was when I came up for some pretrial motions.

Mr. THOMPSON. To the best of your recollection, it was before the trial and not during the trial?

Mr. BARKER. That is the best of my recollection.

Mr. THOMPSON. Let me ask you two or three more specific questions, Mr. Barker and I will be finished. Let me ask you this, I do not know whether or not you have been listening to Mr. McCord's testimony. He testified Tuesday morning to this effect in response to the following questions from Senator Talmadge: "How did Mr. Barker or the other Cuban-Americans ever come to you during the trial—now did Mr. Barker or other Cuban-Americans come to you during the trial and tell you they had been offered Executive clemency by Mr. Hunt?" Mr. McCord says, "Yes, sir." Is that true?

Mr. BARKER. I do not know whether he was saying the truth or not, but I was never offered clemency by anyone.

Mr. THOMPSON. The question is whether or not you——

Mr. BARKER. That is not my recollection.

Mr. THOMPSON. The question is whether or not you came during the trial to Mr. McCord and told him that you had been offered Executive clemency.

Mr. BARKER. I deny that.

Mr. THOMPSON. That is not true?

Mr. BARKER. Our recollections differ, I never discussed this matter with Mr. McCord, to my recollection. I would have no reason to discuss this matter with Mr. McCord.

Mr. THOMPSON. You would remember that, would you not?

Mr. BARKER. I certainly would remember if I had discussed, but I could not remember something I was not offered. I was never offered any kind of clemency whatsoever.

Mr. THOMPSON. It also states that you told him about the pressure stemming from Mr. Hunt and other unnamed individuals to plead guilty and go to prison, and offered, ultimately, executive clemency and financial support for the families while in prison, and that promises were stated concerning help in obtaining a job and rehabilitation.

He says "Mr. Barker spoke to me several times during that week regarding that particular pressure upon him which he described as intense." Is that a true statement?

Mr. BARKER. The only pressure that I had at that time was a disagreement with my attorney, Mr. Rothblatt, as to the plea of guilty. Mr. Rothblatt did not want me to plead guilty at the time.

Mr. THOMPSON. First of all, will you answer my question, is this a true statement?

Mr. BARKER. Not to my recollection. Mr. McCord and I have different recollections.

Mr. THOMPSON. All right. Any further explanation you want to give will be fine.

Mr. BARKER. Mr. Rothblatt refused to represent me if we pleaded guilty. At that time I thought that the decision was up to me. I had to weigh whether pleading guilty and throwing myself at the mercy of the court, and at a time when I had been caught at the Democratic headquarters, when Mr. Hunt said to me that the evidence against us was overwhelming.

Mr. THOMPSON. Mr. Hunt told you that?

Mr. BARKER. Mr. Hunt told me that he had been advised by his attorney that the evidence against us was overwhelming. Mr. Hunt had not been caught inside of the Watergate, I had. I considered him a very intelligent—and still do—capable man, and if Mr. Hunt at the time was going to plead guilty and I was caught inside, I think it would be ridiculous and it has been proven for me to plead anything but guilty, but there was a decision that I had to make, with all due respect to Mr. Rothblatt, and I hope this does not reflect any negation that he conducted himself excellently at the trial, that he was, in my opinion, an excellent attorney, this was my decision, and no one else influenced me in this decision, and I think that it was proven—time has proven that my decision to plead guilty was the correct one.

Mr. THOMPSON. I have no further questions, thank you.

Senator ERVIN. Mr. Barker, you got involved in this at the request of E. Howard Hunt?

Mr. BARKER. That is correct sir.

Senator ERVIN. You had served with E. Howard Hunt at the Bay of Pigs?

Mr. BARKER. That is correct, Senator.

Senator ERVIN. He had been your superior?

Mr. BARKER. That is true.

Senator ERVIN. And all you did in this was at the direction and request of E. Howard Hunt?

Mr. BARKER. Yes, except that I personally was convinced at the time—and I am today too—that what I did at that time was correct.

Senator ERVIN. And Mr. E. Howard Hunt told you this was national security you were working on and was above FBI and CIA?

Mr. BARKER. That is correct.

Senator ERVIN. And you have a code of ethics in work of this kind that you do not tell anything on anybody?

Mr. BARKER. That is correct.

Senator ERVIN. And so if Mr. E. Howard Hunt had pressured you into pleading guilty, you could not tell us that under your code of ethics. [Laughter.]

Mr. BARKER. I do not think that this applies to anything like that of this nature. It was my decision. I think that Mr. Howard Hunt respects me too much to ask me to make that kind of a plea. This is my decision, not Mr. Hunt's.

Senator ERVIN. Well, did you talk to Mr. E. Howard Hunt about this at all?

Mr. BARKER. Yes, at the time—when I spoke to Mr. Hunt, Mr. Hunt told me that in his position, in his condition, he had gone through a terrible ordeal—that with Mrs. Hunt—that he was not physically through that situation and that besides, the evidence in the district attorney's office against us was overwhelming.

Senator ERVIN. Now, Mr. Hunt told you that?

Mr. BARKER. That is correct.

Senator ERVIN. And he told you he was going to plead guilty?

Mr. BARKER. No, he told me what he was pleading. I decided what I would plead. I did not decide at that time.

Senator ERVIN. I know, but Mr. E. Howard Hunt told you that he, Mr. E. Howard Hunt, was going to plead guilty, did he not?

Mr. BARKER. That is correct; yes, sir.

Senator ERVIN. And if Mr. E. Howard Hunt told you the evidence against you was overwhelming——

Mr. BARKER. That is correct.

Senator ERVIN. Yes.

Mr. BARKER. The fact that we were caught, Senator, in the premises itself is indicative that this was overwhelming evidence, to my way of thinking.

Senator ERVIN. So you did consult with Mr. E. Howard Hunt before you pleaded guilty?

Mr. BARKER. It was not a consultation.

Senator ERVIN. Well, it was a discussion.

Mr. BARKER. It was a discussion, certainly.

Senator ERVIN. And he told you that he was going to plead guilty and the evidence against you was overwhelming?

Mr. BARKER. That is true.

Senator ERVIN. And then you decided to plead guilty?

Mr. BARKER. Yes, but this is not pressure. This is my decision—not his decision.

Mr. ERVIN. I know but you were not influenced at all by Mr. E. Howard Hunt?

Mr. BARKER. Influenced?

Senator ERVIN. Yes.

Mr. BARKER. Well, perhaps it could be interpreted so. I consider Mr. Hunt a most intelligent person. He was pleading guilty because this was overwhelming. He had not been caught—I had. It did appear to me that this would be the advisable thing for me to do.

Senator ERVIN. And your lawyer advised you to plead not guilty, did he not?

Mr. BARKER. That is correct.

Senator ERVIN. And you took Mr. Hunt's advice instead of your lawyer's?

Mr. BARKER. No, sir. I made up my own mind without Mr. Hunt or Mr. Rothblatt. This was my decision and I thought that I should do it.

Senator ERVIN. Did you make up your mind before Mr. Hunt told you he was going to plead guilty and that the evidence against you was overwhelming?

Mr. BARKER. I did not make up my mind at that time; no, sir.

Senator ERVIN. No, I thought not.

Senator Baker.

Senator BAKER. Mr. Barker, you are 55 years old.

Mr. BARKER. Fifty-six.

Senator BAKER. You have a real estate business in Miami; you were previously involved in the Bay of Pigs operations for the CIA. You are a veteran of the U.S. Army in World War II where you were a captain in the Army Air Corps, and you were a German prisoner of war for 17 months.

Mr. BARKER. Sixteen months.

Senator BAKER. Mr. Barker, what on earth would motivate you at your station in life, at your age, and with that background, to do something that surely you knew to be illegal?

Mr. BARKER. Senator, E. Howard Hunt, under the name of Edwardo, represents to the Cuban people their liberation. I cannot deny my services in the way that it was proposed to me on a matter of national security, knowing that, with my training, I had personnel available for this type of operation. I could not deny this request at the time.

Senator BAKER. Why?

Mr. BARKER. Because I felt it was my duty to comply with Mr. Hunt's request.

Senator BAKER. Why?

Mr. BARKER. Because it involved a matter of national security.

Senator BAKER. Why?

Mr. BARKER. Because this was a service to my country, sir.

Senator BAKER. What national security?

Mr. BARKER. Discovering information about a person who I had been told by Mr. Hunt was a traitor, who was passing—he or his associates—to a foreign embassy.

Senator BAKER. Who?

Mr. BARKER. Pardon me. [Conferring with counsel.] The Soviet Embassy.

Senator BAKER. Who?

Mr. BARKER. Who? I do not understand. Who what, sir?

Senator BAKER. Who was passing the information to the Soviet Embassy?

Mr. BARKER. At that time Mr. Ellsberg's name was not mentioned. Mr. Ellsberg's name was mentioned to me a half hour before the surreptitious entry; then when I found out the name of the person involved———

Senator BAKER. What was the connection between the allegations of the Ellsberg situation and the imminent and impending break-in into the Democratic National Committee headquarters at the Watergate complex?

Mr. BARKER. At that time, none. After that Ellsberg, we came up on a matter involving security. At the death of Mr. Hoover, the third time———

Senator BAKER. At the request of Mr. Hoover?

Mr. BARKER. At the death of Mr. Hoover.

Senator BAKER. At the what?

Mr. BARKER. At the death of Mr. Hoover.

Senator BAKER. At the death of Mr. Hoover. Why did you come up then?

Mr. BARKER. I came up with about 10 Cubans to infiltrate this group for security reasons.

Senator BAKER. What group?

Mr. BARKER. A group of persons who were demonstrating in front of the Capitol against the war in Vietnam. The group included Mr. Ellsberg, Mr. Kuntsler, and other persons that were not of the same age level as the persons that were there, which were the long-haired hippie type.

Senator BAKER. Why? Why did you do that? What did that have to do with your business in Florida or your loyalty to the United States or freedom of Cuba?

Why were you concerned with infiltration of a group which was demonstrating either against the war or in presence of the last rites for J. Edgar Hoover; why did you do that?

Mr. BARKER. I was following Mr. Hunt's instructions.

Senator BAKER. Did Mr. Hunt say why he wanted you to do that?

Mr. BARKER. As a matter of security. He said that there was, the best that I can recall there was, information that these people would probably desecrate the tomb of Mr. Hoover. It was also told to me that these people would wave a Vietcong flag, and if possible to get that flag away from them. But it was not my decision. At that time I was assisting Mr. Hunt.

Senator BAKER. Mr. Barker, when Mr. Hunt spoke of Ellsberg and the leak to the Soviet Embassy 30 minutes prior to your entry into the Watergate complex and the Democratic headquarters, are you speaking of the first break-in or the second?

Mr. BARKER. No, 30 minutes, the name of Ellsberg was given to me about a half hour before the break-in into the psychiatrist's office.

Senator BAKER. I am sorry, I misunderstood you. May I go back then and ask you why, what was your motivation, what persuaded you to enter the Watergate complex?

Mr. BARKER. Senator, like I said, it started out with Ellsberg, then it came to Hoover, then we came up for these operations which involved not only the break-in at the Democratic national headquarters, but I supposed, the same type of a mission into the McGovern headquarters, and our mission at those times were only to obtain and to try to locate documents that would prove that the Democratic Party and Senator McGovern were receiving contributions nationally, and national and foreign contributions, from organizations that were leftist organizations and inclined to violence in the United States, and also from the Castro government.

Senator BAKER. Did you ever find any such documentation?

Mr. BARKER. No, we did not find these documents; no, sir.

Senator BAKER. Did you have any reason to believe that such documentation existed?

Mr. BARKER. The fact that the Castro government was aiding the Democratic Party had been rumored and had been spoken of freely in Miami from different organizations of personalities that I had confidence in. However, I have no hard evidence at all that this was true.

Senator BAKER. This played some part in your motivation for making the entry into Watergate?

Mr. BARKER. Part, yes. Not the whole motivation.

Senator BAKER. What other part?

Mr. BARKER. As I explained before, we were assisting Mr. Hunt, who was a known factor in the time of the liberation of Cuba. We had hopes that Mr. Hunt's position in the White House would be a decisive factor at a later date for obtaining help in the liberation of Cuba.

Senator BAKER. Mr. Barker, are these reasons that you have just stated the basis for your previous statement a moment ago that you believed what you did was correct?

Mr. BARKER. That is true, sir.

Senator BAKER. Are there other reasons?

Mr. BARKER. No, there are no other reasons that I can think of.

Senator BAKER. When did you first decide to plead guilty?

Mr. BARKER. During the—I hope this is not funny, but at the place and the time when I personally became convinced, I would say, was around—it was after the Dolphins-Redskins game, as far as I can remember.

Senator BAKER. I am sorry, I did not understand you.

Mr. BARKER. I said I hope it did not sound humorous, but I would place the exact time—I do not keep records of time. I would place it just about right after the Dolphins-Redskins game. [Laughter.]

Senator BAKER. The Dolphins and the Redskins game. Do you remember the score, Mr. Barker? [Laughter.]

Mr. BARKER. Thirteen to seven.

Senator BAKER. Mr. Barker, what part did you play in the break-in of the Watergate complex, the Democratic national headquarters, on June 17? What was your assignment and your responsibility?

Mr. BARKER. My assignment and responsibility were, my principal assignment was the location of documents. I entered as a unit with Mr. Martinez, who was the photographer. The first unit was Mr. Sturgis and Mr. Gonzales. They were the entry and the guard, later on became the guard unit. I followed with Mr. Martinez, and I understand that Mr. McCord followed later.

In our entry, I dedicated my time to searching for these documents, passing them to Mr. Martinez. By the time Mr. McCord had finished, the time was over, we left.

Senator BAKER. Did you participate in the taping of the doors?

Mr. BARKER. Never, in either one of the two trips.

Senator BAKER. Do you know who did tape the doors?

Mr. BARKER. On the first one or the second?

Senator BAKER. Both.

Mr. BARKER. Well, they were different in both.

Senator BAKER. Well, tell us if you will, who taped the doors on which occasion?

Mr. BARKER. On the first occasion, the entry team were supposed to tape the doors. Mr. Sturgis would be the person to tape the doors. I would enter with Mr. Martinez and leave the doors taped. Mr. McCord would be the last person in and he would remove the tapes.

Senator BAKER. Did he remove the tapes?

Mr. BARKER. In the first one I assumed; I do not know.

On the second operation, it was handled differently. First, Mr. McCord went in and put—entered by, I do not know what means, and then he taped the doors.

Senator BAKER. After everyone was inside, did someone then remove the tape?

Mr. BARKER. No, no, no.

Senator BAKER. As they did on the first occasion?

Mr. BARKER. No, no, no. First, he went in and taped the doors. Then when he went in, this would facilitate the entry. Then when we went to enter, the tapes had been removed. Then we went into a conference to analyze this at the time. Mr. McCord was of the opinion that this was just the mailman——

Senator BAKER. It was a mailman who had removed the tape?

Mr. BARKER. Who had taken it off. This was his opinion at the time.

Senator BAKER. How many doors were taped?

Mr. BARKER. We are talking about the basement entry door.

Senator BAKER. At what time in the morning?

Mr. BARKER. At night.

Senator BAKER. But it was in the early morning hours, 1:57 in the morning on June 17.

Mr. BARKER. That is right.

Senator BAKER. And Mr. McCord said he thought it was a mailman that had untaped it?

Mr. BARKER. According to Mr. McCord, there was a stack of mail that had been brought down.

Senator BAKER. Was it Mr. McCord who urged you to go ahead despite the fact of discovering that obviously someone had untaped the doors?

Mr. BARKER. Mr. McCord was of this opinion. I am just stating what his opinion was at this time.

Then we proceeded to go back to where Mr. Hunt and Mr. Liddy were and they were the—the information was given to them and that after a while, I was told to proceed.

So I went down and I ordered the entry team to go ahead and enter.

Senator BAKER. Were you apprehensive, knowing that the doors had been taped and some unknown person not of your group had removed the tape? Were you apprehensive about continuing with the burglary?

Mr. BARKER. I was against entry at that time, and to the best of my recollection, so was Mr. Hunt, my superior.

Senator BAKER. Well, who prevailed?

Mr. BARKER. I have no—apparently, somebody prevailed. I have no knowledge. This was not my decision.

Senator BAKER. But somebody decided to go forward with the operation despite the fact that the tape had been removed and you did not think that was a wise decision?

Mr. BARKER. That is generally correct.

Senator BAKER. Do you take any comfort in the fact that your judgment has now been exonerated?

Mr. BARKER. Sir, I followed orders in that sense. I am disciplined.

Senator BAKER. All right, proceed.

Mr. BARKER. Then the team proceeded. To the best of my knowledge, Mr. Sturgis, afrer entering, taped the doors. I went in. There was some problem in the entry upstairs so that, different from the last operation, we joined the entry team that had not been able to open the last door.

After a while, Mr. McCord came. To the best of my recollection, Mr. Martinez asked him if he had taken off the tapes and Mr. McCord replied, "Yes." And after a while from there——

Senator BAKER. You mean Mr. McCord—this is the second entry?
Mr. BARKER. That is correct.
Senator BAKER. And Mr. McCord said he had removed the tape?
Mr. BARKER. To the best of my recollection, this was his answer to Mr. Martinez; yes, sir.
Senator BAKER. And this was after the doors had been taped——
Mr. BARKER. The second time.
Senator BAKER. Oh, I see, the second time, I am sorry.
Mr. BARKER. That is correct.
Senator BAKER. Mr. McCord indicated on the second time that he had removed the tape.
Did you learn later that that was not true?
Mr. BARKER. I don't know.
Senator BAKER. Isn't it true that the police discovered the door still taped?
Mr. BARKER. All I can say is as I remember it. I can't make no assumption on anything else.
Senator BAKER. All right. That is all I have.
Senator ERVIN. Senator Talmadge.
Senator TALMADGE. Mr. Barker, you are an American citizen are you not?
Mr. BARKER. I beg your pardon?
Senator TALMADGE. You are an American citizen, are you not?
Mr. BARKER. I was an American citizen originally by birth, yes.
Senator TALMADGE. And you have never had any other citizenship except American citizenship?
Mr. BARKER. No, at one time, I was citizenless.
Senator TALMADGE. You were what?
Mr. BARKER. I was citizenless.
Senator TALMADGE. How did that happen?
Mr. BARKER. At the time, I joined the Cuban police department in cooperation with Mr. Spears of the Federal Bureau of Investigation who at that time was legal attaché at the Embassy in Havana. This was before CIA.
Then some problem came up of a group of Cubans, of which I was in charge, in the Cuban police department, in cooperation with the Federal Bureau of Investigation, I remember at that time Agents Anderson and Garcia, with whom I worked in cooperation with, at that time.
Then this was denounced to the Embassy and one day I found out that my American citizenship had been taken away from me. At that time, an attorney, a Cuban attorney that represented the Department of Justice in Cuba, Dr. Mario Lazo, took the case up as a matter of personal hardship through Mr. Lazo, I came to the United States and saw the firm of Bennett Williams and they put a bill in Congress for my relief. I never followed it up at that time because I couldn't afford to pay tax to the United States. At that time, I was younger, I didn't have the money for this.
Then I found myself in the position of being citizenless, which I was for some time. Then I became an American citizen, but I have never been anything but an American citizen.
Senator TALMADGE. How long did you live in Cuba before you came to this country?

Mr. BARKER. I was born in Cuba and registered in the American Embassy as a citizen by birth of American parents. Half of my lifetime was spent in Cuba and half of my lifetime was spent in the United States.

Senator TALMADGE. When did you leave Cuba?

Mr. BARKER. I remember going to grammar school in New Rochelle, N.Y., then going back to Cuba, then coming back here. I graduated from Farmingdale High School. I worked for Bethlehem Steel after graduation. I went back to Cuba to the University of Havana. Then I joined the Army Air Force. Half of my lifetime has been spent in Cuba and half of it in the United States. Cuba to me is my second country.

Senator TALMADGE. How long had you been in this country before you joined the Air Force?

Mr. BARKER. I joined—I was the first volunteer in the Second World War from Cuba—the first American volunteer in the Second World War from Cuba.

Senator TALMADGE. You signed up in Cuba for this country?

Mr. BARKER. At the Embassy in Cuba on the Monday after Pearl Harbor.

Senator TALMADGE. Then after you were discharged from the Air Force, where did you locate?

Mr. BARKER. I went back to live in Cuba.

Senator TALMADGE. And remained back there until the Castro assumption of power?

Mr. BARKER. I lived there, stayed there until Mr. Castro overtook the country. Then I had to leave Cuba.

Senator TALMADGE. And you went into the real estate business in Florida after you left Cuba?

Mr. BARKER. After I came to the United States I eventually—after the Bay of Pigs invasion—I went to Chicago, where I worked for Zenith, a subsidiary——

Senator TALMADGE. Worked for who?

Mr. BARKER. A Zenith subsidiary.

Then I went back to Miami. Then I got a job as an assistant manager in G. C. Murphy stores. There I took my—I studied at night until I got my real estate license. Then I became a salesman for E. Valedor Realtor. Then I became a broker and a realtor and I opened my own office.

At the time that Mr. Hunt returned, 10 years to the day of the Bay of Pigs invasion, I returned home and found a note that says, "If you are the same Barker I once knew, contact me." And it was Mr. Hunt.

By that time I had my own office, a new business starting with 10 salesmen, and I was building—had part of three condominium buildings which amounted to—total sales of those three buildings amounted to total sales of close to $3 million.

Senator TALMADGE. And Mr. Hunt recruited you for the Bay of Pigs?

Mr. BARKER. That is correct—no, for the Bay of Pigs?

No, no. I worked inside of Cuba.

Senator TALMADGE. Inside of Cuba?

Mr. BARKER. First.

Senator TALMADGE. How did you get involved in the Bay of Pigs operation?

Mr. BARKER. The same way I got involved in the Ellsberg one. I considered it my duty to help my country.

Senator TALMADGE. Mr. Hunt recruited you?

Mr. BARKER. That is in Cuba. No. In Cuba.

Senator TALMADGE. Who?

Mr. BARKER. At the American Embassy.

Senator TALMADGE. Now, did you ever work for the CIA at any other time except when you were with Mr. Hunt in the Bay of Pigs operation?

Mr. BARKER. Not to my knowledge.

Senator TALMADGE. Not to your knowledge.

Now, I believe you made—you were involved in the Ellsberg break-in in California.

Mr. BARKER. That is correct, sir.

Senator TALMADGE. Have you pled guilty to that and have you been sentenced?

Mr. BARKER. No, that trial is in the future. That trial——

Senator TALMADGE. The trial has not been held?

Mr. BARKER. That I know, no sir, no.

Senator TALMADGE. How many times did you attempt to break into the Democratic National Committee before you succeeded?

Mr. BARKER. To the best of my recollection, there were four tries, two of which were successful.

Senator TALMADGE. Two were successful—the last one when you were arrested. The first one, I believe, was over the Memorial Day weekend last year. Twc previous attempts were unsuccessful?

Mr. BARKER. That is correct.

Senator TALMADGE. How did they happen to prove unsuccessful?

Mr. BARKER. One was—we had a banquet and to the best of my knowledge, someone was staying late in the Democratic headquarters and the mission was aborted.

Senator TALMADGE. In othei words, it was occupied and aborted the first time. What about the second time?

Mr. BARKER. The second time, an entry was tried on just walking into the building on the excuse we were going to another floor. It did not work. We left.

Senator TALMADGE. Were there any other instances except the four times you attempted to break into the Democratic National Committee headquarters, two of which were successful, and the Ellsberg psychiatrist's, that you were involved in the break-in?

Mr. BARKER. We had plans to enter McGovern's headquarters, but they were never actually attempted.

Senator TALMADGE. That was aborted also?

Mr. BARKER. Yes.

Senator TALMADGE. Now, isn't it true that some lawyers showed up immediately after you went to jail following the break-in at Democratic national headquarters?

Mr. BARKER. That is correct.

Senator TALMADGE. And you did not send for them?

Mr. BARKER. No.

Senator TALMADGE. Or any other members of your break-in group?

Mr. BARKER. That is correct.

Senator TALMADGE. Do you have any idea how those lawyers were alerted and came down to attempt to aid you?

Mr. BARKER. I have no idea.

Senator TALMADGE. Were you surprised that they showed up?

Mr. BARKER. No.

Senator TALMADGE. You anticipated that they would?

Mr. BARKER. Yes.

Senator TALMADGE. How did you anticipate that if you had no previous knowledge that they would?

Mr. BARKER. On the philosophy that if you are caught by the enemy, every effort will be made to rescue you.

Senator TALMADGE. Who did you think would attempt to rescue you?

Mr. BARKER. Whoever my backers were.

Senator TALMADGE. Did you know who your backers were?

Mr. BARKER. No, I had no knowledge of anyone by first name, other than Mr. Hunt, who I had known in a previous operation that I dealt with, in this operation, Edwardo, and Mr. Gordon Liddy, who I knew only as George Leonard.

Senator TALMADGE. Who did you think your backers were?

Mr. BARKER. Sir, I was not there to think. I was there to follow orders, not to think.

Senator TALMADGE. You didn't wonder who was giving you the orders?

Mr. BARKER. I beg your pardon.

Senator TALMADGE. Didn't you wonder who was giving you the orders?

Mr. BARKER. No, I had absolute confidence in—as I do now—the people I was dealing with, sir.

Senator TALMADGE. Well, you knew you weren't working for Castro, didn't you?

Mr. BARKER. That I did know.

Senator TALMADGE. Who did you think you were working for?

Mr. BARKER. I was working for Mr. Hunt and those things that Mr. Hunt represents.

Senator TALMADGE. What did he represent?

Mr. BARKER. Edwardo represents the liberation of Cuba, the anti-Communist symbol. It represents the Government of the United States in one form, in its covert form.

Senator TALMADGE. How did you think you could liberate Cuba by participating in a burglary in Washington, D.C.?

Mr. BARKER. If we helped Mr. Hunt and this Government in matters, which I will further add I believe in, it would establish a situation in which, besides the right that the Cuban people have to be free and independent, it would establish us as having aided this Government in this mission. I view that in the same way where hundreds of Cubans have been helping in Africa, in Vietnam, and in other areas of the world, where the people in my particular association are extremely greatful to those sectors of this country who favor our liberation. Mr. Hunt represented this to the greatest degree.

Senator TALMADGE. Now, Mr. Sturgis was with you as a guard in this break-in operation, was he not?

Mr. BARKER. Mr. Sturgis at that time had a mission of lookout and guard, internal guard, that is correct.

Senator TALMADGE. Do you know where he got his CIA identification papers that he had on him?

Mr. BARKER. The CIA identification that Mr. Sturgis had was of Edward J. Hamilton. This identification I was completely familiar with. It is the same identification that E. Howard Hunt, my superior in the Bay of Pigs, used at that time.

Senator TALMADGE. In other words, he got them from Hunt? That was the identification papers he had in the Bay of Pigs, is that correct?

Mr. BARKER. That is correct.

Senator TALMADGE. Now, do you know what the source of the funds was that Mrs. Hunt gave you?

Mr. BARKER. I do not.

Senator TALMADGE. Did she give you $100 bills like she gave everyone else?

Mr. BARKER. I do not exactly remember the denomination of the money that Mrs. Hunt gave me, but I assume that it did include $100 bills, yes.

Senator TALMADGE. Did you ever wonder what the source of that money was?

Mr. BARKER. No, I never did wonder what the source of that money was.

Senator TALMADGE. You made no inquiry as to where it was coming from?

Mr. BARKER. No, I did not.

Senator TALMADGE. And you had no thoughts about the wisdom of passing around $100 bills without knowing what the source was?

Mr. BARKER. This money was given to me to pay attorney fees for expenses and for bondsman. As I have explained before, this seemed natural to me at that time.

Senator TALMADGE. Now, is it true that both your daughter and your attorney urged you to plead not guilty?

Mr. BARKER. Mr. Rothblatt was completely opposed to my plea of guilty. I respect him because this was his conviction. I do not see why my daughter has to be brought into this matter but my daughter coincided with Mr. Rothblatt that I should not plead guilty. My daughter has her own mind. This was one of the things that weighed on my personal decision to a certain extent. But neither Rothblatt nor my daughter nor my wife or anyone or Mr. Hunt or any offer of any kind made any dent on my decision. This was my decision and no one else's.

Senator TALMADGE. Did Mr. Hunt ever talk to you about whether you ought to plead guilty or not?

Mr. BARKER. Mr. Hunt never told me what his opionion—or even his opinion was that I should plead.

Senator TALMADGE. He never suggested one way or another, is that correct?

Mr. BARKER. He never suggested one way or another. Mr. Hunt only told me what his position was and he never even hinted at what my decision should be.

Senator TALMADGE. He told you that he would plead guilty, did he not?

Mr. Barker. That is correct.

Senator Talmadge. Your daughter and your lawyer both urged you not to plead guilty?

Mr. Barker. That is correct.

Senator Talmadge. My time has expired and I yield, Mr. Chairman.

Senator Ervin. Senator Gurney.

Senator Gurney. Mr. Barker, I wonder if we can begin at the very beginning of this Watergate affair or the beginning of your contact with Mr. Hunt. When and how did he contact you?

Mr. Barker. On April 17, 1971, exactly 10 years after the Bay of Pigs—this is the day they commemorate the Bay of Pigs in Miami—there was—I think it was the day before, when I arrived home—there was a note on my door. The note said "If you are the same Barker I once knew——"

Senator Gurney. The note pinned to your door, is that correct?

Mr. Barker. That is correct.

Senator Gurney. Door where?

Mr. Barker. In my home.

Senator Gurney. And it said again, what?

Mr. Barker. "If you are the same Barker I once knew contact me at such and such hotel."

Senator Gurney. And signed by anybody?

Mr. Barker. Howard.

Senator Gurney. What did you do?

Mr. Barker. I immediately contacted him.

Senator Gurney. Where?

Mr. Barker. I do not remember the name of the hotel, it could have been the Tradewinds. I know it was in Miami Beach, and I am not too familiar with Miami Beach, close to, could be, 135 feet in that area.

Senator Gurney. How did you know the name of the hotel?

Mr. Barker. It stated it in the note where I could contact me, or contact him.

Senator Gurney. So it gave the name of the hotel in the note?

Mr. Barker. Yes, sir.

Senator Gurney. You contacted him by phone?

Mr. Barker. Yes, sir, originally by phone and then I immediately drove over there in person.

Senator Gurney. Can you give us an account of the first phone conversation?

Mr. Barker. "Greetings and how are you," and so forth. "It would be nice to see you again," and how—"Well, I am a lot older, a lot fatter," and stuff like that.

Senator Gurney. Did he invite you to come over to the hotel?

Mr. Barker. Yes, sir.

Senator Gurney. And did he give any reason why?

Mr. Barker. No, sir.

Senator Gurney. And then you went to the hotel and met him?

Mr. Barker. That is correct.

Senator Gurney. In his room?

Mr. Barker. I do not recollect. I think Mr. and Mrs. Hunt met me downstairs.

Senator GURNEY. And what transpired—what conversations did you have.

Mr. BARKER. Old times.

Senator GURNEY. Well, I am talking now specifically about what he wanted you to do, of course.

Mr. BARKER. At that time, nothing. It was just he was there to go back to the 10 years after the Bay of Pigs, he would be present incognito at the Bay of Pigs meeting, and asked would I go with him, and I said I would like to.

Senator GURNEY. Why did he not want to be known?

Mr. BARKER. I do not know the nature of the operation at that time. Mr. Hunt was only known to very few persons in Miami, and we did go to this meeting, we did speak in Spanish to two or three persons that were in the old Cuban Revolutionary Council.

Senator GURNEY. Go on; excuse me.

Mr. BARKER. Mr. Martinez joined us. I presented him as Edwardo, and he immediately recognized who Edwardo was, although I think Mr. Martinez had met him previously. Then Mrs. Barker and myself, Mr. and Mrs. Hunt, and Mr. Martinez went to lunch in a Cuban restaurant. Nothing was spoken at that time itself.

Senator GURNEY. This was still just a visit about old times.

Mr. BARKER. Yes, sir.

Senator GURNEY. Well, now, when did he contact you next?

Mr. BARKER. We kept in contact after that without anything special being brought up. I quite frankly waited until Mr. Hunt would tell me if there was any other reason other than social reasons—in the hierarchy, remember that he was my boss—and I expected him in his good time to tell me if there was anything else—and eventually he did.

Senator GURNEY. And when did that take place?

Mr. BARKER. I would say it was approximately—to the best of my recollection—2 weeks before the Ellsberg surreptitious entry.

Senator GURNEY. And what did he tell you?

Mr. BARKER. As I have said before, I think, would I be willing to help him on a matter of national security?

Senator GURNEY. Was this by a phone call?

Mr. BARKER. No, no; personally. He went down to Miami personally, and then after, I would repeat what I said before.

Senator GURNEY. I do not know that we need to go through that.

Mr. BARKER. Then he said that I should recruit two persons for this operation. And then I said I would, and he left. Then I proceeded to sound out two persons, and both of them accepted. The two persons that I had sounded out were Mr. Martinez and Mr. DeDiego. I selected them for their qualifications, not that they were salesmen in my organization. Mr. Martinez had in his record over 300 infiltrations into Castro Communist Cuba, including the obtaining of hard evidence during the missile crisis. I thought it was perfectly justified for a mission of this nature. I consider him one of the greatest heroes of that effort at that time.

Mr. DeDiego had been a member of Operation 40, which had been specially trained to capture documents of the Castro government and the operation was successful. He had received further training as an intelligence officer in the Army of the United States. He also, in my concept, was perfectly qualified for a mission of this nature. I submitted their names and records to Mr. Hunt over the phone—long-distance phone—and some time after that, I do not remember, he called me and said that the two men had been cleared for the mission.

Senator GURNEY. Did he say who and how they were cleared?

Mr. BARKER. No, he did not.

Senator GURNEY. And then go on about the mission and be as brief as possible, because I want to get to the Watergate.

Mr. BARKER. Mr. Hunt then called me one day and said to proceed with my men to Los Angeles and to stay at—I think it was—the Beverly Wilshire Hotel where he would contact me. I bought the tickets, alerted the men, and we took off and went to Los Angeles. I registered in the hotel and Mr. Hunt contacted me. He gave me a brief—he gave me the address of the place where we were to make the entry. I found the place and I went with my men to familiarize myself with the area. I had the exact address at that time. Then the general plan was given to us. We proceeded to the area, and eventually made the entry. I personally searched for those documents.

Senator GURNEY. What documents?

Mr. BARKER. A file of Daniel Ellsberg at his psychiatrist's office. This file was not there. I would search—file from file cabinet. I searched his desk and the file cabinet. The men also helped me in the search. The only thing that I found in connection with him was an address book which had his name. This we photographed, and we also photographed the file cabinet to prove that we had forced them open, and then we left.

Senator GURNEY. Now then let us get to the Watergate: When and where did Mr. Hunt contact you about Watergate?

Mr. BARKER. I do not remember whether—I believe it was in one of the trips down to Miami that he told me of an impending operation—double operation—which would take in length about a week.

Senator GURNEY. Did you say double operation?

Mr. BARKER. I beg your pardon?

Senator GURNEY. Did you say double operation?

Mr. BARKER. That is correct.

Senator GURNEY. What does that mean?

Mr. BARKER. At that time, I did not know but I knew at the time it would involve, after that it was quite evident it was an entry into the McGovern's headquarters as well as an entry into the Watergate headquarters.

Senator GURNEY. Tell us now very carefully what his instructions were.

Mr. BARKER. I would like to explain that Mr. Hunt was our immediate superior in this operation—that we were involved only in the documents that we were to obtain. We had no connection with the electronic part. It is—to the best of my recollection—that the electronic part was not even under the direction of Mr. Hunt, much less of myself. Mr. McCord appeared to be quite capable of that, he handled that. I had no knowledge of that bugging he was going to do. All that my mission—that our team mission was—was the documents to which I have referred, and this was explained to me by Mr. Hunt at that time.

Senator GURNEY. That is what I want to know. I mean he went to Miami, as I understand it, and he got in touch with you and he must have said "Bernard, I have another mission for you."

Mr. BARKER. That is correct.

Senator GURNEY. What did he say, what was the mission?

Mr. BARKER. All he said was a double mission and he would explain to me when we got there, he gave me the general information, as saying, "Get your men in training going up and down stairs. They must be in good physical condition."

This I passed on to my men. I think he mentioned it involved surreptitious entry similar to the one we had done in California, but he did not say anything else specifically to me at that time nor did he have to give me any further explanation.

Senator GURNEY. Did he say to you it was going to be the Democratic national headquarters?

Mr. BARKER. No, he did not, sir.

Senator GURNEY. Did he say to you it was going to be in Senator McGovern's campaign headquarters?

Mr. BARKER. No, he did not.

Senator GURNEY. Now then at some point in time you went to Washington?

Mr. BARKER. That is correct.

Senator GURNEY. Will you tell us about that?

Mr. BARKER. I arrived with my team in Washington, they went to the Hamilton Hotel. I met with Mr. Hunt and there is where Mr. Hunt gave me the general description of our double mission and I asked then, had the mission then—this I did not communicate with the men until just about entry time.

Senator GURNEY. Did he tell you at that time it was the Democratic national headquarters and Senator McGovern's headquarters?

Mr. BARKER. To the best of my recollection this was the time when he said this to me. Previous to this, the only information I had is that we were going to have some kind of a banquet at the Watergate.

Senator GURNEY. A banquet?

Mr. BARKER. Yes.

And we did have that banquet at the Watergate. Then at that time is was explained to me that the banquet in itself was a cover for the entry.

Senator GURNEY. Well, did he tell you at that time what documents you were going to look for?

Mr. BARKER. That is correct.

Senator GURNEY. And what did he say?

Mr. BARKER. He said to look for any documents involving contributors, both foreign and national. If I had any doubts as to the documents I could contact him over our communications.

Senator GURNEY. Now the first and second entries, of course, were unsuccessful, the third entry was, and what documents did you photograph there?

Mr. BARKER. It was quite evident when I searched the documents that this was not the right place to look for the type of documents that we were searching for.

Senator GURNEY. Where did you think was the right place?

Mr. BARKER. I didn't think which was the right place. I just analyzed from the type of documents that I found in the files of the offices that were available to me that it would be very doubtful that these would be the documents we were searching for. So what I did was I took only documents where names of persons were involved, where there might be notations of numbers, and I also came across one document that involved the security of the national—of the Miami convention, and I considered that this document would also be most welcome so I also photographed that document.

Senator GURNEY. Just one or two other questions because my time has expired here but I do want to complete this reason why you went in there.

Now, on the last and fourth attempt why did you go there again if you realized that the documents you were looking for were not there? Didn't it occur to you at this time that perhaps you were doing something that was political rather than national securitywise?

Mr. BARKER. It was then evident that we were not in the office of the chairman. In our second entry we finally came to the office of the chairman of the Democratic National Convention. I believe honestly that there we might find the type of information that we were searching for.

Senator GURNEY. That is when you were discovered?

Mr. BARKER. That is correct.

Senator GURNEY. All right.

I have further questions, Mr. Chairman, but I have used my time up.

Senator ERVIN. Senator Inouye.

Senator INOUYE. Mr. Barker, you have testified that you were recruited by FBI agents who worked for the police department in the government of Fulgencio Batista, is that correct?

Mr. BARKER. No, sir, it was during the government of Dr. Carlos Frio Soccaras who was the last constitutional President of Cuba.

Senator INOUYE. What was your function in the police department?

Mr. BARKER. I entered the police department with a group of veterans in training from the Second World War.

My mission was mostly of a liaison mission in nature. I worked with the treasury department, in cooperation with the treasury department, on drugs and on kidnaping cases and a postal case.

Senator INOUYE. Was it covert-type operations?

Mr. BARKER. No, I was a regular member of the Cuban police force. Some of them were overt. I also escorted VIP's and included a visit of Mrs. Truman and Margaret Truman. Then I did regular police work inside of the Cuban police department.

Senator INOUYE. Mr. Barker, you have testified that you are, well, you are very familiar with CIA discipline and procedure and that you applied all of this discipline and procedure in all of your covert activities, is that correct?

Mr. BARKER. This experience was much later after the—this had nothing to do with my time with the Cuban police department.

Senator INOUYE. I am talking about the Bay of Pigs and later, sir.

Mr. BARKER. That is correct, sir.

Senator INOUYE. You were aware of the CIA discipline in this effort?

Mr. BARKER. Yes, those were the methods we utilized in this matter.

Senator INOUYE. So you realized there was a CIA operation and was carried out in behalf of the Government of the United States.

Mr. BARKER. I don't know the real answer to that question.

Senator INOUYE. Do you think this was a private job of Mr. Hunt?

Mr. BARKER. No, sir. Mr. Hunt——

Senator INOUYE. You have testified, it is on record, that you felt that this was a CIA operation and that you were working for the Government.

Mr. BARKER. I have not testified that I felt it was, that it could or could not be a CIA operation; that the CIA was under national security.

Senator INOUYE. Did you not testify that you were not surprised when expenses for your family were provided, when lawyers appeared?

Mr. BARKER. I testified I believed then and I believe now that——

Senator INOUYE. Because this was part of the CIA procedure.

Mr. BARKER. That this is part of the same procedure, not necessarily that this was a CIA. I surmised that if it was national security or any other organization of the covert type, that the same rules would apply.

Senator INOUYE. And under the CIA procedure, you were assured that everthing would be done to rescue you.

Mr. BARKER. That is correct.

Senator INOUYE. So when the lawyers appeared, you weren't a bit surprised?

Mr. BARKER. No, frankly, I was not surprised, no.

Senator INOUYE. Was clemency part of the recipe?

Mr. BARKER. No, sir. Clemency? The word "clemency" was unnecessary. It had no application in our case whatsoever.

Senator INOUYE. You mean you were told as a CIA undercover operative that once you were captured, you were forgotten?

Mr. BARKER. No, if your families are taken care of, you are not forgotten. If your attorneys are supplied and bail bond money, this is not being forgotten.

Senator INOUYE. And every effort would be made to get you out of it?

Mr. BARKER. That is correct, yes.

Senator INOUYE. Did that include Executive clemency?

Mr. BARKER. I do not see why that should include Executive clemency, no.

Senator INOUYE. As part of your discipline, you have indicated that you never asked questions, you just followed orders. I am quoting you.

Mr. BARKER. Yes, in the spirit of how we organized.

Compartmentation means that you do not speak of these matters with each other. You work on a need-to-know basis. If I do not need to know certain information as to who is above Mr. Hunt, I do not, not only do not need to know, I do not want to know.

Senator INOUYE. So if your leader——

Mr. BARKER. If something goes wrong, I can't be suspected of this. If they would have told me who was above them, I would not have had the confidence I am supposed to have in these people. This would be unnecessary information in the compliance of the mission.

This is the way, also, that the underground worked and this was common to us. This is the way it should be.

Senator INOUYE. So that under this discipline, if a leader told you something, you would never question him?

Mr. BARKER. What leader?

Senator INOUYE. He didn't have to tell you directly. If he suggested something, you took that as an order.

Mr. BARKER. In an operation?

Senator INOUYE. Yes.

Mr. BARKER. That would be correct.

Senator INOUYE. So if Mr. Hunt suggested that you plead guilty, this was an order?

Mr. BARKER. This was not an operation. Pleading guilty was not an operation. Pleading guilty was something that I decided and not Mr. Hunt.

Senator INOUYE. I thought you said that Mr. Hunt had come to you and said that he was going to plead guilty because they caught us with the goods.

Mr. BARKER. That is right. No; because of the overwhelming evidence that there was against all of us.

And may I further observe, in my modest way of thinking, if this was Mr. Hunt's plea and he had not been caught inside the Watergate, it seemed to me intelligent, it seemed to me at that time that this was an intelligent decision for me to make. But does not necessarily indicate that he told me what to do or what not to do in that matter. This was my own decision, sir.

Senator INOUYE. And an important part of the discipline and procedure of covert operators would be silence. Isn't that what you told us?

Mr. BARKER. Would be what, sir?

Senator INOUYE. Silence.

Mr. BARKER. That is correct, yes sir.

Senator INOUYE. Much more important than any other discipline?

Mr. BARKER. To a certain extent, yes, I would say so. Silence is part of the very nature of a covert operation. When you are captured by the enemy, you don't talk.

Perhaps, sir, if I explained the nature of the men that worked with me, I could better explain that.

Senator INOUYE. May we come to that later?

Mr. BARKER. Yes, sir.

Senator INOUYE. The second most important discipline would be not to squeal on your fellow operatives. Would that be correct?

Mr. BARKER. I do not think that the word "squeal" is applicable to a paramilitary operation. I consider that more as a criminal——

Senator INOUYE. Let's use a better word. No to implicate.

Mr. BARKER. Yes, but this is not the case, because implicating—to implicate someone, sir, you have to know who is behind it. The very discipline under which I worked, this was not necessary. I did not know.

Senator INOUYE. Would you, under the code of ethics or code of conduct or code of discipline, implicate members of your team?

Mr. BARKER. No.

Senator INOUYE. And you looked upon Mr. Hunt as a great man. You respected him highly?

Mr. BARKER. Yes.

Senator INOUYE. As one of the key leaders of the Cuban liberation movement.

Mr. BARKER. That is correct.

Senator INOUYE. Would I be correct to assume that under those circumstances, you would never implicate Mr. Hunt and you would forever keep silent

Mr. BARKER. This is a hypothetical question.

Senator INOUYE. No, it is not a hypothetical question, I am asking you.

Mr. BARKER. In this particular case, the answer respectfully, sir, is negative, because there was no need to implicate him. Mr. Hunt was pleading guilty by his own thinking. I was pleading guilty because, and it was proven correct, events that took place after that proved that I was correct in my decision, sir.

Senator INOUYE. But you are a wise man. You know that if Mr. Hunt did in fact tell you to keep silent, he would be guilty of the crime of obstructing justice?

Mr. BARKER. Pardon me if I smile, Senator; if I was a wise man, I would not probably be sitting right here. [Applause.]

I hope this carries no disrespect, sir. sincerely, I mean that.

Senator INOUYE. Well, I am not trying to be disrespectful to you, sir.

But you have also testified, and I quote you directly, sir, that you had "personnel available for this type of operation."

Mr. BARKER. Yes, sir. I had personnel available for this operation.

Senator INOUYE. In other words, you are in this covert business?

Mr. BARKER. Not for the past 10 years.

Senator INOUYE. Then how do you have this personnel available all this time, 10 years?

Mr. BARKER. Sir, I was Edwardo's practically executive arm in the Bay of Pigs invasion. I was his principal assistant. Whether I want to or not, I am a bilingual American-Cuban who is dedicated to the cause of the liberation of Cuba. I have not changed my mentality since that time. I had no need to give any explanation to any of the old teams in Cuba as to what my position was when I called them on these matters—not because I am a leader, which I am not, but because I was part of Mr. Hunt's image.

Senator INOUYE. Would you under the discipline that you have followed, say anything that would injure the Government of the United States?

Mr. BARKER. Although in this case, that is not applicable, because I had no information, I would state that I would never commit an act of that nature.

Senator INOUYE. And you have also said that you would not help the enemy, whoever the enemy is?

Mr. BARKER. Yes; in a general statement, yes, I would say that, sir.

Senator INOUYE. I ask this hopefully in good grace, sir. Do you consider us your enemy, this committee, the enemy?

Mr. BARKER. Sir, of the team that entered the Watergate, Mr. Gonzales and I are Republicans. Mr. Sturgis and Mr. Martinez are Democrats. I do not consider anyone here an enemy of this country, no more than I consider Mr. Martinez or Mr. Sturgis my enemies because they are Democrats.

Senator INOUYE. Did you consider Mr. McGovern and Mr. Muskie your enemies?

Mr. BARKER. I have the greatest respect for Mr. McGovern as a Senator and as a Presidential candidate. I disagree personally with the kind of philosophy that I saw in a similar circumstance turn Cuba into a Communist state.

Senator INOUYE. However, you were willing to place Mr. McGovern in jeopardy, did you not to injure him?

Mr. BARKER. If we were successful in obtaining documents that implicated a foreign government of Cuba in the operation, if this hurt Mr. McGovern, it would be the nature of the evidence, not I. Mr. McGovern, to me, is as impersonal in that aspect as it would be when I was a bombardier in the Second World War in Germany and bombed a town. I have nothing, I do not know Mr. McGovern personally or any of these people. There is no personal grudge in anything, as I interpreted it.

Senator INOUYE. He is not your enemy?

Mr. BARKER. No, no; the man is not.

Senator INOUYE. My final question, sir. In the testimony you have presented to us this afternoon, have you attempted to protect Mr. Hunt?

Mr. BARKER. I have attempted to protect no one in that respect. I would not have to protect Mr. Hunt, sir. I do not understand the question.

If by this you mean—I would like to be clear—that if I am saying that Mr. Hunt asked me to plead guilty and I say that he did not, if this is what I am being asked, I am saying that Mr. Hunt never asked me this. I would not have to protect him in this. I am merely stating the truth.

Senator INOUYE. Did Mr. Hunt ever tell you to remain silent?

Mr. BARKER. No, sir; not in relation to anything concerning the Watergate, or——

Senator INOUYE. Is this not part of the discipline of your organization?

Mr. BARKER. To remain silent on matters regarding an operation, and so forth, yes; this is part of the discipline.

Senator INOUYE. In other words, you are supposed to give name, rank, and serial number—false name, that is?

Mr. BARKER. Yes, sir; that would cover it. False names in a sense that when you do a covert operation it is part of the system not to do it under your own name.

Senator INOUYE. Thank you very much, sir.

Mr. BARKER. Yes, sir.

Senator ERVIN. Senator Weicker.

Senator WEICKER. Mr. Barker, just a very few questions.

In the course of the Watergate operation, did you have in your possession a walkie-talkie?

Mr. BARKER. That is correct.

Senator WEICKER. Were you in communication with anybody over that walkie-talkie?

Mr. BARKER. Yes; I was.

Senator WEICKER. Can you identify who it was you were in communication with?

Mr. BARKER. One station was ours, one was Mr. Hunt's, and the other one was some headquarters.

Senator WEICKER. So, actually, there was you, there was Mr. Hunt with another walkie-talkie, and a third station. Is that correct?

Mr. BARKER. That is correct.

Senator WEICKER. Can you identify the third station?

Mr. BARKER. I cannot.

Senator WEICKER. Just two more questions. Do you look upon your jailing as an honor?

Mr. BARKER. I would like to state that I do not consider my being in jail for that matter or anything else that I have done a dishonor.

Senator WEICKER. And the last question, Mr. Barker. You say that in 1972, you were doing these things in the name of national security. Is that correct?

Mr. BARKER. This is the way it was originally given to me.

Senator WEICKER. And you say that in 1972, you justified these acts in the name of national security?

Mr. BARKER. I do not understand what you mean by justifying these acts. This original situation was never changed. I had no reason to think one way or another on that matter. It was never discussed.

Senator WEICKER. Now, Mr. Barker, it is 1973. Do you still feel that national security is a proper justification for Watergate?

Mr. BARKER. I feel it was a proper justification for Ellsberg and, although not in the same degree, I feel it was a justification for Watergate. But quite frankly, I am just a human being. I get confused about all these things. Sometimes I do not know the answers to these questions. I do not pretend to have all the answers, sir.

Senator WEICKER. Thank you, Mr. Barker.

Senator ERVIN. Senator Montoya.

Senator MONTOYA. Thank you, Mr. Chairman.

Mr. Barker, how long had it been since you had been in touch with Mr. Hunt prior to the time that he went down to Florida and left you a note?

Mr. BARKER. I beg your pardon, sir. I cannot see your face.

Senator MONTOYA. How long had it been since you had seen Mr. Hunt or communicated with him prior to the time that he went to Florida and left you a note?

Mr. BARKER. In the 10 years that passed between the Bay of Pigs invasion and the time that I had this note, I had occasional communications by mail from Mr. Hunt from—mostly from Spain. These were all of a personal nature.

Senator MONTOYA. And since that first visit to Miami, how many times did he go back to Florida to visit with you?

Mr. BARKER. It could have been anywhere between—I would say a dozen—a dozen times at least, in Miami, perhaps—maybe between 10 and 20, 12 or 24.

Senator MONTOYA. Now, did you, during any of those visits, discuss the probability of going into the Democratic National Committee headquarters or the McGovern headquarters or anywhere else other than the Ellsberg psychiatrist's office?

Mr. BARKER. I do not recall that at any visit in Miami, Mr. Hunt discussed with me either the McGovern or the Democratic headquarters. To the best of my recollection, Senator, this took place in Washington.

Senator MONTOYA. Then, why, when he invited you to lunch did you take Martinez with you and DeDiego? You mentioned a luncheon that you had.

Mr. BARKER. In April of 1971, when I went with Mr. Hunt to the area where they were commemorating the Bay of Pigs invasion. They had a statue down there that they were unveiling. Mr. Martinez at the time was with me, a salesman in my organization. He had been in the Bay of Pigs invasion, played a very prominent part in the naval activity. I presented him to Mr. Hunt at that time, to Edwardo at that time.

Senator MONTOYA. What about Mr. DeDiego?

Mr. BARKER. No, Mr. DeDiego was in it at that—I do not remember presenting Mr. DeDiego to Mr. Hunt.

Senator MONTOYA. I believe you mentioned him as one of the people who was at lunch?

Mr. BARKER. No, Mr. Martinez was at lunch.

Senator MONTOYA. All right, who was the other one?

Mr. BARKER. Mr. and Mrs. Hunt, my wife, and Mr. Martinez.

Senator MONTOYA. Now, when did you go to Mr. Martinez and Mr. DeDiego and recruit them for the Washington operation?

Mr. BARKER. Mr. Martinez and Mr. DeDiego were originally recruited for the Ellsberg operation. Subsequently, they participated in the Hoover security operation, and they were brought up with me for the double operation over the weekend of the Labor—the Memorial Day weekend.

Senator MONTOYA. Now, I believe you mentioned that up to that time, Mr. Hunt had not paid you any money?

Mr. BARKER. Mr. Hunt never paid me any money, nor was I ever hired, nor any of my Cubans were ever hired, or paid money in that sense of the word.

Senator MONTOYA. How did you pay for your expenses and how did the other individuals who came in from Florida pay their expenses, and how were the expenses paid when they went to California?

Mr. BARKER. In some cases, I received money before an operation to pay for these expenses. In other cases, I arranged for the tickets for the trip out of my American Express card.

Senator MONTOYA. Well, I am speaking of this: Did you receive any expenses for the two people who went to California or any expenses for them and for yourself to come to Washington?

Mr. BARKER. Well, like I said, in the California operation, to the best of my recollection, these expenses were covered after we got to California and a part of that was sent by mail to me in Miami. This differs from other operations.

I believe that, to the best of my recollection, in the Washington operation, I had been given an amount of money previously by Mr. Hunt and I went with Mr. Martinez to some agency and took out the tickets before. But——

Senator MONTOYA. How much were you given by Mr. Hunt?

Mr. BARKER. I don't remember what I was given for it at that time. I imagine it covered a certain amount of expenses. I have no——

Senator MONTOYA. Was that before the California trip?

Mr. BARKER. No, the California trip, I was not advanced any money. To the best of my recollection, all I did was take—buy the tickets out of my American Express. Then I was refunded.

Senator MONTOYA. Did you buy the tickets for Mr. Martinez and DeDiego and the other people who came in from Miami to Washington with your American Express card?

Mr. BARKER. No, I don't believe so.

Senator MONTOYA. Who paid their expenses?

Mr. BARKER. These expenses came out of the operational money, the accounting of which I would do with Mr. Hunt at the time.

Senator, I would like to explain to you and to the people who may believe that this seems strange. When you are doing a covert operation, a budget or expenses are cleared up at one particular time. They are taken care of and then they are forgotten about. You don't speak about that again. You don't remember them, you don't specify them except that at that time, you give an accounting. To try to remember the exact detail after 2 years, which was the operation where the money was given before that or later, I cannot recall that, sir.

Senator MONTOYA. The question I am asking you is: Did Mr. Hunt give you any money for yourself or for these other people prior to going to California or prior to coming to Washington, D.C.?

Mr. BARKER. In the case of California, to the best of my recollection, I was given no money prior. In the case of the trip to Washington, I believe that a certain amount of money, but I do not remember what amount, was given to me, because in those particular cases when we came to Washington, there was a larger number of people involved. And I don't remember——

Senator MONTOYA. All right.

Now, did Mr. Hunt tell you who he was working for at the time?

Mr. BARKER. Yes.

At the time, Mr. Hunt was a counselor at the White House. On one occasion, I remember that I had met Mr. Hunt at the executive building and went home for lunch with him.

Senator MONTOYA. And he mentioned the internal security aspects of the Ellsberg case with you, and it was with that motivation that you got into that.

Now, what did he mention to you about the Democratic National Committee headquarters and the McGovern headquarters other than the simple objective of going in there to find out what foreign governments had made contributions to either the Democratic National Committee or to Mr. McGovern?

Mr. BARKER. To the best of my recollection, Senator, the operation aspect was never discussed after that.

Senator MONTOYA. Well, didn't he mention to you that the reason that he wanted to go into the Democratic National Committee was to find out whether or not some foreign government had contributed to the Democratic Party?

Mr. BARKER. That is correct, yes, sir.

Senator MONTOYA. And it was your assignment to look at the documents as you went in and for Eugenio Martinez to follow as you gave him the documents with a little photography?

Mr. BARKER. That is correct.

Senator MONTOYA. Now, you stated in response to Senator Baker's question that you found no evidence in those documents that you saw of any contributions to the McGovern campaign or to the Democratic National Committee from any foreign government, and still you pursued the photography of the documents, did you not?

Mr. BARKER. That is correct.

Senator MONTOYA. Why did you?

Mr. BARKER. Because the documents that I uncovered, that I read, included names of persons and in one particular case, there was a series of notations of, they appeared to be money notations and, another document involved security.

Senator MONTOYA. Did it have the name of any foreign country?

Mr. BARKER. No, sir.

Senator MONTOYA. How did you connect it as being something very instrumental with respect to internal security?

Mr. BARKER. I don't understand the question. The documents that I photographed or had photographed were only photographed for the reasons that I believed at that time was the judgment which I had explained. I had stated that it was evident that the type of information that we were searching was not available at that particular office. So I just did the best I could under the circumstances.

Senator MONTOYA. Well, as a matter of fact, Mr. Barker, you went in there for the general purpose of political espionage and not internal security.

Mr. BARKER. Sir?

Senator MONTOYA. Isn't that right?

Mr. BARKER. That is not my honest interpretation.

Senator MONTOYA. Well, in view of the subsequent events and the subsequent disclosures would you agree with me now that it was, in fact, political espionage?

Mr. BARKER. I would respectfully disagree with the Senator.

Senator MONTOYA. Why do you? Now give me your response.

Mr. BARKER. Because, if my motivation was that which I have stated, and it was, there was no—there is no reason now to change that motivation, sir

Senator MONTOYA. All right.

Now, let us go into Mr. Hunt's employment at the White House.

Mr. BARKER. Yes, sir.

Senator MONTOYA. What led you to believe that because Mr. Hunt was working at the White House that this was a covert operation under CIA?

Mr. BARKER. This is stating that I thought this was a covert operation for CIA. I have never stated that this was a covert CIA operation. I have stated, sir, that it could or could not be a CIA operation since it was a national security matter, and the reason that I believe that Mr. Hunt had authority was, first by association, my previous association, with him as the highest Government representative in the Bay of Pigs, and the fact that he was at this time a member of the staff at the White House. I had no reason to think anything else in this matter.

Senator MONTOYA. Well, were you ever told by Mr. Hunt that the CIA would provide technical equipment for the operation?

Mr. BARKER. Mr. Hunt during this operation used equipment that was quite evident the same type used by the CIA. The documents that he had, the certain type of the equipment he informed me at the time that was obtained from CIA sources. But this did not mean that he was a CIA man. This was explained in the fact that the national security organization was above CIA and FBI. To the best of my knowledge, I am not saying that this is true or not, I am just saying as to what my thinking was in regard to the things that were said to me.

Senator MONTOYA. When you had a meeting with Mr. Hunt at the Hamilton Manger Hotel in Washington, D.C., preliminary to going over to the Watergate operation, did you at any time mention the McGovern headquarters and Democratic National Committee or ask him any specific questions as to what the entry into these two places would have—what relevancy it would have, with internal security?

Mr. BARKER. No, I never asked those questions.

Senator MONTOYA. Did you think about it? Did you speculate in your own mind about it?

Mr. BARKER. At that time and place I had no reason to speculate on these matters and I see no reason to change this at this time. I have tried to explain to the best of my ability, Senator, how we conducted these operations. In my concept they were as paramilitary operations as any previous operations I had been involved in, and that is not customary in a hierarchy to question your superiors. You either do it or you don't.

Senator MONTOYA. How can going into a political party office be construed as a paramilitary operation? By what stretch of the imagination do you reach that conclusion?

Mr. BARKER. The paramilitary operations is the procedure that was used.

Senator ERVIN. Senator, we have another witness we have to put on today because we had to get him excused from testifying in a court in Connecticut so he can get here and we want to try to finish.

Senator MONTOYA. I have just one final question, Mr. Chairman. Is it still your opinion that what you did was in the interests of national security?

Mr. BARKER. Today I am confused by all the information but I see no reason to condemn the nature of the assignment as was given to me at that time.

Senator MONTOYA. Thank you, Mr. Chairman.

Senator ERVIN. Your phone area code in Miami is 202?

Mr. BARKER. I think it is 302 or 305. I think it is 305, sir.

Senator ERVIN. Did you make five calls to the phone 202 area code, 333-0362, to the Committee To Re-Elect the President's offices in April and May and June 1972?

Mr. BARKER. To the best of my recollection I think, I could say definitively, but I think yes—those are, to the best of my recollection—those are phones that were included in that.

Senator ERVIN. Now every time that you arranged anything with your commanding officer, Mr. Hunt stayed at a distance, so if anybody was caught in the break-in he would not be one of them?

Mr. BARKER. I didn't understand that question.

Senator ERVIN. Mr. Hunt arranged for the break-ins and then when the time came for breaking in he decided that discretion was the better part of valor and he sent somebody else into danger and stayed away himself.

Mr. BARKER. Senator Ervin, I have the highest concept, personal concept of Mr. Hunt and Mr. Liddy, sir. I say this with all respect to you and the respect I owe my superior.

Senator ERVIN. But he stayed at a distance, didn't he, every time? When you broke into the Watergate every time and when you broke into the psychiatrist's office Mr. Hunt arranged for the breaking in but he never endangered himself, he never placed himself in a position where he would be arrested at the break-in, isn't that so?

Mr. BARKER. Yes, I guess in a way that is correct.

Senator ERVIN. Discretion is the better part of valor.

Any other questions?

You say that Mr. Hunt had not told you to keep silent. Had Mr. Hunt told you to keep silent would you have kept silent and not told us about it?

Mr. BARKER. Had Mr. Hunt told me to keep silent?

Senator ERVIN. Yes, sir.

Mr. BARKER. In what, sir?

Senator ERVIN. If he had told you to keep silent would you have kept silent and not told us that he had told you to keep silent? [Laughter.]

Mr. BARKER. That is a very confusing statement, sir. [Laughter.]

Senator ERVIN. Any further questions, if not, the witness is excused.

Thank you, Mr. Barker, for your testimony. He is excused.

Did you have something further you want to say?

Mr. BARKER. Yes, sir. I think it is only fair before I leave here to say that in a certain way the things that I have said do not represent me as a person. I am part of a team of men of whom I am very proud to have been associated with. Mainly I am speaking of my three associates from Miami. I think I have given a general description of Mr. Martinez. It is only fair now to state that Mr. Frank Sturgis, who by birth was Frank Fiorini, is a devoted anti-communist fighter, who was—who has voted against dictatorship, not only of the left but of the right, that he was the first person to turn against Castro after helping him with his revolution, that he has made innumerable raids over Cuba. That he had been captured in a Honduras Government—by the Honduras Government trying to infiltrate Cuba. That Mr. Gonzales was a member of the OA, Organizacion Authentica which—with an extensive background in the underground of Cuba; that all of these men are devoted family men who feel very deeply in a cause, and that I am not here as a person but as a part of a team, and that it would be unfair, in my concept, that these men were considered in anything but in the true light of the things that they believe in, that we all outside of reprimands by in some cases of Mr. Fiorini for having acted in these matters, your greatest previous crime before the Watergate were just simple photographic violations. That we are not criminal elements. That the word as a newspaper recently said, we are the world's best known burglars, the world's burglars we will have to live with. That we recently, very emotionally is the word, that we were hired. That there was no need to buy our silence. We are not for sale, and that this must be said because this represents our feelings. By this I don't mean that we are perfect, that we are not full of all sorts of defects as persons, that we consider ourselves superior beings to anyone. We are just plain people that very deeply believed that Cuba has a right to be free.

Thank you.

Senator ERVIN. The witness is excused, subject to being recalled later by the committee if it desires.

Thank you very much, Mr. Barker.

Will counsel call the next witness?

Mr. DASH. Will Mr. Baldwin please take the stand?

Senator ERVIN. Do you swear that the evidence that you shall give to the Senate Select Committee on Presidential Campaign Activities shall be the truth, the whole truth, and nothing but the truth, so help you God?

Mr. BALDWIN. I do.

Senator ERVIN. You are accompanied by an attorney. The attorney will please identify himself for the record, giving your name and your place, your office.

Mr. MIRTO. I am Robert Mirto, I practice law at 377 Main Street in Westhaven, Conn.

Mr. DASH. Just for the record, Mr. Baldwin, will you give your full name and address?

TESTIMONY OF ALFRED C. BALDWIN III; ACCOMPANIED BY ROBERT MIRTO, ATTORNEY

Mr. BALDWIN. Yes, sir. It is Alfred C. Baldwin III, 90 Mountainview Terrace, North Haven, Conn. We use a mail address of Hampton, Conn. 06517.

Mr. DASH. Mr. Chairman, I have no questions but I understand that the witness has a short statement to read and then I would like to waive questions and move on.

Will you read your statement, Mr. Baldwin?

Mr. BALDWIN. Thank you. To make a part of the record my understanding of my status in this total affair, I wish to read the following memorandum into the record at this time.

This memorandum was a memorandum prepared by my attorney, Robert Mirto; it is entitled "Memo to the File of Alfred C. Baldwin III."

It is written on July 6, 1972, at 4:40 a.m.

"On July 5, 1972, Robert C. Mirto, Esq., J. Terrance O'Grady, Esq., attorneys known to the Government to be representing Alfred C. Baldwin III, a suspect in the Watergate incident, met with Earl Silkert, Donald Campbell, and Seymour Glanzer, all assistant U.S. attorneys and represented to us to be the assistant U.S. attorneys handling the Watergate incident. A meeting was held at the U.S. district courthouse on the morning of July 5, 1972, at which time it was represented to us by the Government that Baldwin would not be a defendant in the Watergate matter if he cooperated. The Government attorneys stated that if they were satisfied with Baldwin's information he would not be indicted. Negotiations ceased at 12:30 p.m., so that O'Grady and I could talk to Baldwin. At 5:45 p.m., we notified the Government that Baldwin would cooperate. He identified two photographs from photographic spreads and generally told of his Watergate knowledge. He was again told, as we were, he would be a witness, not a defendant. He and O'Grady and I relied on this representation by the Government and plans were made for formal statements in the future. The conference terminated at 7:40 p.m. At the last showup conference were Campbell, Glanzer, Silkert, FBI agents Lanno and McKenna, O'Grady, Baldwin, I and two or three other persons not known to me by name but who I assumed to be either agents or members of the staff of assistant U.S. attorneys handling the matter. Signed, Robert C. Mirto, dated in the lower left-hand corner, July 6, 1972, 4:36 a.m."

Right below on this is an accurate account of the happenings of July 5, 1972, at the U.S. district courthouse room 3600–K and again signed Robert Mirto.

Mr. DASH. I have no further questions.

Mr. BALDWIN. I have one other thing. I am still relying on that promise today as I testify here and from the beginning of my decision to cooperate on June 25 to now, I have attempted to tell the whole truth of this incident to the Government. I believe that as I do now there is only one Government that I have talked truthful to the U.S. attorney, as I will do to this committee. I do not regret this decision, although my life was at that time shattered. I cannot now find employment and I have been without funds. My family has been disgraced. I believe that since I was working for the former Attorney General and White House officials I would not question to do what I was asked to do. Now, I regret only that decision. Regardless of this, I shall now follow through with my commitment to tell the Government and the American people the truth.

Senator BAKER. Mr. Chairman, would the witness read the first sentence of that statement again?

Mr. BALDWIN. To make it part of the record, my understanding of my status in this total affair, I wish to read the following memo into the record.

Senator BAKER. Would you continue?

Mr. BALDWIN. And then I read the memo, sir.

Senator BAKER. Yes, I know you did but you made a statement about the same agreement still obtains. Will you refer to that part of it, read that again for us?

Mr. BALDWIN. Yes, sir, I am still relying on that promise today.

Senator BAKER. What promise?

Mr. BALDWIN. On the promise of the U.S. attorneys that if I cooperated I would be a witness and not a defendant.

Senator BAKER. Do you concede then that you are here as a witness before a committee of the U.S. Senate?

Mr. BALDWIN. Yes, sir.

Senator BAKER. And any testimony you give us you will in effect, have immunity from prosecution by reason of the "agreement" made by the U.S. attorney.

Mr. MIRTO. If I may answer that, Senator, we were not given formal immunity. It was our feeling at the time of the conference with the U.S. attorneys that a promise not to prosecute on which we acted, would be sufficient for our purposes. We do not feel that there is any exposure since Mr. Baldwin has already spoken and testified on the fact which he will testify to today.

Senator BAKER. Well, I just want it clearly understood that no promise by the U.S. attorney is binding on this member of the committee.

Mr. BALDWIN. We realize that. We just, our statement, we feel, there is only one Government, and a promise from the U.S. attorney would bar any prosecution by the Government of the United States, that is our position and that is why we read the statement into the record.

Senator BAKER. Do you understand my position?

Mr. BALDWIN. Yes, I do, Senator.

Senator ERVIN. Your position is that since the Government promised that if you would cooperate that they would make you a witness and not a defendant, and that was the reason why you cooperated on the trial and the reason you are still cooperating.

Mr. BALDWIN. That is correct, Senator. And I also cooperated with other Senate committee members.

Mr. THOMPSON. I would like to defer questioning at the present time, Mr. Chairman.

Senator ERVIN. I will waive questions.

Senator BAKER. Senator Weicker has had an opportunity, Mr. Chairman, to interview this witness on one or more occasion; he is from Connecticut, and I would recommend, if I may, we defer to him from the outset.

Senator ERVIN. I certainly agree with you that would be an advisable course.

Senator WEICKER. Thank you, Senator Baker, Mr. Chairman, and members of the committee.

Mr. Baldwin, on May 1, 1972, you were contacted by James McCord with regard to employment, is that correct?

Mr. BALDWIN. That is correct, Senator.

Senator WEICKER. When Mr. McCord called you did he say how he had obtained your name?

Mr. BALDWIN. I do not recall if it was during the first conversation or a subsequent conversation the following day but he told me he had obtained my résumé from the Society of Ex-FBI Agents in New York City.

Senator WEICKER. Did he describe the work he wanted you to do?

Mr. BALDWIN. In the initial phone call he did not go into explicit details, said it was a matter of urgency and if it was possible to come to Washington where he would like to interview me but he did basically inform me that it would involve security work for the Committee To Re-Elect the President, and that particular time—in specific some services with Mrs. Martha Mitchell, the wife of the Attorney General.

Senator WEICKER. And did you go to Washington then on the next day, May 2?

Mr. BALDWIN. No, I went to Washington that night.

Senator WEICKER. That evening?

Mr. BALDWIN. That evening, yes sir.

Senator WEICKER. And you met with Mr. McCord on May 2?

Mr. BALDWIN. I met with him the following morning on May 2, that is correct.

Senator WEICKER. Now, on May 2, did you visit the Committee To Re-Elect the President?

Mr. BALDWIN. That is correct, I did.

Senator WEICKER. And as a result of that visit were you employed by the committee?

Mr. BALDWIN. Yes, I was.

Senator WEICKER. Would you describe to this committee your visit of May 2 to the Committee To Re-Elect the President?

Mr. BALDWIN. Well the early morning hours, I did not know at that time Mr. Hoover had passed away that morning and there was some confusion at the Committee To Re-Elect headquarters. What I had been told by Mr. McCord was the fact that Mrs. Mitchell would be departing that day for a trip to the Midwest. For approximately 2 hours or so it was undetermined whether or not she would make the trip. After it was determined that she would, Mr. McCord then took me to the office of Mr. LaRue. He——

Senator WEICKER. I beg your pardon, can you speak into the microphone more directly, Mr. Baldwin?

Mr. BALDWIN. After it was determined that Mrs. Mitchell would make the trip, I was taken to the office of Fred LaRue who, I was told, would have the final say whether or not I was hired.

Senator WEICKER. Did you meet Mr. LaRue?

Mr. BALDWIN. That is correct. I had a very brief interview with Mr. LaRue that lasted approximately 2 or 3 minutes.

Senator WEICKER. And was the decision to hire you made in your presence, or was it the moment you had met Mr. LaRue, or did you leave the room and become informed of the decision later?

Mr. BALDWIN. It was not in my presence, Mr. LaRue asked if I would mind waiting outside the office where Mr. McCord joined me in the outer office and he said, "It is all set, you are all set to go." I believe he might even have mentioned "You are on board," something like that.

Senator WEICKER. Would it be fair to describe your hiring as having been accomplished by a combination of initially Jim McCord with the final say-so by Mr. LaRue?

Mr. BALDWIN. Well, I was interviewed by Mr. McCord but Mr. McCord in the presence of Mr. LaRue it was obvious Mr. LaRue was making the decision.

Senator WEICKER. Now, at the time that or after you were hired, on that particular day, were you given a weapon?

Mr. BALDWIN. That is correct, I was issued a .38 snub-nosed revolver, Smith and Wesson.

Senator WEICKER. Would you describe to the committee that particular event, was that on the same day of May 2?

Mr. BALDWIN. That is correct, after we left Mr. LaRue's office. This occurred in the security office adjacent to the main reception room on the third floor of the Republican headquarters there on Pennsylvania Avenue.

Mr. McCord went over to a file cabinet and removed the weapon either from the first or second drawer of the file cabinet and stated "You will need this while you are with Mrs. Mitchell. You know how to use one of these."

Senator WEICKER. So, in other words, it is your testimony to this committee that Mr. McCord gave you the .38.

Mr. BALDWIN. That is correct, he did.

Senator WEICKER. Now, can you tell me what actually happened to that weapon?

Mr. BALDWIN. I retained possession of that weapon through the trip. When I returned to Washington, I had possession of that weapon. There was another scheduled on the Thursday of the week we returned, I believe we returned on May 8 and I think, I believe Mrs. Mitchell was scheduled to go out on another trip that Thursday. I was told that the decision whether or not I would go with her had not been reached yet but in all likelihood would be going with her to keep the weapon in my possession. I had to leave to go back to Connecticut to get more clothing so the weapon stayed with me back to Connecticut. When I returned from Connecticut, Mr. McCord advised me that Mr. LaRue would be going with Mrs. Mitchell and he had other work for me to do, and at that time he said, I believe, it was "Have you still got the weapon?" I said, "Yes." We went downstairs to the Roger Smith Hotel. Outside the barber shop he took it.

Senator WEICKER. So the weapon was returned then to Mr. McCord?

Mr. BALDWIN. That is correct.

Senator WEICKER. On May 2, were there any others that you were introduced to, any individuals that you were introduced to at the Committee To Re-Elect the President?

Mr. BALDWIN. Yes, Mr. LaRue's office is in a cubicle where I believe Mr. Magruder's office is and I also met Mr. Odle. As Mr. Magruder passed through from his office, I was introduced to Mr. Magruder. I do not believe I was introduced to Mr. Odle, but I believe Mr. McCord pointed him out to me and he pointed out several other individuals. I was being introduced mainly to the security force that was at the headquarters. I met some people in Mr. Mitchell's law offices. I was taken around to Mrs. Mitchell's office, introduced to different people at each one of these offices, as I would be going with Mrs. Mitchell as her bodyguard, I was coming aboard. Several individuals were pointed out to me.

Senator WEICKER. Was it indicated to you at that time, as to the terms of your appointment, specifically how you would be paid?

Mr. BALDWIN. That question came up originally, Senator, on the night Mr. McCord telephoned me, because on the résumé that was submitted with the Ex-Agents Society, I had listed the general salary for the year. Mr. McCord—I asked him about the salary. He told me because of the fact that I mentioned to him that there would be no sense in wasting your time and my time if the employment was not in the salary range that I was seeking, he did say there would be a discrepancy, that it would involve a matter of approximately $70 a day while I was with Mrs. Mitchell and there would be a different rate when I was not working with Mrs. Mitchell. However, I was paid the same rate at all times.

Senator WEICKER. Did you believe at that time that your employer was the Committee To Re-Elect the President?

Mr. BALDWIN. Absolutely.

Senator WEICKER. Do you have any documents in your possession which you believe to be supportive of that opinion?

Mr. BALDWIN. No, I have documents in my possession that are contradictory of that position. It was my understanding prior to the criminal trials that efforts were being made to disown me from the committee and as a matter of fact, I have a——

Senator WEICKER. I intend to get into that—I am just trying to keep this in the logical sequence.

Mr. BALDWIN. No, all the application forms——

Senator WEICKER. Do you have in your possession a check from the Finance Committee To Re-Elect the President, or rather, a Xerox copy of a check issued by the Finance Committee To Re-Elect the President?

Mr. BALDWIN. That is correct. I received the check and cashed it and I did make a photostat of the check.

Senator WEICKER. Would you go ahead and present that to the committee?

Mr. BALDWIN. Yes.

Senator WEICKER. Is there any other document that you have in your possession which again would indicate your employment by the Finance Committee To Re-Elect the President?

Mr. BALDWIN. I have what is entitled schedule D, itemized expenditures, personal service, loans, and transfers, and under events, it says, "The Finance Committee To Re-Elect the President", itemized listing, for a period of, I believe it is August 1 through August 8, 1972, and on that, my name appears.

Senator WEICKER. All right, and what is the amount listed beside your name?

Mr. BALDWIN. It is listed $429.84.

Senator WEICKER. For travel expense?

Mr. BALDWIN. That is what the purpose of the expenditure under the column "Purpose of expenditure," that is correct.

Senator WEICKER. What travel expense do you believe that to refer to?

Mr. BALDWIN. I was told this was reimbursement for traveling expense incurred while with Mrs. Mitchell. This figure coincides with a figure that I submitted regarding her expenditures, spent on the trip.

Senator WEICKER. So in other words, you believe this figure listed on schedule D and also set forth on the check from the Finance Committee To Re-Elect the President as coinciding with a voucher which you submitted for travel expenses attendant to your trip with Mrs. Mitchell, is that correct?

Mr. BALDWIN. That is correct, a combination of her expenses and my expenses.

Senator WEICKER. Have you presented a copy of schedule D to the committee?

I would appreciate it, Mr. Chairman, if both of these items could be in the record.

Senator ERVIN. Let the record show that Xerox copies of the check and voucher are made exhibits with appropriate numbers.

[The documents referred to were marked exhibits Nos. 14 and 15*]

Senator WEICKER. As your first assignment, did you make a trip to Detroit and Westchester County as a bodyguard for Mrs. Mitchell?

* See pp. 455, 456.

Mr. BALDWIN. That is correct.

Senator WEICKER. And returned from that trip on May 8?

Mr. BALDWIN. That is correct, we did.

Senator WEICKER. On that trip on May 8, or at any other time, were you informed by anyone that you had been fired by the Committee To Re-Elect?

Mr. BALDWIN. I have never received any official notification from anyone up to this date.

Senator WEICKER. Did you at any time return to the office of Mr. LaRue and receive from him notification of termination of appointment?

Mr. BALDWIN. No, I did not.

Senator WEICKER. Now, then, to move to May 12, Mr. Baldwin, did you return to Connecticut at that time?

Or rather, did you return from Connecticut after the 8th?

Mr. BALDWIN. I returned approximately on the 9th to Connecticut, yes sir.

Senator WEICKER. And back to Washington on May 12?

Mr. BALDWIN. That is correct.

Senator WEICKER. Would you briefly describe your assignments between May 12 and May 23, when you again returned to Connecticut?

Mr. BALDWIN. On my return to Washington, I was advised that Mr. LaRue would be going with Mrs. Mitchell on the trip to Nebraska and that Mr. McCord wanted me to perform other functions in the Washington, D.C., area which would cover surveillance activity. At that time, I do not believe there was any specific organization, but on a day-to-day basis, he would give me instructions where to go and what type of activities to perform.

Senator WEICKER. Where were you housed at this time?

Mr. BALDWIN. On my return back, I stayed at the—I believe it is the Roger Smith, a block up from the committee headquarters. Mr. McCord advised me that he would like me then to move to the Howard Johnson, where he had obtained a room, and that to cut down expenses, I should stay in the Howard Johnson.

Senator WEICKER. I do not want to have us get ahead of ourselves here.

On May 12, you were still at the Roger Smith Hotel, is that correct?

Mr. BALDWIN. On my return from Connecticut, I stayed at the Roger Smith, that is correct.

Senator WEICKER. And Mr. McCord would come to the Roger Smith and give you instructions?

Mr. BALDWIN. That is correct. We had breakfast meetings.

Senator WEICKER. What did those instructions consist of?

Mr. BALDWIN. The first instructions were to move to the Howard Johnson and he would brief me. There was a planned news conference on that Friday when Rennie Davis was due in town and he wanted me to go to the news conference and obtain any information I could.

Senator WEICKER. In order that we not take overly much time, would it be fair to state that during the period between May 12 and May 23, you were principally engaged in surveillance of various activities, organizations, and occurrences in the Washington, D.C., area?

Mr. BALDWIN. That is correct, sir.

96-296 O—73——bk. 1—26

Senator WEICKER. Now, at any time, were you sent to the Capitol area to conduct these surveillances?

Mr. BALDWIN. I believe it was the day after Governor Wallace was shot that I was instructed to go to the Capitol rotunda, where there were planned sit-ins.

Senator WEICKER. During this period of time, were you sent to areas outside the offices of various Senators and Congressmen to observe persons in those areas?

Mr. BALDWIN. That is correct.

Senator WEICKER. Now, Mr. Baldwin, would you try to the best of your ability to recall these areas or the specific offices to which you went in order to observe persons?

Mr. BALDWIN. I am going to do some great injustice to some of the Representatives, I am sure, with their names. But I know I went to Senator Kennedy's office.

Senator WEICKER. Why did you go to Senator Kennedy's office?

Mr. BALDWIN. On one particular day at the Capitol, a large number of demonstrators had been receiving Senate passes to the gallery area. This was also the day that the three astronauts appeared and the information circulating amongst the different security officers up there was that the passes were being issued by, I believe it was Senator Kennedy's office, and I am not sure he—it might have been Senator Gravel's office at that time. On one of my phone calls to Mr. McCord, I advised him of this and he then advised me to go to the Senator's office to determine what groups were in the area, how the passes were being handed out and distributed, who was doing it, obtain any literature that was being handed out, basically try to determine what groups were in the area of the Senator's office. That is on that particular day.

Senator WEICKER. Now, you mentioned Senator Kennedy's office and possibly also Senator Gravel's office. Were there any other Representatives or Senators whose offices you recall going to in order to observe persons moving about on that day?

Mr. BALDWIN. Representatives from New York. I believe it was Bella Abzug—I do not know if my pronunciation is correct on that—and Representative Chisholm. I believe——

Senator WEICKER. At any time, did you visit the office of Senator Muskie?

Mr. BALDWIN. To the best of my recollection, I do not recall being in the area of Senator Muskie's office.

Senator WEICKER. Senator McGovern?

Mr. BALDWIN. No; those names I do not recall.

Senator WEICKER. Senator Javits?

Mr. BALDWIN. That is correct, because it is Mr. Javits of New York.

Senator WEICKER. Senator Proxmire?

Mr. BALDWIN. That is correct.

Senator WEICKER. Congressman Koch?

Mr. BALDWIN. If he is the gentleman from New York, I believe that possibly is one of the other gentlemen from New York.

Senator WEICKER. All right. Aside from that type of surveillance, did you also engage in the surveillance of demonstrations in the Capitol area?

Mr. BALDWIN. I participated in the demonstrations in the Capitol; that is correct.

I am sorry. My attorney reminded me there was also Representative McCloskey.

Senator WEICKER. Representative McCloskey's office was another one?

Mr. BALDWIN. That is right.

Senator WEICKER. You have already mentioned Rennie Davis' news conference, the surveillance on the Hill. At any time, did you leave Capitol Hill to engage in surveillance activities?

Mr. BALDWIN. There was a planned demonstration at Andrews Air Force Base the day that the President was leaving for Moscow, on a Saturday morning.

Senator WEICKER. Who instructed you to go to Andrews Air Force Base?

Mr. BALDWIN. Mr. McCord.

Senator WEICKER. Did you receive, in other words, your instructions from Mr. McCord as to your surveillance activities and where they should take place?

Mr. BALDWIN. That is correct.

Senator WEICKER. Now, at the time of your return on May 12, you have already stated you moved to room 419 at the Howard Johnson's on Virginia Avenue, across from the Watergate. In whose name was the room registered?

Mr. BALDWIN. I did not know that—McCord had just advised me that he had a room there, but subsequently, when I went downstairs to ask for mail, I was told it was under the name of McCord Associates, and I gave the desk clerk my name and asked if any mail was received, to put it into McCord Associates' room.

Senator WEICKER. Now, there have been reports that in fact, you are not employed by the Committee To Re-Elect the President, and you have stated here already that you believe you were employed by the Committee To Re-Elect the President. Did any event during this period of time serve to confirm that belief in your mind?

Mr. BALDWIN. Well, I was instructed that if at any time I was stopped by any Government agency or law enforcement body regarding the weapon or regarding my presence in a particular area, that I was to do two things: No. 1, advise them that I worked for the Committee To Re-Elect the President; that I was in the security office of that department; and if that did not work, to go on and say that I was working for former Attorney General Mitchell. Then, as a last resort, I had Mr. McCord's business card that said, "James McCord, Director of Security, Committee To Re-Elect the President," and a telephone number. I was to give the person that card and they would call and verify it.

So, on at least three or four occasions, that process had to be followed, where I had to identify myself.

Senator WEICKER. When you say three or four occasions, can you state to the committee several of those occasions when you had to use Mr. McCord's card and telephone number as a means of identifying yourself?

Mr. BALDWIN. I had no authority to carry the weapons, so when I flew home to Connecticut, I would declare the weapon and I was flying Allegheny Airlines. So every time I would fly, I would have to declare the weapon. They would verify the fact, they would call right in front of me the ticket agent, and the manager would come out, usually from the office, and they would make a call. They would say, no problem and hand the gun back to me.

Another time I was questioned by the FBI liaison officer on Capitol Hill. He verified it.

Then the day at Andrews Air Force Base, I was stopped by the air security police and they had to call down to committee headquarters and verify. On all occasions, I was told I was OK, all my items of identity were returned to me and I was on my way.

Senator WEICKER. Were you given any sort of identification pin as belonging to the Committee To Re-Elect the President?

Mr. BALDWIN. Yes, I was. I was issued a lapel pin. It was red and white in appearance, had an eagle on it. This pin allowed me——

Senator WEICKER. Where is that pin now?

Mr. BALDWIN. That was turned over to the U.S. attorney prior to the criminal trial.

Senator WEICKER. Now, Mr. Baldwin, to keep on giving the continuity here, you interrupt me or state if I am incorrect, you returned to Connecticut on May 23 and came back to Washington on May 26, is that correct?

Mr. BALDWIN. That is correct, Friday.

Senator WEICKER. And you returned to room 419 of the Howard Johnsons on May 26. Now, when you entered room 419 on May 26, what did you see?

Mr. BALDWIN. When I entered the room, there were numerous items of electronic equipment in the room. When I entered the room, it was approximately 2 in the afternoon, I believe, about that hour. Mr. McCord was in the room and operating one of the receiver units. At that time, I did not know what it was. He explained it.

Senator WEICKER. In other words, this was the first time that you had seen electronic equipment in room 419 of the Howard Johnsons?

Mr. BALDWIN. This particular piece of equipment that he was working on, that was the first time I had seen that. On the couch there was a piece of electronic equipment which was containing the briefcase that had been described to me, that I had previously seen at the Committee To Re-Elect the President headquarters. This was called the debugger, had a monitoring unit.

Senator WEICKER. In other words, you had seen a portion of the equipment?

Mr. BALDWIN. A portion I had seen previous.

Senator WEICKER. At the Committee To Re-Elect the President?

Mr. BALDWIN. That is correct. But the equipment he was working on when I entered the room, I had never seen that before.

Senator WEICKER. And as you entered the room, Mr. McCord was in the process of what—experimenting with this equipment? What did he indicate to you at the time you entered the room?

Mr. BALDWIN. He was tuning this equipment. The unit was operating and he was working the tuning dials. There are several tuning dials on the piece of equipment.

Senator WEICKER. Did you have any questions of him as to exactly what was going on at that time?

Mr. BALDWIN. No, I had just driven approximately 6 hours and he said, "As soon as you get unpacked and relaxed, I will explain this." I said, "All right, I will take a shower and shave and join you."

Senator WEICKER. Now, Mr. Baldwin, was there a sequence of events leading up to a visit by other persons to the room that afternoon?

Mr. BALDWIN. Well, I was told that some other individuals would be coming into the room. They were part of the security force and in view of their position, they would be introduced under aliases to me and that I would also be introduced in this way. He said, there is no reflection on you, but because of the nature of the work you are involved in, I am going to use an alias for you and an alias for them. I will be introducing them——

Senator WEICKER. What was the alias he gave to you?

Mr. BALDWIN. He asked me to use the alias of Bill Johnson, the alias I used when I was calling in reports on my surveillance operation.

Senator WEICKER. Would you like to continue your narrative to the committee as to what happened that afternoon?

Mr. BALDWIN. Are you asking me regarding the introductions of the individuals that came to the room, Senator?

Senator WEICKER. I gather from what you told the committee, that you were already told there would be a visit by individuals from the Committee To Re-Elect the President?

Mr. BALDWIN. That is correct. Two individuals came into the room and when they entered the room, Mr. McCord turned to me and he said at this point—he introduced me. "Al," he said, and I believe he said "Ed," and then he got all confused because he had not used the aliases.

Senator WEICKER. He had not used the aliases which you were supposed to use?

Mr. BALDWIN. That is correct. He said—I do not know if he said at that point, "Ed, go in—" he had to retract. Then he had to introduce me under my alias and he could not remember, then he just introduced us under our personal names.

Senator WEICKER. Now, subsequently, have you identified who those two men were who came in the room?

Mr. BALDWIN. That is correct, and at the FBI photographic display, they were identified as Mr. Liddy and Mr. Hunt.

Senator WEICKER. That same evening, May 26, was there a trip to McGovern headquarters?

Mr. BALDWIN. That is correct; there was.

Senator WEICKER. Would you describe to the committee that trip and the evening's activity at McGovern headquarters?

Mr. BALDWIN. Well, the purpose of my returning from Connecticut was to work that weekend. Mr. McCord advised me that we would have to work that weekend. I did not know we were going into McGovern headquarters until we arrived at the scene. Prior to arriving there, we stopped to buy some batteries. He sent me in to buy them, then we proceeded to McGovern headquarters.

As we went by the McGovern headquarters, he pointed to a building, said, this is what we are interested in, we have got to meet some people here. Then he proceeded to explain that we have to find our individual; one of our men is here. He will be in a yellow Volkswagen, keep your eyes open for the Volkswagen, for the man sitting in it—I believe he even mentioned "boy." I do not think he said "man"; he said there is a boy sitting in a Volkswagen.

He said, "We have one of our people inside the headquarters." The problem was there was a man standing outside the headquarters, which was a second-story headquarters above—I believe there were stores—there was a chain across them.

This individual was there. This was late in the evening, approximately 1 or 2 o'clock in the early morning hours, and Mr. McCord was quite upset by the fact that this individual was standing in front of the door. He had no business being there, according to Mr. McCord. He should not have been there.

Senator WEICKER. Did you meet any other individuals at that particular address?

Mr. BALDWIN. That is correct. Mr. McCord had been in communication over a walkie-talkie unit with some other individuals and at one point, as we proceeded down the same street that McGovern's headquarters is located on, we stopped adjacent to a light-colored car. An individual alighted from the car, came into the front seat of Mr. McCord's car. I slid over so I was between Mr. McCord and this individual.

Senator WEICKER. Can you tell me who that individual was?

Mr. BALDWIN. That was Mr. Liddy.

Senator WEICKER. And did you succeed in getting into the McGovern headquarters on that evening?

Mr. BALDWIN. No, they drove around. Mr. McCord and Mr. Liddy did all the talking and they drove around, I do not know the exact length of time. But it was over a half hour. As a matter of fact, we drove up the alleyway adjacent to the building. There was a problem of lights. They discussed whether or not their man was inside. There were several problems. Mr. McCord said, we will abort the mission.

Senator WEICKER. What was your primary job during the first 2 weeks of June? We have moved now from the end of May to the first week of June.

Mr. BALDWIN. I was instructed to monitor all telephone conversations that were being received over these units that were in the Howard Johnson room and to make a log of all units.

Senator WEICKER. With reference to overheard telephone conversation and excluding anything to do with personal lives of those who were overheard, can you tell the committee the content of any conversations of a political nature?

Senator ERVIN. Senator? I am afraid we made a mistake when we passed the Omnibus Crime Act. It may be illegal for him to say anything about the conversation. I think maybe we were very foolish when Congress passed that law, but I believe it is the law.

Mr. BALDWIN. I will decline to answer that respectfully, Senator, based on 18 section 2515, prohibition of the use of evidence of intercepted wire or oral communications, which specifically states under this Federal statute that if I divulge those contents, I am subject to possible prosecution.

Senator ERVIN. On that basis I would suggest you not ask him.

Senator WEICKER. About how many calls did you monitor?

Mr. BALDWIN. Approximately 200.

Senator WEICKER. Will you describe how you recorded them?

Mr. BALDWIN, Initially, the first day, it was on a yellow legal pad. Mr. McCord took the actual log and copy that I had made. Subsequently, he returned to the room, I believe it was on Labor Day Monday, with an electric typewriter. He asked me to transcribe my notes into typewritten form, making up duplicate copies, an original and an onionskin. That is what I proceeded to do.

Senator WEICKER. Then, who would you transmit those logs to, Mr. McCord?

Mr. BALDWIN. Mr. McCord received both the original and onionskin, that is correct.

Senator WEICKER. At any time, did you hand those logs to individuals other than Mr. McCord?

Mr. BALDWIN. The one incident where I was telephoned from Miami and told to deliver the logs to the Republican headquarters, the Committee To Re-Elect the President, on Pennsylvania Avenue, which I did.

Senator WEICKER. Now, during these first 2 weeks in June, did you engage in any other activities? Physically, did you go over to the Democratic National Committee?

Mr. BALDWIN. That is correct, I did.

Senator WEICKER. Would you describe that particular incident?

Mr. BALDWIN. Mr. McCord appeared in the room on Monday, I believe it was the 12th of June, and advised me that—well, he furnished me a $100 bill and said, you are going to have a ball this week, here. I am going to go over to the restaurant. I want you to hang around in the cocktail lounge, the restaurant, do visual surveillance of anybody from the Democratic headquarters. He gave me a pretext to take a tour of the Democratic headquarters.

I did not agree with his approach and I asked him if I could do it a different way. I followed that way and I was given a tour of the Democratic headquarters that day.

Senator WEICKER. Prior to the weekend of June 16 did Mr. McCord discuss the plans for the rest of that weekend and any subsequent plans?

In other words, what was the schedule of events for the weekend of June 16?

Mr. BALDWIN. Well, after the tour, Senator, of the McGovern headquarters it was obvious that Mr. Lawrence O'Brien was not in the Washington area, that he had been to Miami and was working in Miami.

Senator WEICKER. May I ask you this question, Mr. Baldwin, are you talking about McGovern headquarters or the Democratic National Committee?

Mr. BALDWIN. I am talking about the Democratic National Committee headquarters. After my tour there part of the information I received there Mr. O'Brien had not been in Washington for the past month or so or longer. He had been in Miami and Mr. McCord was quite pleased to hear this. And it appeared to me that it called for a rescheduling of the timetable because he got quite upset with the fact that I would have to, he would try to make some arrangement for me to go to Miami. He had already discussed with me the fact that I would be going to both the Democratic and the Republican Conventions but in view of this information that Mr. O'Brien was in Miami, this seemed to change his timetable for the rest of the week. That week at several different points he told me he would like to get my identification sewed up and get me down to Miami. He had to confer with some other individuals regarding this, so if I was approved I would be going to Miami.

Senator WEICKER. Now, on June 16, at around 4:30 p.m., did Mr. McCord appear in the room at the Howard Johnson?

Mr. BALDWIN. Yes, he appeared at Howard Johnson.

Senator WEICKER. What were your activities and his activities between 4:30 in the afternoon and 10 o'clock in the evening?

Mr. BALDWIN. Do you want every detail, Senator?

Senator WEICKER. I would like you to tell in a broad narrative sense the committee as to what he did.

Mr. BALDWIN. He gave me several instructions to buy some items for him, which I did, try to obtain some batteries, regular flashlight batteries, and what he called speaker wire which is regular wire.

I couldn't get the wire, so subsequently he left the room and went out. Part of the activity, he tested some type of a device on the phone. He tested a freestanding device next to the television, the—it has on it, fire alarm unit on it, I believe. So based—and I did some soldering of some batteries together during the course of that time.

He made phone calls, I believe, received one or two phone calls in the room. It was that general activity up to the point where he decided—the difficulty was there was a gentleman working in the Democratic committee.

Senator WEICKER. Did you know at that time he had planned to go into the Democratic National Committee?

Mr. BALDWIN. No, not until he was on the phone at one point that he said, "We still can't go over there because there is somebody working," and then I looked across and there was somebody working in the Democratic headquarters. He then told me, "We don't know whether we are going to abort." Approximately a half hour or so later this individual left and the decision was made to go across the street.

Senator WEICKER. At 10 p.m., then, was it your contention that Mr. McCord left the room?

Mr. BALDWIN. I don't know the exact time—no, no, he left later than 10 p.m.; you mean to go to the Democratic headquarters?

Senator WEICKER. Yes.

Mr. BALDWIN. He left at one point to go buy some equipment at a radio discount store or some place and then returned and then subsequent to that he again went across, then he left to go to the—across the street to the Democratic National Committee.

Senator WEICKER. Did he give you any instructions as to what your role would be on that particular evening?

Mr. BALDWIN. The only instructions that I received was just prior to him leaving, he removed a walkie-talkie unit, I believe hooked onto his belt or he had it inside a belt loop, put it on the table next to the television set and he said:

> I am going across the street, we have got some people over there, I want you to watch. If you see anything, anything at all, any activity get on this unit and let us know.

That was it. He didn't tell me any type of a radio call to use. He didn't tell me any type of a code name. That was the sum extent of his instructions.

Senator WEICKER. In other words, would it be safe to say that he asked you to report over the walkie-talkie any unusual activity but without specifying what it was that he was going to do or what the operation in the Watergate was going to be?

Mr. BALDWIN. He said: "Anything you see, any activity you see, across the street you just get on this unit and let us know," and with that he walked out of the room.

Senator WEICKER. Now, Mr. Baldwin, in your own narrative, describe to the committee your role and what you observed in the early morning hours of June 17.

Mr. BALDWIN. The first thing I observed was, while I was on the balcony, just standing on the balcony, it was a beautiful night, I was out there——

Senator WEICKER. Is this balcony, Mr. Baldwin, as we take a look at the picture, on the seventh floor?

Mr. BALDWIN. Room 723, that is correct.

Senator WEICKER. Of the Howard Johnson Motel?

Mr. BALDWIN. That is correct.

Senator WEICKER. Please continue.

Mr. BALDWIN. And I observed the guard, there was a guard standing in front of the building at 2600 directly across the Watergate complex. I was watching this individual when a car stopped and three men alighted and proceeded inside the headquarters. I didn't really pay any attention. The gentlemen——

Senator WEICKER. Mr. Baldwin, again I don't want you to get ahead of yourself, you were out on the balcony?

Mr. BALDWIN. That is correct.

Senator WEICKER. Following the general instruction——

Mr. BALDWIN. That is correct.

Senator WEICKER [continuing]. Of Mr. McCord to observe anything unusual, is that correct?

Mr. BALDWIN. That is correct.

Senator WEICKER. The walkie-talkie was inside the room?

Mr. BALDWIN. That is correct.

Senator WEICKER. Now, did you hear any conversations, prior to the arrival——

Mr. BALDWIN. No, sir.

Senator WEICKER [continuing]. Of any car or any individual?

Mr. BALDWIN. No, sir, I did not.

Senator WEICKER. You did not.

Did you observe anything across the way that was unusual?

Mr. BALDWIN. No, sir.

Senator WEICKER. In the way of lights going on or off?

Mr. BALDWIN. No, sir.

Senator WEICKER. Did you see any individuals?

Mr. BALDWIN. I saw lights go on, I believe it was just at about, subsequent to or just around, the time of the arrival of the three gentlemen. I do remember observing the three gentlemen leaving the car and going into the building.

Senator WEICKER. All right. Pick it up from there. There were no observations up until the time the car arrived and these three gentlemen got out, right?

Mr. BALDWIN. The first thing that really stuck in my mind was the eighth floor of the building the lights went on on the entire eighth floor and when the lights went on on the eighth floor I went inside and I picked up the walkie-talkie, and not knowing whether to say, "Unit 1 to base 1" or how to call I just picked up the walkie-talkie and I believe I used both designations, you know, unit 1, I might have even said, "Base headquarters, base 1, to any unit, do you read me?" And the voice came on, back, "I read you, go on. What have you got."

I said, "The lights just went on on the entire eighth floor."

They said, "We know about that that is the 2 o'clock guard check." They said, "OK, let us know if anything else happens."

I put the walkie-talkie down and I proceeded out on the balcony again. I noticed the light flicker on the sixth floor of the Democratic headquarters to the extreme right. They just went on briefly and went off. I went back inside and picked up the walkie-talkie and was standing in the doorway when I observed these individuals coming out on the balcony of the Democratic National Committee.

Senator WEICKER. Which individuals are you referring to?

Mr. BALDWIN. There were two individuals. Do you want me to describe them?

Senator WEICKER. I want you to describe to the committee what you saw that night.

Mr. BALDWIN. One individual had on what I would call a windbreaker, appeared to have a university emblem and a university written across one of the pockets, the chest area. The other individual had a weapon out and, both of them were casually dressed. One individual had sort of long blond hair, a stocky built individual.

As I observed them I called over the walkie-talkie again "Base 1, unit 1, are our people in suits or are they dressed casually?" And the call came back, "Our people are dressed in suits. Why?"

I said, "You have some trouble because there are some individuals out here who are dressed casually and have got their gun out," and the guy on the other end went a little bit frantic. [Laughter.]

I put the walkie-talkie down and I continued to hear "Are you reading us? Are you telling us? Hello, hello."

I knew they were not calling me, I stood out on the balcony and watched as they continued to search the building, a third individual had turned the lights on and there were three now searching.

Senator WEICKER. Were you able to observe anyone else on the street below?

Mr. BALDWIN. I don't directly recall at that specific point, Senator, in time right now.

Senator WEICKER. Why don't you continue your narrative then?

Mr. BALDWIN. Well, the individuals then went into the office and proceeded to the left of the building and as they passed through, the corridor light was on and as they passed by various office doors eventually they went out of sight and I didn't see them.

I believe it was about this time that a voice came over the unit that said, "They have got us," a whisper something like, "They have got us," and then what I believe was Mr. McCord's voice in the distance saying, "Are you gentlemen metropolitan police?" or something to that effect.

Then another voice came on, he said, "Are you still across the street?" and I thought if somebody is listening, you know, I didn't know what was going on, I said, "Yes, I am," and they said, "Well, we will be right over."

Subsequently to that I saw two individuals walking out between the Watergate building directly across and the one closest to the Capitol Building, they came out an alleyway.

Senator WEICKER. Can you identify those two individuals?

Mr. BALDWIN. One of the gentlemen looked up at me, I was still on the balcony, he was Mr. Sturgis. The other individual was dressed in a windbreaker and I believe casual shirt. The other gentleman was dressed in a suit and from my observation he didn't look up but I had the belief it was Mr. Liddy.

Senator WEICKER. Did you see Mr. Hunt go over to the Howard Johnson Motel?

Mr. BALDWIN. They walked up in front of this far complex, almost directly in front of that lobby, got into a car and proceeded up the street and as soon as they went in the car another voice came over the walkie-talkie and said, "I am on my way," and approximately 2 or 3 minutes later Mr. Hunt came into the room.

Senator WEICKER. All right, Mr. Hunt came into the room.

Will you describe Mr. Hunt's entry into the room?

Mr. BALDWIN. Everything?

Senator WEICKER. Everything.

Mr. BALDWIN. Well, he proceeded over and I was standing there in the balcony area and he crouched down behind a table and said, "What is going on, what is going on?" And just about this time they were leading Mr. McCord and the other gentleman out of the lobby and there were all kinds of police cars there and I was standing on the balcony, "C'mon, see."

He says, "I have got to use the bathroom."

He went into the bathroom and he came out and he said, "I have got to call a lawyer, where is your phone?" I said, "It is right there." And he went over, he dialed a direct dial number because in the motel room if you want to place a long distance call you have to go through the desk, so he dialed 8 as I would do when I would dial a local number and he dialed a direct number. I paid no attention to the conversation. I proceeded to the balcony, continued to watch and, I did hear him say, "I have $5,000 cash on me now, Al, for bail or bonds if you need it," and something to the effect, "will you go right down or should I go down," and I believe that was it. He then proceeded to give me instructions what to do with the equipment.

Senator WEICKER. What were those instructions?

Mr. BALDWIN. Well, he removed a walkie-talkie, put it on the bed, and told me to pack up everything, I believe his expresstion was "Get it the hell out of here, get yourself the hell out of here, go somewheres. Where are you going to go?"

I said, "Well, I am going to Connecticut."

He said, "Well, go." He said, "We will be in touch, you will get further instructions." He said, "I want you to take all of this equipment to Mr. McCord's house."

I had a little debate with him about that, I said, "Well, there are two of you and there is only one of me. Why can't somebody drive you back if you go out there? I have no way to get back."

He said, "Mrs. McCord or somebody will drive you back. You work that out," and he proceeded to go out the door and he went down to the elevator.

Senator WEICKER. You say now he went out the door, and was he running down the hall or walking?

Mr. BALDWIN. Yes, he was. He was departing——

Senator WEICKER. Did you say anything to him as he went running down the hall?

Mr. BALDWIN. Yes, I did.

Senator WEICKER. What did you say to him?

Mr. BALDWIN. I asked him if this meant I wasn't going to Miami? [Laughter.]

Senator WEICKER. Now, Mr. Baldwin, did you accidentally in the course of cleaning up the room, did you accidentally pick up certain memos from Mr. McCord's bag and, if so, could you describe the nature of those memos?

Mr. BALDWIN. That is correct. After I was given the instructions to pack up everything and get out, which meant putting all the electronic equipment away, Mr. McCord's briefcase was open, he had left his wallet, I didn't see him leave his wallet. He had put his wallet, all his change, his car keys, all his personal effects were on the bed. I proceeded to put those inside his briefcase, inside his briefcase, and attaché case, and then I proceeded to collect all of the logs, not the logs of, I believe there was one, might have been one, call that day that was still in the room on the logsheet and I put that with all the yellow pad into his briefcase and at the time I did I took everything off the table that was the work area, and along with that went an insurance book that had the dates in it, that I had been keeping for myself, and I threw all that material into Mr. McCord's briefcase, and when I realized I had put my own personal notebook in there, and the yellow pad, I proceeded to remove those and I didn't stop to separate the papers, I just threw them into my attaché case and when I arrived back in Connecticut I had some memorandums that belonged to Mr. McCord. I immediately wrote him a letter telling him that.

Senator WEICKER. You still have these memorandums?

Mr. BALDWIN. That is correct. I have those memorandums.

Senator WEICKER. Would you care to turn those over to the committee at this time?

Mr. Chairman, these are memorandums, in most instances, of a rather routine nature.

By way of identification, I would identify them as follows, and the originals are now being given to the committee.

Senator ERVIN. Would you like to have them marked for identification?

Senator WEICKER. I would very much like to have them marked for identification and ultimately as exhibits. There are two memorandums which are personnel reports on individuals who had made application to work at the Committee To Re-Elect the President. There is further a memorandum which is on a Committee for the Re-Election of the President heading. It is to Mr. Robert Odle from James McCord, and it describes or relates to security at the Republican Convention.

Then also, there is a group of papers, a group of papers which I would best describe as relating to Jack Anderson. The memorandum at the top is "Confidential, subject: Jack Anderson", and it is signed James McCord. This group of papers relates to Mr. Anderson.

Senator ERVIN. Let the record show that each paper writing identified by the witness will be appropriately numbered and received as an exhibit, the reporter assigning the appropriate number.

[The documents referred to were marked for identification, committee exhibits Nos. 15A, 15B, 15C, and 15D (in camera) and are not for publication. They will be retained in the files of the committee.]

Mr. BALDWIN. The committee can retain them, I have no use for them at all.

Senator WEICKER. Am I correct, Mr. Baldwin, that these are all of the memorandums which you accidentally took from Mr. McCord's effects and have held in your possession? Are there any others aside from the ones I have mentioned here?

Mr. BALDWIN. No, sir. There are no others.

Senator WEICKER. Now, recently there have been suggestions, Mr. Baldwin, you were a double agent working for the Democrats.

Senator ERVIN. I believe that counsel doubts whether the memorandum relating to Jack Anderson should be made public.

Senator WEICKER. I have not tried to reveal the contents of any of these memorandums but just for identification purposes, I have turned them over to the committee.

Senator ERVIN. Mark them for identification rather than exhibits.

Senator WEICKER. Recently there have been——

Senator ERVIN. They will not be printed in the record unless the committee orders it at a subsequent time.

Senator WEICKER. I think what I have tried to do here, Mr. Chairman, is to make sure that names are protected but whatever memorrandums this man had in his possession that came to him that night will come to the committee and not be embarrassing.

Senator ERVIN. They will not be publicly released or printed in the record but they will be marked for appropriate identification purposes rather than as exhibits.

Senator WEICKER. Now, again to repeat, Mr. Baldwin, recently there have been suggestions that you were a double agent working for the Democrats. I want you to describe to this committee, first of all, any incidents that may have led to such comments being made.

Mr. BALDWIN. Well, I believe the No. 1 incident may be the fact that I was not a defendant in the criminal action that preceeded this incident. There have also been incidents in the paper that Mrs. Mitchell has attributed to the fact that I had stated to her on several occasions that I was a Democrat. I do have Democratic friends, I would not deny that. [Laughter.]

But I have been a registered Republican since I have been old enough to vote, so I do not know if that makes any difference, and, at the time of the trial, the criminal trial I am speaking of, of the defendants, during the course of the days that we were roomed at the U.S. Attorney's Office, the conversation was initiated on several occasions by one or two of the detectives that the only way I could have gotten away was the fact I was a double agent. There was some kidding back and forth amongst police officers, and that, to the best of my knowledge, is the only indication that I have of other than the fact that I heard statements made by different individuals that I was a double agent.

Senator WEICKER. Was there not one additional incident which actually came to the attention of Mr. McCord?

Mr. BALDWIN [conferring with his attorney]. I believe, Senator—are you referring to during the course of my employment in Washington where I had a date with an individual young lady that happened to work for the Democratic—for an official of the Democratic Party?

Senator WEICKER. Yes.

Mr. BALDWIN. I do not believe that would have led Mr. McCord to believe I was a double agent. As a matter of fact, he wanted me to exploit that and obtain all the information I could obtain from her. [Laughter.]

And I kind of refused to go along with that.

Senator WEICKER. But just so your entire story is complete, Mr. Baldwin, it is true that you were with a young lady who was in the employ of an official of the Democratic Party, is that correct?

Mr. BALDWIN. Well, she was in the employment of an attorney who had an affiliation with the Democratic Party organization in the Washington, D.C., area. I do not mean to imply that he was an official working at the Democratic National Committee offices. He had a law office in the Washington, D.C., area and she worked for him. She was going to the convention for the Democratic Party. I mean, she told me that, thought we might see each other down there.

Senator WEICKER. Right. But, in other words, these are the only three incidents that you can bring to mind that might have given rise to any speculation as to your being a double agent in this matter, is that correct?

Mr. BALDWIN. That is correct.

Senator WEICKER. Now, would you state to the committee your own feelings on this matter?

Have you received, at any time, any promise of payment, any income, from anyone associated with the Democratic Party?

Mr. BALDWIN. Absolutely none. As a matter of fact, I have 3 weeks of pay from the Republican committee that I have not been paid for either. [Laughter.]

Senator WEICKER. And lastly, Mr. Baldwin, would you just give the committee a very brief description of your professional background prior to being employed by the Committee To Re-Elect the President? Specifically, did you work for the Federal Bureau of Investigation?

Mr. BALDWIN. Correct. I graduated from the Fairfield University in 1957. I entered the U.S. Marine Corps. I was a member of the Marine Corps Reserve with the rank of captain. I am no longer a member of the Reserve. I then entered law school in 1960. Upon graduation from law school I entered the Federal Bureau of Investigation as a special agent. I resigned from the Federal Bureau of Investigation. I worked for the circuit court system in the State of Connecticut and, at the same time, I was also an instructor in police science at a local university.

Senator WEICKER. You testified here today that you took an active role in what you must have known were illegal phone taps or breaking in and, as you have just stated, you are a former FBI agent, graduate of a law school, associated with various law enforcement agencies, and my final question is: Why did you, with this type of background, take part in such activities?

Mr. BALDWIN. Well, with this background, Senator, I have been in organizations where I have always taken orders. I did not question the legality of the operation because of several factors. I had come down from Connecticut to work for the Committee To Re-Elect the President, and that was the President's organization, as far as I was concerned. Mr. Mitchell was head of the organization. Every individual that I was introduced to or that was pointed out to me I was advised "This is a White House consultant, this is a White House aide, they are on loan. As soon as the election is over in November they go back to the White House, Al, if we do a good job here." My sole goal was to obtain permanent employment, and Mr. McCord had been, I knew that he was, an ex-FBI agent, that he had been in the CIA and, based on the credentials of all these people I did not question—possibly that was a wrong assumption on my part, not to have questioned, but I did not—the legality of it. I have been asked if it entered my mind whether I thought it was illegal. I realize that there are wiretaps that are illegal but I also realize that under certain conditions such a wiretap can be ordered or authorized by specific individuals, and I felt that I was in no position to question John Mitchell or anyone else under his command, including Mr. McCord.

Senator WEICKER. But it is also true, Mr. Baldwin, you never received any direct order from Mr. John Mitchell relative to that phone tap?

Mr. BALDWIN. Other than reference to Mr. Mitchell if I obtained—if I was involved in any difficulty establishing my authority for being in a certain place or the fact of the weapon I was to mention John Mitchell.

Senator WEICKER. With the exception, with the exception of the time when you took a trip to Chicago, Detroit, and Westchester County with Mrs. Mitchell, you received all your orders from Mr. McCord, isn't that correct?

Mr. BALDWIN. That is correct.

Senator WEICKER. Now, just to finish up on the time sequence, you left the Howard Johnson on the morning, early morning of the 17th of June, is that correct?

Mr. BALDWIN. That is correct.

Senator WEICKER. And where did you go to from the Howard Johnson?

Mr. BALDWIN. I proceeded to Connecticut.

Senator WEICKER. Did you first go to the McCord home?

Mr. BALDWIN. Oh, I assumed, Senator, you had covered the fact that I had delivered the items of equipment to Mr. McCord's home. Mrs. McCord drove me back to Washington. I then took my own personal car and returned to Connecticut.

Senator WEICKER. All right.

Mr. Chairman, this is all the questioning I have for Mr. Baldwin. There are events of which counsel knows that transpired after Mr. Baldwin's arrival in Connecticut which is something that the committee should go into further.

I have no further questions.

Senator ERVIN. Did you ask Mr. Baldwin about what he did with the information he got from the wiretap?

Senator WEICKER. Mr. Chairman, I could have possibly missed such a question, I will ask him again in any event. To whom did you gave this information, the information on the wiretaps?

Mr. BALDWIN. Other than the time I delivered it to the Committee To Re-Elect the President, I gave it to James McCord at all times. The onionskins were still in his briefcase the night I locked his briefcase. Some of them, I can't specify that every single copy of the logs were in his briefcase, but the night I delivered the logs to his home copies of quite a few of the conversations were in his briefcase.

Senator WEICKER. It is your testimony then that you gave these items to Mr. McCord with the exception of one time when you delivered them to the Committee To Re-Elect the President?

Mr. BALDWIN. That is correct.

Senator WEICKER. Whom did you give them to on that occasion?

Mr. BALDWIN. I left them with a guard that was in the lobby. I arrived after 6 o'clock and the guard was stationed in the lobby, the offices had been closed.

Senator ERVIN. I don't know whether it was brought out in what form he put them in.

How did you take the information which you gave to Mr. McCord with the exception of that one occasion—what form was it in?

Mr. BALDWIN. I am sorry, Senator, do you mean the actual way of transcribing?

Senator ERVIN. The information you got while you were at the Howard Johnson from the Democratic headquarters, what form was it in when you gave it to Mr. McCord?

Mr. BALDWIN. The initial day, the first day that I recorded the conversations was on a yellow sheet. On Memorial Day, I believe it is Memorial Day, on the holiday of May, I believe it was, 28th when he returned to the room he brought an electric typewriter, he instructed me in the upper left-hand corner to print, or by typewriter, the unit, the date, the page and then proceed down into the body and in chronological order put the time and then the contents of the conversation.

I used, as unit I used, the exact frequency that we were monitoring and after about 2 days Mr. McCord came back and said change that, anybody reading these things is going to know the frequency.

Senator ERVIN. And you typed a summary of the conversations you overheard?

Mr. BALDWIN. Well, they weren't exactly a summary, I would say almost verbatim, Senator.

Senator ERVIN. Almost verbatim.

And the names of the people who, as far as you could identify them, were using the phones?

Mr. BALDWIN. Well that is correct. Initially, it was very hard to establish names for maybe the first day or two. But subsequent to that you see the problem was I had never worked one of the units before and after Mr. McCord instructed me on how to operate it, I could tune it so that the minute the call was either going out or coming in I would then be in on the beginning but prior to that I would receive a little indication on the scope and I would be into the conversation so I would not know who they asked for or who was calling. Professional, that was correct.

Senator ERVIN. Then you gave all the typewritten transcriptions of what you heard to Mr. McCord except on one occasion you mentioned?

Mr. BALDWIN. That is correct, Senator.

Senator ERVIN. You did not keep any carbon copies?

Mr. BALDWIN. No. Mr. McCord had the onionskins and they were still in his briefcase the night I locked it.

Senator BAKER. Mr. Baldwin, it is 10 minutes after 5 in the afternoon. Rather than proceed much further with the questioning, I am going to ask you a question or so, or rather, a few questions about a topic or so. Counsel and other members of the committee necessarily will defer their questions until later. May I assume you are agreeable to returning at the committee's pleasure to answer questions?

Mr. BALDWIN. Yes.

Senator BAKER. The first witness we have had in a long time who has been able to smile.

On the night in question, or, rather, the morning of June 17, 1972, when you were standing on the balcony of Howard Johnson's, you testified that you saw the lights come on on the eighth floor, you saw two men on the balcony of the sixth floor, you called on your walkie-talkie on the second occasion and said, are your men dressed casually? Someone replied, no, they are dressed in business suits. Did you know whom you were talking to?

Mr. BALDWIN. No, I did not, Senator.

Senator BAKER. Who had you been talking to previously inside the Democratic National Convention?

Mr. BALDWIN. With the walkie-talkie? Well, I hadn't used the walkie-talkie with anybody. Mr. McCord had used the walkie-talkie at all times. As I say, he had gone across the street.

Senator BAKER. Could you distinguish from the quality of the reception whom you were talking to? Could you recognize the voice?

Mr. BALDWIN. McCord's voice I could recognize. My assumption that I had to make was that there were two other units besides mine in operation, one unit that was turned on and the other unit that was turned off, because it was very obvious that one of the units was not on at a particular point.

Senator BAKER. All I am striving for is to know if you could identify the person you were communicating with when you asked, are your men dressed casually?

Mr. BALDWIN. I would be taking a—I am not positive of it, but at this point, I would not want to implicate somebody without being positive of it. I would recognize the voice subsequently as being Mr. Hunt's, since I have heard it on several occasions.

Senator BAKER. Hunt was inside the Democratic National Committee?

Mr. BALDWIN. Senator, I did not know where any of the individuals were other than Mr. McCord, when he walked across the street. I had no knowledge how many or who were across the street.

Senator BAKER. The voice who replied, "No, our men are in business suits," was not Mr. McCord's?

Mr. BALDWIN. Absolutely. I would know Mr. McCord's.

96-296 O—73——bk. 1—27

Senator BAKER. And it is your best judgment that it was Mr. Hunt's voice?

Mr. BALDWIN. Having heard it subsequently, yes, sir.

Senator BAKER. Have you subsequently learned that Mr. Hunt was not inside the Democratic National Committee but rather was in the Howard Johnson Hotel?

Mr. BALDWIN. No, I learned Mr. Hunt was in the Watergate Hotel directly behind the Watergate Office Building.

Senator BAKER. That is what I mean to say. He was inside the Watergate Hotel, but not in the Democratic National Committee?

Mr. BALDWIN. That is right, he was in that part of the hotel that was to the rear of the Democratic National Committee.

Senator BAKER. So as far as you can tell, your inquiry about clothing never reached anyone within the Democratic National Committee headquarters?

Mr. BALDWIN. That is correct. The only indication I had of any communication was when the gentleman got on and said, "They have got us," in a whisper. Then, what I would definitely describe as Mr. McCord's voice saying, "Are you gentlemen metropolitan police?"

Senator BAKER. Did you know the officers who arrested——

Mr. BALDWIN. I did not at the time. I do now.

Senator BAKER. Had you ever known any of them before?

Mr. BALDWIN. No, sir. I had—during the course of the trial, we communicated. Mr. Shoffler and I had observed each other in several of the demonstrations, I believe. I remember observing him and I think he remembers observing me. We were both using the same phone to call in.

Senator BAKER. What do you mean you were using the same phone to call in?

Mr. BALDWIN. Well, you have to make reports every 2 or 3 hours. Mr. McCord wanted activity reports, whether or not any groups were moving or what groups were there, who was there. And several times, I was the only one there.

Senator BAKER. Are you speaking about Mr. Shoffler using the same phone?

Mr. BALDWIN. No, the day of the Capitol demonstrations, and I believe before the march to the Capitol, there were several days of preparation for the march and there was gatherings around the Washington Monument, several campsites set out. I think we crossed paths on several occasions, because both of us were dressed in fatigue jackets. We sort of remembered each other.

And he finally said, oh, now I know who you were.

Senator BAKER. Did you recognize him on the balcony——

Mr. BALDWIN. I did not, no. He was the gentleman on—you see, on this subsequent date, it was Sergeant Leeper, I believe. The sergeant, when he came out, stood there and observed Detective Shoffler. He was the gentleman who was proceeding along the balcony in a rather dangerous situation, so he was more or less looking around the side of the building. He had a flashlight, but I could not say for a fact, at that time, at that time it was the same man. We did not realize this until we were at the trial that we had been at demonstrations, after we got talking together.

Senator BAKER. Mr. Baldwin, the hour is late and I have other questions as Senator Weicker probably does, and the chairman, but I am going to stop now with your assurance already given that you will return when we meet.

Mr. BALDWIN. Yes, sir.

Senator ERVIN. It is satisfactory to excuse the witness, with the understanding that he will return when we meet again.

We will adjourn until Tuesday morning, June 5, at 10 a.m., in this room.

[Whereupon. at 5:15 p.m., the hearing was recessed, to reconvene at 10 a.m., Tuesday, June 5, 1973.]

MATERIAL SUBMITTED FOR THE RECORD

By SENATOR ERVIN

Rules of Procedure

FOR THE

SELECT COMMITTEE ON

PRESIDENTIAL CAMPAIGN ACTIVITIES

WITH

GUIDELINES, and

S. RES. 60 (93d Cong.)

S. RES. 278 (91st Cong.)

United States Senate

PRINTED FOR THE USE OF THE SELECT COMMITTEE

SENATE SELECT COMMITTEE ON PRESIDENTIAL CAMPAIGN ACTIVITIES

Established by S. Res. 60

93D CONGRESS, 1ST SESSION

★

SAM J. ERVIN, Jr., N.C., *Chairman*
HOWARD H. BAKER, Jr., Tenn., *Vice Chairman*

HERMAN E. TALMADGE, Ga. EDWARD J. GURNEY, Fla.
DANIEL K. INOUYE, Hawaii LOWELL P. WEICKER, Jr., Conn.
JOSEPH M. MONTOYA, N. Mex.

SAMUEL DASH, *Chief Counsel and Staff Director*
FRED D. THOMPSON, *Minority Counsel*
RUFUS L. EDMISTEN, *Deputy Counsel*

CONTENTS

RULES OF PROCEDURE

FOR THE

SELECT COMMITTEE ON PRESIDENTIAL CAMPAIGN ACTIVITIES

1. Preliminary investigations may be initiated by the committee staff with the approval of the Chairman or at his direction.

2. Committee hearings or meetings shall be conducted by the Chairman or member designated by the Chairman.

3. The Chairman shall give each member written notice of the subject of and scope of any hearings 24 hours prior to the time such hearing is to begin within the District of Columbia; otherwise 48 hours prior thereto. No hearings shall then be held if any member objects unless upon the subsequent approval of the majority of the committee.

4. The Chairman shall have authority to call meetings of the committee which authority he may delegate to any other member. Members shall have at least 24 hours notice of any meeting of the committee within the District of Columbia; otherwise 48 hours prior thereto.

Should a majority of the members request the Chairman in writing to call a meeting of the committee and should the Chairman fail to call such meeting within 10 days thereafter, such majority may call a meeting by filing a written notice with the Clerk who shall promptly notify each member of the committee in writing. If the Chairman is not present at any such meeting, and has not designated another member to conduct the meeting, the ranking majority member present shall preside.

5. A quorum for the transaction of committee business shall consist of a majority of the committee members. Unless otherwise specified in these rules, decisions of the committee shall be by a majority of votes cast. For the purpose of hearing witnesses, taking testimony, and receiving evidence, a quorum will consist of one Senator.

6. No person shall be allowed to be present during a hearing or meeting held in executive session except members and employees of the committee, the witness and his counsel, stenographers, or interpreters of the committee. Other persons whose presence is requested or consented to by the majority of the members of the committee present may be

admitted to such sessions.

7. It shall be the duty of the Clerk and staff director to keep or cause to be kept a record of all committee proceedings, including the record of votes on any matter on which a record vote is taken and of all quorum calls together with all motions, points of order, parliamentary inquiries, rulings of the chair and appeals therefrom. The record shall show those members present at each meeting. Such record shall be available to any member of the committee upon request.

8. A vote by any member of the committee with respect to any measure or matter being considered by the committee may be cast by proxy providing the proxy authorization is in writing to the Chairman, designating the person who is to execute the proxy authorization, and is limited to a specific measure or matter and any amendments pertaining thereto. Proxies shall not be considered for the establishment of a quorum.

9. Subpenas for attendance of witnesses and the production of memoranda, documents, and records may be issued by the Chairman or any other member designated by him, and may be served by any person designated by such Chairman or member. Authorization for the issuance of a subpena shall be

given by the Chairman or Vice Chairman of the committee, or both, or by the majority of the members of the committee present at a meeting, if either the Chairman or Vice Chairman or both requests that the authorization for the issuance of any particular subpena or subpenas be decided by the committee.

10. Each subpena shall be accompanied by a copy of the Senate resolution authorizing the investigation with respect to which the witness is summoned to testify or to produce papers.

11. Witnesses shall be subpenaed at a reasonably sufficient time in advance of any hearing in order to give the witness an opportunity to prepare for the hearing, employ counsel should he so desire, and/or produce documents, books, records, memoranda, and papers called for by a subpena *duces tecum*. The committee shall determine, in each particular instance, what period of time constitutes reasonable notice; however in no case shall it be less than 24 hours.

12. Except when publication is authorized by the Chairman, no member of the committee or staff shall make public the name of any witness subpenaed before the committee or release any information to the public relating to a witness under subpena or the issuance of

a subpena prior to the time and date set for his appearance.

13. All witnesses appearing before the committee, pursuant to subpena, shall be furnished a printed copy of the rules of procedure of the committee.

14. All witnesses at public or executive investigative hearings shall give all testimony under oath or affirmation which shall be administered by the Chairman or a member of the committee.

15. The time and order of interrogation of witnesses appearing before the committee shall be controlled by the Chairman. Interrogation of witnesses at committee hearings shall be conducted by committee members and authorized committee staff personnel only.

16. Any objection raised by a witness or his counsel to procedures or to the admissibility of testimony and evidence shall be ruled upon by the Chairman or presiding member and such rulings shall be the rulings of the committee, unless a disagreement thereon is expressed by a majority of the committee present. In the case of a tie, the rule of the Chair will prevail.

17. Any witness desiring to make a prepared or written statement for the records of the proceedings shall file a copy of such state-

ment with the counsel of the committee 24 hours in advance of the hearings at which the statement is to be presented, unless the Chairman waives the requirement. All such statements or portions thereof so received which are relevant and germane to the subject of investigation may, at the conclusion of the testimony of the witness and with the approval of a majority of the committee members be inserted in the official transcript of the proceedings.

18. A witness may make a statement, which shall be brief and relevant to the subject matter of his examination, at the beginning and conclusion of his testimony. Each such statement shall not exceed three minutes unless an extension of time is authorized by the Chairman. However, statements which take the form of personal attacks by the witness upon the motives of the committee, the personal character of any members of the Congress or of the committee staff, and intemperate statements, are not deemed to be relevant or germane, shall not be made, and may be stricken from the record of the proceedings.

19. All witnesses at public or executive hearings shall have the right to be accompanied by counsel. Any witness who desires

counsel but who is unable to secure counsel may inform the committee at least 24 hours in advance of his appearance of his inability to retain counsel and the committee will endeavor to secure voluntary counsel for the witness. However, failure to secure counsel will not excuse the witness from appearing.

20. Counsel retained by any witness and accompanying such witness shall be permitted to be present during the testimony of such witness at any public or executive hearing. The sole and exclusive prerogative of the counsel shall be to advise such witness while he is testifying of his legal rights and constitutional rights. Provided, however, that any Government officer or employee being interrogated by the staff or testifying before the committee and electing to have his personal counsel present shall not be permitted to select such counsel from the employees or officers of any Government agency.

21. A witness shall not be excused from testifying in the event his counsel is not present or is ejected for contumacy or disorderly conduct; nor shall counsel for the witness coach the witness, answer for the witness, or put words in the witness' mouth. The failure of any witness to secure counsel shall not excuse such witness from attendance in re-

sponse to subpena.

22. At the conclusion of the interrogation of his client, counsel shall be permitted to make such reasonable and pertinent requests upon the committee, including the testimony of other witnesses or presentation of other evidence, as he shall deem necessary to protect his client's rights. These requests shall be ruled upon by the committee members present.

23. Counsel for witnesses shall conduct himself in a professional, ethical, and proper manner. His failure to do so shall, upon a finding to that effect by a majority of the committee members present, subject such counsel to disciplinary action which may include warning, censure, removal of counsel from the hearing room, or a recommendation of contempt proceedings.

24. There shall be no direct or cross-examination by counsel appearing for a witness. However, the counsel may submit in writing any questions he wishes propounded to his client or to any other witness. With the consent of the majority of the members present, such question or questions shall be put to the witness by the Chairman, by another member or by counsel of the committee either in the original form or in modified language. The

decision of the committee as to the admissibility of questions submitted by counsel for a witness, as well as their form, shall be final.

25. Any person who is the subject of an investigation in public hearings may submit to the Chairman questions in writing for the cross-examination of the witnesses. Their formulation and admissibility shall be decided by the committee in accordance with rule 25.

26. Any person whose name is mentioned or who is specifically identified, and who believes that testimony or other evidence presented at a public hearing, or comment made by the committee member or counsel, tends to defame him or otherwise adversely affect his reputation, may (a) request to appear personally before the committee to testify on his own behalf, or, in the alternative; (b) file a sworn statement of facts relevant to the testimony, or other evidence or comment complained of. Such request and such statement shall be submitted to the committee for its consideration and action.

27. No testimony taken or material presented in an executive session, or any summary or excerpt thereof shall be made available to other than the committee members and committee staff and no such material or

testimony shall be made public or presented at a public hearing, either in whole or in part, unless authorized by a majority of the committee members or as otherwise provided for in these rules.

28. No evidence or testimony, or any summary or excerpt thereof given in executive session which the committee determines may tend to defame, degrade, or incriminate any person shall be released, or presented at a public hearing unless such person shall have been afforded the opportunity to testify or file a statement in rebuttal, and any pertinent evidence or testimony given by such person, or on his behalf, is made a part of the transcript, summary, or excerpt prior to the public release of such portion of the testimony.

29. A complete and accurate stenographic record shall be made of all testimony at all public and executive committee hearings.

30. A witness shall, upon request, be given a reasonable opportunity before any transcript is made public to inspect in the office of the committee the transcript of his testimony to determine whether it was correctly transcribed and may be accompanied by his counsel during such inspection. If the witness so desires, the committee will furnish him a copy of his testimony, at no expense to the witness.

31. Any corrections in the transcription of the testimony of the witness which the witness desires to make shall be submitted in writing to the committee within 5 days of the taking of his testimony. However, changes shall only be made for the purpose of making minor grammatical corrections and editing, and not for the purpose of changing the substance of the testimony. Any questions arising with respect to such editing shall be decided by the Chairman.

32. A copy of the testimony given in public session or that part of the testimony given by the witness in executive session and subsequently quoted or made part of the record in a public session shall be made available to any witness at his expense, if he so requests. Any witness shall be given a reasonable opportunity to inspect any such public testimony in the committee office.

33. Whenever the Chairman so permits, any committee hearing that is open to the public may be covered, in whole or in part, by television broadcast, radio broadcast, and still photography, or by any other media coverage, provided that such coverage is orderly and unobtrusive.

34. The coverage of any hearing of the committee by television, radio, or still

photography shall be under the direct supervision of the Chairman, who may for good cause terminate such media coverage in whole or in part, or take such other action as the circumstances may warrant.

35. A witness may request, on grounds of distraction, harassment, or physical discomfort, that during his testimony, television, motion picture, and other cameras and lights shall not be directed at him, such requests to be ruled on by the committee members present at the hearing.

36. No recommendation that a witness be cited for contempt of Congress shall be forwarded to the Senate unless and until the committee has, upon notice to all its members, met and considered the alleged contempt and by a majority of the committee voted that such recommendation be made.

37. All staff members shall be confirmed by a majority of the committee. After confirmation, the Chairman shall certify staff appointments to the financial clerk of the Senate, in writing.

38. The Chairman shall have the authority to utilize the services, information, facilities, and personnel of the departments and establishments of the Government, and to procure the temporary or intermittent services of

experts or consultants or organizations thereof to make studies or assist or advise the committee with respect to any matter under investigation.

39. In preparing for or conducting the investigation and study authorized and directed by the resolution creating this committee the committee is empowered to exercise the powers conferred upon committees of the Senate by sections 6002 and 6005 of title 18 of the United States Code or any other act of Congress regulating the granting of immunity to witnesses.

40. All information developed by or made known to any member of the committee staff shall be deemed to be confidential. No member of the committee staff shall communicate to any person, other than a member of the committee or another member of the committee staff, any substantive information with respect to any substantive matter related to the activities of the committee. All communications with the press and other persons not on the committee or committee staff in respect to confidential substantive matters shall be by members of the committee only. Official releases of information to the press on behalf of the committee shall be made only with the express consent of the Chairman and Vice

Chairman.

41. These rules may be modified, amended, or repealed by a decision of the committee, provided that a notice in writing of the proposed change has been given to each member at least 48 hours prior to the respective action.

GUIDELINES
OF THE
SELECT COMMITTEE ON PRESIDENTIAL CAMPAIGN ACTIVITIES

STATEMENT OF
SAM J. ERVIN, JR., CHAIRMAN
HOWARD H. BAKER, JR., VICE CHAIRMAN

On Monday, April 16, 1973, the Select Committee on Presidential Campaign Activities met and unanimously adopted guidelines regarding testimony and appearances of prospective witnesses before the Select Committee. The text follows.

In investigating the matters mentioned in S. Res. 60, the Senate Select Committee on Presidential Campaign Activities will observe its standing rules, its previously established procedures for staff interviews of prospective witnesses, and these guidelines:

1. The committee will receive oral and documentary evidence relevant to the matters S. Res. 60 authorizes it to investigate and matters bearing on the credibility of the witnesses who testify before it.

2. All witnesses shall testify before the committee on oath or affirmation in hearings which shall be open to the public and the news media. This guideline shall not abridge, however, the power of the committee to take the testimony of a particular witness on oath or affirmation in an executive meeting if the committee would otherwise be unable to ascertain whether the witness knows anything relevant to the matters the committee is authorized to investigate.

3. All still and motion picture photography will be completed before a witness actually testifies, and no such photography shall occur while the witness is testifying. Television coverage of a witness and his testimony shall be permitted, however, under the provisions of the Standing Rules of the Committee.

4. In taking the testimony of a witnesses, the committee will endeavor to do two things: First, to minimize inconvenience to the witness and disruption of his affairs; and, second, to afford the witness a fair opportunity to give his testimony without undue interrup-

tion. To achieve the first of these objectives, the committee will honor the request of the witness to the extent feasible for advance notice of the time and place appointed for taking his testimony, complete the taking of of his testimony with as much dispatch as circumstances permit, and release the witness from further attendance on the committee as soon as circumstances allow, subject, however, to the power of the committee to recall him for further testimony in the event the committee deems such action advisable. To afford the witness a fair opportunity to present his testimony, the committee will permit the witness to make an opening statement not exceeding 20 minutes, which shall not be interrupted by questioning, and a closing statement summarizing his testimony, not exceeding 5 minutes, which will not be interrupted by questioning: Provided, however, questions suggested by the closing statement may be propounded after such statement is made.

5. The committee respects and recognizes the right of a prospective witness who is interviewed by the staff of the committee in advance of a public hearing as well as the right of a witness who appears before the committee to be accompanied by a lawyer of his own

choosing to advise him concerning his constitutional and legal rights as a witness.

6. If the lawyer who accompanies a witness before the committee advises the witness to claim a privilege against giving any testimony sought by the committee, the committee shall have the discretionary power to permit the lawyer to present his views on the matter for the information of the committee, and the committee shall thereupon rule on the validity of the claim or its application to the particular circumstances involved and require the witness to give the testimony sought in the event its ruling on the claim is adverse to the witness. Neither the witness nor any other officer or person shall be permitted to claim a privilege against the witness testifying prior to the appearance of the witness before the committee, and the committee shall not rule in respect to the claim until the question by which the testimony is sought is put to the witness.

7. The committee believes that it may be necessary for it to obtain the testimony of some White House aides if the committee is to be able to ascertain the complete truth in respect to the matters it is authorized to investigate by S. Res. 60. To this end, the committee will invite such White House aides as

it has reason to believe have knowledge or information relevant to the matters it is authorized to investigate to appear before the committee and give testimony on oath or affirmation in open hearings respecting such matters. In this connection, the committee will extend to such aides the considerations set forth in detail in guideline No. 4 and the right to counsel set forth in detail in guidelines Nos. 5 and 6. In addition to these considerations and rights, the committee will permit the White House to have its own counsel present when any White House aide appears before the committee as a witness, and permit such counsel to invoke any claim that a privilege available to the President forbids a White House aide to give the testimony sought by the committee, and the committee shall thereupon rule on validity of such claim or its application to the particular testimony sought in the manner and with the effect set forth in guideline No. 6 in respect to a claim of privilege invoked by a witness or his counsel. The committee will not subpena a White House aide to appear before it or its staff unless such aide fails to make timely response to an invitation to appear.

8. The committee may require the Sergeant at Arms of the Senate, or any of his assist-

ants or deputies, or any available law enforcement officer to eject from a meeting of the committee any person who willfully disrupts the meeting or willfully impedes the committee in the performance of its functions under S. Res. 60.

9. Whenever the committee takes testimony through the agency of less than the majority of the members of the committee, as authorized by its standing rules, the member or members of the committee taking the testimony shall be vested with the powers set forth in these guidelines and shall be deemed to act as the committee in exercising such powers.

S. RES. 60

93D CONGRESS, 1ST SESSION

IN THE SENATE OF THE UNITED STATES

FEBRUARY 5, 1973

Mr. ERVIN (for himself and Mr. MANSFIELD) submitted the following resolution; which was ordered to be placed on the calendar.

FEBRUARY 7, 1973

Considered, amended, and agreed to

RESOLUTION

To establish a select committee of the Senate to conduct an investigation and study of the extent, if any, to which illegal, improper, or unethical activities were engaged in by any persons, acting individually or in combination with others, in the presidential election of 1972, or any campaign, canvass, or other activity related to it.

Resolved, SECTION 1. (a) That there is hereby established a select committee of the Senate, which may be called, for convenience of expression, the Select Committee on Presidential Campaign Activities, to conduct an investigation and study of the extent, if any, to which illegal, improper, or unethical activities were engaged in by any persons, acting either individually or in combination with others, in the presidential election of 1972, or in any related campaign or canvass conducted by or in behalf of any person seeking nomination or election as the candidate of any political party for the office of President of the United States in such election, and to determine whether in its judgment any occurrences which may be revealed by the investigation and study indicate the necessity or desirability of the enactment of new congressional legislation to safeguard the electoral process by which the President of the United States is chosen.

(b) The select committee created by this resolution shall consist of seven Members of the Senate, four of whom shall be appointed by the President of the Senate from the majority Members of the Senate upon the recommendation of the majority leader of the Senate, and three of whom shall be appointed

96-296 O - 73 - bk. 1 - 28

by the President of the Senate from the minority Members of the Senate upon the recommendation of the minority leader of the Senate. For the purposes of paragraph 6 of rule XXV of the Standing Rules of the Senate, service of a Senator as a member, chairman, or vice chairman of the select committee shall not be taken into account.

(c) The select committee shall select a chairman and vice chairman from among its members, and adopt rules of procedure to govern its proceedings. The vice chairman shall preside over meetings of the select committee during the absence of the chairman, and discharge such other responsibilities as may be assigned to him by the select committee or the chairman. Vacancies in the membership of the select committee shall not affect the authority of the remaining members to execute the functions of the select committee and shall be filled in the same manner as original appointments to it are made.

(d) A majority of the members of the select committee shall constitute a quorum for the transaction of business, but the select committee may fix a lesser number as a quorum for the purpose of taking testimony or depositions.

SEC. 2. That the select committee is author-

ized and directed to do everything necessary or appropriate to make the investigation and study specified in section 1(a). Without abridging or limiting in any way the authority conferred upon the select committee by the preceding sentence, the Senate further expressly authorizes and directs the select committee to make a complete investigation and study of the activities of any and all persons or groups of persons or organizations of any kind which have any tendency to reveal the full facts in respect to the following matters or questions:

(1) The breaking, entering, and bugging of the headquarters or offices of the Democratic National Committee in the Watergate Building in Washington, District of Columbia;

(2) The monitoring by bugging, eavesdropping, wiretapping, or other surreptitious means of conversations or communications occurring in whole or in part in the headquarters or offices of the Democratic National Committee in the Watergate Building in Washington, District of Columbia;

(3) Whether or not any printed or typed or written document or paper or other material was surreptitiously re-

moved from the headquarters or offices of the Democratic National Committee in the Watergate Building in Washington, District of Columbia, and thereafter copied or reproduced by photography or any other means for the information of any person or political committee or organization;

(4) The preparing, transmitting, or receiving by any person for himself or any political committee or any organization of any report or information concerning the activities mentioned in subdivision (1), (2), or (3) of this section, and the information contained in any such report;

(5) Whether any persons, acting individually or in combination with others, planned the activities mentioned in subdivision (1), (2), (3), or (4) of this section, or employed any of the participants in such activities to participate in them, or made any payments or promises of payments of money or other things of value to the participants in such activities or their families for their activities, or for concealing the truth in respect to them or any of the persons having any connection with them or their activities,

and, if so, the source of the moneys used in such payments, and the identities and motives of the persons planning such activities or employing the participants in them;

(6) Whether any persons participating in any of the activities mentioned in subdivision (1), (2), (3), (4), or (5) of this section have been induced by bribery, coercion, threats, or any other means whatsoever to plead guilty to the charges preferred against them in the District Court of the District of Columbia or to conceal or fail to reveal any knowledge of any of the activities mentioned in subdivision (1), (2), (3), (4), or (5) of this section, and, if so, the identities of the persons inducing them to do such things, and the identities of any other persons or any committees or organizations for whom they acted;

(7) Any efforts to disrupt, hinder, impede, or sabotage in any way any campaign, canvass, or activity conducted by or in behalf of any person seeking nomination or election as the candidate of any political party for the office of President of the United States in 1972 by infiltrating any political committee or

organization or headquarters or offices or home or whereabouts of the person seeking such nomination or election or of any person aiding him in so doing, or by bugging or eavesdropping or wiretapping the conversations, communications, plans, headquarters, offices, home, or whereabouts of the person seeking such nomination or election or of any other person assisting him in so doing, or by exercising surveillance over the person seeking such nomination or election or of any person assisting him in so doing, or by reporting to any other person or to any political committee or organization any information obtained by such infiltration, eavesdropping, bugging, wiretapping, or surveillance;

(8) Whether any person, acting individually or in combination with others, or political committee or organization induced any of the activities mentioned in subdivision (7) of this section or paid any of the participants in any such activities for their services, and, if so, the identities of such persons, or committee, or organization, and the source of the funds used by them to procure or finance such activities;

(9) Any fabrication, dissemination, or publication of any false charges or other false information having the purpose of discrediting any person seeking nomination or election as the candidate of any political party to the office of President of the United States in 1972;

(10) The planning of any of the activities mentioned in subdivision (7), (8), or (9) of this section, the employing of the participants in such activities, and the source of any moneys or things of value which may have been given or promised to the participants in such activities for their services, and the identities of any persons or committees or organizations which may have been involved in any way in the planning, procuring, and financing of such activities.

(11) Any transactions or circumstances relating to the source, the control, the transmission, the transfer, the deposit, the storage, the concealment, the expenditure, or use in the United States or in any other country, of any moneys or other things of value collected or received for actual or pretended use in the presidential election of 1972 or in any related campaign or canvass or activities

preceding or accompanying such election by any person, group of persons, committee, or organization of any kind acting or professing to act in behalf of any national political party or in support of or in opposition to any person seeking nomination or election to the office of President of the United States in 1972;

(12) Compliance or noncompliance with any act of Congress requiring the reporting of the receipt or disbursement or use of any moneys or other things of value mentioned in subdivision (11) of this section;

(13) Whether any of the moneys or things of value mentioned in subdivision (11) of this section were placed in any secret fund or place of storage for use in financing any activity which was sought to be concealed from the public, and, if so, what disbursement or expenditure was made of such secret fund, and the identities of any person or group of persons or committee or organization having any control over such secret fund or the disbursement or expenditure of the same;

(14) Whether any books, checks, canceled checks, communications, corre-

spondence, documents, papers, physical evidence, records, recordings, tapes, or materials relating to any of the matters or questions the select committee is authorized and directed to investigate and study have been concealed, suppressed, or destroyed by any persons acting individually or in combination with others, and, if so, the identities and motives of any such persons or groups of persons;

(15) Any other activities, circumstances, materials, or transactions having a tendency to prove or disprove that persons acting either individually or in combination with others, engaged in any illegal, improper, or unethical activities in connection with the presidential election of 1972 or any campaign, canvass, or activity related to such election;

(16) Whether any of the existing laws of the United States are inadequate, either in their provisions or manner of enforcement to safeguard the integrity or purity of the process by which Presidents are chosen.

SEC. 3. (a) To enable the select committee to make the investigation and study authorized and directed by this resolution, the Senate hereby empowers the select committee as an agency of the Senate

(1) to employ and fix the compensation of such clerical, investigatory, legal, technical, and other assistants as it deems necessary or appropriate;

(2) to sit and act at any time or place during sessions, recesses, and adjournment periods of the Senate;

(3) to hold hearings for taking testimony on oath or to receive documentary or physical evidence relating to the matters and questions it is authorized to investigate or study;

(4) to require by subpena or otherwise the attendance as witnesses of any persons who the select committee believes have knowledge or information concerning any of the matters or questions it is authorized to investigate and study;

(5) to require by subpena or order any department, agency, officer, or employee of the executive branch of the United States Government, or any private person, firm, or corporation, or any officer or former officer or employee of any political committee or organization to produce for its consideration or

for use as evidence in its investigation and study any books, checks, canceled checks, correspondence, communications, document, papers, physical evidence, records, recordings, tapes, or materials relating to any of the matters or questions it is authorized to investigate and study which they or any of them may have in their custody or under their control;

(6) to make to the Senate any recommendations it deems appropriate in respect to the willful failure or refusal of any person to appear before it in obedience to a subpena or order, or in respect to the willful failure or refusal of any person to answer questions or give testimony in his character as a witness during his appearance before it, or in respect to the willful failure or refusal of any officer or employee of the executive branch of the United States Government or any person, firm, or corporation, or any officer or former officer or employee of any political committee or organization, to produce before the committee any books, checks, canceled checks, correspondence, communications, document, financial records, papers, physical

evidence, records, recordings, tapes, or materials in obedience to any subpena or order;

(7) to take depositions and other testimony on oath anywhere within the United States or in any other country;

(8) to procure the temporary or intermittent services of individual consultants, or organizations thereof, in the same manner and under the same conditions as a standing committee of the Senate may procure such services under section 202(i) of the Legislative Reorganization Act of 1946;

(9) to use on a reimbursable basis, with the prior consent of the Government department or agency concerned and the Committee on Rules and Administration, the services of personnel of any such department or agency;

(10) to use on a reimbursable basis or otherwise with the prior consent of the chairman of any other of the Senate committees or the chairman of any subcommittee of any committee of the Senate the facilities or services of any members of the staffs of such other Senate committees or any subcommittees of such other Senate committees whenever

the select committee or its chairman deems that such action is necessary or appropriate to enable the select committee to make the investigation and study authorized and directed by this resolution;

(11) to have access through the agency of any members of the select committee, chief majority counsel, minority counsel, or any of its investigatory assistants jointly designated by the chairman and the ranking minority member to any data, evidence, information, report, analysis, or document or papers relating to any of the matters or questions which it is authorized and directed to investigate and study in the custody or under the control of any department, agency, officer, or employee of the executive branch of the United States Government having the power under the laws of the United States to investigate any alleged criminal activities or to prosecute persons charged with crimes against the United States which will aid the select committee to prepare for or conduct the investigation and study authorized and directed by this resolution; and

(12) to expend to the extent it determines necessary or appropriate any moneys made available to it by the Senate to perform the duties and exercise the powers conferred upon it by this resolution and to make the investigation and study it is authorized by this resolution to make.

(b) Subpenas may be issued by the select committee acting through the chairman or any other member designated by him, and may be served by any person designated by such chairman or other member anywhere within the borders of the United States. The chairman of the select committee, or any other member thereof is hereby authorized to administer oaths to any witnesses appearing before the committee.

(c) In preparing for or conducting the investigation and study authorized and directed by this resolution, the select committee shall be empowered to exercise the powers conferred upon committees of the Senate by section 6002 of title 18 of the United States Code or any other Act of Congress regulating the granting of immunity to witnesses.

SEC. 4. The select committee shall have authority to recommend the enactment of any new congressional legislation which its investigation considers it is necessary or desirable to safeguard the electoral process by which the President of the United States is chosen.

SEC. 5. The select committee shall make a final report of the results of the investigation and study conducted by it pursuant to this resolution, together with its findings and its recommendations as to new congressional legislation it deems necessary or desirable, to the Senate at the earliest practicable date, but no later than February 28, 1974. The select committee may also submit to the Senate such interim reports as it considers appropriate. After submission of its final report, the select committee shall have three calendar months to close its affairs, and on the expiration of such three calendar months shall cease to exist.

SEC. 6. The expenses of the select committee through February 28, 1974, under this resolution shall not exceed $500,000, of which amount not to exceed $25,000 shall be available for the procurement of the services of individual consultants or organizations thereof. Such expenses shall be paid from the contingent fund of the Senate upon vouchers approved by the chairman of the select committee. The minority members of the select committee shall have one-third of the professional staff of the select committee (including a minority counsel) and such part of the clerical staff as may be adequate.

S. RES. 278

91ST CONGRESS, 1ST SESSION

(Report No. 91–515)

IN THE SENATE OF THE UNITED STATES

NOVEMBER 5, 1969

Mr. CANNON, from the Committee on Rules and Administration, reported the following resolution; which was ordered to be placed on the calendar

NOVEMBER 11, 1969

Considered and agreed to

RESOLUTION

Relating to fees of witnesses appearing before Senate committees.

Resolved, That witnesses summoned to appear before the Senate or any of its committees shall be entitled to a witness fee rated at not to exceed $25 for each full day spent in traveling to and from the place of examination and for each full day in attendance. A witness shall also be entitled to reimbursement of the actual and necessary transportation expenses incurred by him in traveling to and from the place of examination, in no case to exceed 20 cents a mile for the distance actually traveled by him for the purpose of appearing as a witness if such distance is not more than six hundred miles or 12 cents a mile if such distance is more than six hundred miles.

By ROBERT C. ODLE, Jr.

Committee for the Re-Election of the President and Finance Committee for the Re-Election of the President

Name	Dates of service	Former employment*
Abbott, Karla	July–Nov. 1972	San Diego Federal Savings & Loan, San Diego, Calif.
Abrahams, Albert	July–Nov. 1972	Cost of Living Council.
Abrams, Michael	May–Nov. 1972	Justice Department.
Adams, Joseph	June–Nov. 1972	Civil Aeronautics Board.
Adams, Mary	Feb.–Nov. 1972	Minnesota Republican State Committee, Minneapolis, Minn.
Agnich, Victoria	Feb.–Nov. 1972	Wagner & Baroody.
Allen, David	Feb.–Nov. 1972	U.S. Army.
Allen, Yvonne	Feb. 1972–Jan. 1973	Arista Trading Co.
Almaguer, Frank	June–Nov. 1972	OEO.
Amborse, Elaine	June–Nov. 1972	Potomac Temporary Girl.
Amolsch, Arthur	Feb.–Nov. 1972	State Department.
Anderson, Stanton	Sept.–Nov. 1972	White House.
Anderson, Stephen	Apr. 1972–Feb. 1973	Dart Drug Co.
Armao, Robert	June–Nov. 1972	Stuart Porter Agency, New York City.
Armendaris, Alex	June-Nov. 1972	OEO.
Arsht, Leslie	Apr. 1972–Mar. 1973	White House.
Asbell, Fred	June–Nov. 1972	Student.
Atwood, Dorothy	Apr.–Nov. 1972	St. Louis Post Dispatch, St. Louis, Mo.
Au, Susan	July–Nov. 1972	Cushman, Darby & Cushman, Attorneys.
Auchincloss, Eve	Mar.–Nov. 1972	George Washington University.
Austin, Timothy	Sept.–Nov. 1972	RNC.
Barbieri, Janice	Aug.–Nov. 1972	State Department.
Barbour, Joyce	Apr. 1972–Apr. 1973	Department of Labor.
Barnard, Bailey	June–Nov. 1972	Borel Restaurant Corp., San Mateo, Calif.
Barnett, Louis	Feb.–Nov. 1972	Los Angeles County Republican Committee, Los Angeles, Calif.
Barrick, Paul	Apr. 1972–Present	Susquehanna Corp., Alexandria, Va.
Battles, Roy	Aug.–Nov. 1972	Unknown.
Beitzel, Irma	Sept.–Nov. 1972	None.
Bell, Thomas	Feb.–Nov. 1972.	Student.
Belt, Gail	Mar.–Nov. 1972	Steiger & Associates, Vienna, Va.
Bennett, James	Mar.–Nov. 1972	Student.
Beverly, Barbara	Aug.–Nov. 1972	Action.
Bigninatti, Mildred	May–Nov. 1972	Unknown.
Black, Katherine	Mar.–Nov. 1972	Unknown.
Blackman, Ann	July–Nov. 1972	Unknown.
Blackman, Robert	Apr.–Nov. 1972	Grainger County, San Jose, Calif.

*Place: Washington, D.C., unless otherwise indicated.

Committee for the Re-Election of the President and Finance Committee for the Re-Election of the President—Continued

Name	Dates of service	Former employment*
Blair, Nancy	Feb.–July 1972	RNC.
Bourbonnais, Suzanne	June–Nov. 1972	Exotech Systems.
Bourne, Beebe	June–Nov. 1972	Unknown.
Bowen, Maura	May–Nov. 1972	Student.
Boyd, Richard	June–Sept. 1972	Student.
Braafladt, Ann	Nov. 1972	White House.
Brataas, Nancy	Feb.–Nov. 1972	J. Irwin Miller, Columbus, Ind.
Braydon, Walter	Apr.–May 1972	CIA.
Broadus, Constance	July–Nov. 1972	Federal Aviation Administration.
Broccoletti, Peter	June–Nov. 1972	Unknown.
Bronson, Michael	June–Nov. 1972	E. N. Hay & Associates, Philadelphia, Pa.
Bryan, Alice	Aug.–Nov. 1972	Unknown.
Brookshire, Joan	May–May 1972	Unknown.
Brown, Raymond	July–Nov. 1972	Attorney, Pascagovla, Miss.
Bruner, Gary	Aug.–Nov. 1972	Reagan for Governor Committee, Texas.
Buchanan, Angela	July–Nov. 1972	Francisco's, Bethesda, Md.
Buchanan, Carol	Sept.–Nov. 1972	Unknown.
Buchanan, Ronald	May–Nov. 1972	Guardian Security, Silver Spring, Md.
Bullard, Susan	Sept.–Nov. 1972	Emberton for Governor Committee, Kentucky.
Bungato, Monico	Feb. 1972–June 1973.	U.S. Navy.
Burhop, Gary	May–Nov. 1972	U.S. Army.
Butler, Barbara	June–Nov. 1972	Unknown.
Byers, Buckley	May–Nov. 1972	Unknown.
Caldiero, Raymond	July–Nov. 1972	Marriott Corp.
Callaway, Elizabeth	Apr.–Nov. 1972	Student.
Calloway, Maxwell	Feb.–Nov. 1972	Fulton County Board of Education, Atlanta, Ga.
Capone, Jerome	May–Oct. 1972	Student.
Carlisle, Margo	July–Nov. 1972	None.
Carpenter, Frank	Apr.–Nov. 1972	Penn Valley Community College.
Carroccio, A. Thomas	June–Nov. 1972	Federal Communications Commission.
Carroccio, Charles	July–Nov. 1972	Student.
Caulfield, John	Mar.–Apr. 1972	White House.
Chern, Victoria	Oct. 1971–Nov. 1972	Senator Robert Griffin.
Chew, David	June–Nov. 1972	Student.
Chadwell, John	May–June 1972	Treasury Department.
Chambers, Arden	Apr. 1972–Present	Commerce Department.
Chase, Warren	May–Nov. 1972	Unknown.
Christian, Paul	June–Nov. 1972	Lien for Senate Comm., South Dakota.
Clifton, Geraldine	July–Nov. 1972	Appalachian Regional Comm.
Cochran, Patricia	Feb.–Nov. 1972	Golightly & Co., New York City.
Cohen, Beryl	Apr.–June 1972	Unknown.
Coleman, Lois	Feb.–Nov. 1972	International Systems & Controls Corp., Houston, Tex.
Collins, Marvin	Aug.–Nov. 1972	River City Inn, Austin, Tex.
Cooper, James	Feb.–Nov. 1972	Dart Drug Co.
Corbet, Dallas	Oct.–Oct. 1972	Unknown.
Corby, Connie	July–Nov. 1972	Student.

*Place: Washington, D.C., unless otherwise indicated.

COMMITTEE FOR THE RE-ELECTION OF THE PRESIDENT AND FINANCE COMMITTEE FOR THE RE-ELECTION OF THE PRESIDENT—Continued

Name	Dates of service	Former employment*
Cowling, Edward	Mar.–Nov. 1972; Apr. 1973–Present	Federal Communications Commission and Inaugural Committee.
Cox, Marianne	Feb.–Nov. 1972	Congressman William Harsha.
Cram, Sandra	Mar.–Nov. 1972	American Air Lines.
Creighton, Josephine	Feb.–Mar. 1972	Carl Davis, Attorney.
Croft, Jean	Sept.–Nov. 1972	Veterans' Administration.
Crouch, Nancy	Feb.–Nov. 1972	Van, Arkel & Kaiser.
Crouch, Tom	Aug.–Nov. 1972	Attorney, Dallas, Tex.
Cudd, Connie	July–Nov. 1972	Unknown.
Daley, Ray	June–Nov. 1972	Automobile Association.
Dankworth, June	Feb.–May 1972	None.
Dannenhauer, Jane	Apr.–Dec. 1972	Senator George Murphy.
Daoust, Elizabeth	Sept.–Nov. 1972	Student.
Davis, Susan	Feb.–Nov. 1972	Cost of Living Council.
Davis, Thomas	Mar.–Nov. 1972	U.S. Army.
Deane, John R	Aug.–Nov. 1972	White House.
DeFalco, Anthony	Apr.–June 1972	Department of Transportation.
DeLury, Bernard	June–Nov. 1972	New York State Department of Labor, New York City.
Devlin, Maureen	Apr. 1972–Jan. 1973	E. F. Hutton Co., New York City.
Dexter, Charles	Apr.–Nov. 1972	RNC.
Dey, Thomas	Mar.–Sept. 1972	Student.
Dickey, Gordon	July–Nov. 1972	Student.
Dietrick, Bruce	Sept.–Nov. 1972	Clark County Republican Committee, Las Vegas, Nev.
Donnelly, Joan	Mar.–Nov. 1972	Senator Lowell Weicker.
Dooley, James	Apr.–June 1972	Unknown.
Dore, Ann	Feb.–Nov. 1972	Myers Infoplan, New York City.
Dorminy, Yolande	Apr. 1972–Feb. 1973	Senator Murphy.
Dunaway, Margo	July–Nov. 1972	University of Arkansas, Little Rock, Ark.
Duncan, Martha	June 1971–Jan. 1973	White House.
Ebner, Stanley	July–Nov. 1972	U.S. Senate.
Eden, Charles	July–Nov. 1972	U.S. Navy.
Edwards, Mary	Sept.–Nov. 1972	RNC.
Ehman, Richard	Sept.–Nov. 1972	Unknown.
Ehrlichman, Jam	June–Nov. 1972	Student.
Ehrlichman, Peter	Aug.–Sept. 1972	Student.
Elliott, Morgan	Feb.–Oct. 1972	U.S. Army.
Emge, David	June–Aug. 1972	Student.
Engebretson, Margaret	July–Nov. 1972	Unknown.
Ernst, John	Mar. 1972–Feb. 1973	Dart Drug Co.
Evans, Daniel	Feb.–Nov. 1972	City of Indianapolis, Ind.
Failor, Edward	June–Nov. 1972	Department of Interior.
Fangboner, Harold	Feb.–Nov. 1972	C & P Telephone Co.
Farnham, Timothy	Sept.–Nov. 1972	Fairfax County Republican Committee, Fairfax, Va.
Felgner, Karen	July–Nov. 1972	Tucker, Anthony & Day, New York City.
Finkelstein, Arthur	Feb.–Nov. 1972	Unknown.
Flanagan, Judy	Aug.–Sept. 1972	Student.
Flemming, Harry	Feb.–Nov. 1972	White House.
Florence, David	July–Nov. 1972	State of California, San Francisco, Calif.
Flynn, Timothy	May–Nov. 1972	Student.

*Place: Washington, D.C., unless otherwise indicated.

COMMITTEE FOR THE RE-ELECTION OF THE PRESIDENT AND FINANCE COMMITTEE FOR THE RE-ELECTION OF THE PRESIDENT—Continued

Name	Dates of service	Former employment*
Fokine, Peter	May 1972–Present	Pepsi Cola Corp., New York City.
Foltz, John	Feb.–Nov. 1972	Department of Agriculture.
Ford, John	May–Nov. 1972	Student.
Fore, Richard	Feb.–Nov. 1972	Hal Short & Assoc.
Forsberg, Kristin	Feb.–Nov. 1972 Mar. 1973–Present	Department of Interior and Inaugural Committee.
Foster, Carl	Mar.–Nov. 1972	U.S. Air Force.
Foust, John	Apr.–Nov. 1972	White House.
Fowler, Judy	June–Nov. 1972	Student.
Frankfort, Paul	May–Nov. 1972	FBI (retired).
Frederick, Laura	Feb. 1972–Present	White House.
Fuller, John	Feb–Nov. 1972	Self-employed writer.
Funke, Baiba	Sept.–Nov. 1972	RNC.
Gallagher, Robert	Oct.–Nov. 1972	Continental Advisors, Coral Gables, Fla.
Gaillard, Jeanne	June–Sept. 1972	Unknown.
Garcia, Sylvia	Aug.–Nov. 1972	Department of Labor.
Garner, Ronald	Sept.–Nov. 1972	Connor for Congress Committee, Wausau, Wis.
Garrish, Theodore	Feb.–Nov. 1972	Assistant U.S. Attorney, Detroit, Mich.
Gavigan, Thomas	July 1972	Unknown.
Genader, Robert	Sept.–Nov. 1972	Security Pacific National Bank, Los Angeles, Calif.
Gibson, Roy	Feb.–May 1972	U.S. Army.
Gillespie, Bernard	Aug.–Nov. 1972	California Delegation Committee, San Rafael, Calif.
Gillis, Sharon	Feb.–Nov. 1972	Congressman James Fulton.
Girard, Thomas	Feb.–May 1972	Metromedia Corp.
Gleason, Millicent	Apr.–Nov. 1972	Dart Drug Co.
Goldberg, Lawrence	Feb.–Nov. 1972	American Leisure Products, Providence, R.I.
Goldstein, Tony	Mar.–Nov. 1972	Student.
Gonzalez, Betty Jean	May–Nov. 1972	Edoc McGrant Worker Project, San Antonio, Tex.
Gooch, Gordon	Aug.–Nov. 1972	Federal Power Commission.
Goodspeed, Rebecca	Mar.–Nov. 1972	Office of Lieutenant Governor, Sacramento, Calif.
Gorton, George	Feb.–Nov. 1972	Wilson for Mayor Committee, San Diego, Calif.
Graham, Ann Margaret	Feb.–Apr. 1972	RNC.
Graham, Diane	Apr.–Sept. 1972	Auto Club of Southern California, Los Angeles, Calif.
Green, Jerome	Aug.–Oct. 1972	Austin Youth Foundation, Chicago, Ill.
Greenwald, Ronald	Apr.–Nov. 1972	YM–YWJA, Williamsburg, N.Y.
Groom, Ruth	May–June 1972	RNC.
Haggart, Veronica	Feb.–Nov. 1972	RNC.
Haldeman, Harry	June–Nov. 1972	Student.
Hall, Dan	May–Sept. 1972	Fuller Brush Corp., Sunnyoak, Calif.
Hall, Elaine	Apr.–Dec. 1972	Unknown.
Harbaugh, Judith	June 1972–Jan. 1973	RNC.
Harlowe, Jayne	Apr.–Nov. 1972	White House.
Harmony, Sally	Apr.–Sept. 1972	Congressman Clarence Miller.
Harper, William	Feb.–Nov. 1972	Amphenol Sams, Calif.
Harris, Mary Angela	Feb.–Nov. 1972	Congressman Roger Zion.
Harris, Sharon	Apr.–Nov. 1972	Student.

*Place: Washington, D.C., unless otherwise indicated.

COMMITTEE FOR THE RE-ELECTION OF THE PRESIDENT AND FINANCE COMMITTEE FOR THE RE-ELECTION OF THE PRESIDENT—Continued

Name	Dates of service	Former employment*
Hauser, Rita	Feb.–Nov. 1972	Unknown.
Healy, Helen	Sept.–Nov. 1972	Quaker Hill Development Corp., San Rafael, Calif.
Herge, J. Curtis	Feb.–Nov. 1972	Mudge, Rose, Guthrie & Alexander, New York City.
Herndon, Michael	June–Nov. 1972	Student.
Herrell, Gregory	July–Sept. 1972	Student.
Herron, Orley	July–Nov. 1972	President, Greenville College, Greenville, Ill.
Higgins, Barbara	Aug.–Nov. 1972	Murray Chotiner, Attorney.
Hill, Kathy	Apr.–Nov. 1972	Senator Carl Mundt.
Hirschel, Anne	Oct.–Nov. 1972	Unknown.
Hoback, Judith	Apr. 1972–Jan. 1973	Councilor, Buchanan & Mitchell.
Hoeppner, Carmen	Mar.–Nov. 1972	Gelco Leasing.
Holmes, Constance	July–Nov. 1972	Student.
Holmes, Peter	Apr.–Nov. 1972	Department of Commerce.
Holton, Carol	Apr.–Nov. 1972	Unknown.
Hooker, Joyce	June–Nov. 1972	Congressman Jack Kemp.
Horacek, Joseph	Feb.–Nov. 1972	Mitchell & Silberberg, Los Angeles, Calif.
Houston, George	May–Nov. 1972	Student.
Houston, Robert	Feb. 1972–Feb. 1973	U.S. Army.
Howard, Ronald	Apr.–Nov. 1972	Unknown.
Hristakos, Christine	June 1972–Feb. 1973	Student.
Hudson, Geoffrey	Mar.–Nov. 1972	Student.
Hughes, William	July–Nov. 1972	Unknown.
Humphrey, Katherine	July–Nov. 1972	White House.
Hunger, Merlyn	Mar.–Nov. 1972	National Alcoholic Beverage Cont. Assoc.
Hunt, Gary	July–Nov. 1972	Assemblyman John Stull, Sacramento, Calif.
Hurley, Elizabeth	July–Nov. 1972	Unknown.
Hutar, Patricia	Feb.–Nov. 1972	Self-employed P.R. consultant, Chicago, Ill.
Hyde, Eveline	Apr. 1972–Present	
Jablonsky, Lea	Mar.–Nov. 1972	Justice Department.
Jacobini, Lois	Aug.–Nov. 1972	U.S. Postal Service.
Joanou, Phillip	Feb.–Nov. 1972	Doyle, Dane, Bernbach, Los Angeles, Calif.
Johansen, Elizabeth	Feb.–Nov. 1972	U.S. Savings & Loan League.
Johnson, Brenda	June–Nov. 1972	Burkhalter & Hickerson, Architects, Nashville, Tenn.
Johnson, Marilyn	Feb.–Nov. 1972	RNC.
Jones, Billie	Aug.–Nov. 1972	Georgetown University.
Jones, Jerry	Apr.–Nov. 1972	White House.
Jones, Paul	Feb.–Nov. 1972	Peace Corps.
Kalin, Diane	Apr. 1972–Jan. 1973	American Airlines.
Kantzer, Noelle	Feb. 1972–Apr. 1973	American International School, Nigeria.
Kaupinen, Allen	Feb.–Nov. 1972	White House.
Karalekas, Christine	Feb.–Nov. 1972	Kennedy Center.
Karem, Fred	Aug.–Nov. 1972	Emberton for Governor Committee, Kentucky.
Kayser, Paul	Feb.–Nov. 1972	Golightly & Co., New York City.
Keesling, Karen	July–Nov. 1972	University of Kansas, Lawrence, Kans.
Kekker, Michael	Apr.–Nov. 1972	Student.
Kerwan, Margaret	June–July 1972	Unknown.

*Place: Washington, D.C., unless otherwise indicated.

COMMITTEE FOR THE RE-ELECTION OF THE PRESIDENT AND FINANCE COMMITTEE FOR THE RE-ELECTION OF THE PRESIDENT—Continued

Name	Dates of service	Former employment*
Kihl, Erik	Aug.–Nov. 1972	Self-employed management consultant.
King, Eugenia	Aug.–Nov. 1972	Republican Central Committee, Texas.
King, Stephen	May–Nov. 1972	FBI, U.S. Senate.
Kinnear, Edward	Oct.–Nov. 1972	Canteen Vending Corp., Logansport, Ind.
Knox, Thomas	June–Nov. 1972	Household Finance Corp., New York City.
Knudsen, Robert	July–Aug. 1972	Student.
Koeze, Marybeth	Mar.–Nov. 1972	Market Opinion Research, Detroit, Mich.
Kolstad, James	Aug.–Nov. 1972	Unknown.
Koob, Mary Catherine	Feb.–Nov. 1972	Republican National Finance Committee.
Koon, Karen	Feb.–Nov. 1972	White House.
Kopperman, Diane	May–Nov. 1972	State Department.
Kos, Michael	Aug.–Nov. 1972	Attorney in private practice, Chicago, Ill.
Krattli, Robert	June–Nov. 1972	Unknown.
Kreitler, Joan	Aug.–Nov. 1972	Gourmet Magazine, New York City.
Krueger, Herbert	Feb.–Nov. 1972	Student.
Krueger, Judith	Mar.–Nov. 1972	State of Illinois, Chicago.
Kuhn, Loughrey	Feb.–May 1972	Commonwealth Services, Inc.
Lallmang, Sue	Aug.–Nov. 1972	Public Health Services, Rockville, Md.
Lamke, Judith	Aug.–Nov. 1972	Unknown.
Lamont, William	Mar.–Nov. 1972	Lone Star Cement, Dallas, Tex.
Lampe, Virginia	June–Nov. 1972	None.
Lang, Michael	Aug.–Nov. 1972	Price Commission.
Lasky, Patricia	May–Nov. 1972	None.
Laughlin, Alexander	Feb.–Nov. 1972	Student.
Lawrence, G. Andrew	June–Nov. 1972	Office of the Vice President.
LeDonne, Susan	May–Nov. 1972	State Department.
Lehman, Harry	June–Nov. 1972	Unknown.
Leonard, Frank	Feb.–Nov. 1972	Unknown.
Letendre, Andre	May–Nov. 1972	Commerce Department.
Lewis, Mary	May–Aug. 1972	Student.
Licata, Judy	July–Nov. 1972	White House.
Liddy, G. Gordon	Dec. 1971–June 1972	White House.
Lommason, Lucinda	July 1972–Present	Student.
Lozano, Diana	July–Nov. 1972	Cabinet Committee for Spanish Speaking.
Lyeth, Charlotte	Apr. 1972–Mar. 1973	U.S. Postal Service.
Lynch, Jane	Aug.–Nov. 1972	White House.
Madison, Dolly	Aug.–Nov. 1972	Washington Hilton Hotel.
Madson, Gary	Apr.–Nov. 1972	Congressman Paul Findley.
Magruder, Jeb	Feb. 1972–Mar. 1973	White House.
Mallon, Neille	May–Nov. 1972	Justice Department.
Manning, Kenneth	Mar.–Sept. 1972	Manning Construction Co., Hacienda Heights, Calif.
Mardian, Robert	Apr.–Nov. 1972	Justice Department.
Marik, Robert	Feb. 1972–Feb. 1973	Department of Health, Education, and Welfare.
Marshall, Carol	June–Dec. 1972	WRC–TV.
Mason, Jeanne	Feb.–Sept. 1972	Mellon Collection Agency.
Masse, Michael	May–Nov. 1972	Woodward & Lothrop.
Malek, Frederic	July–Nov. 1972	White House.

*Place: Washington, D.C., unless otherwise indicated.

COMMITTEE FOR THE RE-ELECTION OF THE PRESIDENT AND FINANCE COMMITTEE FOR THE RE-ELECTION OF THE PRESIDENT—Continued

Name	Dates of service	Former employment*
Mallicoat, Marlene	Sept.–Nov. 1972	IBM Corp., San Francisco Calif.
MacGregor, Clark	July–Nov. 1972	White House.
Mandato, Joseph	Sept.–Nov. 1972	U.S. Army.
Maxwell, Frank	Sept.–Nov. 1972	Unknown.
McCann, Robert	July–Nov. 1972	Student.
McDonald, Dian	Aug.–Nov. 1972	Price Commission.
McKenzie, Sally	July–Nov. 1972	Unknown.
McPhee, Henry	Aug.–Nov. 1972	Student.
Mehocic, George	Sept.–Nov. 1972	Standard Oil Corp., New York City.
Mena, Armando	July–Nov. 1972	Jobs for Progress, Inc.
Miller, Arlene	July–Nov. 1972	None.
Miller, Bruce	Aug.–Nov. 1972	Unknown.
Millican, Manyon	July–Nov. 1972	University Hospital, Birmingham, Ala.
Minor, Karen	Sept.–Nov. 1972	Federal City College.
Minton, Larry	Aug.–Nov. 1972	State Farm Insurance, Birmingham, Ala.
Moore, Kimberly	July–Nov. 1972	Patrick Gorman, Consultant.
McAdoo, Richard	Apr.–Nov. 1972	Security Pacific National Bank, Los Angeles, Calif.
McAuliffe, Wyn	Apr.–Nov. 1972	Justice Department.
McCord, James	Feb.–June 1972	Self-employed security consultant.
McCormack, Georgina	Feb.–June 1972	Charles Dana, Jr., New York
McClung, Margaret	Feb.–Aug. 1972	Mudge, Rose, Guthrie & Alexander.
McDonald, Anthony	June–Nov. 1972	Unknown.
McDonald, Dorothy	June–July 1972	Washington Hospital Center.
McGlone, Ann	Apr.–Nov. 1972	Cogressman Paul Findley.
Meade, Forest	June–Nov. 1972	Student.
Metcalf, Martha	June–Nov. 1972	Student.
Meyers, Ed	June–Nov. 1972	Student.
Miller, Angela	Feb.–Nov. 1972	Student.
Miller, Michael	June–Sept. 1972	Unknown.
Milligan, Robert	June–Nov. 1972	Unknown.
Milliken, Justine	Feb.–Nov. 1972	Student.
Mills, James	Feb.–Nov. 1972	Aging & Older Americans, Inc.
Minshall, William, III	Feb.–Nov. 1972	Student.
Mintz, Daniel	Feb.–Nov. 1972	University of Maryland, College Park, Md.
Mitchell, Jeanne	Feb.–Nov. 1972	Unknown.
Mitchell, John	Apr.–June 1972	Justice Department.
Moeller, William	June–Nov. 1972	First National City Bank, New York.
Moore, Powell	May–Nov. 1972	Justice Department.
Morgan, Robert	Feb.–Nov. 1972	Reuben H. Donnelley Corp., Houston, Tex.
Mosiman, Donald	Apr.–Nov. 1972	Environmental Protection Agency.
Mumford, John	June–Nov. 1972	FBI (retired).
Murdock, Dustin	Apr.–Nov. 1972	District of Columbia Public Schools.
Murphy, Pat	May–Sept. 1972	Student.
Murray, Richard	July–Nov. 1972	Unknown.
Muse, Carolyn	May–Nov. 1972	White House.
Myers, Judith	Feb.–Nov. 1972	Herbert Fierst, Attorney.
Myers, Marcia	Sept.–Nov. 1972	OEO.
Nadeau, Christine	June–Nov. 1972	Student.

*Place: Washington, D.C., unless otherwise indicated.

COMMITTEE FOR THE RE-ELECTION OF THE PRESIDENT AND FINANCE COMMITTEE FOR THE RE-ELECTION OF THE PRESIDENT—Continued

Name	Dates of service	Former employment*
Naylor, Frank	Apr.–Nov. 1972	Department of Agriculture.
Neubauer, Richard	July–Nov. 1972	Colorado Farm Bureau, Denver, Colo.
Newman, Jacqueline	Feb. 1972–Present	Governor Maurice H. Thatcher.
Niedzwiecki, Rosalie	Sept.–Nov. 1972	Connecticut Mutual Life Insurance Co., Hartford, Conn.
Nixon, Deborah	May–Nov. 1972	Student.
Nixon, Edward C	Feb.–Nov. 1972	Oceanographic Engineer, Lynwood, Wash.
Nolan, Betty	Feb.–Nov. 1972	Wagner & Baroody.
Nostrand, Stephen	June–Sept. 1972	Greater Miami Chamber of Commerce, Miami, Fla.
Novelli, William	Feb.–Nov. 1972	Action.
Nunn, Lee	Apr.–Dec. 1972	Republican Senatorial Campaign Committee.
Ochs, Valerie	Aug.–Nov. 1972	White House.
Odle, Robert	Feb. 1972–June 1973	White House.
O'Donnell, Michael	Feb.–June 1972	Republican State Central Committee, California.
O'Gara, Molly	June–Nov. 1972	Student.
O'Gorman, Elaine	June 1972–Mar. 1973	Russell Reynolds Assoc., N.Y.
Olson, Glenn	Apr.–Nov. 1972	Student.
O'Melia, Kathleen	Feb.–Nov. 1972	White House.
O'Neal, Lacey	Oct.–Nov. 1972	District of Columbia Public Schools.
Orr, Lorraine	July–Nov. 1972	Unknown.
Palmer, Elizabeth	Aug.–Nov. 1972	White Collar Girls of America, Inc., Mount Prospect, Ill.
Panarites, Sylvia	Feb.–Nov. 1972	National Journal.
Parish, William	Feb.–Nov. 1972	World Publishing Co., N.Y.
Parker, Anthony	Aug.–Nov. 1972	U.S. Navy.
Parker, John	May–Nov. 1972	Cargill, Inc., Chesapeake, Va.
Pashayan, Charles	June–Dec. 1972	GSA.
Passell, Joyce	June–Sept. 1972	Katz & Salmon, Attorneys, Miami Beach, Fla.
Peters, Scott	Apr.–Nov. 1972	United Press International.
Peters, Virginia	Apr.–Nov. 1972	Department of Interior.
Peterson, June	Mar.–Nov. 1972	Carey Corp.
Pettross, Brenda	Nov. 1972	Federal City College.
Piliero, Daniel	May–Nov. 1972	Unknown.
Pinkerton, Ann	July–Nov. 1972	First National City Bank, N.Y.
Plesner, Judith	Apr. 1972	Filmakers Group, Universal City, Calif.
Podesta, Robert	Feb.–Nov. 1972	Student.
Porter, Herbert	Feb.–Nov. 1972	White House.
Powell, Gregory	Aug.–Nov. 1972	Richman Bros. Records, Philadelphia, Pa.
Pratt, Gliere	Aug.–Nov. 1972	Bridal Shop, Tysons Corner, Va.
Presock, Patricia	Aug.–Nov. 1972	Unknown.
Price, Patricia	Feb.–Nov. 1972	University of North Carolina, Chapel Hill, N.C.
Prokop, Judith	May–Nov. 1972	Congressman E. B. Forsythe.
Putts, Margaret	June–Nov. 1972	Toms River Board of Education, Toms River, N.J.
Randall, James	May–Nov. 1972	Lieutenant Governor of Massachusetts, Boston, Mass.
Ratajski, Magda	Aug.–Nov. 1972	USIA.
Rausch, Doris	July–Nov. 1972	White House.
Reiley, Susan	July–Nov. 1972	Student.

*Place: Washington, D.C., unless otherwise indicated.

COMMITTEE FOR THE RE-ELECTION OF THE PRESIDENT AND FINANCE COMMITTEE FOR THE RE-ELECTION OF THE PRESIDENT—Continued

Name	Dates of service	Former employment*
Reilly, Sandra	Aug.–Nov. 1972	Virginia Squires, Norfolk, Va.
Reisler, Charles	July–Nov. 1972	White House.
Reisner, Robert	Feb.–Nov. 1972	Environmental Protection Agency.
Rezabek, Lois	June 1972–Present	
Richards, Richard	May–Nov. 1972	Unknown.
Richter, Jean	June–Nov. 1972	Unknown.
Richmond, Lee	Mar.–May 1972	Teledyne Ryan Aeronautical, San Diego, Calif.
Rietz, Kenneth	Feb.–Nov. 1972	Unknown.
Roberts, Gene	May–Nov. 1972	White House.
Rocchio, Peter	Feb.–Nov. 1972	National Alliance of Businessmen.
Rogers, Bruce	Feb.–Mar. 1972	Department of Housing and Urban Development.
Rogers, Ronald	July–Sept. 1972	Air National Guard.
Rosenker, Mark	June–Nov. 1972	U.S. Air Force.
Rossi, Lora	Aug.–Nov. 1972	Automotive Trade Association.
Rushing, Albert	May–Nov. 1972	FBI (retired).
Ryales, Barry	Sept.–Nov. 1972	Unknown.
Santarelli, Ann	Feb. 1972–Mar. 1973	Careers Unlimited, Alexandria, Va.
Sawers, Peter	Sept.–Nov. 1972	Unknown.
Sawicki, John	June–Nov. 1972	State of California, Sacramento, Calif.
Schjeldrup, Susan	Feb.–Nov. 1972	Young & Rubicam, New York.
Schrager, Patricia	Feb.–Nov. 1972	None.
Scott, Thomas	May–Nov. 1972	Massachusetts Mutual Life Insurance Co., New York.
Scully, Michael	Feb.–Nov. 1972	Senator Lowell Weicker.
Sedam, Glenn	Feb.–Nov. 1972	RNC.
Sedlak, Pauline	Feb.–Nov. 1972	White House Conference on Aging.
Shanks, George	May 1972	Advance Industrial Security, Falls, Church, Va.
Shearer, Charles	May–Nov. 1972	Export-Import Bank.
Sheedy, Laurelle	Sept.–Nov. 1972	Senator James Buckley.
Shem, Carl	June–Nov. 1972	Unknown.
Shem, Story	Mar.–Nov. 1972	RNC.
Shepherd, Katherine	Aug.–Nov. 1972	Congressman Thomas Foley.
Sheridan, Richard	Mar.–Nov. 1972	Unknown.
Sholer, Michael	June–July 1972	Great Western Equities, Englewood, Calif.
Shriver, Richard	Apr.–Nov. 1972	R. Shriver Assoc., Denville, N.J.
Shuemake, Joyce	July–Nov. 1972	Unknown.
Shull, Edward	Aug.–Sept. 1972	Guiffe Distributing Co., Virginia.
Shumway, DeVan	Feb. 1972–Present	White House.
Skladany, Barney	Aug.–Nov. 1972	Unknown.
Slivinski, Thomas	May–Nov. 1972	McCormack for Congress Committee Pennsylvania
Sloan, Hugh	Apr.–July 1972	White House.
Smith, James C	May–Nov. 1972	Veterans' Administration, Lincoln, Nebr.
Smith, Joseph	Feb. –Nov. 1972	U.S. Air Force.
Smith, Kenneth	Feb. –Nov 1972	White House.
Snyder, Anne	Sept.–Oct. 1972	None.
Sorg, Leslie	Aug.–Nov. 1972	North Shore Hospital Manhasset, N.Y.

*Place: Washington, D.C., unless otherwise indicated.

COMMITTEE FOR THE RE-ELECTION OF THE PRESIDENT AND FINANCE COMMITTEE FOR THE RE-ELECTION OF THE PRESIDENT—Continued

Name	Dates of service	Former employment*
Sotirhos, Michael	May–Nov. 1972	Aristol Interior Designers, Inc., New York City.
Stans, Maurice	Apr. 1972–Present	Department of Commerce.
Stein, Nancy	May 1972	Unknown.
Steorts, Nancy	Feb.–Nov. 1972	Department of Agriculture.
Stickle, Frank	Unknown	Unknown.
Stone, Roger	May–Nov. 1972	Congressman Robert Steele.
Stover, William	Mar.–Nov. 1972	Senator George Murphy.
Straker, Shirley	June–Nov. 1972	Kaiser Engineers.
Strunk, Patricia	Feb.–Nov. 1972	Student.
Suiter, William	July–Nov. 1972	Collins, Knaggs & Assoc., Austin, Tex.
Sullivan, Susan	Apr.–Sept. 1972	Republican State Central Committee of California.
Sykes, Robert	June–Nov. 1972	Unknown.
Szmagala, Taras	Aug.–Nov. 1972	Senator Robert Taft, Jr.
Talmage, Kenneth	Apr. 1972–Feb. 1973	Ambassador John Humes, Vienna, Austria.
Tarone, Michael	July–Nov. 1972	Unknown.
Teeter, Robert	Feb.–Nov. 1972	Market Opinion Research, Detroit, Mich.
Taylor, George	Sept.–Nov. 1972	U.S. Postal Service.
Terrar, Celine	Apr.–Nov. 1972	St. Leo Golf Course, St. Leo, College, Fla.
Terrar, David	Aug.–Nov. 1972	Self-employed antique dealer.
Thayer, Teri	Feb.–Nov. 1972	Student.
Thompson, Florence	Apr.–July 1972	Thompson Funeral Home, Paw Paw, Mich.
Thompson, James	Aug.–Nov. 1972	Office of the Vice President.
Tim, Terry	July–Nov. 1972	Student.
Tochilin, Sharon	Sept.–Nov. 1972	Systems Industries, Inc., Sunnyvale, Calif.
Todd, Christine	Mar.–Nov. 1972	State of New York.
Todd, Webster	Feb.–Nov. 1972	Civil Aeronautics Board.
Tooze, Frank	Aug.–Nov. 1972	International Brotherhood of Electrical Workers.
Townsend, Carol	June–Nov. 1972	Prince Georges' County School System, Maryland.
Triplett, Larry	Aug.–Nov. 1972	Department of Labor.
Ulman, Delores	Feb.–Nov. 1972	Paul Mellon.
Underwood, Laura	Feb. 1972–Jan. 1973	Zoecon Corp., Palo Alto, Calif.
Van Buren, Valerie	Aug.–Sept. 1972	Federal City College.
Vandersommen, Nora	Feb.–Nov. 1972	White House.
Venuto, Michael	July–Nov. 1972	Action.
Visceglia, Richard	Feb.–Mar. 1972	Student.
Wagner, Carrie	Feb.–Nov. 1972	RNC.
Wagner, Ellen	June–Nov. 1972	Export-Import Bank.
Wagoner, Lucille	Feb.–May 1972	Student.
Walker, Laura	June–Nov. 1972	Skitch Henderson, N.Y. City.
Wallace, Anne	June–Nov. 1972	Senator Robert Dole.
Wallach, Elizabeth	Aug.–Nov. 1972	Student.
Wangenheim, Walter	June–Nov. 1972	FBI (retired).
Warner, Harry	May–Nov. 1972	Jerry Reed Enterprises, Nashville, Tenn.
Washburn, John	Apr.–Nov. 1972	Student.
Washburn, C. Langhorne	May–Nov. 1972	Department of Commerce.
Watona, Pauline	Sept.–Nov. 1972	Environmental Protection Agency.
Watson, Benjamin	Sept.–Nov. 1972	U.S. Army

*Place: Washington, D.C., unless otherwise indicated.

COMMITTEE FOR THE RE-ELECTION OF THE PRESIDENT AND FINANCE COMMITTEE FOR THE RE-ELECTION OF THE PRESIDENT—Continued

Name	Dates of service	Former employment*
Weber, George	Sept.–Nov. 1972	Federal Power Commission.
West, Edward	Apr. 1972	Unknown.
Whitbeck, Elizabeth	July–Nov. 1972	First National Bank, Minneapolis, Minn.
White, James	Aug.–Nov. 1972	Unknown.
Whittier, Susan	Feb.–Nov. 1972	S. G. Whittier, Wumetta, Ill.
Wiesmann, Peggy	Apr.–Nov. 1972	Mudge, Rose, Guthrie & Alexander.
Wigger, Theodore	July–Nov. 1972	Student.
Wilks, John	Aug.–Nov. 1972	Department of Labor.
Williams, John	Mar.–May 1972	Unknown.
Williams, Sylvester	Aug.–Nov. 1972	Unknown.
Willis, Carol	Mar.–Nov. 1972	Republican Party of Alabama, Birmingham, Ala.
Wilson, Michael	June–Nov. 1972	Justice Department.
Wince, Tom	Feb.–Nov. 1972	U.S. Army.
Windon, Bernard	Aug.–Nov. 1972	G.D. Searle & Co., Chicago, Ill.
Wirth, John	June–Nov. 1972	Avon Products, N.Y. City.
Wise, Thomas	May–Nov. 1972	Sears, Roebuck Co., Silver Spring, Md.
Woodruff, Patricia	July–Nov. 1972	Unknown.
Woodley, Clarice	July–Nov. 1972	Unknown.
Yeutter, Clayton	Feb.–Nov. 1972	Department of Agriculture.
Youngs, Ruby	May–Nov. 1972	White House.
Zapp, Barbara	Jan.–Nov. 1972	RNC.
Zier, Linde	Mar.–Nov. 1972	American Campus Management Corp.
Zingale, Salvatore	Aug.–Nov. 1972	City of Lakewood, Lakewood, Ohio.

*Place: Washington, D.C., unless otherwise indicated.

By JAMES W. McCORD, Jr.

Accounting of How $76,000 was Spent

Reconstruction of Technical Equipment and Related Receipts and Expenditures, Approximations

	Amount
Receipts:	
April 12, 1972	$65, 000
May 8, 1972	4, 000
May 26, 27, 1972	2, 000
June 1972	5, 000
Total receipts	76, 000
Expenditures:	
Equipment:	
Bell and Howell Co., Conn	3, 800
Watkins Johnson Co., Rockville	3, 500
Stevens Laboratory, Chicago	5, 400
Miles Wireless Guitar Co., New York City	3, 000
Unidentified company, New York City—purchase of 1 transmitter	1, 000
Unidentified company, Chicago—purchase of 1 brief-case recorder	700
Olden Optical Co., New York City ($700 plus $400)	1, 100
Business Equipment Center, Washington, D.C	2, 000
Hechingers, Washington area stores	500
Lafayette Radio, Washington and Maryland area stores	1, 000
Miscellaneous purchases, tools and equipment, Washington, D.C., Chicago, and New York City	12, 750
Unidentified store, New York City—recorders	700
Unidentified store, New York City—recorders and accessories	2, 600
Total	38, 050
Truck	4, 500
Rentals:	
Howard Johnson Motel	900
Gatti Mortgage Co	1, 750
Total	2, 650
Overhead	12, 000
Subtotal	57, 200
Balance remaining, used for legal fees	18, 800
Total expenditures	76, 000

EXHIBITS

EXHIBIT No. 1

CITIZENS FOR THE RE-ELECTION OF THE PRESIDENT

WASHINGTON

SUITE 272
1701 PENNSYLVANIA AVENUE, N.W.
WASHINGTON, D.C. 20006
(202) 333-0920

July 3, 1971

CONFIDENTIAL

MEMORANDUM FOR THE ATTORNEY GENERAL

SUBJECT: Grantsmanship

Enclosed is a copy of a proposal to insure that the President and his Congressional supporters get proper credit for Federal Government programs. This proposal was written by Bill Horton in Fred Malek's office with the assistance of Bill Gifford, OMB, and Peter Millspaugh in Harry Dent's office.

If implemented this should be an effective method of insuring that political considerations are taken into account.

JEB S. MAGRUDER

Enclosure

CONFIDENTIAL

EXHIBIT NO. 2

GEMSTONE

date________

source______________

Exdis
No Disem

WARNING: This information is for intelligence purposes only. Exploitation may compromise source and terminate flow of information.

EXHIBIT NO. 3

MEMORANDUM

Copy #1 of 2

THE WHITE HOUSE

WASHINGTON

CONFIDENTIAL

February 9, 1972

EYES ONLY

MEMORANDUM FOR: JEB MAGRUDER

FROM: FRED MALEK FVM

SUBJECT: Coordinating Functions for the Campaign Organization

I have given further thought to our conversation of last night and to your February 7 memorandum to the Attorney General. Since I do not yet have an in-depth knowledge of the campaign operation, it is difficult for my observations to be precise. Nevertheless, I do have some reservations about the recommendations contained in that memorandum which can best be expressed in writing.

PLANNING

My reservations on your recommendations pertain mainly to the suggested planning process, but also to the responsibility for implementation.

Planning Process. As you know, the Attorney General has asked me to devise a management audit system by which he can track overall progress and identify major problem areas for corrective action. Naturally, an integral part of such a system is the establishment of benchmarks by which progress is to be judged, or in short, a plan. Based upon my preliminary thinking on this, I have tentatively concluded that the planning system should incorporate the following characteristics:

-- The principal focal points of the planning should be the States (with the emphasis given to key States) rather than the functional areas such as voter bloc activities, telephone, direct mail, etc. Planning by State will help to highlight and direct management attention to progress on building voter support to carry individual States -- the key to victory.

-- Planning of the functional activities within a State should be based upon a clearly defined strategy for obtaining the needed votes for carrying that State, spelling out, for example, the needed vote margin by distinctive geographical areas and the organizing and persuasion tactics which will be utilized.

-- As is implicit in the above two points, the planning should provide a sound basis for tracking progress and identifying problem areas for corrective action.

-- The line officials who will be held accountable for results, principally the State Chairmen, should feel as though they have the lead in developing the plans affecting their areas of responsibility. Naturally, exercising quality control, the national campaign organization must ensure the plans fit the overall re-election strategy and capitalize upon polling information.

From our conversation, I would say you generally agree with this. However, from reading your memorandum your position on these principles is not clear. I believe they should be clarified prior to proceeding with development of a planning system.

Responsibility for Implementation. I believe there is a strong argument for having Bob Marik perform this function in view of his sound knowledge of the campaign operations and his access to research information. However, it is also important for the "controller" to be intimately involved since these plans will provide the basis for tracking progress and identifying problems. To do this effectively, the "controller" must ensure that the plans provide a sound basis for monitoring campaign effectiveness. Also, he must be thoroughly familiar with their content. Perhaps we can meet the needs and capitalize on the strengths of both individuals by also giving the "controller" a definite part of this responsibility.

FORMAL DECISION-MAKING PROCESS

I really wonder whether the sort of staff secretariat operation which you suggest is necessary. Such a procedure has undoubtedly been helpful up to now, since the Attorney General has not been present and responsibilities have been shifting with the growth of the organization. However, with the Attorney General coming on board full-time soon, with him taking a more direct supervisory role over field operations, and with the division of responsibilities between the principals being clarified, I question the need for a staff secretariat system.

In fact, it may be counterproductive. Such systems are inevitably cumbersome and therefore not conducive to the need for fast decisions as the campaign heats up. Also, due to the sensitivity of the information and the need for speedy action, many of the decisions will undoubtedly be handled verbally, particularly toward the end of the campaign. This would undermine the staff secretariat's ability to coordinate effectively.

I recognize the abuse which can be perpetrated without such a system. However, given the nature of campaign management the answer lies in appointing competent division managers and making sure they have a clear understanding of their respective responsibilities rather than creating a cumbersome staff secretariat system. Of course, the Attorney General should, and will decide this matter. I believe it would be a disservice, however, to try to persuade him to lean on a staff secretariat system rather than bringing in the most competent managers possible, clearly laying out their responsibilities and then holding them fully accountable for results.

These are, of course, my initial reactions based on quite limited knowledge. Please note I am not stating how it should be done, but merely laying out possible problems that need to be addressed before we get locked in.

Because of the above reservations, I recommend you either pull back the memorandum or ask the Attorney General to delay acting on it pending further coordination with me. Another option would be for me to inform the Attorney General of my reservations and ask him to defer the decision. However, I do not think this is desirable and would prefer that you and I work it out in the spirit of cooperation that must become our trademark.

Frankly, I was taken by surprise last night. After our discussion on Friday about the need for teamwork and my openly discussing my role, I was surprised that you unilaterally submitted to the Attorney General recommendations having a profound impact on my area of responsibility and my working relationship with him. This was the reason for my rather vigorous reaction. In any case, we covered that ground fairly thoroughly last night, and I am confident that in the future we can work together on matters of this sort and resolve or spell out any differences prior to submitting recommendations.

EXHIBIT NO. 4

SAMPLE

COMMITTEE FOR THE RE-ELECTION OF THE PRESIDENT

MEMORANDUM January 17, 1972

CONFIDENTIAL

MEMORANDUM FOR: MR. H. R. HALDEMAN

FROM: JOHN N. SMITH

SUBJECT: Memoranda

This is the form for all memoranda addressed to members of our staff, people at the White House, and the RNC. Memorandum paper, rather than stationery, should be used. If the memo is confidential, it should be so marked at the top and bottom. The word "Mr.", "Mrs.", or "Miss" should precede the addressee's name, but not the writer's. Mr. Haldeman is always "Mr. H. R. Haldeman," never "Bob" or "Robert Haldeman" -- which is not his name. Middle initials should always be used in both lines.

The names of both the writer and the addressee are always all in capital letters. The subject line is in both upper and lower case and the subject is always underlined. However, you need not necessarily use a subject line.

Paragraphs should not be indented. The left margin should begin under the last letter ("m") of the word "Memorandum" on the paper. The typist's initials should never appear on the memo. Carbon copies should be addressed to a person using his full name, e.g., "Mr. John D. Ehrlichman," never "John Ehrlichman," or "Mr. Ehrlichman."

Check with Gene Roberts for the number and kind of file copies you should make if the memo is for Mr. Magruder's signature. Always mark the copies.

Thank you.

cc: Mr. John D. Ehrlichman

CONFIDENTIAL

EXHIBIT NO. 14

FINANCE COMMITTEE TO RE-ELECT THE PRESIDENT
1701 Pennsylvania Ave. N. W., Suite 272
WASHINGTON, D. C. 20006

7785

15-4
540

PAY Four hundred twenty-nine & 84/100 DOLLARS

DATE	CHECK NUMBER	AMOUNT
8-7-72	7785	429.84

TO THE ORDER OF Alfred C. Baldwin III
90 Mt. View Terrace
Hamden Conn.

FINANCE COMMITTEE TO RE-ELECT THE PRESIDENT
Judith G Hoback
Kenneth K. Talmadge

THE FIRST NATIONAL BANK OF WASHINGTON-WASHINGTON, D. C.

⑆0540⑈0004⑆ ⑈026 407 5⑈

Exhibit No. 15

PERIOD 08-01-72 THRU 08-09-72 — S C H E D U L E D — PAGE 14

ITEMIZED EXPENDITURES - PERSONAL SERVICES, LOANS, AND TRANSFERS

FINANCE COMMITTEE TO RE-ELECT THE PRESIDENT — PART NO. 7

DATE	PAYEE NAME PAYEE MAILING ADDRESS	PAYEE OCCUPATION PAYEE PLACE OF BUS.	PURPOSE OF EXPENDITURE	EXPENDITURE AMT THS PER
08-04-72	WILLIAMS SYLVESTER E 11209 SCHUYLKILL RD ROCKVILLE MD 20853	FIELD REPRESENTATIVE COMM TO REELECT THE PRES WASHINGTON DC	TRAVEL EXPENSE	200.00
08-05-72	CRAWFORD JACK 1407 L ST NW WASHINGTON DC	OWNER JACK CRAWFORD CONSTRUCTION CO WASHINGTON DC	TRAVEL EXPENSE	192.22
08-05-72	CRONK C ROBERT 5349 WHEATON ST LA MESA CALIF 92041	EXECUTIVE DIRECTOR PROJECT CONCERN LA MESA CALIF	REIMB TRAVEL EXPENSE	310.00
08-05-72	GROVES MARILYN 14899 VALLEY VISTA BLVD SHERMAN OAKS CALIF 91403	CHAIRMAN AREA 1 YOUTH FOR NIXON SHERMAN OAKS CALIF	TRAVEL EXPENSE	164.54
08-05-72	STURM CLARENCE L MANAWA WISC 54949	PAST PRESIDENT LIONS INTERNATIONAL MANAWA WISC	REIMB TRAVEL EXPENSE	186.00
08-05-72	WIRTH JOHN C JR 36 S FERRIS ST IRVINGTON N Y 10533	ETHNIC DIRECTOR COMM TO REELECT THE PRES WASHINGTON DC 20006	TRAVEL EXPENSE	209.67
08-07-72	BAILEY ROBERT H 433 E CENTER ST KINGSPORT TENN 37660	ATTORNEY ROBERT H BAILEY LAW OFFICE CHURCHILL TENN	TRAVEL EXPENSE	100.99
08-07-72	BALDWIN III ALFRED C 90 MT VIEW TERRACE HAMDEN CONN	SECURITY GUARD SELF-EMPLOYED HAMDEN CONN	TRAVEL EXPENSE	429.84
08-04-72	ROBINSON JOHN 2121 8th AVE BIRMINGHAM ALABAMA	SOUTH EAST ATTRACTIONS, INC. BIRMINGHAM ALABAMA	ENTERTAINMENT EXPENSE	750.00